VN £10.00

VERDI'S *OTELLO* and *Simon Boccanegra* (revised version)
IN LETTERS AND DOCUMENTS

'Uno splendor che non avrà tramonto'
    (*Opprandino Arrivabene to Verdi, 31 October 1886*)

VERDI'S
OTELLO
AND
Simon Boccanegra
(revised version)

IN LETTERS AND DOCUMENTS

EDITED AND TRANSLATED
BY
HANS BUSCH

Foreword by Julian Budden

VOLUME I
LETTERS AND TELEGRAMS

CLARENDON PRESS · OXFORD
1988

Oxford University Press, Walton Street, Oxford OX2 6DP

Oxford   New York   Toronto
Delhi   Bombay   Calcutta   Madras   Karachi
Petaling   Jaya   Singapore   Hong Kong   Tokyo
Nairobi   Dar es Salaam   Cape Town
Melbourne   Auckland
and associated companies in
Berlin   Ibadan

OXFORD is a trade mark of Oxford University Press

Published in the United States
by Oxford University Press, New York

The author and publishers gratefully acknowledge
the contribution of the late Dr Mimi Rudulph
towards the costs of publication

British Library Cataloguing in Publication Data
Verdi, Giuseppe
Verdi's Otello and Simon Boccanegra
(revised edition) in letters and documents.
1. Verdi, Giuseppe, 1813–1901. 2. Composers
—Italy—Biography.
I. Title.   II. Busch, Hans
782.1'092'4   ML410.V4
ISBN 0–19–313207–9

Library of Congress Cataloging-in-Publication Data
Verdi's Otello and Simon Boccanegra (revised version) in letters and
documents/collected and translated by Hans Busch ; foreword by
Julian Budden.
Includes correspondence by Giuseppe Verdi.
Bibliography:
Includes index.
1. Verdi, Giuseppe, 1813–1901. Otello. 2. Verdi, Giuseppe,
1813–1901. Simon Boccanegra. 3. Verdi, Giuseppe, 1813–1901–
–Correspondence. 4. Boito, Arrigo, 1842–1918—Correspondence.
5. Ricordi, Giulio, 1840–1912—Correspondence. 6. Opera.
I. Verdi, Giuseppe, 1813–1901. II. Busch, Hans, 1914–
ML410.V4V36   1988   782.1'092'4—dc19   87–34474
ISBN 0–19–313207–9

Set by Latimer Trend & Co. Ltd, Plymouth.
Printed in Great Britain by
Biddles Ltd, Guildford and King's Lynn

MIMI RUDULPH

IN MEMORIAM

FOREWORD

THIS volume can be seen as a follow-up to the same author's admirable *Verdi's Aida: The History of an Opera* (Minnesota, 1978), and its interest is, if anything, greater: for, if the revised *Simon Boccanegra* is a milestone in the progress of Verdi's self-renewal, *Otello* remains one of the outstanding cultural happenings of the century.

Most of the material presented here is known to scholars, but it is scattered among various publications. Of the letters relating to the genesis of both operas only those exchanged with Boito are currently available in a single publication (the *Carteggio Verdi–Boito* ed. Mario Medici and Marcello Conati (2 vols.; Parma, 1978); and of these only the ones concerned with the revision of *Boccanegra* have been translated into English in their entirety in Frits Noske's *The Signifier and the Signified* (The Hague, 1977). The composer's correspondence with the publisher, Giulio Ricordi, will shortly be brought out by the Istituto di Studi Verdiani, Parma edited by Pierluigi Petrobelli and Franca Cella. For the rest it is a matter of sifting collections of letters to friends—Count Arrivabene, Deputy (later Senator Piroli), Clarina Maffei—not to mention Verdi's own *Copialettere*, for references which in isolation can easily pass unnoticed but which spring into significance when placed in chronological context. The advantage of an epistolary 'pull-together' such as this, already demonstrated in Professor Busch's *Aida* monograph, is that it brings a sharper focus to the events described, while the addition of miscellaneous documents bearing on them serves to set them in a wider perspective.

As the author readily admits, scholars will always want to consult the original sources in the original language. The object of the present work is to bring a fascinating story to a wider public in all its detail and in readable form. The translations nicely capture the tone and manner of the correspondents—Verdi, always terse and to the point; Boito, stylishly elegant with a penchant for the neat antithesis; Giulio Ricordi, infinitely wordy and repetitive, and never more so than when fearful of incurring the Maestro's wrath. Verdi's concern with every aspect of production—voices, scenery, and costumes, disposition of the orchestra—is everywhere apparent; nor did it cease with the two premières. Time and again Ricordi is belaboured with objections to this or that revival and with suggestions for remedying this or that defect ('Damnedest *Otello*!—If only I had never written it!'). Yet Verdi could be very tactful and considerate with his singers, notably the unfortunate Romilda Pantaleoni.

Among the documents particular importance attaches to the two production manuals (*disposizioni sceniche*), here translated for the first time; both are required reading for modern producers, if only as a starting point for their own ideas. The intellectual climate of the time is well illustrated by a number of reviews, among which I particularly commend to the reader

Camille Bellaigue's brilliant notice of the first performance of *Otello* at the Paris Opéra.

The entire compilation, amply footnoted and furnished with valuable appendices, bears witness to years of careful study and research. But with Professor Busch devotion to Verdi runs in the family. With a famous performance of *La forza del destino* in Dresden in 1926 his father, Fritz Busch, is generally held to have launched the Verdi renaissance in Germany; and no one who was privileged to hear the same opera directed by him at Glyndebourne and Edinburgh in 1951 is ever likely to forget the experience. It is heartening to see the same tradition carried on by the son.

JULIAN BUDDEN

PREFACE

The letters, documents, and appendices presented on these pages shed new light on Verdi's *Otello* as well as on the revision of *Simon Boccanegra*. A similar book of mine on *Aida*,[1] which closed an apparent gap in Verdi literature, was welcomed with such unexpected appreciation that I felt encouraged, in fact almost obliged, to collect and translate the same kind of material with regard to *Otello*. The choice of this particular work was prompted by my good fortune of finding, in 1972, 141 autographs of Verdi's letters to Arrigo Boito, the librettist of *Otello* and *Falstaff*; they were in the possession of Boito's heirs, Countess Elena Carandini Albertini and her brother Leonardo Albertini, in Rome. A year later, at my suggestion, they donated these treasures to the Istituto di Studi Verdiani in Parma. This rare generosity moved Dr Gabriella Carrara Verdi and her family, Verdi's heirs at St Agata, to give photocopies of 121 letters from Boito to Verdi to the Institute, which published the entire Verdi–Boito correspondence in an exemplary Italian edition in 1979.[2]

While I was working on the book on *Aida*, Dr Gabriella Carrara Verdi enabled me to translate and publish some of the most important letters and documents from the archives at St Agata for the first time. In December 1978 she also allowed me to photocopy the autographs of Boito's letters to Verdi,[3] as well as photocopies of the replies from Verdi which I had discovered in Rome. A few weeks later I began to translate these invaluable autographs into German, resulting in the first edition in West and East Germany of Verdi's entire correspondence with Boito.[4]

The more I became involved with these projects, the more I became convinced that the present volume on *Otello* should include the twenty-two letters and two telegrams that Verdi exchanged with Boito about their revision of *Simon Boccanegra*. The link in their collaboration on these two operas was the publisher Giulio Ricordi. In November 1979 Dr Gabriella Carrara Verdi generously permitted me to photocopy, translate, and publish hundreds of his letters to Verdi, including a few apparently unpublished ones. Also, the House of Ricordi made available to me photocopies of many letters from Verdi to Ricordi. While some facts about the Verdi–Boito–Ricordi triumvirate are known, only their letters can tell the complete story of their personal and working relationship.

[1] Busch, *Aida*.
[2] *Carteggio*.
[3] The special order in which Verdi himself kept these letters according to subjects and years testifies to the importance he attributed to them.
[4] *Verdi–Boito Briefwechsel*, ed. and trans. Hans Busch (Berlin: Henschelverlag, 1986; Frankfurt am Main: S. Fischer Verlag, 1986). Frank Walker, the eminent English Verdi scholar, who had access to the Albertini family's safe in Parella, Piedmont, translated parts of Verdi's letters to Boito in *The Man Verdi*.

The nucleus of this volume is Verdi's correspondence with these two men. Letters of various others are included. The 656 letters, three Pro Memoria notes, and seventeen telegrams collected and translated here represent a careful selection from the wealth of published and unpublished correspondence relating to *Otello* and the revised *Simon Boccanegra*. They were exchanged over a fifteen-year period, from the inception of *Otello* in 1879 up to its première at La Scala in 1887 and its first performance at the Paris Opéra, which came about only in 1894. The delay of the French première complicated the selection of these letters, for in the meantime *Falstaff* had been composed; the first performance of the French *Otello* followed the first French *Falstaff* by six months. While the correspondents' writings on matters beyond their collaboration on *Otello* and *Simon Boccanegra* deepen the human background of their artistic activities and have been included, later letters such as those concerning Franco Faccio's tragic death relate more closely to the creation of *Falstaff* and as such do not belong to this volume.

Inevitably there are gaps in the chronological sequence of a correspondence that spans fifteen years. Some letters, and particularly telegrams, which are missing, were obviously lost or thrown away by the recipients. At times correspondence was rendered unnecessary by frequent visits to St Agata, Milan, or Genoa. Some letters which do not pertain to *Otello* or *Simon Boccanegra*, nor to the times of their creation and early performances, are omitted; still other letters are, sadly, unavailable.

Long ago, 266 of the approximately 1,700 letters that Verdi addressed to his publishers between 1844 and 1900 disappeared mysteriously from the Ricordi Archives in Milan. A remarkable coincidence in 1972 led me to these treasures, which were in the care of the music antiquarian Hans Schneider in Germany; I attempted immediately to save them, for the sake of research, from commercial exploitation. In 1981, through my intervention, these autographs were finally purchased by the Italian government and deposited in the Biblioteca Palatina in Parma.[5] Rights of first publication are reserved by the Istituto di Studi Verdiani in that city. However, photocopies of some of these letters, which Verdi sent to Giulio Ricordi between 1881 and 1890, were on display at La Scala in the autumn of 1981 and published in a catalogue edited by Franca Cella and Pierluigi Petrobelli.[6] These letters deal mainly with *Don Carlos*, the revised *Simon Boccanegra*, and *Otello*, and provide information regarding the interpretation of these works as well as Verdi's involvement in the vicissitudes of the times.

As scholars, no doubt, will wish to refer to these letters in the original, the locations of autographs and some published sources are given in the List of Letters and Telegrams. However, these translations should make this correspondence accessible to a wider readership.

[5] See Hans Schneider (ed.), *Katalog Nr. 170* (1972); *Katalog Nr. 172* (1972); *Katalog Nr. 180* (1973); *Katalog Nr. 192* (1975) (Tutzing: Musikantiquariat Hans Schneider).
[6] *Giuseppe Verdi–Giulio Ricordi: Corrispondenza e immagini 1881–1890*, Catalogo della mostra a cura di Franca Cella e Pierluigi Petrobelli (Milan: Edizioni del Teatro alla Scala, 1981).

The section of documents and appendices includes the Production Books for *Simon Boccanegra* and *Otello*, compiled by Giulio Ricordi with a few previously unpublished corrections and annotations in Boito's hand, which I recently discovered at the Conservatorio Arrigo Boito in Parma. These *disposizioni sceniche* are now out of print, but since they represent Verdi's and Boito's own ideas about the staging of their works, they appear here in translation. Any producer involved with operas should study them, for certain basic principles which the authors know better than their interpreters deserve to be respected, regardless of changes in time and taste. Meticulous descriptions and illustrations of costumes, jewellery, and properties, however, seem too outdated to warrant inclusion. Parts of a third production book written in French by the celebrated Victor Maurel, Verdi's first Jago and Falstaff, are translated here, apparently for the first time in English, because a number of Maurel's personal thoughts about the *mise-en-scène* of *Otello*, old-fashioned as they are, merit equal consideration.

The autographs of Boito's libretti for *Simon Boccanegra* and *Otello* are not included: permission for publication of these documents in their entirety is still withheld by Verdi's heirs. But I was privileged to study the autographs, as well as the libretto for *Falstaff*, at St Agata. Piero Nardi, however, describes the autographs of the *Otello* and *Falstaff* libretti and publishes excerpts from the *Otello* libretto with Boito's original text.[7] Alessandro Luzio, too, reveals some of their most interesting secrets.[8]

Among the other documents and appendices, some opinions of distinguished contemporary critics in their reviews of the revised *Simon Boccanegra* and *Otello* premières will surprise, and perhaps amuse, today's reader. And Francis Robinson's television essay on St Agata and *Otello*, broadcast one hundred years later, reflects my own admiration and gratitude for the man and artist, Giuseppe Verdi.

Chronologies of Verdi's and Boito's lives follow the appendices. As the genesis and initial productions of *Otello* span so many years, this volume offers an ideal opportunity to publish full chronologies, providing a broad basis of Verdi's and Boito's interdisciplinary activities and associations; but several facts that can be ascertained from the correspondence have not been duplicated. Verdi's chronology alone required a great deal of research that, while still incomplete, is nevertheless more accurate than any others I have seen. For example, I have included even Verdi's frequent trips to St Agata, proofs of his extraordinary energy and concern for his farmers. Much of Boito's life, on the other hand, is still shrouded in mystery; because of his great personal reserve, his activities and even his whereabouts are often uncertain, and in many instances could be established only through his correspondence, which to a large extent is either lost or yet to be found.

In 1940, in Buenos Aires, I discovered the autograph of a particularly

---

[7] Nardi, *Scritti*, pp. 1536–41.
[8] *Carteggi*, ii. 108–22, 126.

revealing letter which Verdi wrote about his *Macbeth* in 1865. Thirty years later I began to realize the dream of a lifetime and study Verdi's correspondence in depth. Verdi was a prolific letter-writer, addressing himself to an immensely wide range of topics, but above all he emerges as his own best interpreter: he makes his intentions about his own works unmistakably clear, and expresses his thoughts about the battles he fought for their productions in no uncertain terms. However, the thousands of letters that he wrote are scattered over many parts of the world, and are difficult to obtain. Some of the most important appear in out-of-print Italian publications; in addition, many unpublished autographs are hidden in inaccessible archives. Transcriptions of Verdi's handwriting, which is not always easy to decipher, are frequently erratic and unreliable, even offering incorrect dates.

This volume attempts to surmount such obstacles. It should open up new perspectives, while also serving conscientious professionals and interested laymen alike. I am grateful for the privilege of presenting the pages that follow.

HANS BUSCH

October 1986

ACKNOWLEDGEMENTS

A fellowship from the National Endowment for the Humanities in Washington, DC, has turned this volume from an idea into a reality, and grants from Indiana University have also been gratefully received. I am particularly indebted to Dr Harold Cannon, Dr Eugene Eoyang, Dr Paul Horgan, J. Hellmut Freund, Professor Corrado Mingardi, and Dr Mimi Rudulph for their encouragement and faith in this project.

The completion of this book during the past eight years required so much help that I cannot possibly name all the friends, colleagues, and acquaintances who have aided my labours in so many ways. But I would like to express sincere appreciation to the following for their assistance in my research, for providing photocopies, and for permission to publish: Dr Gabriella Carrara Verdi, at St Agata; Signora Luciana Pestalozza, Signora Mimma Guastoni, Signor Carlo Clausetti, and Maestro Fausto Broussard at the Ricordi Archives, Milan; Dr Giampiero Tintori at the Museo Teatrale alla Scala, Milan; Professor Corrado Mingardi at Busseto; Professor A. Giovanni Da Pozzo of the Boito Institute at the University of Padua; Dr Giovanni Bergonzi in Parma; Dr Stefano Zamboni at the Conservatorio Arrigo Boito in Parma; Dr Martin Chusid at the American Institute for Verdi Studies, New York, and the staffs at the Indiana University libraries, the Bibliothèque Nationale and the Bibliothèque de l'Opéra in Paris, the Conservatory in Bologna, the Library of Congress in Washington, DC, and the Arturo Toscanini Collection of the New York Public Library.

I am especially obliged to Dr John Cullars and Donald Wilson, who have steadfastedly assisted my research, translations, and writing; in addition, Brian Hart has come to the rescue during the final proofing. I also thank Martial Singher, a prominent successor to Victor Maurel's Jago at the Paris Opéra, and his wife, my sister Eta, for their advice concerning French texts and biographical investigations in France; Giuliana Busch for interpreting several enigmatic Italian expressions; Giovanni Bria for transcribing the musical examples that appear intermittently in the correspondence, and two distinguished Verdi historians, George Martin and Dr Mary Jane Phillips Matz, for contributing their scholarship to these pages, as well as the ninety-year-old Mieczysław Horszowski for his vivid reminiscences of Arrigo Boito, whose friendship he cherished as a young pianist from Poland in Milan.

Giulio Ricordi's Production Book for *Simon Boccanegra* was translated by Giuliana Busch, his Production Book for *Otello* by Dr Michael Pisoni. Giuliana Busch, Martial and Eta Singher, Dr John Cullars, and Donald Wilson provided literal translations of Victor Maurel's French Production Book for *Otello*, which was then freely adapted by Dr Mimi Rudulph. I am responsible for the final editing and all other translations in this book.

I should also express appreciation for the varied published works of Verdi scholarship which have enlightened and reinforced my research. In particular

I would like to record my respect for Gaetano Cesari, Alessandro Luzio, Carlo Gatti, Piero Nardi, Frank Walker, Julian Budden, Mario Medici, Marcello Conati, Marisa Casati, Andrew Porter, and William Weaver.

To three distinguished lawyers, my late friend Alfredo Amman, Giorgio Jarach, and Dr Ferdinand Sieger, I am grateful for clear and definite answers to complex international copyright questions which were confirmed by the appropriate Italian agency, the Società Italiana degli Autori ed Editori in Rome.

For permission to reproduce illustrations, I thank the Museo Teatrale alla Scala, Milan, and the Bibliothèque de l'Opéra, Paris.

To the Delegates and staff of the Oxford University Press, I offer my thanks, for the honour of appearing under the OUP imprint, and for appointing Hilary Walford, the ideal copy-editor. No words can tell how grateful I feel for her infinite patience and splendid advice.

Beyond her unflinching encouragement and faith in my research, Dr Mimi Rudulph became my most active and dedicated collaborator. Alas, she did not live to see the ultimate result of our labour, but will be assured forever of my gratitude.

CONTENTS

LIST OF ILLUSTRATIONS

ABBREVIATIONS

Abbreviations used in the List of Letters and Telegrams

AUTOGRAPH LOCATIONS

AC	Accademia Nazionale dei Lincei, Rome
Br.	Biblioteca Nazionale Braidense, Milan
Bo.	Conservatorio di Musica 'G. B. Martini', Bologna
Bus.	Biblioteca della Cassa di Risparmio e Monte di Credito su Pegno, Busseto
Ch.	Collezione Enrico Olmo, Chiari
HA	Historisches Archiv, Cologne
IP	Istituto di Studi Verdiani, Parma
Op.	Bibliothèque de l'Opéra, Paris
Pa.	Biblioteca Palatina, Parma
Ri.	Archivio Ricordi, Milan
SA	Collezione Carrara Verdi, St Agata
Sc.	Museo Teatrale alla Scala, Milan
To.	Arturo Toscanini Collection, New York Public Library

PUBLISHED SOURCES

Abb.	Abbiati, Franco, *Giuseppe Verdi* (4 vols.; Milan: G. Ricordi, 1959)
Al.	*Verdi intimo: Carteggio di Giuseppe Verdi con il Conte Opprandino Arrivabene (1861–1886),* ed. Annibale Alberti (Milan: A. Mondadori, 1931)
As.	Ascoli, Arturo di (ed.), *Quartetto milanese ottocentesco* (Rome: Archivi Edizioni, 1974)
Cart.	*Carteggi Verdiani,* ed. Alessandro Luzio (vols. i and ii: Rome: Reale Accademia d'Italia, 1935; vols. iii and iv: Rome: Accademia Nazionale dei Lincei, 1947)
Cart. V–B	*Carteggio Verdi-Boito,* ed. Mario Medici e Marcello Conati con la collaborazione di Marisa Casati (2 vols.; Parma: Istituto di Studi Verdiani, 1978)
Cop.	*I copialettere di Giuseppe Verdi,* ed. Gaetano Cesari and Alessandro Luzio (Milan: Comune di Milano, 1913)
De R.	*Franco Faccio e Verdi: Carteggi e documenti inediti,* ed. Raffaello De Rensis (Milan: Fratelli Treves, 1934)
Ga.	Gatti, Carlo, *Verdi nelle immagini* (Milan: Garzanti, 1941)
Mor.	*Verdi: Lettere inedite,* ed. Giuseppe Morazzoni (Milan: La Scala e il Museo Teatrale e Libreria Editrice Milanese, 1929)
Nar.	Nardi, Piero, *Vita di Arrigo Boito* (Verona: A. Mondadori, 1942)
Oth.	*Othello* piano-vocal score (London: G. Ricordi & Co.)
Wa.	Walker, Frank, *The Man Verdi* (London: J. M. Dent & Sons, 1962; University of Chicago Press, 1982)
We.	Weaver, William, *Verdi: A Documentary Study* (London: Thames and Hudson, 1977)

xx

Abbreviations

Abbreviations used in the footnotes

AUTOGRAPH LOCATIONS

Braidense   Biblioteca Nazionale Braidense, Milan
Chiari   Collezione Enrico Olmo, Chiari
Istituto Par-   Istituto di Studi Verdiani, Parma
ma
Palatina   Biblioteca Palatina, Parma
Paris Opéra   Bibliothèque de l'Opéra, Paris
Ricordi   Archivio Ricordi, Milan
Scala   Museo Teatrale alla Scala, Milan
St Agata   Collezione Carrara Verdi, St Agata

PUBLISHED WORKS

Abbiati   Abbiati, Franco, *Giuseppe Verdi* (4 vols.; Milan: G. Ricordi, 1959)
Adami   Adami, Giuseppe, *Giulio Ricordi e i suoi musicisti* (Milan: Fratelli Treves, 1933)
Alberti   *Verdi intimo: Carteggio di Giuseppe Verdi con il Conte Opprandino Arrivabene (1861–1886)*, ed. Annibale Alberti (Milan: A. Mondadori, 1931)
Ascoli   Ascoli, Arturo di (ed.), *Quartetto milanese ottocentesco* (Rome: Archivi Edizioni, 1974)
Busch, *Aida*   Busch, Hans (ed. and trans.), *Verdi's Aida: The History of an Opera in Letters and Documents* (Minneapolis: University of Minnesota Press, 1978)
Carteggi   *Carteggi Verdiani*, ed. Alessandro Luzio (vols. i and ii: Rome: Reale Accademia d'Italia, 1935; vols. iii and iv: Rome: Accademia Nazionale dei Lincei, 1947)
Carteggio   *Carteggio Verdi-Boito*, ed. Mario Medici e Marcello Conati con la collaborazione di Marisa Casati (2 vols.; Parma: Istituto di Studi Verdiani, 1978)
Copialettere   *I copialettere di Giuseppe Verdi*, ed. Gaetano Cesari and Alessandro Luzio (Milan: Comune di Milano, 1913)
Depanis   Depanis, Giuseppe, *I concerti popolari ed il Teatro Regio di Torino: Quindici anni di vita musicale: Appunti-Ricordi* (2 vols.; Turin: STEN, 1915)
De Rensis, *Faccio e Verdi*   *Franco Faccio e Verdi: Carteggi e documenti inediti*, ed. Raffaello De Rensis (Milan: Fratelli Treves, 1934)
De Rensis, *Lettere di Boito*   *Lettere di Arrigo Boito*, ed. Raffaello De Rensis (Rome: Società Editrice di 'Novissima', 1932)
Hanslick, *Aus dem Opernleben*   Hanslick, Eduard, *Die moderne Oper*, iii. *Aus dem Opernleben der Gegenwart* (Berlin: Allgemeiner Verein für Deutsche Litteratur, 1884)
Hanslick, *Aus meinem Leben*   Hanslick, Eduard, *Aus meinem Leben* (2 vols.; Berlin: Allgemeiner Verein für Deutsche Litteratur, 1894, 1911)
Levi   Levi, Primo, *Domenico Morelli nella vita e nell'arte* (Rome and Turin: Casa Editrice Nazionale Roux e Viarengo, 1906)

Martin, *Verdi*   Martin, George, *Verdi: His Music, Life and Times* (New York: Dodd, Mead, 1963)

Maurel   Maurel, Victor, *Dix ans de carrière 1887–1897* (Paris: Imprimerie Paul Dupont, 1897; New York: Arno Press, 1977)

Nardi, *Vita di Boito*   Nardi, Piero, *Vita di Arrigo Boito* (Verona: A. Mondadori, 1942)

Nardi, *Scritti*   *Arrigo Boito: Tutti gli scritti*, ed. Piero Nardi (Verona: A. Mondadori, 1942)

Noske   Noske, Fritz, *The Signifier and the Signified: Studies in the Operas of Mozart and Verdi* (The Hague: Martinus Nijhoff, 1977)

Roosevelt   Roosevelt, Blanche, *Verdi: Milan and 'Othello'* (London: Ward and Downey, 1887)

Walker   Walker, Frank, *The Man Verdi* (London: J. M. Dent & Sons, 1962; University of Chicago Press, 1982)

Weinstock   Weinstock, Herbert, *Rossini* (New York: Alfred A. Knopf, 1968)

EDITORIAL GUIDE

List of Letters and Telegrams

The List of Letters and Telegrams on pp. xli–lx gives details of the correspondence in this volume. The majority of the letters and telegrams were written in Italian; the few that were written in French are indicated by an asterisk (*). A telegram is indicated by a dagger (†). A reference to 'Ricordi' is always to Giulio Ricordi.

The destination of letters and telegrams is listed wherever possible, taken either from extant envelopes or from corroborative evidence in the correspondence or chronologies; a question mark indicates any doubt.

The correspondence is listed in chronological order. Brackets indicate that details in the dates have been supplied, a question mark that there is still some doubt.

The location of the original autographs is given when known. Major existing publications are listed, even if incomplete; the abbreviations used are on pp. xix–xxi.

Letters and Telegrams

The letters and telegrams appear in chronological order. There is an indication below the first heading of any written originally in French, and of telegrams.

Places and dates are given at the head of each letter. Details which have been supplied are in brackets, with a question mark indicating any doubt. Such information has been taken from extant envelopes, and from the correspondence and chronologies; false dates appearing in other publications have been silently corrected; any special explanations are in footnotes.

Translations are from autographs wherever possible: this includes the Verdi–Boito correspondence; Verdi's, Boito's, Faccio's, and Muzio's letters to the House of Ricordi, which are in the publishers' archives in Milan; and Ricordi's letters, which are at St Agata.

When autographs were unavailable, translations originate mainly from Cesari's and Luzio's *I copialettere di Guiseppe Verdi* and Luzio's four-volume *Carteggi verdiani*. *I copialettere*, originally published, with the help of Boito, for the centenary of Verdi's birth, are based on letters Verdi drafted and copied in five simple copy-books, together with all kinds of financial annotations, additions, and subtractions scribbled in between the letters. These books, approximately 9½ inches long and 7 inches wide, together with five others of his wife, are kept at St Agata. Luzio's *Carteggi*, a major source of information are, unfortunately, out of print.

Translations of Verdi's telegrams to Boito are from Medici's, Conati's, and Casati's *Carteggio Verdi–Boito*. These telegrams were transcribed by Piero Nardi. Frank Walker left these transcriptions to the Istituto di Studi Verdiani, Parma, upon his premature death.

Translations have not been given for the many titles of operas, books, etc., which appear in their original languages. Phrases in languages other than Italian, and in dialect, have been left as in the original, to give some flavour of the letters as written. Translations have been provided in only a few instances, in which the text seemed particularly obscure. Quotations of libretto have been translated, following the Italian text as closely as possible.

The translations of letters aim to adhere to the original style of the writers: Verdi direct and unaffected; Boito diffident at first, but increasingly confident; Ricordi long-winded and verbose.

Unfortunately, subtle yet important nuances in the Italian forms of address—the formal 'Lei', the more personal 'Voi', the intimate 'tu'—cannot be rendered in English. In Verdi's letters, the old friend Tito Ricordi is addressed as 'tu', but Giulio Ricordi as 'Voi'; the formal 'Lei' to Boito changes to 'Voi' after Boito's 'ravioli' letter of 21 January 1884. Both Boito and Ricordi always address Verdi as 'Lei'.

Verdi's scratchy handwriting is sometimes difficult, in rare instances impossible, to decipher. Dates are often abbreviated, and also salutations: for example, 'C. Giulio' for 'Caro Giulio', spelled out in these translations as 'Dear Giulio'. Greetings at the end of letters, including the usual 'addio', are frequently illegible, and have had to be guessed. But his signature, even to friends, is invariably 'G. Verdi'; and several letters, especially to strangers, are headed 'Busseto' rather than the nearby 'St Agata' where he lived from spring 1851.

In contrast, Boito's and Ricordi's letters are, with rare exceptions, easily legible. However, Boito seldom dates his letters completely, but he always signs his full name, except in a single letter of 25 July 1886.

Many of Ricordi's letters are too long to be quoted in full in this volume, and his Italianate nineteenth-century style needed simplifying in translation.

In presenting the letters, every effort has been made to follow the original text. Therefore, such matters as paragraph breaks, misspelling of names, idiosyncratic punctuation, and groups of dots and dashes are reproduced as they appear in the autographs. But rules indicating a break in the text are indicated by a line space.

Any emphasis in the original letter is indicated by italic type. Italics are also used if a foreign word or phrase is left untranslated. However, changes have been made to avoid ambiguity between titles of operas and plays and names of characters: titles are always in italics, names of characters in roman.

The distinction of different spellings in different languages has been maintained; thus the Italian *Otello* becomes *Othello* in the French translation; the French *Don Carlos* becomes *Don Carlo* in Italian. This is particularly relevant to distinguish, for example, between productions in France of the original Italian opera and of the French translation. References to Shakespeare's play are always to *Othello*; to his character, Othello.

There have been some problems translating some technical words. For example, Verdi uses the term '*stampati*', 'printed', to refer also to something which may be proofed, engraved, or typeset, but not actually printed. Such uses are translated according to the sense.

English spelling and terminology have been adopted throughout. So references are to producer, not stage director; to films, not movies.

There are some draft letters which have no signature. Any enclosures with the letters are set in small type immediately after the letters.

The letters contain many extracts of libretto, and these are quoted in the original Italian, with English translations. Except in a few cases where a literal translation appeared outlandish, the English text follows the original Italian as closely as possible. When space allows, these translations are set beside the original; where there is not enough room for two columns, they appear below the Italian. As elsewhere in the letters, the emphasis of the original has been maintained: if the libretto is underlined in the autograph, then the Italian and English translation are both printed in italic type; if the libretto is not underlined, the Italian and the English are both in roman type.

In transcribing the extracts from the libretto some conventions have been adopted for clarity: for example, characters' names are always in small capitals and followed by a full stop; stage directions are in parentheses; words or phrases which were ruled through in the autograph are indicated by double brackets.

Footnotes have been kept to a minimum: where possible information has been incorporated into documents, appendices, chronologies, or biographical notes. But footnotes are used for the following information: details of letters which are at present missing or unavailable; cross references to other letters (by name of correspondents and date; a reference to 'Ricordi' is always to Giulio Ricordi); cross references to other sections in this volume; references to Shakespeare's text; bibliographical details. There is a list of abbreviations on pp. xix–xxi for autograph locations and published works which appear frequently in the footnotes. Other works are cited in full at the first footnote in each section of the book, and thereafter are referred to by author's surname and a short title.

Documents and appendices

The documents and appendices collect together the original production books, reviews of first performances, and other relevant material to avoid an excessive number of footnotes.

The documents are all directly concerned with the two operas; they consist mainly of quoted text with brief introductions by the editor. The appendices contain rather more peripheral material, which, although not directly concerned with the two operas, yet sheds light on various aspects of the correspondence.

Quotations from the libretto are translated in the reviews. However, in the Production Books it was not thought necessary to translate the frequent references to the libretto.

In both the documents and the appendices, the editor's footnotes are indicated, as usual, by superior figures. Foonotes of the original author are indicated by asterisk, dagger, etc.

The Production Books do not follow the exact use of bold and italic type of the original. These are printed works, not autographs, and this volume seemed to offer the opportunity to correct a few errors and impose some consistency in the presentation of the books.

Victor Maurel's effusive writing, and to a lesser extent Camille Bellaigue's elaborate writing, required a freer translation than was needed for the letters and the other documents.

Biographical Notes

Biographical details on all correspondents and the vast majority of names mentioned in the introduction, letters, documents, appendices, and chronologies are gathered together in the Biographical Notes. All but the most well known are included: it was not thought necessary, for example, to provide details for Shakespeare, Mozart, or Boccaccio. The correspondents, and a few other important figures, are differentiated typographically: their names are in small capitals rather than italics; also places, as well as dates, of their birth and death are supplied. In some instances, places and dates are missing, having defied extensive and careful research. A very few biographical footnotes remain in the text, usually just one line on someone who appears only once in the whole volume.

Select Bibliography

In view of the enormous growth of Verdi literature internationally, the bibliography is very selective. Works by Boito and Verdi are given first, then editions of letters and correspondence, and finally a selection of works of reference and criticism.

INTRODUCTION

*It is in these wide spaces that certain men are destined to meet
and understand each other.*

Giuseppina Verdi to Giulio Ricordi, 7 November 1879

The history of *Otello* and of the revised *Simon Boccanegra* is rooted in
Giuseppe Verdi's encounter with Arrigo Boito, which evolved into an almost
unparalleled artistic union, but only after it had passed through a curious
sequence of preliminary stages: an initial contact, followed by a cautious
distance, and, in the end, a genuine accord, brought about by Giulio Ricordi.

Death had robbed Verdi of his wife and children at an early age. Boito's
father, an Italian painter, had abandoned his wife, a Polish countess, and
their two sons. In the shadow of such personal tragedies, the old composer
and his young librettist eventually grew as close as father and son, while their
dedication to Shakespeare united them in the spirit and the creation of lyric
drama.

They first met in Paris in 1862, when Verdi invited Boito to write the text to
his *Inno delle nazioni* on the occasion of the World Exhibition in London.
Verdi thanked his young poet with a gift, accompanied by these lines:

Paris, 29 March 1862

Grateful for the beautiful work you have done for me, I take the liberty of
offering you, as a token of my esteem, this modest watch. Accept it with your heart,
as I offer it to you from the heart. May it remind you of my name and of the value
of time.

Greetings to Faccio, and to both of you, glory and good fortune!

G. Verdi[1]

'The value of time'—a prophetic warning! The prudent Maestro had already
recognized a problem with which Boito was to struggle all his life: the timing
of his work, the dissipation of his talents through the frequent digressions
caused by his notorious generosity and his concern for others, which made it
difficult for him to focus on his own creativity. His selflessness, which was to
reach its peak in his later service to Verdi, bordered on self-denial. Forever
torn between music and literature, Boito felt he was an Italian of his native
Padua, yet he was strongly attracted to the North, to France, Poland, and
German romanticism. Caught between contrasting cultures, he was a 'rare
mélange de Latin et de Slave, de précision meridionale et de poésie du Nord'[2]
and one of the noblest and purest spirits of the whole romantic movement, in
fact the only true Romantic in Italian literature.[3] Under Wagner's spell,

---

[1] Autograph: Istituto Parma. Facsimile and transcription precede *Carteggio* i. 1. The
autograph of Boito's answer has been found at St Agata years ago, but still awaits first
publication by the Istituto in Parma.

[2] In a letter from Camille Bellaigue to Arrigo Boito, 15 Nov. 1904 (Autograph: Scala; Nardi,
Vita di Boito, p. 661).

[3] Benedetto Croce supposedly expressed this opinion. See Appendix IV.

Boito translated several of his works, but he felt ambivalent about the German master. 'Il faut méditerraniser la musique,' he said, quoting Nietzsche[4]—his home was the Mediterranean, and Dante as well as Bach, and Shakespeare were his heroes.

Boito's earliest poems were influenced by Baudelaire and by the *scapigliatura*,[5] a movement of writers, painters, and musicians in the 1860s in Milan, somewhat comparable to the French *Bohème*. The principal leaders of the group were Emilio Praga (1839–75), Giovanni Camerana (1845–1905), Igino Ugo Tarchetti (1830–69), Carlo Righetti (1830–74), Carlo Dossi (1849–1910), Giuseppe Rovani (1818–74), Antonio Ghislanzoni (1824–93), and Arrigo Boito. Under the pen-name Cletto Arrighi, Carlo Righetti described the *scapigliatura* as a kind of mystic association of eccentric geniuses. Disappointed by the erosion of the Risorgimento, the period of the liberation and unification of Italy in the nineteenth century, they attacked the bourgeoisie, frowned on the church and religion, indulged in sexual freedom, alcohol, and drugs. Deprived and impoverished, Camerana committed suicide; Praga became a victim of alcohol; Tarchetti died of consumption. Incapable of replacing the social and cultural institutions of their time with a concrete programme, the *scapigliati* longed for acceptance by a future society that favoured artistic genius.

Boito's *Libro dei versi* opens with *Dualismo*, in which the poet speaks of his own light and shadow. The fantasy tale *Re Orso* is rich in wit and irony, mad puns and whimsical rhymes that foreshadow *Otello* and *Falstaff*. Boito was intrigued by 'le génie du mal' as it appeared in the figures of Mephistopheles, Nero, Iago, and Barnaba, the villain in *La gioconda*. The eternal battle between Good and Evil is the dominant theme of his bold opera *Mefistofele*, based on both parts of Goethe's *Faust*, of *Nerone*, involving the conflict of decadent paganism and dawning Christianity, and of *Otello*, whose original title was *Jago*.

Mefistofele was a resounding fiasco when first performed at La Scala in 1868. Boito destroyed most of the score, then revised and shortened it by an entire act. He rewrote the baritone part of Faust for a tenor and inserted a duet from his sketch for *Ero e Leandro*, another opera that he never finished. In 1875 the new *Mefistofele* was enthusiastically applauded by the avantgarde in Bologna. A year later Boito enriched the score for Venice with Margherita's final scene, and it is in this version that the opera continues to be performed throughout the world.

The unfinished manuscript of *Nerone*, preserved in the Ricordi Archives, testifies to the torment Boito endured behind the closed curtains of his apartment in Milan, a torment that ended only with his death. His merciless self-criticism and anguished doubts recall Verdi's comment to Domenico Morelli, 'In the arts too much (I say too much) reflection stifles inspiration.'[6]

---

[4] From Friedrich Nietzsche (1844–1900), *Der Fall Wagner*, in a letter to Camille Bellaigue in late April 1894 (Autograph: Scala; De Rensis, *Lettere di Boito*, p. 316). Nietzsche wrote these words in French.

[5] Italian for loose-living, dissoluteness, profligacy.

[6] 28 Mar. 1884.

No psychologist, however, could have analysed Boito's complex nature more keenly than Giuseppina Verdi did in her letter to Giulio Ricordi of 7 November 1879. Aware of his own weaknesses, Boito himself wrote in 1902 to Eugenio Tornaghi, the secretary of the House of Ricordi:

> We don't have to regret the slowness of my work, and even less to deplore it, for even if it is slow, it is incessant and entirely directed to the goal shown me by my artistic and personal conscience. If I had a great deal more talent than I have, I would study less and work faster; if I were a bit more of an animal, I would study less and work faster; but I can only work with the brain that God has given me and in the manner that my brain allows. [. . .][7]

The obsessive working habits of this highly intellectual artist were in no way due to the lack of either emotional response or temperament. Once, in Naples, when his challenge to a duel was refused, Boito flew into a rage, smashing the furniture in his hotel room. This was far from being his only such outburst, although in all likelihood it was the worst. For the most part, Boito was uncommonly amiable in his behaviour, and his air of aristocratic elegance was quite in keeping with his nature, as was his impressive height. The restless Eleonora Duse found peace with him, while he himself was torn by inner strife. After their separation, in 1898, he became increasingly drawn to his friends and acquaintances, among them several French and Italian writers whose prominence continued beyond their own era. His beloved brother Camillo, also a man of genius, became a widower in the same year. Having protected and supported the younger Arrigo in his early days, Camillo lived in the same building as his brother—in Milan's Principe Amedeo No. 1—until he died, four years earlier, in 1914. A bachelor throughout his life, the ageing Arrigo Boito found warmth and harmony, along with enlightening discourse, amid the families of Camille Bellaigue and Paul Dubois. In the peace of Verdi's St Agata he felt at home.

Upon Boito's death, in 1918, his one-time protégé Ferruccio Busoni, who had much in common with his mentor, expressed these sad and honest thoughts:

> Now he is gone, without ever seeing his *Nero* come to life on the stage. Even on his deathbed, it is said, he was still announcing his intention of seeing to certain changes in the score. [. . .] His sense of responsibility for his promised *Nero* grew and grew until it had become an enormous burden upon his shoulders, like back-payments that are accumulating interest. After twenty years of shouldering this burden he found that tastes and tendencies in art had changed. [. . .] In the interim, renowned composers had grown to maturity and were producing success after success.
>
> Boito, who once had a strong thirst for the new, had slowly turned his back on the present and faced the past. Always in a state of inner torment, always trying to come to terms with himself, he made change after change in the work. He was mature now, and he had left the young Boito behind. The craftsmanship of the first act that he once wrote could no longer satisfy him; the younger generation of composers had outstripped him. He studied Johann Sebastian Bach, the last

---

[7] 11 May 1902 (Autograph: Ricordi; De Rensis, *Lettere di Boito*, p. 99).

quartets of Beethoven. But he would sooner remain an Italian, so it was with good reason that he placed himself in the service of the patriarch Verdi. He wanted to be part of the consummation of Italian opera. His subconscious wish was clearly to play the trump card on Richard Wagner no less than to set an example for the 'new breed' and let them see just how small they were. He rewrote his work again and again, while the time for its première drew ominously closer. On one or two occasions a firm date was set, and widely publicized. [...] At the last moment the performance was cancelled, Boito withdrew his score—if he ever submitted it at all—and began his 'revision' all over agian. [...] Whenever I visited Boito in the last fifteen years, he was 'just then' busy putting the finishing touches on the score. But to return to the here and now: how is one ever to find a rational explanation for what is highly irrational in this artist's life? What, in the end, was the cause of Boito's colossal problems? [...][8]

Arturo Toscanini, who kept night-time vigil at Boito's coffin, related eleven years afterwards:

Poor Boito! Long before he died, he announced to me on several occasions the completion of *Nerone* and expressed the hope that it might be performed at La Scala under my direction. But each time, there were delays—his dissatisfaction was by now legendary—with scenes and entire acts either modified or completely rewritten. When he died, the entire opera was found sketched out in a piano score,[9] although the orchestration was incomplete. Boito's annotations were numerous and precise enough, however, to allow the orchestration to be completed in full accord with his intentions. Maestro Tommasini and I undertook this task with the greatest care. How strange, how utterly amazing that the mind of this unforget-table artist suffered so much self-inflicted torment! Boito's notes concerning the harmony and orchestration were exactly right, because his tonal intuition almost never abandoned him. But when it came to giving actual shape to his ideas, to realizing his intentions fully, he shied away from his intuition and could not bring himself to achieve the effects he had aimed for. Thus the feelings of doubt, the periods of depression, the reams of paper that ended up in the wastebasket—and the endless postponements. [...][10]

On 1 May 1924 Toscanini gave the première of his late friend's monumen-tal *Nerone* at La Scala. It was a critical success only, and not even Toscanini's loyal and stubborn support was enough to keep it in the repertoire. Boito the composer was defeated in the end, but his greatness as Verdi's poet remains for the ages.

We owe Verdi's collaboration with Boito to Giulio Ricordi and Giuseppina Verdi. On her advice, Ricordi pursued this goal with perseverance and diplomacy against perilous odds. On 31 July 1863 Verdi had expressed his concern for the young Boito and his friend Faccio to Clara Maffei:

In Paris last year I often saw Boito and Faccio. Certainly they are two very gifted young men, but I cannot say anything about their musical talent, since I have never

[8] *Neue Zürcher Zeitung*, 18 June 1918.
[9] According to Julian Budden, Boito had sketched only four of the five acts and his manuscript was in an appalling state of confusion.
[10] Interview in *il giornale d'Italia*, 18 Dec. 1929.

heard anything by Boito, and only a few things by Faccio, which he let me hear one day. Besides, since Faccio is having an opera performed, the audience will pronounce judgement. These two young men are accused of being ardent admirers of Vagner [*sic*]. There is nothing wrong with that, as long as their admiration doesn't degenerate into imitation. Vagner is made, and it's useless to remake him.

Vagner is no ferocious beast, as the purists claim, nor a prophet, as his apostles claim. He is a man of great genius, who likes rough roads because he cannot find easy and more direct ones. The young must not fool themselves; there are so many who make believe that they have wings, because really they have no legs to stand on. [. . .][11]

Three months after this warning Faccio's *I profughi fiamminghi* had a successful première at La Scala, and Boito saw fit to recite an exuberant poem he had conceived for the occasion, an *Ode all'arte italiana*. It contained this bow to Faccio: 'Forse già nacque chi sovra l'altare / Rizzerà l'arte, verecondo e puro, / Su quell'altar bruttato come un muro / Di lupanare.' ['Perhaps the one has already been born who will revive true and pure art on its altar, which is soiled like the wall of a brothel.'] Understandably, Verdi wondered whether the young poet, in his outburst of *Sturm und Drang*, was including the twenty-four operas he had created by then. Thus he wrote to Tito Ricordi: 'If among others I, too, have soiled the altar, as Boito says, let him clean it, and I will be the first to light a little candle.'[12] About one month later, on 13 December 1863, Verdi commented on the same affair to Clara Maffei:

> I know that there has been a lot of talk about this [Faccio's] opera, too much, I believe; I have read a few newspaper articles where I found big words about *art, aesthetics, revelations*, the *past*, the *future*, etc., etc., and I confess that (ignorant as I am!) I haven't understood a thing. On the other hand, I neither know Faccio's talent nor his opera; and I don't want to know it, either, since I don't want to discuss it or give a judgement of it, a thing I detest, because it's one of the most useless ones in this world. *Discussions* don't persuade anyone; *judgements* are in most cases wrong. If Faccio has found new ways, after all, as his friends say, if Faccio is destined to raise art on the altar that is now as ugly *as the wall of a brothel*, so much the better for him and the public. If he is *led astray*, as others say, let him find the right way, if he believes in it and it seems so to him. [. . .][13]

While Faccio, encouraged by Clara Maffei, had respectfully reported the success of his opera to Verdi along with Boito's greetings, Boito himself remained silent. Reviews that he wrote in early 1864, however, prove that— critical as he was—he never counted Verdi among the artists who had 'soiled the altar' in his thoughtless ode:

> *Lombardi* is an opera that no longer holds up too bravely and securely.
> Time has put its first layer of dust on it; Verdi's later discoveries, and also those of others, have revealed to the public the existence of a more serious, a more accomplished, a more truthful art.

---

[11] Autograph: Braidense; *Carteggi* iv. 83; Ascoli, p. 131.

[12] Presumably St Agata, Nov. 1863 (Autograph: Ricordi; Carlo Gatti, *Verdi* (2 vols.; rev. edn., 1981), ii. 101).

[13] Autograph: Braidense; Gatti, *Verdi*, ii. 101–3. Ascoli, pp. 136–8.

Certainly there are marvellous traces of eternal beauty here and there, but on the whole, the *Lombardi* has aged and become a bit gray. [. . .]

'One must squint,' Verdi said when writing the *Lombardi.* 'One must squint, looking with one eye at the public, with the other at art.' This was a bold statement at that time, for there were many looking with both eyes at the public, which is pernicious to the eyesight, and a little bit also to art. [. . .] Therefore the *Lombardi* has aged, while *Rigoletto* is still young. [. . .][14]

On the evening of St Stephen, Milan reversed the severe judgement it had given this opera [*Un ballo in maschera*] two years ago. The audience corrected its error and warmly applauded the same music of which it had previously disapproved. This is art's eventful story: it is full of these errors and these repentances. [. . .][15]

Even though on the whole somewhat colourless, this opera [*I vespri siciliani*] is admirable in its details; it has the most exquisite harmonic and rhythmic elegance, which is not too frequent in the other operas of the great composer. [. . .]

To list all the tender and robust qualities of this solemn opera would lead too far, for one would then have to dwell on every single one in admiration. [. . .][16]

Four years after Boito had written these reviews, the situation was the exact opposite, as Giulio Ricordi published his critical comments on the disastrous première of *Mefistofele*:

Since our friendship is a deep and sincere one, I can in all candour tell him [Boito] to his face: 'You may be a poet and a distinguished man of letters, but you will never be a composer of theatre works.' [. . .][17]

Despite the successful revision of *Mefistofele*, Ricordi had put his finger on Boito's great weakness. But he was also well aware of Verdi's dissatisfaction with most of the librettists of his 'galley years'. He knew, too, that Verdi, having grown financially independent, was no longer compelled to write operas and could afford to make increasing demands on a librettist. As early as 1853 the composer had confided to his friend Cesare De Sanctis that he wanted

nothing more than to find a good libretto and along with it a good poet (and we need one so badly!); but I cannot hide from you that I read the libretti that are sent to me with great reluctance. It is impossible, or almost impossible, for another man to sense what I want. I want subjects that are *new, great, beautiful, different, bold . . .* and bold to the core . . . with *new forms* that are *novel*, and so on and on— yet at the same time suitable for music. [. . .][18]

While writing *Aida* in 1870 and 1871 Verdi became fascinated with the very subject of Boito's tragic obsession, and Giulio Ricordi informed him that

Boito would consider himself the *most fortunate*, the *most blissfully happy* of men if he could write the libretto of *Nerone* for you; he would gladly give up the idea at

[14] Nardi, *Scritti*, pp. 1094–5.

[15] Ibid., p. 1095.

[16] Ibid., p. 1119.

[17] *La gazzetta musicale*, 9 Mar. 1868. Quoted in full in Julian Budden, *The Operas of Verdi* (3 vols.; London: Cassell; New York: Oxford University Press, 1973–81), iii.296, where a slightly different interpretation is offered.

[18] Rome, 1 Jan. 1853 (Autograph: Accademia Nazionale dei Lincei, Rome; *Carteggio* i. 16).

once of composing the music himself. [. . .] Boito maintains that there has never been a subject so great, so beautiful and so well suited to Verdi's genius as *Nerone*. [. . .][19]

'I need not repeat how much I love this subject,' Verdi replied, 'nor do I have to add how much I would enjoy working with a young poet whose enormous talent I admired so deeply in his recent *Amleto*.'[20]

How much easier Boito's existence might have been, if Verdi had set 'the instrument of his torture'[21] to music! It was not in the stars, but Giulio did not waver in his determination to unite the gruff, crusty, yet kindly farmer of St Agata, 'one of the most virile characters ever to appear in the history of art',[22] with the polished, highly literate intellectual. In the spring of 1878 Ricordi sent Verdi the revised *Mefistofele* score and received this acknowledgement:

> Paris, 1 June [1876]

> Dear Giulio,
>   You who have sent me *Mefistofele*:
>   Thank my 'one-time poet' for still remembering me for a moment.
>   Addio and believe me.

>> Yours,
>> G. Verdi[23]

Two letters to Opprandno Arrivabene[24] give testimony to Verdi's unceasing interest in Boito, but also reveal some reservations:

> Genoa, 21 March 1877

> [. . .] Certainly you will tell me honestly about *Mefistofele!*[25] At this time it's difficult to say whether Boito can give Italy masterpieces. He has a great deal of talent, aspires to originality, but the result is rather strange. He lacks spontaneity and he lacks impulse: great musical qualities. With these tendencies one can more or less succeed in a strange and theatrical subject like *Mefistofele*, but less so in *Nerone!* [. . .]

> Genoa, 30 March 1879

> [. . .] You speak to me of music, but by my word of honour, it seems to me that I have almost forgotten it; a proof of this is that a few nights ago I went to hear *Mefistofele*,[26] and I understood everything in the wrong way.

[19] Milan, 26 Jan. 1871 (Autograph: St Agata; *Carteggio* i, p. xxvi).

[20] Genoa, 28 Jan. 1871 (Autograph: Ricordi; *Carteggio* i, p. xxvi).

[21] Boito's reference to *Nerone* in a letter to Camille Bellaigue from Sirimone, 5 Jan. 1902 (Autograph: Scala; De Rensis, *Lettere di Boito*, p. 333).

[22] Paul Bekker, *The Changing Opera*, trans. Aurthur Mendel (New York: W. W. Norton, 1935), p. 193.

[23] Autograph: Ricordi. (In the Ricordi Archives and in Abbiati, iv. 82, this letter is listed 1 June 1879 instead of 1876. Verdi's dating can easily be misread, but he was not in Paris at that time and obviously received the piano–vocal score following *Mefistofele*'s successful revision in 1875. Preserved at St Agata, this score is inscribed 'To Giuseppe Verdi, the master of us all, from his one-time poet as a token of deep veneration. Arrigo Boito.')

[24] Alberti, pp. 201 and 226.

[25] After the first performance of this opera on 4 Apr. 1877 in Rome. See also Arrivabene to Verdi, 26 Mar. 1882, n. 2, and Appendix IV.

[26] In Genoa.

For example: I had always heard and read that the Prologue *in Heaven* was a perfect whole, and of genius . . . but when I heard the harmonies of this time piece, based on dissonances almost all the time, it seemed to me that I was . . . certainly not in *Heaven*. [. . .]

Only a few months after this appraisal, the composer of *Mefistofele* submitted the first draft of his libretto for *Otello* to Verdi, seventeen years after their first encounter in Paris.

Giulio Ricordi persuaded Verdi to conduct his *Requiem* at a benefit concert held for victims of floods in northern Italy on 29 June 1879 in Milan. On that occasion, during a memorable dinner with Verdi and his wife, he and Faccio raised the question of creating an *Otello*.[27] The Maestro's lingering reluctance to commit himself to the 'chocolate' (the nickname they gave to the opera about the tragic Moor of Venice) pervades much of the subsequent correspondence. Meanwhile, in the spring 1880, Verdi conducted a triumphant *Aida* at the Paris Opéra. Yet his letters to Domenico Morelli and those of Emanuele Muzio to Giulio Ricordi during this period show to what extent the characters of Otello and Jago, unbeknownst to others, had begun to germinate and take shape in Verdi's mind. Shortly after he returned from Paris, in April 1880, his 'Pater noster' and 'Ave Maria' were performed at La Scala.

Giulio's dream of *Otello* seemed thwarted. Apart from all idealistic considerations, the publisher was in need of cash; in lucrative terms, these sacred pieces did not suffice. For years he had tried in vain to have Verdi revise *Simon Boccanegra* (1857), whose première, in the composer's own words, had been 'almost as great a fiasco as that of *Traviata*'.[28] Verdi refused to accommodate Giulio, and this appeared to be his final reply:

St Agata, 2 May 1879

[. . .] Yesterday I received a large package which, I assume, contains a score of *Simone*! If you come to St Agata in six months, a year, or two or three, you will find it unopened, just as you sent it to me. I told you in Genoa that I detest things that are useless. It's true that I have done nothing else in my life, but there were extenuating circumstances in the past. There would be nothing more useless to the theatre at this time than one of my operas . . . And then, and then, it's better to end with *Aida* and the Mass than with a *rehash*. [. . .][29]

Giulio Ricordi did not subscribe to this view, but he abandoned *Simon Boccanegra* and, four weeks later, again brought up *Otello*. When, still in the summer of the following year, Verdi put the Moor aside, Ricordi once more urged him to revise *Boccanegra*. It seems doubtful that this revival was just La Scala's idea, as Giulio claimed in his letter of 19 November 1880. Whatever the case might have been, his persistent diplomacy furthered the development of one of Verdi's most noble works.

---

[27] See Verdi to Ricordi, 4 Sept. 1879, and Giuseppina Verdi to Giuseppina Negroni Prati Morosini, 18 Dec. 1879.

[28] Remark in a letter to Clara Maffei of 25 Mar. 1857 (Autograph: Braidense; Ascoli, p. 109).

[29] Autograph: Ricordi; Abbiati, iv. 82; *Carteggio* ii. 289.

The original version of *Simon Boccanegra* had suffered an unfortunate history. At that time Francesco Maria Piave, who was to write the text, resided in Venice, while Verdi was staying in a suburb of Paris, from where he wrote:

Enghien, 3 September 1856

Dear Piave,

What good can it do to finish the Simon Boccanegra story before the end of this month? Don't the police [i.e. the censors] and the presidency [of the theatre] have a detailed enough programme? It's not merely a programme, but a totally completed drama. Not one word or idea in the libretto will be changed. What does it matter whether, for now, it's in prose or in verse? And as you have so well observed, there is something original in this Simone. Thus the style of the libretto and the various pieces, etc., etc., must be as original as can be. This cannot be done unless we're together; therefore it would now be time wasted.

Tell Torniello,[30] our friend Torniello, that he should calm down and leave us alone, since we can handle our business quite well; and that, if he wants something to do, to look for it elsewhere. Let him think about the scenery and the costumes. Oh, the scenery could be so beautiful in this Simone! In three [scenes] especially, a painter should and could do very well. But the sets should have double and triple drops, and the *platforms* should not be stools like those in *Guglielmo Tell*,[31] but real *platforms*. And as for the costumes . . . . Enough! . . . Enough. [. . .]

PS Prepare yourself for St Agata and plan to stay there until Boccanegra is finished.[32]

Only by mid-January 1857 was Verdi able to return to St Agata, but Piave did not appear. Meanwhile, before leaving Paris, the composer had been compelled to look for another writer. He found him in Giuseppe Montanelli,[33] an exiled Tuscan poet living in Paris, and Piave received the following undated letter from St Agata, presumably in late January or early February 1857:

[. . .] Here you have the shortened and reduced libretto more or less the way it must be. As I told you in one of my letters, you may put your name to it or not. If you regret what has happened, I regret it, too, and perhaps more so than you, but I can only tell you that 'it was a necessity'.

I am dragging myself along as well as possible. Thanks to my good intentions I am pulling ahead, and the opera would already be finished if my stomach would let me work when I want to. In any case I hope that *Simone* will be performed on the 7th! . . .

Take great care over the sets. The directions are exact enough; in spite of this I will allow myself a few observations. In the first scene, the Fieschi Palace, if it's on the side, must be clearly visible to the entire audience, since everybody must see Simone entering the house, going to the balcony, and taking down the little lantern; I think I have obtained a musical effect [here], which I don't want to lose on

---

[30] Tornielli, president of the Teatro Fenice in Venice.
[31] Opera in 5 acts by Rossini.
[32] Autograph: Scala; Abbiati, ii. 371–2.
[33] See Frank Walker, 'Verdi, Giuseppe Montanelli and the Libretto of *Simon Boccanegra*', *Bollettino quadrimestrale dell'Istituto di Studi Verdiani*, 1. 3 (1960), 1767–89.

account of the set. Furthermore, in front of the Church of San Lorenzo I would like to see a little staircase, a real one with 3 or 4 steps, with some columns, which would serve now Paolo, now Fiesco, etc., to lean on and to hide behind. This scene must have a deep background.

The Grimaldi Palace in the first act need not have a deep background. Instead of one window I would have several down to the ground, and a terrace; I would put in a second backdrop showing the moon, whose rays would shine on the sea; the sea would be a shimmering, slanted drop. If I were a painter, I would certainly make a beautiful, simple set with great effect.

I attach great importance to the scene in which the Doge orders Pietro to open the balconies; one must see the rich and broad illumination taking up a great deal of space, so that the lights can clearly be seen as they are gradually extinguished, one after the other, until at the Doge's death everything is in deep darkness.

It's a very effective moment, I believe, and Heaven help us if the scene is not well done. The first drop need not be very far in the background, but the second, the drop with the illumination, must be very far away. Addio, addio.

G. Verdi

PS Tomorrow I hope to receive your letters; if there is anything important I'll answer straightaway. Addio, addio.[34]

The ill-feeling between the old friends did not last. All the same, the première of *Simon Boccanegra*, in Venice on 12 March 1857, was a failure. The reaction to the libretto was hostile, and 'the music in general was considered so serious that it could not be judged at first hearing, so that the audience left the theatre undecided'.[35]

Shortly before the opera's next production, at Reggio Emilia in May, Verdi wrote to Tito Ricordi:

I am sending you a little change for the orchestra. In the Introduction, at the 6/8 tempo in F-sharp minor, at the 68th bar, I have changed the orchestration for the duration of ten bars in order to avoid a difficult passage for the cellos and violas; since these instruments are almost always *a pack of dogs* in our orchestras, it's better to change it straightaway in the score to avoid a messy performance. [. . .][36]

Under Verdi's personal supervision *Simon Boccanegra* fared better in Reggio Emilia, Naples, and Rome, but after twelve performances at La Scala in 1859, the opera disappeared from the repertoire.

At this time, during the rehearsals for *Un ballo in maschera* in Rome, Verdi wrote to Tito Ricordi, on 4 February 1859:

Boccanegra in Milan [on 24 January] had to be and has been. A *Boccanegra* without *Boccanegra*!![37] Cut off the head of a man, and then recognize him, if you can. You wonder about the 'improper behaviour of the audience?' It doesn't surprise me at all. They are always happy when they bring about a scandal! When I was 25 years old, I, too, had illusions, and believed in its courtesy; a year later, light

[34] Autograph: Scala; Abbiati, ii. 375.
[35] Marco Marcelliano Marcello (1820–65), librettist and music critic, in the Venetian journal *L'arte*, 18 Mar. 1857.
[36] Autograph: Ricordi.
[37] The role had been taken by Sebastiano Ronconi (c. 1814–1900), mediocre baritone, brother of the famous Giorgio Ronconi (1810–90), the first Nabucco.

dawned upon me, and I saw with whom I had to deal. I don't mean to condemn them; I admit their severe judgement, I accept their boos, as long as I don't owe them anything for their applause. We poor gypsies, charlatans, and whatever you wish, are forced to sell our efforts, our thoughts, our raptures for money—the audience, for three Lire, buys the right to boo or applaud us. Our destiny is to resign ourselves: that's all! And yet, in spite of what friends or enemies might say, *Boccanegra* is not inferior to many fortunate operas, since it probably calls for a more refined performance and an audience that wants to listen. A sad thing is the theatre!! [. . .][38]

Thereafter *Un ballo in maschera*, two versions of *La forza del destino*, the revision of *Macbeth, Don Carlos, Aida,* and the *Requiem* had all appeared. Why, then, did Verdi once more take up the ill-fated *Simon Boccanegra* so many years later, despite his doubts and perpetual reluctance? His letters suggest an answer. It seems that he was still fascinated by the greatness and tragedy of the hero and by the love between father and daughter, a theme that held very personal meaning for him and that occurs in so many of his operas. Moreover, he was no doubt intrigued by his favourite motives of honour[39] and patriotism, and also by the atmosphere of Genoa, the port city in which he felt at home.

The alterations to this opera, done with Boito's assistance, resulted in the most thorough revision that Verdi undertook of any of his works. He rewrote about one third of the score. As in the case of *Macbeth*, however, he had no time to compose a completely new opera, and—having *Otello* on his mind— he may even have lacked the interest. This would explain the mixture of styles in the second version of *Simon Boccanegra*. In any case, this further collaboration with Boito provided a crucial test for their later work.

Simón Bocanegra, like *El trovador*, was a Spanish play in a prologue and four acts by Antonio García Gutiérrez, who was fond of exchanging infants in their cradles, of placing characters in disguise, and of creating impossible situations that neither Piave nor Boito could make believable. In spite of Boito's help, the action became even less logical, and even more unclear, than it had been before. Still, an unnecessary scene change was eliminated in Act I, and the scene at the beginning of Act II was added in which Paolo pours the poison into the Doge's cup. Boito also improved a number of poor rhymes in the original text and injected into Paolo a substantial dose of Jago's satanic blood. But his most important contribution was the new finale of Act I in the Senate. He lacked enthusiasm, however, for repairing a text that was not his own (and which he described as 'a wobbly table'); his desire was rather to promote further the idea of collaborating on *Otello* with the Maestro, to whom he was becoming increasingly attached. Nevertheless, the letters clearly indicate that it was only sheer lack of time that prevented an even more thorough revision of *Simon Boccanegra*.

[38] *Copialettere*, pp. 556–7.

[39] See Guglielmo Barblan, 'Il sentimento dell'onore nella drammaturgia verdiana', in *Atti dell III° Congresso Internazionale di Studi Verdiani* (Parma: Istituto di Studi Verdiani, 1974), 2–13.

In view of Verdi's recurring interest in Schiller, the figure of Fiesco—also referred to as Fieschi—might have been inspired by Schiller's *Die Verschwörung des Fiesko zu Genua*. In the appendix to his Italian edition of Arthur Pougin's Verdi biography, Folchetto actually claimed that Verdi had planned to revise *Simon Boccanegra* after attending a performance of Schiller's drama in Cologne (in 1875).[40] But Verdi himself denied this assertion in a letter to Giuseppina Negroni Prati Morosini dated 1 August 1881:

> [. . .] What Folchetto says about the new *Boccanegra* is not true. I actually did hear *Fieschi* in German in Cologne, but it could not have suggested anything for the *Boccanegra* just performed at La Scala. This opera derives from a Spanish drama by Gutiérrez, and Boito has made the final changes. [. . .][41]

The original libretto differs considerably from the Gutiérrez play; the second one, discussed in the correspondence that follows, shows radical changes, although Simone Boccanegra's Spanish first name was kept. The action is based on a chapter from the turbulent history of the Italian Renaissance in which the people of the city-state of Genoa rebelled against the excesses of the aristocracy. From 1257 until 1262 Genoa was ruled by Guglielmo Boccanegra, a wealthy man of the people. As *capitano del popolo* he tried in vain to curb the power of the nobles. They banished him, and the struggle between people and nobility continued on and off for four years. The nobles ruled over the city-state until the event of Simone Boccanegra in 1339. As in Venice, the office of doge was originally established with the provision that he could not be an aristocrat. Coming from the rank-and-file of the people, Simone Boccanegra was elected the first Doge of the Republic of Genoa. He was no corsair as in the opera, although his brother Egidio fought daring battles at sea and destroyed African pirates who threatened the shores of the city.[42] In historical reality—even more so than in the opera—Simone Boccanegra was a powerful statesman and crafty politician, desiring peace not only between his fellow citizens but also between Genoa and all her Mediterranean neighbours. In the spirit of Petrarch he strove for an end to the civil wars and for the brotherhood of all Italy. Intrigues of his adversaries and even of his own people led to Boccanegra's abdication and a self-imposed, twelve-year exile in Pisa. In 1356 he returned to Genoa and ruled once more as doge until his death by poisoning in 1363.[43]

Five centuries later, with their common fatherland still in the heat of the struggle for unity and liberation, Verdi found himself moved by the character and fate of this noble patriot. Nineteenth-century Italian audiences, however, preferred the popular melodies and stirring rhythms in the equally confusing *Trovatore* to the rich, subtle, yet sombre orchestration of *Boccanegra*. Close as this work was to Verdi's heart, even after the successful première of its

[40] Presumably in May 1877, when he conducted the *Requiem* in that city.
[41] Autograph: Scala; *Copialettere*, p. 560 n.
[42] See Biographical Note on Egidio Boccanegra.
[43] See Appendix I.

revision on 24 March 1881 it seemed once more destined to oblivion. As in the case of *Macbeth*, the somewhat dark, gripping magic of this tragedy was discovered in Northern Europe and America only decades later. A number of enlightening papers on *Simon Boccanegra* read at the Fourth International Verdi Congress, held at Chicago in 1974, are still awaiting publication. For an appreciation of the complex differences between the two versions, the extensive comparative analyses by Frits Noske and Julian Budden are strongly recommended. These distinguished musicologists, on the other hand, consider Wolfgang Osthoff's study, *Die beiden 'Boccanegra'—Fassungen und der Beginn von Verdis Spätstil*, the most thorough work of its kind. Budden sums up the opera's ambiguity:

> The subject, the complex and often illogical plot, the preponderance of lower male voices, the comparative rarity of true bassi profondi such as are needed for Fiesco, and not least the heavy demands made on the acting ability of the singers ('In *Forza* the characters are ready made; in *Boccanegra* you have to make them')[44]—all these factors inevitably militate against its popularity. But it remains for the Verdian connoisseur a pearl of immeasurable price.[45]

Work on *Otello* resumed only after the rehabilitation of Boito's *Mefistofele* at La Scala on 25 May 1881, but, following Verdi's letter to his librettist of 27 August 1881, their dialogue in writing was interrupted for and entire year. Although *Otello* continued to be on Verdi's mind, he withdrew to his fields, entertained other thoughts, and engaged in various non-musical activities reflected in his correspondence. Due to unpropitious circumstances and the revision of *Don Carlos*, the writing of *Otello* extended over six years—far longer than any other of his operas. Depressed by the state of his country and of the Italian theatre in particular, while being financially independent, Verdi showed a greater reluctance than any other composer to compose and to have his works performed. He defended Italian music from Wagner's influence, yet he had more in common with him than has traditionally been acknowledged. The *Gesamtkunstwerk*, the total work of art, was also very much of Verdi's concern, and he praised Wagner's concept of the invisible orchestra. Boito contributed to Verdi's critical interest in his 'adversary', but it was their love of Shakespeare which united them.

Since his early youth Verdi, himself an avid reader, had been attracted to Shakespeare, although his interest was on a more intuitive level than that of Boito, the intellectual. The underlining and annotations that appear in Boito's volumes of François-Victor Hugo's French translations of Shakespeare[46] indicate intensive studies. Verdi valued his *Macbeth* more highly than any of his nine previous operas; and for many years he had attempted to compose *King Lear*. Boito's first libretto was *Hamlet*, and even after *Falstaff*

[44] See Verdi to Ricordi, 2 Dec. 1880.
[45] Julian Budden, *The Operas of Verdi* (3 vols.; London: Cassell; New York: Oxford University Press, 1973–81), ii. 334.
[46] Five of these volumes (iii, v, xi, xiii, xiv) are in the library of the Museo Teatrale alla Scala in Milan. (See Boito Chronology, 1911.) François-Victor Hugo (1828–73) was son of Victor Hugo (1802–85).

he began to write a *King Lear* for Verdi. Because of her husband's old age, however, Giuseppina Verdi dissuaded him from proceeding.[47] Neither the three complete libretti for *Lear* preserved at St Agata (one in Verdi's own handwriting) nor Boito's text have ever been set to music.

In the early nineteenth century Shakespeare was so little known in Italy that Verdi's *Macbeth*, which was premièred in Florence in 1874, preceded the first Italian performance of Shakespeare's play by several years. Verdi read Shakespeare in Italian and French translations that had been made under the influence of Germany's great Shakespeare tradition, which, inspired by Lessing, Wieland, Herder, Goethe, Schiller, and Schlegel, enlightened all of Europe during the early years of the nineteenth century. The Shakespeare lectures that August Wilhelm Schlegel gave in Vienna in 1808 appeared in Milan as early as 1817. In view of Verdi's broad literary interests, it seems quite probable that he was well acquainted with this publication. Two important Italian Shakespeare scholars, Giulio Carcano and Andrea Maffei, were among his closest friends. Carcano offered him a *Hamlet* libretto in 1850 and, between 1875 and 1882, published translations of all of Shakespeare's plays in Italian verse. Maffei, who had been educated in Munich, not only translated Schiller but also—with that poet's *Die Räuber* as his source—wrote the text to Verdi's *I masnadieri* and added verses to his *Macbeth*, which was based on Schiller's German version. The first Italian translation, in prose, of all of Shakespeare's works was by Carlo Rusconi and appeared in 1838; to this day these books remain in Verdi's library alongside Carcano's later translations. In fourteen of his thirty-seven volumes, Rusconi quotes from Schlegel's Vienna lectures. There is thus no doubt that Verdi read Shakespeare in the German romantic tradition.

Just how close Verdi was to Shakespeare—even though he consistently misspelled his name—is proved, by his protest against a Parisian review of *Macbeth* in 1865: 'That I do not know Shacpearce, that I do not understand and feel him—no, by God, no. He is one of my favourite poets, whose works I have held in my hands since early youth, and whom I read again and again.'[48] Verdi's letter to Boito of 8 May 1886 further verifies this sentiment, and reflects his precise and conscientious literary investigations. When Verdi, whose dramatic instinct failed him at no other time, for once lost his bearings (in his letter to Boito of 15 August 1880), the librettist's adherence to Shakespeare set him straight in the very first letter he dared to address to the Maestro (18 October 1880). The same Boito eliminated the entire first act of Shakespeare's *Othello*, borrowing only a few lines; his idea of replacing Shakespeare's long exposition with the unleashing of nature's elements at the height of the fiercest battle is as admirable as the compression of the tragedy into the shortest period of time. The 'Credo' he wrote for Jago was welcomed, in Verdi's words, 'in the true spirit of Shakespeare'.[49]

[47] Nardi, *Vita di Boito*, p. 594.
[48] In a letter from Verdi to his publisher and producer, Léon Escudier (1828–81) in Paris (*Carteggi* iv. 159).
[49] See Verdi to Boito, 3 May 1884.

The Maestro's incessant drive for ideal performances is clearly apparent in many of his letters even after the opening night of *Otello* at La Scala on 5 February 1887. Despite his distaste for the conventions of the Paris Opéra, with its traditional ballets, he wisely compromised and forced himself to research and write the required interpolation for the Paris première. He even made important changes in the finale of Act III, which caused him and Boito more concern than any other part of the opera.[50] The compact structure of the libretto presented a far more serious challenge than had *Don Carlos* and *Aida* with their great finales. In this ensemble, how could, and how can, one follow Jago's relentless intrigue, set as it is with so many contrasting thoughts and emotions? Verdi himself seems never to have been quite satisfied with the solution. His most unorthodox decision, in favour of the text,[51] should be of particular interest not only to conductors, but to producers, designers, and singers, as well.

A very human drama unfolds in these pages. It reveals the interplay of strongly contrasting personalities and the tact and diplomacy required in their common pursuit of a cherished goal. In this collection we are privileged to enter the workshop of the two craftsmen and their zealous partner; to marvel at their genius as well as at their infinite patience and attention to detail, and trace the development of *Otello* from its hesitant beginnings to a glorious culmination.

[50] See, *inter alia*, Verdi to Boito, 17 July 1886, as well as his letters to Ricordi of 3, 9, and 10 Feb. 1889 regarding a revival of *Otello* at La Scala on 19 Feb. For the first French production of *Othello* at the Paris Opéra on 12 Oct. 1894, Verdi revised the concerted finale of Act III as described by Julian Budden, *Operas*, iii. 399–413.

[51] See Verdi to Ricordi, 9 Feb. 1889, para. 4.

LIST OF LETTERS
AND TELEGRAMS

(PH) indicates a photocopy of an autograph; (FAC) indicates a facsimile of a letter; an asterisk (*) indicates that a letter was written in French; a dagger (†) indicates a telegram. For other abbreviations, see pp. xix–xxi.

From	To	Destination	Date	Autograph location	Published source
Verdi	Ricordi	Milan	18 July 79	Ri.	Abb. iv. 86
Ricordi	Verdi	St Agata	23 July 79	SA	
Boito	Tornaghi	Milan	[?] July 79	Ri.	*Cart. V–B* i, p. xxvii
Verdi	Hiller	Cologne	31 July 79	HA; IP (PH)	*Cart.* ii. 330–1; Abb. iv. 75–6
Boito	Tornaghi	Milan	24 Aug. [79]	Ri.	*Cart. V–B* i, p. xxvii
Verdi	Ricordi	Milan	4 Aug. [Sept.] 79	Ri.	*Cop.* 311; Abb. iv. 86–7; Wa. 474; We. 237; *Cart. V–B* i, p. xxvii
Ricordi	Verdi	St Agata	5 Sept. 79	SA	*Cart.* iv. 200–2; Abb. iv. 90–3; *Cart. V–B* i, p. xxviii
Verdi	Hiller	Cologne	8 Sept. 79	HA; IP (PH)	*Cart.* ii. 331
Ricordi	Verdi	St Agata	17 Sept. 79	SA	*Cart.* iv. 202; Abb. iv. 94
Boito	Tornaghi	Milan	[21 Sept. 79]	Ri.	*Cart. V–B* i, p. xxviii
Verdi	Ricordi	Milan	28 Sept. 79	Ri.	Abb. iv. 98–9
Ricordi	Verdi	St Agata	29 Sept. 79	SA	*Cart.* iv. 203; Abb. iv. 94–5
Verdi	Ricordi	Milan	4 Oct. 79	Ri.	
Ricordi	Verdi	St Agata	7 Oct. 79	SA	*Cart.* iv. 203; Abb. iv. 95
Boito	Ricordi	Milan	[7 Oct. 79]	Ri.	*Cart.* iv. 203; Abb. iv. 95–6; Wa. 475
Ricordi	Giuseppina Verdi	St Agata	4 Nov. 79	SA	
Giuseppina Verdi	Ricordi	Milan	7 Nov. 79	Ri.	Abb. iv. 113; Wa. 476; We. 237; *Cart. V–B* i, p. xxix
Ricordi	Giuseppina Verdi	St Agata	8 Nov. 79	SA	*Cart. V–B* i, p. xxix
Ricordi	Verdi	St Agata	13 Nov. 79	SA	
Verdi	Ricordi	Milan	18 Nov. 79	Ri.	*Cart. V–B* i, p. xxix
Verdi	Ricordi	Milan	[after 20 Nov. 79]	Ri.	
Giuseppina Verdi	Negroni Prati Morosini	Milan	18 Dec. 79	Sc.	*Cart.* ii. 47–8; *Cart. V–B* i, p. xxix

From	To	Destination	Date	Autograph location	Published source
Ricordi	Verdi	Genoa	19 Dec. 79	SA	
Giuseppina Verdi	C. De Sanctis	Naples	5 Jan. 80	AC; IP (PH)	*Cart.* i. 190–1
Ricordi	Verdi	Genoa	6 Jan. 80	SA	
Verdi	Morelli	Naples	6 Jan. 80	IP (PH)	*Cop.* 692–3
Verdi	Hiller	Cologne	7 Jan. 80	HA; IP (PH)	*Cart.* ii. 333–4
Verdi	Faccio	Milan	8 Jan. 80	?	De R. 224
Morelli	Verdi	Genoa	8 Jan. 80	?	*Cart.* i. 290–1
Verdi	Morelli	Naples	7 Feb. 80	IP (PH)	*Cop.* 693–4
Muzio	Ricordi	Milan	[25 Feb. 80]	Ri.	Abb. iv. 176
Muzio	Ricordi	Milan	[4 Mar. 80]	Ri.	Abb. iv. 176
Verdi	Morelli	Naples	19 Apr. 80	IP (PH)	*Cop.* 694
Verdi	Morelli	Naples	12 May 80	IP (PH)	*Cop.* 694
Ricordi	Boito	Monaco?	24 July 80	Ri.	Abb. iv. 169; *Cart. V–B* i, p. xxx
Boito	Tornaghi	Milan	[3 Aug. 80]	Ri.	
Boito	Tornaghi	Milan	[4–5? Aug. 80]	Ri.	
Ricordi	Giuseppina Verdi	St Agata	5 Aug. 80	SA	*Cart. V–B* i, p. xxxi
Boito	Ricordi	Milan	[? Aug. 80]	Ri.	
Verdi	Boito	Milan	15 Aug. 80	IP	Nar. 466–7; Abb. iv. 170; Wa. 477–8; We. 238–9; *Cart. V–B* i. 1–2
Hiller*	Verdi	St Agata	2 Sept. 80	SA	*Cart.* ii. 336–7
Boito	Giuseppina Verdi	St Agata	[4 Sept. 80]	SA	*Cart. V–B* i. 2–3
Boito	Ricordi	Milan?	[4 Sept. 80]	Ri.	*Cart. V–B* ii. 287
Giuseppina Verdi	Ricordi	Milan?	7 Sept. 80	Ri.	Abb. iv. 171; *Cart. V–B* ii. 288
Verdi	Hiller	Cologne	14 Sept. 80	HA IP (PH)	*Cart.* ii. 337
Verdi	Arrivabene	Rome?	14 Sept. 80	?	Al. 259–60; Abb. iv. 127
Verdi	Boito	Milan	14 Oct. 80	IP	Nar. 468; *Cart. V–B* i. 3
Boito	Verdi	St Agata	[18 Oct. 80]	IP	Nar. 469–71; Abb. iv. 172–4; Wa. 478–9; We. 239; *Cart. V–B* i. 4–6
Verdi	Arrivabene	Rome	18 Oct. 80	?	Al. 260–2; Abb. iv. 127
Ricordi	Verdi	Genoa	19 Nov. 80	SA	*Cart. V–B* ii. 290
Verdi	Ricordi	Milan	20 Nov. 80	Ri.	*Cop.* 559; Abb. iv. 132–3; *Cart. V–B* ii. 290–1
Ricordi	Verdi	Genoa	24 Nov. 80	SA	*Cart.* iv. 204–6; Abb. iv. 135–6; *Cart. V–B* ii. 291

From	To	Destination	Date	Autograph location	Published source
Verdi	Ricordi	[Draft]	[25 Nov. 80?]	SA	*Cart.* ii. 49; Abb. iv. 130–1
Ricordi	Verdi	Genoa	26 Nov. 80	SA	
Ricordi	Verdi	Genoa	27 Nov. 80	SA	*Cart.* iv. 204; Abb. iv. 134–5
Verdi	Ricordi	[Draft]	[after 27 Nov. 80]	SA	*Cart.* iv. 204; Abb. iv. 134–5
Ricordi	Verdi	Genoa	30 Nov. 80	SA	*Cart. V–B* ii. 291
Verdi	Ricordi	Milan	2 Dec. 80	Ri.	Abb. iv. 137
Ricordi	Verdi	Genoa	2 Dec. 80	SA	
Verdi	Boito	Milan	2 Dec. 80	IP	Nar. 471; Wa. 480; *Cart. V–B* i. 6
Ricordi	Verdi	Genoa	4 Dec. 80	SA	
Ricordi	Verdi	Genoa	5 Dec. 80	SA	
Verdi	Ricordi	Milan	5 Dec. 80	Pa.	
Boito	Verdi	Genoa	[8 Dec. 80]	SA	*Cart. V–B* i. 7–12
Ricordi	Verdi	Genoa	11 Dec. 80	SA	
Verdi	Boito	Milan	11 Dec. 80	IP	*Cop.* 315–16; Abb. iv. 137–8; Wa. 480–1; We. 239; *Cart. V–B* i. 12–13
Ricordi	Giuseppina Verdi	Genoa	14 Dec. 80	SA	
Verdi	Piroli	Rome	18 Dec. 80	AC; IP (PH)	*Cart.* iii. 149
Ricordi	Verdi	Genoa	20 Dec. 80	SA	
Ricordi	Verdi	Genoa	22 Dec. 80	SA	*Cart. V–B* ii. 294
Locatelli	T. Ricordi	Milan	23 Dec. 80	SA	
Ricordi	Verdi	Genoa	25 Dec. 80	SA	*Cart. V–B* ii. 294
Verdi	Boito	Milan	28 Dec. 80	IP	Wa. 481; *Cart. V–B* i. 14–15
Verdi	Arrivabene	Rome	6 Jan. 81	?	Al. 268–71
Verdi	Boito	Milan	8 Jan. 81	IP	Wa. 482; *Cart. V–B* i. 15–16
Verdi	Boito	Milan	9 Jan. 81	IP	*Cart. V–B* i. 17
Boito	Verdi	Genoa	[8–9 Jan. 81]	SA	*Cart.* ii. 80–4; Abb. iv. 138–9; *Cart. V–B* i. 18–24
Boito	Verdi	Genoa	[9 Jan. 81]	SA	*Cart.* ii. 80; *Cart. V–B* i. 24
Verdi	Boito	Milan	10 Jan. 81	IP	Wa. 483; *Cart. V–B* i. 25–6
Verdi†	Boito	Milan	11 Jan. 81	IP	*Cart. V–B* i. 26
Verdi	Boito	Milan	11 [Jan. 81]	IP	*Cart. V–B* i. 27
Boito	Verdi	Genoa	14 Jan. [81]	SA	*Cart.* ii. 85–7; Abb. iv. 140–1; *Cart. V–B* i. 28–31

List of Letters and Telegrams

From	To	Destination	Date	Autograph location	Published source
Verdi	Boito	Milan	15 [Jan.] 81	IP	Abb. iv. 140; Wa. 484; *Cart. V–B* i. 31–2
Boito	Verdi	Genoa	[16 Jan. 81]	SA	*Cart.* ii. 89–91; Abb. iv. 143; *Cart. V–B* i. 32–5
Verdi	Boito	Milan	[17 Jan. 81]	IP	Wa. 484; *Cart. V–B* i. 35
Muzio	Ricordi	Milan	[17 Jan. 81]	Ri.	Abb. iv. 177
Boito	Ricordi	Milan	21 Jan. 81	Ri.	Abb. iv. 175; We. 239
Verdi	Boito	Padua	[24 Jan. 81]	IP	Wa. 484; *Cart. V–B* i. 35–6
Boito	Verdi	Genoa	31 Jan. [81]	SA	*Cart.* ii. 91–2; *Cart. V–B* i. 36–7
Faccio	Verdi	Genoa	31 Jan. 81	SA	De R. 190–1
Ricordi	Giuseppina Verdi	Genoa	1 Feb. 81	SA	
Ricordi	Verdi	Genoa	2 Feb. 81	SA	
Verdi	Faccio	Milan	2 Feb. 81	SA	De R. 192; Abb. iv. 146
Verdi	Boito	Milan	2 Feb. 81	IP	*Cart.* iv. 47; Wa. 484. *Cart. V–B* i. 38
Verdi	Boito	Milan	5 Feb. 81	IP	*Cart.* iv. 48–9; Wa. 484; *Cart. V–B* i. 38–9
Boito	Verdi	Genoa	[5 Feb. 81]	SA	*Cart.* ii. 92; Abb. iv. 144; *Cart. V–B* i. 40
Verdi	Boito	Milan	[6 Feb. 81]	IP	Wa. 484; *Cart. V–B* i. 40–1
Verdi	T. Ricordi	Milan	6 Feb. 81	Ri.	Abb. iv. 145; *Cart. V–B* ii. 300
Faccio	Verdi	Genoa	6 Feb. 81	SA	De R. 193
Boito	Verdi	Genoa	[7 Feb. 81]	SA	*Cart.* ii. 87–9; Abb. iv. 141–3; *Cart. V–B* i. 41–4
Verdi	Tornaghi	Milan	[7 Feb. 81]	Ri.	
Tornaghi	Verdi	Genoa	7 Feb. 81	SA	
Verdi†	Boito	Milan	8 Feb. 81	IP	*Cart. V–B* i. 44
Verdi	*Pro Memoria* Tornaghi		[8 Feb. 81]		*Cart. V–B* ii. 300
Faccio	Verdi	Genoa	11 Feb. 81	SA	De R. 193–4
Ricordi	Verdi	Genoa	12 Feb. 81	SA	
Faccio	Verdi	Genoa	13 Feb. 81	SA	De R. 194–5
Tornaghi	Verdi	Genoa	14 Feb. 81	SA	
Verdi	Faccio	Milan	[14?] Feb. 81	?	De R. 195–6
Verdi	Boito	Milan	15 Feb. 81	IP	Wa. 485; *Cart. V–B* i. 45

From	To	Destination	Date	Autograph location	Published source
Boito	Verdi	Genoa	15 [Feb. 81]	SA	*Cart.* iv. 92–3; Abb. iv. 144; *Cart. V–B* i. 46–7
Faccio	Verdi	Genoa	16 Feb. 81	SA	De R. 196–8
Verdi	Faccio	Milan	17 Feb. 81	SA	De R. 198–9
Verdi	Ricordi	Milan	[18 Feb. 81]	Pa.	
Ricordi	Verdi	Genoa	[19 Feb. 81]	SA	*Cart. V–B* ii. 302
Verdi	Ricordi	Milan	21 Feb. 81	Ri.	Abb. iv. 147–8; *Cart. V–B* ii. 302
Verdi	Ricordi	Milan	[22 Feb. 81]	Pa.	
Ricordi	Verdi	Genoa	22 Feb. 81	SA	*Cart. V–B* ii. 302–3
Faccio	Verdi	Genoa	22 Feb. 81	SA	De R. 199–200
Verdi	Ricordi	Milan	[23 Feb. 81]	Pa.	
Ricordi	Verdi	Genoa	23 Feb. 81	SA	
Verdi	Hiller	Cologne	24 Feb. 81	?	*Cart.* ii. 338
Ricordi	Verdi	Milan	25 Feb. 81	SA	
Verdi	Arrivabene	Rome	25 Mar. 81	?	*Cop.* 560; Al. 283
Boito	Verdi	Genoa	[31 Mar. 81]	SA	*Cart.* ii. 93–4; Abb. iv. 163; *Cart. V–B* i. 47–8
Verdi	Boito	Milan	2 Apr. 81	IP	*Cop.* 512–13; Abb. iv. 164; *Cart. V–B* 1. 48–9
Verdi	Arrivabene	Rome	2 Apr. 81	?	*Cop.* 560; Al. 285–6
Boito	Verdi	Genoa	[4 Apr. 81]	SA	*Cart.* ii. 138; *Cart. V–B* i. 49
Verdi	Waldmann	Ferrara	5 Apr. 81	Bo.	*Cart.* ii 253
Verdi	Ricordi	Milan	[14 Apr. 81]	Ri.	Abb. iv. 148
Ricordi	Verdi	Genoa	18 Apr. 81	SA	
Verdi	Ricordi	Milan	1 May 81	Pa.	
Arrivabene	Verdi	St Agata	11 May 81	SA	Al. 286–7
Verdi	Ricordi	Milan	11 May 81	Pa.	
Ricordi	Verdi	St Agata	13 May 81	SA	
Ricordi	Verdi	St Agata	22 May 81	SA	
Boito	Verdi	St Agata	[25 May 81]	SA	*Cart.* ii. 106; Abb. iv. 178; *Cart. V–B* i. 50
Verdi†	Boito	Milan	26 May 81	IP	*Cart. V–B* i. 51
Verdi	Arrivabene	Rome	27 May 81	?	*Cop.* 607–8; Al. 288–9
Arrivabene	Verdi	St Agata	29 May 81	SA	Al. 289–91
Verdi	Torelli	?	17 June 81	?	*Cop.* 627–8
Boito	Verdi	St Agata	17 June [81]	SA	*Cart.* ii. 107–8; Abb. iv. 179–80; *Cart. V–B* i. 51–7

From	To	Destination	Date	Autograph location	Published source
Verdi	Boito	Milan	23 June 81	IP	Nar. 480–1; Abb. iv. 180; Wa. 485; *Cart. V–B* i. 57
Boito	Tornaghi	Milan	10 July 81	Ri.	*Cart. V–B* ii. 308
Ricordi	Verdi	St Agata	12 July 81	SA	
Verdi	Ricordi	Milan	17 July 81	Ri.	Abb. iv. 167
Morelli	Verdi	St Agata	10 Aug. 81	?	*Cop.* 694; Abb. iv. 181–2
Verdi	Morelli	Naples	20 Aug. 81	IP (PH)	*Cop.* 694
Boito	Verdi	St Agata	[24 Aug. 81]	SA	*Cart.* ii. 112–15; Abb. iv. 256–8; *Cart. V–B* i. 58–61
Verdi	Boito	Monticello	[27 Aug. 81]	IP	Wa. 486–7; *Cart. V–B* i. 61–2
Verdi	Morelli	Naples	1 Sept. 81	IP (PH)	*Cop.* 695
Morelli	Verdi	St Agata	[?] Sept. 81	?	*Cop.* 695–6; *Cart.* i. 292–3; Abb. iv. 182–3; We. 239
Verdi	Morelli	Naples	24 Sept. 81	IP (PH)	*Cop.* 317–18; Abb. iv. 183; We. 239–40
Verdi	Maffei	Milan	29 Oct. 81	Br.; IP (PH)	*Cop.* 513; Abb. iv. 116; As. 387; *Cart. V–B* ii. 311
Ricordi	Verdi	St Agata	2 Nov. 81	SA	
Verdi	Ricordi	Milan	5 Nov. 81	Ri.	
Ricordi	Verdi	?	10 Nov. 81	SA	
Ricordi	Verdi	St Agata	18 Nov. 81	SA	
Verdi	Ricordi	Milan	24 Nov. 81	Pa.	
Ricordi	Verdi	Genoa	26 Nov. 81	SA	
Verdi	Ricordi	Milan	3 Dec. 81	Pa.	
Ricordi	Verdi	Genoa	4 Dec. 81	SA	
Verdi	Ricordi	Milan	5 Dec. 81	Pa.	
Ricordi	Verdi	Genoa	6 Dec. 81	SA	
Verdi	Arrivabene	Rome	8 Dec. 81	?	Al. 291–2
Verdi	Arrivabene	Rome	23 Dec. 81	?	Al. 294
Ricordi	Giuseppina Verdi	Genoa	31 Dec. 81	SA	
Giuseppina Verdi	Ricordi	Milan	1 Jan. 82	Ri.	Abb. iv. 189–90
Verdi	Arrivabene	Rome	5 Jan. 82	?	Al. 295
Verdi	Morelli	Naples	5 Jan. 82	IP (PH)	*Cop.* 697
Ricordi	Verdi	Genoa	18 Jan. 82	SA	
Verdi	Ricordi	Milan	8 Feb. 82	Ri.	
Ricordi	Verdi	Genoa	27 Feb. 82	SA	
T. Ricordi	Verdi	Genoa	2 Mar. 82	SA	
Ricordi	Verdi	Genoa	13 Mar. 82	SA	

From	To	Destination	Date	Autograph location	Published source
Verdi	Ricordi	Milan	14 Mar. 82	Ri.	
T. Ricordi	Verdi	Genoa	17 Mar. 82	SA	
Ricordi	Verdi	Genoa	25 Mar. 82	SA	
Arrivabene	Verdi	Genoa	26 Mar. 82	SA	Al. 297–9
Ricordi	Giuseppina Verdi	Genoa	6 Apr. 82	SA	
Verdi	Maffei	Milan?	23 Apr. 82	Ch.; IP (PH)	As. 389
Ricordi	Verdi	St Agata	27 May 82	SA	
Boito	Verdi	St Agata	10 Aug. [82]	SA	*Cart.* ii. 132–3; *Cart. V–B* i. 63–4
Verdi	Boito	Villa d'Este	16 Aug. 82	IP	Nar. 482–3; *Cart. V–B* i. 65
Boito	Verdi	St Agata	[17–18 Aug. 82]	SA	*Cart.* ii. 133–4; *Cart. V–B* i. 66
Ricordi	Verdi	St Agata	14 Oct. 82	SA	
Verdi	Hofmann	Vienna	31 Oct. 82	?	*Cop.* 319
Ricordi	Verdi	Genoa	17 Nov. 82	SA	
Ricordi	Verdi	Genoa	10 Dec. 82	SA	
Verdi	Maffei	Milan	16 Dec. 82	Br.; IP (PH)	Abb. iv. 203; As. 392–3
Verdi	Ricordi	Milan	25 Dec. 82	Ri.	*Cart. V–B* ii. 314
Muzio	Ricordi	Milan	[25?] Dec. 82	Ri.	Abb. iv. 205–6
Giuseppina Verdi	Ricordi	Milan	[25?] Dec. 82	Ri.	Abb. iv. 205
Muzio	Ricordi	Milan	29 Dec. 82	Ri.	Abb. iv. 206
Ricordi	Giuseppina Verdi	Genoa	29 Dec. 82	SA	
Ricordi	Verdi	Genoa	23 Jan. 83	SA	
Ricordi	Verdi	Genoa	2 Feb. 83	SA	
Verdi	Piroli	Rome	2 Feb. 83	AC; IP (PH)	*Cop.* 319–21
Boito	Ricordi	Milan	[? Feb. 83]	Ri.	
Verdi	Baccelli	Rome?	4 Feb. 83	?	*Cop.* 321–2
Verdi	Ricordi	Milan	15 Feb. 83	Ri.	*Cop.* 323 (FAC); Abb. iv. 208; We. 240
Ricordi	Verdi	Genoa	17 Feb. 83	SA	
Boito	Tornaghi	Milan	4 Mar. 83	Ri.	*Cart. V–B* ii. 315
Verdi	Florimo	Naples	12 Mar. 83	IP (PH)	*Cop.* 322–3
Verdi	Arrivabene	Rome	15 Mar. 83	?	*Cop.* 698; Al. 300
Ricordi	Verdi	Genoa	16 Mar. 83	SA	
Verdi	Piroli	Rome	16 Mar. 83	AC; IP (PH)	*Cart.* iii. 163–4
Verdi	Ricordi	Milan	24 Mar. 83	Ri.	*Cop.* 699
Ricordi	Verdi	Genoa	24 Mar. 83	SA	
Boito	Verdi	Genoa	5 Apr. [83]	SA	*Cart.* ii. 139; *Cart. V–B* i. 67
Verdi	Boito	Milan	7 Apr. 83	IP	Nar. 489; *Cart. V–B* i. 68
Arrivabene	Verdi	Genoa?	7 Apr. 83	SA	Al. 301–2
Verdi	Ricordi	Milan	3 Sept. 83	Pa.	
Verdi	Ricordi	Milan	18 Sept. 83	Pa.	

From	To	Destination	Date	Autograph location	Published source
Verdi	Ricordi	Milan	[?] Sept. 83	Pa.	
Verdi	Maffei	Milan	11 Oct. 83	Ch.; IP (PH)	Abb. iv. 226; As. 398; We. 241
Verdi	Ricordi	Milan	12 Oct. 83	Pa.	
Verdi	Ricordi	Milan	[13 Oct. 83]	Pa.	
Verdi	Ricordi	Milan	27 Oct. 83	Ri.	
Muzio	Verdi	St Agata	30 Oct. 83	?	*Cart.* iv. 224
Ricordi	Verdi	Genoa	5 Dec. 83	SA	
Faccio	Verdi	St Agata	[? Nov. 83?]	?	Abb. iv. 223
Boito	Verdi	Genoa	[21 Jan. 84]	SA	*Cart.* ii. 137; *Cart. V–B* i. 68
Verdi	Arrivabene	Rome	29 Jan. 84	?	Al. 305–6
Verdi	Maffei	Milan	29 Jan. 84	Ch.; IP (PH)	Abb. iv. 231; As. 399; We. 241
Verdi	Boito	Nervi?	7 Feb. 84	IP	Nar. 490; *Cart. V–B* i. 69
Verdi	Arrivabene	Rome	12 Feb. 84	?	Al. 310
Boito	Tornaghi	Milan	13 [Feb. 84]	Ri.	*Cart. V–B* ii. 318
Boito	Tornaghi	Milan	28 Feb. 84	Ri.	*Cart. V–B* ii. 318
Muzio	D'Ormeville	Milan	9 Mar. 84	Bus.	
Boito	Ricordi	Milan	[20 Mar. 84]	Ri.	We. 241; *Cart. V–B* ii. 318
Morelli	Verdi	Genoa	[23 Mar. 84]	?	*Cart.* i. 294; Abb. iv. 245; *Cart. V–B* ii. 321–2
Verdi	Faccio	Milan	27 Mar. 84	IP (PH)	*Cop.* 324–5; Abb. iv. 236; Wa. 489; We. 241
Verdi	Morelli	Naples	28 Mar. 84	IP (PH)	*Cop.* 697–8; *Cart. V–B* ii. 322
Faccio	Verdi	Genoa	4 Apr. 84	SA	De R. 225–7; Abb. iv. 237–8
Verdi	Faccio	Turin?	20 Apr. 84	IP (PH)	De R. 227; *Cart. V–B* ii. 320
Boito	Verdi	Genoa	[26 Apr. 84]	SA	*Cart.* ii. 100–3; Abb. iv. 239–43; Wa. 489–90; We. 241; *Cart. V–B* i. 69–73
Verdi	Boito	Milan	26 Apr. 84	IP	*Cop.* 325–6; Abb. iv. 243–4; *Cart. V–B* i. 73–4
Faccio	Ricordi	Milan	27 Apr. 84	Ri.	
Faccio	Verdi	Genoa	29 Apr. 84	SA	De R. 227–8; Abb. iv. 238–9

From	To	Destination	Date	Autograph location	Published source
Boito	Verdi	Genoa	[end Apr.–2 May 84]	SA	*Cart.* ii. 110; Abb. iv. 253–4; Wa. 490; We. 241–2; *Cart. V–B* i. 74–6
Verdi	Boito	Milan	3 May 84	IP	Nar. 496; Wa. 490; We. 242; *Cart. V–B* i. 76
Verdi*	Blaze de Bury	Paris	6 May 84	?	Abb. iv. 233
Verdi	Faccio	Turin?	6 May 84	IP (PH)	*Cop.* 326 n; Abb. iv. 244; *Cart. V–B* ii. 324
Faccio	Ricordi	Milan	21 May 84	Ri.	
Verdi	Ricordi	Milan	23 May 84	Pa.	
Faccio	Ricordi	Milan	4 Aug. 84	Ri.	
Verdi	Maffei	Milan	2 Sept. 84	Br.; IP (PH)	*Cop.* 526–7; Abb. iv. 246; As. 401–2
Boito	Verdi	St Agata	25 [Sept. 84]	SA	*Cart.* ii. 138; *Cart. V–B* i. 77
Verdi†	Boito	Milan	26 Sept. 84	IP	*Cart. V–B* i. 77
Verdi	Boito	Milan	26 Sept. 84	IP	*Cart. V–B* i. 78
Verdi	Maffei	Milan	16 Nov. 84	Ch.; IP (PH)	As. 404
Verdi	Boito	Milan?	9 Dec. 84	IP	Nar. 498; We. 242; *Cart. V–B* i. 78–9
Boito	Verdi	Genoa	[after 9 Dec. 84]	SA	*Cart.* ii. 108–9; Abb. iv. 254–5; *Cart. V–B* i. 79–81
Verdi	Arrivabene	Rome	24 Dec. 84	?	Al. 317
Boito	Verdi	Genoa	7 Feb. [85]	SA	*Cart.* ii. 127; *Cart. V–B* i. 82
Verdi	Boito	Nervi	[18 Feb. 85]	IP	*Cart. V–B* i. 82
Verdi	Ricordi	Milan	12 Mar. 85	Pa.	
Boito	Verdi	Genoa	[5 Apr. 85]	SA	*Cart.* ii. 138; *Cart. V–B* i. 83
Ponchielli	Brambilla	?	[end Apr.–early May 85]	?	Abb. iv. 261–2; *Cart. V–B* ii. 331–2
Verdi	Arrivabene	Rome	2 May 85	?	Al. 319–20
Ricordi	Verdi	St Agata	8 May 85	Pa.	
Verdi	Ricordi	Milan	10 May 85	Pa.	
Arrivabene	Verdi	St Agata	24 May 85	SA	Al. 322–5
Boito	Verdi	St Agata	[9 Sept. 85]	SA	*Cart.* ii. 122; Wa. 492; We. 242; *Cart. V–B* i. 84

From	To	Destination	Date	Autograph location	Published source
Verdi	Boito	Milan	10 Sept. 85	IP	Nar. 489; Wa. 492; We. 242; *Cart. V–B* i. 84–5
Verdi	Boito	?	[Sept.–Oct. 85?]	IP	*Cart. V–B* i. 283
Verdi	Boito	Villa d'Este	5 Oct. 85	IP	*Cart.* ii. 122 (FAC); *Cart. V–B* i. 85–9 (FAC)
Verdi	Maffei	Milan	9 Oct. 85	Ch. IP (PH)	As. 410–11
Boito	Verdi	St Agata	9 Oct. [85]	SA	*Cart.* ii. 123; Abb. iv. 260; We. 242; *Cart. V–B* i. 89–90
Verdi	Boito	Villa d'Este	11 Oct. 85	IP	*Cart. V–B* i. 91
Boito	Verdi	St Agata	23 [Oct. 85]	SA	*Cart.* ii. 123–4; *Cart. V–B* i. 91–2
Verdi	Boito	Milan	27 Oct. 85	IP	*Cart. V–B* i. 92
Verdi	Ricordi	Milan	6 Nov. 85	Ri.	
Verdi	Boito	Milan	8 Nov. 85	IP	*Cop.* 236 n; *Cart. V–B* i. 93
Arrivabene	Verdi	St Agata	16 Nov. 85	SA	Al. 325–6
Verdi	Arrivabene	Rome	20 Nov. 85	?	Al. 326–7
Maffei	Verdi	Genoa	7 Dec. 85	?	*Cart.* ii. 298
Arrivabene	Verdi	Genoa	9 Dec. 85	SA	Al. 327–9
Maurel*	Verdi	Genoa	22 Dec. 85	?	*Cop.* 330
Verdi	Maurel	Paris	30 Dec. 85	?	*Cop.* 331; Abb. iv. 267–8; We. 242
Verdi	Waldmann	Ferrara	1 Jan. 86	Bo.	
Giuseppina Verdi	G. De Sanctis	Naples	1 Jan. 86	IP (PH)	*Cart.* i. 203
Leduc*	Verdi	Genoa	1 Jan. 86	?	*Cop.* 331–2
Verdi*	Leduc	Paris	[? Jan. 86]	?	*Cop.* 332
Maurel*	Verdi	Genoa	10 Jan. 86	?	*Cop.* 336–9
Ricordi	Verdi	Genoa	11 Jan. 86	SA	
Verdi	Boito	Milan	11 Jan. 86	IP	Nar. 501; *Cart. V–B* i. 93–4
Verdi	Boito	Milan	14 Jan. 86	IP	*Cart. V–B* i. 95
Boito	Verdi	Genoa	[16 Jan. 86]	SA	*Cart.* ii. 124; *Cart. V–B* i. 96
Boito	Verdi	Genoa	[18 Jan. 86]	SA	*Cart.* ii. 124–5; *Cart. V–B* i. 96–7
Verdi	Ricordi	Milan	18 Jan. 86	Ri.	*Cart. V–B* ii. 340–1
Ricordi	Verdi	Genoa	19 Jan. 86	SA	
Verdi	Maurel	Paris	19 Jan. 86	?	*Cop.* 341
Verdi	Ricordi	Milan	20 Jan. 86	Ri.	*Cart. V–B* ii. 338
Boito	Verdi	Genoa	[20 Jan. 86]	SA	*Cart.* ii. 128–9; *Cart. V–B* i. 97–8
Verdi	Boito	Milan	21 Jan. 86	IP	Nar. 501–2; *Cart. V–B* i. 99–100

From	To	Destination	Date	Autograph location	Published source
Verdi	Ricordi	Milan	[22 Jan. 86]	Ri.	
Ricordi	Verdi	Genoa	23 Jan. 86	SA	
Boito	Verdi	Genoa	[23 Jan. 86]	SA	*Cart.* ii. 129–30; *Cart. V–B* i. 100–1
Ricordi	Verdi	Genoa	26 Jan. 86	SA	
Muzio	Ricordi	Milan	28 Jan. 86	Ri.	Abb. iv. 277; *Cart. V–B* ii. 343
Verdi	Piroli	Rome	29 Jan. 86	AC; IP (PH)	*Cart.* iii. 175
Tamagno	Verdi	Genoa	29 Jan. 86	?	*Cop.* 342
Verdi	Ricordi	Milan	31 Jan. 86	Pa.	
Verdi	Tamagno	Madrid	31 Jan. 86	?	*Cop.* 342–3
Muzio	Ricordi	Milan	1 Feb. 86	Ri.	Abb. iv. 277–8; *Cart. V–B* ii. 343
T. Ricordi	Verdi	Genoa	3 Feb. 86	SA	
Verdi	Ricordi	Milan	4 Feb. 86	Pa.	
Ricordi	Verdi	Genoa	5 Feb. 86	SA	
Verdi	Masini	?	[early Feb. 86]	?	*Cop.* 344
Verdi	Ricordi	Milan	7 Feb. 86	Ri.	*Cop.* 343–4
Muzio	Ricordi	Milan	11 Feb. 86	Ri.	Abb. iv. 278; *Cart. V–B* ii. 343
Stolz	Pantaleoni	?	[mid-Feb. 86]	?	Abb. iv. 291–2
Ricordi	Verdi	Genoa	18 Feb. 86	SA	
Pantaleoni	A. Pantaleoni	?	27 Feb. 86	?	*Cart. V–B* ii. 344
Tamagno	Verdi	Genoa	27 Feb. 86	?	*Cop.* 344–5
Muzio	Ricordi	Milan	14 Mar. 86	Ri.	Abb. iv. 279; *Cart. V–B* ii. 344
Verdi	Arrivabene	Rome	17 Mar. 86	?	*Cop.* 699; Al. 331–2; *Cart. V–B* ii. 345
Verdi	Piroli	Rome	4 Apr. 86	AC; IP (PH)	*Cart.* iii. 176
Verdi	Ricordi	Milan	7 Apr. 86	Pa.	
Verdi	Piroli	Rome	7 Apr. 86	AC; IP (PH)	*Cart.* iii. 176
T. Ricordi	Verdi	Genoa	16 Apr. 86	SA	
Boito	Tornaghi	Milan	16 Apr. 86	Ri.	
Ricordi	Verdi	Genoa	23 Apr. 86	SA	
Boito	Ricordi	Milan	24 Apr. 86	Ri.	*Cart. V–B* ii. 345
Boito	Verdi		6 May [86]	IP	Nar. 502; *Cart. V–B* i. 101–2
Verdi	Boito	Quinto	8 May 86	IP	*Cart. V–B* i. 103
Boito	Verdi	St Agata	10 May [86]	SA	*Cart.* ii. 125–6; Abb. iv. 289; *Cart. V–B* i. 104
Verdi	Boito	Quinto	14 May 86	IP	*Cart.* ii. 104; *Cart. V–B* i. 105
Boito	Verdi	St Agata	16 [May 86]	SA	*Cart.* ii. 103–4; Abb. iv. 284–5; We. 242–3; *Cart. V–B* i. 106–8

From	To	Destination	Date	Autograph location	Published source
Boito	Verdi	St Agata	4 June [86]	SA	*Cart. V–B* i. 280
Verdi	Ricordi	Milan	28 June 86	Ri.	
Ricordi	Verdi	Montecatini	30 June 86	SA	
Verdi	Ricordi	Milan	[4 July 86]	Pa.	
Ricordi	Verdi	Montecatini	6 July 86	SA	
Faccio	Ricordi	Milan	14 July 86	Ri.	
Verdi	Boito	Villa d'Este?	17 July 86	IP	*Cart. V–B* i. 108–10
Boito	Verdi	St Agata	21 July [86]	SA	*Cart.* ii. 116–17; Abb. iv. 289–90; *Cart. V–B* i. 111
Verdi	Boito	Villa d'Este	[22 July 86]	IP	*Cart. V–B* i. 112
Verdi	Waldmann	Ferrara	23 July 86	Bo.	
Boito	Verdi	St Agata	25 July [86]	SA	*Cart.* ii. 117; *Cart. V–B* i. 113
Boito	Tornaghi	Milan	28 July 86	Ri.	*Cart. V–B* ii. 350
Verdi	Piroli	Rome	7 Aug. 86	AC; IP (PH)	*Cart.* iii. 178–9; We. 243
Ricordi	Verdi	St Agata	10 Aug. 86	SA	
Faccio	Ricordi	Milan	14 Aug. 86	Ri.	
Ricordi	Verdi	St Agata	18 Aug. 86	SA	
Ricordi	Verdi	St Agata	26 Aug. 86	SA	
Verdi	*Pro Memoria* Boito	Villa d'Este?	[*c.*29 Aug. 86]	IP	*Cart. V–B* i. 113–14
Verdi	Faccio	Brescia?	2 Sept. 86	To.	
Boito	Verdi	St Agata	[6 Sept. 86]	SA	*Cart.* ii. 105–6; Abb. iv. 290–1; *Cart. V–B* i. 114–15
Ricordi	Verdi	St Agata	7 Sept. 86	SA	*Cart. V–B* ii. 350
Faccio	Verdi	St Agata	7 Sept. 86	SA	Abb. iv. 292
Verdi	Ricordi	Milan	[7 Sept. 86]	Pa.	
Verdi	Boito	Villa d'Este	[9 Sept. 86]	IP	*Cart. V–B* i. 115–16
Ricordi	Verdi	St Agata	9 Sept. 86	SA	*Cart. V–B* ii. 350
Verdi	Ricordi	Milan	[12 Sept. 86]	Pa.	
Ricordi	Verdi	St Agata	15 Sept. 86	SA	
Verdi	Ricordi	Milan	[17 Sept. 86]	Pa.	
Ricordi	Verdi	St Agata	20 Sept. 86	SA	*Cart. V–B* ii. 352
Verdi	Piroli	Rome	1 Oct. 86	AC; IP (PH)	*Cart.* iii. 179
Verdi	*Pro Memoria* Ricordi		[*c.*1 Oct. 86]	Ri.	Abb. iv. 305
Ricordi	Verdi	St Agata	3 Oct. 86	SA	*Cart. V–B* ii. 352
Ricordi	Verdi	St Agata	5 Oct. 86	SA	
Ricordi	Verdi	St Agata	8 Oct. 86	SA	
Faccio	Ricordi	Milan	9 Oct. 86	Ri.	
Verdi	Ricordi	Milan	[13 Oct. 86]	Ri.	*Cart. V–B* ii. 352

From	To	Destination	Date	Autograph location	Published source
Pantaleoni	A. Pantaleoni	?	14 Oct. 86	?	*Cart. V–B* ii. 353
Ricordi	Verdi	St Agata	18 Oct. 86	SA	*Cart. V–B* ii. 353
Verdi	Ricordi	Milan	18 Oct. 86	Pa.	
Ricordi	Verdi	St Agata	19 Oct. 86	SA	*Cart. V–B* ii. 352
Verdi	Ricordi	Milan	21 Oct. 86	Pa.	
Ricordi	Verdi	St Agata	23 Oct. 86	SA	
Verdi	Ricordi	Milan	[24 Oct. 86]	Ri.	Abb. iv. 293–4; *Cart. V–B* ii. 353
Tornaghi	Verdi	St Agata	25 Oct. 86	SA	
Verdi	Ricordi	Milan	[26 Oct. 86]	Pa.	
Verdi	Tornaghi	Milan	[26 Oct. 86]	Ri.	Abb. iv. 294
Tornaghi	Verdi	St Agata	28 Oct. 86	SA	
Pantaleoni	A. Pantaleoni	?	29 Oct. 86	?	*Cart. V–B* ii. 354
Verdi	Boito	Milan	29 Oct. 86	IP	Nar. 503; Abb. iv. 294; *Cart. V–b* i. 116–17
Verdi	Faccio	Milan	29 Oct. 86	To.	Mor. 45
Faccio	Verdi	St Agata	31 Oct. 86	SA	De R. 231–2; Abb. iv. 295
Arrivabene	Verdi	St Agata	31 Oct. 86	SA	Al. 333–4
Verdi	Boito	Milan	[1 Nov. 86]		*Cop.* 700; Ga. 118 (FAC); *Cart. V–B* i. 117
Verdi	Ricordi	Milan	1 Nov. 86	Ri.	Abb. iv. 294; *Cart. V–B* ii. 355
Ricordi	Giuseppina Verdi	St Agata	2 Nov. 86	SA	
Ricordi	Verdi	St Agata	3 Nov. 86	SA	
Verdi	Ricordi	Milan	[3 Nov. 86]	Pa.	
Verdi	Ricordi	Milan	4 Nov. 86	Ri.	
Verdi	Arrivabene	Rome	4 Nov. 86	?	Al. 334
Giuseppina Verdi	G. De Sanctis	Naples	5 Nov. 86	IP (PH)	*Cart.* i. 203–4; *Cart. V–B* ii. 355
Ricordi	Verdi	St Agata	6 Nov. 86	SA	
Muzio	Ricordi	Milan	9 Nov. 86	Ri.	Abb. iv. 296; *Cart. V–B* ii. 357
Ricordi	Verdi	St Agata	9 Nov. 86	SA	
Verdi	Ricordi	Milan	11 Nov. 86	Ri.	
Ricordi	Verdi	St Agata	12 Nov. 86	SA	
Ricordi	Verdi	St Agata	13 Nov. 86	SA	
Verdi	Tornaghi	Milan	13 Nov. 86	Ri.	
Tornaghi	Verdi	St Agata	15 Nov. 86	SA	
Ricordi	Verdi	St Agata	15 Nov. 86	SA	
Verdi	Ricordi	Milan	16 Nov. 86	Ri.	*Cart. V–B* ii. 357

List of Letters and Telegrams

From	To	Destination	Date	Autograph location	Published source
Ricordi	Verdi	St Agata	18 Nov. 86	SA	
Ricordi	Verdi	St Agata	18 Nov. 86	SA	
Verdi	Ricordi	Milan	[19 Nov. 86]	Ri.	*Cart. V–B* ii. 357
Ricordi	Verdi	St Agata	20 Nov. 86	SA	
Ricordi	Verdi	St Agata	22 Nov. 86	SA	
Muzio	Ricordi	Milan	22 Nov. 86	Ri.	Abb. iv. 296–7
Torlonia†	Verdi	St Agata	27 Nov. 86	SA	
Muzio	Ricordi	Milan	2 Dec. 86	Ri.	Abb. iv. 297; *Cart. V–B* ii. 357
Ricordi	Verdi	St Agata	2 Dec. 86	SA	
Verdi	Ricordi	Milan	2 Dec. 86	Pa.	
Ricordi	Verdi	St Agata	4 Dec. 86	SA	*Cart. V–B* ii. 357
Ricordi	Verdi	St Agata	7 Dec. 86	SA	
Verdi	Du Locle	Rome	10 Dec. 86	Op.; IP (PH)	*Cart. V–B* ii. 357
Ricordi	Verdi	Genoa	10 Dec. 86	SA	
Ricordi	Verdi	Genoa	14 Dec. 86	SA	
Verdi	Ricordi	Milan	15 Dec. 86	Ri.	
Verdi	Ricordi	Milan	[15 Dec. 86]	Ri.	
Boito	Verdi	Genoa	[16–17 Dec. 86]	SA	*Cart.* ii. 127; *Cart. V–B* i. 117–18
Ricordi	Verdi	Genoa	17 Dec. 86	SA	
Verdi	Boito	Milan?	18 Dec. 86	IP	*Cop.* 700; *Cart. V–B* i. 118
Verdi	Ricordi	Milan	[18 Dec. 86]	Ri.	Abb. iv. 293
Ricordi	Verdi	Genoa	19 Dec. 86	SA	*Cart. V–B* ii. 358
Boito	Verdi	Genoa	[21 Dec. 86]	SA	*Cart.* ii. 128; *Cart. V–B* i. 119
Verdi	Ricordi	Milan	24 Dec. 86	Ri.	*Cart. V–B* ii. 359
Ricordi	Verdi	Genoa	25 Dec. 86	SA	
Verdi	Ricordi	Milan	26 Dec. 86	Pa.	
Verdi	Waldmann	Ferrara	26 Dec. 86	Bo.	*Cop.* 700
Ricordi	Giuseppina Verdi	Genoa	29 Dec. 86	SA	
Ricordi	Verdi	Genoa	30 Dec. 86	SA	
Giuseppina Verdi	G. De Sanctis	Naples	2 Jan. 87	IP (PH)	*Cart.* i. 204
Tornaghi	Verdi	Genoa	[c.2 Jan. 87]	SA	
Ricordi	Verdi	Genoa	2 Jan. 87	SA	*Cart. V–B* ii. 358
Verdi	Waldmann	Ferrara	7 Jan. 87	Bo.	
Verdi	Piroli	Rome	[9] Jan. 87	AC; IP (PH)	*Cart.* iii. 180; We. 243
Verdi	Morelli	Naples	11 Jan. 87	IP (PH)	*Cop.* 631
Verdi	Waldmann	Ferrara	12 Jan. 87	Bo.	
T. Salvini	Verdi	Genoa	24 Feb. 87	?	Abb. iv. 512
Verdi	President of International Artistic Circle	Rome	7 Mar. 87	?	*Cop.* 345

From	To	Destination	Date	Autograph location	Published source
Ricordi	Verdi	Genoa	11 Mar. 87	SA	
Verdi	Piroli	Rome	12 Mar. 87	AC; IP (PH)	*Cart.* iii. 181; *Cart. V–B* ii. 360
Verdi	Ricordi	Milan	[14 Mar. 87]	Ri.	*Cart. V–B* ii. 360
Ricordi	Verdi	Genoa	15 Mar. 87	SA	*Cart. V–B* ii. 360
Verdi*	Bellaigue's parents	Paris	15 Mar. 87	?	*Cart.* ii. 299–300
Giuseppina Verdi	G. De Sanctis	Naples	21 Mar. 87	IP (PH)	*Cart.* i. 205
Verdi	Ricordi	Milan	25 Mar. 87	Ri.	*Cart. V–B* ii. 360
Ricordi	Verdi	Genoa	26 Mar. 87	SA	*Cart. V–B* ii. 360
Verdi	D'Ormeville	Milan	28 Mar. 87	Sc.; IP (PH)	Mor. 46
Bellaigue*	Verdi	Genoa	29 Mar. 87	SA	*Cart.* ii. 300–1
Verdi	Muzio	Paris	2 Apr. 87	?	Abb. iv. 330
Verdi†	Boito	Nervi	14 Apr. 87	IP	*Cart. V–B* i. 120
Boito	Tornaghi	Milan	14 Apr. [87]	Ri.	
Chilesotti	Verdi	Genoa	15 Apr. 87	?	Abb. iv. 330
Verdi†	Boito	Nervi	17 Apr. 87	IP	*Cart. V–B* i. 120, ii. 361
Verdi	Faccio	Rome	19 Apr. 87	SA	De R. 235
Verdi	Ricordi	Milan	22 Apr. 87	Ri.	
Verdi†	Boito	Nantes?	22 Apr. 87	IP	*Cart. V–B* i. 120
Verdi	Boito	Paris?	[26 Apr. 87]	IP	*Cart. V–B* i. 121
Verdi	Ricordi	Milan	27 Apr. 87	Pa.	
Verdi	Ricordi	Milan	29 Apr. 87	Pa.	*Cart.* iv. 87–8
Verdi	Pantaleoni	[Draft]	[after 29 Apr. 87]	SA	*Cart.* iv. 86
Verdi	Faccio	Milan?	29 Apr. 87	SA	De R. 235–7
Verdi	Faccio	Milan?	1 May 87	?	De R. 237
Verdi	Ricordi	Milan	1 May 87	Ri.	
Ricordi	Verdi	St Agata	2 May 87	SA	
Verdi	Ricordi	Milan	2 May 87	Pa.	
Verdi	Ricordi	Milan	5 May 87	Ri.	
Verdi	Ricordi	Milan	11 May 87	Ri.	
Verdi	Ricordi	Milan	15 May 87	Pa.	
Verdi	Pantaleoni	Milan?	15 May 87	?	Mor. 45
Ferrarini	Ricordi	Milan	16 May 87	SA	
Ricordi	Verdi	St Agata	18 May 87	SA	
Verdi	Ricordi	Milan	19 May 87	Ri.	
Verdi	Vigna	Venice	22 May 87	?	Abb. iv. 338
Verdi	Ricordi	Milan	22 May 87	Pa.	
Verdi	Boito	Milan	24 May 87	IP	Nar. 505; *Cart. V–B* i. 121
Boito	Verdi	St Agata	26 May [87]	SA	*Cart.* ii. 134–5; Abb. iv. 339; *Cart. V–B* i. 122
Verdi	Boito	Milan	27 May 87	IP	Nar. 505; *Cart. V–B* i. 123

From	To	Destination	Date	Autograph location	Published source
Boito	Verdi	St Agata	30 May [87]	SA	*Cart.* iv. 206; Abb. iv. 339; *Cart. V–B* i. 123–4
Vacquirie*†	Verdi	St Agata	30 May 87	Ri.	
Verdi*†	Vacquirie	Paris	[31 May 87]	Ri.	*Cart. V–B* ii. 367–8
Verdi	Ricordi	Milan	31 May 87	Ri.	Abb. iv. 340–1
Tamagno	Verdi	St Agata	7 June 87	SA	*Cart.* iv. 88–9
Boito	Verdi	St Agata	9 June [87]	SA	*Cart.* ii. 137; *Cart. V–B* i. 124–5.
Verdi	Boito	Milan	[12 June 87]	IP	*Cart. V–B* i. 125
Verdi	Piroli	Rome	28 June 87	AC; IP (PH)	*Cart.* iii. 188; Abb. iv. 341–2
Hueffer	Boito		July 87	?	*Cart. V–B* ii. 363–7; *Oth.*
Verdi	Ricordi	Milan	9 July 87	Pa.	
Ricordi	Verdi	Montecatini	14 July 87	SA	
Ricordi	Verdi	St Agata	[29 July 87]	SA	
Verdi	Ricordi	Milan	1 Aug. 87	Pa.	
Verdi	Tornaghi	Milan	12 Aug. 87	Ri.	
Verdi	Tornaghi	Milan	13 Aug. 87	Ri.	*Cart. V–B* ii. 368
Verdi	Faccio	Brescia	19 Aug. 87	IP (PH)	*Cop.* 701; Abb. iv. 343–4
Ricordi	Verdi	St Agata	24 Aug. 87	SA	
Verdi	Ricordi	Milan	[after 24 Aug. 87]	Pa.	
Ricordi	Verdi	St Agata	30 Aug. 87	SA	
Ricordi	Verdi	St Agata	6 Sept. 87	SA	
Verdi	Faccio	Parma	16 Sept. 87	?	*Cart.* iv. 89–90
Verdi	Boito	Villa d'Este?	16 Sept. 87	IP	*Cart. V–B* i. 126
Ricordi	Verdi	St Agata	1 Oct. 87	SA	
Boito	Verdi	St Agata	4 Oct. [87]	SA	*Cart.* ii. 140–1; Abb. iv. 344–5; *Cart. V–B* i. 127–8
Verdi	Boito	Villa d'Este	5 Oct. 87	IP	*Cop.* 632–3; Abb. iv. 346; *Cart. V–B* i. 129–30
Ricordi	Verdi	St Agata	12 Oct. 87	SA	
Boito	Verdi	St Agata	31 Oct. [87]	SA	*Cart.* ii. 141; Abb. iv. 347; *Cart. V–B* i. 131
Verdi	Ricordi	Milan	5 Dec. 87	Ri.	*Cop.* 346; Abb. iv. 349
Verdi	Ricordi	Milan	26 Dec. 87	Pa.	
Verdi	Faccio	Milan	2 Jan. 88	SA	*Cart.* iv. 90
Verdi	Faccio	Milan	[? Jan. 88]	?	Abb. iv. 352
Verdi†	Boito	Milan	5 Jan. 88	IP	*Cart. V–B* i. 131
Verdi	Ricordi	Milan	22 Jan. 88	Ri.	Abb. iv. 356
Ricordi	Verdi	Genoa	23 Jan. 88	SA	
Verdi	Ricordi	Milan	26 Jan. 88	Pa.	

From	To	Destination	Date	Autograph location	Published source
Tornaghi	Verdi	Genoa	11 Feb. 88	SA	
Verdi	Tornaghi	Milan	13 Feb. 88	Pa.	Abb. iv. 352–3
Tornaghi	Verdi	Genoa	14 Feb. 88	SA	
Ricordi	Verdi	Genoa	16 Feb. 88	SA	
Giuseppina Verdi	G. De Sanctis	Naples	18 Feb. 88	IP (PH)	*Cart.* i. 207
Tornaghi	Verdi	Genoa	22 Feb. 88	SA	
Verdi	Tornaghi	Milan	23 Feb. 88	Ri.	Abb. iv. 353
Ricordi	Verdi	Genoa	25 Feb. 88	SA	
Delfico	Verdi	Genoa	[1 Mar. 88]	?	*Cart.* i 319–20; Abb. iv. 356–7
Verdi†	Boito	Nervi	3 Mar. 88	IP	*Cart. V–B* i. 132
Ricordi†	Verdi	Genoa	15 Mar. 88	SA	
Verdi	Delfico	Portici	[22 Mar. 88]	?	*Cart.* i. 319–20
Verdi	Boito	Milan	[8 Apr. 88]	IP	*Cart. V–B* i. 132
Tornaghi	Verdi	Genoa	2 May 88	SA	
Verdi	Ricordi	Milan	[? May 88?]	Ri.	Abb. iv. 351
Verdi†	Pantaleoni	Buenos Aires	[? May 88?]	IP (PH)	Abb. iv. 351
Ricordi	Verdi	St Agata	16 June 88	SA	
Ricordi†	Verdi	St Agata	7 Sept. 88	SA	
Verdi	Faccio	?	23 Sept. 88	SA	*Cart.* iv. 90
Ricordi	Verdi	St Agata	24 Sept. 88	SA	
Boito	Verdi	St Agata	9 Oct. [88]	SA	*Cart.* ii. 163–9; *Cart. V–B* i. 132–3
Verdi	Boito	S. Giuseppe	14 Oct. 88	IP	*Cart. V–B* i. 133–4
Ricordi	Verdi	St Agata	18 Oct. 88	SA	*Cart. V–B* 11. 375
Verdi	Ricordi	Milan	9 Nov. 88	Ri.	*Cop.* 347–8; Abb. iv. 362; *Cart. V–B* ii. 377
Verdi	Ricordi	Milan	[after 9 Nov. 88]	Ri.	
Boito	Verdi	Genoa	6 Dec. [88]	SA	*Cart.* ii. 164; *Cart. V–B* i. 134
Verdi	Ricordi	Milan	14 Dec. 88	Pa.	
Verdi	Ricordi	Milan	1 Jan. 89	Ri.	
Verdi	Ricordi	Milan	6 Jan. 89	Ri.	*Cop.* 348
Ricordi	Verdi	Genoa	7 Jan. 89	SA	
Verdi	Ricordi	Milan	7 [8] Jan. 89	Ri.	
Verdi	Ricordi	Milan	9 Jan. 89	Ri.	
Ricordi	Verdi	Genoa	12 Jan. 89	SA	
Verdi	Boriani	Villanova	16 Jan. 89		*Cop.* 350; We. 244
Verdi	Ricordi	Milan	22 Jan. 89	Ri	
Ricordi	Verdi	Genoa	25 Jan. 89	SA	
Verdi	Ricordi	Milan	2 Feb. 89	Ri.	
Verdi	Ricordi	Milan	3 Feb. 89	Ri.	*Cart. V–B* ii. 454
Verdi	Ricordi	Milan	5 Feb. 89	Pa.	
Ricordi	Verdi	Genoa	8 Feb. 89	SA	
Verdi	Ricordi	Milan	9 Feb. 89	Ri.	*Cart. V–B* ii. 455

From	To	Destination	Date	Autograph location	Published source
Verdi	Faccio	Milan	10 Feb. 89	?	Abb. iv. 354–5
Verdi	Piroli	Rome	10 Feb. 89	AC; IP (PH)	*Cart.* iii. 190–1; Abb. iv. 359–60
Ricordi	Verdi	Genoa	15 Feb. 89	SA	
Verdi	Boito	San Remo	17 Feb. 89	IP	*Cop.* 351–3; Abb. iv. 363–4; *Cart. V–B* 135–6
Verdi	Ricordi	Milan	18 Feb. 89	Ri.	
Boito	Verdi	Genoa	20 Feb. [89]	SA	*Cart.* ii. 139–40; *Cart. V–B* i. 137
Verdi	Boito	San Remo	21 Feb. 89	IP	*Cart. V–B* i. 137–8
Verdi	Faccio	Milan	24 Feb. 89	?	Abb. iv. 373
Verdi	Ricordi	Milan	3 Mar. 89	Ri.	
Verdi	Boito	Milan	6 Mar. 89	IP	*Cop.* 356; Abb. iv. 375–6; We. 244–5; *Cart. V–B* i. 138
Boito	Verdi	Genoa	[7 Mar. 89]	SA	*Cart.* ii. 184; Abb. iv. 376; We. 245; *Cart. V–B* i. 139
Ricordi	Verdi	Genoa	10 Mar. 89	SA	
Verdi	Ricordi	Milan	11 Mar. 89	Ri.	
Verdi	Boito	Milan	11 Mar. 89	IP	*Cop.* 702; Nar. 510; Abb. iv. 376; *Cart. V–B* i. 139–40
Boito	Verdi	Genoa	[13 Mar. 89]	SA	*Cart.* ii. 130–1; *Cart. V–B* i. 140–1
Giuseppina Verdi	G. De Sanctis	Naples	19 Mar. 89	IP (PH)	*Cart.* i. 209
Verdi	Ricordi	Milan	28 Mar. 89	Ri.	
Giuseppina Verdi	G. De Sanctis	Naples	29 Mar. 89	IP (PH)	*Cart.* i. 209–10
Giuseppina Verdi	G. De Sanctis	Naples	11 Apr. 89	IP (PH)	*Cart.* i. 210
Ricordi	Verdi	St Agata	30 Apr. 89	SA	
Ricordi	Verdi	St Agata	8 May 89	SA	
Verdi	Ricordi	Milan	10 May 89	Ri.	
Muzio	D'Ormeville	Milan	6 July 89	Bus.	
Verdi	Faccio	London	14 July 89	IP (PH)	*Cop.* 702
Verdi	Ricordi	Milan	17 Jan. 90	Pa.	
Ricordi	Verdi	Genoa	18 Jan. 90	SA	
Muzio	Verdi	St Agata	[22 Oct. 90]	?	*Cop.* 359 n; We. 246
Verdi	Ricordi	Milan	4 Nov. 90	Ri.	*Cop.* 358–9; We. 246
Verdi	Mayor of Villanova	Villanova	16 Nov. 90	?	*Cop.* 360
Verdi	Durot	Madrid	5 Jan. 91	?	*Cop.* 361
Verdi	Ricordi	Milan	11 Mar. 91	Ri.	
Verdi	Ricordi	Milan	15 Mar. 91	Ri.	
Verdi	Ricordi	Milan	21 Mar. 91	Pa.	

From	To	Destination	Date	Autograph location	Published source
Ricordi	Verdi	Genoa	31 Mar. 91	SA	
Verdi	Boriani	Villanova	22 Apr. 91	?	*Cop.* 367–8
Ricordi	Verdi	St Agata	22 May 91	SA	
Verdi	Ricordi	Milan	25 May 91	Ri.	*Cart. V–B* ii. 409
Ricordi	Verdi	Montecatini	18 July 91	SA	
Verdi*	Bertrand	Paris	27 Oct. 91	?	*Cop.* 371
Verdi	Ricordi	Milan	26 Jan. 92	Ri.	
Ricordi	Verdi	Genoa	29 Jan. 92	SA	
Verdi	Ricordi	Milan	31 Jan. 92	Ri.	*Cart.* ii. 131–2
Ricordi	Verdi	Genoa	1 Feb. 92	SA	
Verdi	Ricordi	Milan	2 Feb. 92	Ri.	
Ricordi	Verdi	Genoa	5 Feb. 92	SA	
Ricordi	Verdi	Genoa	9 Feb. 92	SA	
Ricordi	Verdi	Genoa	16 Feb. 92	SA	
Verdi	Darclée	?	29 May 93	?	Abb. iv. 510
Ricordi	Verdi	St Agata	31 July 93	SA	
Verdi	Ricordi	Milan?	4 Aug. 93	Ri.	
Ricordi	Verdi	St Agata	10 Sept. 93	SA	
Verdi	Ricordi	Milan	[14 Sept. 93]	Ri.	
Ricordi	Verdi	St Agata	20 Sept. 93	SA	
Verdi	Ricordi	Milan	21 Sept. 93	Ri.	
Verdi	Ricordi	Milan	21 [22] Sept. 93	Ri.	
Ricordi	Verdi	St Agata	29 Sept. 93	SA	
Verdi	Ricordi	Milan	2 Oct. 93	Ri.	
Verdi	Ricordi	Milan	4 Dec. 93	Ri.	
Ricordi	Verdi	Genoa	7 Dec. 93	SA	
Verdi	Ricordi	Milan	14 [12] Jan. 94	Ri.	
Verdi	Ricordi	Milan	12 Jan. 93 [94]	Ri.	
Ricordi	Verdi	Genoa	[13 Jan. 94]	SA	
Verdi	Ricordi	Milan	14 [13] Jan. 94	Ri.	
Tornaghi	Verdi	Genoa	14 Jan. 94	SA	
Boito	Verdi	Genoa	[18 Jan. 94]	SA	*Cart.* ii. 135–6; *Cart. V–B* i. 222–3
Verdi	Boito	Milan	19 Jan. 94	IP	*Cart. V–B* i. 223
Verdi	Ricordi	Milan	19 Jan. 94	Ri.	
Ricordi	Verdi	Genoa	19 Jan. 94	SA	
Verdi	Tornaghi	Milan	25 Jan. 94	Ri.	
Tornaghi	Verdi	Genoa	26 Jan. 94	SA	
Verdi*	Gailhard	Paris	31 Jan. 94	?	*Cop.* 388
Verdi	Ricordi	Milan	31 Jan [94]	Ri.	
Verdi	Du Locle	Paris	8 Feb. 94	?	*Cop.* 389
Verdi†	Ricordi	Milan?	8 May 94	IP	*Cart. V–B* i. 227
Verdi	Ricordi	Milan	10 May 94	Ri.	*Cart. V–B* ii. 448
Boito	Verdi	St Agata	11 May [94]	SA	*Cart.* ii. 136; *Cart. V–B* i. 227–8
Verdi	Boito	Milan	12 May 94	IP	*Cart. V–B* i. 228
Boito	Verdi	St Agata	14 May [94]	SA	*Cart.* ii. 176; *Cart. V–B* i. 229
Verdi	Boito	Milan	16 May 94	IP	*Cart. V–B* i. 229
Verdi	Boito		[c.17 May 94]	IP	*Cart. V–B* ii. 450–1

From	To	Destination	Date	Autograph location	Published source
Verdi	Boito	Milan	25 May [94]	IP	*Cart. V–B* i. 230
Verdi	Boito	Milan	[26 May 94]	IP	*Cart. V–B* i. 230
Ricordi	Verdi	St Agata	9 June 94	SA	
Chilesotti	Ricordi	Milan	10 June 94	SA	
Ricordi	Verdi	St Agata	11 June 94	SA	
Verdi	Ricordi	Milan	[12 June 94]	Ri.	
Verdi	Boito	Milan	12 June 94	IP	*Cart. V–B* i. 231
Boito	Verdi	St Agata	[13 June 94]	SA	*Cart.* ii. 177; *Cart. V–B* i. 232
Verdi	Ricordi	Milan	13 June 94	Ri.	
Ricordi	Verdi	St Agata	[15 June 94]	SA	
Ricordi	Verdi	St Agata	15 June 94	SA	
Verdi	Ricordi	Milan	16 June 94	Ri.	
Ricordi	Verdi	St Agata	21 June 94	SA	
Verdi	Boito	Paris	23 [22] June 94	IP	Nar. 596; *Cart. V–B* i. 232–3
Verdi	Ricordi	Milan	23 [22 June 94]	Ri.	
Ricordi	Verdi	St Agata	23 June 94	SA	
Verdi	Ricordi	Milan	3 July 94	Ri.	
Ricordi	Verdi	Montecatini	9 July 94	SA	
Verdi	Ricordi	Milan	9 July 94	Ri.	*Cart. V–B* ii. 454
Verdi	Ricordi	Milan	10 July 94	Ri.	*Cart. V–B* ii. 455
Ricordi	Verdi	Montecatini	11 July 94	SA	
Verdi	Ricordi	Milan	12 July 94	Ri.	*Cart. V–B* ii. 455–6
Verdi	Ricordi	Milan	17 July 94	Ri.	
Ricordi	Verdi	St Agata	18 July 94	SA	
Verdi*	Gailhard	Paris	19 July 94	?	Abb. iv. 550–1
Verdi	Ricordi	Milan	[19 July 94]	Ri.	
Verdi	Ricordi	Milan	20 [21] July 94	Ri.	
Ricordi	Verdi	St Agata	23 July 94	SA	
Verdi	Ricordi	Milan?	[26 July 94]	Ri.	
Ricordi	Verdi	St Agata	29 July 94	SA	
Verdi	Tornaghi	Milan	5 Aug. 94	Ri.	*Cart. V–B* ii. 456
Verdi	Ricordi	Milan	21 Aug. 94	Ri.	*Cart. V–B* ii. 456
Ricordi	Verdi	St Agata	22 Aug. 94	SA	
Ricordi	Verdi	St Agata	14 Sept. 94	SA	
Verdi	Ricordi	Milan	17 Sept. 94	Ri.	*Cart. V–B* ii. 457
Verdi†	Boito	Milan	19 Sept. 94	IP	*Cart. V–B* i. 233
Verdi	Ricordi	Milan	[19 Sept. 94]	Ri.	*Cart. V–B* ii. 457
Verdi	Ricordi	Milan	20 Sept. 94	Ri.	
Verdi	Crispi	Rome	13 Oct. 94	?	*Cart.* ii. 51–2
Verdi	Ricordi	Milan	[21 Oct. 94]	Ri.	
Verdi	Ricordi	Milan	[22 Oct. 94]	Ri.	
Ricordi	Verdi	Genoa	24 Oct. 94	SA	

Giuseppe Verdi (Ricordi Archive, Milan)

Arrigo Boito (Ricordi Archive, Milan)

Giulio Ricordi (Ricordi Archive, Milan)

LETTERS AND TELEGRAMS

VERDI TO GIULIO RICORDI

Genoa, 18 July 1879

[. . .] Giuditta[1] has written to Peppina[2] about the chocolate,[3] you write to me about the cocoa[4] . . . Listen well . . . I warn you once more that I have not made the slightest commitment, do not want to make any, and that I wish to keep all my freedom . . . Do you understand? . . . .

Addio and believe me

Yours,
G. Verdi

GIULIO RICORDI TO VERDI

Milan, 23 July 1879

[. . .] As for the chocolate and the cocoa, consider them jokes, and keen anticipation! . . . . Our veneration for you is too great, and our respect too deeply felt, to abuse your habitual kindness toward us.

A single fact, however, is incontestable!! . . . . Without you, theatres, publishers and art rush into precipitous ruin! . . . . . . There will be—there can be—there shall and must come—a composer, but meanwhile there is none; we are dying of starvation and agony!! . . . awaiting the Messiah! [. . .]

BOITO TO EUGENIO TORNAGHI

[Milan?, ?] July 1879

[. . .] Tell Giulio that I am preparing the chocolate.

Yours,
Arrigo

VERDI TO FERDINAND HILLER

Busseto, 31 July 1879.—St Agata

Dear Hiller,

Upon my return from Genoa, imagine my surprise in seeing an original work of yours on my desk! And the surprise was multiplied a thousand times when I read *De profundis*, translated by Dante. The funny thing is that last winter I myself was thinking of composing this psalm, but fortunately I changed my mind, and then decided to do the *Pater noster* for five voices, in

---

[1] Giuditta Ricordi (1838–1916), wife of Giulio Ricordi. Her letter is missing.
[2] Giuseppina Verdi Strepponi (1815–97), Verdi's second wife.
[3] The nickname Verdi, Boito, and Giulio Ricordi gave to *Otello*.
[4] In a letter of 17 July 1879.

Dante's own precise translation in his Minor Works, from which you took your *De profundis*. Reading and rereading this piece of yours—apart from its having much character and great beauty, like your other things—I could not help exclaiming, 'This devil Hiller writes just like an Italian! ... he writes as we do, and better than many of us! ....' I would have given anything to find some error of prosody or some mistaken accent ... Vain hopes! I repeat again: *better than us*! Excellent, excellent!

As I told you above, I was in Genoa with my wife for some two weeks on the occasion of the Agricultural Exhibition. It was poor and little; still, there was something good in the livestock and the flowers. A month before that I was also in Milan (you see what a wanderer I have become!) for some ten days. You know that in late spring we had floods in Italy which have destroyed entire provinces. Everyone—cities and individuals—sent help. Milan, among many other things, had arranged for a great concert in which the Mass was performed.[1] With a very good orchestra, a very good chorus, and first-rate singers,[2] the performance could only be excellent. But more than with the artistic result, I was content with the material one, which surpassed even my hopes. The receipts were 37,000 Lire. So the assistance was not ephemeral.

And here I am again in my fields, from which I won't move until I go to Genoa in November. [. . .]

BOITO TO EUGENIO TORNAGHI

Venice, 24 August [1879]
Hôtel de l'Univers

[. . .] Tomorrow or the day after tomorrow I'll tackle the opening verses of the last act. *All will be ready on time.* [. . .]

VERDI TO GIULIO RICORDI

St Agata, 4 August [September] 1879[1]

[. . .] A visit from you will always be welcome in the company of a friend, who now would be Boito, of course. Permit me, however, to speak to you very clearly and without ceremony about this matter.—A visit from him would commit me too much, and I absolutely do not want to commit myself.—You know how this *chocolate* project came about ... You were dining with me together with a few friends. There was talk of *Otello*, of Sheaspeare,[2] of

---

[1] Verdi had conducted the *Requiem Mass* at the Teatro Dal Verme in Milan on 29 June. (See Introduction, p. 00.)

[2] The orchestra of La Scala, a chorus including the *Cappella del Duomo* and students of the Conservatory, Teresa Stolz, Maria Waldmann, the tenor Enrico Barbacini, and the bass Ormondo Maini.

---

[1] In a misdated answer to a letter from Giulio Ricordi of 28 Aug. 1879.

[2] Verdi's frequent misspelling (see Editorial Guide).

Boito. The following day Faccio came with Boito to my hotel.[3] Three days later Boito brought me the sketch of *Otello*, which I read and found good. Write the poetry, I told him; it will always be good for you, for me, for someone else, etc., etc. .[4]

If you come here with Boito now, I shall inevitably be obliged to read the finished libretto he will bring along with him.

If I find the libretto thoroughly good, I'll find myself committed in some way.

If I find it good and suggest modifications which Boito accepts, I'll find myself committed even more.

If I don't like it, however, even if it is very beautiful, it would be too hard to tell him this opinion to his face!

No, no . . . You have already gone too far, and we must stop before gossip and annoyances arise.—In my view it would be best (if you think so and Boito agrees) to send me the finished poem so that I can read it and calmly express my opinion without committing any of the persons involved.[5]

Once these rather touchy problems have been resolved, I'll be very happy to see you come here with Boito.

Believe me in the meantime

Yours,
G. Verdi

GIULIO RICORDI TO VERDI

Milan, 5 September 1879

[. . .] Ever since *Aida* was performed at La Scala,[1] Faccio, Boito and I have talked a good deal about how happy Boito would have been to write a libretto for Verdi. Unfortunately, several years have gone by, but this idea has never left us! . . . and we have hoped in vain for a favourable circum-

---

[3] Grand Hôtel et de Milan in Via Manzoni in Milan.

[4] Giuseppe Adami, Giulio Ricordi's biographer, gives this account of the occasion:

'The idea of the opera, said Signor Giulio, came up during a dinner with friends, where I casually directed the conversation to Shakespeare and Boito. At the mention of *Otello*, I saw Verdi look hard at me with distrust, but with interest. He had certainly understood, he was certainly stirred. I thought the matter was ripe. My able accomplice was Franco Faccio. I hoped too much. The next day, when, upon my advice, Faccio brought Boito to Verdi with the project of the already outlined libretto, the Maestro, having examined it and having found it excellent, did not want to commit himself. [. . .]' (Adami, p. 64.)

[5] Verdi's reluctance to study a libretto in the presence of its author, his hesitation to commit himself, are reflected also in two of his letters to the French playwright Adolphe Dennery (1811–99). On 19 June 1878 he wrote to Dennery that 'it would be useless to do business if the poetry—even though very beautiful, as I do not doubt—were not to my taste'. On 9 July 1878 Verdi added that 'the reading of a poem by the author—his very presence, I am afraid—might influence me toward an impression which might then be less when I reread the poem in the silence of my room'. (Busch, *Aida*, pp. 411–12.)

---

[1] 8 Feb. 1872.

stance! .... Boito had *Mefistofele*[2] performed and then undertook *Nerone*;[3] he wrote to me at that time[4] that he would do no more libretti for anyone .... but he would give up all other work to write a libretto for Verdi, for such an honour and such good fortune.—But the opportunity has still not presented itself! ...., nor have I ever had the courage to mention it to you ...., because when I find myself in front of Verdi I become so intimidated I lose my bearings and my train of thought! .... And then, to tell you the truth, the publisher's fate [...] always makes me fear you might think it is the *conniver* who speaks!! .... and that disgusts me. It certainly would be extremely naïve to tell you that an opera by Verdi would not be a real fortune in material terms!! .... But this idea is considered a hundred times and, so to speak, eclipsed by the immense, indescribable emotion for a work that would make your name even more glorious, if that is possible, and would permit our beloved Italian art to shine in a new light .... and remain forever in musical history. Furthermore these ideas of mine are shared by Boito and Faccio; during their daily visits we never fail to look at the picture I have in my studio, exclaiming: 'But is he really not to write any more? ...' And thereupon talk, and more talk, only serves to make me more excited and to keep my hopes alive. This may explain the true, heartfelt, honest friendship that ties Boito, Faccio, and me together; and how much it pains me that a man like you, Maestro, could not know Boito as he really is. I know, if my memory does not fail me, that Boito once committed a wrong against you;[5] but since he is a nervous, bizarre character, I will wager he was not aware of offending you—or never found a way to make it up to you. The fact is that in our frequent meetings Boito has always spoken of Verdi with veneration and enthusiasm; otherwise he could not be my friend; and I can tell you from my experience in many personal and professional matters that Boito has always displayed a frank and loyal nature, and that he is a perfect gentleman. When he went to Genoa[6] I encouraged him to visit you; he was afraid to bother you, etc., etc., but finally he took his courage in both hands and told me that he had gone to see Verdi and tried to discuss a matter that for a long time has been on our minds. In fact, he wrote to me at that time:[7]

I went to see him yesterday morning; I did not dare to bring up the matter that is close to our hearts, because after not seeing him for so many years, it seemed far too familiar to discuss matters he did not raise himself. He was most cordial to me, and I am extremely grateful for the perfect way he received me, and could not expect any more. Among the greatest musicians I have known (among them Rossini, Meyerbeer, Wagner) Verdi is the one who excites me most deeply.

   [2] Opera in a prologue, 4 acts, and an epilogue, based on both parts of Goethe's *Faust*. Unsuccessfully premièred at La Scala in Milan on 5 Mar. 1868. Revision premièred at the Teatro Comunale in Bologna on 4 Oct. 1875. See Introduction and Boito Chronology.
   [3] Unfinished opera in 4 acts, premièred at La Scala on 1 May 1924. See Introduction and Boito Chronology.
   [4] Missing.
   [5] Boito's ode 'All'arte italiana'. See his Chronology, 1863.
   [6] For the first performance of *Mefistofele* at the Teatro Carlo Felice in Mar. 1879.
   [7] The following quotation—within Giulio Ricordi's letter—is not in his own handwriting.

Your coming to Milan,[8] which was a hundred-thousand times blessed, was the happy occasion for which we had ultimately hoped. No need to tell you what it brought about. Everything I have told you is proved by the fact that, since the day of your departure,[9] Boito has halted all other work and has occupied himself only with the libretto. Having gone to Venice for reasons of health, he wrote to me:[10]

Don't worry, I have tried to work again these past few days, taking advantage of the morning hours, in which I have some respite from the neuralgia. Even without much effort the work shall be finished in August. The hardest thing in this opera is condensing the boundless sublimity of the text into fast-paced dialogues. Regarding what I wrote in Milan, I find much to cut, much to reduce, much to reshape into smoother forms. I know for whom I am writing, and want to do the best I can.

Yesterday morning Boito's latest letter arrived:[11]

I am applying to this work a certain rhythmic construction (in the lyric part), and I believe this will deeply interest our Maestro; it will be no small surprise to you and will be a powerful incentive to realize this project, which is so close to our hearts. But this idea came late to me, and now I must do all the lyric parts of the second and third acts over again. My health is perfectly restored and I can have the entire work reconstructed and completed by the 9th or 10th of this month. I seem to have found a form that can wonderfully serve Shakespeare's text and its musical interpreter! ...

But you will tell me: it seems to me that all of you are making up the bill without the host!! .... No, Maestro ..... if we speak and write this way to each other, it's because we speak and write about something we have been discussing for years, and because we have such an intense hope of changing fantasy into reality. This is the goal, but it never occurred to any of us to take advantage of past talks with you, and consider them promises of a commitment! .... That would be a lack of respect for you! .... Nor has Boito undertaken this work with the idea of a sure and accomplished fact; this is perfectly clear to him.

The Maestro, however, will ask me: Why, then, so much haste? .... And here, too, I can tell you the reason. Boito hoped to finish by early August; but being in bad health, he went to Venice, and there was a delay. The conspirators who would have come to Busseto were three; Boito, Faccio, and I. Faccio is engaged in Madrid for the fall and is leaving, I think, on the 15th or 16th of this month. He also had high hopes of going to St Agata to greet Verdi before his departure, and of leaving with the consolation of great and happy news!! .... should this be the case, or at least of having the pleasure of seeing you!! [...]

Meanwhile, if you find the time and the means to address only a few words

[8] To conduct a benefit performance of his *Requiem Mass* at the Teatro Dal Verme in Milan on 29 June 1879.

[9] On or about 4 July 1879.

[10] The following quotation—within Giulio Ricordi's letter—is not in his own handwriting.

[11] Again, the following quotation—within Giulio Ricordi's letter—is not in his own handwriting.

to me: 'I received your letter and it's all right,' it will be an immense satisfaction and comfort to me, because it will mean that none of us—even in his dreams—has done anything that might displease you in the slightest! . . .

But in the meantime, I can tell you that my nerves are in a state of convulsion. It is hard to keep wearing a mask and to refrain from speaking of all the hopes that are racing through my head! . . .

A devoted greeting to Signora Peppina, and believe me always

Yours most devotedly,
Giulio Ricordi

VERDI TO FERDINAND HILLER[1]

[St Agata] Busseto, 8 September 1879

[. . .] Imagine how happy I would be to see my name on a frontispiece next to a composer and friend like you! But what can I say—as a matter of principle I have for many years refused dedications offered to me by artists, professors, dilettantes, and even by some worthy composers. I understand that you are you, and there are not very many like you. This is incontestable, but you could not save me from being stoned if I accepted your dedication. Tell me if in spite of this you want me to talk to Ricordi about the printing of this piece. [. . .]

GIULIO RICORDI TO VERDI

Milan, 17 September 1879

Illustrious Maestro,

Boito has written to me today from Venice[1] that he has finished the work and is recopying it, but with such trepidation that he would like to begin all over again! . . . . since the thought of submitting it to you gives him no peace of mind and he fears that he will not succeed in doing anything worthwhile. Anyway, he will be in Milan next week and will deliver his manuscript to me.—Depending on your plans, I shall forward it to you so that you can examine it at your convenience and with full freedom. If I had the good fortune to be devout, this would be the time to light candles to the Madonna and prostrate myself before God so that our most ardent vows might be heard! . . . . Mary is such a lovely celestial figure that she might even accept a non-believer's prayer!! [. . .]

---

[1] In answer to a missing letter.

---

[1] Missing.

BOITO TO EUGENIO TORNAGHI

[Venice]
Hôtel de l'Univers
Sunday [21 September 1879]

[. . .] If I don't deliver the strangled Desdemona to Giulio this week, I fear he'll strangle me. [. . .]

VERDI TO GIULIO RICORDI

St Agata, 28 September 1879

Dear Giulio,
  I am sending you Hiller's *De profundis* and thank you, etc., etc. . . [. . .]
  Look at those harmonies! The funny thing is that he is hostile to Wagner, etc., etc. But in this piece he is more advanced than Wagner, even than *Goldmark*! . . I like this in a German, as I deplore such a thing in an Italian. With them it is natural; with us it is forced and artificial. Among their excesses, once in a while one finds a strong passage; in us, the distorted, the trite, the conventional. A pity, a pity! And in the meantime, bent on the study of their absurdities, we are losing the qualities that are ours, essentially ours. [. . .]

GIULIO RICORDI TO VERDI

Milan, 29 September 1879

Illustrious Maestro,
  Confirming my last letter, I advise you that Boito arrived last night with the finished work. I am not sending it right away, since he is recopying it and at the same time will rewrite two scenes that do not fully satisfy him. He is a little late, having been bothered by a rather nasty facial neuralgia that kept him from working. He hopes that he has faithfully followed and condensed Shakespeare's concepts and that he will win your approval.
  In the meantime I find myself between heaven and earth, anxious, panting between life and death!!! . . . Make us live, Maestro!!!! . . . .
  The most cordial greetings from

Yours always most gratefully,
Giulio Ricordi

VERDI TO GIULIO RICORDI

St Agata, 4 October 1879

[. . .] You can do whatever you wish with the libretto, since no one has commitments to me just as I have commitments to no one. [. . .]

GIULIO RICORDI TO VERDI

Milan, 7 October 1879

[. . .] Saturday, in agreement with Boito, I telegraphed you that I would send the manuscript on Thursday; but Boito fell ill again, and this morning I wrote a few lines to him[1] telling him how distressed I was by this delay, how I regretted breaking my word to a man like Verdi—who, on the other hand, might have different thoughts about the reasons for the delay and consider it a lack of respect; therefore he should try to finish the work on the day promised, dead or alive! . . . Boito answered my letter.[2] I was very much in doubt whether or not to enclose the letter. By sending it to you I would have fully justified myself, but it might also have seemed inappropriate. It could have created other impressions, too, since it was a card written to me in complete confidence and under the pressure of my rebukes—right on the one hand, wrong on the other! . . . . However this may be, realizing that there is a certain man called Verdi, who likes matters to be clear and clean and likes to know the truth *intus et in cute*, I am enclosing Boito's reply. If I was wrong, the fault and the penalty are mine. In any case, I beg you to return the letter to me. As you see, there is a delay of a few days which should not be attributed to the ill will of the poet, who will take up his work again as soon as he is given some respite from his pain. [. . .]

BOITO TO GIULIO RICORDI

[Milan, 7 October 1879]

Dear Giulio,

 I am far more distressed than you; today I got up at half past seven and sat at my desk working as much as I could; but until noon yesterday the abscess that torments me had not burst, and I could not work with that hell in my mouth. I hope that abscess was the definite *cadenza* of my ills. I have nothing else in mind except to finish the work well, as well and as quickly as I can. No other enterprise in my life has caused me the restlessness and agitation that I have felt in these months of mental and physical battle.

Don't think that the libretto can be finished until after tomorrow. The abscess has made me lose three days; I only returned to work today, so three days must be added to Thursday. The bad luck that dogs this work shall be vanquished.

But whatever may happen, even if V. no longer wishes to be my collaborator, I shall finish the work in the best way possible, to give him proof that—even battered by physical ailments—I dedicated four months of my life to him with all the affection that he inspires in me. For this I would not demand, heaven knows, any material compensation, either from him or

---

[1] Missing.
[2] See the letter that follows, apparently delivered by a messenger the same day.

from you, if nothing comes of it. It would be enough for me to give V. proof
that I am far more devoted to him than he thinks.

Your
Arrigo

GIULIO RICORDI TO GIUSEPPINA VERDI

Milan, 4 November 1879

[...] Now on to another matter about which I ask your advice.

Boito had promised me the third and fourth acts for today. He came to me
and told me that he had finished the third, but not yet the fourth, and that he
did not want to send the one without the other.

I have never seen Boito in such a state of agitation, so much so that it
makes me take pity on him. He says that he doesn't know himself any more!
. . .

Another time he confided to me:

If only I could have done in twelve hours the work of twelve days. The idea of
submitting a work to Verdi excites me so much that I remain as in a daze. For several
nights I stayed up until 3 o'clock, almost without putting down my pen, totally
absorbed in my work and excited by its purpose. What more can I tell you! . . . I live in
constant fear of doing something that will not please Verdi and omitting something
that might please him instead! . . . I am writing and rewriting. Should I find strength in
the thought that I might succeed with a libretto which might finally induce the
Maestro to write? . . . And then what? . . . . . all my boldness goes up in smoke. If I'd
been able to confer with Verdi about general guidelines, I would have gone on
quickly, since the questions of detail amount to nothing: one changes, one cuts, one
arranges. But Shakespeare's tragedy is immense; in this immensity I must work out a
general line that should conform to Verdi's ideas. Will I succeed? . . . Here is the
problem that robs me of my strength! . . . I could have asked the Maestro for
permission to see him; but even if I had received a courteous yes from him, I was
afraid that my request might have made it seem that I was pressuring him—and this I
absolutely would not want! . . . . . I know that Verdi can think ill of my hesitations; I
might also fear he will run out of patience! . . . . but I cannot do violence to myself; to
a man like Verdi I want to send something that leaves me with a clear conscience, even
if it should fail. . . . . .

In short, it seemed to me as if a five-year-old boy were standing before me.
I comforted him, telling him how sorry I was that he was so upset. He left me,
went back home to work, and begged me to find a way of asking for the
Maestro's patience—not for need of the libretto, but to keep him from being
annoyed by its delay and from judging this a lack of respect.

Now I am asking for your advice. If it were possible to let Boito speak to
Verdi, I think all of this would be over . . . . . . and the libretto finished in a
few hours. . . . . But the Maestro, understandably, sees a moral commitment
in this; Boito, on the other hand, also understandably, fears to exert pressure.
So we have two negative poles! . . . . Is there no way to change the current,

transforming them to positive ones? . . . How beautiful this would be! . . . But to do this, the idea of a commitment would have to be totally eliminated on the one side, and the fear of pressure on the other. Well, with all of this, I bear all the blows in the meantime, and my nerves feel like an electrical wire . . . . . . I have no peace, I cannot sleep! . . . . . My head is an erupting volcano. In a word, this blessed Verdi gives everybody the shivers! . . . . . . great and small alike.

So I conclude; that is, I don't conclude, but ask you what to do under these circumstances? . . .

Ask the Maestro for permission to come? . . . . But at the same time persuade him that this means no pressure on *anybody's* part? . . . . and if this is the best solution, in what manner, by what means can I tell him this and persuade him? . . . . Because here, I think, is the knot of the question; once this idea is eliminated and this fear put aside, nothing else should stand in the way.

So please help me, peerless Signora Peppina, and tell me what is the best thing to do. I no longer have an hour's peace, and am walking on hot coals! . . .

Ah! the day I might drink the famous chocolate! . . . . That will be the most beautiful chocolate in all my life! . . . .

With warmest good wishes and thanks from

Yours most gratefully,
Giulio Ricordi

GIUSEPPINA VERDI TO GIULIO RICORDI

St Agata, 7 November 1879

[. . .] I don't know Boito very well, but I think I have deciphered him. A nervous, most excitable nature! When overwhelmed with admiration he is capable of endless enthusiasms and sometimes—perhaps 'for the sake of contrast'—of excessive antipathies as well! All this, however, comes in brief paroxysms, and only when there is a battle between the mind and the heart, or better, between contrasting passions or powers. The loyalty, the fairness of his character must then predominate quickly, and re-establish the balance of all his faculties. He is firm in friendship and, at the same time, gentle and docile as a child, as long as he is not 'stung', so to speak. I am saying all this to make you *understand* that I think I have *understood the man*. Therefore his feverish state of mind at present does not surprise me. In the hope of bringing a bit of calm, I shall whisper a little confidence into Giulio's ear, on the condition that it doesn't become the secret of Pulcinella.

Towards the 20th of this month we shall be spending a few days in Milan; I think we should wait for that moment as being the most opportune to let Boito talk quietly and at length with Verdi without attracting the attention of the curious.

Inter nos: What he [Boito] has written of the *African* so far seems to be to his [Verdi's] taste and done very well; he is sure that the rest will be done equally well. He [Boito] should, then, abandon himself to his fantasy and calmly finish the poem (without torturing himself); as soon as he has finished it he should send it without hesitation or delay to Verdi before he comes to Milan, so that he can quietly read it in case he wishes to make observations beforehand. I repeat: the impression is good; the modifications and the polishing will come later.

I hope, and am confident, that we shall be able to say, 'All's well that ends well', and so may it end. Don't write or speak, then, to Verdi of fears, wishes, uncertainties. Let me add: Do not even tell Verdi that I have written to you about this matter. I believe this to be the best way not to arouse the idea of even the remotest pressure in Verdi's mind. Let the stream flow straight on its way to the sea. It is in these wide spaces that certain men are destined to meet, and understand each other. [. . .]

GIULIO RICORDI TO GIUSEPPINA VERDI

Milan, 8 November 1879

Kindest Signora Peppina,

I received your most welcome letter just as I was sending off the post. A few lines, therefore, to tell you of the immense pleasure it has given me! . . . . Life as a whole is a very ugly thing! . . . . . But certain joys compensate for great sorrows! [. . .]

So as not to bother the Maestro unnecessarily, I am transcribing for you a note that Boito sent me a short while ago;[1] too bad that no telegraph wire has been established between me and him!!

Yesterday I worked on the fourth act and am content. There is still the trio of the third act, a pivotal piece that makes me despair! . . . Every once in a while I let it alone and go ahead with some other scene; then I return to the trio, and find it more awkward than ever! . . Yet I don't despair, but am sure I'll be seeing you shortly with the chocolate warm and ready . . . . . . and how content we shall be! . . . .

So the chocolate is boiling, boiling, boiling!! . . . . . And I am, too! [. . .]

GIULIO RICORDI TO VERDI

Milan, 13 November 1879

[. . .] Yesterday I drank the third cup of chocolate![1] . . . The fourth is almost ready, and on Saturday or Sunday I hope to send you a complete chocolate bar made of good cocoa, properly roasted and concentrated! . . . Then . . . . *à la grâce de Dieu*! [. . .]

---

[1] Missing.

---

[1] The third act of Boito's *Otello* libretto.

VERDI TO GIULIO RICORDI

St Agata, 18 November 1879

[...] I have just received the chocolate. I'll read it tonight, since at the moment I have other things on my mind.
  Addio, addio

G. Verdi

VERDI TO GIULIO RICORDI

[Milan, shortly after 20 November 1879]

Dear Giulio,
  I am not feeling too well and want to postpone the talk with Boito until tomorrow.

G. Verdi

GIUSEPPINA VERDI TO GIUSEPPINA NEGRONI PRATI MOROSINI

Genoa, 18 December 1879

[...] By coincidence, the conversation one day in Milan[1] drifted towards Sheakspeare's marvellous drama and how the bungler,[2] reducing it for the stage (that is, 'to the form of an operatic libretto') had not done it in any poetic, dramatic, much less Sheakspearean way. The conversation was mentioned to Boito, who warmed to his fantasy, presenting a draft two days later, and then the entire libretto in verse. Verdi read it, and one must say he liked it, since he acquired the rights ... but he put it beside Somma's Re Lear,[3] who for twenty years has been lying deeply and undisturbedly asleep in his briefcase. What will become of this Otello? Who knows? I wish Verdi could let him sleep for another twenty years like Re Lear and might then feel strong and courageous enough to set him to music. Of course, I, too, would like to be strong enough then to drag myself at least to the first performance! [...]

GIULIO RICORDI TO VERDI

Milan, 19 December 1879

[...] Every day I am (literally) besieged by people who want to know

---

  [1] See Introduction, p. 00, and Verdi to Ricordi, 4 Aug. [Sept.] 1897.
  [2] Marquis Francesco Berio di Salsa (1767–1820), librettist of Rossini's opera in 3 acts, *Otello ossia il Moro di Venezia*, which had its première in Naples on 4 December 1816.
  [3] See Introduction, p. 00.

something about *Otello*. The level of general interest is extraordinarily high.
[. . .]

GIUSEPPINA VERDI TO CESARE DE SANCTIS

Genoa, 5 January 1880

[. . .] For the time being, at least, *Otello* is in the mind of God. Beware of
believing the papers. The only thing certain is the performance of a *Pater
noster* and *Ave Maria* at Milan in the spring.[1] [. . .]

GIULIO RICORDI TO VERDI

Milan, 6 January 1880

[. . .] If I were impertinent I would ask for news of the chocolate . . . but I obey
the orders received! . . Therefore: *drink up the water!* . . . not being able to say:
drink up the chocolate. [. . .]

VERDI TO DOMENICO MORELLI

Genoa, 6 January 1880

[. . .] How beautiful is this sketch of *King Lear!*[1] As desolate as the subject.
The figure of old Kent must have a very powerful expression, I suppose.

Why don't you create the counterpart of this sketch with a scene from
Otello?

For instance, when Otello strangles Desdemona; or better yet (this would
be more original), when Otello, tortured by jealousy, faints and Jago, gazing
at him, says with a diabolical smile: 'Work on, my medicine'[2] . . . .

What a figure, this Jago!!!

Well, then? What about it?

Write to me, work—which is even better—and give me a hearty handshake, since I embrace you with the greatest admiration.

G. Verdi

---

[1] On 18 Apr. 1880, Franco Faccio conducted the first performance of these works in Verdi's
presence at La Scala (see Introduction, p. xxxiii). Composed in 1879–80, these two sacred pieces
preceded the *Pezzi sacri*, which Verdi wrote years later.

---

[1] See two reproductions in Levi, p. 227.

[2] Verdi quotes in Italian from Shakespeare, *Othello*, IV. 44–5: 'Work,/My medicine,
work . . .—'opera, farmaco mio'. In Boito's final text (III, 9) Jago sings, 'Il mio velen lavora' [My
poison works], as well as in an earlier aside (II. 5). Morelli sketched some ideas (reproduced in
Levi, p. 226) for this scene, but never executed them.

VERDI TO FERDINAND HILLER

Genoa, 7 January 1880

Dear Hiller,

How many times have I taken my pen in hand to write to you, but do not think of this as one of the usual meagre excuses of those singers who are late for rehearsals and blame their watch! No! My watch is accurate, and the delay only came about because, returning from Milan, I found here many very urgent matters to take care of, and then I was forced to make a trip to St Agata for no less urgent business. Now here I am with you, and first of all let me tell you that it is not certain that I shall go to Paris. I have so little desire to get involved in the Babel of that pretentious *Opéra*, where music is performed so poorly, that as of now I really don't know whether or not I shall make this journey.[1] [. . .]

My *Pater noster* will be performed during Lent in Milan at a benefit concert with about 300 voices. It is written in five vocal parts, without accompaniment, in the style of Palestrina, with modern modulations and harmonies, of course, perhaps even with too many modulations, especially in the beginning. However, it is not too difficult. It will be published as soon as it has been given at the concert, so that you can easily perform it at your *Festival*; I shall even tell you my opinion, which will be more frank and sincere than those you might read in the papers. [. . .]

VERDI TO FRANCO FACCIO[1]

Genoa, 8 January 1880

Dear Faccio,

It's a little late, I know, but accept anyway the sincere and most cordial wishes which Peppina and I both send you. The patient whom you mention to me is very gravely ill, and perhaps no doctor can heal him now. An *Otello*, even if successful, would make the patient live a few more days and nothing more. Of very little use, without any satisfaction to the doctor. The public in general, and yours in particular, is led astray and no longer loves the theatre with abandon as in the past—in fact, they say, it affects contempt out of fashion! Seduced by big words that make no sense, elsewhere it swallows boredom under the title of *Great Art*; as if Italian opera, on the whole the true, well-made opera, did not belong to *Great Art*! And how much music is admired under this pretext of *Great Art*! It's forced, little music, extravagant, orchestrated for the accordion, with affected little harmonies, without

---

[1] The production of *Aida* in French that Verdi directed and conducted at the Opéra on 22 Mar. 1880 was the greatest success the work had ever enjoyed.

[1] In answer to a New Year's letter from Faccio, in which he referred to Verdi's work for the poor, adding: 'Think, however, that another poor one needs help, a sick one, whom you can heal with the cure of the chocolate: the Italian lyric theatre.' (De Rensis, *Faccio e Verdi*, p. 224.)

honesty, without spontaneity, and without the slightest trace of an idea! An art that lacks naturalness and [any] ideas of art? Addio, addio. Some other time I'll tell you the rest.

Devotedly,
G. Verdi

DOMENICO MORELLI TO VERDI

Naples, 8 January 1880

Dearest Maestro,

Jago gazing at the fainted Otello—what a beautiful situation. Jago with the face of a righteous man. I have found a priest who seems to be exactly like him. If I can manage I'll send him to you—not the priest, but a canvas full of my scrawls. But! What music you will have found for this situation! When I think of it I feel very, very small and would far prefer being a singer to working with colours, so that I could make a whole theatre tremble, even if it were full of stupid people. [. . .]

VERDI TO DOMENICO MORELLI[1]

Genoa, 7 February 1880

Dear Morelli,

Good, very good, excellent, most, most excellent! Jago with the face of an honest man!

You have hit upon it exactly! Ah, I knew you would; I was sure of it. I seem to see this *priest*, that is, this Jago with the face of a righteous man! Quickly, then; set down four strokes of the brush and send me this 'canvas full of scrawls'. Set it down, down . . quickly, quickly . . with inspiration . . . Let it come as it comes . . . . don't do it for the painters . . do it for a musician! — —

Don't be so modest, telling me that you feel *small, very small*, because it's useless, I don't believe you. When a man has done what Domenico Morelli has done, he doesn't raise his voice and talk like a common mortal, but looks inside and says to himself: '*I* am *I* and *I* again.' . . . .

So let's get on with this 'scrawl'.!

How beautiful is the scene of the kneeling monks: *La Vergine degli Angeli*, etc., but it's a *subject* from opera.[2] This Jago is *Shaspeare*, he is *humanity*—a part of humanity, that is, the ugly part. [. . .]

[1] This translation is based on a facsimile published by Levi, pp. 229–32. The facsimile, representing the actual letter, differs slightly from Verdi's copy in *Copialettere*, pp. 693–4.
[2] A painting by Morelli, *Il Venerdì Santo*, reminded Verdi of the 'Virgin of the Angels' Chorus in *La forza del destino*. Act II. For a sketch and study of this painting, see Levi, pp. 233–4.

EMANUELE MUZIO TO GIULIO RICORDI

[Paris, 25 February 1880]

[. . .] Speaking of *Otello*, he [Verdi] told me[1] that he has already begun to set it to music; I will come with him to Milan and will then be able to tell you more. For now, he must be left alone; if you were to come, it would seem as though you wished to keep him from writing an opera in French, which he won't do; for he told me, 'I want to write in Italian.' What I am telling you is for the good of all of us, and we must keep quiet while the water is flowing. [. . .]

EMANUELE MUZIO TO GIULIO RICORDI

[Paris, 4 March 1880]

[. . .] The first performance of *Aida* won't be given on the 12th, but on the 15th ... Verdi has added a most beautiful musical idea for a *da capo* in the dance [section] of the march, a little *bijou*![1] How many motives, how much melody, and how much *cantabile* music that great man has in his head. By God, *Jago*[2] has been started, and now that he has started it, he will finish it. [. . .]

VERDI TO DOMENICO MORELLI

Milan, 19 April 1880

[. . .] Think a bit about finding a Jago face. [. . .]

VERDI TO DOMENICO MORELLI

St Agata, 12 May 1880

[. . .] And Jago? Have you found this scoundrel with the face of a righteous man? [. . .]

---

[1] In Paris, while preparing *Aida* at the Opéra.

[1] This addition involves fifty-two bars of new music, followed by the recapitulation of the theme in F minor, the total amounting to eighty-eight bars. (See Partitura d'Orchestra, Ricordi 1958, PR 153, from the last two bars on p. 172 until the entire page 188.)

[2] Verdi and Boito decided to name the opera *Otello* rather than *Jago* only in 1886 (see Verdi to Boito, 21 Jan. 1886). Victor Maurel, quite obviously, pressed for the title *Jago* (see his letter to Verdi, 22 Dec. 1885).

GIULIO RICORDI TO BOITO

[Milan?] 24 July 1880

[. . .] We need to wake up our Verdi a bit! . . . Remember—I wrote to him at your request[1] that upon your return you would work on the finale you had already drafted, in which only the verses were still missing! . . . Don't make an ass out of me!! [. . .] I have the feeling that Verdi has put the Moor to sleep for a while!! . . . and the electrical shock of your verses would now be a godsend!! . . . So do me the blessed favour of sending your confounded finale to Busseto. [. . .]

BOITO TO EUGENIO TORNAGHI[1]

[Monaco, 3 August 1880]

[. . .] The new finale of the third act, along with a letter of mine,[2] went off to B. [Busseto] as I was leaving for Monaco. I give you this news to reassure you. [. . .]

BOITO TO EUGENIO TORNAGHI

[Monaco, 4–5? August 1880]

[. . .] I have no news from Busseto, but the Maestro must have received the scene [the third act finale] at least five or six days ago. I expected an answer, which should have been sent to me on these shores. [. . .]

GIULIO RICORDI TO GIUSEPPINA VERDI

[Cernobbio on Lake Como?] 5 August 1880

[. . .] Boito is trying some sea-bathing to restore his health. I am glad to hear that he fulfilled his promise to the Maestro as soon as he returned from London. This time he was no poet.—Since I must write to him in a few days, I shall be honoured to give him your and the Maestro's message,[1] which will make him very happy and proud.—By the way, I must share a little confidence with you. A few days ago, when I spoke with Boito about you,

---

[1] Missing.

---

[1] While Giulio Ricordi was vacationing at Cernobbio on Lake Como.
[2] Missing.

---

[1] Presumably in reference to the new third act finale and Boito's lines to Tornaghi of 3 Aug.

Verdi, and Busseto, he remembered the excursion planned for there last year and regretted that various circumstances had made it go up in smoke. From that conversation I gather that Boito's wish to pay you a visit at St Agata is still alive; but as I know his character and way of thinking, I am sure that he will fear his visit might be considered an act of tactless curiosity, and that this will keep him from making any direct reference, so that he will just mention it to me in a few words and ask if I have no occasion to go to Busseto.

Since for special reasons the Maestro, too, might now welcome such a visit, I am asking you confidentially whether I should drop the matter in the event that it comes up again, or behave differently [. . .] .

BOITO TO GIULIO RICORDI

[Monaco ?, ? August 1880]

[. . .] Give me news of the Moor if you have any. [. . .]

VERDI TO BOITO

St Agata, 15 August 1880[1]

Dear Signor Boito,

Giulio will have told you that I received your verses several days ago, and that I wanted to read and study them well before I answered you.

They are certainly of greater warmth than the earlier ones, but in my opinion the dramatic part is still missing; and it is missing because it cannot be there. Once Otello has insulted Desdemona there is nothing more to be said. At the most a phrase, a reprimand, a curse upon the *barbarian* who has insulted a lady! And here either we let the curtain fall or we come up with a *device* beyond Shakspeare. For example (I'm merely thinking aloud), after the words '*Demonio taci*' ['Demon, be still'], Lodovico, with all the pride of a patrician and the dignity of an ambassador, might boldly address Otello—'*Indegno Moro*, tu osi *insultare una Patrizia Veneta, mia parente, e non temi l'ira del Senato!*' ['*Unworthy Moor*, you dare *insult a Venetian noblewoman, my relative, and you do not fear the wrath of the Senate!*'] / strophe of *4* or *6* lines.

Jago is pleased with his work / also a strophe
Desdemona laments / also a strophe
Rodrigo / strophe
Emilia and Chorus / strophe
Otello silent, immobile, terrible, says nothing . . .

Suddenly drums, trumpets, *cannon shots*, etc., etc., are heard far off. . . . '*I Turchi! I Turchi!*' ['*The Turks! The Turks!*'] Populace and soldiers rush on-stage. Surprise and fear in all! Otello rouses himself and rises up like a

---

[1] Not knowing Boito's address, Verdi only posted this letter two days later with a letter to Giulio Ricordi of 17 Aug. 1880 (Palatina).

lion; he brandishes his sword and turns to Lodovico—'*Andiamo vi condurrò di nuovo alla vittoria. Venezia mi compenserà poi* con una destituzione!' ['*Let's go, I'll lead you again to victory. Then Venice will reward me* with impeachment!'] . . .

Everyone leaves the stage except Desdemona. Meanwhile the women in the crowd rush in from all sides; terrified, they throw themselves on to their knees while the shouts of the warriors, cannon shots, drums, trumpets, etc., and all the furor of the battle are heard from backstage. Desdemona, in the middle of the stage, isolated, immobile, gazing up at the sky, prays for Otello.

The curtain falls.

The musical part would be there, and a composer could be content. The critic would have many observations to make. For example: If the Turks have been defeated (as is said in the beginning), how could they return to fight now? This would not be a serious criticism, however, because it might be supposed, and said in two words, that the Turks had been hurt and scattered by the storm but not destroyed.—There would be a more serious criticism. Otello, overcome with grief, consumed with jealousy, crushed, sick in mind and body—could he suddenly rouse himself and return as the hero he was before? If he can, and if he is still lured by glory, and if he can forget love, grief, jealousy—why does he kill Desdemona and then himself?

Are these doubts, or serious observations? I wanted to tell you what is going through my head. Who knows, maybe you'll discover a germ in this nonsense from which to create something!

Think about it, write me, and believe me

Most devotedly,
G. Verdi

PS Allow me to send you my sincerest congratulations on the happy outcome of *Mefistofele* in London[2]—

FERDINAND HILLER TO VERDI
[In French]

Sassnitz,[1] 2 September 1880

[. . .] And you, dear Maestro, are you occupied with the new opera that is already more talked about before its appearance than are those of other composers afterwards? I hope so; you really are still too young in mind, heart and body not to compose any more for the millions of people enthusiastic about your works. [. . .]

---

[2] At Her Majesty's Theatre on 6 July (see Harold Rosenthal (ed.), *The Mapleson Memoirs: The Career of an Operatic Impresario, 1858–1888* (London: Putnam, 1966, pp. 137–44).

[1] Seaside resort on the German island of Rügen in the Baltic Sea, where Hiller was on vacation.

BOITO TO GIUSEPPINA VERDI[1]

> Monaco (Alpes maritimes)
> Hôtel des bains
> Saturday [4 September 1880]

Most gracious Signora,

I really must thank you for the deep gratification I have derived from the lovely words you wrote to our friend Giulio,[2] words concerning me which have been faithfully conveyed to me. Today I received a most interesting letter from the Maestro,[3] which I have already read and reread ten times over, and given much thought to. I shall have no peace with myself until I realize the ideas in this letter. But in order not to bore the Maestro with empty words when he expects results, I am withholding my answer until I can give him the fruit of the germ he has put in my head. And this shall certainly be soon, since fortunately I am not plagued this year by the demon of neuralgia, the enemy of all work. Bathing in the sea, which one can do very well in this gulf, has greatly restored my health, on which, I believe, any good state of mind depends.

I beg you to pay my respects to the Maestro and to accept, with your innate, genuine courtesy, the expression of my devoted friendship.

> Yours most devotedly,
> Arrigo Boito

BOITO TO GIULIO RICORDI

> [Monaco, 4 September 1880]

Dear Giulio,

I have done what you wanted: I have just written to Signora Verdi. The chocolate seems to be in the oven. [. . .]

GIUSEPPINA VERDI TO GIULIO RICORDI

> St Agata, 7 September 1880

[. . .] I am very, very late in answering your last letter;[1] and this time not only from the sin of laziness, but because I was ill, as Maestro Muzio can tell you, and because your question embarrasses me very much! But I must begin the matter *ab ovo*.

You know how this business of the wicked Jago came about.[2] One can say

---

[1] Giulio Ricordi had forwarded Verdi's letter of 15 Aug. 1880 to Boito and probably suggested this letter to Giuseppina Verdi.
[2] Presumably on 7 Nov. 1879.
[3] Verdi's letter of 15 Aug. 1880, forwarded by Giulio Ricordi to Monaco.

---

[1] Of 5 Aug. 1880.
[2] See Introduction, p. xxxiii, Verdi to Giulio Ricordi, 4 Sept. 1879, and Giuseppina Verdi to Giuseppina Negroni Prati Morosini, 18 Dec. 1879.

that Verdi entered blindly and unwillingly into this kind of net. One thing led to another and out of *nothing*, out of a simple word, cheerfully dropped with a wineglass in the hand, a *libretto* was born. Verdi accepted it, though *without committing himself*, and I heard him say several times, not without a touch of bad humour: 'I let myself be tied down too much—things are going too far ahead and I absolutely don't want to be forced to do what I don't want to do,' etc., etc.

You see that if you came here with Boito—no matter how dear to us your visit might be—the papers, whose bells are constantly ringing, would chatter about this (far distant) Jago with twice the number of bells! All this would lead to even stronger ties, a greater commitment to do this *Otello*, of whom Verdi still has no really sharp and clear ideas, in spite of the very beautiful verses. And without clear ideas . . . Verdi would never write, not now or later, not in any event!

After all that I have told you quickly, I frankly consider it best, at least for the moment, to leave things as they are, and to maintain the greatest possible silence about the Moor! Besides, Verdi's activities and concerns are so many and varied at this time that it would be impossible for him to occupy himself with the Moor even if everything should move him to compose.

Boito has written me a very kind letter, from which I learn with pleasure how greatly his health has benefited from the sea bathing. Health is a precious gift for everyone, and particularly for strong talents like Boito, able to enrich the world with masterworks of art and literature. Please, dear Giulio, assure him of my esteem. [. . .]

VERDI TO FERDINAND HILLER[1]

St Agata, 14 September 1880

[. . .] As for myself, I am occupied only with buildings and agriculture.

The music is locked up in my piano, and, since you ask about it, Otello sleeps peacefully and so far has murdered neither Desdemona nor any audience. You know that since this past spring I have had the libretto from Boito,[2] the author of *Mefistofele*. I have bought the libretto; I have put it with my papers and have not written a note. That's all. [. . .]

VERDI TO OPPRANDINO ARRIVABENE

St Agata, 14 September 1880

Dear Arrivabene,

Lucky you, if you can breathe good, healthy air and admire the masterworks of ancient Italian art. Here I am breathing all the air I want, but I have nothing else to admire besides my cows, my oxen, horses, etc., etc.,

---

[1] In answer to Hiller's letter of 2 Sept. 1880.
[2] Verdi had already received Boito's *Otello* libretto from Giulio Ricordi on 18 Nov. 1879.

being a peasant, mason, carpenter, and a labourer when necessary. Let me explain. I have many farmhouses in ruin, as they all are around here. I have made up my mind to repair them, as long as there is time, and to build some so that sooner or later somebody or other isn't killed. So I am architect, master mason, blacksmith, a bit of everything. Therefore, goodbye books, goodbye music; I feel that I have forgotten and don't know notes any more.

Of the wicked Jago there is no talk at this time. Boito has made the book for me, I have bought it, but I haven't written a note. [. . .]

VERDI TO BOITO[1]

Busseto, 14 October 1880
St Agata

Dear Boito,

I received the third [act] finale today.[2] I have read it: divine! . . . And now, what do you think about the doubts I expressed in my last letter?[3] What do you think about the character of Otello?

Drop me a line.

My wife thanks you[4] and sends her regards. I take your hand and beg you to forgive me for causing so many problems—

Affectionately,
G. Verdi

BOITO TO VERDI[1]

Milan, Monday [18 October 1880]
Via Principe Amedeo 1.

Dear Maestro,

Your letter has filled my heart with joy. So, we have the third [act] finale. So, I had the good fortune to find a suitable form for the concepts you had in mind. Through my handiwork, you now recognize the ideas that you indicated to me, that I transcribed without being disturbed by any doubts, not even the doubts you raised yourself. Working in this way, I have shown

---

[1] Verdi addressed this letter only 'Arrigo Boito *Milano*' and posted it to Giulio Ricordi together with a letter of the same date (Palatina). On 17 Oct. 1880 Ricordi informed Verdi that he had forwarded these lines to Boito's address in Milan: Via Principe Amedeo No. 1.

[2] According to his letter to Giuseppina Verdi of 4 Sept. 1880, Boito intended to send Verdi a second version of this finale.

[3] Of 15 Aug. 1880.

[4] Presumably for Boito's letter to her of 4 Sept. 1880.

---

[1] Boito addressed this letter 'Giuseppe Verdi—Busseto per St Agata' (postal stamp: MILANO 18/10/80). The autograph was among Verdi's letters to Boito in the possession of the Albertini family.

you that I gave far greater weight to the feelings which made you speak out
than to the arguments reflected in that feeling. But now you ask my opinion
of those arguments as well, and that is gravely embarrassing to me, since, as
you have seen, I have proved by my actions that I agree with [Verdi,] the
artist, the composer, and now my words must agree with [Verdi,] the critic.
When you say (I am repeating the words of your letter to me in Monaco):[2]
'Otello, overcome with grief, consumed with jealousy, crushed, sick in mind
and body—could he suddenly rouse himself and return as the hero he was
before? If he can, and if he is still lured by glory, and if he can forget love,
grief, jealousy—why does he kill Desdemona and then himself?' When you
argue this way I find no further words to contradict you; but later on, when
you ask me (rather, when you ask yourself): 'Are these doubts, or serious
observations?' then I answer: *they are serious observations.* You have put
your finger on the wound. Otello is like a man who is wandering through a
nightmare, and under the fatal, growing domination of this nightmare he
thinks, acts, suffers, and commits his tremendous crime. Now, if we imagine
an event that must necessarily shake Otello and distract him from such a
gripping nightmare, then we destroy all the sinister enchantment created by
Shakespeare, and we cannot logically come to the conclusion of the action.
That attack of the Turks gives me the impression of a fist breaking the
window of a chamber in which two people are about to die of asphyxiation.
That intimate sense of death, so carefully created by Schakespeare, suddenly
vanishes. Life-giving air flows once again into our tragedy, and Otello and
Desdemona are safe. To make them re-enter upon the road of death, we must
lock them up once more in that lethal chamber, recreate the nightmare,
patiently lead Jago back to his prey—and we have but a single act left in
which to redo the whole tragedy from the start. In other words: *we have found
the end of an act, but we have lost the effect of the final catastrophe.* Everyone
knows that *Othello* is a very great masterpiece and *perfect* in its greatness.
This perfection derives (you know this better than I) from the prodigious
harmony of the whole and its details, from the profound delineation of the
characters, from that most rigorous and *fatal* logic by which all the events of
the tragedy unfold, from the way in which all the passions that are stirred in
it—and above all the dominating passion—are observed and portrayed. All
these virtues contribute to make *Othello* an artistic masterpiece. A work of
such beauty and wisdom cannot be retouched, even at a single point, without
diminishing its perfection. Now, if we diminish its perfection from the
psychological point of view, with respect to the events, and also with respect
to the characters, then the tragedy is no longer as logical or as complete or as
harmonious or as fatal as Schakespeare intended. Thus Otello's character
suffers, as does Jago's; the immediate, direct action on his [Jago's] part
leading to the catastrophe is suddenly interrupted by an event that he has not
brought about, by the *only* event, the *single* incident beyond his influence: a
sudden attack by the enemy. After this altogether new, unforeseen event,

[2] Of 15 Aug. 1880.

Otello no longer acts under Jago's incessant domination, and instead of appearing miserably wretched, appears cruel.

We wanted to retouch the *perfection*, and we have destroyed it. This is the *critic's* reasoning. And it is right. But an opera is not a legitimate drama; our art lives by elements unknown to spoken tragedy. An atmosphere destroyed can be created all over again; eight measures are enough to revive a feeling; a rhythm can remake a character. Music is the most omnipotent of all the arts; it has a logic of its own, more rapid and more free than the logic of the spoken word, and far more eloquent. You, Maestro, can reduce the critic's most compelling arguments to silence with a stroke of your pen. You have said: the third act 'is divine'. You are right, then, because this exclamation of yours is nothing but a clear indication to me of how, in your mind, you already see your ideas taking strong and clear shape.

But I have already rattled on too much.

To you, my dear Maestro, and to your Signora, my most cordial and respectful regards. I am always at your command, ready to revise, cut, and add—and please remember this—always happy if I succeed in pleasing you.

Your
Arrigo Boito

VERDI TO OPPRANDINO ARRIVABENE

St Agata, 18 October 1880

Dear Arrivabene,

I thank you for the article about Bellini. All in all, I think that Florimo does his late friend a disservice. In the meantime he has provoked a letter from Romani's wife that brings a very, very petty Bellini before the public; and who knows what else will come forth later on. But what need is there to go and drag a composer's letters out into the open? They're always written in haste, without care, without any importance [being attached to them], since the composer knows that he has no reputation to uphold as a writer. Isn't it enough that they boo him for his music? No, Sir! The letters, too! Oh, fame is a great nuisance! The poor little great famous men pay dearly for popularity! Never an hour of peace for them, neither in life nor in death!

I leave you now and go to my fields. That is my present occupation. The weather is nice and I'm on the go from morning till night. It's a very prosaic life, but it keeps me very fit.

Peppina is in Cremona at her sister's,[1] and I'll pick her up tomorrow. Keep well and believe me

G. Verdi

---

[1] Barberina Strepponi.

GIULIO RICORDI TO VERDI

Milan, 19 November 1880

Illustrious Maestro,

Forgive me if I come to bother you a bit! .. but that is my .... profession.

The management of La Scala insistently requests *Simon Boccanegra* from us for next season. Apart from the keenest desire to make this opera known, the management tells me that it is spurred on by the recollection of all that the tenor Patierno said about this opera, which he had performed in a revival at the San Carlo in Naples.

In fact, I recall that you, illustrious Maestro, repeatedly told me that *Boccanegra*, in your staging, was completely successful at that very same San Carlo.[1] Do you think that the forces at La Scala's disposal this year could bring about the performance you would desire?

They all have the most beautiful voices, namely—D'Angeri—Tamagno—Salvati—De Reszke.

You will recall that we talked at length about this opera in Genoa; as a matter of fact, you still had the autograph score! ... And I don't know what keeps me from starting a suit against Maestro Verdi for illegal possession of precious objects!!!! ..

You concluded that you either had to make radical changes .... which in this case meant writing a new opera (may God will it!!), or you had to leave *Boccanegra* as it was.

Don't you think that this is a case just like that of *La forza del destino*?[2]

In a matter of such weight I have given no positive reply to the management of La Scala; and pretending that I did not remember the opera too well, I said that I wanted to reread the libretto and would give an answer in two or three days.

And so I am asking you, illustrious Maestro, to tell me with your usual candour what you think about this matter, and to give me your advice, or to make your recommendations, which shall become laws for us. [...]

VERDI TO GIULIO RICORDI

Genoa, 20 November 1880

Dear Giulio,

Either *the operas for the singers* or *the singers for the operas*—an old axiom that no manager has ever known how to practise, and without which no success is possible in the theatre.

You have made a good company for La Scala, but it's not suitable for

---

[1] On 30 Nov. 1858.
[2] The successful revision of that opera at La Scala on 27 Feb. 1869.

Boccanegra.—Your baritone must be a young fellow.[1] He may have all the voice, talent and feeling you want, but he will never have the calm, the composure, and that certain authority on-stage that is indispensable for the part of Simone. It's an exhausting part, like Rigoletto, but a thousand times more difficult. In *Rigoletto* the *part is made*, and with a little voice and feeling one can manage well. For Boccanegra voice and feeling are not enough.

For Fieschi[2] a deep voice would be needed, one audible in the low notes down to the F, with something inexorable, prophetic, sepulchral in the voice; everything that De Restke's somewhat empty, baritonal voice does not have. Also la D'Angeri—precisely because of the power of her voice and personality—would not be right for the part of a modest, withdrawn maiden who is rather like a young nun. I think la D'Angeri herself would not be happy with this part.

Furthermore the score is not possible as it is. It's too sad, too desolate! Nothing must be retouched in the first or last act,[3] or in the third, either, except for a few bars here and there. But the entire second act[4] must be redone to give it relief, variety, and greater life.—From a musical viewpoint the prima donna's cavatina, the duet with the tenor, and the other duet between father and daughter should be kept, even though there are cabalettas!! *Open up, earth!*[5] I am not so terrified of the cabalettas, however, and if tomorrow a youngster came along who could write me some effective ones, such as '*Meco tu vieni o misera*'[6] ['*With me you come, O poor one*'], for instance, or '*Ah, perchè non posso odiarti*'[7] ['*Ah, why can I not hate you*'], I'd be delighted to hear them and renounce all the harmonic quibbles, all the affectations of our learned orchestrations ... Ah, the progress, the science, the realism ... Ugh, ugh ... [be a] realist all you want, but ... Shaespeare was a realist,[8] but he didn't know it. He was a realist through inspiration; we are realists by intention, by calculation; system for the sake of system, it's all the same. Better yet the cabalettas. What a fine thing, then, that with all this

---

[1] Victor Maurel, then 32 years old. He had sung Amonasro under Verdi's own baton in the first performance of *Aida* at the Paris Opéra on 22 Mar. 1880.
[2] Frequent spelling of Fiesco in this correspondence.
[3] By the first act, Verdi means the Prologue; by the last act, the third.
[4] The first act.
[5] Cynical reaction to criticisms of his cabalettas as in the case of 'that horrible one' in the third act of *Aida*, 'which has attracted so much advice, so much wisdom, and so much benevolence from your critics!!' (Verdi to Ricordi, 6 Apr. 1872.)
[6] Valdeburgo's cabaletta in the second act of Bellini's *La straniera*.
[7] Elvino's cabaletta in the second act of Bellini's *La sonnambula*.
[8] Verdi shared similar thoughts with Clara Maffei on 20 Mar. 1876:

'To copy truth can be a good thing, but *to invent the truth* is better, much better. There seems to be a contradiction between the two words 'to invent the truth', but ask Papa [Shakespeare] about it. He, Papa, might have met some Falstaff, but he will have hardly met such a villain as Iago, and never, never such angels as Cordelia, Imogene, Desdemona, etc., etc., who are so true! ... To copy truth is a beautiful thing, but it's photography, not *painting*.' (Autograph: Braidense; Ascoli, pp. 331–2; *Copialettere*, p. 624. The date of 20 Oct. 1876 given in both publications is in error. In this letter Verdi refers to Piave's death on 5 Mar. 1876 as well as his departure, for Paris, on 20 Mar. See also Verdi Chronology, 1876.)

progress art turns backwards. Art lacking spontaneity, naturalness and simplicity is no longer art.

Let's go back to the second act.[9] Who could redo it? In what way? What could be found? I said in the beginning that in this act something must be found that would give variety and a little liveliness to the excessive darkness of the drama. How? For example:

Stage a hunt?

That wouldn't be theatrical.

A feast? Too ordinary.

A fight with the corsairs of Africa?

That would scarcely be diverting.

Preparations for war with Pisa or Venice? . . .

In this connection, I recall two stupendous letters by Petrarch,[10] one written to the Doge Boccanegra,[11] the other to the Doge of Venice, telling those who were about to embark upon a fratricidal war that they were both born of the same mother: Italy, etc., etc. A sublime sentiment for the Italian fatherland at that time!—All this is political, not dramatic; but a man with talent could well dramatize this event. For example: . . Boccanegra, struck by this thought, would follow the poet's advice: he convenes the Senate or a private council to expose the letter, and his own feeling about it . . . Horror on everyone's part, rhetorical speeches, fits of anger, even accusations of treason against the Doge, etc., etc.. The struggle is interrupted by Amelia's abduction. . I am only talking off the top of my head. . If you discover the way to adjust and smooth out all the difficulties I have outlined to you, I am ready to do this act over, after all . . .

Think about it and answer me.

Addio
G. Verdi

GIULIO RICORDI TO VERDI

Milan, 24 November 1880

[. . .] I need not tell you, illustrious Maestro, what joy your answer has brought me; as always, your idea for the change to be made is certainly a most fortunate one.—

Last night I was able (don't laugh!! . .) to read *Boccanegra* attentively! . . What beautiful music. . . . . and what a pity that it is not known . . . . But I had to persuade myself that what you say about la D'Angeri is very well founded. It is true that I have seen her achieve wonders and 'on occasion squeeze blood from a turnip'. As far as vocal equipment is concerned, I could not find anyone more suitable than la D'Angeri; regarding the expression of her voice and personality, I would not know how much could be got out of

---

[9] The first act.

[10] In *Delle cose familiari* (*Familiarium rerum*) by Francesco Petrarca.

[11] See Introduction, p. xxxvii, and Appendix I.

her . . . . and if you knew this artist better you could decide. As for Salvati, I believe he has the talent and the voice to succeed in even the most difficult parts, such as Simone; above all, if well directed he could, I think, satisfy any demand. De Reszke, whom you may not have heard for some time, has made great vocal progress and is always a magnificent actor.

I would see only a single artist as right for Amelia . . . . la *Borghi-Mamo*: she is ugly, yet adorable on-stage . . . a beguiling timbre, first-rate talent! . . . . With all these precious qualities, however . . . . . we are in trouble . . . . the overall tessitura of the opera is too high for her. If you think this might be remedied, certainly *no one else* would be better able to interpret your music with the adjustments you could make.

And la Patti? . . . . There are many *pros and cons*: first, the hairdresser, Nicolini! . . . As for the range of her voice, we have the very same case as with Borghi-Mamo—maybe even worse; for by now la Patti lowers her part in every opera; and although in fast passages she can still risk high notes, she can no longer sustain them in dramatic and expressive phrases.[1] Furthermore she now demands 15,000 fr. . . . per performance!! . ., an absolutely impossible sum, for Italian theatres not to be suggested to any manager.

These are problems concerning the performance that are to be solved; . . . . to me they do not seem hard to solve: for if you consider La Scala's present company absolutely unsuitable, fortunately we shall have many good opportunities to give the performance in the spring or fall of next year; and it will not be difficult to put together a company of artists whom you yourself may choose to your satisfaction. I am saying this on the assumption that you think it *absolutely impossible* to use artists whom La Scala's present company has to offer.

As for the libretto, this seems even more certain to succeed; *most of it you have already done* . . . . by hitting upon the *basic idea*, which strikes me as magnificent and interesting. All that is missing is the form; and the day before yesterday, just after receiving your letter, Boito came to see me on business of his own; and as our talk went along I asked him—without going into detail— whether he might see to the retouching of a libretto by Verdi if this needed to be done. He replied that he was always ready to do anything Verdi requested. And while on this subject he mentioned another matter to me. He obliged me not to say another word about the matter and not to bring it up in any way, and I have faithfully carried out his orders! . . But in battle, too, generals have sometimes disobeyed orders, and risked their necks if their audacity was not crowned with victory. I break the promise . . . . . and I hope you will not be so cruel as to ask for my head; that truly is the case with *Rigoletto*: '*che far di tal testa?*' ['*what to do with that head?*']². .

Boito asked me for news of you, whether you were in Genoa, etc., etc., and told me:

---

[1] Other sources (Hanslick, Shaw, Klein, Clara Louise Kellogg) indicate that la Patti's high register was reliable until *c*.1893.
[2] The title character's question to the Duke in *Rigoletto*, I. i.

Since my last letter I haven't heard anything more from the Maestro; I would regret it if Verdi did not approve my observations about a change that he not only proposed to me, but also adopted and carried out. Since he asked me, I meant to give him my ideas frankly, being somewhat encouraged by a few words of his, which gave me the impression that he might partly concur. Meanwhile I have studied, and believe that I have come up with something else that will satisfy the Maestro's demands and will also be faithful to the play.

—But why didn't you write this to the Maestro? ... I asked him.

And there we are again. ... Boito is afraid of becoming a nuisance to you .... As he left he repeated to me that he was always ready to do, undo, and change anything that Verdi thought necessary.

I thought I should inform you of the above. If I have done wrong ... here is my head ... and with the head, my entire self, always at your disposal, everywhere and for everything! ... as long as I may have the pleasure of finding you satisfied, no matter how small my part ...... and the consolation of seeing that the poor art [of opera], sent to wrack and ruin by the government and the city halls, is always sustained by an omnipotent hand. You alone can exclaim: *Fiat lux*, which, in my blundering manner, I am in this case translating: *May he do it!* ... and that shall be good fortune.

I await your orders anxiously, then, as you can well imagine.

G. Ricordi

PS I apologize for the disorder of the pages .... and the inelegance of the writing.

VERDI TO GIULIO RICORDI

Genoa [25 November 1880?][1]

A few short words in haste, in reply to your letter about *Boccanegra*. It is necessary:

1. That I be content with Boito's adjustments, which, by the way, I have not yet received.

2. That I be content with myself regarding the work I shall do.

3. That the artists be suitable for the parts they are to perform.

Engage Tom, Dick, etc. The management may let them make their débuts. I'll hear them first, and if I don't like them we'll do nothing.

I shall be demanding about everything else, and not as easygoing as I have been at other times. [...]

---

[1] In apparent reaction to Giulio Ricordi's letter of 24 Nov. 1880, Verdi drafted these lines without ever posting them.

GIULIO RICORDI TO VERDI

Milan, 26 November 1880

Illustrious Maestro,

The Signori Corti, managers of La Scala, are going to Genoa on business and have expressed to me their desire to have the honour of greeting you and paying their respects to you, since they would much regret leaving the city in which you currently reside without the satisfaction of having seen you.

They ask me, therefore, to send you a few lines so that you may be kind enough to receive them.

I thank you and have the honour to remain

Yours most devotedly and gratefully,
Giulio Ricordi

GIULIO RICORDI TO VERDI

Milan, 27 November 1880

[. . .] Boito has begun work right away and has told me that he will soon be sending the new finale[1] as you conceived it, in the hope that you may like it; that would be a great comfort to him.

I shall write to you tomorrow or the day after tomorrow, and in a calmer state of mind, about everything concerning *Boccanegra*. The other night I reread the whole opera! . . . Really, really, Maestro, it is a crime to neglect it. We will search . . . we will find . . by Jove! . . . and we will succeed in pleasing and persuading you about what can be done. But I shall have no more peace unless I hear: Yes . . . . I am persuaded. [. . .]

VERDI TO GIULIO RICORDI

[Genoa, shortly after 27 November 1880][1]

Corti brought me your card, but I divined quickly what it was all about. With less diplomacy we would have accomplished something. Now we are still in the clouds, and standing on high we don't see lowly, mundane matters. I descend from the clouds to tell you:

1. No commitments to the public. I am no militant artist any more; I am one who is *more*; what I am doing is for *more*, what I shall do will be *more*. Therefore no poster, no obligation on my part to anybody. In spite of this, I will hold all the rehearsals (and you shall see with what rigour). I will have the singers go through their parts so that they will not sing by their method,

---

[1] *Otello*, Act III.

[1] Verdi drafted this letter with many corrections, but apparently did not post it. (See also Julian Budden, *The Operas of Verdi*, ii. 256 n.)

but as I wish. We'll give the opera when we see that it's healthy and strong, and I shall leave when I please.

2. A prima donna (on la D'Angeri we all agree) who suits this part. I ask again: what is this Monale like?[2]

3. De Reztke too nice, too beautiful a voice, too good, too whatever you like, but find another Fieschi. Give me a low F; the high notes don't matter, I'll take them all out, if necessary, but a low F.

4. I again repeat that a young artist cannot do the part of Simone well.[3] Corti told me about Berardi.[4] I don't believe anything.

For instance, it's useless to tell me: Tizio, Paolo, Pietro, etc., etc., have heard him. I don't believe it! Artists are not judged in a room but in the theatre; and not even in the theatre when it is empty, when it is not illuminated, and when the orchestra does not play; the acoustics change. Besides, I would prefer an Italian.

These are the most difficult rocks to steer past.

As for the libretto, the text of the finale[5] requires a vast idea, one of grandiose form and colour; for the rest, little needs to be done.

I say *text*, because Amelia's narrative must be kept; I would change a good deal of the music, yet keep many things in the Stretta, especially the beginning.

Writing one of the usual ensembles for the moment when Amelia suddenly appears does not seem appropriate. But I would let the Doge say four or eight verses in which he thanks Heaven for his daughter's rescue from dishonour.

Four verses as Boito can do them—to be set, as well as possible, to a broad musical phrase. I would like to repeat this phrase, with some different words, at the point in the middle of the Stretta where the harps come in.

That will make a great finale, if Boito can provide me with a nice beginning, and if I can come up with a few notes that aren't senseless.

GIULIO RICORDI TO VERDI

Milan, 30 November 1880

Illustrious Maestro,

Confirming my telegram of today,[1] I am enclosing what Boito has just brought me; he has written a few lines on the back of the little sheets[2] and asks you to forgive him for not making lengthy remarks about what he has done. It is unnecessary, he thinks, since you will judge better than anybody else whether the new idea can work.

[2] An unknown soprano, described by Giulio Ricordi in his letters of 30 Nov., 2 and 5 Dec. 1880.

[3] Victor Maurel's success in this part proved even Verdi's judgement to be wrong.

[4] Unknown.

[5] *Simon Boccanegra*, I. ii.

---

[1] Missing.

[2] Missing revision of the finale in *Otello*, Act III.

He thinks the contrast is excellent; terribly dramatic, and with a rapid conclusion to the act in this way. I have said enough.

Having finished this piece, which was very close to his heart, Boito is starting right away on *Boccanegra*; I informed him of the ideas you were kind enough to write to me about, and he does not think it will be difficult to find something *ad hoc*; besides, one idea leads to another; and the greatest part is now done. As for all the rest, you know very well that you have only to *say the word, whatever it may be*; all we have to do is obey you; and furthermore you need not exhort me to work for something that has been *my dream for many, many years* and now fills me with joy . .

To come to your last letter in particular, I reply

1. Everything you request regarding absolute freedom towards the public, management, etc., etc., is all right.

2. I think la Monale is a fair mediocrity; but I shall hear her at the Dal Verme[3] and let you know. As for la D'Angeri, it seems to me that, as you say, we do not all agree. You will recall that in the first letter, a few days ago, in which I spoke of *Boccanegra*, I considered la D'Angeri excellent; have you heard her? . . . Whatever you may say, I am convinced, totally convinced that once you have heard her you will say: all right! . . . But more about this when the time comes; meanwhile I shall hear this Monale and also think about the others.

3. I am taking care about the bass, as well; you mention the low F to me, but apart from the voice we also need an *excellent* singer, since Fieschi's prayer in the prologue and the Andante with Boccanegra in the last act require, I think, a flexible voice, one that blends well, is on pitch, and has a singing quality.

I am seeing to all of this right away. What is most urgent above all is that Boito puts something on paper that will completely satisfy you; *that is the question.*[4] [. . .]

VERDI TO GIULIO RICORDI

Genoa, 2 December 1880

Dear Giulio,

Alas, alas! If we start discussing the merits of this or that artist, we'll waste precious time and won't accomplish a thing. To avoid argument, I declare right away that I am wrong, that the fault is all mine when I see things from a different point of view from yours. But in this instance who obliges us to give *Boccanegra*? What interest could I have in wearing myself down once more with this opera? With an opera to be given out of *convenience*, after all! . . I also add that this opera was born in sin, and that we shall hardly find water to baptize it. You will recall that you came to St Agata ten years ago

[3] Teatro Dal Verme in Milan.
[4] Giulio Ricordi quotes Hamlet in English.

proposing that I devote myself to *Boccanegra* for La Scala. *No*, I replied, *Forza del destino* is *better*!. I was not too wrong. *Boccanegra* lacks *theatricality*! In *Forza* the parts are made; in *Boccanegra* they all have to be made. Therefore, first of all, great actors. A voice of steel for Fieschi. A young, modest, quiet, thin, tender lady for Amelia. A most passionate, ardent, proud soul, outwardly dignified, solemn, serene (quite difficult to portray) for Boccanegra. These we won't find, I know well; but at least something approaching them. [. . .]

GIULIO RICORDI TO VERDI

Milan, 2 December 1880

Illustrious Maestro,
    I hasten to report to you my impressions of la Di Monale, whom I went to hear last night.
Voice: Good in the top notes, and with sufficient colour—mediocre in the middle—weak in the low notes.
Figure: Neither pretty nor ugly, but not sympathetic.
Actress: Cold, in fact downright clumsy.
    All in all, a good little singer for second-rank theatres.
    Boito is working indefatigably, and I myself will make sure that the project is presented to you shortly. [. . .]

VERDI TO BOITO

Genoa, 2 December 1880

Dear Boito,
    A happy find, the third [act] finale! I like Otello's fainting better in this finale than where it was before. I just cannot find, or feel, the *ensemble piece*! But this can even be done without. We'll talk about it later, since now, as Giulio must have told you, we have other things to think about.—I believed that there was a lot to do in this *Boccanegra*, but I have noticed that if we can find a *good beginning* for the finale,[1] one that will give variety, much variety, to the excessive uniformity of the drama, then what remains to be done is reduced to only a few verses here and there, with the aim of changing some musical phrases, etc.
    So think about it a bit and write to me as soon as you have found something.
    A good handshake in haste from

your affectionate
G. Verdi

[1] *Simon Boccanegra*, I. ii.

GIULIO RICORDI TO VERDI[1]

Milan, 4 December 1880

Illustrious Maestro,

For heaven's sake, Maestro, don't scare me with this tremendous *Alas!* . .
alas! at the beginning of your last letter! [. . .]

Even granting that precious time is being wasted, I *absolutely* cannot
stomach that nasty word 'convenience'!! . . . No, by Jove—*Boccanegra* was
requested not once but 20, 30, 100 times; and I believe . . . I have been . . . . . a
damned nuisance to you . . . several times! [. . .]

I am in perfect agreement with you about Maurel; but this artist has
already sung three times at La Scala; the audience received him extremely
well and found him sympathetic, but his voice was always insufficient for the
large size of the threatre. Do you think, though, that I should find out about
him! [. . .]

I sent your brief letter to Boito[2] straight away; I saw him for a moment last
night; I think he will write to you;[3] from a few words he said I gather that he
has already come up with something; one idea would correspond to what you
wrote to me[4] and what I related to him; the other—without touching the first
and last acts at all—would be more radical, but he is afraid it would involve
more work than the first idea. But Boito himself will report this to you. [. . .]

GIULIO RICORDI TO VERDI

Milan, 5 December 1880

Illustrious Maestro,

Last night I heard la Di Monale again, in *Carmen*; I liked her better than in
L'Étoile du nord,[1] but as for her voice I confirm what I have already written to
you; and as for the actress, she is always ice. [. . .]

VERDI TO GIULIO RICORDI

Genoa, 5 December 1880

[. . .] For *Boccanegra* we need not search for *midi à 14 heures*.[1] It's best to
leave it as it is, redoing only the finale. Certainly I shall change some phrases

---

[1] In answer to Verdi's letter, 2 Dec. 1880.
[2] Verdi's lines to Boito, 2 Dec. 1880.
[3] See Boito to Verdi, 8 Dec. 1880.
[4] On 20 Nov. 1880.

---

[1] Opera in 3 acts by Giacomo Meyerbeer, adapted from his German opera *Ein feldlager in
Schlesien*.

---

[1] French saying, meaning 'not complicate matters'.

and some pieces, and here and there I'll need verses and strophes; but a radical change would carry me too far. That would amount to writing another opera. [...]

There is no better singer and actor than Maurel. But I would not dare to request him and impose him on the management. He is crazy, or to be more precise, so temperamental as to make you lose a première, as he did for *Aida* in Paris.[2]

And the bass?.. I repeat once again, the two parts of Fieschi and Boccanegra are harder to perform than all the others; and if these parts are weak the opera cannot hold up. Let's not try to avoid the difficulties with *but* and *if*. This opera is risky in itself. With two good actors for these parts and two good voices for the others, the opera can work; otherwise not. So we'd better consider this well before we go to the ball.

Do everything quickly.

Addio
G. Verdi

PS [...] On my return[3] I, too, shall go to work in earnest. But the real obstacles are the artists suitable for those parts. Mind you, for many reasons I will not be easily satisfied. I repeat again: De Reszke no .. absolutely not. All the considerations of success, of sympathy in Milan are of no interest to me ...

The same goes for the Doge: a young artist is impossible! If a young one could do this part well it would be a miracle! I do not believe in miracles.

One must also think about Amelia. —

Meanwhile addio. Talk with Boito.

Addio
G. Verdi [...]

BOITO TO VERDI[1]

[Milan] Wednesday. [8 December 1880][2]

Dear Maestro,

One idea gives birth to another, and just two ideas are enough to generate doubt, which is the natural enemy of action. That is why I am turning to you to help me out of this hesitation and to point out to me the path to follow. Truly the path was very clearly indicated in the letters that you wrote to

---

[2] Verdi seems to have considered as malingering Maurel's claim of a sore throat, which had postponed the opening of *Aida* at the Paris Opéra by a week until 22 Mar. 1880. In several letters about that performance, however, he had only the highest praise for Maurel. (Busch, *Aida*, pp. 420–3.)

[3] From St Agata where Verdi went from 12 to 19 Dec. 1880.

[1] In answer to Verdi's letter of 2 Dec. 1880.

[2] The date of this letter, which Boito apparently wrote in close association with Giulio Ricordi in Milan, is inferred from Verdi to Boito, 2 and 11 Dec. 1880.

Giulio,[3] and this should have been enough to enable me to get down to work without asking anything else, but man is not always the master of his own brain.

Here, then, is how I would develop the Senate scene:

The most accurate representation, from the historical point of view, would be the following:

Council chamber in the Palace of the Abati.

The Doge. The Mayor. The noble councillors. The councillors of the people. The consuls of the sea, the High Constables.

An attendant announces a woman who begs to speak to the Doge. The Doge orders that the woman be received, but only after the affairs of state have been discussed. The Doge announces to the Council that Toris, the King of the Tartars, is sending an ambassador to seek peace with the Genoese. (See *Annals of the Genoese Republic* by Giustiniani, vol. ii, bk iv.[4]) The entire Council unanimously agrees to peace. Then the Doge calls upon them to cease the war with the Republic of Venice. Rejections by the Council, uproar. The Doge exclaims, 'With barbarians, with infidels you consent to peace, yet you want war with your brothers. Don't your triumphs satisfy you? And the blood that has been shed on the waters of the Bosporus—*has it not yet exhausted your ferocity? You have carried your victorious standard on the waves of the Tyrrhenian, the Adriatic, the Black Sea, the Ionian and the Aegean,*' and here we can use some of the most beautiful passages of Letter V, Book XIV of *Petrarch's Letters*. Especially where he says, '*Beautiful it is to overcome a foe by the test of the sword; most beautiful it is to conquer him by the magnanimity of the heart,*' and where he speaks so lyrically of the splendours of the seashore (provided this last digression doesn't prolong the scene too much), but it is so beautiful where he says, '*and the boatman, admiring the novelty of the scene, let the oars fall from his hands and stopped the boat in mid-course*'. The Doge's peroration, however, must finish proudly, interrupted here and there by cries from the crowd; the people want peace, the nobles war. Very vigorous antagonism between the nobles and the plebeians.—A disturbance at the door of the chamber; the arrest of a noble who, sword in hand, had wanted to force his way into the Council, is announced. The nobles and the people vehemently want this noble to come in. Enter Gabriello Adorno, who accuses the Doge of having caused the abduction of Amelia Grimaldi. Surprise and indignation of the nobles; the Doge stands as if thunderstruck and orders that the woman, who shortly before had sought help and asylum in the palace, be made to appear. The woman is introduced. It is Amelia, who throws herself at the feet of the Doge and announces that she has saved herself. Here a place might be found for some lines in which the Doge thanks Heaven for saving Amelia, and the act would end as it does in the already existing opera.

Let us go on to explore another idea:

---

[3] Particularly in Verdi to Ricordi, 20 Nov. 1880.
[4] Agostino Giustiniani (1470–1536), Genoese historian (see Appendix I).

It is based on this concept: to fuse into a single act the main sections of the two middle acts, omitting entirely Scenes x, xi, and xii, which now conclude the second act (or the first, counting the prologue), and finishing this entire (recast) act with the *trio* that ends the present penultimate act. Having done this, we would add an entire act—new, not long—and put it in place of the original penultimate act.

Let us talk first of all about the means of bringing about the fusion of the two intermediate acts. Above all the events should be simplified. Give up the abduction of Amelia. Let us see.

Act I
The Garden of the Grimaldi

Scene i—Amelia alone

Scene ii—Amelia and Gabriele

Scenes iii, iv, vi, vii as they are now. We would do without Scene v, thus allowing Scenes iv and vi to follow without interruption and without a scene change, and [allowing them to be followed by] the duet between the Doge and Amelia. After the duet Amelia moves slowly away, while Scene viii, between the Doge and Paolo, follows very quickly; in this scene we need to add a threat from Paolo, who is the guiding spirit of the popular faction and who will foment a revolt if the Doge does not surrender Amelia to him. Adamant, the Doge accepts the challenge and refuses to give Amelia up to Paolo. Paolo exits. Amelia is still in the garden not very far off, and the Doge calls her to bid her farewell and embrace her in this hour of danger. During the embrace of father and daughter Gabriele enters, drawing his sword to attack the Doge. Amelia defends her father. This is followed by the trio; the act closes as it does now, with shouts of '*All'armi*' ['*To arms*'].

Act II (penultimate)
Inside the Church of S. Siro, adjacent to the houses of the Boccanegras (the ancient cloister of the Benedictines)

The church is full of armed men, on the balconies are crossbowmen, and at the front, by the central rose-window, a catapult[5] is being loaded. Outside, cries and the noise of attackers, trumpets; within, at the altar, a priest blesses the combatants. Gabriele is on the central balcony next to the catapult, on the look-out; Boccanegra is giving orders; some scouts enter; the Fieschi, the D'Oria and the Grimaldi have joined forces with that part of the popular factions which is attacking the church. Remaining loyal to Boccanegra are the maritime consuls, together with all the navy, the crossbowmen, and the greater part of the people. Gabriele repeatedly asks if he may launch the catapult (the Genoese of old called catapults *trabocchi*), but the Doge forbids it. As the doors of the church are loudly struck, the *great bell* sounds the alarm. A messenger arrives with the news that the attackers have been surrounded by a powerful band of crossbowmen from one of the Boccanegra houses (the messengers enter and exit by a door that leads to Simone's

---

[5] A machine of ancient warfare for throwing stones, spears, or arrows.

house). The door of the church threatens to collapse; Boccanegra stands in front of the door with a group of crossbowmen; the door collapses; Fiesco enters at the head of a surging mass of nobles and common people and wounds Boccanegra in the hand, but suddenly, seeing the church full of armed men ready to fall upon them, the attackers stop, intimidated. Boccanegra, wounded, shows Fiesco the catapult, which looms threateningly over the heads of the attackers, and swears that he will not release it and that no assault shall be made against the insurgents if, in the sacred place where they are, they will solemnly promise peace. A moment of silence. Meanwhile Paolo, the leader of the revolt, quietly asks Pietro, who is among Boccanegra's supporters (in order to betray him), whether there is any hope left for the insurgents. Pietro answers that they are surrounded by crossbowmen and that Boccanegra has them completely caught in his snares. Thereupon Paolo tears off the sash from his sword, and after putting on the sash some drops of poison that he draws from his jerkin, he throws the sword at Boccanegra's feet and, kneeling before him, asks to dress the bloody wound on his hand. Then all the attackers put their swords in their sheaths. Boccanegra allows Paolo to bandage his hand, tells him to rise, and pardons him. Meanwhile Amelia comes in through the door by which the messengers had exited. Gabriele has come down from the balcony. Boccanegra solemnly makes them swear peace, utters the ceremonial phrases of the oath, and expresses the wish that this peace between the nobles and the plebeians be consecrated by the marriage of Adorno with his daughter Amelia.—An *Oath* that will have the necessary proportions for an ample and powerful musical passage. Thus would the act end.—Let us look now at the advantages of this second idea: to present the poisoning of the Doge—an occasion that ties in with the final catastrophe, consequently making it more evident and more tragic. Second advantage: to present a fact (recorded in the *Annals* of Giustiniani, Bk IV, for the year 1356) that will lend a little historical and local colour to the drama. (In Genoese history, one encounters these churches that are suddenly transformed into front-line fortresses.) It will show Boccanegra to the public as he is struck down by Paolo's treachery, at the very moment he accomplishes a deed of great power and magnanimity, an act of greatness and generosity. Yet another advantage: to make the marriage derive logically from the action that precedes it.

But will the tenor have no scene in which to display his virtuosity? This scene could take place at the beginning of the last act.

There, I have said everything that has passed through my mind these past few days while I ploughed through the literature about Genoese history. I can guess the criticisms that you will make regarding the first as well as the second idea.

The Senate scene could seem cold unless the patriotic and political theme that animates it is treated with enough ardour, and in the right form, to make it dramatic. Then again, if this theme succeeds in touching the emotion of the drama and in interesting the listener, another obstacle confronts us—the arrival of Gabriele (and then Amelia) interrupts this theme before its full development, and the question of Venice, which raises so many impressions in the beginning, remains unresolved because of the new incident. So [the effect of] this new incident will be lost, and the end of the act along with it. The criticism of the second idea is far from obscure: the war in the church could perhaps seem novel enough, but the theatrical effect could seem very problematical. We already have a plot black enough in itself, and the act that we would add would not modify the overall hue. The armed church is certainly neither serene nor merry.

Our task, my Maestro, is arduous. The drama that we are working with is lopsided, like a table that wobbles, but no one knows which leg is the cause, and whatever is done to steady it, it still wobbles. I don't find in this drama a single character of which one can say: It's sharply delineated! No event that is really *fatal*, that is indispensable and potent, generated by tragic inevitability. I make an exception of the prologue, which is truly beautiful and, in its dark quality, powerful, a shadowy yet solid object, like a piece of basalt. But the prologue (still speaking of the tragic plot, not having had the opportunity to hear again the music of *Boccanegra* for many, many years), the prologue is the straight leg of the table, the only one that is solidly placed; the other three, as you know better than I, are all rickety. There is much intrigue but not much structure. Everything in this drama is superficial—all these events seem thought up on the spur of the moment, as material to fill up the stage; there are neither deep roots nor strong connecting links; there is only the *semblance of real events* without relation to the characters. To correct such a drama, this must be changed.

If, my Maestro, you could read my mind (not that I should be reticent, or lie) you would see a strong aversion to taking up this play again and presenting it in performance, this drama that lacks as much in profound virtues as it does in superficial merits, this drama that (aside from the prologue) lacks tragic power as much as it lacks *theatricality*.

Still, I will submerge my desires in yours, and now that I have bared my soul to you, I tell you that I will do whatever you think must be done, seeing that the supreme judge in such a matter is you, not I.

So I am awaiting your decision to do the Senate or the Church of S. Siro—or to do nothing at all.

You don't hear the connection in the third act of *Otello*; actually, I don't either. We'll do all the better without it; the important thing is for us to feel that the act has reached a fitting conclusion. I must change a few lines in this ending.

I don't want to end this *little book* without telling you of the grateful affection that you awoke in my soul by making a certain remark last winter in Paris to Baron Blaze de Bury, a remark that does me high honour and that I read with emotion in one of the latest musical reviews in the *Revue des deux mondes.*[6] I have withheld these thanks for over a month in order not to bore you, but now that I have the opportunity to write to you, I am giving my gratitude free rein.

Many, many regards to your wife.

Your most affectionate
Arrigo Boito

GIULIO RICORDI TO VERDI

Milan, 11 December 1880

[. . .] I hope that you have received a letter from Boito. I think it unnecessary to repeat that if need be I am always ready to come to Genoa as soon as I receive a signal from you—to spare you from writing in case you should have instructions to give me. [. . .]

VERDI TO BOITO

Genoa, 11 December 1880

Dear Boito,

Either the Senate . . . or the Church of S. Siro . . . or do nothing . . .

To do nothing would be best, and yet reasons not financial but, I should say, professional prevent me from abandoning the idea of revising this *Boccanegra*, at least not without first having tried to do something about it. Parenthetically, it is in everyone's interest that *La Scala should survive!*—The repertory for this season, alas, is deplorable![1] Ponchielli's opera is very fine, but the rest? Eternal gods!!!! There is an opera that would awaken great interest in the public, and I don't understand why the Author and Publisher stubbornly persist in refusing it!—I'm talking about *Mefistofele.* The moment would be propitious, and you would render a service to Art and to everyone.[2]

The act that you have envisioned in the Church of S. Siro is stupendous in every respect. Beautiful in its novelty—beautiful in its historical colour—beautiful on the musico-dramatic side; but it would demand too much of me, and I could not subject myself to so much work.

While, unfortunately, renouncing this act, we must keep the Senate scene,

---

[6] ' "Watch out for Boito," the Maestro tells us. "He is not only a musician but also a dramatic poet, in fact one of the most remarkable ones." ' (*Revue des deux mondes*, 15 Oct. 1880. Blaze de Bury signed his Verdi interview with the pen-name F. de Lagenevais.)

---

[1] The final repertoire of the 1880–1 season consisted of Ponchielli, *Il figliuol prodigo*; Marchetti, *Ruy Blas*; Verdi, *Ernani*; Weber, *Der Freischütz*; Verdi, *Simon Boccanegra*; Mozart, *Don Giovanni*; Bellini, *La sonnambula*; Boito, *Mefistofele*; Rossini, *La semiramide*; Gomes, *Il Guarany*.
[2] Ten performances of Boito's revised *Mefistofele* were to be given beginning 25 May 1881.

which as done by you will no doubt prove anything but cold. Your criticisms are just, but engulfed by more elevated labours, having *Otello* in mind, you aim at a perfection that would be impossible to attain. I look lower and, more optimistic than you, do not despair. I agree that the table is wobbly, but by adjusting some of the legs I believe we can make it stand firm. I also agree that there are none of those characters (always very rare!) that make you say, '*It's sharply delineated!*'; nevertheless it seems to me that there is something in the roles of Fiesco and Simone that could be used to good advantage.

Let's try, then, and let's write this finale with that Tartar ambassador, with the letters of Petrarch, etc., . . etc., . . . etc., . . . Let's try. I repeat: We are not so inexperienced after all that we don't understand even beforehand what will succeed in the theatre.—If it's no burden to you, and if you have time, go right to work. Meanwhile I shall see to straightening out, here and there, the many crooked legs of my notes, and . . . we'll see!

With affection, I am

Your
G. Verdi

GIULIO RICORDI TO GIUSEPPINA VERDI

Milan, 14 December 1880

[. . .] As you can imagine, I am in turmoil on account of this *Boccanegra* affair—for the enormous joy in such a happy artistic event as well for the trepidation that I feel about satisfying our great Maestro! [. . .]

VERDI TO GIUSEPPE PIROLI

St Agata, 18 December 1880

[. . .] I have been here since Sunday to look after my affairs a bit and to give all the instructions for the work to be done during the rest of the winter. The season has been good here, too, until today. Now it is raining, and tomorrow I go back to Genoa. Otherwise nothing new. I am not working and I don't feel like working later on, even though there is the idea in the air of having me put on *Boccanegra* again in Milan. [. . .]

GIULIO RICORDI TO VERDI

Milan, 20 December 1880

Illustrious Maestro,

In answer to your most recent esteemed letters,[1] I related to Boito right away what you wrote me concerning the women's chorus in the finale; he will think about it immediately, and he told me that tomorrow or, at the latest,

---

[1] Probably in the Biblioteca Palatina.

the day after tomorrow he will send his work, since he is ahead of schedule. [. . .]

Meanwhile I am taking the necessary steps for the baritone and the bass. [. . .]

GIULIO RICORDI TO VERDI

Milan, 22 December 1880

Illustrious Maestro,

Boito should have posted his work today;[1] I only hope it satisfies you! . . . What a feast that would be.

Meanwhile I have been looking for a baritone; I have three names to submit to you:

Maurel—Aldighieri—Kaschmann.

Maurel: is only free in the Carnival season, but it might not be difficult to obtain his leave for Lent, as well. I have made enquiries in Florence and am told that his voice has greatly deteriorated; therefore it is feared it would now be insufficient for a big theatre like La Scala. He is, however, always the distinguished artist you know. He makes great demands, but not at all insuperable ones. To be more certain still, I am making further enquiries of another person in Florence.

Aldighieri: Do you know him? . . . Always has an excellent voice, is a distinguished, very well-educated person, but a slow learner, and so you would have to arm yourself with patience.

Kaschmann: is in Madrid, but I think we could have him during Lent; most intelligent, good on stage, distinguished actor, good musician; I would consider him the most suitable one. He has already sung in *Don Carlos* at La Scala with complete success, and he has taken Lassalle's part in *Le Roi de Lahore*,[2] also with excellent success. He enjoys great sympathy with the audience. [. . .]

Tomorrow or the day after tomorrow I shall know something about the bass.

The affairs of La Scala, in my modest opinion, are in a bad way. Yesterday I spoke with the editor of *Il corriere della sera*,[3] who promised to keep silent about *Boccanegra* for now. I was also invited by the Commission of the Theatre, since they wanted to be reassured about the condition of the theatre itself. I described the state of affairs frankly and precisely, as well as the resulting impossibility of making an announcement to the public at this time, an announcement that is awaited with the greatest anxiety; and just let me say that it would be the only thing to ensure the fate of our poor theatre! . . . . The Commission would have liked to write to you directly, if only to thank you for giving hope concerning the possibility of *Boccanegra*. [. . .]

[1] Missing.
[2] Opera in 5 acts by Jules Massenet.
[3] The leading newspaper of Milan.

A. LOCATELLI[1] TO TITO RICORDI

Florence, 23 December 1880

Concerning your telegram of today:[2]

Maurel possesses a dramatic talent of unsurpassed perfection. In his voice, however, pleasant and sonorous as it is, I have not noticed the vibrato that I had been led to believe it possessed. Yet if the baritone Maurel could arouse such a frenzy in an aristocratic and intelligent audience such as this—despite the poor acoustics of the Pergola[3]—it is evident that at La Scala he would achieve the same effect, if not a greater one. As for the quality of his voice, I observed perfect homogeneity from the low to the high notes. The low notes such as the B, B flat and A are stupendous, but not to be compared with those of Lassalle. The middle voice is strong and vibrant, while the notes from the high F to the G are a little weak and tight, leaving something to be desired. His singing, however, is noble in expression and sentiment. Italian pronunciation correct and clear. All agile passages and trills are easy for him, while he is always on pitch, even in the difficult transition from full voice to *mezza voce*. The impression he made on the audience was excellent. In a word: Maurel is inferior to Lassalle in the volume of his voice, but very superior to Kaschmann, and he exceeds both of them artistically and in theatrical action. [. . .]

GIULIO RICORDI TO VERDI

Milan, 25 December 1880

Illustrious Maestro,

I am replying right away to your most esteemed letter of yesterday,[1] quite surprised and sorry that you still have not received Boito's verses. He told me that he posted them on Monday or Tuesday. If they have not been lost or gone astray, this means that he disliked something and consequently delayed. I have not seen Boito for 5 or 6 days, but I will find out today.

Even though you know Maurel thoroughly and can judge him better than anyone else, I am enclosing a letter from our House in Florence just to give you an idea of the impression this artist is making on an Italian audience today. With this news in hand I pushed the negotiations forward right away, with the result that Maurel is free during Lent. He is completely disposed not only to accept La Scala engagement, but if needed he would be very happy to make his début in *Ernani*, which would thus have a *non plus ultra* cast. Of course, he makes enormous pretences, but these would be no obstacle

[1] Representative of the House of Ricordi in Florence.
[2] Missing.
[3] Teatro alla Pergola in Florence, built in 1656 and renovated several times.

[1] Probably in the Biblioteca Palatina.

whatsoever if this engagement were another step toward the goal we desire so much!! [. . .] If it is no bother may I ask you to telegraph me simply: *All right.*[2] [. . .]

VERDI TO BOITO[1]

Genoa, 28 December 1880

Dear Boito,

This scene in the Senate is very beautiful, full of movement, of local colour, with very elegant and forceful lines such as you usually write. It's all right to change the lines at the beginning of the third act,[2] and the poisoning of the Doge is very good this way. But to my misfortune, the piece is very vast, difficult to set to music, and I don't know, now that I'm no longer *dans le mouvement*, whether I have time to get back in the saddle to do this and to arrange all the rest.

Permit me now to make some observations just for my own clarification.

1. Do you think it necessary to have it known from the beginning that Amelia is safe, and *invokes justice*?

2. Do you believe that the matter of the Tartars alone is sufficient to unite the Senate? Couldn't some other affair of State be added—for example, an attack of Corsairs, or even the war with Venice that is cursed by the poet [Petrarch]? Everything, of course, in passing, in a very few lines?

3. If Adorno says, '*Ho ucciso Lorenzino perchè mi rapia la sposa*' ['*I killed Lorenzino because he abducted my fiancée*'], and Amelia says, '*Salva lo sposo mio*' ['*Save my fiancé*'], the scene in the third act[3] between the Doge and Amelia will be destroyed. Not a very important scene in itself, but one that prepares very well for the Doge's sleep and for the trio. It seems to me that the action would lose nothing if, when the Doge says, '*Perchè impugni l'acciar?*' ['*Why do you grip your sword?*'], Gabriele responded, '*Tu facesti rapire Amelia Grimaldi . . . Vile Corsaro coronato muori*' ['*You had Amelia Grimaldi abducted . . . Vile crowned Corsair, die*'].

D[OGE]. Ferisci . . .	[Strike . . .
G[ABRIELE]. Amelia	Amelia
T[UTTI]. Amelia	Amelia
DOG. *Adorno: tu la vergin difendi; t'am-*	*Adorno: you defend the maiden: I admire*
miro, e t'assolvo .... Amelia, dì come	*you, and I absolve you . . . Amelia, tell you*
tu fosti rapita et., et.?	*how you were abducted*, etc., etc?]

The rest very good. Stupendous from '*Plebe, Patrizi, Popolo*' ['*Plebeians,*

---

¹ In answer to Boito's important, but unfortunately missing letter mentioned in Giulio Ricordi's letters to Verdi of 22 and 25 Dec.

² Read 'second act'.

³ Again, read 'second act'.

Patricians, People'] until the end, where we shall close with '*Sia maledetto!*' ['*May he be accursed!*'].

Answer me as quickly as possible.

> Most sincere wishes.
> G. Verdi

VERDI TO OPPRANDINO ARRIVABENE

Genoa, 6 January 1881

[. . .] I'm not killing myself with fatigue, but I am working. I'm about to mend the legs of an old dog who got a good thrashing in Venice and is called *Simon Boccanegra*. Nothing has been decided, however; first, because I want to be sure to have the legs well adjusted; second, because I also want to be sure that he will be in good hands and well directed. [. . .]

VERDI TO BOITO

Genoa, 8 January 1881

Dear Boito,

Don't feel remorseful about having wasted my time.[1] I haven't busied myself at all with music up to now. However, I am beginning to think about it; in fact, I've thought all day long about this *Boccanegra*, and here, it seems to me, is what could be done:

I pass over the prologue, of which I may change the first recitative and a few bars here and there in the orchestra.

In the first act, I would take out the cabaletta of the first piece, not because it is a cabaletta, but because it is very ugly. I would change the prelude, to which I would join the prima donna's *cantabile*, changing its orchestration, and I would make a *unified piece* of it. I would take up again, at the end, an orchestral passage from the prelude, during which Amelia would say, '*Spuntò il giorno ... Ei non vien!*' ... ['*Day has dawned ... He has not come!*'], or something similar. So arrange for me a few short lines in broken phrases . . . I wouldn't like those words of jealousy from Amelia!

The off-stage romanza for the tenor would stay as it is.

In the duet that follows, I would change the form of the cabaletta; you would have nothing to do . .

In Scene v, between Fieschi and Gabriele, I would like a few more words of recitative after the line '*A nostre nozze assenti?*' ['*Do you consent to our marriage?*']. If the public loses the word '*Umil*' ['*humble*'], it will understand nothing more. If he said, for instance, '*Ascolta ... alto segreto*' ['*Listen ... a*

---

[1] These words and Verdi's request of 28 Dec. to 'answer me as quickly as possible' suggest the loss of another letter from Boito.

deep secret'], etc., etc.—These are words that always make the audience's ears prick up. Add a couple of lines, then, if you think so, or don't, as you wish. What matters to me is to change the duet between Fieschi and Gabriele, '*Paventa o Doge*' ['*Fear, O Doge*']. It is too fierce and says nothing. Instead, I would like Fieschi, [who is] practically Amelia's father, to bless the future young couple. It could give rise to a touching moment, which would be a ray of light amid so much gloom. To maintain the colour, introduce also a bit of *patriotic feeling.* Fieschi can say, '. . . *ama quell'angelo* . . . *Ma dopo Dio* . . . *la Patria*' ['. . . *love that angel* . . . *but after God* . . . *your Country*'], etc. . . All good words for making the ears prick up . . . Eight beautiful lines, then, for Fieschi and an equal number for Gabriele, affectionate, moving, simple, in order to make a bit of melody, or something that at least has the semblance of one. If only it were possible to have Amelia return to the stage, and to write a little trio for solo voices! What a nice thing, to write for three voices! . . . Amelia and Gabriele kneeling, Fiesco standing in the middle, tall, blessing them! . . . But I am aware that, apart from the difficulty of making Amelia return to the stage, we would have a scene almost identical to the finale of the last act . . .

Have I explained myself?—I'm not quite sure. Try to guess what I haven't known how to say, and meanwhile send me these few lines as quickly as possible; tomorrow or the day after I'll tell you the rest. In the meantime, I will begin work on the first piece of this first act, if for no other reason than to put myself *dans le mouvement* before coming to the finale. I would like to do everything in sequence, just as if a new opera were concerned.[2]

I am waiting, and believe me your

G. Verdi

VERDI TO BOITO

Genoa, 9 January 1881

Dear Boito,

I continue my letter of the other day[1] . . .

I don't know whether I told you not to make the lines too long for me in the little duet between Gabriele and Fiesco.

In Scene vi, in place of the trumpets that announce the Doge, I would prefer a distant chorus of Huntsmen. What do you say?

In the new finale, the first two lines of the Doge, '*Il nuovo dì* . . .' ['*The new day* . . .'], etc. are useless. Adjust the rest that follows, and let's leave the duet between father and daughter[2] as it is. Only at the end, instead of the four lines

---

[2] Frits Noske considers this statement 'of great importance, since it proves that Verdi set his libretti in a "chronological" order, in contrast to his predecessors who conceived of their works in a mosaic-like way". (Noske, p. 353.)

---

[1] Obviously yesterday, 8 Jan.
[2] Act I, Scene i.

Non di regale orgoglio	[*Instead of the ephemeral*
L'effimero splendor	*Splendour of royal pride*
Mi cingerà d'aureolo	*I will be encircled*
Il raggio dell'amor	*By the golden ray of love*]

I would like to have Amelia speak another four lines of equal length, '*Vivrò nel mistero perchè tu non sia bersaglio all'odio dei nemici*' ['*I will live in mystery lest you be the target of your enemies' hatred*'].[3] In this way I would give greater development to the so-called cabaletta, and I would not repeat it.

Moreover, I would ask you to change the line or lines of the father to avoid the word '*aureola*'.[4] I'm not difficult about words, but in a vocal line, those *au . . . eo* sounds give a nasal, guttural, unpleasant tone.

Very little, indeed almost nothing, will have to be done in the other acts.

I have put myself to work in earnest.—Try to send me, as soon as possible, what I asked you for yesterday, and what I ask you for today.

In haste

Your
G. Verdi

BOITO TO VERDI

[Milan, 8–9 January 1881][1]

VARIANTS FOR ACT I
ACT I
Before the romanza for the tenor

· ·

S'inalba il ciel, ma l'amoroso canto
Non s'ode ancora. . .
Ei mi terge ogni dí, come l'aurora
La rugiada dei fiori, del ciglio il pianto.

[. ·

The sky grows bright, but the amorous song
Is not yet heard . . .
Each day it dries the tears on my cheek
As the dawn dries the dew on the flowers.]

---

[3] See Boito to Verdi, 14 Jan. 1881 for the final text.
[4] Verdi writes the correct form of the word, which is feminine.

---

[1] The date of this writing is inferred from Verdi's answer of 10 Jan. Obviously, Boito posted these variants from Milan in haste. Unless otherwise indicated, all of Boito's following variants represent the final text.

Addition to the dialogue between Gabriello² and Fiesco Scene V

.   .   .   .

GAB. A nostre nozze assenti?
ANDREA.   Alto mistero [[cupo arcano]]
   Sulla vergine incombe.
GAB.   E qual?
AND.   Se parlo
   Forse tu piú non l'amerai.
GAB.   Non teme
   Ombra d'arcani l'amor mio!—T'ascolto.
AND. Amelia tua d'umile stirpe nacque . . .
GAB. La figlia dei Grimaldi?!
AND.   No—la figlia
   Dei Grimaldi morí fra consacrate
   Vergini in Pisa ecc ecc ecc . . .

[.   .   .   .   .
GAB. Do you consent to our wedding?
ANDREA.   A great mystery [A dark secret]
   Looms over the maiden.
GAB.   What is it?
AND.   If I speak
   Perhaps you will no longer love her.
GAB.   My love
   Does not fear the shadow of mysteries!—I listen to you.
AND. Your Amelia was born of common stock . . .
GAB. The daughter of the Grimaldi?!
AND.   No—the daughter
   Of the Grimaldi died among consecrated
   Maidens in Pisa, etc., etc., etc. . . .]

ACT I

End of Scene V³

after the blank verses

.   .   .   .

ANDREA. Pio guerrier, del tempo antico
   L'alta fede in te rampolla;
   No, la spada tua non crolla
   Per nemico odio crudel.
   Vieni a me,
   (abbracciandolo) [[Baldo eroe]] ti benedico
   Nell'amore e nella guerra,
   Sii fedele alla tua terra,
   L'angiol tuo ti sia fedel.

² Gabriele.
³ See Boito to Verdi, 14 Jan. 1881 for Andrea's and Gabriele's lines in the final text.

GABR. Del tuo labbro il sacro detto
    Come balsamo raccolsi,
    Saldi son pel brando
    [[Forti ho già le vene e]] i polsi,
    M'empie il petto un vasto ardor.
    Se da te fui benedetto
    L'alma mia piú in me non langue,
    Freme e m'agita nel sangue
    Odio immenso e immenso amor.

[.   .   .   .

ANDREA. Pious warrior, the great faith
    Of ancient times lives in you;
    No, your sword falls not
    By the cruel hate of the enemy.
    Come to me,
    (embracing him) [[Gallant hero]] I bless you
    In love and in war.
    Be faithful to your country,
    May your angel be faithful to you.
GABR. From your lips the sacred word
    I received like balsam,
    Strong for the sword are
    [[Ever strong are my veins and]] my pulses,
    A great ardour fills my breast.
    If by you I have been blessed,
    My spirit no longer languishes in me,
    My blood boils and is agitated
    By immense hatred and immense love.]

Variant for the scene in the Senate.

SIM. Messeri il re di Tartaria vi porge
    Pegni di pace e ricchi doni e annunzia
    Schiuso l'Eusin alle liguri prore
    Acconsentite?
TUTTI.   Sí.
SIM. *(dopo una pausa)* Ma d'altro voto
    Piú generoso io vi richiedo.
ALCUNI.   Parla.
SIM. La stessa voce che tuonò su Rienzi
    Vaticinio di gloria e poi di morte
    Or su Genova tuona. *(s'incomincia ad udire un tumulto lontano)*.
                                Ecco un messaggio
    Del romito di Sorga, ei per Venezia
    Supplica pace ...
PAOLO *(interrompendo)* Attenda alle sue rime
    Il cantor della bionda Avignonese.
SIM. *(con forza)*. Messeri! ...   *(il tumulto s'avvicina)*
PIETRO.   Qual clamor?!
ALCUNI.   D'onde tai grida?
               ecc ecc ecc ecc.

[SIM. My Lords, the king of Tartary sends you
   Tokens of peace and rich gifts, and declares
   The Eusin open to Ligurian ships.
   Do you agree?
ALL.   Yes.
SIM. *(after a pause)* But another vote,
   More generous, I request from you.
SOME.   Speak.
SIM. The same voice which thundered over Rienzi
   Prophecies of glory and then of death[4]
   Now thunders over Genoa. *(a distant uproar begins to be heard)*.
                                      Here is a message
   From the hermit of the Sorgue,[5] he pleads for peace
   On behalf of Venice . . .
PAOLO *(interrupting)*.   Let the singer of the fair
   Avignonaise[6] attend to his rhymes.
SIM. *(forcefully)*. My Lords! . . .
                              (the uproar draws nearer)
PIETRO. What is that noise?!
SOME.   From where such screams?
                    etc., etc., etc., etc.]

Further variant to the scene in the Senate before Amelia's entrance.

. . . .

SIM. *(a Gabr.)* Perché impugni l'acciar?
GAB.   Ho trucidato
   Lorenzino.
POP.   Assassin.
FIESCHI.   Ei la Grimaldi
   Avea rapita.
SIM.   (Orror!)
POP.   Menti!
GAB.   Quel vile
   Pria di morir disse che un uom possente
   Al criminè l'ha spinto.

PIETRO *(a Paolo)*.   (Ah! Sei scoperto [[perd]])

   [4] The voice of Petrarch, who had expected Cola di Rienzi to become the *condottiere* and unifier of Italy.
   [5] Boito followed Verdi's suggestion to Giulio Ricordi of 20 Nov. 1880, by alluding to 'the hermit of the Sorgue,' i.e. Petrarch, who stayed at the source of the river Sorgue in the mountains of south eastern France.
   [6] Petrarch's beloved Laura, whom he met at Avignon and praised in his *Canzoniere*.

SIM. *(con agitazione).* E il nome suo?
GAB. *(fissando il Doge con tremenda ironia).*
                                        T'aqueta! il reo si spense
  Pria di svelarlo.
SIM.   Che vuoi dir?
GAB. *(terribilmente).*   Pel cielo!!
  Uom possente tu sei!
SIM. *(a Gabriel).*   Ribaldo!
GAB. *(al Doge slanciandosi).*   Audace
  Rapitor di fanciulle!
ALCUNI.   Si disarmi!
GAB. *(disvincolandosi e correndo con Fiesco per ferire il Doge).* Empio corsaro
  incoronato! muori!
AMELIA *(entrando e interponendosi fra i due assaltatori e il
  Doge).* Ferisci.
SIM.   ⎫
FIESCO   ⎬   Amelia!
GABR.   ⎭
TUTTI. Amelia! . .
AM.   O Doge! (o padre!)
  Salva l'Adorno tu.
SIM *(alle guardie che si sono impossessate di Gabriello per disarmarlo).* Nessun
  l'offenda!!
  Cade l'orgoglio e al suon del suon dolore
  Tutta l'anima mia parla d'amore.
  Amelia dí come tu fosti rapita
  E come ecc ecc ecc ecc.

  .   .   .   .

  [.   .   .   .   .

SIM *(to Gabr.).* Why do you grip your sword?
GAB.   I have slain
  Lorenzino.
PEOPLE.   Assassin.
FIESCHI.   He had abducted
  The Grimaldi.
SIM.   (Horror!)
PEOPLE.   You lie!

GAB.   That villain
  Said before dying that a powerful man
  Had driven him to the crime.
PIETRO *(to Paolo)*
  (Ah! You are discovered [[lost]])
SIM. *(agitated).* And his name?
GAB. *(glaring at the Doge with tremendous sarcasm).*
                              Stay calm! The culprit died
  Before revealing it.
SIM.   What do you mean?

GAB. *(terrifying)*.   By Heaven!!
   You are a powerful man!
SIM. *(to Gabriel)*.   Scoundrel!
GAB. *(rushing at the Doge)*.   Audacious
   Abductor of girls!
SOME.   Disarm him!
GAB. *(freeing himself and rushing with Fiesco to stab the Doge)*. Vile crowned
   corsair! Die!
AMELIA Strike.
       (entering and throwing herself between the two assailants and the Doge.)
SIM.   ⎫
FIESCO   ⎬   Amelia!
GABR.   ⎭
ALL.   Amelia! . .
AM.   O Doge! (O Father!)
   You save the Adorno.[7]
SIM *(to the guards who have seized Gabriello to disarm him)*.
                              Let no one touch him!!
   Pride succumbs and at the sound of her grief,
   My whole soul speaks of love.
   Amelia, tell how you were abducted,
   And how, etc., etc., etc., etc.
·]

A very small variant for my use and consumption and for the peace of
my *timorous conscience*.

Finale Act I

Stanza for	Il suo commosso accento	[His voice so moved knows
the Chorus:	Sa l'ira in noi calmar;	How to calm our anger;
	Vol di soave vento	A breeze of gentle wind
	Che rasserena il mar.	That smooths the sea.]

(in the first manuscript I did not like those two images of *altare* [altar] and *mare* [sea]
heaped together, since they annulled each other. This variant isn't beautiful, no, but it
has a bit more common sense.)

VARIANTS FOR ACT II

Variant in Act II, Scenes i and ii

Scene i

Palazzo degli Abati.
Camera del Doge. ecc ecc. Seggiolone, tavola,
un alcova. Sul tavolo un anfora e una tazza.

Paolo e Pietro.

PAOLO. Quei due vedesti?

---

[7] '*O Doge! Ah! Salva.* / *Salva l'Adorno tu.*' ['O Doge! Ah! Save. / You save the Adorno'] in the
final text.

PIE.   Sí.
PAO.   Li traggi tosto
Dal carcer loro per l'andito ascoso
Che questa chiave schiuderà.
PIE.   T'intesi.
              (esce)

[*The palace of the Abati.*
Chamber of the Doge, etc., etc. A large chair, a table,
an alcove. On the table a carafe and a cup.

Paolo and Pietro.

PAOLO. You saw the two of them?
PIE.   Yes.
PAO.   Have them brought at once
From their prison by the secret passage,
Which this key will open.
PIE.   I heard you.

                                        (exits)]

            Scene ii

            Paolo alone

Me stesso ho maledetto!! ...
E l'anatema
M'insegue ancor ... e l'aura ancor ne trema!
Vilipeso ... rejetto
Dal Senato e da Genova, qui vibro
L'ultimo stral pria di fuggir, qui libro
La sorte tua, Doge, in quest'ansia estrema.
Tu che m'offendi e che mi devi il trono
Qui t'abbandono
Al tuo destino
In quest'ora fatale.
        (estrae un ampolla, ne versa il contenuto nella tazza)
Qui ti stillo una lenta atra agonía,
Là t'armo un'assassino.
Scelga Morte sua via
Fra il tosco ed il pugnale.

[I have cursed myself!! ...
And the anathema
Still follows me ... and the air still shudders with it!
Vilified ... rejected
By the Senate and all Genoa, here I free
The last dart before my flight, here I seal
Your fate, Doge, in this extreme desire.
You who offends me and owes the throne to me,
Here I leave you
To your destiny
In this fatal hour.
        (he pulls out a flask, pours its contents in the cup)

Here I pour for you a slow dark agony,
There I arm your assassin.
Let Death choose its path
Between the poison and the dagger.]

ACT II

Scene iii (brief variant)

The same, Andrea, Gabriele led on from the right by Pietro.

FIE. Prigioniero, in qual loco m'adduci? [[mi trovo]]
PAO. Nelle stanze del Doge, e favella
  A te Paolo.
FIE.   I tuoi sguardi son truci!
PAO. Io so l'odio che celasi in te.
  Tu m'ascolta.
FIE.   Che brami?
PAO.   Al cimento
  Preparasti de' Guelfi la schiera
  ecc ecc ecc ecc.
[FIE. Where do you take me [[I find myself]], as a prisoner?
PAO. In the rooms of the Doge, and Paolo
  Speaks to you.
FIE.   Your glances are fierce!
PAO. I know the hatred which you hide within you.
  Listen to me.
FIE.   What do you want?
PAO.   For the riot
  You prepared the forces of the Guelphs
  etc., etc., etc., etc.]

ACT II

Variant for Act II, Scene viii.[8]

Doge e Gabriele nascosto.
Il Doge entra meditabondo, siede.
DOGE. Doge!—Ancor proveran la tua clemenza
  I due ribelli?—Di paura segno
  Fora il castigo—M'ardono le fauci . . .
    (versa dall'anfora nella tazza e beve.)
  Perfin l'onda del fonte è amara al labbro
  Dell'uom che regna . . . ho l'alma oppressa . . . infrante
  Dal duol le membra . . . già . . . mi vince il sonno . . .
  Oh Amelia . . . ami . . . un nemico . . .
    (s'addormenta)
  ecc ecc ecc ecc

---

[8] A few slight changes were made in the final text: *'Doge! Ancor proveran la tua clemenza | I traditori'* [The traitors']?, etc. *'Perfin l'acqua* [the water] *del fonte è amara al labbro | Dell'uom che regna! O duol! La mente è oppressa* . . . [O grief! My mind is oppressed] | *Stanche le membra* . . . *ohimè!* [Tired the limbs . . . alas!] . . . *mi vince il sonno. | O Amelia . . . ami un nemico! (S'addormenta,* etc.)'

[*The Doge, and Gabriele hidden.*
The Doge enters, lost in thought, and sits down.
DOGE. Doge!—Do the two rebels againt test
Your clemency!—Punishment would be
A sign of fear.—My throat is burning . . .
     (he pours from the carafe into the cup and drinks.)
Even the wave of the fountain is bitter to the lips
Of the man who rules . . . my soul is oppressed . . . broken
By grief my limbs . . . already . . . sleep overcomes me . . .
Oh Amelia . . . you love . . . an enemy . . .
     (he falls asleep)
etc., etc., etc., etc.]

Dear Maestro,
   Have I guessed your ideas correctly? I don't know.—I await your
instructions, and limit myself today to sending a cordial greeting to
you and your wife.

Your
Arrigo Boito

BOITO TO VERDI

[Milan, 9 January 1881][1]

Dear Maestro,
   Here you see the effects of myopia combined with absentmindedness:
On my desk I find this sheet,[2] which belongs to the variants of the first act.
Little harm done. I hope that you will receive it with the rest.
         Affectionate greetings

Arrigo Boito

VERDI TO BOITO

Genoa, 10 January 1881

Dear Boito,
   The two registered letters with the variants have reached me at just the
right moment. With the four lines '*S'inalba il Ciel*' ['*The sky grows bright*'],
etc., I'll finish the first piece, which is, in fact, as good as finished.
   The few lines added to the scene that follows between Andrea and Gabriele
are good—The little duet, I'm afraid, comes out long and too powerful.
Precisely at this moment I would like something calm, solemn, religious. It

---

[1] Presumably, Boito wrote these undated lines in Milan on this day. Verdi received them by
registered post on 10 Jan. as he had the preceding ones.
[2] We do not know which particular sheet Boito had forgotten to post with the preceding
variants. Therefore, it is included in the preceding pages.

deals with a marriage. He's a father who is blessing his adopted children. I don't much like the rhythm of the eight-syllable lines because of those damned notes on the upbeat.

but I'll avoid them and, so as not to waste time, I'll set to work right away on the four lines of Andrea in this duet

Vieni a me, ti benedico   [Come to me, I bless you]

. . . .

. . . .

. . . .

Meanwhile I'll throw together another four words [*sic*] for Gabriele, so as to go on with the work until your lines arrive.—Four lines for each are enough.—To make myself clearer, I'd like Gabriele to be able to sing his stanza on his knees; therefore something religious. Apart from this, it seems to me that nothing is spoiled; this calm, and that of the following scenes, would help to make the commotion of the finale stand out better. You tell me that the *little duet* would start *after the unrhymed lines* ... All of them? It seems to me that the little duet should start after '*In terra e in ciel ...*' ['*On earth and in heaven*'] or else after

Ma non rallenti amor   [But may love not lessen
La foga in te de' cittadini affetti   *Your   ardour   for   your   compatriots'
                                                     affections[1]*]

adjusting the rhymes and the lines, of course, as you think best. ... Then, if you think so, we could put in the lines

Il doge vien. Partiam   [*The doge is coming. Let us leave*
. . — — — —   . . — — — —

Fiesco in Andrea   *Fiesco in Andrea*]

after the little duet, during the fanfare *of the trumpets* or the Chorus of Huntsmen ..

   All the other changes very fine, and the recitative of the *poison* is very beautiful.—We may find ourselves a bit embarrassed as to the staging, at the words of Amelia

O Doge (o padre)   [O Doge (O Father)
Salva l'Adorno tu ...   *Save Adorno ...*]

How will she sing these words? ... *sotto voce* to the Doge? ... That wouldn't be very nice ... But these are trifles that will look after themselves, by a gesture on stage or by a word.

   Courage, then, my dear Boito, and make me these four lines of eight

---

[1] These lines were eliminated from the final text.

syllables for Gabriele. Not more than four lines each. That's enough. Send them as soon as possible. In the meantime, I am working . . .

Greetings also from my wife.

G. Verdi

VERDI TO BOITO
[Telegram]

Genoa, 11 January 1881

DO NOT DO HUNTSMEN CHORUS—WILL WRITE

VERDI

VERDI TO BOITO

[Genoa] Tuesday 11 [January 1881][1]

Dear Boito,

I believe it is useless, as I said in the telegram sent to you this morning,[2] to do the Chorus of the Huntsmen. It would be another piece of music, and in this act (counting the prelude, aria for soprano, and romanza for tenor as a single piece) we would still have six pieces, one of which, the finale, is very long. A *blast* of trumpets of *12* or *16* bars will suffice for the Doge's entrance.

Yesterday evening I did the duet between Andrea and Gabriele. The additions have forced me to redo, in part, the recitative, and I have stopped at the words '*In terra e in Ciel*' ['*On earth and in Heaven*'].

However, I can also add

.. Ma non rallenti amore	[*.. But may love not lessen*
La foga in te de'cittadini affetti	*Your ardour for your compatriots' affections.*]

Adjust the end of this recitative as you think best.

For the cantabile, I have used the four lines of Andrea

Vieni a me ti benedico . . .	[*Come to me, I bless you* . . .]
. . . .	. . . .
. . . .	. . . .
. . . .	. . . .

and I have made up another strophe for Gabriele just to finish. I only need 4 lines for Andrea (and the four cited above can serve) and another four lines for Gabriele [which are] still to be written. The piece has a calm, solemn character, a bit religious, a bit old-fashioned .. I ask you, then, for this strophe; meanwhile, I am going forward in order to get to the finale. After the

---

[1] Postmark: GENOVA 12/1/81.
[2] Since Verdi had addressed his telegram erroneously to Via Principe Umberto instead of Principe Amedeo, Boito might have received it with one day's delay.

Andrea–Gabriele duet the trumpets will begin off stage and meanwhile, if necessary, the lines

Il Doge vien . . Partiam et.   [*The Doge is coming . . Let us leave*, etc.]

can be sung.
   Tell me where I must stop . .
   I greet you in haste.

G. Verdi

BOITO TO VERDI

[Milan] 14 January [1881]
Via Principe Amedeo 1

My Maestro,
   I waited for the letter that you announced to me in your telegram before sitting down at my desk for the new variants. I received the letter yesterday, and here is the result of an attentive reading of all that you have written to me in the last few days.[1] It seems to me that the recitative in the scene of Andrea and Gabriele should go up to the words '*In terra e in ciel*' ['*On earth and in heaven*'], completing the lines, as I shall explain and beginning the lyrical part at once; for example:

    ANDREA. Di lei sei degno!
    GABRIELE.   A me fia dunque unita!
    ANDREA. In terra e in ciel.
    GABRIELE (*con effusione*).   Ah! mi ridai[2] la vita!
    ANDREA. Vieni a me, ti benedico
      Nella pace di quest'ora;
      Lieto vivi e fido adora
      L'angiol tuo, la patria, il ciel.

    [ANDREA. You are worthy of her!
    GABRIELE.   Then let her be united with me!
    ANDREA. On earth and in heaven.
    GABRIELE (*with effusion*)   Ah! You give me back my life!
    ANDREA. Come to me, I bless you
      In the peace of this hour;
      Live happily and worship faithfully
      Your angel, your country, and heaven.]

(See an *alternative* on the back of this sheet.)[3]

    GABRIELE. Eco pia del tempo antico
      La tua voce è un casto incanto;

[1] On 9, 10, and 11 Jan.
[2] '*Ah! tu mi dai la vita!*' ['Ah! You give me life!'] in the final text.
[3] See the (discarded) alternative in a postscriptium to this letter.

Serberà ricordo santo
Di quest'ora il cor fedel.
    (*squilli di trombe*)
Ecco il Doge—Partiam. Ch'ei non ti scorga.
ANDREA. Ah! presto il dì della vendetta sorga.

[GABRIELE. Holy echo of ancient times,
  Your voice is a chaste enchantment;
  My heart ever faithful will
  Keep the sainted memory of this hour.
    (*sounds of trumpets*)
  The Doge is coming—We must go. Don't let him see you.
ANDREA. Ah! may the day of vengeance soon appear.]

Do you think it is enough?.. It seems sufficient to me; it is better, I think, not to speak about the plot of the Guelphs;[4] it would perhaps confuse the minds, always a bit lazy, of the audience and would ruin the clarity of the finale. If, however, you think that it should be mentioned, nothing prevents you from keeping as they are the six lines of the original libretto that come immediately after the fanfare.

One observation. It would be desirable to avoid a scene change at this point. Three scenes in one act are, in my opinion, too many; they destroy the impression of unity that is so necessary for the well-organized life of the act. Consider that in the whole drama, this garden is the only cheerful scene. All the others are grave, solemn, or dark. There are too many *interiors*: Council Chamber, Room of the Doge, Ducal Hall. Since in this beginning of the first act we are in the open air, let's stay there as long as we can. On one side, at the back of the garden, there can be a pair of columns representing the entrance to the Grimaldi palace. Amelia would come to meet the Doge on the threshold of the palace, and the scene that follows would find the garden a sufficiently natural setting. Besides, if the scene were changed there would be no reason to remove Fiesco and Gabriele from a place where the Doge, whom they are fleeing, should not set foot. But let's not waste time.

SCENE vi

Doge, Paolo, etc., etc.

DOGE.   Paolo
PAOLO.   Signor.
DOGE.   Ci spronano gli eventi.
  Di qua partir convien, ecc., ecc.

[DOGE.   Paolo
PAOLO.   My Lord.
DOGE.   Events are pressing.
  We must leave from here, etc., etc.]

---

[4] Members of a political faction opposed to the Ghibellines (see Appendix I, n. 4).

with what follows.

This way, the line about the *festive day* would be patched up *well and even better*.

SCENE vii

I move on to the au ... eo ...
Shall we put *gloria* instead of *aureola*?

| Di mia corona il raggio | [The splendour of my crown |
| La gloria tua sarà? | Will be your glory?] |

And then, in transcribing them, let's see if the four new lines sound right with the old ones where Amelia replies to her father:

AMELIA. Padre, vedrai la vigile	[Father, you'll see your vigilant
Figlia tua sempre accanto;	Daughter always at your side;
Nell'ore melanconiche	In hours of melancholy
Asciugherò il tuo pianto ...	I'll dry your tears ...
Avrem gioie romite	We'll have solitary joys
Note soltanto al ciel:	Known only to Heaven:
Io la colomba mite	I'll be the gentle dove
Sarò del regio ostel.	Of the royal dwelling.][5]

Well, for today I seem to have finished my assignment; ready to begin again if anything about it doesn't suit you.

I advise you, dear Maestro, that Thursday I leave Milan to go to Padua. I'll stay a week in that city to help with the cooking of *Mefistofele*[6] and to serve it hot to my fellow citizens. Until Wednesday evening I can receive your letters at Milan, afterwards at *Padua, Albergo della Croce d'Oro*. But by the 29th I'll have returned home.

Giulio Ricordi was sick in bed for many days; he's still not up but is feeling better.

Many, many greetings

Your
Arrigo Boito

Alternative:

La tua voce un'eco, un canto	[Your voice seems almost an echo,
Quasi par del tempo antico,	A song of ancient times;
Serberà ricordo santo	My faithful heart will
De' tuoi detti il cor fedel.	Keep a sainted memory of your words.]

These damned eight-syllable lines, you're right, are the most annoying

[5] In the final text, the third line reads '*Nell'ora melanconica*' ['In the hour of melancholy'], and the sixth line '*Soltano note al ciel*' ['Only known to heaven'].

[6] At the final rehearsals in Boito's native city. The successful opening night on 25 Jan. was conducted by Alessandro Pomè (1853–1934). Boito informed Tornaghi of his return to Milan on 26 Jan.

rigmaroles in our poetic metre. I have chosen them out of desperation. I didn't want seven-syllable lines because almost all of the libretto in its lyrical parts is in seven-syllable lines; I didn't want five-syllable lines because just at this point the old text was written in five-syllable lines, and I thought that perhaps you would return grudgingly to the old rhythm.

VERDI TO BOITO

Genoa, 15 [January] 1881

Dear Boito,

Everything works well, and I am doubly happy not to have to change the first scene of the second act.[1]

Do you, dear Boito, imagine that you have finished? Quite the contrary! We'll have finished after the dress rehearsal, if indeed we get that far. Meanwhile, in the duet between the father and daughter there is something that should be given greater emphasis. If the audience loses the poor little line '*Ai non fratelli miei*' ['*To brothers not my own*'], it won't understand anything more.

I would like them to say, for example:

D[OGE]. *Paolo!*	[*Paolo!*
A[MELIA]. *Quel vil nomasti!* ...	*You've named that vile one!* ...
Ma a te buono, generoso devo dire *il vero*	*But to you*, so kind, so generous, I must tell *the truth*
[[D[OGE]. *Che!*]]	[[What!]]
A[MELIA]. *I Grimaldi non sono i miei fratelli*	*The Grimaldi are not my brothers*
D[OGE]. *Ma e tu?*	*But what about you?*
A[MELIA]. *Non sono una Grimaldi*	*I am not a Grimaldi*
D[OGE]. *E chi sei dunque?.*	*And who are you, then?.*][2]

Thus the attention is fixed, and something is understood. . . . If you think so, make me three or four unrhymed lines, clear and neat. You will always write beautiful lines, but here it would not matter to me even if they were ugly. Pardon the heresy; I believe that in the theatre, just as it is sometimes praiseworthy for composers to have the talent not to make music and to be able *s'effacer*,[3] so also for poets, instead of a beautiful line a plain and theatrical word is sometimes better. I say this only for my part.

Another observation about the finale. Among the 2000 spectators on the first evening, there may be scarcely more than twenty who know the two letters of Petrarch. Unless we include a footnote, Simone's lines will prove obscure to the public. I would like, almost as a comment, just after the line

---

[1] The first act.

[2] See Boito's following letter for the final text.

[3] On 17 August 1870, Verdi had expressed the same idea to his librettist for *Aida*, Antonio Ghislanzoni: 'Unfortunately, it is sometimes necessary in the theatre for poets and composers to have the talent *not* to write poetry or music.' (Busch, *Aida*, p. 50.)

Il cantor della bionda Avignonese
[*The poet of the fair Avignonaise*]

everyone to say

Guerra a Venezia!	[War against Venice!
DOGE. È guerra fratricida. Venezia e Genova hanno una patria comune: Italia.	It is a war of fratricide! Venice and Genoa have a common homeland: Italy.

TUTTI. Nostra patria è Genova
    (*Tumulto interno, et.*)
	Our homeland is Genoa
	    (*Uproar within, etc.*)]

[[But do as you think best.]]
   Answer me before you leave. Meanwhile I wish you a good trip and good luck . . .

Affectionately,
G. Verdi

PS I am sorry about Giulio. I believed it was something more slight. I'm very glad to hear that he's getting better.

BOITO TO VERDI

[Milan] Sunday [16 January 1881][1]

I fully agree with you, dear Maestro, about the idea of sacrificing, when necessary, the euphony of poetry and music to the effectiveness of dramatic accentuation and theatrical truth. You wanted three or four lines, unrhymed, even ugly, but clear, instead of the line

dei non fratelli miei

[*of brothers not my own*]

which isn't beautiful. I wrote the four lines (I wasn't able to do only three), but I didn't think it wise to make them unrhymed, since I was afraid that between the seven-syllable rhymed lines that precede them and the eight-syllable rhymed lines that follow, the abandoning of rhyme for only four lines would seem feeble when read:

·   ·   ·   ·   ·   ·   ·   ·   ·   ·   ·

DOGE. Paolo!
AM.   Quel vil nomasti . . . E poichè tanta
   Pietà ti move dei destini miei
   Vo' svelarti il segreto che mi ammanta:
      (*dopo breve pausa*)
   Non sono una Grimaldi.
DOGE.   O ciel! Chi sei?

[1] Postmark: MILANO 16/1/81.

[DOGE. Paolo!
AMELIA.   You've named the fiend ... And since so much
   Pity for my destiny moves you
   I want to reveal to you the secret that surrounds me:
        (*After a short pause*)
   I am not a Grimaldi.
DOGE.   O Heaven! Who are you, then?]
        . . . .

Let's go on to the Council chamber:

        . . . .

PAOLO (*ridendo*) . . . . . . Attenda alle sue rime
   Il cantor della bionda Avignonese.
   Tutti i Consiglieri
        (poi Paolo ferocemente)
                    Guerra a Venezia!
DOGE.   E con quest'urlo atroce
   Fra' due liti d'Italia erge Caino
   La sua clava cruenta!—Adria e Liguria
   Hanno patria comune.
TUTTI.   È nostra patria
   Genova!
PIERO.   Qual clamor?
ALCUNI.   D'onde tai grida?
   ecc ec ecc.

[PAOLO (*laughing*) . . . . . . Let the poet of the fair
   Avignonaise attend to his rhymes.
   All Councillors
        (*then Paolo fiercely*)
                    War against Venice!
DOGE.   And with this horrible cry
   Between two factions of Italy, Cain
   Raises his bloody club!—The Adriatic and Ligurian shores
   Have a common homeland.
ALL.   Our homeland is
   Genoa!
PIETRO. What is this noise?
SEVERAL.   Whence these screams?
   etc., etc., etc.]

        . . . .

I have avoided the word *fratricidal* war, indicated in your letter, so as not to take away from the effect of the exlamation '*Fratricidi!*' ['*Fratricides!*'], which bursts forth before the words of the Doge.

        DOGE. *Plebe, patrizi!* ... ecc.
            [*Plebeians, patricians!* ... etc.]

Certainly there will be no more than twenty persons in the theatre sufficiently cultured to recognize the allusion that the Doge makes to the two letters Petrarch wrote to the Prince of Rome,[2] but heaven keep us far from the temptation to use footnotes and comments. Still, if you want the 20 persons to become two hundred or more, it is enough to change the allusion and, instead of the letters (today known to few, whereas to Petrarch's contemporaries they were very well known) allude to the song that everyone learns at school,[3] changing it thus:

La stessa voce che [[*tuonò*]] *innegiò su Roma*	[*The same voice that* [[*thundered*]] *extolled over Rome*
Pria che recasse tutta alle sue mani	*Before the insolent Rienzi in his*
Rienzi protervo la civil possanza,	*Own hands assumed all civil power,*
Or su Genova tuona ...	*Now thunders over Genoa ...*]

But the sentence turns out too prolix and too contorted for the clarity and speed needed for musical accentuation.

On the other hand, the first version is not historically exact; instead of

Vaticino di gloria e poi di morte

[*Prophecy of glory and then of death*]

it would be more correct to say:

Vaticino di gloria e poscia d'onta

[*Prophecy of glory and then of shame*].

But this way the line is ugly; however, this makes no difference to you or me. I leave you as arbiter in the decision.[4] The public, moreover, is an animal that swallows everything and doesn't give a damn about these scruples, and in this it isn't so wrong.

If you need any more drops of ink from my pen, I could receive another letter from you before my departure, still set for Thursday.

Many cordial greetings,

Your
Arrigo Boito

Giulio was worse yesterday, not so bad today; he has congestion in his lungs, for which they had to apply vesicatories to his chest; it's a situation that keeps us a little alarmed, not so much for now as for the future—.

---

[2] Cola di Rienzi.
[3] Probably '*Spirito gentil*' ['Gentle spirit'] in Donizetti's *La favorita*.
[4] Verdi decided on the first version.

VERDI TO BOITO

[Genoa] Monday [17 January 1881][1]

Dear Boito,

Just a word to tell you that this morning I received your lines, and they work very well.

Enough for now . . . .

Later, however, I don't know . —

Affectionate greetings,

. . [illegible]
G. Verdi

EMANUELE MUZIO TO GIULIO RICORDI

[Genoa?, 17 January 1881]

[. . .] I don't have the slightest doubt about the final result of *Simon Boccanegra* and then of *Otello*, since Verdi has returned the two very beautiful libretti[1] to the Opéra [. . .] And so he will occupy himself only with *Otello*, whose music, I think, is all alive in his mind. [. . .]

BOITO TO GIULIO RICORDI

Padua, 21 January 1881

[. . .] When the management of La Scala decides to publish the additional poster announcing *Boccanegra*, make sure that neither my name nor my pseudonym is printed by mistake, or through an indiscretion of the management.

You know that I have agreed to give a hand to the libretto of *Boccanegra* because I am devoted to Verdi's wishes; you know that I have always been opposed to the idea of giving this opera at La Scala at this time; you know that I don't attribute any artistic or literary merit to the patchwork I have made from poor Piave's libretto.

Therefore I beg you to watch out for this; the new *Boccanegra* shall clearly and plainly run under F. M. Piave's name, and mine is not to be added in any way. [. . .]

[1] Postmark: GENOVA 17/I/81.

---

[1] Unknown.

VERDI TO BOITO[1]

[Genoa], *Monday* [24 January 1881][2]

Dear Boito,

Again I need another drop of your ink. I say *another* . . . I don't say the *last*!

Without wanting to, I've written an *ensemble piece* in the new finale. It is understood that Simone sings, first *alone*, all of his sixteen lines.

> *Plebe! Patrizi! Popolo*
>
> . . . .
>
> [*Plebeians! Patricians! People*
>
> . . . .]

Afterwards comes this *ensemble piece*, which is hardly an ensemble piece but is one nonetheless. In general I'm not fond of *asides*, since they force the artist into immobility; and I would at least like Amelia to turn to Fieschi, recommending '*Pace . . . perdono . . . oblìo . . Sono fratelli nostri! . . .*' ['*Peace . . . pardon . . . oblivion . . They are our brothers! . . .*'] This way the little phrase written for Amelia would prove warmer for me. In this new little stanza, don't forget the word '*pace*' ['*peace*'] . . . which to me works very well.

In Amelia's narrative earlier, I have never been able, am not able, and never shall be able to have declaimed properly the line '*Non egli è di tanto misfatto il più reo*' ['*He is not the most guilty of such a great crime*'], and it is true enough that in the old score, I wrote (misjudging the line and rhyme)

> *Di tanto misfatto, il più reo non è*
>
> [*Of such a great crime, the most guilty he is not.*]

To avoid so much disgrace, see if you can't adjust the line for me, placing an accent on the first as well as the second *six-syllable line*.

I've finished . . . for now! I greet you from the heart.

> [illegible]
>
>   G. Verdi

BOITO TO VERDI

Milan, 31 January [1881]

My dear Maestro,

I received your letter at Padua, but not until today, in Milan, was I able to make the changes you expected of me. I calmed myself with the thought that you, meanwhile, were working on some other part of the opera.

From the words that you wrote to me, I understood that in this ensemble

---

[1] Verdi addressed this letter: Arrigo Boito *Padova*.
[2] Postmark: GENOVA 24/1/81.

piece the role of Amelia has proved to be musically the most important after
that of the Doge, and I deduced from this that just four lines would perhaps
not be enough, and so I wrote eight. See if they are suitable:

Amelia to Fiesco[1]

Pace! l'altero sangue   [Peace! Restrain your noble blood
Doma e l'orgoglio piega!   And yield your pride!
Pace! la patria langue   Peace! The country languishes
Per l'ira tua crudel.   Through your cruel wrath.
Col labro mio ti prega   Through my lips she pleads with you—
L'alma fra gli astri assunta   The soul of the gentle departed,
Della gentil defunta   Who, now risen among the stars,
Che ti contempla in ciel.   Watches you from Heaven.]

I would have liked to give the role of Gabriele a bit of action, but it didn't
work out, and the reason is clear: If the Doge speaks to everyone and if
Amelia implores Fiesco, then Gabriele no longer has anyone to talk to, since
Pietro and Paolo also are talking together, and he is necessarily condemned
to stand motionless.

And now, dear Maestro, in place of that bad line in the old libretto, try to
put the following line:

AM. *V'è un uom più nefando—*   [*There is a man more wicked—*
   Che illeso ancor sta.   *Who is still unsullied.*]

I was aware that here you need a broken [*tronca*] line, and I had to search
through several lines above for a broken ending that would lead to any
rhyme whatsoever.

Now I have taken up my accustomed life in Milan and am at your disposal
for anything that you shall find necessary. Cordial greetings

from your
Arrigo Boito

FRANCO FACCIO TO VERDI

Milan, 31 January 1881

Illustrious Maestro,

Only a few lines in the hope that the news of the first performance of
Ernani[1] may not displease you. First of all, I will tell you that the audience's
interest in this revival was such that the other night, it seemed to be attending
the opening night of *Aida* . . . or of *Simon Boccanegra* . . . or of *O* . . . (You

---

[1] These lines are not included in the final text. See Boito to Verdi, 7 Feb. 1881 for their
substitution.

---

[1] A revival of Verdi's *Ernani* conducted by Franco Faccio at La Scala on 29 Jan. 1881. The
same principal artists—D'Angeri, Tamagno, Maurel and Edouard De Reszke—were to appear
in *Simon Boccanegra* on 24 Mar. 1881.

will laugh and interrupt me, exclaiming, 'How many *ors*!!!') Well then, let's change the 'ors' to zeros, and let me say that [. . .] the box office made the excellent sum of 9,000 lire. The opera had a splendid success, and it was unfortunate that an indisposition on Maurel's part prevented last night's second performance, for which all the seats had already been grabbed. La D'Angeri sang very well and had real ovations. [. . .] Tamagno very good, with his exceptional voice and his *extremely powerful* effects, and De Retzke very good, who might only be reproached for singing too well! [. . .] As for Maurel, I must tell you that his vocal indisposition was already apparent in the first performance [. . .] but everybody admired the distinguished talent also of the actor and singer. [. . .] I would like to speak very well also of the chorus and the orchestra, if such an assertion were not up to others rather than up to me. There's no use concealing from you that all the choruses and finales were greeted with resounding applause, including that of the conspiracy, '*Si ridesti il Leon di Castiglia*' ['*Let the Lion of Castile awaken*'], which by tradition (I was told in rehearsals) should be performed at a slightly faster tempo than I had taken; therefore I bothered you with a telegram[2] dictated by an artistic scruple with which you will sympathize. Costumes magnificent, historical, sumptuous; the sets so-so. And now I am writing to you directly, that we would like to announce *Simon Boccanegra*, and that the management, the committee (including the insignificant undersigned), the public—in short, all those who care about the dignity and glory of Italian art—wait upon your decision. [. . .]

GIULIO RICORDI TO GIUSEPPINA VERDI

Milan, 1 February 1881

[. . .] Thursday I hope to make a trip to Genoa, and from there we shall go to the Riviera for 4 or 5 days.[1] But we will not leave Genoa without first having the pleasure of greeting you.

You will have heard about the enormous success with which *Ernani* was received. I was desperate because I had to stay at home! [. . .]

Going by the general opinions of musicians and non-musicians, dilettantes and laymen, the order of merit is

Reske
Maurel
D'Angeri
Tamagno

But Maurel will certainly take first place when he is well again, and Tamagno, who had never sung the opera before, and faltered a good deal, will move up next to la D'Angeri. [. . .]

2 Missing.

---

1 To recover from his recent illness.

GIULIO RICORDI TO VERDI

Milan, 2 February 1881

[. . .] As for Maurel, he has now left Florence, where he has always sung with complete success and been in the best of health; in this regard I have exact information. On the night train to Milan he caught the devil of a cold. [. . .]

Despite all of this, he was applauded throughout the opera,[1] and when he did not take his bow with all the others after the third act, the entire audience called for him and gave him an ovation.

Faccio, who had told me very nice things about Maurel at the rehearsals (the orchestra was enthusiastic about him, too), completely confirmed the above to me. [. . .]

As for the papers!!. . What can I tell you, illustrious Maestro, that you don't already know! . . . What can I tell you about these *stupid reporters* (may God strike them) who pick up the first news they hear[2] . . . . boasting that they are well informed! . . .

Before I became ill I managed, by dint of entreaties, friendships, and influence, to restrain all those scribbling nitwits. [. . .]

What matters to me is that you will not be upset by all these little miseries; the day after tomorrow I shall have the pleasure of seeing you and giving you all the details you may wish to hear. [. . .]

VERDI TO FRANCO FACCIO

Genoa, 2 February 1881

Dear Faccio,

A thousand thanks for the news of *Ernani*, and a thousand congratulations.

You press me too much, and you, who know what the theatre is like, will understand that in the present circumstances I cannot answer anything about *Boccanegra*. First of all, there are *ifs* and *buts*, many, very many of them, about which one must come to a very clear understanding. I have written from the beginning that the performance of *Boccanegra* should be considered as 'an encore'. Therefore I did not ask and oblige the management to engage anyone (let's understand each other well, anyone), in order to be free from any commitment, reserving for myself the right to choose the artists who would be agreeable to me. Now I ask you, can you say that you have a dependable baritone at La Scala? Can you tell me when the indispositions will end? He had to sing on Sunday, then Tuesday, then . . . Saturday! Who knows! Let's understand each other well, and I repeat again, I have no commitments of any kind with anyone. Corti will remember that I told him some two weeks ago, in precisely these words, 'I am working on *Boccanegra*,

---

[1] *Ernani*.
[2] About the revision of *Simon Boccanegra*.

but I am not far along; I cannot assure you of anything now; if you have another score on hand, do it, and it will be in your interest.' I still say the same, all the more so because of the prolonged indisposition of the baritone. I am sorry I cannot give a more satisfactory answer, but the circumstances are such that it is impossible for me. My wife sends her greetings, and I say addio.

G. Verdi

VERDI TO BOITO[1]

[Genoa] 2 February 1881

Dear Boito,

First of all, my sincere congratulations on the success of *Mefistofele* at Padua.

Eight lines are too many for Amelia. After all, the piece is none other than a *Grand Solo* for the Doge, with other parts added. Amelia has only a little phrase. To me, the first four [lines] work very well, but you may want to change the second for the rhyme.

The line for the narrative will work well.

And now we come to the last act.—The first chorus of this act no longer has its reason for being, and, with the curtain closed, I would have the orchestra repeat the music of the *revolt* with which the preceding act ends, with off-stage cries of '*Vittoria Vittoria!*' ['Victory, Victory!']. With the curtain up, the Doge would begin.

> *Brando guerrier, et., et.*
>
> [*Sword of war, etc., etc.*]

Does the scene which follows between Pietro, Paolo, and Paolo-Fieschi remain?

If only we were finished! I greet you from the heart.

Your
G. Verdi

VERDI TO BOITO

Genoa, 5 February 1881

Dear Boito,

We're not finished!!!!

In the first scene of the first act, after the off-stage stanzas for Gabriele, some bars for the orchestra should be added to give him time to enter; I would prefer a brief, agitated phrase for Amelia. Indeed, I myself have made four broken [*tronchi*] lines of five syllables:

[1] In answer to Boito's letter of 31 Jan. 1881.

È desso! O Ciel!	[*It is he! O Heaven!*
Mi manca il Cor	*My strength fails me*]

. . . .

. . . .

and I have written the musical phrase. I ask you for these four lines. Six will be better still, but no more than six.

For the *revolt* scene of the new finale, in spite of an agitated movement in the orchestra, I have made sure that all the words will be clearly heard: the orchestra rages, but rages softly. At the end, however, even the orchestra must make its formidable voice heard, and I want to make a great *forte* after the Doge's words *'Ecco le plebi. . . . . .'* ['*Here are the plebeians. . . . . .*']. Here the orchestra would break forth in full force, to which would be added, as soon as they enter, '*Popolo, Patrizi, Donne*' ['*People, Patricians, Women*'] etc. etc. Therefore I would need two lines so as to have the whole world shouting. Don't let the word '*Vendetta!*' ['*Vengeance!*'] be missing from these lines! I am composing for Paolo the beautiful recitative you have added to the beginning of the second act. What a pity! Those lines, which are so powerful, in the mouth of a common scoundrel! I have, however, made arrangements for this Paolo to become a scoundrel of the less rascally sort.

And now tell me.

Would it be an unforgivable sin if to the final chorus of Act II '*All'armi, all'armi Liguri*' ['*To arms, to arms, Ligurians*'] I added the women?. .

Would it be another sin if in the last scene, the Doge's death, Maria, having become Gabriele's wife, entered followed by several female attendants? *Several* would mean the whole *Women's Chorus*?

After this perhaps we'll be finished.

Believe me always

Your
G. Verdi

BOITO TO VERDI[1]

Saturday—Milan [5 February 1881][2]

Dear Maestro,

I return to my old analogy of the table; now it is the fourth leg that wobbles. We must steady it, and in this operation we must be very clever so as to prevent the others from starting to wobble again once this leg is set straight. For two days I have been thinking over and over again about the fourth act.[3] The idea of the orchestral introduction with the curtain closed and shouts off stage pleases me a lot; it is very useful, since it is a wonderful link between the end of the third act and the beginning of the fourth[4] and

---

[1] In answer to Verdi's letter of 2 Feb. 1881.
[2] This date is inferred from Verdi's following answer.
[3] The third act.
[4] The second act and the beginning of the third.

unites the events of the last two acts into a unity of time, rapid, compressed, and very dramatic. But this idea isn't enough. The scene between Fiesco and Paolo can no longer remain as it is.

Some aspects of the scene between the Doge and Fieschi should be changed. (Fieschi and the Doge have already been found in a violent encounter two acts earlier, that is, in the ensemble.) From the very first words of the Doge in the fourth[5] act we must foreshadow the catastrophe. In the old libretto Simone, when he says '*brando guerrier*' ['*sword of war*'], looks much too healthy. In short, tomorrow I shall send you a tentative remedy in verse, and you can judge.

I thank you, my dear Maestro, for the kind words with which you began your letter.

Until tomorrow. A greeting from the heart.

Your
Arrigo Boito

VERDI TO BOITO

[Genoa] Sunday [6 February 1881][1]

Dear Boito,

Let's adjust the fourth leg, as well ... but you frighten me by saying that we need to change the scene between Fieschi and the Doge! If it concerns some little thing, that's fine; but if it is necessary to rewrite, there is an impossible obstacle, time. Enough: I wait impatiently for tomorrow's letter.

And tell me: couldn't the whole first scene be avoided? Thus the Doge would be seen in this act only once, when he enters poisoned ... '*M'ardon le tempia*' ['*My temples are burning*'], etc. The act would begin with the orchestral prelude and the off-stage cry '*Vittoria*' ['*Victory*'] ... When the curtain rises the *Wedding Chorus* would be heard from off stage, and those two Saints, Pietro and Paolo, could say that the Doge has won and that Gabriele is marrying Amelia...

Now I am waiting for those four or six verses of broken five-syllable lines which I asked you for yesterday. Send them as soon as possible.

In haste,

Your
G. Verdi

PS You've written me nothing about the stanza for Amelia in the new finale—

[5] The third act.

[1] Postmark: GENOVA 6/2/81.

VERDI TO TITO RICORDI[1]

Genoa, 6 February 1881

Dear Tito,

I have received two telegrams,[2] one of which is not signed but is, I believe, from the management — —

Thereupon I told Giulio that I would come to hear the performance and then decide; I am sorry that there will be no *Ernani* before Wednesday. This way time is lost, and if it is not too late to give it on Tuesday, a day is gained, which is a lot in our case.—I also told Giulio that it's not a question of *Maurel* alone, but that I must hear the others, especially *De Restke*, whom I do not consider good for this part, in spite of all the good things that are said about him. I said from the start that someone else should be considered, but nothing has been done. Now it's late and there is no time left to find anyone, and so I won't give the opera if I don't find everyone suitable for these roles.

I told Giulio, too, that the baritone who sings Paolo must be an actor above all else. Find him right away, since I absolutely want to hear him. If all the parts are not cast before the rehearsals, I will not give the opera.

Let's conclude: When you give *Ernani*, I'll come to hear it and we'll make a decision right away. If the decision is positive you will let me hear the Paolo, and we shall plan everything for the rehearsals, for the copying, etc., etc. . . Otherwise I shall leave directly the following morning . .

To avoid so many, many things, I want no one to come to the station; I shall take a carriage, leave my bag at the hotel, and be in Tornaghi's studio at about 1 o'clock.

Advise Faccio and Boito to come to the same studio a little later, about 2 o'clock, and we shall arrange everything that can be arranged . .

I know it will be impossible to keep my visit from being noticed, but tell no one about it, and reserve a box that is high up but where one can still hear and see well. I want *Tornaghi* and someone else to be with me when I come to the theatre, because I don't want to be subjected to demonstations *under any circumstances*.

One last word

The Maurel Question!! . . This will take care of itself if Maurel has the high and low notes he has had until now. If he behaves as he did in Paris there will be trouble in Simone — — And tell me, why did he leave out two or three pieces the other night, even though he was in the best of voice? — —

Let's be careful not to cause *publicity*. Already the papers have talked about your archaeological research to *launch the opera!* — — Oh, that really is too much!

To launch the opera!! — —

Do I really need that?

G.V.

[1] During Giulio's convalescence on the Riviera (see his letter to Giuseppina Verdi, 1 Feb. 1881).

[2] Missing.

FRANCO FACCIO TO VERDI

Milan, 6 February 1881

Illustrious Maestro,
I am responding to the precious letter with which you have honoured me
by telling you that the second performance of *Ernani* dispelled the legitimate
doubt about the baritone Maurel's complete success. Having regained his
health and his voice, this distinguished artist received a general ovation for
each of his pieces, and one can certainly assert that Maurel is enjoying the
sympathies of the audience, which is proved by the long applause at his
appearance on stage [. . .] I know that the management has telegraphed; 'We
are in your hands' is the phrase. You hear it very well, it is exact, and I repeat
it with trepidation . . . and confidence. [. . .]

BOITO TO VERDI[1]

[Milan, 7 February 1881][2]

Dear Maestro,
This time it is I who say that we're not finished yet. I am keeping your last
three letters on my desk, and I consult them at each step, but my ideas are
still in a jumble about the first scenes of the last act. Various attempts have
turned out badly. Today, however, you make a suggestion that seems very
practical to me: to open the act with the wedding song far off (a fine contrast
after the martial vigour of the prelude), while on stage the very rapid but
indispensable dialogue between Fiesco and Paolo is taking place (the other
apostle, Pietro, we can forget; no one will notice it), and this dialogue should
assume a different character from what appears in the old libretto. Paolo
must have taken an active part in the uprising of the Guelphs to overthrow
the Doge, and to have been captured, imprisoned, and condemned to death
by the Doge himself. It's good that the Doge should finally condemn
someone, and since we have in our hands a scoundrel who has betrayed the
people's faction to join the Guelphs and has committed every sort of villainy,
let's condemn him to the gallows and have nothing more said about him.
Quite the opposite for Fiesco: at the very moment Paolo is passing between
the guards on the way to his execution, Fiesco, I'm saying, is liberated by
order of the Doge; and it is right that he should be, because obviously he has
not taken part in the uprising, since he was in prison; so the condemned man
and the freed man meet while the wedding hymn is going on, and in their
dialogue Paolo reveals the affair of the poison, and from the words of the two
the facts are clarified which need clarifying. Some fifteen lines, not in verse,
will be enough. We now come to the scene between the Doge and Fiesco.
Don't be alarmed, dear Maestro—I understand the importance of that scene,

[1] In answer to Verdi's letter of 6 Feb. 1881.
[2] Postmark: MILANO 7/2/81.

which, among other things, is the most beautiful in the drama. I said that some aspects of that dialogue had to be changed; some is to say too much; one is enough, the one that is summarized in the words '*risorgon dalle tombe i morti*' ['*the dead rise from their tombs*']. But I also understand, too, the great importance of these words; I won't remove them, but will add perhaps a line or two so as to introduce them into the dialogue in a more logical manner, since we have now, in the first act, created some facts and some discords that didn't exist in the old version. Therein lies the need for the changes.

But as for Fiesco, before I forget, I must propose two very minuscule changes in the scene between Fiesco and Paolo in the penultimate act, and this for the sake of clarity. Instead of the word that Paolo says, '*Stolido, va*' ['*Fool, go away*'], which is very rough and could seem ridiculous to the audience for its vulgarity (let's say even *verismo*), I would say:

> FIESCO. Osi a Fiesco proporre un misfatto?
> PAOLO. Tu ricusi? (*dopo una pausa*) Al tuo carcer ten va.[3]
>
> [FIESCO. Do you dare to propose a crime to Fiesco?
> PAOLO. You decline? (*after a pause*) Go to your cell.]

In this way, this fact is clarified: *Fiesco, rather than consent to a betrayal, returns to prison.* This fact is indispensable for a world of reasons. The old text said at this point: '*Fieschi parte dalla destra*' ['*Fieschi exits to the right*']. And when he exits to the right, where does he go? To prison? It doesn't appear so. Thus he accepted not the cowardly pact with Paolo but the freedom that was, it seems, the reward of that pact. And that was not Fiesco's way. It's useful to us that Fiesco does not take an active part in the rebellion of the Guelphs, so that he's not burdened with yet another offence against the Doge, and I repeat that the best way to prevent this is to keep him under lock and key.

Meanwhile here are the scraps of poetry for which you asked me:

Act I.

Scene i.

(Five-syllable broken [*tronchi*] lines after the off-stage song of Gabriele)

AM. Ei vien! ... l'amor	[He's coming ... love
M'avvampa in seno (sen)	Fills my breast
E spezza il freno	And the throbbing heart
L'ansante cor.	Bursts its confines.]

I'll wager that the ones you wrote are much better, but these five-syllable broken [*tronchi*] lines are enemies of the pen.

Variant for the entrance of the Chorus in the Senate scene.

---

[3] In the final text, Paolo says 'Tu rifiuti?' ['You refuse?'], and Fiesco answers 'Si' ['Yes']. Paolo then says 'Al carcer ten va' ['Go to the cell'].

DOGE. Ecco le plebi!
LA FOLLA.   Vendetta! Vendetta!
   Spargasi il sangue del fiero uccisor! .
DOGE (*ironicamente*). Questa è dunque del popolo la voce?!
   Da lungi tuono d'uragan, da presso
   Gridío di donne e di fanciulli . . .
[DOGE. Here are the plebeians!
THE CROWD.   Vengeance! Vengeance!
   Let the fierce murderer's blood be spilled! .
DOGE (*sarcastically*). This, then, is the voice of the people?
   From afar, the thunder of a hurricane, from
   Nearby, screams of women and children . . .]

            . . . .

You notice that you can repeat not only '*Vendetta*' as much as you want, but also the eleven-syllable line that follows. Thus the outburst of the orchestra and chorus can make its appearance, and if the strident notes of the women in the upper register can find their place in this outburst, then the wish of your poet is fulfilled and the sarcastic line of the Doge is explained. I have put the line there so as to confront bravely the first difficulty that preoccupied us: how to have the women appear in the Senate. If we make the audience notice that the women are there, and do so courageously, no one will dream of making the least objection. Moreover, it is a well-known fact that women play a principal role in people's riots; think of the *Commune* in Paris. But where the devil am I headed? Let's get back to the libretto. Here are the four lines for Amelia at the end of the lyric fragment of the same act:

AMELIA (*a Fiesco*): Pace! lo sdegno   [(*to Fiesco*). Peace! restrain your im-
   immenso   mense
   Raffrena[4] per pietà!   Scorn, for pity's sake!
   Pace! t'ispiri un senso   Peace! let a sense of patriotic
   Di patria carità   Love inspire you.]

And now I respond to two half-serious questions you ask: The observation made earlier shows you that I don't believe it objectionable to add female voices to the warlike chorus

All'armi! All'armi o liguri.   [*To arms! To arms, o Ligurians.*]

A few more lines and I'll be finished for today. In the last act, why can Amelia not be followed by her female attendants? She is returning from the church, from her wedding, with her retinue of women and also, if you like, of pages.
   Most cordial greetings.

---

[4] 'Nascondi' ['Hide'] in the final text.

I don't think I'm deluding myself if I promise you another discussion for tomorrow.[5]

Your most affectionate
Arrigo Boito

VERDI TO EUGENIO TORNAGHI[1]

[Genoa] Monday [7 February 1881][2]

Dear Signor Tornaghi,

Well then, if by tomorrow evening I receive the telegram,[3] I'll leave Wednesday morning on the *through train*. Thus we can discuss many, many things, and among the many, there is also the fact that I haven't finished the opera. I wrote this to Faccio,[4] and I repeat it again so that you will say it quite clearly to the management, and so that I will not be made to *say* and *promise* what I have never *said* and *promised*. Well, we'll talk, and we'll be able to come to some resolution. In the meantime you have almost *48* hours to search for and find this baritone for Paolo. I am most anxious about this; and in the event the opera can be given, I want to hear him first . . .

I repeat again: nobody shall come to the station. I will be at the studio after the hour. Wait for me. I repeat again: notify Faccio and Boito for 2 o'clock—not before. Don't forget to notify the hotel about a warm room . . .

A box in a good location, and with two *guardian angels*.

Addio, addio
G. Verdi

EUGENIO TORNAGHI TO VERDI[1]

Milan, 7 February 1881

[. . .] I agreed with Faccio to inform the management that we would wait for a decision until after the performance on Wednesday. In the meantime we must search for a good artist for the part of Paolo; on Thursday a decision will certainly be made. Tomorrow Faccio will hear several artists and will choose the best to submit to your most esteemed judgement.

I shall obey you by not coming to the station, but by remaining at the studio, instead. At 2 o'clock Boito and Faccio will come to my studio, too.

[5] Another discussion in writing was obviously replaced by an oral one during Verdi's short stay in Milan on 9 and 10 Feb., of which Boito was advised by Tornaghi. See the following letters and Verdi's telegram of 8 Feb.

[1] In Giulio Ricordi's absence.
[2] This date is inferred from Verdi's departure for Milan on 9 Feb.
[3] Presumably a missing telegram confirming the arrangements for Verdi's brief stay in Milan on 9 and 10 Feb.
[4] On 2 Feb. 1881.

[1] In answer to Verdi to Tito Ricordi, 6 Feb. 1881.

For the evening I have taken Box no. 12 in the third row left, so that it can be reached through the entrance in the Via Filodrammatici, where only the accountant of the House [of Ricordi] and I myself shall be. A box of the House [of Ricordi], also located in the third row, would be at your disposal, as well, but I think it would be harder to keep the secret there. [. . .]

VERDI TO BOITO[1]
[Telegram]

Genoa, 8 February 1881

EXCELLENT—BUT BEWARE TIME IS SHORT—TORNAGHI WILL TELL YOU

VERDI

VERDI

[Genoa?, 8 February 1881][1]

Pro Memoria Tornaghi

Examine *Forza del destino* contract
No commitment to the management, and in any case I am free to withdraw the score, even at the dress rehearsal, as I did
           for *Forza del destino*[2]
The sum is . . . . . and half, or the 40
           for first rental
All the same singers for the entire season

   Faccio
Ask if De Restke has an audible low F
Understanding regarding rehearsals and [illegible]
Hear the Paolo
Run a telegraphic wire from the conductor
       to the stage for the finale, etc.

   Boito! . .
Settle everything that must be
       done and establish everything
          While I am in Milan . .

[1] In answer to Boito's letter of 7 Feb. 1881.

---

[1] Verdi made these notes before his conferences in Milan on 9 and 10 Feb.

[2] Supposedly in reference to the cancellation of *Forza* on account of the illness of the prima donna in St Petersburg in Dec. 1861. No other reason caused the postponement of that production to Nov. 1862.

FRANCO FACCIO TO VERDI[1]

Milan, 11 February 1881

Illustrious Maestro,

I have the honour of repeating in writing what I told you this morning by telegram.[2] The only points in the part of Boccanegra where Maurel was afraid he would not succeed because of the difficult tessitura are exactly the ones that you have changed; and so this likeable artist now feels reassured and is longing for the moment to start studying. And believe me, illustrious Maestro, I have not failed to stop at those passages in particular where Maurel's voice might have met some obstacle; for example, in the duet with Amelia, with the change at the end and with the variants of the principal motive that you have already made, Maurel has been relieved of every fearful preoccupation, and in the finale of the opera, too, where he believes he can carry out the moving scene of the benediction *as it stands and sans être gêné.* [...] We are fervently preparing the prologue and are impatiently awaiting the first act. [...]

GIULIO RICORDI TO VERDI

Mentone, 12 February 1881

Illustrious Maestro,

I have just received detailed news from Tornaghi about your trip to Milan; I cannot tell you how happy I am about your decision, not only because *Boccanegra* will be given, but because I am *deeply convinced* that certain unfavourable impressions of the artists (which, by the way, I knew you would have) will change a great deal at the rehearsals. [...]

We shall be back in Genoa Monday afternoon and will have the pleasure of coming to greet you in the evening, while I shall reserve Tuesday to receive all necessary instructions from you. [...]

FRANCO FACCIO TO VERDI

Milan, 13 February 1881

Illustrious Maestro,

Yesterday, the moment I came back from the *Freyschüstz* rehearsal, I examined the tenor aria, but there was no more time left to answer you that day. The tessitura of this piece is excellent for Tamagno, and I am sure that on the climactic phrase his voice will fill out with the greatest effect. Therefore I would think it opportune for you to delay your decision for or against the transposition until after the experiment that you yourself will

---

[1] Verdi had apparently returned to Genoa in the evening of 10 Feb.
[2] Missing.

make by rehearsing the aria with Tamagno in the two different keys; all the more so since, in the case of the transposition, I think it could be done without making any changes in the accompaniment, and therefore without causing you to lose time, which in the *future* will be more precious than ever. [...] Meanwhile, last night a notice in the lobby of La Scala announcing *Simon Boccanegra* made a fine display, and the atmosphere of satisfaction and enthusiasm now reigning in our theatre is beyond words. [...]

EUGENIO TORNAGHI TO VERDI

Milan, 14 February 1881

In answer to your esteemed lines of yesterday,[1] I have the honour to inform you that the vocal score of the prologue has already been printed and that the parts are ready. Work is proceeding on the first act, and the vocal score and the parts are being engraved anew, since no time should be lost in comparing and reviewing the first edition. I received your telegram[2] with the request to send the second act. As soon as I have it I shall telegraph you.[3]

Faccio asked me if you had sent me the parts of the new finale so that he could give them to the artists. Please discuss this with Giulio, who will be there [in Genoa] tomorrow. Would you also arrange with Giulio for me to keep the libretto, which is needed here to review the proofs of the vocal score.

Faccio asks me to give you his regards and is pleased to inform you that Maurel can do the benediction in the final quartet well. [...]

VERDI TO FRANCO FACCIO

Genoa [14?] February 1881

Dear Faccio,

I am pleased to hear that Tamagno can sing the aria in the original key. I'd certainly be the last to enjoy making him try it a half tone higher (he would love that), but I would rather transpose some notes in the second part of the *cantabile*. For Maurel the part cannot be bad as it is now adjusted. Only the third bar of the final tempo in the duet with Amelia will not go too well for him. I wouldn't know how to adjust that one without making the lowering of the notes obvious. I have sent the second act today, and I hope to send the last the day after tomorrow. Meanwhile, as soon as you can, hold a few section rehearsals of the music for me. Let's go ahead with the music, since there will be much, very much, so very much to be done for the rest. The opera is dramatic ... even too much so. It's true that its legs are a bit wobbly, as Boito says, but it is dramatic. [...] But it's done. I don't know, however,

[1] Probably in the Biblioteca Palatina.
[2] Missing.
[3] Missing.

whether it's done well! The part of the apostle S. Paolo[1] has become a very important one dramatically. Keep me informed about our affairs, and believe me yours most affectionately

G. Verdi

VERDI TO BOITO

Genoa, 15 February 1881

Dear Boito,

We're not finished yet! The beautiful, most beautiful finale you have made for me[1] has done a bit of damage to the scene in the last act between Fieschi and the Doge. In the old libretto, after the Prologue, they did not meet each other again. Twenty-five years have passed since Boccanegra was elected Doge, in 1339, and he died in 1364.—Now, the Doge knows Fieschi too well, and he cannot '*apparirgli come un Fantasima*' ['appear to him like a Phantom'] any more. It seems to me, however, that it won't be difficult to fix everything if we avoid

1. saying '*accanto ad esso combatte il Fiesco*' ['*at his side Fiesco is battling*'].
2. Fieschi should stay hidden as long as possible disguised as Andrea[2] and should not say '*Ei la Grimaldi aveva rapita*' ['*He had abducted the Grimaldi*'], nor should he rush against the Doge, etc.
3. In Scene viii of the second act, it would be well to avoid the words '*i Due ribelli*' ['*the two rebels*'] and to say [instead] '*i traditor*' ['*the traitors*'] in general.
4. In the new scene of the last act, I wouldn't say '*Libero il Doge ti proclama!*' ['*The Doge proclaims you free!*'], but . . . '*Il Doge perdona a tutti: Tu sei libero!*' ['*The Doge pardons everyone: You are free!*'].[3]

And many, many other little things.

Think about it a bit and you'll find something better. Write me at once. Just in case, we still have time to discuss it in person.

Believe me

your affectionate
G. Verdi

[1] Cf. Verdi to Boito, 6 Feb. 1881, where he jokingly refers to Pietro and Paolo as Saints.

[1] Boito's verses for the finale of the last act cannot be found in his letters. Apparently, Boito never posted the 'tentative remedy in verse' mentioned at the end of his letter to Verdi of 5 Feb. We may surmise that he handed these verses to Verdi in Milan on 9 or 10 Feb. (See *Carteggio* ii. 301.)
[2] In the finale of the opera.
[3] See Boito's following letter, para. 2, for the change of this line.

BOITO TO VERDI

[Milan] Tuesday, 15 [February 1881][1]

Dear Maestro,

We're not finished! —The same scruples that tormented you tormented me, too. I accept and approve all the expedients that you suggest. We'll say, '*Accanto ad esso combatte un Guelfo*' ['*At his side a Guelph is battling*']. Or: '*Accanto ad esso pugna un vegliardo*' ['*At his side an old man is fighting*']. Or else: '*Accanto ad esso pugna un patrizio*' ['*At his side a Patrician is fighting*']. You choose.[2] The words '*Ei la Grimaldi avea rapita*' ['*He has abducted the Grimaldi*'] we'll have said by Adorno or by a part of the chorus.[3] Instead of '*due ribelli*' ['*two rebels*'], we'll say '*i traditori*' ['*the traitors*'] or '*i rivoltosi*' ['*the rioters*'], whichever you like best.[4]

We'll no longer say, '*Libero il Doge ti proclama*' ['*The Doge proclaims you free*'], but instead, '*Libero sei; ecco la spada*' ['*You are free; here is the sword*'].[5] Or: '*Libero sei; quest'è il tuo brando*' ['*You are free; this is your sword*'] . . . and the officer hands over the sword to Fiesco.

I believe that these little touches will suffice to set things right.

In one of my last letters,[6] when I spoke of the need for changes in the scene between Fiesco and the Doge, I was alluding to precisely the points that you raised; I even sounded the alarm, in that I believed we needed to change some aspects of the scene in question, but I understand, on the other hand, that this solution could prove damaging to the last act. I thought that I could kill two birds with one stone by having Fiesco exclaim this (always very useful) line:

alfine
È giunta l'ora di trovarci a fronte!

[*at last*
The hour has come to meet each other face to face!]

With this line I had intended to explain that the two antagonists, even if they had met in a tumultuous crowd in the scene in the *Palazzo degli Abati*, had never, in all the years which have passed since the scene of the Prologue, found themselves *in a confrontation*, that is, *face to face*, alone, masters of their own actions and their own words, isolated and free from extraneous influences, from extraneous events; or, to use a favourite phrase of our Schakespeare, they had never found themselves *beard to beard*. And this is true, and the line about the *phantom* could, with strict logic, stand up *quand*

---

[1] Without any doubt, Boito fulfilled Verdi's request at the end of the preceding letter to answer 'at once'. The envelopes of both letters are missing. Presumably, Verdi sent his letter— clearly dated 15 Feb. 1881—by special delivery, unless he wrote it on 14 Feb.

[2] This line was omitted, as Verdi suggested in his preceding letter.

[3] Gabriele Adorno says these words in the Senate scene.

[4] See Boito to Verdi, 8–9 Jan. 1881, n. 8.

[5] In the final text, these are the Captain's words at the beginning of Act III.

[6] Of 7 Feb.

même.[7] Still, the brief word substitutions that we have set down today work very well in clarifying our concerns.

And so, dear Maestro, till we see each other soon in Milan. A greeting from the heart

from your most affectionate
Arrigo Boito

FRANCO FACCIO TO VERDI

Milan, 16 February 1881

Illustrious Maestro,

I refer to your last, most precious letter[1] to tell you that *everything* is coming along in order; and one might say that everyone is penetrated by a bit of the fever that is in your great soul. The chorus has already been given the Prologue, and by the end of the week the Prologue and the first act will be given to the singers. [. . .] While they are meditating and sweating over the notes, I am pushing forward with the performance of *Freyschüstz*, of which I held the first orchestra rehearsal this morning. Early next week I'll devote myself body and soul to that *Bocca* (so-called) *Negra*,[2] which will be rosy instead, fresh and full of promises like the mouth of a young bride. And now I beg you to resolve a doubt that came about in the reduction of Paolo's recitative from your orchestra score. The old manuscript says:

and the new one:

Instead of the first two quarter-rests (in the new manuscript), are the preceding quavers not resolved to C minor like this?

Another doubt: the new orchestra score, after the words '*l'aura ancor ne trema*' ['*the air still trembles from it*'], says:

---

[7] Fiesco's line in the final text is: 'Come fantasima Fiesco t'appar' ['Like a phantom Fiesco appears to you'].

---

[1] Of 14 Feb. 1881.
[2] Play on words, *Bocca* meaning 'mouth', *Negra* 'black'.

That trumpet, it seems, must play in octaves with the trombone, and in this case the return to E flat would not work; could it be a trumpet in A? Today I talked with the esteemed Magnani, who is leaving for Genoa tonight; so you can give him the necessary scenic instructions. I hear that the excellent Giulio is there with his wife; I look forward very much to seeing him again completely recovered. [. . .]

VERDI TO FRANCO FACCIO

Genoa, 17 February 1881

Dear Faccio,

I am in the midst of sets and costumes[1] and can only reply in two words to your very dear letter. At the beginning of the second act my intention would be to suspend the orchestra at

since Paolo recalls the scene of the curse, which you don't know. The E of the trumpet is a slip of the pen. In order not to change the A slide, write in B flats. I thank you, and will thank you even more if you will carefully go through the piano–vocal score and inform me of the many mistakes in the key changes in the horns, clarinets, and trumpets, and of the millions of sharps and flats that will be missing.

How is it that you are distributing the parts so late? I urge you not to lose time. Today I hope to hand over the fourth act[2] to Giulio; and so I'll only have to write out the parts of the chorus and the singers in the long finale and send them to be copied and distributed. Then in Milan I'll do the orchestration. And so no time will be lost on my account . . . How are your Ernani and Carlo V? Are the grudges and jealousies over?[3] Yes? Won't they be renewed? Addio, my dear Faccio, and till we see each other.

G. Verdi

VERDI TO GIULIO RICORDI

[Genoa] Friday [18 February 1881]

Dear Giulio,

It's about 5 p.m., and by this time you will have seen Boito and, who

---

[1] With the designer Girolamo Magnani, probably together with Giulio Ricordi, who, according to his letter of 19 Feb., returned to Milan only on the 18th.

[2] The third act.

[3] Between Tamagno and Maurel in the roles of Ernani and Carlo V (see Ricordi to Verdi 19 and 22 Feb., and Faccio's letter of 22 Feb. 1881).

knows, perhaps also arranged for the *Sea of Lights*.[1] In any case, I will tell you what is going on in my mind regarding this matter in order to save time—and because often even in the *very worst* ideas there can be the germ of something good.

1. After the prelude of the last act, at the very moment the shout of '*Vittoria Vittoria!*' ['*Victory Victory!*'] is heard, the curtain should quickly rise, the balcony doors of the Ducal Palace be opened wide, and the whole city and the port should be seen illuminated. The scene between the Captain, Fiesco, and Paolo stays as it is. At the words ... '*degno era il tuo fato*' ['*worthy was your fate*'], I would have the Captain return with a Trumpeter and have them go straight to the balconies; after the trumpet has sounded three times, the Captain should shout '*D'ordine del Doge spegnete le faci ... Non vuole s'insulti ai caduti*' ['*By order of the Doge, put out the lights ... He does not want the fallen to be insulted*'].[2] A great many of the lights nearby should be extinguished right away ... The Doge should enter ... '*M'ardon le tempia*' ['*My temples are burning*'], etc.., omitting, of course, '*Chi turbare degli estinti*' ['*Who disturb the dead's*'], etc., etc. *Otherwise* ... As the curtain rises I would have a roughly painted set, very shallow, not more than two metres away from the curtain. A corridor on one side leading to the prisons, on the other to the street; somewhere in the middle, a door leading to the Doge's apartment. The Captain and Fiesco should enter . .

FIESCO. Dove siamo? [Where are we?
CAPIT. Questa è la porta delle stanze del [This is the door to the rooms of the
Doge ... Là è Genova Tu sei libero ... Doge ... There is Genoa
Prendi,[3] ecc. You are free ... Take, etc.]

The scene as follows until '*era degno il tuo fato*'.

FIESCO. Dunque là dentro è il Doge?[4] [Then is the Doge there?
È giunta l'ora di trovarsi[5] a fronte The hour has come to meet face to face].

He enters the apartment of the Doge ...
Here the curtain should rise[6] and the Sea of Lights appear from the great balconies of the Doge's room. The Doge should be on stage with his head on the table, fallen or prostrate with fatigue and torment[7]

---

[1] In all probability, Verdi had discussed this matter with Magnani and Giulio Ricordi in Genoa; it was very close to his heart. (See his letter to Piave of late Jan. or early Feb. 1857 in the Introduction, p. xxxv, Ricordi to Verdi, 19 and 22 Feb. and 18 Nov. 1881, as well as Verdi's letters to him of 21, 22, and 23 Feb. and 24 Nov. 1881.)

[2] In the final text: '*Cittadini! per ordine del Doge / S'estinguano le faci e non s'offenda / Col clamor del trionfo i prodi estinti.*' ['Citizens! By order of the Doge / The lights be extinguished, and with the clamour of triumph / The valiant dead shall not be offended.']

[3] These lines were omitted from the final text.

[4] These lines also were omitted.

[5] '*trovarci*' ['meet each other'] in the final text, as Boito wrote to Verdi on 15 Feb. 1881.

[6] In accordance with later production decisions, there was no change of scene in the last act; Fiesco did not leave the stage, and the Doge entered as indicated in the libretto and scores.

[7] The remainder of the letter is missing.

GIULIO RICORDI TO VERDI

[Milan] Saturday evening [19 February 1881]

Illustrious Maestro,

The journey, the change of climate, and so many other little problems caused me to spend a very bad night on Friday, so that today I had to stay in bed until 4. That may explain why everything took some time and why I am writing you only late after dinner. Besides, you will have seen from my telegram[1] that no time has been lost—that the difficulties (foreseen, by the way) concerning the delivery of the theatre's material to Magnani were immediately resolved by my sending a request to the Mayor that he take care of the matter; and in fact, without any fuss he had the engineer called and ordered him to send the necessary drops right away. Tomorrow I shall submit the costume list, since the tailor is entitled to 18 days after the order to prepare all the costumes. Today I talk with the chorus master to see what female voices are needed. Tonight I deliver the singers' parts that have been sent, minus, of course, the third act received yesterday, which will be ready in a couple of days. So therefore, Maestro, everything proceeds according to your plans.

Now on to two important matters:

Tamagno–Maurel Question: It's absolutely over and done with; besides, I had guessed it! ... It was just a matter of some remarks by Maurel that busybodies quoted to Tamagno! .... the cause of the quarrel. Now everything is going well; Tamagno really did have a cold and had to stay in bed; but he is already on the road to recovery. *Amen!* ....

Sea-of-Lights Question: Great confabulation with Boito—let me explain his ideas:

—He likes best of all what already exists in the old libretto, but he does not think this would prevent a fine Sea of Lights. He proposes the big openings in the background, but enclosed by windows through which the illumination would be seen perfectly well; so that there is the scenic effect at the rise of the curtain.

The Doge, who surely has assisted in the wedding of his daughter, cannot completely ignore this Sea of Lights; he comes on stage, oppressed, gasping for breath, and Boito finds great beauty in the Doge's own words:[2]

Alle marine aure il veron dischiudi.   [To the sea breeze open the balcony.]

These words not only go well as spoken by the old Corsair, but tie in very well with the following:

Oh! refrigerio! ... la marina brezza! ...   [Oh! relief! ... The marine breeze! ...
Il mare! ..... Il mare! .....   The sea! ..... The sea! .....]

The scene is thus more logical, more moving.

---

[1] Missing.
[2] However, these words were eliminated from the final text.

For Pietro[3] it is enough, then, to open a single wide window in the centre, and it is natural that the Doge should turn around and approach the window to take a breath; at this point it is logical that he should see the illuminated city in all its splendour, and that he should exclaim in surprise: '*Qual fulgore*'[4] ['*What brilliance*']. Also, the order to extinguish is, according to Boito, more beautiful in Simone's words than in others'![5] [. . .]

Of the two versions you propose, Boito absolutely discards the one involving another scene, which he considers harmful to the drama; if anything, he believes the other one is better, in which the Captain enters and gives the order from the balcony. But all in all, from his point of view it seems better to leave it as it is, since this is a question of staging more than anything else; and to replace the *curtains* (which he, too, maintains are difficult to open, and which, on top of this, would distract the audience) with large windows of transparent glass; it is more natural that this great opening which leads to a hall should be enclosed by windows rather than curtains . . . . no matter how pleasant and mild the climate might presumably be; therefore it is enough that only one of these windows be opened by Pietro on the order of the Doge. Boito, however, is at your command, should you wish to adopt the proposal of letting the Captain enter. Besides, I think there will be time to decide this on your next visit; and whatever your preference, we shall have an understanding with Magnani, who, by the way, must also come to Milan for all the scenic details to be studied in the theatre. [. . .]

Give me your orders, then, and you will make me very happy. Anxious to see you again shortly, believe me

Always yours gratefully,
Giulio Ricordi

Faccio has received your last letter;[6] he assures you that he will take care of everything as you wish.

VERDI TO GIULIO RICORDI

[Genoa] Monday, 21 February 1881

Dear Giulio,

I was surprised to learn from your letter that the parts are to be distributed only two days from now. I thought that the moment you arrived in Milan you would have the parts copied by hand and distributed the following day. The slight expense of the copying would have saved a great deal of time.

I was even more surprised to see *Freischüz* announced only for [this coming] Saturday, and I telegraphed you that this would leave no more time for the rehearsals of *Simone*. I told you orally and now *formally* repeat that I

---

[3] Pietro does not appear at all in the last act.
[4] Not in the final text.
[5] This order is announced by the Captain (see Verdi's preceding letter).
[6] Of 17 Feb. 1881.

will give the opera only on the condition of being able to give a series of performances. Now, then, *Boccanegra* requires from *25* to *30* days of rehearsal, without calculating the days of illnesses; so I ask you whether there will still be time to put on at least *8* or *10* performances?—

I have finished the finale and could even bring it along tomorrow, but it makes no sense for me to come to Milan if at this hour, so to speak, nothing is settled.

Mind you, I will make no more concessions; I have made enough for this opera and regret it. I request *30* days and the time to put on *8* or *10* performances if the audience wants them.

Decide what is to be done. I am ready; but I repeat what I said to the management in Milan, that it is in no one's interest to give this opera; and since there was talk about the *Huguenots*,[1] [I said] give the *Huguenots*, an opera that will be better received than *Simone* by your so-called two columns of the theatre.

If we agree on this, don't read what *follows*:

I know well that it's better to leave things in the last act as they are; and I know that the *Sea of Lights* is a matter of the *mise-en-scène*. But that's exactly what I don't trust, and so I looked for *ficelles* [tricks] to cover up the flaw of our *mise-en-scène*. You don't share my opinion, my dear Giulio, but what can I say! I have never had the good fortune to see an opera of mine well staged at La Scala. . Even *Aida* was better produced in a little provincial town, Parma,[2] than in Milan.

Make the *Sea of Lights* as you please, then, and let's not talk about it any more, while I reserve the right, however, always to state my opinion or make clear my will at the rehearsals.

Write me, or better yet, telegraph me so that we don't waste time. Don't work so hard, and take better care of your health.

Addio, addio
G. Verdi

Have Tornaghi inform the hotel that I don't mind not getting the usual apartment, but would rather have a single well-heated bedroom, even on the second floor; and don't let them say anything to anybody.

Inform me by telegram a day earlier, sometime before evening . .

Addio

Cordially,
G. Verdi

---

[1] Opera in 5 acts by Giacomo Meyerbeer.
[2] Under Verdi's supervision on 20 Apr. 1872.

VERDI TO GIULIO RICORDI

[Genoa] Tuesday [22 February 1881][1]

Dear Giulio,

I repeat what I said in the telegram just sent:[2] *Saturday too late to begin rehearsals*. And how will you manage to put on 12 performances! But we are at the ball.[3]

We arrive Thursday night after *11*. For Heaven's sake don't stand on ceremony. Take care of yourself and go to bed instead of coming to the station. At most send Tornaghi. But there is absolutely no need of anyone.

Do me the favour of having the hotel-keeper notified about the apartment for the two of us.[4] I want a good half grand piano and a fairly large writing-table. You will send me a sufficiently comfortable desk.

Friday morning at about 9 a copyist can come to me for the *questions* regarding the notes and the *stage directions*. Later on we'll talk about the rest. If Magnani could also come on Friday at noontime we could settle everything. You all will take care of the *Sea of Lights*.

We are agreed, then. Thursday night. Addio

G. Verdi

GIULIO RICORDI TO VERDI

Milan, 22 February 1881

Illustrious Maestro,

Further to my telegram,[1] I shall try to reply as briefly as possible to what you wrote to me in your esteemed letter of yesterday.

I arrived in Milan on Friday; I immediately gave the order for the singers' parts to be hand-copied by the best copyists so as to complete what had been engraved; work was done on this on Saturday, Sunday and part of Monday, and *this morning* the artists have received complete: Prologue—first part, first act—and the entire second. The third act is being copied and will be ready *tomorrow*, and so all the singers' parts will be *complete*, with the exception of the new Grand Finale.

The chorus has already studied the Prologue. Today they received and read the finale Act II; tomorrow they will have the entire third act; and so the chorus will be complete, except for the new first [act] finale. Today I complete the list of the costume orders, props, etc., etc., which I shall hand over tomorrow morning.

[1] Postmark: GENOVA 22/2/81.
[2] Missing.
[3] 'and must dance', Verdi added on other occasions when, as now, there was no alternative.
[4] Note Verdi's obvious change of mind in this request since his postscript to the preceding letter.

[1] Missing.

This morning Faccio came to me, and I think he will also write to you; meanwhile I telegraphed to you that *Freyschutz* is being given tomorrow, or Thursday at the latest, and not Saturday; I don't know where you could have heard that rumour. Actually, it was to be given on Saturday, but on last Saturday and not the coming one; the delay was caused by the illness of the bass. Faccio added that he has really tried to do his very best with this *Freyschutz*, because a fiasco would require putting on another opera with the second company! . . . . . If it goes fairly well it will be possible to go ahead calmly with the performances, and no other work will have to be done except for *Boccanegra*. Therefore, while occupying himself with *Freyschutz* these days, his intention has been to act not only in the interest of the theatre, but also in that of *Boccanegra*, who will thus remain the absolute master of the theatre. Today he held a short rehearsal of details; tonight is the dress rehearsal. Tomorrow he will assume the direction of the *Boccanegra* reading rehearsals for the orchestra—and therefore I telegraphed you that you could start on Saturday. I repeat that if you came even sooner the time would not be lost; it is also urgent that you decide on the various sets as a guide to Magnani. There are still some doubts about notes and stage directions; and to tell you of only one example, in your orchestra score, when the Doge's return from the hunt is announced to Amelia, there is written: '*Un'ancella*' ['*A handmaid*']; I believe that '*Un servo*' ['*A servant*'] had been decided upon, instead, who would also be the *Capitano de' Balestrieri* [*Captain of the Crossbowmen*] in the last act. Little things, which, however, must be settled *as soon as possible*.

I repeat, also in Faccio's name, that no more anger and strife exists between Maurel and Tamagno. Tamagno really was ill, not vocally, but with a strong head cold, along with bloodshot eyes and a splitting headache. He sang to keep the theatre from staying closed on Saturday and Sunday, asking to leave out a few things for fear of becoming seriously ill; this, and this alone, is the truth; and not only because I gave you my word, but out of duty to my conscience, I would have written you right away if things had been different.

With regard to the scene of the *Sea of Lights*, I think there will be time for you to decide here [in Milan]; I merely outlined to you the reasons Boito gave me, which by no means exclude a beautiful staging and a great *Sea of Lights*; furthermore, Boito said that we would do better to adopt the idea of the Captain's announcing the order to extinguish; as for the other, you can discuss it again—one idea leads to another—better than by writing; and since this will be the last set Magnani will do, a delay of two or three days will do no one any harm. [. . .]

In any event you have only to command, and we all will go out of our way, we will cut ourselves into tiny pieces just to see one of your *nice* smiles . . . and to keep those tempests far off which make everyone shudder.

I don't know which paper has announced the *launching* of the opera!! . . . . It must have been some *idiot*, the most common kind of journalist. In Genoa I spoke with no one; and here in Milan I stayed in bed for one day, at home for another, and only yesterday before dinner did I go out to catch a breath of air. For my part, I don't *launch* anything! . . . . . Rest assured.

To move on to another matter: I spoke with Boito about the costumes of the noble and popular councillors. He thinks they need not have special costumes; yet something distinctive, if only for the nobles, would, I think, serve to set them apart from one another. This, too, is an urgent matter for discussion and decision. Edel has found other materials in the Melzi library that will be quite useful. [. . .]

FRANCO FACCIO TO VERDI

Milan, 22 February 1881

Illustrious Maestro,

I have the honour of informing you that tonight the dress rehearsal of *Freyschüstz* takes place; it will be performed tomorrow, Wednesday, allowing for the usual unforeseen accidents. Today the parts of *Simon Boccanegra* were handed out to the artists, and tomorrow at noon I shall hold the first piano rehearsal; as for the chorus, I advise you that the greater part of the opera is in their hands and that they have already had three rehearsals; tomorrow they will have the *fourth*. From tomorrow morning onwards I shall rehearse with the artists every day, and I should think that by Saturday you could personally take over the direction of the ensemble. Believe me, illustrious Maestro, much work has been done these last few days, and without losing a minute. We don't talk about grudges and jealousies; everything is proceeding most regularly; Carlo V is in the best of health and voice, and only Ernani was a bit ill the last few days, making the management lose a performance. Giulio has given me hope for your forthcoming arrival, and I am overjoyed at the idea of seeing you again and of putting myself at your service. [. . .]

VERDI TO GIULIO RICORDI

[Genoa] *Wednesday* [23 February 1881]

Dear Giulio,

Only a line in answer to your letter.

The rumour about *Freyschütz* I got close at hand . . . from your *Corriere della sera*.

The other one, about the *launching*, was reported here by another paper of Milan, I think the *Ragione*. [. . .]

As for the Sea of Lights, which I feel—and already foresee—will not be good, do it as you see fit. I said this in my previous letter, too . . And as for the costumes, I'll give you my opinion later . . .

I repeat once more: I shall be in Milan tomorrow night by *11.35*.

I ask you again, don't stand on ceremony, and excuse the troubles I have caused you and shall continue to cause you during this new sojourn in Milan. Believe me always

Yours,
G. Verdi

PS I don't recall if, besides the piano, I asked you yesterday to arrange for a little desk at the hotel.

GIULIO RICORDI TO VERDI

Milan, 23 February 1881

Illustrious Maestro,

In haste, to answer your esteemed letter—

I went right away to Signor Spatz,[1] who is desperate because he is unable to place the usual apartment *immediately* at your disposal, since the sitting-room is being renovated. He had hoped to do it in time, believing that you would not come before the end of the month; but your arrival has upset his plans. Therefore he wishes to give you another apartment temporarily, for 6 or 7 days. I saw two of them: one on the first floor, the other one directly above on the second, where you stayed once before, for *La forza del destino*; as soon as you have received this letter, I beg you to telegraph me whether you prefer the first floor (fairly nice apartment along the Red Cross) or the second, which is more cheerful and sunny. Of course, the customary sitting-room will be at your disposal as always, as soon as it is in order. The piano is ready; and I am only awaiting your telegram so I may know where to put it and when to order the heating of the rooms. Anticipating the pleasure of seeing you, I remain

Yours gratefully,
Giulio Ricordi

This morning, chorus rehearsal and of the whole company. Last night the dress rehearsal of *Freyschutz* went well; I did not go, since I am not yet ready to face the theatre at night; the bass Ordinas[2] was stricken by severe stomach pains in the middle of the rehearsal! . . . . Let us hope he *gave birth* during the night and will no longer delay the performance of the opera.

VERDI TO FERDINAND HILLER

Genoa, 24 February 1881

[. . .] Must I tell you that I have worked a lot of late? I have rewritten many parts of an old opera of mine that was an outright fiasco in Venice when I gave it for the first time, *Simon Boccanegra*. A new version of this opera will

---

[1] Owner of the Grand Hôtel et de Milan, presumably of Swiss origin, since 1896 father-in-law of the composer Umberto Giordano (1867–1948).

[2] In the role of Kaspar, in which he appeared at La Scala next to Ramfis, Alvise in *La gioconda*, and Mefistofele in *Faust* between 1879 and 1881.

be given in Milan, for which I am departing tonight. Yesterday they began the rehearsals, and I hope that around 20 March we can have the performance—barring any unforeseen delays. [. . .]

GIULIO RICORDI TO VERDI[1]

Milan, 25 February 1881

—Maestro!—

You will understand that I am in such a state that I don't know where my head is any more! . . . . . It is the most horrible thing that has happened to me in my whole life! . . . . I will come to you later, when my nerves are calmer and I am able to reason! . . . . . . Now, in the midst of anger, mortification, desolation, my brains are boiling; and an idea comes to me; I submit it to you for what it is worth. You did not want to give *Boccanegra* in the spring. You did not tell me why; but maybe you did not want to find yourself in Milan at the time of the unveiling of your statue;[2] if this is the obstacle, it is removed right away. I promise you that I will put together in a few hours a company of *gentlemen* and true artists who will give you not only deference but also the satisfaction of obtaining all the effects—

Mariani
Marconi
Moriami
another baritone to be chosen
and maybe Nannetti, who I think could still be engaged.

Take what I write for what it is worth, for I'm not only most desolate, but I'm in a rage that upsets me more every moment.

Always yours most devotedly,
Giulio Ricordi

VERDI TO OPPRANDINO ARRIVABENE

Milan, 25 March 1881

Dear Arrivabene,

Even before last night's performance, if I had had the time to write to you, I would have told you that the broken legs of this old *Boccanegra* seemed well mended to me.

The success of last night confirmed my opinion. So then: very good performance on everyone's part; stupendous on the part of the protagonist; excellent success.[1] [. . .]

[1] At his first *Boccanegra* rehearsal at La Scala, Verdi clashed with the artists. Apparently he threatened to leave and withdraw the score. Thereupon he received these lines at his hotel.

[2] Verdi objected to placing his statue in the entrance hall of La Scala. (See Boito to Verdi, 31 Mar. and 4 Apr. 1881 and Verdi to Boito, 2 Apr. 1881.)

---

[1] Under Franco Faccio's baton, the cast consisted of Victor Maurel (Simon Boccanegra), Anna D'Angeri (Amelia), Edouard De Reszke (Fiesco), Francesco Tamagno (Gabriele Adorno), Frederico Salvati (Paolo Albiani), Giovanni Bianco (Pietro). Alfredo Cairati was the chorus master, Girolamo Magnani the scenic designer, Alfredo Edel the costume designer.

BOITO TO VERDI

Milan, Thursday [31 March 1881][1]

Dear Maestro,

There is a delicate question that is disturbing the sleep of some gentlemen who sleep lightly. They had already turned to Giulio so that he might help them sleep calmly, but Giulio does not care to satisfy them and has directed them to me. I suggested chloral [hydrate] to these insomniacs as an excellent soporific, but they did not want to drink it, and they do not allow themselves any peace, and rob me of it, too. Will you see, dear Maestro, if you can find a way to calm them, since their fate is in your hands.

They have set their minds on having Verdi's name read in the list of the donors of Bellini's statue[2] and already are looking forward with emotion to this event. I do not know who gave them hope that after the appearance of *Boccanegra* at La Scala, and not before, their desire would be realized; now they are waiting, staying awake, and visibly losing weight, and they do not want to take the chloral [hydrate]; Giulio washes his hands, and they prod me, who does not want to be prodded, to speak to you. Yesterday I said yes, but took advantage of your departure not to speak to you about this and bother you with this chatter during the last hours of your stay in Milan. Today I will say that you have left, and will add that I shall *not* write to you; however, I am writing to you, since it is fitting, after all, that you do not ignore this state of affairs. Now then, without their (the insomniacs') knowledge I advise you of this matter—so that you can judge its worth and solve the problem as it seems best to you. It is only fair for me to add that all this zeal has arisen in the hearts of persons who feel the most ardent admiration for you, and that it is the zeal of love.

I have spoken. When will we begin that correspondence? Keep me a little in your kind thoughts.

Your most affectionate
Arrigo Boito

VERDI TO BOITO

Genoa, 2 April 1881

Dear Boito,

Last year at this time I was departing from Milan,[1] and the train had scarcely started when I realized the error that I and everybody else had

---

[1] This date is inferred from Verdi's departure for Genoa the day before, as mentioned in this letter and reported by *La gazzetta musicale di Milano* of 3 Apr. 1881.
[2] By the sculptor Ambrogio Borghi (1849–87) in the entrance hall of La Scala.

---

[1] On 20 Apr. 1880, after the première of his *Pater noster* and *Ave Maria*, conducted by Faccio at La Scala on 18 Apr. 1880.

committed in erecting that statue, etc., etc ... I tried with Giulio to remedy the fault, but without success. I thought it best, therefore, to abstain utterly and entirely from everything in regard to this affair.—The way things are at this point, don't you think, dear Boito, that if I offered a sum for Bellini's statue, one might believe, or claim, that I made the offer for the one, provided the other one was erected?[2] You will answer that the necessary sum for the first statue was collected right away; and so it may be. The fact is, however, that I would have contributed to the simultaneous placing of the statues. The fact being what it is, many would not make a distinction as to whether the offer was made for Bellini's statue, for mine, or for both!

In May or June of last year I wrote to Ricordi[3] that I was disposed to offer a sum of ....., if a way could be found not to speak any more of the two statues and to convert all the money into a work of charity. That would still be the best, the most useful, and to me the most welcome thing to do. Nevertheless, if this cannot be done, I am disposed, in fact am authorizing you, dear Boito, to tell the commission that I will put *my name on the list of the donors of the statue of Bellini*, offering the sum still needed to erect it, but on the condition that for now, my own not be erected and that it will not be erected in the future without my permission.

Answer me in this matter as soon as possible, and believe me always

Affectionately,
G. Verdi

PS I am leaving tomorrow morning for a few days at St Agata. Address the letter in [this] case
to Busseto.

VERDI TO OPPRANDINO ARRIVABENE

Genoa, 2 April 1881

Dear Arrivabene,

From what they write to me it seems that *Boccanegra* received the same applause on the fourth night as on the others, if not more. What pleases me most is that the theatre was more crowded than at the second and third performances. Everybody was frightened by the disaster in Nice.[1]

Now, if you care to know, I'll tell you that *Boccanegra* can make the tour of the theatres like so many of his sisters, although the subject is very sad.

It is sad because it must be sad, but it has interest. In the second act the effect seems to diminish; but if the first [act] finale were less successful in

[2] Verdi's own statue by Francesco Barzaghi (1839–92) in the entrance hall of La Scala. It was erected against Verdi's wishes and unveiled together with Bellini's statue on 25 Oct. 1881. Both statues survived the destruction of La Scala in the Second World War.
[3] Presumably letter of 30 Apr. 1880 which is possibly in the Biblioteca Palatina.

[1] The Théâtre Municipal in Nice burned down as the result of a gas explosion on 23 Mar. 1881, causing 120 deaths.

another theatre, one would not be surprised if this second act were as successful as the others. Things of this world . . . . that is, of the theatre! We'll see, and meanwhile we hope. [. . .]

BOITO TO VERDI

[Milan] Monday [4 April 1881][1]

Dear Maestro,

I perfectly understand the way in which you judge the question, and others have understood it along with me. I shall explain it to the committee exactly as you have explained it to me, and you won't be bothered with the statues any more. This is resolved; yet the two statues will be erected, and no one can prevent this from taking place; *the matter is closed.* They will be erected, and you personally can stay away from this event without anyone's objecting to it any more.

A cordial greeting from your

Arrigo Boito

All the best to your wife.

VERDI TO MARIA WALDMANN

Genoa, 5 April 1881

[. . .] You gave me hope that you would come to Milan for the opening night of *Boccanegra.* You can well imagine how pleased I, first of all, Peppina, and everybody would have been! You would have heard ugly music, but a good performance and a superb singing actor in the part of Simone (Maurel)! Truly an artist! I don't have to tell you about the success, of which you are already aware. It was good the three nights when I was present, and I am told that it held up afterwards, too. [. . .]

VERDI TO GIULIO RICORDI

[Genoa] Thursday [14 April 1881][1]

All is well! Repeated ovations don't mean a thing if the box-office isn't full to overflowing. When the box-office is full, it means that many people go to the theatre.

If many people go to the theatre, it means that the audience is interested in the show.

If the audience is interested in the show, it means that the work is *valid.*
This is the purpose!

---

[1] This date is inferred from Verdi's request at the end of his letter of 2 Apr. to answer 'as soon as possible'.

---

[1] Postmark: GENOVA 14/4/81.

It may very well be the disaster in Nice that frightened the audience, but (an excuse can always be found) the fact is that the ten performances of *Boccanegra* have brought little money, and that is what I regret. [. . .]

GIULIO RICORDI TO VERDI

Milan, 18 April 1881

Illustrious Maestro,

I received your kind letter, to which I can reply with great pleasure that your observations are absolutely right; I wish to confirm that the success of *Boccanegra* was one of the most *complete* that has ever been at La Scala, and I will tell you that the audience gradually increased; the last three performances were magnificent not only because of the success of the music, but also because of the crowd, with hardly an empty box or seat!!! . . . . . If it had been possible to give 3 or 4 more performances, it would have meant a great fortune for the theatre and the management.

All the newspapers (including the famous *Ragione*!), which you will find quoted in today's *Gazzetta musicale*, will confirm this.

Since I [began to] frequent the theatres I have never happened to notice such continuing interest on the part of an Italian audience, intense from the beginning to the end of the opera; it was a real satisfaction. And I will also say, with *Il corriere della sera*: a pity that Verdi was not in the theatre!! Because *de visu et de auditu* you would have concurred with what I am saying now, and have already telegraphed you.

All the performances, without exception, were excellent on everyone's part; I won't speak of Maurel; but, for example, you cannot believe what an immense improvement you would have found in Tamagno, who by singing the opera again and again has better understood his part both musically and dramatically; on the last nights he had exceptionally beautiful moments and aroused the enthusiasm of the audience. [. . .]

VERDI TO GIULIO RICORDI

Genoa, 1 May 1881

Dear Giulio,

I stayed a day longer to hear la *Nevada*.[1] Very, very good; extremely good. She really has exceptional qualities of voice and sentiment. She has the reputation now of being only a bravura singer, but believe me, she has remarkable dramatic presence and will go very *far*! .. There is also a tenor with a splendid voice,[2] who sings As, Bs, and Cs you won't believe; he can execute a *diminuendo* and, without knowing it, has a most beautiful *mezza voce*; but his singing is so coarse; he does such atrocious things that he should

---

[1] In a performance of *La sonnambula* at the Teatro Paganini in Genoa.

[2] Giuseppe Cantoni was the Elvino in this *Sonnambula* but is otherwise unknown.

be shot right away. But what a pity!—And what murderers his voice teachers were! He also has a figure!—coarse, like his singing. All the same, keep your eye on him. [. . .]

Forgive me for the troubles I caused you in Milan. Peppina sends best regards to Giuditta, and I say

Addio.
G. Verdi

OPPRANDINO ARRIVABENE TO VERDI

Rome, 11 May 1881

[. . .] It would please me if Maurel could succeed in having your *Simon Boccanegra* given at the Opéra. But I wouldn't like to see it treated as they now treat everything Italian in France. They have always had little love for us, and now they don't even pretend to respect us. [. . .]

VERDI TO GIULIO RICORDI

St Agata, 11 May 1881

Dear Giulio,

You must have known about the telegram which the employees of your firm have sent me.[1] If so, you should have acted as a friend by preventing it. You know that I detest showing myself in public. Let it be a sign of 'modesty'; let it be a sign of pride; let it be whatever you want, the fact is that I do not like publicity. When I work for the theatre in Italy, it's a miserable necessity to show myself, but other than that I, too, am a man like everyone else. [. . .]

GIULIO RICORDI TO VERDI

Milan, 13 May 1881

[. . .] The telegram that was sent to you was entirely the idea of the employees of the firm; and it is a natural idea. Briefly, this is what it is about: with small weekly contributions they have established an emergency fund to pay for a physician on an annual basis, and for sick leave. [. . .]

If you want to do a good deed, would you send a gift of 100 or 200 lire to the fund? [. . .]

The final rehearsals of *Mefistofele* are beginning; I believe the performance will be truly excellent; and then? . . . . We shall see. Boito is half-sick; he told me that in spite of the rehearsals he was also busy with something else! . . and that he would write to you soon. [. . .]

---

[1] Missing.

GIULIO RICORDI TO VERDI

Milan, 22 May 1881

[. . .] Let me inform you that we are negotiating with Barcelona for *Boccanegra*; Faccio, Maurel, and Nannetti have already been engaged; if we complete the company well, I think the performance will be excellent; in any case I shall write to you first to get your instructions. [. . .]

Next Wednesday *Mefistofele* will be performed; the staging seems to me to be well done; orchestra, chorus, la Mariani and Nannetti all excellent. Marconi sings well . . . but he is a tenor, which means a clod! . . . This is the privilege of tenors today! . . . As for the success of the opera, I can't predict anything. [. . .]

BOITO TO VERDI

[Milan] Wednesday [25 May 1881][1]

Dear Maestro,

Don't think that I have forgotten about the Moor of Venice; I have thought about him, but until now I have lacked the necessary tranquillity to work at my desk. No matter what happens tonight I will get it back in a couple of days—the time needed to take leave of my friends who have come over from Turin. This Mefisto has made us sweat; the one who has sweated more than all the others is Faccio, who has obtained splendid results; but Giulio and I, too, have both had our share of this toil.

In three hours the theatre will open; I am using this half hour of rest to assure you that in a couple of days I shall be working efficiently on the Moor.

I don't know whether the Secretary of the Committee for the Congress of Musicians[2] has posted the circular to St Agata or to Genoa.[3] In any case I put it to you: dear Maestro, see if you would like to give us some good advice. You can contribute a great deal to the practical outcome of the Congress. You will have time, until 14 June, to let us know your ideas.

See how stupid the rehearsals of Mefisto have made me: for quite some time I have had a diploma from the *Concert Society of Barcelona*[4] which I have been meaning to send you, and only now do I find the time to prepare this parcel.

And on this little enclosed page, dear Maestro, you may read my affectionate greetings.

Your
Arrigo Boito

[1] The first performance of the revised *Mefistofele* at La Scala, mentioned in this letter, took place on this date. In view of the fiasco of the opera's original version at La Scala on 5 Mar. 1868, this performance was of vital importance to Boito. His handwriting and some orthographical errors in this letter betray his nervous condition. A few hours later he enjoyed a decisive success.
[2] Held in Milan from 16 to 22 June 1881.   [3] Missing.   [4] Missing.

VERDI TO BOITO
[Telegram]

Busseto, 26 May 1881

VERY HAPPY ABOUT SUCCESS—I SEND MOST HEARTFELT SINCERE
CONGRATULATIONS—AND SOON NERONE

VERDI

VERDI TO OPPRANDINO ARRIVABENE[1]

St Agata, 27 May 1881

Dear Arrivabene,
   You're crazy!! Give *Boccanegra* in Paris?!!
   Do you think I want to go to that country at this time? Never! . . . not for
all the gold in the world! We have received a big slap in the face![2] Oh, it's true
that the fault is ours, all ours! It's impossible that there has ever been, that
there is, that there can be in the future a government so . . . You add the
epithet. [. . .]

OPPRANDINO ARRIVABENE TO VERDI

Rome, 29 May 1881

Dearest friend,
   Your anger has given me immense pleasure. A good citizen, a gentleman,
cannot watch with indifference a band of scoundrels that mistreats the
country and covers it with shame. As for the French, you know that I have
always believed them to be our enemies, and now, too, about their insolent
behaviour, I agree with you. [. . .]
   It seems to me that the papers are wrong in saying that Milan has changed
its mind about Boito's opera. He has changed his mind, if he rewrote half of
it. I don't think it's an *extraordinary success*. [. . .]

VERDI TO ACHILLE TORELLI

St Agata, 17 June 1881

[. . .] You who are still young, write, write, write! Don't mind the public. You
do your job; let them do theirs. It's well known that the public never goes to
the theatre to admire. *Amusement* is the word for them (an odious word for
an author). However it may be, don't ever leave time for the public to
abandon itself to mirth; gradually you will pull it up to you. [. . .]

---

   [1] Verdi's reaction to Arrivabene's proposal of 11 May 1881.
   [2] Italy had hoped to appropriate Tunisia which, in early 1881, was occupied by France.

BOITO TO VERDI

Milan, 17 June [1881]

Dear Maestro,

The foreign assault has still not ended. The poor, unhappy people living in Milan in these times of the Exhibition[1] and the Congresses are subjected to the torture of courtesies and social expediencies, the most stupid and cruel moral torture imaginable. For more than three weeks I have been a martyr to this barbaric state of affairs; my day is ruined, and the evening comes without my having written even half a page.

Yesterday, however, irritated by this silly fate, and thinking of what you expect of me, I set to work (after closing doors and windows) and tried to put down on paper the ideas that have been going through my head for a long time concerning the chorus in the second act. Here is where I have found it opportune to place this chorus: towards the end of the first fateful conversation between Jago and Otello,[2] where Jago cleverly pushes the Moor's thoughts to the brink of jealousy, after Otello's words:

Amore e gelosia vadan dispersi insieme!

[*Love and jealousy must be dispelled together!*[3]]

The audience hears a lovely chorus backstage that gradually draws nearer as Jago continues his infernal work. Soon after this, through the rather large opening centrestage that leads to the garden, Desdemona, in a gracefully arranged group, should be seen surrounded by women and children who are singing serenely and throwing flowers and branches in her path and all around her. In this fateful moment of the drama, the songs and flowers surrounding the beautiful and innocent Desdemona will be like a chaste and tender apotheosis. It would be nice if the chorus and Desdemona could remain framed by the arch of the central opening during the whole piece. You, Maestro, will recall the ground plan of this scene:[4] it is octagonal and surrounded by flats:

and it is a shallow set. The chorus (with Desdemona) should therefore stay on the other side of the opening, in view of the audience and tightly grouped, but no one should cross the threshold. Since they are a bit far from the

[1] The *Esposizione Nazionale di Milano* had opened on 5 May 1881.
[2] Act II, Scene iii.
[3] Cf. Shakespeare, *Othello*, III. iii. 196: 'Away at once with love and jealousy!'
[4] Years in advance of the completion and production of *Otello*, what kind of ground plan can Boito mean? It would appear that he and Verdi made up their own for the creation of the opera.

orchestra, they might be accompanied by harps, which could even be visible; the text also speaks of *mandolas*,[5] so the *mandolin* could be used, too.

Jago and Otello remain on stage, that is, on this side of the door, towards the proscenium, while the sweet apotheosis of Desdemona continues.

At the beginning and at the end, and in the refrains of this chorus, I have tried a six-syllable verse, not accented like the usual ones, but uniformly, with one strong and one weak accent; the rhythm of the verse suggests three-quarter time. But it's time to copy down the strophes:[6]

CORO

(interno avvicinandosi)

Dove guardi splendono
    avvampan cuori,
Raggi, [[echeggian Cori]]
Dove passi scendono
Nuvole di fiori.
Qui fra gigli e rose
Come a un casto altar,
Padri, bimbi, spose
Vengono a cantar.

FANCIULLI

(spargendo al suolo fiori di giglio)

T'offriamo il giglio
Soave stel
Che in man degli angeli
Fu assunto in ciel,
Che abbella il fulgido
Manto e la gonna
Della Madonna,
E il santo vel.

DESDEMONA

Splende il cielo, danza
L'aura intorno ai fior.
Gioja, Amor, Speranza
Cantan nel mio cor.

DONNE E MARINARI

(mentre cantano i fanciulli, accompagnando e armonizzando)

(Mentre all'aure vola
Lieta la canzon,
L'agile mandòla
Ne accompagna il suon)

---

[5] Medieval string instrument, a small lute, also called mandora, quinterna, or pandurina.

[6] Except for minor corrections, this copy corresponds to the final text. Desdemona, however, sings only at the end of the chorus: 'Splende il cielo, danza / L'aura, olezza il fior. / Gioia, amor, speranza / Cantan nel mio cor.' ['The sky is sparkling / The air is dancing 'round the flowers. / Joy, Love, Hope / Are singing in my heart.']

MARINARI

(offrendo a Desdemona dei monili di corallo e di perle)

A te le porpore
Le perle e gli ostri,
Nella
[[Dalla]] voragine
Colti del mar.
Vogliam Desdemona
Coi doni nostri
Come un imagine
Sacra adornar.

FANCIULLI E DONNE

(mentre cantano i marinari, accompagnando e armonizzando)

(Mentre all'aure vola
Lieta la canzon,
L'agile mandòla
Ne accompagna il suon.)

LE DONNE

(spargendo rami e fiori)

Per te la
[[La messe]] florida
[[A te del salice]]
Messe dai
[[Dai nostri]] grembi
[[La molle fronda,]]
A nembi, a nembi,
[[Amor dell'onda]]
Spargiamo al suol.
[[Dei carmi Amor]].
L'April circonda
La sposa bionda
[[A te il ciclame
Tua testa bionda
Dal fragil stame,]]
D'un etra rorida
[[Dal tenue calice]]
Che vibra al sol
[[D'azzurro e d'or]]
FANCIULLI E MARINARI
OPPURE MARINARI SOLI

(mentre le donne cantano accompagnando e armonizzando)

(Mentre all'aure vola
Lieta la canzon
L'agile mandola
Ne accompagna il suon.)

CORO.

§ Vivi felice! Addio. Qui regna Amor.

TUTTI.

Dove guardi splendono
　　avvampan cuori,
Raggi, [[echeggian Cori,]]
Dove passi scendono
Nuvole di fiori.
Qui fra gigli e rose,
Come a un casto altar,

Padri, bimbi, spose
Vengono a cantar.

DESDEMONA.

Splende il cielo, danza
L'aura intorno ai fior
Gioja, Amor, Speranza
Cantan nel mio cor.

e, mentre questo Coro dura, Otello, fin dal principio, mormora:

Eccola!
　　　　　　　Vigilate.

e JAGO.
(gli mormora
e gli ripete
mentre canta
il Coro)

e OTELLO.
(soavemente
commosso)

Quel canto mi conquide:
No, no, s'ella m'inganna, il ciel sé stesso
[irride.

[CHORUS.

Wherever you look, rays
Shine, hearts are enflamed;
　　　　　　　[[choruses echo]]
Wherever you pass, clouds
Of flowers descend.

(backstage
drawing
nearer)

Here, midst lilies and roses,
As at an altar pure,
Come fathers, children,
Wives to sing.

CHILDREN

(scattering lilies on the ground)

We offer you the lily's
Tender stem
Which in the angel's hands
Was raised up to Heaven,
To adorn the Madonna's
Gleaming gown and mantle,
And her sacred veil.

WOMEN AND SAILORS

(while the children are singing, accompanying and harmonizing)

(As our song soars,
Joyously on the air,
The agile mandola
Accompanies the sound.)

SAILORS

(offering Desdemona jewelry of coral and pearls)

To you the purple,
The pearls and the corals,
Gathered in [[from]]
The deep sea.
With our gifts
We wish to adorn Desdemona,
Like a sacred image.

CHILDREN AND WOMEN

(while the sailors are singing, accompanying and harmonizing)

(As our song soars
Joyously on the air,
The agile mandola
Accompanies the sound.)

DESDEMONA.

The sky is sparkling,
The air is dancing 'round the flowers.
Joy, Love, Hope
Are singing in my heart.

WOMEN

(strewing branches and flowers)

For you, the
[[The harvest]] flourishing
[[To you the willow's]]
Harvest from the
[[From our]]   laps
[[The soft, leafy branch,]]
In clouds, in clouds,
[[Love on the wave]]
We scatter on the ground
[[Some poems of Love.]]
April surrounds
The blond bride
[[To you the cyclamen
Your fair head
From the fragile stamen]]
With etheral dew
[[From a slender cup]]
That shimmers in the sun
[[Of blue and gold.]]

CHILDREN AND SAILORS,
OR SAILORS ALONE

(while the women are singing, accompanying, and harmonizing)

(As our song soars
Joyously on the air,
The agile mandola
Accompanies the sound.)

ALL

Wherever you look, rays
Shine, hearts are enflamed;
        [choruses echo,]
Wherever you pass, clouds
Of flowers descend.
Here, midst lilies and roses,
As at an altar pure,

Come fathers, children,
Wives to sing.

§ Live happily! Farewell. Here Love reigns. CHORUS.

DESDEMONA.

The sky is sparkling,
The air is dancing 'round the flowers.
Joy, Love, Hope
Are singing in my heart. §

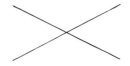

And while this chorus is going on, Otello, from the very beginning, whispers:[7]

> There she is!

and JAGO.   Watch her.
(whispering to
him and repeating
while the
chorus sings)

and OTELLO: That song conquers me.
(gently moved)   No, no, if she deceives me, heaven mocks itself.]

When the chorus ends Desdemona kisses the heads of some of the children, and some of the women kiss the hem of her dress. She hands a purse to the sailors, the chorus disperses, and (followed by Emilia) she enters the room, approaches Otello, and the following scene begins: DESD. '*D'un uom che geme sotto il tuo disdegno, la preghiera ti porto* ...' ['*From a man who is suffering your disdain, this prayer I bring you* ...'],[8] etc., etc., etc. The moment Desdemona mentions the name of Cassio, the memory of the chorus that has enchanted Otello ceases, and the terrible drama resumes its inexorable course.

Now I must give you the reason I have chosen the six-syllable verse accented in two parts. I didn't do it for the love of novelty at all, but because I was looking for a rhythm capable of accompanying the single five-syllable stanzas that are interpolated with the frequency of notes.

I will resort to an example because I can't explain myself in any better way.[9]

3/4	Mĕntrĕ	all'ăură	vŏlă	lĭetă	lă	cănzōn	ecc.
3/4	Ā	tē	dēl	sā	lī	cē	ecc.

If this chorus seems good to you, the most arduous part of the *Otello* revisions is over; I'll get to work on the ensemble. Then I'll try a few more cuts in Otello's part, in addition to the ones I have already made. It would be almost indispensable, however, to discuss this last point together in person.

I also want to thank you for the telegram you sent me after the first performance of *Mefisto*. I shall never be able to tell you what noble joy I felt in your words.

Mefisto at La Scala was like one of those fireworks that start out with a big bang and end up with a miserable little pop. The public didn't fill the theatre very well. My competition was too serious to overcome—I mean the

---

[7] In the final text it is Jago who says 'Eccola' ['There she is'] and 'vigilate' ['watch her']. During Otello's words 'Quel canto mi conquide...' ['That singing conquers me...'] Jago is saying aside: 'Beltà ed amor in dolce inno concordi! / I vostri infrangerò soavi accordi.' ['Beauty and Love, harmonizing in sweet song! / Your gentle chords I will break.'] (Shakespeare, *Othello*, II. i. 199–200: 'IAGO. (Aside) O, you are well tun'd now! / But I'll set down the pegs that make this music, / As honest as I am.') Cf. Verdi to Ricordi, 15 Dec., and Boito to Verdi, 16–17 Dec. 1886.

[8] Cf. Shakespeare, *Othello*, III. iii. 44: 'A man that languishes in your displeasure.'

[9] See *Carteggi* ii. 108 n.

Amazons of the Renz Circus.[10] But I am also very happy with the fate that is mine.

Many friendly greetings to your Signora. For you, an affectionate handshake. Write and tell me whether the chorus impresses you, since I could, if necessary, come up with another idea before I leave for the country.

                    Your devoted

                                                      Arrigo Boito

VERDI TO BOITO

                                            St Agata, 23 June 1881

Dear Boito,

Don't throw stones at me for not answering your very dear and important letter until now.

The chorus you sent me will do very well, I think. I say 'I think' because, not having the second act in front of me, I am not fully aware of the place the chorus must occupy. In any case this chorus couldn't be more charming or more elegant or more beautiful. And then, what a flash of light in the midst of so much darkness! Go ahead with the finale, then, and make it fairly well developed, I'd say, even *broad*. The theatre demands it, but more than the theatre, the colossal power of the drama calls for it. The idea (which still appeals to me) of setting an *Otello* to music without a chorus was, and perhaps is, a crazy one!

As for the cuts in Otello's part, I agree, we'll make them together.

I send you my wife's regards and affectionately shake your hand.

                                                        G. Verdi

BOITO TO EUGENIO TORNAGHI

                                          Monticello,[1] 10 July 1881

[. . .] Giulio will have told you that, although our visit to St Agata was useless for Catalonia,[2] it was most useful for the chocolate. We settled the last doubtful point of the work very well with the Maestro, and now I am busy applying the result of that exchange of ideas, and with all of this before me I think I shall be exhausted. [. . .]

---

[10] Founded by Ernst Jakob Renz (1815–92), later Circus Schumann.

[1] Village near Monza to the north of Milan.
[2] In early July, Giulio Ricordi, Franco Faccio, and Boito had proposed a production of *Simon Boccanegra* in Barcelona, to which Verdi objected.

GIULIO RICORDI TO VERDI

Milan, 12 July 1881

[...] Mancinelli told me that the people in Bologna hope to have *Boccanegra* in Verdi's own production. [...] Tell me what you think of this. [...]

VERDI TO GIULIO RICORDI

St Agata, 17 July 1881

[...] Let's not think of Bologna. I won't go there! They have done so many operas of mine without ever thinking of me, and now!! . What does this mean? It's true ... I am, together with Gobati,[1] an honorary citizen of Bologna, but .... I will not go to Bologna to stage *Boccanegra.*—

Are we agreed? Enjoy yourself in the country, and *addio.*

G. Verdi

DOMENICO MORELLI TO VERDI

[Naples] 10 August 1881

[...] You know that I have painted a row of monks in church on Good Friday![1] A stupendous theme! ... Everyday I went to my studio with the intention of doing Jago and Otello—as you wrote to me—and then the brushes painted the monks. [...]

VERDI TO DOMENICO MORELLI

St Agata, 20 August 1881

[...] It's really true: When I received your letter I cried out: Finally he remembers us! All these stories of yours. What do I care if you're thinking of *La Vergine degli Angeli*! ... Those notes are one thing, and I am another! If only they had excited you enough to put down four scratches, four rough strokes of the brush for Jago or for another, and send them to me! ... But nothing, always nothing! [...]

---

[1] The composer Stefano Gobatti.

[1] See Verdi to Morelli, 7 Feb. 1880.

BOITO TO VERDI

[Milan] Wednesday [24 August 1881][1]

Dear Maestro,

You had already begun to believe that, together with my hat, the sponge, and the brush, I had forgotten the finale of [the third act of] *Otello*.[2] It wasn't like that. I thought and thought about this finale, and since it was a very big mouthful, I never succeeded in assimilating it into the *essence of the form*, if I may express myself in this way, and I have spared no small pain to obtain the result that is already known to you by now. I think it is the outcome of all the talks we had at St Agata.

As we had planned it, the *ensemble piece* has its lyric and dramatic parts *fused together*. Therefore it is a lyric–melodic piece interwoven with dramatic dialogue. On the lyric side, the principal character is Desdemona; on the dramatic side, the principal character is Jago. Thus, after being overwhelmed for only a moment by an event beyond his control (the letter recalling Otello to Venice), Jago immediately ties all the threads of the tragedy together again with incomparable swiftness and energy. He continues to bring about *his* catastrophe, even taking advantage of the unforeseen event to accelerate the course of the final disaster at breakneck speed. All of this was in Schakespeare's mind; all of this appears clearly in our work. Jago passes from Otello to Rodrigo,[3] the two instruments left to him for his crime; then he has the last word and the last gesture in the act.

See whether the two parts, the lyric and the dramatic, seem well fused to you. See also whether the length of each part is well calculated. I did not economize in the lines, because I remembered your advice: '*Say everything that is useful to say, and everything should be explained.*' In giving this advice you felt that the dialogue of the lyric part had to be developed in order to be tragic; and you understood very well, and I have done it that way. Actually, in case the dialogue between Jago and Rodrigo should seem a bit incomplete and not too clear to you, here are four lines which, if needed, will complete and finish it.

> JAGO. *A notte folta io la sua traccia vigilo*
> *E il varco e l'ora scruto, il resto a te.*
> *Sarò tua scorta. A caccia, a caccia! Cingiti*
> *L'arco.*
> RODR. *Si. T'ho venduto onore e fè.*[4]

---

[1] The place and date of this letter are inferred from Boito's mention of his trip to Monticello and his return from there, as well as from Verdi's visit to Milan to which he refers, mentioned in the following letter.

[2] Apparently, Boito had paid a recent visit to St Agata, for which he thanks Verdi at the end of the letter.

[3] Roderigo in the final text as in Shakespeare's *Othello*.

[4] See Verdi to Boito, 17 July 1886. (Cf. Shakespeare, *Othello*, IV. ii.)

[JAGO. *In the thick of night I watch for his tracks*
    And search for his passage and the hour; the rest is up to you.
    I will be your escort. To the hunt, to the hunt! Gird on
    The bow.
RODR. *Yes. I have sold you my honour and faith.*]

One thing must be observed. The Jago–Otello, Jago–Rodrigo dialogues
follow one another; first the one, then the other. During the Jago–Otello
dialogue, what does Rodrigo do? Nothing. Yet his voice could create another
real part at the beginning of the melodic ensemble and he could sing the fifth
part until the time came for his dialogue with Jago. In this case I offer you
four lyric lines that Rodrigo could sing with the others while Otello is
speaking with Jago and at the start of the ensemble piece:

RODRIGO. (*Per me s'oscura il mondo,*   [(*The world grows dark for me,*
  S'annuvola il destin,   *My fate is clouded,*
  L'angelo casto e biondo   *The chaste and blond angel*
  Fugge dal mio cammin.)[5]   *Flees from my path.*)]

One might object to this: We have taken care of Rodrigo during the *Jago–*
Otello dialogue, so why don't we take care of Otello during the *Jago–Rodrigo*
dialogue? No. Otello's position is indicated, is determined by the dramatic
action. We have seen him collapse at the side of the table after the words '*A*
terra! e piangi!' ['*To the ground! and cry!*'], and so he must remain collapsed,
and must not lift himself up, not even while answering Jago, as long as the
whole *ensemble piece* lasts. He has no need to *speak* or *sing* while Jago is
speaking to Rodrigo. By remaining silent he is greater, and more terrible,
more three-dimensional. He rises only to scream, '*Fuggite!*' ['*Go!*'], and then
crashes to the floor.

It's good this way. Up to now, I hope, we are in perfect agreement. But
perhaps you will note that Desdemona (being, as I said, *the principal*
character of the lyric part of the piece) needs four lines more than the others.
Moreover, her first four lines do not lend themselves to being developed
musically and melodically. In that case, here are four lines that should end
Desdemona's stanza; but in order to read them, and also to write them down,
I see, you will have to turn the page over:

DESDEMONA.. .   .   .   .

   .   .   .   .   .

  .   .   .   .   .

   .   .   .   .   .

  .   .   .   .   .

   .   .   .   .   .

  .   .   .   .   .

   .   .   .   .

Sole sereno e vivido   [*You sun serene and bright*
Che allieti il cielo e il mare,   *That gladdens sky and sea,*
Tergi le stille amare   *Dry the bitter drops*
Che sparge il mio dolor![6]   *That are shed by my grief!*]

[5] See the final text (III. viii) in Verdi to Boito, 17 July 1886.
[6] Ibid.

We had agreed that the lyric part of the piece should have one metre and the dialogue part (including the chorus) should have another. And I have done it that way. The metre of the *dialogue* is an eleven-syllable line that can be divided as you wish and can, if it is divided, resolve itself into so many five-syllable lines from beginning to end. Therefore you can use either one of the two metres; I had to do it this way because an eleven-syllable line, extended in a lyrical phrase (a strict eleven-syllable line), might have come out too heavy, and a five-syllable line too light. I did not want to mix the two metres openly, preferring the device that you see; besides, it seems to me that its effect is impressive.

At this point I don't think there is anything else left for me to tell you, except to thank you again for the beautiful day at St Agata, which I shall never forget and which has reinforced all the good will I feel towards you. Many regards to Signora Giuseppina and to your sister-in-law.[7] Tomorrow I leave for *Monticello*. Here is the address: *Monza per Monticello*. That is enough; if you write to me, your letter will arrive. But in a week I'll be back in Milan again, and afterwards I am going to Lake Como. Please don't spare me, make me work! When I am working for you, I am happy.

Your most affectionate
Arrigo Boito

VERDI TO BOITO

[Milan, 27 August 1881][1]

Dear Boito,

I am in Milan, and your two letters have been forwarded to me here from Busseto.[2]—The [third act] finale is very good, extremely good. What a difference between this and the first one!

I'll add the four lines for Rodrigo.

The other four for Desdemona may be unnecessary.

It is so true that by remaining silent Otello is greater, and more terrible, so I would not let him speak at all during the entire ensemble piece. It seems to me that Jago, by himself, could say more briefly all that need be said for the audience to understand, without having Otello give an answer.

> JAG. *T'affretta! Il tempo vola! All'opra ergi tua mira! all'opra sola! Io penso a Cassio .. L'infame anima ria gli svellerò. Lo giuro. Tu avrai le sue novelle a mezzanotte.*[3]

---

[7] Barberina Strepponi.

[1] Boito's biographer Piero Nardi has unquestionably seen the postmark 'MILANO 27/8/81' on the missing envelope of this letter mailed to Monticello (see *Carteggio* ii. 309). According to *La gazzetta musicale* of 4 Sept. 1881, Verdi and his wife went to see the *Esposizione Nazionale* in Milan between the end of Aug. and 2 Sept. On 30 Aug. Verdi studied various brass instruments built by the firm of Pelitti which he visited together with Boito and Giulio Ricordi.

[2] Only Boito's letter of 24 Aug. 1881 has been found at St Agata.

[3] See Verdi to Boito, 17 July 1886. (Cf. Shakespeare, *Othello*, IV. i. 206–7.)

[JAG. *Make haste! Time flies! Set your sights on the task! Only on the task! I think about Cassio . . I'll pluck the infamous guilty soul out of him. I swear it. You will have his news at midnight.*]

(adjusting the lines, of course)

After the *ensemble* and after the words '*Tutti fuggite Otello!*' ['*Everyone flee from Otello!*'], it seems to me that Otello doesn't speak and shout enough. He is quiet for four lines, and it seems to me that (dramatically speaking) after '*Che d'ogni senso il priva*' ['*That he has been stripped of all sense*'], Otello should shout one or two lines . . . '*Fuggite. Io detesto voi, me, il mondo intero*' ['*Away. I detest you, myself, the entire world*'][4] . .

And it also seems to me that some lines could be spared when Otello and Jago remain alone.

[OTELLO.] Fuggirmi io sol non so.[5] . . . Ah l'idra! Signor vederli insieme avvinti. Ah maledetto pensiero . . Sangue Sangue . .
    (*un grido e sviene*) Il fazzoletto.

[4] In the final text (III. viii): 'Chi non si scosta è contro me rubello.' ['Who does not withdraw is rebellious against me.']
[5] In the final text (III. ix) in which Otello recalls Jago's first words 'ciò m'accora!' ['That saddens me!'] in Act II, Scene iii of the opera. (Cf. Shakespeare, *Othello*, III. iii. 35: 'Ha, I like not that.')

OTELLO (*sempre più affannoso*). Fuggirmi io sol non so! . . . Sangue! Ah! l'abbietto
  Pensiero! . . . ciò m'accora!
    (*convulsivamente, delirando*)
  Vederli insieme avvinti. . . il fazzoletto! . . .
  Ah! (*Sviene*)
JAGO. (Il mio velen lavora.)
FANFARE E VOCI (*dal di fuori*). Viva Otello!
JAGO (*ascoltando le grida, poi osservando Otello disteso a terra tramortito*). L'eco della vittoria
  Porge sua laude estrema.
    (*dopo una pausa*)
  Chi può vietar che questa fronte io prema
  Col mio tallone?
FANFARE E VOCI (*esterne più vicine*). Evviva Otello! Gloria
  Al Leon di Venezia!
JAGO (*ritto e con gesto d'orrendo trionfo, indicando il corpo inerte d'Otello*). Ecco il Leone! . . .

[OTELLO (*ever more breathless*). Only I cannot flee from myself! . . . Blood! Ah! The vile
  Thought! . . . That saddens me!
    (*convulsively, raving*)
  To see them embracing together. . . The handkerchief! . . .
  Ah! (*He faints*)
JAGO. (My poison works.)
FANFARES AND VOICES (*from without*). Long live Otello!
JAGO (*hearing the shouts, then observing Otello stretched out on the ground unconscious*)). The echo of victory
  Brings its last praise,
    (*after a pause*)
  Who can keep me from pressing upon this forehead
  With my heel?
FANFARES AND VOICES (*outside, nearer*). Long live Otello! Glory
  To the Lion of Venice!
JAGO (*standing erect and with a gesture of horrible triumph, pointing at the inert body of Otello*).
  There is the Lion! . . .]

[JAGO.] Il mio velen lavora
   Viva l'eroe di Cipro
   Chi può vietar che questa fronte io prema
   Col mio tallone
                 Gloria
   Al Leon di Venezia
                 Ecco il Leone!

[OTELLO. Only I cannot flee from myself. ... Ah, the hydra! Lord, to see them
   together embracing. Ah, cursed thought .. Blood, blood ..
      (*a scream and he faints*) The handkerchief.
JAGO. My poison works
   Long live the hero of Cyprus
   Who can keep me from pressing upon this forehead
   With my heel?
                 Glory
   To the Lion of Venice
                 Behold the Lion!]

A choked scream on the word '*fazzoletto*' would seem more terrible to me
than a scream on the common exclamation '*Oh Satana*' ['*O Satan*']. The
words '*Svenuto ... Immobil .. muto*' ['*Fainted ... Immobile .. silent*'] hold up
the action a bit. One thinks, one reflects, but here it must end rapidly. Tell me
your opinion.

I'm not finished yet! The chorus has little to do—in fact nothing. Couldn't
a way be found for them to move a bit? E.g., after the words ... '*In Cipro
elegge un successor ...... Cassio!*' ['*In Cyprus he elects a successor ......
Cassio!*'], a chorus with four lines, I wouldn't say *in revolt*, but *in protest* ...
'*Nò Nò .. noi vogliano Otello*' ['*No, no .. we want Otello*'].[6]

I know quite well you will answer me right away ... 'Dear Signor Maestro,
don't you know that no one ever dared to breathe after a decree by the
Serenissima?[7] and that sometimes the mere presence of the *Messer Grande*[8]
was enough to disperse the crowd and to quell a riot?'

I would dare to counter with the reply that the action is in Cyprus, that the
Serenissimi[9] were far away, and that because of this the Cypriots perhaps
dared more than the Venetians.

If you come to Milan I hope to see you. I don't know, but I think you have
all the poetry of the third act.

In haste addio, addio.

                                                                    G. Verdi
                                                                    Hôtel Milan

   [6] These words are not in the final text, nor is any other protest of the chorus.
   [7] The Venetian Republic.
   [8] Presumably the Doge. (Messer, literally 'My Sir', is an old Italian title awarded to eminent
clerical and secular personalities until the seventeenth century.)
   [9] The rulers of the Venetian Republic.

VERDI TO DOMENICO MORELLI

Milan, 1 September 1881

[. . .] And have you given no more thought to Jago?

I am leaving for St Agata tomorrow morning. The *Industrial* Exhibition is very beautiful and does our country much honour. The *Artistic* one is like so many others: a few nice things and many ugly ones. [. . .]

DOMENICO MORELLI TO VERDI

[Naples,?] September 1881

[. . .] Jago, easier said than done! How to paint him? Now I think that I have found him in a type of figure, in a certain face, in a proportion of, so to speak, underdeveloped limbs; then I think that he is not the Jago of the author; and I must forget the one I have cherished for so long and find another one. If Shakespeare had not made him a soldier, or at least had not made him say that he had been in a war, I would be more free to give him the stamp of a Jesuit in face and figure. And then? There is more to it: the true dramatic action of one who observes with (apparent) concern a man who is suffering. The more hypocritical he is in his iniquity, the more hidden it is, the less visible; and in painting, where everything is apparent, you know how difficult this is! [. . .]

Imagine how glad I would have been if I could have sent you a sketch made with gunpowder. But—. Now I find another problem: I had imagined this scene in a room of the fortress, since Michel's[1] translation says: *Un appartement dans le château.* And it seemed right to me that most delicate and secret matters should be discussed in a secluded place. For my painting, this is really stupendous. I would have put only a floor in the picture, and on the floor I would have had Otello stretched out. It's terrible to see a man stretched out on the ground from above. On the pavement of a street he can at first sight seem to be killed, fallen, drunk; not so in a room. And especially not so on the floor of a stately room with colourful carpets, and Otello should not be dressed as a Turk, which is an error; it's all right for him to wear something oriental, but the style should be Venetian; that is very handsome, in bright colours—(the Moors always choose bright, loud colours, never black, for their clothes). Jago is dressed in black, bending over him, about to help him, feeling sorry, but, but you understand more of what I am saying. Well then, I found in the original English text that the scene is set *before the fortress*, and in Hugo's translation *devant le château*. What shall we do? In the theatre it doesn't matter; the audience is used to considering certain changes necessary for the performance. But in a painting, the same changes might be called hideous. [. . .] What do you say to that? [. . .]

---

[1] Francisque Xavier Michel.

VERDI TO DOMENICO MORELLI

St Agata, 24 September 1881

Dear Morelli,

'What do you say to that?' are the last words of your last letter. I say that if my name were Domenico Morelli and I wanted to do a scene from *Otello*, and precisely the one where Otello faints, I wouldn't rack my brains one bit over the stage direction '*Before the fortress*'. In the libretto Boito has made for me this scene takes place *inside the castle*, and I am quite content with this. *Inside* or *outside* isn't important. In this matter one mustn't have so many scruples, since in Shaspeare's times the *mise-en-scène* was known . . . . as God wanted it!

Jago dressed in black, black as his soul—nothing could be better; but I don't understand why you would dress Otello in Venetian style! I know quite well that this general by the name of Otello in the service of the Serenissima was none other than the Venetian Giacomo Moro.[1] But since Signor William wanted to commit the bad mistake to make him a Moor, let Signor William worry about it. Otello dressed as a Turk will not do; but why not dressed as an Ethiopian without the customary turban? For the type of Jago's figure, the matter is more difficult. You would like a small figure, with underdeveloped limbs (you say), and if I understand clearly, one of those sly, malicious figures, one, I would say, 'sharp as a knife'. All right: you feel this way, do it this way. But if I were an actor and had to portray Jago, I would want to have a rather haggard, slender figure, thin lips, and small eyes close to the nose, like those of apes, a high forehead that slants backward, with the head well developed at the back. He appears distracted, nonchalant, indifferent to everything, incredulous, caustic. He speaks good and evil kind of lightly, as if not even thinking of something other than what he is saying. If anyone were to reproach him: 'What you are saying, what you are proposing is infamous!', he might answer, 'Really? I don't think so . . . , let's not talk about it any more! . . .' A figure such as this can deceive anybody—even his wife, up to a point. A small, malicious figure arouses suspicion in everyone and deceives no one! *Amen.*

You are laughing, as I am laughing, too, about this long *chatter*! But short or tall as Jago may be, and Otello as a Turk or Venetian, do as you like; it will always go well. Only don't think too much. Get on, get on, get on with it. . . . . . and quickly. . . . . .

I send you greetings from my wife, and remain

most affectionately
G. Verdi

---

[1] Verdi obviously confused the relatively insignificant Cristoforo Moro (fl. 1500)—possibly the model of Cinzio Giraldi's hero, on whom Shakespeare based *Othello*—with the historically more important procurator Giacomo Moro who died in 1377. (See Boito to Verdi, 6 and 16 May 1886, and Appendix II.)

VERDI TO CLARA MAFFEI

St Agata, 29 October 1881

Dear Clarina,

A thousand thanks for your note of 25 October![1] But do you know what 25 October means at La Scala? It means that I am old (and that is unfortunately true) and a veteran put among the invalids! Be that as it may ... It was an error on my part, and on the part of others! I deplored it and I still deplore it[2] ... [...]

Here all is going as usual. I am occupied with fields, buildings, and land, and so the day goes by without, perhaps, my doing anything useful, spending a lot of money ... and without anyone's thanking me for it! ... So goes the world, so did it go, and so did it always go; and I let it go ... [...]

GIULIO RICORDI TO VERDI

Milan, 2 November 1881

Illustrious Maestro,

Poor Maestro! ... I have just returned from the country, and here I am already tormenting you with telegrams and letters; my office is absolutely destined to have you regard it as a nuisance!!

Now then, to get down to business: as I telegraphed you,[1] the management of La Scala insists upon the revival of *Boccanegra*, a revival most hoped for by the public, as well. The cast seems good to me, and I repeat, the only point to be considered is the comparison with Maurel.

For the soprano, la Borelli would be well worth engaging, since she gave a very fine account of herself in the recent autumn season; she has a lovely voice, is quite intelligent, and would altogether gain by comparison with la D'Angeri.

Tenor: Marin,[2] first-rate artist.

Bass: Nannetti—id. id.

Two baritones have been engaged: Aldighieri and Battistini. We need not talk about the first; the second is young, intelligent, with a beautiful voice: in Rome, Turin, Florence he has had real success; Ponchielli, who heard him, tells me a lot of good things about him; if I remember well, he came to two performances of *Boccanegra* last year. All the information I have agrees with this, and as a person, as well as for the quality of his voice, he is generally judged superior to Kaschmann. He is now in Buenos-Ayres. [...] Moriami:

[1] In reference to the unveiling of Verdi's statue together with Bellini's in the entrance hall of La Scala on 25 Oct.
[2] Verdi stayed away from the ceremony, of course. (See Boito to Verdi, 31 Mar. and 4 Apr., and Verdi to Boito, 2 Apr. 1881.)

[1] Missing.
[2] Sang Manrico in a single performance of *Il trovatore* at La Scala in 1883.

as an actor he would be splendid, but is his voice suitable for the role? . . . For another theatre Moriami, very good; but for La Scala? . . There are pros and cons.

I do not know if I told you that *Boccanegra* has been requested of us for Naples and Turin; in Naples they don't have a cast and have a very poor conductor; in Turin there might be a cast; but, alas, I would not be happy with Pedrotti grown old and nervous by now; yet even Pedrotti would work out very well if Maestro Verdi were there to direct; but dare I make such a proposal?

In these circumstances *Boccanegra* would have to be given up for next season, should it not be feasible for La Scala. This would be a real pity from an artistic point of view, of course! . . .

What is your view of all this? . . . And what would you say is the best advice for us to follow?

If *Boccanegra* were decided upon, this year's season at La Scala might be assured, as well, with *Guglielmo Tell, Boccanegra, Hérodiade, Nabucco*,[3] *Sonnambula*, and perhaps a new opera by a young fellow, Smareglia from whom I do not expect much of anything. [. . .]

VERDI TO GIULIO RICORDI

St Agata, 5 November 1881

Dear Giulio,

I, too, have heard good things about Battistini, and if it's really as you say, I would not hesitate to compare him with Maurel. La Borelli, for what little she may be, will always be better than la D'Angeri. For the *Maria*, I believe the part is too high, and I would not like to embark upon the systems of transposing, which is as ugly a practice as one can find in theatrical performances. Let's not talk about Nanetti. But you have forgotten the most important parts! I say *important*, and I'm not joking. Pietro and Paolo[1] are parts for two actors who really should be actors. At La Scala these parts were very badly performed, as were all the others except Boccanegra. Somehow the Paolo managed to get through; but the Pietro was very poor, in his singing as well as his acting. So let me know in any case who the two *apostles* would be. Let's conclude: If you cannot get *Kaschmann* or this Battistini (after new information, however), don't think about *Boccanegra* at all. Moriami an excellent Barnaba, perhaps a good Jago; never, never a Boccanegra at La Scala or any other theatre. It would be bad for him, too!! My dear Giulio, come on! Just think for a moment of the cantabili in the

---

[3] Replaced by *Les Huguenots*.

---

[1] Verdi had already written to Piave on 9 Feb. 1857 concerning the original version of *Simon Boccanegra*: 'The role of Paolo is very important; there is absolute need for a baritone who should be a good actor; bad casting of that role could jeopardize the opera. He must absolutely be found!' (*Carteggi* ii. 352.)

prologue, of the duet with the daughter, the solo in the finale .. the trio, the entire scene '*il mare il mare*' ['the sea, the sea'] .. the duet with Fieschi, the benediction when he dies! Good heavens!! .

To sum up, *Boccanegra* was so poorly given last year, with inappropriate artists,[2] that I would not hesitate to revive it this year, provided that this time the artists, even with lesser names, are more suitable for the parts they must perform.—

If you give *Boccanegra*, why give *Nabucco*? The Old Testament with the New Testament! One Testament is enough!! Then again, *Nabucco* is not so easy. The part of Abigaille is most difficult to perform. It's not enough to have soul and sentiment; a real actress is needed. As for the *Boccanegras* in Naples and Turin, I wouldn't know what advice to give you. Certainly I would go neither to Naples nor to Turin. I am really tired of putting myself on display and showing my face to the audience. And now that you have put me among the dead, they would take me for a ghost. [. . .]

GIULIO RICORDI TO VERDI

Milan, 10 November 1881

Illustrious Maestro,

I waited a couple of days to answer your most esteemed letter in order to accomplish things better and to deal with your comments.

About Battistini all the information is in agreement, and he absolutely seems to be an artist worthy of La Scala; so there we are.

Marin's repertoire in particular consists of *Lucia, Hugueonots, Guglielmo Tell*, and this artist would even have wanted to make his début in either of the last two of these operas; in this case he could easily sing the part of Gabriele. As for Paolo, I think I have found an excellent interpreter in De Bernis,[1] incomparably better than Salvati, and I hope I still have time to have him engaged. Concerning the part of Pietro you are perfectly right, and I maintain that it will be easy to find a better one than last year's *clod*. As for the production, we shall follow exactly what you have done, but I will see if it is possible to improve the scene in the last act and give it greater effect, after the experience of the past season. [. . .]

PS To return to Moriami, I had the very same ideas as you; yet on his account I heard *Boccanegra* this summer, and I was surprised, since I didn't think that Moriami would be able to phrase so well; I also noticed that he is a very learned man! [. . .]

---

[2] Verdi refers to the revision of *Simon Boccanegra* at La Scala on 24 Mar. 1881, the same year of this writing. His negative judgement of that première is a sharp contradiction to the praise he expressed to Arrivabene in his letter of 25 Mar. 1881.

---

[1] Appeared at La Scala in 1881 as Gonzales in *Il guarany*.

GIULIO RICORDI TO VERDI

Milan, 18 November 1881

Illustrious Maestro,

[. . .] For *Boccanegra* I have taken, and will continue to take, all imaginable precautions. La Borelli has been engaged; De Bernis (Paolo), who I feared would run away, was also engaged the day before yesterday; only Pietro is lacking. In any event I reserve for myself full freedom in the contract not to make final decisions regarding the artists until all the companies (first and second) have made their début—then I shall choose. In principle only these performers are being considered: Borelli, Marin, Battistini, De Bernis and Nannetti.

Regarding the *staging* of the last act, I do not mean the action on stage, but rather the lighting. Oil-lamps—which take a long time to be prepared, stink when extinguished, and are dangerous—would be replaced by gas, improving the entire effect of the lighting of the city and the ships. You will recall that this last scene did not fully satisfy you; but with the limited time we had it was not possible to change or improve it; so that this time, I hope, your wishes shall be better realized.[1] All the other sets are in good order, and I am especially pleased with the very beautiful council chamber. [. . .]

VERDI TO GIULIO RICORDI

Genoa, 24 November 1881

Dear Giulio,

I have been here for two days. If you need to write to me, use the address Genoa.

Settle everything before putting *Boccanegra* on the boards. Don't be trusting.

The lighting of the fourth act was very poor! If you change it you will be doing a very good thing! As for the *mise-en-scène*, don't clutter the stage any further.—Let's hope you will have somewhat better actors than last year! Then you can succeed in doing something, especially during the off-stage chorus in the third act finale. The tenor and soprano have something to do. They must be made to move more! With the others it was impossible!

It's not unlikely that I shall come with Peppina to Milan one of these days . .

1. Because I have various bills to settle;
2. Because Peppina will have some rags to mend . . .

And even in Faccio's absence I would like to establish (I don't mean *establish*), I would like to find out what will be done to reform the orchestra of La Scala. If there is something to be done, or better, if there is something that one wants to do, it would be well to do it now. I would not want to be

---

[1] See the following letter and Verdi to Ricordi, 18 Feb. 1881, n. 1.

compelled to speak up later on! Never, never! I would sooner renounce everything!

With you and Boito as members of the Commission we could understand each other.

Yours,
G. Verdi

GIULIO RICORDI TO VERDI

Milan, 26 November 1881

Illustrious Maestro,

It goes without saying how much pleasure I have taken in your announcement that you are likely to be travelling to Milan with the splendid Signora Peppina; it is always a feast for us to see you.

On the question of the orchestra I have, in fact, been awaiting Faccio's arrival; but nothing could be better than to settle it right away, together with Boito, while you are here. I am sure that there will be no obstacle on the part of the management, which would have to engage some musicians or increase salaries, or on the part of the Board of Directors; very much to the contrary. You will remember that La Scala owes to you a good big drum and excellent kettledrums; now it will owe to you this improvement in the orchestra, too, and if it does not want this to be known, we shall keep it *inter nos*! [. . .]

VERDI TO GIULIO RICORDI

Genoa, 3 December 1881

Dear Giulio,

Tuesday, just when we wanted to come to Milan, Peppina was hit hard by her usual stomach cramps. She is better now, but is still in bed. Strict diet, and therefore extreme weakness. I couldn't tell you when she might be recovered enough to undertake this little trip, nor do I know if she will be able to make it. I am sorry, because even in Faccio's absence, as I told you, I would have liked to talk with Boito and you about the changes to be made in the orchestra. Either they are made now or not at all.—In all that was said in the Committee there was too much theory and too little practice. It was pointless to spend so much time, and so many words, on those *four* vibrations of the diapason. By splitting hairs in this way only new problems are created. In the theatre problems arise at every step, and woe betide him who does not have the talent to ward them off.

I am not happy with the Committee's provisions
  1. For the double-basses
  2. For the French horns
  3. For the trombones, etc.—
I would have comments on other matters, but those mentioned above are

the principal ones, and instead of correcting old abuses you have done nothing else but add new ones.

I repeat that this was the moment to deal with them, also because it's the first time the orchestra will meet again after the Committee's deliberations. Later on we would no longer be in time, nor would I want to have my say later on. Either now or never! *Never* would be bad, after the stir that has been made about the need to change the orchestra; a great, enormous need. [. . .]

GIULIO RICORDI TO VERDI

Milan, 4 December 1881

Illustrious Maestro,

Your letter, with its news that Signora Peppina's indisposition still persists, has brought us the deepest regret. Let us hope for her early and complete recovery [. . .] and that your trip to Milan may soon be realized.

Your coming would really be most useful in settling the matter of the orchestra. If I am not mistaken, two points are especially important for the orchestra: that of the bass-trombone (already approved by you at Pelitti's) and that of the double-basses with 4 strings. One of the good musicians, Mottelli,[1] has already played the double-bass with 4 strings and owns a large instrument that formerly, *in illo tempore*, had 4 strings, then was reduced to 3. I have since talked with Mottelli, who arranged right away to have his instrument changed back to 4 strings. [. . .]

You already know that Boito and I are completely at your disposal; I also think that Faccio will be here on the 10th of the month, which is not very far off. [. . .]

VERDI TO GIULIO RICORDI

Genoa, 5 December 1881

Dear Giulio,

I am replying to your letter at once, because I see that I did not make myself clear.

It's a question of far more than the bass-trombone and Mottelli's double-bass.—It's a question of *all* the double-basses. It's a question of *all* the trombones. It's a question of the *French horns*. It's a question of the *tuning*, and other matters of lesser importance.

I will not hear Mottelli's double-bass, because I know what double-basses with four strings are like; and because I must not, nor do I want to, concern myself with the orchestra of La Scala. I can express my opinion privately to

[1] Unknown.

Boito or Faccio, but nothing more than that. If I come to Milan we'll talk about it, even though I can already see that nothing will be done.

Peppina is much better. She thanks you and greets you.

In haste, addio

G. Verdi

GIULIO RICORDI TO VERDI

Milan, 6 December 1881

Illustrious Maestro,

I see that I, too, to my great regret, did not make myself clear; after the first session of the Congress I was sick in bed and no longer took part in any discussions; from you and Boito I found out only what concerned the bass-trombone; I therefore ignored any other changes you might have advised. I spoke of the bass-trombone because I believe that the other 3 trombones are already equal to the established ones in the orchestra; an easy thing to check.

Since I know what your other ideas are, in the unfortunate event that you do not come to Milan, I could give you an exact answer on the subject; and I repeat again that it is neither difficult nor impossible to introduce all desirable improvements into the orchestra. [. . .]

VERDI TO OPPRANDINO ARRIVABENE

Genoa, 8 December 1881

[. . .] I know that you have been in Urbino, and I envy you. For a long time I, too, have wanted to see these little towns like Urbino, Loreto, Arezzo, Perugia, etc., where there are so many artistic wonders; but I have never been able to find the time. I'm not doing a thing, absolutely nothing (I see many Jagos, but I'm not working on one of my own); in spite of this, the day goes by, and I couldn't tell you how it goes by and how it can go by in this way. [. . .]

The last page of your letter[1] gave me the shivers. The German is right, absolutely right. Yes, we no longer have any literature or art or sciences of our own. Everything is foreign, and already we are two-thirds not Italian any more, not even politically. I feel real desolation when I think about our condition; and a symptom of our decadence is the indifference with which insults from everybody are tolerated! .. Hated by France, scorned for now, and later on hated, by Germany, not liked by anyone, what can we hope for? [. . .]

[1] Missing.

VERDI TO OPPRANDINO ARRIVABENE

Genoa, 23 December 1881

Dear Arrivabene,

I have been in Milan, just for three days, without carrying music with me, without writing any, and without even talking about it, although I saw Faccio, Boito, Ricordi, and the whole musical coterie! . . . What do you say to that? It doesn't seem true, but it is so. Meanwhile, it seems, the slight exertion of the trip has been rather good for Peppina, and she almost doesn't feel her stomach cramps any more. Last night I came back from St Agata, where I had been for two days. You will say, what the devil am I doing in the country? But you know (I don't know, by the way, if I ever wrote this to you) that I am building; that last year I built a dairy, this year two that are even larger; and that there are about two hundred labourers who have been working up to now, and to whom I have had to give instructions for future work, as soon as the frost permits. These are useless works for me, since these buildings won't give me another cent of income from the land, but in the meantime the people are earning money and aren't emigrating from my village.

I won't speak or respond to you about the electoral reform, the Senate, the Chamber, etc. . . . These things give me the shivers! . . . And for my part, I hope for nothing any more, even in our rotten days! [. . .]

GIULIO RICORDI TO GIUSEPPINA VERDI

Milan, 31 December 1881

[. . .] What, then, will this blessed '82 be like, on whose doors we are about to knock? . . . For myself I can make only a single wish, since it would include all the happiest and dearest wishes I could hope for; and that is to see our Verdi at the *Hôtel de Milan*! . . . But alas! . . . it seems to me that the chocolate is still not prepared; and for me this idea makes a bad ending to the dying '81, and a worse beginning of the new '82! [. . .]

GIUSEPPINA VERDI TO GIULIO RICORDI

Genoa, 1 January 1882

[. . .] I don't know if Verdi will come to the Hôtel Milan, but as for preparing the chocolate needed for the Hôtel, although there seems to be nothing wrong with the wood, the will to light the fire is missing . . . and even if there were a grain of will, it disappears upon reading certain observations about such things, for instance, as agricultural activities, lawyers, a suit to obtain water rights, etc., etc.

Perhaps these pressures of yours are flattering, but in the long run they are still pressures. Apparently the writer does not know Verdi, who states that he is sixty-eight years old and, having worked so much, thinks he has the right to enjoy a life of retirement.

Let the water run down the slope, and who knows whether one day or another, without pressure, he might not present the newborn child (including the missing piece) in the dark little baby[1] whose delicious contours we are gobbling up. [. . .]

VERDI TO OPPRANDINO ARRIVABENE

Genoa, 5 January 1882

Dear Arrivabene,

I'm anxious to tell you that it was not I who established that pension for the poor of Busseto. My wife had a house in Busseto[1] and running it became an annoyance to her; she sold it and assigned a part of that sum for pensions to be given *in perpetuo* to several poor people.

I don't have time to answer you at length about Berlioz and *L'Hérodiade*[2] . . . Berlioz was a poor sick man, angry with everybody, acid and malign. A great and keen mind; he had a feeling for orchestration and preceded Wagner in many orchestral effects. (The Wagnerians don't agree, but it is so.) He had no moderation and lacked that calm and, I would say, that balance which produces complete works of art. He always went too far, even when he did laudable things. The present successes in Paris are largely just and deserved, but there is still a great deal of reaction in them. He was so mistreated when he was alive!!! Now he is dead! Hosanna!!! I don't think that *L'Hérodiade* is of greater value than the *Roi de Lahore*.[3] There is no greater degree of invention. Good workmanship and scenic pomp. There is an obstacle that in my opinion is hard to overcome: *St John* making love to *Salomé*. This I can't stomach! But the audience sometimes drinks heavy stuff! We'll see! . . .

I greet you in haste. Affectionately

G. Verdi

[1] The Ricordi family had sent the traditional *panettone*, a Milanese cake, to the Verdis for Christmas. This time the cake was topped with a chocolate figure representing Otello, a piece of whose anatomy was missing.

[1] Verdi had sold the Palazzo Dordoni-Cavalli, which he had bought in 1845, to Giuseppina Strepponi before she became his wife. He had lived there with her on and off between 1849 and 1852, but absolutely reliable dates of their occupancy have not been established. (See Verdi Chronology, 1845 and 1849–51; see also the Biographical Note on Giuseppina Verdi Strepponi.) The former Palazzo Dordoni-Cavalli, now Palazzo Orlandi, has recently been restored to its neoclassical splendour.

[2] Opera in 4 acts by Jules Massenet (1842–1912).

[3] Opera in 5 acts by Jules Massenet.

VERDI TO DOMENICO MORELLI

Genoa, 5 January 1882

[...] And Jago? What have you done with him? Have you thought about him? Yes, you did think about him, since you've also written to me concerning him. I answered you in the oddest of all my past and future letters![1] I expressed ideas that certainly weren't yours; but I believe, and hope, that you paid no attention to them and went straight ahead down your own path. Only I'd like to know whether you have walked down this path; and I'd also like to know how many steps—no, how many metres and how many kilometres—you have covered. I'm afraid of the answer, but let me have it anyway.

Yours most affectionately,
G. Verdi

GIULIO RICORDI TO VERDI

Milan, 18 January 1882

Illustrious Maestro,
   Two lines to let you know that the string for the piano was posted today, and to tell you that last night 5 double-basses with 4 strings made their triumphal entry into the orchestra, and that they work very well. [...]

VERDI TO GIULIO RICORDI

Genoa, 8 February 1882

[...] You are proceeding too slowly with the reforms of the orchestra! Is the bass-trombone still not ready?
   For God's sake, let's leave the *chocolate* and Desdemona and Jago in peace. [...]

GIULIO RICORDI TO VERDI

Milan, 27 February 1882

[P.S.] Today the *Boccanegra* rehearsals begin;[1] in a few days I shall give you exact news.

[1] On 24 Sept. 1881.

---

[1] For a reprise at La Scala on 18 Mar.

TITO RICORDI TO VERDI

Milan, 2 March 1882

[. . .] Heaven help me if Verdi does not compose! He is the only one to follow the straight and narrow path, the only one who interests and moves us. In short, as my wife puts it so well: Only from you do we await the resurrection of music. How right my Giulio is to be worried about the future in every respect, if you should not allow your immense [illegible] genius to shine once more!

For pity's sake, then, send me to the devil if you want; but let me once again, with hands clasped, implore you to make the decision to compose. Only then will there be any life for us all. I am not asking for any promise whatsoever—just a little hope is enough to free us from this discouragement.

Now I am anxious to enjoy your *Boccanegra*, which shall certainly heal the wounds of the poor management. [. . .]

GIULIO RICORDI TO VERDI

Milan, 13 March 1882

[. . .] I am happy to give you the very good news that the *Boccanegra* rehearsals are proceeding in full sail, and with such *entrain* that it seems as though the opera was performed only eight days ago. The first performance is planned for Saturday; kindly tell me if you will be in Genoa on Sunday so that I can send you exact news right away.

This morning and evening, stage rehearsals. Maurel is in good voice; all the others are doing very well, above all Nannetti, who will be a first-rate Fiesco. The Signori Pietro and Paolo good! [. . .]

VERDI TO GIULIO RICORDI

Genoa, 14 March 1882

[. . .] Well then, you are so far ahead with the rehearsals for *Boccanegra*? I wish you good luck . . . but this theatre of yours is so run-down, so badly set up, in such a *sad state of decay* that it cannot be trusted. . Let it be as you wish, but at least a decisive success or fiasco. Today this most pretentious audience can no longer *boo* or *applaud*. It's supposed to become knowledgeable, and it becomes . . . you say it.

Write or telegraph here directly. I'll let you know if I leave. Addio, addio

Yours,
G. Verdi

TITO RICORDI TO VERDI

Milan, 17 March 1882

[. . .] Yesterday I was at the rehearsal of your *Simon Boccanegra*. My God, what music! I really felt as if I'd been reborn to a new life, and noticed the same feeling in everybody who attended the rehearsal. Maurel is even better than last year; he is really sublime! Nannetti very good and also Mierzwinski. La Borelli sang well but was a bit cold. Let us hope she will do as she did in *Hérodiade*, where she was impassive at the rehearsals but in the performance showed herself a passionate and intelligent artist. Paolo also good. Orchestra and chorus excellent. In short, I do not doubt one bit that tomorrow night we shall attend a feast of the very kind that the unique Verdi alone can produce! [. . .]

GIULIO RICORDI TO VERDI

Milan, 25 March 1882

[. . .] I am confirming my telegrams[1] concerning *Boccanegra*, and repeat: *great, genuine triumph*! . . . *absolute.*
   Tonight, third performance, and perhaps tomorrow fourth. [. . .]
   Bass-trombone very good.

OPPRANDINO ARRIVABENE TO VERDI

Rome, 26 March 1882

[. . .] Is it true that they sent you a cake from Milan with a nice question mark on top? If that mark is real, it will ask you what *point Jago* has reached. You will certainly not be working on it for as long as Boito is taking for his *Nerone*. You have already shown that you don't need to wait for inspiration for entire years. The new and most incontestable triumph that your *Boccanegra* has now achieved in Milan must be an incentive for you to respond before long to that very sweet interrogative.
   As for Boito: I hear with regret that he is not very well. If the definition he gave is true that he is a Sarah Bernhardt[1] of a different sex, what will happen if he is ill? As for his intrinsic merit as a composer I have heard many opinions, in each of which I have found an observation that has remained in my mind. I see that almost all these observations of intelligent and also benevolent men are wrapped up now in an *if*, now in a *but*; I see them summarized on the opinion I am enclosing of a highly esteemed German critic.[2] Of course, I would like the German to be wrong, and [I wish] that we

---

[1] Missing.

[1] The celebrated French actress was known to be a flighty and temperamental hypochondriac.
[2] The enclosure is missing; Verdi probably discarded it. The German critic seems to have been Eduard Hanslick. (See Appendix IV.)

could await some noble and great creation from Boito, and not just a work of one who is *crazy about the project*; but unfortunately I fear that the German is right. [. . .]

GIULIO RICORDI TO GIUSEPPINA VERDI

Milan, 6 April 1882

[. . .] I am confirming my telegram of this morning;[1] these have been ten really memorable nights,[2] also in view of the greatest interest and enthusiasm on the audience's part.

To tell the truth, the Corti brothers, for all their faults, have done themselves honour, scrupulously fulfilling their obligations throughout a very difficult season. [. . .]

VERDI TO CLARA MAFFEI

St Agata, 23 April 1882

Dear Clarina,

Your letter has been forwarded to me here in my desert, where *je m'amuse* by being a bit of an architect, a bit of a mason, and much of a farmer. In the midst of these everyday things, your letter had to be doubly welcome to me. [. . .]

Peppina is in Genoa to put the house in order, and it's not certain, but very likely, that upon my return to Genoa we'll leave for Paris. Oh, I'm not going there to enjoy myself!

[You ask] if I remember Manzoni[1] and when I saw him for the first time?

Sarah[2] is truly an artist. She has an extraordinary talent. Herself, and again herself, and always herself, even in the defects some people think they find.

Addio, my dear Clarina. Think always kindly of your old friend.

G. Verdi

GIULIO RICORDI TO VERDI

Milan, 27 May 1882

[. . .] Concerning *Boccanegra*, the two managers in Turin and Naples came to Milan expressly to negotiate, and I would not have bothered you with this if I had not seen the possibility of agreements. . . . Of course, there is no point in telling you that they have consulted me about Turin as well as Naples, and

---

[1] Missing.

[2] Of performances of *Simon Boccanegra* at La Scala.

---

[1] On 30 June 1868 Clara Maffei had brought about Verdi's one and only meeting with Alessandro Manzoni (1785–1873), Italy's great poet of the Risorgimento. Verdi spoke of him as a saint and wrote the *Requiem* in his memory.

[2] Sarah Bernhardt.

especially about Naples—because your presence would be required; therefore I did not want to assume any obligation whatsoever. I believe it to be my duty, however, to tell you this, in case you might have instructions to give me in the matter.

To return to *Boccanegra*, let me also inform you that there is talk of it for Rome, at the Costanzi in the autumn, and for Genoa, at the Carlo Felice during the Carnival season; in regard to this latter theatre please tell me whether I may negotiate, if the management should be in touch with us, or whether I should decline straight away—this, because I would not like you to suffer nuisances of any kind during the time your home is in Genoa.

So if no problems arise, *Boccanegra* would start on his own triumphal way. Now I await your decisions, that I may know how to proceed. [. . .]

BOITO TO VERDI

Villa d'Este (Lago di Como)
10 August [1882][1]

Dear Maestro,

As early as two months ago the Baron Blaze de Bury made a request of me through his wife, whom I had known in Paris. The request amounts to this (I transcribe): '*Un jour ou l'autre le* Jago *existera et par conséquant sera donné içi* [in Paris] *sur la scène de l'Opéra*' etc. . . . To get to the point, Blaze de Bury charges his wife, the Baroness,[2] to ask me to ask you, Maestro, to give him, on that '*jour ou l'autre*', the right to make the French translation of *Otello*.

'*Vous trouverez je pense Verdi très favorable à cet arrangement dont Vous pouvez lui parler tout de suite*'. So continues the Signora, but the '*tout de suite*' has been such that her letter is dated 22 June, and I am carrying out the mission today (11 August).

For a number of reasons I haven't been in any hurry to fulfil Blaze de Bury's wish. First of all, Maestro, I did not know where you would be during this period; I only knew that you were no longer in Genoa and that you weren't at St Agata, either,[3] and this I wrote truthfully to the Baroness to explain my delay. Another reason: for all the value of this proposal, which comes from a highly cultured man and an artist at heart, whom I esteem and consider the most authoritative critic in France, I thought that the proposal was ill-timed, and therefore I was in no hurry to carry out my mission. But I didn't mention this consideration to the Baroness, since I did not feel authorized to judge for the Signora whether the proposal was opportune or inopportune; you, Maestro, are the only judge of this. In another letter, however, [the Baroness] Blaze de Bury repeats the request, and this time . . . , and this time, in order to answer, I must go to the source, and I can no longer say that I do not know where Verdi is staying.

[1] Postmark: CERNOBBIO 11/8/82.
[2] See Biographical Note on Henry Blaze de Bury.
[3] From 18 June until early July, Verdi and his wife were at the Montecatini spa in Tuscany.

Therefore, I beg you, Maestro, to drop me a line about this question; or if you prefer, to drop a line to Blaze de Bury himself, who lives in Paris, *rue Oudinot 20*. To me it's all the same, as long as a *yes* or *no*, or *later*, or *perhaps* is said. I would not want this renowned French writer to think I have shown bad faith in this matter. Actually I have, but not in the sense that he (whom I admire) might think, since I have shown *good faith* by not bothering you, Maestro; for I know from experience that when a work is not finished, any word or act is annoying which seems to come with the intention of forcing that work out of the mind, which is itself examining and measuring and which alone knows the way that points to its goal. Yet from all these indications one sees with how much feverish desire this opera is awaited in France; and if this is so in France, the haughtiest of nations and the least of our friends, think what it must be here and elsewhere. Enough, however; I have said too much already.

By the way, you complained about a line that contained the word *arce* as being too contrived. Unless my memory fails me, the line read:

E l'*arce* ascesa alla breccia fatal   [And the *fortress* climbed to the fatal gap].

I believe this is easily corrected by changing the word *ascesa* to a noun, e.g.:

E l'aspra ascesa e la breccia fatal   [*And the rough ascent and the fatal gap*].[4]

See if this would go with the sense of the preceding line.

Giulio Ricordi is in Trescorre[5] for the treatment of a hand that is bothering him.

I'll be staying at the Villa d'Este until the 28th of this month; then I'll pay a visit to a Benedictine brother by the name of Guido d'Arezzo.[6] I still do not know Tuscany (what a shame!), and this will be a good occasion to get to know it.

Many affectionate greetings to the House of St Agata and to its dear inhabitants.

Your
Arrigo Boito

VERDI TO BOITO

Busseto, 16 August 1882
St Agata

Dear Boito,

'*Un jour ou l'autre* Jago (it isn't *Jago*) *existera*' .... I am surprised that the Baron can be so sure, since I ... I personally do not know if it '*existera*'. I am

[4] In the final text (I. iii): 'E il vol gagliardo alla breccia mortal' ['And the bold flight into the deadly breach']. (Cf. Shakespeare, *Othello*, I. iii. 136: 'Of hair-breadth scapes i'th'imminent deadly breach.')

[5] Presumably Trescorre Balneario, a thermal spa near Bergamo. (See *Carteggio* ii. 312.)

[6] For celebrations in honour of the music theorist and inventor of the musical staves (c.990–1050), Luigi Mancinelli composed a hymn tune to a text by Boito and conducted *Mefistofele* in Arezzo. He also introduced his 16-year-old protégé Ferruccio Busoni to Boito on that occasion.

also greatly surprised that a man of letters of Blaze de Bury's distinction, the most authoritative critic in France, as you say, wants to condemn himself to a real chore by translating an opera from Italian into French, which is even harder than from French into Italian. We have unrhymed verse, while they are bound to rhyme and to the masculine–feminine couplet, one after the other, so that they can hardly keep the literary sense together with the musical phrase and accent. For that matter, a few months ago I said to the translator of one of my operas, '*Why do you make the lines rhyme in the recitatives and the dramatic moments?*' But the nature of their poetry doesn't allow them—or at least no one dares—to use *vers blanc*.[1]

But I repeat, why talk about an opera that doesn't exist? An opera that will be Italian in scale and will have who knows how many other (Earth, open wide!) things Italian? . . Perhaps a couple of melodies . . (if they can be found) . . And the melody will always be Italian, essentially Italian, and it cannot be anything but Italian, no matter where it may come from. Furthermore: it's an opera that will have no *mise-en-scène*! and no ballet! Imagine: an opera at the *Opéra* without a ballet!!![2] I add yet another opinion of mine, and this one is particularly my own, and it is that I am convinced, completely convinced, that a real success with a new kind of music is impossible at the *Opéra* as that theatre is at present. The reason lies, I think, in the acoustics, the splendour, the beauty of that monument. Am I wrong? Possibly, but until I see a success I won't change my mind.

Meanwhile, write to the Baron as you think best. Happy to have your news after such a long time, I remain

Ever yours affectionately,
G. Verdi

BOITO TO VERDI

Villa d'Este [17–18 August 1882][1]

Dear Maestro,

There is telepathy in the air: just before I received your letter, I was writing to my French translator[2] the same criticisms you have about the prosody of those neighbours of ours, and in almost the same words, talking about *vers blanc* in the very same way and about the masculine and feminine endings, and coming to the same conclusion.

I also felt the same astonishment you did at the Baron's proposal. I shall answer him this very day, without mentioning this astonishment; I shall limit my answer to a pure and simple sentence, like the order of the day in our

---

[1] Blank, i. e. unrhymed verse.
[2] The ironclad tradition of the Paris Opéra required a ballet in every opera.

---

[1] Presumably Boito did not delay this answer to Verdi's preceding letter.
[2] The co-librettist of Massenet's *Werther* and *Thaïs* Paul Milliet (1858–?), who translated *Mefistofele*.

worthy chamber. The sentence will be: '*The Maestro is writing* Otello (or
Jago, whatever) *especially with a view towards Italy, such a vigorously Italian
subject.*' .... No, here the sentence goes awry; if I mention Italy once more
the good relations between the two countries could also go awry. I will simply
say that you do not think the opera you are writing will ever have the
necessary scale and form that are traditional at the *Opéra*. And that is
enough.

Forgive the trouble I have caused you. Having guessed how you would feel
about it, I did all I could to save you from it, but in the long run I wasn't able
to do so. I am consoled by the thought that if this nuisance has struck you
once, it has struck me three times in three letters which (including today's) I
have written to the Baron's wife, who is certainly a very intelligent lady, but
not beautiful, and not young, either. And to me the writing of letters is
always a most tormenting nuisance, except when I write to St Agata ... or to
the Palazzo d'Oria,[3] or to my brother, or some rare, good and faithful friend.
Then this chattering with the pen might never end, but continue as easily as
now, and as pleasantly.

Give my very, very best regards to Signora Giuseppina.

Your most affectionate
Arrigo Boito

GIULIO RICORDI TO VERDI

Milan, 14 October 1882

[. . .] *Simon Boccanegra* will now be given in Naples, Rome and Turin; and if
the miserable subsidies to other theatres had not prevented the engagement
of at least fairly good artists, it could have been arranged in a few other cities,
too; but really! .... not a single acceptable name was presented to me! [. . .]

VERDI TO BARON LEOPOLD FRIEDRICH VON HOFMANN

St Agata, 31 October 1882

Most gratified by your very esteemed letter,[1] I consider it my duty to
confirm what Signor Ricordi has written to you. I am actually working on
the changes to *Don Carlos*, reducing it to shorter proportions, in four acts. It
is a tedious and rather long task, but it will soon be completely finished, and
you may have it performed when you think it opportune and convenient.

I will be extremely grateful to you for the telegram that you promise me
after the first performance of *Simon Boccanegra*.[2] [. . .]

---

[3] The Palazzo Doria in Genoa, where the Verdis occupied an apartment during the winter
months from 1874 until 1896. See Appendix I, n. 19 for Boito's antique spelling.

---

[1] Missing.
[2] The Hofoper in Vienna gave the first performance of *Simon Boccanegra* in German on 18
Nov. 1882, but no such telegram has been located.

GIULIO RICORDI TO VERDI

Milan, 17 November 1882

[. . .] I am waiting for news about the *Boccanegra* rehearsals in Rome, where I had planned to go to assure myself that all goes well; I am not sure as yet whether I can realize this plan, depending on my doctor's permission; but if I go on like this I hope to be able to go to Rome to insist that the opera be performed and staged in the best possible way. [. . .]

GIULIO RICORDI TO VERDI

Milan, 10 December 1882

[. . .] The financial catastrophe of the Costanzi[1] prevented the performance of *Boccanegra*, which was for the best, in view of the troubles of the management. [. . .]

Yesterday Maurel arrived; it seems to me that this management [of La Scala] is over-confident in counting on him to open the theatre on a given day! . . . and even on St Stephen's Day.[2] Great artist! . But you know his caprices better than I, his whims, etc., etc.! [. . .]

VERDI TO CLARA MAFFEI

Genoa, 16 December 1882

Dear Clarina,

Oh, the papers, the papers!! Some of what they have said is true, and much is false. Since you mention it to me, I think I should tell you how things are; the simple truth.

1. It is not at all true that for two years I have been having a building constructed for a hospital. In these last years I have had several farm buildings built, but it would take much good will to believe that the barns and big sheds would serve as a hospital.

2. Busseto does not need a hospital. It has one of its own, which would also be well provided for, if it were well administered.

So this does not concern Busseto, but the tiny little community of Villanova, which consists of four villages, among them St Agata, where I live, with a total population of about six thousand inhabitants. The little community is part of the Province of Piacenza, and the poor people who get sick have only the hospital in Piacenza. The distance is 34 or 36 kilometres, and the poor sick people (not all, but many) die on the way.

I proposed to the mayor of this little community that he buy, at my

---

[1] The Teatro Costanzi in Rome, named after its wealthy builder and inaugurated on 27 Nov. 1880; renovated in 1926 and renamed Teatro Reale dell'Opera, it was reopened with Boito's *Nerone* on 28 Feb. 1928 and became the Teatro dell'Opera in 1946.

[2] 26 Dec., at that time the traditional opening night of La Scala's opera season.

expense, a small piece of land in a suitable location, where I would have a little building constructed, a shelter, something, I don't know what, for these people, with no pretence of doing anything of importance and of the proportions described by the papers: first, because it would be useless for such a small population; second, because I really, really, really couldn't do it. To you I can say frankly that my fortune, about which I don't complain at all, is not as great as the papers have sometimes reported. Oh, always the papers!!

I wanted to write about it to *La perseveranza* or ask Giulio to speak with the directors about it; but thinking it over, I thought it would be better not to say a thing. A newspaper article is talked about for 24 hours. A second article would have been talked about for another 24. Altogether, 48 hours. Better, therefore, to stay with the 24! [. . .]

VERDI TO GIULIO RICORDI

Genoa, 25 December 1882

Dear Giulio,

Received last night, just in time . . . . at *seven* . . . the well-known,[1] etc., and this morning, the telegram.—I thank you for the one and the other. And you really do believe that only the legs are missing? I believe, instead, that legs, head, chest, arms—all, all, all are missing. You will see that I am right! But if I never have time! And now this blessed *D. Carlos*—which is a harder nut to crack than I had thought—is keeping me very busy.[2] [. . .]

It's not true that for the past two years I've been having a hospital built. Busseto has a hospital for the poor of its own community.

Instead, it's for the community where I live, and where there is no hospital; the poor who get sick there go to Piacenza (a city about 36 kilometres away). The unfortunate ones often die on the way! I have had, and still have, the intention of building (not in co-operation with the community, as has been said) some modest place to remedy these abuses somewhat. By no means a hospital of the proportions described by the papers: first, because it would be of no use to the small population of this community; second, because my finances would not permit it. The papers make atrocious jokes when they talk of my *immense* wealth! *Immense*?!! And how can it be such? No one can know better than you that when I wrote a lot, little was paid for the operas; now that they are well paid and bring good returns, I hardly write any more. [. . .]

EMANUELE MUZIO TO GIULIO RICORDI

Genoa [25?] December 1882

[. . .] What a beautiful *panettone*, and just in time for dessert. During the day the Maestro said, 'It hasn't arrived yet,' and I replied that it would arrive.

---

[1] *Panettone.*
[2] See Verdi to Baron Leopold Friedrich von Hofmann, 31 Oct. 1882.

Returning home from a walk: 'You see, it hasn't come yet'; and the same reply: 'It will arrive.'

At 7 o'clock the bell rings; the Maestro and I exclaim, 'The panettone!' Signora Peppina and De Amicis[1] say no; so the Maestro and I bet a penny, and the servant announces the famous box. The Maestro sees it and exclaims: 'There is a statue'; we all say: 'It's a statue of Otello.'

After the box has been very carefully opened, the monster is placed on the table; Verdi unties the knots, lifts the lid, and *half an Otello* is discovered. There was a cry of amazement; then we drank a toast that a year from now he may have legs and stand up, and I myself hope to be present at the great ceremony of *Otello* in chocolate and music. [. . .]

GIUSEPPINA VERDI TO GIULIO RICORDI

Genoa [25?] December 1882

[. . .] That poor little Moor, mutilated in what battle I don't know, won't get his legs back until Judgment Day! . . . the breath of the Eternal has not yet hovered over the chaos to divide the elements and create (after all the rest) the white man and the black. Let us hope that Verdi may become bored with his present activities and decide to take care of the Moors. [. . .]

EMANUELE MUZIO TO GIULIO RICORDI

Genoa, 29 December 1882

[. . .] I gave the Maestro your letter[1] to read; at first he said nothing, then he wanted to speak, and finally said, 'Nothing has been done, and I'm not going to think about it now.' I answered that he should finish *Otello*, and that this would be a good way to pay for the hospital he wants to build,[2] and also for the endowment.[3] Thereupon he made some calculations, and then nothing more was said until this morning, when I saw some sheets of music on the piano, and others with poetry for *Otello* that weren't there last year. [. . .]

GIULIO RICORDI TO GIUSEPPINA VERDI

Milan, 29 December 1882

[. . .] As an optical, magnetic, or chemical effect, whatever it may be, you will have noticed that for quite some time a black face—and therefore one negative to light—has transformed itself for me into a luminous point, from which I can turn neither my eyes nor my thoughts! [. . .]

I know that the Maestro has lately been very busy with business matters, as

---

[1] Giuseppe De Amicis.

[1] Missing.
[2] At Villanova near St Agata (see Verdi to Clara Maffei, 16 Dec., and Ricordi, 25 Dec. 1882).
[3] For the Casa di Riposo per Musicisti [House of Rest for (old) Musicians], which Verdi had built in Milan (see Chronology, 1888, 1889, 1895, 1896, 1897, 1899, and 1901).

well as *Don Carlo*, which he wrote to me was a harder nut to crack than he had thought! ...... In view of this: We! ..... grant him a well-deserved rest! ..... And we hope he will take our kindness into account! ...... But! ..... but! ..... what can I say! ..... the right moment will come .... and certain bottles of champagne. [...]

GIULIO RICORDI TO VERDI

Turin, 23 January 1883

Illustrious Maestro,

I am writing to you from Turin, where your letter of Sunday[1] was forwarded to me. [...] I am in Turin for the final rehearsals of *Boccanegra*, which will be performed tomorrow evening. Last night the dress rehearsal took place, with truly outstanding success from every point of view concerning the music and the staging. There are no great celebrities, it is true, but all the performers have good voices and sing in tune, with intelligence and good will. They are: La Borelli and Ortisi, Menotti,[2] Tamburlini, Marescalchi; the two comprimarii, Pietro and the Captain of the Crossbowmen, excellent. Orchestra and chorus very good. [...]

GIULIO RICORDI TO VERDI

Milan, 2 February 1883

[...] Please know that *Boccanegra* is having a triumphant run in Turin: success for the music and at the *box-office*. *Boccanegra* has literally saved the theatre from a *catastrophe*. [...]

VERDI TO GIUSEPPE PIROLI

Genoa, 2 February 1883

Dear Piroli,

I admire our minister's[1] wish to reform our music schools, but I don't think it is possible to succeed. Today there are neither composers nor students who are not attacked by Germanism, and one could not even form a commission free from the malady—a malady that, like any other, must take its course, and which at this time cannot be cured by commissions, programmes, or regulations. (Remember the regulation made in Florence during the Correnti Ministry.)[2]

[1] Probably in the Biblioteca Palatina.

[2] Delfino Menotti sang major roles, including Jago under Toscanini, at La Scala between 1883 and 1900.

[1] Guido Baccelli.

[2] Invited by Cesare Correnti (1815–88), Baccelli's predecessor, Verdi presided over a Commission for the Reform of the Conservatories, which met in Florence in March 1871 (see Verdi to Giuseppe Piroli, 20 Feb. 1871 in Busch, *Aida*, pp. 138–9).

A remedy for this evil might be:

1. A new young man, an artist of genius, not influenced by schools;
2. Theatres in a flourishing condition.

Our music, unlike the German—which can live in halls with symphonies and in apartments with quartets—ours, I say, is mainly located in the theatre. Now, the theatres cannot last without the help of the government. It's a fact that cannot be denied; all of them must necessarily close, and a few exceptional ones can only drag themselves along with difficulty.—The *Scala*, the very *Scala* might close next year.

With these convictions of mine, it is not possible for me to be part of a commission that in my opinion would bring no help to art.

Make my most sincere excuses to the minister, to whom I shall write two days from now, in order to give you time to inform him beforehand, and tell him that I am truly sorry to respond in this way to such a kind and courteous invitation. Yours affectionately

BOITO TO GIULIO RICORDI

[Madrid?, ? February 1883]

[...] Certainly I shall see Verdi in Genoa and strike the key.[1] [...]

VERDI TO GUIDO BACCELLI

Genoa, 4 February 1883

Excellency!

It is painful for me to have to reply to Your Excellency's honourable invitation as the circumstances and my convictions oblige me; and permit me, Excellency, to tell you that commissions and regulations cannot arrest the evil that we deplore.

This invasion of a foreign art has blinded us all in a manner that prevents us from seeing like the Germans, who truly make German music, and are right. We, however, who imitate them, have been renegades to our own nature, making music without an Italian character, hybrid and crossbred.

The only remedy for this evil might be:

1. A new man, an artist of genius, not influenced by schools;
2. Protection by the government, that is: Subsidies to the theatres and not taxes! With the conditions in which theatres of all kinds presently find themselves, the poor impresarios cannot face the demands of the artists and the public. Instead of serving art with dignity, having uselessly fought against a thousand difficulties, they are quite often forced to back out, to fail, and worse, to disgrace this art with productions that certainly give rise neither to splendour nor to higher public morale!

These deep convictions of mine about the present state of the theatre and

[1] To depress a note on the keyboard of the piano, i.e. remind Verdi of *Otello*.

music in Italy will, I hope, excuse me in Your Excellency's eyes, if I am firm in my resolution not to be part of any commission. [. . .]

VERDI TO GIULIO RICORDI

Genoa, 15 February 1883

The score paper is excellent, the first kind as well as the second; maybe the thinner one, R.B., is better, but make sure that the colour of the staffs is not too dark.

Sad, sad, sad!
Wagner is dead![1]
When I read the dispatch yesterday, I can say I was horrorstruck! Let's not argue.—It's a great personality that vanishes! A name that leaves a most powerful mark on the history of art!

GIULIO RICORDI TO VERDI

Milan, 17 February 1883

[. . .] The topic of the day is Wagner's sudden death. Filippi told me that it did not surprise him, since when he saw him in Venice some 2 months ago, he gave him the impression of a real walking corpse. For many years he suffered from heart disease; now, in Venice, he committed extravagances and excesses of all kinds! . . and I thought it advisable not to publicize this, although the correspondents wrote all sorts of stories about it!! . . I think that the diseased heart from which he suffered also afflicted his brain, and those of people who were close to him, too. All things considered . . . . he impresses me as the musical Garibaldi . . . . . with the notes proper for our Italian Garibaldi going to a German! . . .
Peace be with him anyway! [. . .]

BOITO TO EUGENIO TORNAGHI

Nervi, 4 March 1883

[. . .] In an hour I go to Genoa to see Verdi. [. . .]

VERDI TO FRANCESCO FLORIMO

Genoa, 12 March 1883

Dear Florimo,
At this moment I am reading in Ricordi's *Gazzetta musicale* that in early April a book of yours will come out, in which there will also be published 'a

---

[1] On 13 Feb. in Venice.

programmatic letter from Gius. Verdi to Florimo regarding the Neapolitan conservatory,[1] etc. . .'

You know that I have never liked publicity . . . .; nowadays it is distasteful and almost irritating to me. I would be most grateful to you if you could leave the place of that letter blank; if you cannot, be kind enough to add a note in your book expressing my wish. [. . .]

VERDI TO OPPRANDINO ARRIVABENE

Genoa, 15 March 1883

[. . .] I have been busy, it's true, and have toiled more than I had thought. *Don Carlos* is now reduced to 4 acts and will be more suitable, and also, I believe, better, from an artistic point of view.

More concision and more vigour.

As for the other one[1] . . . it hasn't been baptized yet, I haven't thought, am not thinking, and don't know whether I will think about him in the future. But at this point the theatres are in such bad shape that it's useless to write operas! You are unsure about my opinion; but you will see that all the theatres will close, one after the other! . . .

All of them! Composers and the public don't know what they want. Singers make impossible demands. The government gives no subsidies. An impossible credit balance, and therefore ruin and death. Who knows if after a while something might not come out of *nothing*. [. . .]

GIULIO RICORDI TO VERDI

Milan, 16 March 1883

[. . .] Our lawyer in Vienna, Dr Eirich, has written to me that *Boccanegra* was revived with the *greatest*, the *most complete* success, and asks me to give you this news. [. . .]

VERDI TO GIUSEPPE PIROLI

Genoa, 16 March 1883

[. . .] Today it's no longer Caesar, but Nero, [. . .] no longer Faust, but Mephistopheles, no longer Otello, according to what they say, but Jago!!

And recently the Milan papers actually announced *Jago* for 1884!!

I recall that when we talked you protested against this rumour, but why doesn't Ricordi seize the opportunity to rectify this error. [. . .]

---

[1] Verdi's letter of 5 Jan. 1871 (see *Copialettere*, pp. 232–3).

[1] *Otello*.

VERDI TO GIULIO RICORDI

Genoa, 24 March 1883

Dear Giulio,

This morning I read in *La fanfulla*:[1] 'Maurel also told us that Verdi is preparing the greatest surprises for the musical world and the greatest lessons for the young avant-garde with his *Jago*,' etc., etc.

God help me!

It has never been my intention, and never will be, to give lessons to anybody. I admire without scholarly prejudices all that I like; I compose as I feel and let everybody compose what he wants.

Besides, until now I haven't written a thing of this *Jago*, or better, *Otello*, and don't know what I will do later on.

Believe me always yours,

G. Verdi

PS Arrange a little article[2] on this subject; or publish my own words in a big paper as soon as possible.

GIULIO RICORDI TO VERDI

Milan, 24 March 1883

[...] Today I am sending you two acts of the staging of *Boccanegra*.[1] [...]

BOITO TO VERDI

[Milan] 5 April [1883]

Dear Maestro,

On 22 March[1] the anniversary of the death of Manzoni, Milan will inaugurate the monument in the Piazza Manzoni,[2] and on the same night at La Scala—if for that period worthy singers are found (and there is much hope that they will be found)—the municipality of Milan would like to have Verdi's Mass performed. If I am not mistaken, Masini, la Teodorini, and Nannetti do not have engagements at the end of May; with the orchestra and chorus of La Scala as mighty auxiliaries, this time, too, the Mass would have

[1] A Roman newspaper.
[2] '[...] We do not have the slightest notion of *Jago* or *Otello* [...],' the editors of *La gazzetta musicale* declared on 8 Apr. 1883 below a report of 2 Apr. 1883 by their Paris correspondent A.A.

[1] See Document I.

[1] 22 May.
[2] A monument of Alessandro Manzoni by Francesco Barzaghi, who also created Verdi's statue at La Scala. Manzoni's monument stands in the Piazza S. Fedele.

a perfect performance. The occasion is a solemn one. The 22 May 1883 will glorify the name of Alessandro Manzoni; at that glorification the Mass you wrote for him must not be missing, and so that nothing may be missing from the nobility of the celebration, you, Maestro, *should come to conduct it in person*. So thinks the municipality, and so think I. Nobody knows anything about this as yet; not even Giulio Ricordi knows that I am writing to you today. Our excellent Negri, municipal alderman (you know that Negri is one of the most capable men in Milan)—Negri asked me yesterday to ask you officially, and to beg you graciously for this, and I obey with all my heart. If we find perfect singers,[3] will you say yes? I am waiting for an answer of two lines from you.

I was so sorry to have missed the feast of St Joseph[4] in your home; I had to leave, but the snow had me worried, and I stayed in Nervi for another four or five days. I almost had *the impertinence* to appear as an unexpected guest at the Palazzo Doria, but then I lacked the *nerve*. The next day I reached Milan, where we have now had spring for three days. Yesterday I spent the whole evening with Edmondo De Amicis, and we talked a great deal about you and Signora Giuseppina, to whom you will give my affectionate regards.

And you, Maestro, even when I bore you every once in a while, may keep me in your good friendship.

Your
Arrigo Boito

VERDI TO BOITO

St Agata, 7 April 1883

Dear Boito,

I received your very dear letter here, forwarded from Genoa.

The occasion is certainly a solemn one, but . . . . it would be an encore—I detest encores—you are an artist and you will understand me.—[1]

A bit of *nerve* is good every once in a while! If I could have imagined that on the feast of St Joseph you were still in Nervi, I would have come personally to drag you here by the legs.—

Just continue to write to me, without fear that your very dear letters might bore me.

In all friendship

Yours,
G. Verdi

---

[3] With the exception of the tenor Eugène Durot, Faccio conducted the *Requiem* with less than perfect singers at La Scala on 22 May 1883.

[4] In Italian San Giuseppe, Giuseppe and Giuseppina's patron saint, whose feast-day is 19 Mar.

---

[1] Upon receipt of this letter, Boito wrote to Gaetano Negri on 9 Apr. from Milan: 'We have had a fiasco.—Verdi answers me politely that he cannot, and he advances serious reasons for his inability.'

OPPRANDINO ARRIVABENE TO VERDI

Rome, 7 April 1883

[. . .] The papers say that Maurel sings *Rigoletto* very well,[1] and that by slowing the tempo of '*sì vendetta!*' ['*yes, revenge!*'], he has truly interpreted your intention. Others say, however, that he slows down because he lacks the breath, and that *Rigoletto* is not a score for him. Who is right?[2] [. . .]

VERDI TO GIULIO RICORDI

St Agata, 3 September 1883

Dear Giulio,

I received the two booklets you sent me by *Hanslick*[1] and by *Marcello*.[2] It was about fifty years ago that I read the booklet by the latter. It seemed dull to me at that time!

I won't read the one by Hanslick. It would be useless! The 'beautiful in music!!!'

Where is it? What is it? . . . If you ask Filippi or Boito about Bach, they will exclaim . . . 'Beautiful! Beautiful!' Others would say, 'Dry, hard, cold, boring!' Who would be right?

Useless, then, so many words; *useless* to read them;

Useless to write this letter; but it would be more *useless* to write another one.

Addio

Yours,
G. Verdi

VERDI TO GIULIO RICORDI

St Agata, 18 September 1883

Dear Giulio,

I promised to write you before the 20th, the day of Signor Corti's departure for Paris. You may tell him, then, that I cannot give a different answer from the one I gave him orally here at St Agata a few days ago. I am truly distressed that this opera is running into so many difficulties[1] (strange, I

---

[1] At the Teatro Apollo in Rome on 6 Apr.
[2] Verdi's answer is missing.

---

[1] Hanslick's *Vom Musikalisch-Schönen*, published in 1854, probably in French or Italian translation.
[2] Benedetto Marcello (1686–1739), the Venetian composer, is also known by his treatise *Il teatro alla moda* (1722), to which Verdi probably refers.

---

[1] Under the management of the Corti brothers, the Italian Theatre in Paris was to be reopened with *Simon Boccanegra*.

never ran into so many, even when I was thirty years old!!); and if it can't be given as it stands . . . . the dilemma is quickly solved!—They shall think about it, and we shall think about it! [. . .]

VERDI TO GIULIO RICORDI

St Agata, [?] September 1883

Dear Giulio,

Boccanegra goes badly. He is a little bowlegged. I would think that by saying this out loud, as you propose, you would run the risk of crippling him altogether.

In haste

Addio
G. Verdi

VERDI TO CLARA MAFFEI

St Agata, 11 October 1883

Dear Clarina,

I have known it all;[1] I have admired your courage and can understand, now that the first nervous excitement is over, the whole despondency of your soul. There are no words that can give comfort in a misfortune of this sort. And I will not say to you the usual stupid word '*courage* . . .', a word that has always made me angry when addressed to me. There is need for something else! Comfort you will only find in the strength of your soul and in the soundness of *your* mind. My obolus[2] will not be missing. I thank you for 9 October.[3] We spent a rather cheerful day with the family. There was also la Stoltz, who has left for Milan.

I wish you good health in your mountains, and get a good supply to take back with you to Milan. Ah, health! I didn't think about it for many years, but I don't know what it will be in the future. The years are really beginning to be too many, and I think . . . I think that life is the most stupid and, what is even worse, the most useless thing! What does one do? What have we done? . . . What shall we do? . . . To sum it all up, there is one . . . humiliating . . . very sad answer!

Nothing!

Addio, my dear Clarina. Let's avoid and keep away from sad things as long as we can, and let's be friends as long as can be. Addio, addio.

Affectionately,

G. Verdi

PS Peppina sends you all the very best.

[1] Carlo Tenca (1816–83), writer, journalist, and politician, passionately fighting for Italy's liberation, had been Clara Maffei's companion since 1846 and had died on 4 Sept.
[2] A pious commemorative offering to the dead.
[3] Apparently for birthday congratulations.

VERDI TO GIULIO RICORDI

St Agata, 12 October 1883

Dear Giulio,

From the enclosed telegram[1] you will see that Signora Devries does not wish to sing *Boccanegra* without the addition of that well-known cabaletta.[2] She is right.

I took out that cabaletta because I did not like it and because the scene required the tenor to enter without waiting for the prima donna to finish her *cock-a-doodle-do*. I think that I, too, am right.

If Corti has planned everything for the opening of *Boccanegra*[3] and is in despair if he can't give it, he, too, is right. And you, too, will be right if you don't authorize *Boccanegra* without a guarantee that it shall be performed by better artists — — — —

We all are right, then; and if, in spite of this, we don't reach an agreement, it's because everything has been spoiled, and was badly based to begin with — —

You will do as you think best; and you will do me the favour of liberating me from this *Boccanegra*, which has become almost tedious to me.

Addio

Yours,
G. Verdi

VERDI TO GIULIO RICORDI

[St Agata] Saturday [13 October 1883][1]

Dear Giulio

Oh, this *Boccanegra* in Paris is a real torture!

Today I have written giving the authorization to do the old cabaletta if they want. It's an outrage!! But let's get it over with! — —

For your part, you will do what you think best — —

I received your letter today. I have no time to answer.

Addio
G. Verdi

---

[1] A missing telegram from Paris.
[2] In Act I, Scene i of the original version. See third paragraph in Verdi to Boito, 8 Jan. 1881.
[3] The first in France on 27 Nov. 1883 at the Italian Theatre in Paris with Fidès Devriès, Victor Maurel, and Édouard De Reszke under Faccio's baton. The revived theatre was inaugurated with this performance attended by Victor Hugo, Gounod, and others of equal prestige.

---

[1] Postmark: BUSSETO 13/10/83.

VERDI TO GIULIO RICORDI

St Agata, 27 October 1883

Dear Giulio,

I have never liked publicity; now I detest it, and I detest it to the point of feeling ill. Imagine the pleasure I take from reading, for example: 'Costume sketches and scenic designs have been sent to Maestro Verdi ... Maestro Verdi has orchestrated the cabaletta of *Boccanegra* ... Maestro Verdi will come to Milan, will not come . . has disapproved [illegible]. [. . .] Furthermore this lumping together of everything and everybody—operas, song, sound, dances—seasoned with *blague*, is unbearable to me. It may suit the others; it absolutely does not suit me, absolutely not.— You will say, 'What does this have to do with me?' . . . Yes: however, the matter of the costume sketches and the cabaletta of *Boccanegra* can only come from the House of Ricordi! — — — — — — — —

If I had not [already] promised, I would promise neither *Boccanegra* for Paris nor *D. Carlos* for Milan. Now I declare that I will not make a new orchestration of the cabaletta, and that I don't have the old one. When I rewrote [the opera], I cut the old sheets and threw them into the fire, and probably that useless cabaletta, too.

As for *D. Carlos*, it would be a real consolation for me if it could not be done, and I would almost make a *sacrifice*, so to speak ... Anyway, I won't take on any obligation for rehearsals and other things. Later we'll see what is to be done; in the meantime, let me catch my breath, and do me the favour of not talking to me any more about sets, costume sketches, *D. Carlos* and theatres ... I really can't stand it any more—

Addio, addio

G. Verdi

EMANUELE MUZIO TO VERDI

Paris, 30 October 1883
4 Rue des Capucins

My dearest Maestro,

Ricordi telegraphed me yesterday as follows:

'Orchestration of cabaletta no longer exists, neither with author nor me; grave difficulty.'

It's more than serious, most serious, because it destroys everything and one returns once again to the tortured and the tormented.

I have copied the cabaletta, because I think that you do not have it, and so I send it to you.[1]

Omitting the first four bars and the final cadenzas, only 42 bars would have to be orchestrated. If you don't do it, who would dare to put a hand to your music? ... Nobody.

---

[1] The text of the enclosed cabaletta in the original version of *Simon Boccanegra* reads:

Ah, Il palpito deh frena   [Ah, hold your beating,
  O core innamorato   Oh heart in love.

In Venice I myself wrote the reduction, and since I heard the rehearsals and the first three performances, and then at St Agata continued to work on the reduction for four hands, I remember the orchestration.

The arpeggio was executed by Mirco[2] on the clarinet, the pizzicato of the double-basses was followed on the second fourth by the violas and violins, and I still remember the extraordinary, magic effect at the repeat when the voice was accompanied by the flute and oboe, ending with the chromatic scale amid thunderous applause. If once again you deny and sacrifice yourself, it will be the height of your kindness. [. . .]

GIULIO RICORDI TO VERDI

Milan, 5 December 1883

[PS] Maestro Cairati returned from Paris repeating and confirming the *complete* success of *Boccanegra* in the fullest way.[1]

FRANCO FACCIO TO VERDI

[Milan?, ? November 1883?][1]

[. . .] With deep sadness I have read that part of your precious letter[2] mentioning the 'chocolate', and with great interest that other which speaks of 'too' long legs.[3] The word 'too' is yours and is accepted, up to a point. Those so-called legs were in proportion with the broad chest, in which a great heart was beating, and shall beat eternally. If you shorten them you do so because you wish to adapt them to that part of the audience which is shortsighted—that is all.

As for the 'chocolate': it is a great misfortune that you cannot bring yourself to start. I have heard you say several times: 'I have done my duty, now it's up to the young fellows.' But consider, Maestro, that the ray of eternal youth shines upon your head, that all eyes are turned toward your genius. [. . .]

In questo dì beato	On this blessed day
Oh, non vorrei morir.	Oh, I would not wish to die.
Qual Iride somiglia	How like Iris
La dolce sua parola,	Is his sweet word.
Dal cielo mio s'invola	From my heaven flies away
La nube dei sospir.	The cloud of sighs.
Il palpito deh frena (*bis*)	Hold your beating (*repeated*)]

Verdi probably asked Muzio to orchestrate the cabaletta for Madame Devriès. (See Verdi to Ricordi, 12, 13 and 27 October 1883.)
  [2] Unknown.

  [1] See Verdi to Ricordi, 12 Oct. 1883, n. 3.

  [1] Abbiati (IV. 223) gives no date for this letter, but only suggests Nov. 1883. Therefore, it seemed permissible for once to break the chronological sequence of the correspondence by placing this letter after the last one concerning *Simon Boccanegra* in Paris.
  [2] Missing.
  [3] *Don Carlos.*

BOITO TO VERDI
                                                    Nervi
                                              Hôtel Victoria
                                      Monday [21 January 1884][1]

Dearest Maestro,
    The ravioli in Genoa are excellent. I adore them, and I'd like to devour
them at your table next Thursday. If I haven't chosen the day well, you'll
have time to answer me: no.
    But I think that if ravioli are on the table I'll eat too many of them; you'll
eat them, too, and we'll have trouble digesting them. I think that whatever
intrigues the stomach, doesn't go to work in the brain, and this reminds me of
the phrase you spoke to me concerning the *Moor of Venice*: 'It's all a question
of the stomach.'
    And so *no ravioli*. We shall dine together Thursday (I believe you have
dinner at *six* in Genoa, too)—we'll dine, but without the temptation of the
ravioli. We shall have a little meal, one that's wise, healthy, and altogether
intellectual.
    Well then, with your permission (if you don't answer me it will be a sign of
your permission), till we see each other on Thursday at six.
    My best regards to Signora Peppina. An affectionate handshake

                                                    Your
                                                    Arrigo Boito

VERDI TO OPPRANDINO ARRIVABENE

                                        Genoa, 29 January 1884

Dear Arrivabene,
    I am really obliged to you for your dear letter.[1] A hundred times I wanted
to send you a word from Milan, but as we know, when one is in the midst of
that damned shop they call the theatre, one never finds time for anything.[2] As
for my *impassiveness*, I'll tell you that even this time I wasn't much moved. I
know what that so-called good reception for me was trying to say. It wasn't
either for *Don Carlos* or for the author of the previous operas. That clapping
meant to say, 'You, who are still in this world, as old as you are, go kill
yourself with fatigue, but make us dance once more . . .' Go ahead, buffoon,
and long live the glory!
    However, *D. Carlos* was altogether well executed and very well staged. In
spite of this, I believe that the theatre is poorly attended.
    The cuts do not spoil the musical drama and actually, by shortening it,
they make it livelier. Those who plan on being dissatisfied—always the
subscribers—complain that there is no first act any more, in which they say

---

[1] Postmark: NERVI 21/I/84.

[1] Of 25 Jan. 1884 (see Alberti, pp. 304–5).
[2] In reference to rehearsals for *Don Carlo*, which opened at La Scala on 10 Jan., conducted by
Faccio.

the music was very beautiful. Now it's very beautiful; before they didn't realize, perhaps, that it existed. It's a discovery! [. . .]

VERDI TO CLARA MAFFEI

Genoa, 29 January 1884

Dear Clarina,

How can you say that![1] I'm the one who must thank you and be grateful to you for the sincere affection you always have for me, and for the welcome you give me each time I have the pleasure of seeing you in Milan. A pity, that in this latest circumstance I couldn't come to you more frequently and stay with you for a longer time. But what can you say! When you have to deal with that galley[2] which others call the theatre, you are never master of your own time. Poor artists, whom many people have the . . . kindness, I'd say, to envy, slaves of a public that is ignorant most of the time (not so bad), capricious and unfair. I must laugh that I, too, was once fond of it—I was 25 years old—but it didn't last long. A year later, light dawned upon me; and when I was involved later on, I armed myself with a breastplate and, prepared for the shots, said, '*Hit us!*' In fact, there always were battles! Battles that never did one any good . . . even when one was victorious!! . . . Sad. Sad!!

Now let's talk about us. I imagine and I hope that you are well. Our health isn't bad, either. We have splendid sunshine, but it's a bit windy and chilly. Twice I have seen Boito, who is having a nice quiet rest in Nervi. [. . .]

VERDI TO BOITO

Genoa, 7 February 1884

Dear Boito,

How quickly you have [done this]![1] If only I could do likewise! All right. Till we see each other then.

Affectionately,
G. Verdi

VERDI TO OPPRANDINO ARRIVABENE

Genoa, 12 February 1884

[. . .] Good operas have always been rare at all times; now they are almost impossible . . . Why? you will say! Because we make too much music! Because we search too much! Because we look in the dark and neglect the sun! Because we have exaggerated the little things! Because we are making big things, not great things! And from the big comes the small and the perverse! . . . There we are! [. . .]

[1] In response to a missing letter after Verdi's sojourn for *Don Carlo* in Milan.
[2] Verdi refers to the early years when he felt like a galley slave, forced to write to earn a living.

[1] Judging from Boito's letter to Tornaghi of 13 Feb. 1884, Verdi refers to some revisions in the first act of *Otello*.

BOITO TO EUGENIO TORNAGHI

Nervi, 13 [February 1884]

[. . .] I leave for Naples Saturday night;[1] I shall probably stay at the Hôtel Bristol in the Via V. E. [Vittorio Emanuele], where it seems the typhus hasn't arrived. I want to know the conditions of the contract in order to judge how much of a free hand I shall have to act and do and, just in case, also to undo, in my own way. [. . .] If you or Giulio have any particular instructions to give me on how to behave in that country of gangsters, write to me and instruct me.

It seems to me that this time Verdi has given serious thought to setting about his work. I have made some revisions in a section of the first act of the Moor. I have also worked on my libretto, which, as you know, is the great problem of the opera that occupies me.[2] [. . .]

BOITO TO EUGENIO TORNAGHI

Nervi, 28 February 1884

[. . .] As I told you, I leave on 3 March; I'm no longer going to the Bristol Hôtel—it's too far from the centre; I'll go to the Hôtel Roma, where I hope to find a couple of rooms available. [. . .]

Today I am going to Genoa to see our Maestro, whom I have not seen since my return from Naples. [. . .]

EMANUELE MUZIO TO CARLO D'ORMEVILLE

Paris, 9 March 1884
5 rue des Capucines

[. . .] *Inter nos* (absolutely) it is quite true that Verdi wrote to me *that for now he has no desire whatsoever to occupy himself with Otello*; this is not a denial. Since Verdi always used to indicate the artists he wanted for his new operas, I would not find it at all out of place if Signor Ferrari paid him a diplomatic visit to ask him what his ideal would be for the interpreters of the future *Otello. Verdi will never accept artists for a limited number of performances*; this is a matter that should not even be mentioned. [. . .]

---

[1] On 16 Feb. for rehearsals of *Mefistofele* at the San Carlo. These rehearsals were so far behind schedule, however, that Boito returned to Nervi. '*Errare humanum est*,' he wrote good-naturedly to Tornaghi from there on 23 Feb. enclosing the bill for the unnecessary journey and reminding him of orchestra parts and costume designs required in Naples. On 26 Feb., Boito informed Tornaghi that he would return to Naples on 3 Mar. for rehearsals on the 5th.
[2] *Nerone.*

BOITO TO GIULIO RICORDI

[Naples, 20 March 1884]

[. . .] Once again we have been victorious[1] . . . But what an effort to obtain this result! I'm so tired I won't be able to help with the rehearsals in Florence.[2] To triumph is nice—but not to drop dead in the process. [. . .]

Next Tuesday I'll be back in Nervi. I have good news for you, but for Heaven's sake don't talk to anyone about it, don't talk about it even in your home, don't talk about it even to yourself; already I fear that I am committing an indiscretion: The Maestro is writing, has in fact already written a good part of the beginning of the 1st act, and seems to be enthusiastic. I shall see him in a few days. [. . .]

DOMENICO MORELLI TO VERDI

[Naples] Studio, 4 pm Sunday [23 March 1884]

Dearest Maestro,

Boito left just a moment ago; he was here in my studio for a few minutes, is leaving tomorrow, and will bring you a photograph of a painting I have sent to Milan.[1]

We talked about Jago; I showed him a colour sketch and told him about the problem that kept me from continuing. You have reason to complain about me—that is, about the painter, because he still could not find the essence of the situation. A few days ago I thought I had captured a part of it, and if I am able to see all of it, I'll make a mess of a canvas and send it to you.

Thinking of you—and I am always, always thinking of you—certain notes, certain *sounds*, when remembered, are transformed into colours; but these colours must express particular, *material* things, and thus I lose the vision that is so dear, and a battle takes place which I always lose. The remains are left on the canvas, without transparency, without anybody's being able to see what I saw in my mind.

Oh, I wish no one could see what I have painted, and you least of all. You frighten me.

Providence has caused my delay, by not allowing my painting to spoil the vision you have of Otello and Jago.

Boito will tell you how I am putting Desdemona into the setting of that scene. Oh, I hope to send you something when there will be no more danger of harming you.

A thousand affectionate greetings to Signora Peppina. Will she also be angry with me? I shall come to see you in Genoa; will you be staying there much longer?

Always your
Morelli

[1] In the first performance of *Mefistofele* at the Teatro San Carlo on 19 March, conducted by Raffaele Kuon (1831–85). "This most fortunate Neapolitan campaign," Boito reported to Tornaghi from Nervi on 2 April 1884, was a climax in his life.

[2] These dates have not been ascertained.

[1] Not identified. (See Boito to Verdi, 26 Apr. 1884, n. 5.)

VERDI TO FRANCO FACCIO

Genoa, 27 March 1884

Dear Faccio,

Two words to thank you for the kindness you showed towards the person I recommended to you.[1] Two other words about a matter that concerns me personally.

Il pungolo[2] quotes these lines from *Il piccolo* in Naples: 'Concerning *Jago*, Boito said that he treated the subject almost against his will; but that when it was finished he regretted not having been able to compose it himself.'[3] .. Admittedly those words, spoken at a banquet, are of no great importance; but unfortunately they are subject to comment. It might be said, for example, that I forced him to treat the subject. This by itself would not be so bad; in any case, you know how things went.

The trouble is that when Boito *regrets* not being able to compose the opera himself, it must be supposed, of course, that he could not hope to see it composed by me the way he would like it. I perfectly agree with this, I completely agree; and therefore I address myself to you, Boito's oldest, most steadfast friend, so that upon his return to Milan you may tell him in person, not in writing, that—without the shadow of resentment, without any deep-seated anger—I return his manuscript to him intact. Furthermore, since the libretto is my property, I offer it to him as a gift, for whenever he intends to compose it. If he accepts this I will be happy—happy in the hope of having furthered and served the art we all love.

Forgive the trouble I am causing you, but this is a matter that must be handled discreetly. There is no one better suited to take care of this than you.

Take care of your health, and believe me

Yours
G. Verdi

VERDI TO DOMENICO MORELLI

Genoa, 28 March 1884

Dear Morelli,

I've had no news from you for so long that I am very glad to receive this very dear letter of yours[1] and the photograph Boito has brought me[2] of your

[1] Unknown.

[2] A newspaper in Naples with editions in Rome and Milan. (See Boito to Verdi, 26 Apr. 1884.)

[3] Before publishing this letter in *Copialettere*, the editors Gaetano Cesari and Alessandro Luzio asked Boito to explain its contents. Boito responded: 'After the first performance of *Mefistofele* at the San Carlo in 1884, the professors of the Conservatory offered me a banquet where, when asked about the libretto of *Otello*, I expressed very different feelings from those that were coarsely interpreted by *Il piccolo*.' (*Copialettere*, p. 324 n.)

[1] Of 23 Mar. 1884.

[2] According to Morelli's letter of 23 Mar., Boito left Naples on the 24th. The newspaper *Roma* of the same date reports that he planned to visit his brother in Rome. In his letter to Verdi

latest painting. That must be a most beautiful painting! Extremely beautiful and new! In spite of my great admiration, however, I am a little annoyed, because you always find time to do these beautiful things and never time to do a bit of Jago for me.

Boito came to see me for a few minutes and explained nothing, or almost nothing, of the sketch that you had shown him. I don't understand how you have Desdemona entering in this scene! Never mind, I'll understand later on. But with or without Desdemona, you will do it well in any case; and you'll always do it better if you don't think too much. Too much is always too much! In the arts too much (I say too much) reflection stifles inspiration. [. . .]

FRANCO FACCIO TO VERDI[1]

Milan, 4 April 1884

[. . .] Sunday night, just back from Trieste, and having gone to La Scala for the performance of *Le Prophète*, I found your letter, which I read with the greatest emotion. [. . .] The reflections and the conclusions of your letter prove once again the immense kindness and sensitivity of your soul, a kindness and a sensitivity that appear in even the most hidden acts of your private life and that are in perfect balance (something which, allow me to say, is not always found in illustrious personages) with the greatness of mind that gave birth to so many immortal works in the field of art. Will you permit me now to respectfully, but frankly, express an opinion of mine? In transcribing the words that Boito supposedly uttered in Naples, you add that 'Admittedly those words, spoken at a banquet, are of no great importance;' and perhaps you did not think that even more was made of them because they were reported in a newspaper, which could have and must have misunderstood them. If Boito spoke of 'regret', I would swear by all that is holy to me that he alluded to what he, Ricordi, I, and all who love and long for the glory of Italian art would feel if you really were to resolve not to write *Otello*. Do you think it possible that Boito would have let three years go by (for that many have passed, I believe, since the *Otello* libretto was written), do you think he would have talked a thousand times with me, his old and most intimate friend, about you and the music you will write, which we long for so much, without at least mentioning that regret, if there had been a regret, which I cannot and will not admit? Instead, there were countless times when he spoke to me of the immense honour and satisfaction he had felt while, working only for Verdi he gave musical and dramatic form to that powerful and difficult subject which *Verdi alone* may set to music.

---

of 26 Apr. 1884, Boito mentions only an encounter with Signora Giuseppina, presumably the morning of 26 Mar. on his return from Naples via Rome and Genoa to Nervi. We may surmise that 'for a few moments' he also saw Verdi at that time, and that Verdi had not yet read the newspaper mentioned in his preceding letter to Faccio of 27 Mar.

[1] In answer to Verdi's letter of 27 Mar.

Of course, when Boito is back I shall speak with him (I won't write, as you so rightly say) about this incident, which for me is in every way most unfortunate; and I shall do so in a way that, having confirmed the truth, will spare him undeserved distress. Even at this time, I am sure, he doesn't know about the article in *Il piccolo* and the reprint in *Il pungolo*, since he left Naples the morning after the banquet; anyone wishing to find him now would have to take the road to Nervi. When the very delicate task is done, I shall write to you about it. [. . .]

VERDI TO FRANCO FACCIO

Genoa, 20 April 1884

[. . .] When Boito arrives in Milan[1] you will perhaps already have left for Turin. In any case, when you return you will still have time to speak to him about the matter I mentioned to you in my letter of 27 March. The libretto is always at his disposal. [. . .]

BOITO TO VERDI

Milan, Saturday [26 April 1884][1]

Dear Maestro,

I ran over to Turin to see the medieval castle,[2] which is wonderful, and arrived in Milan yesterday. For many reasons I am glad I made this trip. In Turin I saw my brother and several good friends, among them Giacosa, who was my guide, and Faccio, who was rehearsing his Cantata,[3] which (especially in the beginning and the cadenza) made the great impression on me that I had expected. But the main reason my trip turned out to be even more fortunate than I had hoped—the unpredictably favourable reason—lay in the confidences Faccio revealed to me concerning a letter you had written to him. Had I not gone to Turin, who knows for how many months I might not have known what you wanted me to know from my friend's own lips.

---

[1] Presumably returning from Nervi without having seen Verdi in Genoa.

[1] Presumably, Boito wrote this letter—perhaps by special delivery—the same Saturday on which Verdi answered him. The envelope is missing. In all probability, Verdi answered this important letter without delay, but might have misdated his reply, i.e. have written it on 27 instead of 26 Apr. Also Faccio's lines to Giulio Ricordi of 27 Apr. seem to establish this date for Boito's letter to Verdi.

[2] A Piedmont castle of the fifteenth century was recreated for the National Exhibition in Turin.

[3] A *Cantata inaugurale* for the opening of the exhibition on 25 Apr. 1884 (Depanis, ii. 218–23).

With all my heart, thank you, my Maestro, thank you, but it seems really
too much to have to answer you seriously that I do not accept—that I do not
accept your great, your noble offer. These journalists must be of quite a
different sort from honest people; I don't say all of them, but most. Here is
one who manages to misunderstand my words in such a bestial manner as to
produce a sentence that is precisely the opposite of my feelings, and he prints
this sentence, and other journalists repeat it, and thus the work of foolish,
indiscreet people creates, at my expense, a foolish and indiscreet situation
between you and me, a situation from which I find myself set free only today.
And if I find myself set free from this unreal situation, Maestro, the credit is
yours. For that more than for the offer itself I thank you fervently, because
through this my heart finds the occasion to open itself to you with complete
confidence.

I read this tasteless report in the *Roma*, a Neapolitan newspaper[4] I had
with me while travelling to Genoa. I cannot tell you how indignant and
disturbed I was. Throughout the trip I thought how I might remedy the
journalist's silly talk. My first impulse was to write to the editor of the *Roma*
myself; then I hesitated to write about you without your consent, and I
decided to ask you for it. In order to get it, I dropped in at the Palazzo Doria
in Genoa the very morning of my arrival; I resolved to do this because I also
had the excuse of bringing you Morelli's photograph.[5] When Signora
Giuseppina suddenly entered the room, I didn't have the nerve to bore your
wife with talk that concerned such a silly thing, and couldn't have done so
without showing my annoyance. A few days went by, and I calmed down; I
began to think that the *Roma* was a paper known only in the Neapolitan
provinces and that no other paper would have published this blunder; I
thought that corrections and the writing of letters to papers were almost
always vain, and always fruitless. I soon regained my composure, strong
though I was in my feelings. I thought the public would have read the report
in the *Roma* with indifference, and since this was the case, I hoped that you
would never have seen it. But human foolishness has long legs. *Il piccolo* in
Naples reproduced the report (I only learned of this in Turin the day before
yesterday), and so did *Il pungolo*. This surprises me, because Fortis knows me
too well to have believed what he printed; and as soon as I see him I shall ask
him in confidence whether he read the galleys of his paper that day, and he
will tell me no. The Italian public has little faith in the papers, however, and
this enables me not to worry about the public's impression. But I cannot help
worrying about the effect this report might have had on you, Maestro. This
letter is getting long; forgive me, but now that I have started I must tell you

[4] On 24 Mar. 1884, this paper reported:

The banquet for the illustrious Arrigo Boito offered last night by the professors of our
Conservatory in a room of the *Caffè di Napoli* was a most cordial celebration of brothers-in-
art. , , , Asked about *Jago*, which he has written for Verdi, he [Boito] mentioned that at first he
had treated such a subject reluctantly, but that, having finished the libretto, he regretted that
he himself could not be the composer destined to set it to music.

[5] See Morelli to Verdi, 23 Mar. and Verdi's reply to Morelli, 28 Mar. 1884.

everything. This is the origin of the misunderstanding. (Blessed are you who have such glory and authority that you can decline dinners. I cannot afford this luxury, since I would be accused of being presumptuous and nothing else.) At the supper which some colleagues offered me after the *Mefistofele* in Naples, a polite journalist, a cultivated and courteous man, Signor Martino Caffiero, made this observation to me point-blank: '*Otello* would have been a subject for you, too.' (This proves that a well-mannered man is capable of saying words that embarrass the one who listens to them.) I answered by denying this, adding that I had never thought of *Otello* for myself. But realizing then that by persisting in this negative answer, without any explanation, I was leaving myself open to the interpretation that I had brought little love to the work that Verdi was to compose, I explained my answer. I said that I had never thought about it, because I felt too passionately about Schakespere's masterwork in its *tragic* form to be able to express it in *operatic* form (and this is partly true). I added that I had never thought it possible to transform Schakespeare's tragedy into a good libretto until I did this work for you, Maestro, and with you (and this is true), and that only now, after much retouching, was I satisfied that the work I had undertaken with great trepidation possessed, in the end, the eminently lyrical qualities and forms which lend themselves perfectly to composition and which are suited in every way to the demands of opera. I spoke these words with the emphasis of profound conviction, and Signor Caffiero, who understood them correctly, did not publish them, because he is not one of those who publish conversations that take place at the dinner table. Somebody else, to whom, obviously, I had not addressed my remarks, and who understood them in the most distorted manner, published them in the *Roma* after his own fashion, perhaps without any malicious intent, but with a twisting of the sense and with the attribution to me of a desire that offends me and is precisely the opposite of my great desire—which is to have you set to music a libretto that I have written solely for the joy of seeing you take up your pen once more *per causa mia*, for the glory of being your collaborator, for the ambition of hearing my name coupled with yours, and ours with Schakespeare's, and because this theme and my libretto have been transferred to you by the sacred right of conquest. Only you can compose *Otello*. The entire world of opera you have given us affirms this truth; if I have been able to perceive the Schakespearean tragedy's enormous capability of being set to music (which I did not feel at first), and if in fact I have been able to prove this with my libretto, it is because I placed myself within the sphere of Verdian art. It is so because, in writing those verses, I felt what you would feel when illustrating them with that other language—a thousand times more intimate and mighty—sound. And if I have done this it is because I wanted to take the opportunity in the prime of my life, at an age when [one's] faith no longer wavers, to take the opportunity to show you, better than by praises thrown in your direction, how much I love and am moved by the art that you have given us.

    You must now answer me whether you thought the report by the editor of the *Roma*, [as] reported by *Il piccolo* and *Il pungolo*, was true. I hope not. Yet the report existed, and because you read it you felt the same need I felt, to untie a tangled knot, to resolve a delicate question, and you have resolved it in the most exquisitely suitable manner that was possible. You addressed yourself confidentially to my most trusted friend so that in speaking to me he could question my intentions, and had he detected even a germ of truth in the journalist's report, you would have been ready to give *Otello* to me so that I might set it to music.

For a moment you doubted me, like the wise man who recognizes the weakness of Adam in men, but this doubt within you changed into a kind and generous offer. What you cannot suspect, Maestro, is the irony which this offer seemed to possess for me, without your being at fault. Look: for the past seven or eight years, perhaps, I have been working on *Nerone* (put the *perhaps* where you want it, attached to the word *years* or to the word *working*), and I live in that nightmare. On the days I don't work, I pass the hours like a lazybones; on the days I do work, [I work] like an ox. Thus life goes on and I continue to carry on, slowly asphyxiated by an ideal that is too high for me. Unfortunately I have studied my historical period (that is, the period of my subject) too well, and I am terribly attached to it. No other subject on earth, not even Schakespeare's *Othello*, could distract me from my theme; it corresponds in every way to my artistic temperament and to my concept of the theatre. I may or may not finish *Nerone*, but I will certainly never give it up for another work. If I do not have the strength to finish it, I won't complain, but will spend my life neither sad nor happy, with that dream in mind.

Now you may judge if, with this obstinacy, I could accept your offer. But for Heaven's sake don't abandon *Otello*, don't abandon it. It is predestined for you. You must set it to music; you had already begun work on it, and I was already quite encouraged, and was hoping to see it finished on some not-too-distant day.

You are healthier than I, stronger than I. We engaged in a test of strength, and my arm bent under yours. Your life is tranquil and serene—take up your pen again and write me soon: 'Dear Boito, do me the favour of changing these lines,' etc., etc., and I will change them right away, with joy. I'll know how to work for you, I, who cannot work for myself, because you live the real and true life of art, while I live in the world of hallucinations. But I must end. Many regards to Signora Giuseppina.

An affectionate handshake.

> Your
> Arrigo Boito

VERDI TO BOITO

Genoa, 26 April 1884

Dear Boito,

Seeing that you do not accept [my offer], the letter I wrote to Faccio no longer has any meaning or purpose.

I read quickly and don't believe everything in the papers. If something strikes me I stop, reflect, and try to get to the bottom to see it clearly. The question you were asked point-blank, and in that manner, at the banquet in Naples, was at the very least ... curious, and it certainly had hidden intentions which your answer did not express. Perhaps you could not have answered differently than you did—I agree; but it is also true that the entire conversation did lead to those comments which I mentioned in my letter to Faccio.

But it's useless to talk about this any more, since you absolutely do not want to accept the offer I have made you. Believe me, and without any trace of irony.

You say, '*I may or may not finish* Nerone!!' ... I, too, repeat your words with regard to *Otello*. There has been too much talk about it! Too much time has gone by! Too many are my years of age! And too many my YEARS OF SERVICE!!!! May the public not have to say to me all too obviously, '*Enough!*'

The result of all this is that something cold has spread over this *Otello* and has stiffened the hand that had begun to jot down a few measures! What will happen next? I don't know! Meanwhile I am very glad about your explanation, which, however, would have been better the moment you returned from Naples. I take your hand affectionately and greet you in Peppina's name.

Your
G. Verdi

FRANCO FACCIO TO GIULIO RICORDI

Turin, 27 April 1884

[. . .] You will know that Boito was in Turin and that I gave him the delicate message . . . . It's only a misunderstanding, which Boito will explain to our Maestro in a letter with the simple and most noble words which he has already spoken to me, while showing that he is quite upset about the unfortunate incident. [. . .]

FRANCO FACCIO TO VERDI

Turin, 29 April 1884

[. . .] Good fortune brought your Boito to me here, and I have had the expected and delicate talk with him. By now, no doubt, you will have received a letter from him; I will limit myself to reporting with fraternal gratification that the words Boito expressed to me were as I had expected, worthy in every way of his frank and most noble character. It is a pity that this incident (in which, as Boito himself observed with deep emotion, there appears the immense kindness of your soul) has perhaps made you slow down the work on *Otello*, which you must, really must, bring to an end for the glory of Italian art. I know well that for some time you have taken up the deplorable habit of mentioning the date of your baptism. Remember, however, that it used to be said of the eighty-year-old Antaeus[1] that he was four times twenty years, and that you lack another ten to reach that fourth youth. [. . .]

BOITO TO VERDI

[Milan, end April–2 May 1884][1]

Dear Maestro,

Your letter, although wise and kind, left me (I do not know why) with an uneasy feeling, and I found no peace until I went to work for you again. I recalled that you were not satisfied with a scene of Jago's in the second act that was in double five-syllable lines, and that you desired a more broken, less lyrical form. I suggested making a kind of *evil Credo*, and have tried to write it in a broken, unsymmetrical metre. The link between this piece and the preceding recitative[2] is missing, but I don't have the manuscript in front of me and therefore I cannot do this; but the gap will only amount to two or three lines. If I have done badly in this attempt, ascribe it to haste and

---

[1] In Greek legend, a giant wrestler, invincible whenever he touched the earth; crushed by Hercules, who lifted him into the air.

---

[1] The envelope is missing, but the approximate date can be inferred from Verdi's letter of 26 Apr. and his following one of 3 May 1884.

[2] It exists in Boito's handwriting on a little paper in the autograph of his libretto at St Agata:

JAGO *solo*

(*seguendo coll'occhio Cassio*) [[che]]
   Vanne; la tua mèta già vedo.
Ti spinge il tuo dimone
E il tuo dimon son io,
E me trascina il mio, nel qual io credo,
[[Inesorato Iddio:]]

[JAGO *alone*

(*following Cassio with his eyes*) [[who]]
   Go on; I already see your end.
Your demon forces you,
And I am your demon,
And my [[inexorable]] God,
In whom I believe, drags me on:]

See *Carteggi* ii. 110 for Boito's first draft, presumably conserved in the unavailable autograph of his libretto at St Agata.

excitement; I'll do it again better when you want it. Meanwhile, if you don't think it a complete mistake, please put this piece together with the other pages of *Otello*. I have done it for my own consolation and for my personal satisfaction, because I felt the need to do it. Interpret this as you wish: as childishness, as sentimentality, as superstition; it doesn't matter. Only I beg you not to answer me with even a *thank you* (which this page does not deserve), or I'll become uneasy all over again.

Here it is, then. I quote *Jago's Credo* for you.

JAGO.

. . . .

—Credo in un Dio crudel che m'ha creato
   Simile a sé, e che nell'ira io nomo.
   [[E che nell'ira io nomo.]]
—Dalla viltà d'un germe o d'un atòmo
   Vile son nato;
   Son scellerato
   Perché son uomo,
   E sento il fango originario in me.
—Sí! questa è la mia fè!
—Credo con fermo cuor, siccome crede
   La vedovella al Tempio,
   Che il mal ch'io penso e che da me procede
   Per mio destino adempio.
—Credo che il giusto è un istrïon beffardo
   E nel viso e nel cuor,
   Che tutto è in lui bugiardo,
   Lagrima, bacio, sguardo,
   Sacrificio ed onor.
—E credo l'uom [[gioco]] giuoco d'iniqua sorte
   Dal germe della culla
   Al verme dell'avel.
—Vien dopo tanta irrisïon la Morte!
—E poi?—La Morte è il Nulla,
   E vecchia fola il Ciel.

[JAGO.

. . . .

—I believe in a cruel God who has created me
   In his likeness, and whom I name in anger.
   [[And whom I name in anger.]]
—From the baseness of a germ or an atom
   Vile I was born;
   I am a villain
   Because I am a man,
   And I feel the original filth in me.

—Yes! This is my faith!
—I believe with a firm heart, as
    The little widow believes in church
    That the evil I conceive and that proceeds from me
    I accomplish by my fate.
—I believe that the righteous man is a mocking actor
    Both in his face and in his heart,
    That all in him is a lie,
    Tear, kiss, glance,
    Sacrifice and honour.
—And I believe that man is the toy of iniquitous destiny
    From the germ of the cradle
    To the worm of the tomb.
—Comes, after so much derision, Death!
—And then?—Death is Nothingness,
    And Heaven is an old tale.]

See how much devilishness I've made him speak.
An affectionate greeting to you and Signora Giuseppina

from your
Arrigo Boito

VERDI TO BOITO

Genoa, 3 May 1884

Dear Boito,
    Since you don't want it, I won't say thank you; but I will say bravo.
    This Credo is most beautiful, most powerful, and Shaespearean in every way,[1] Of course, you must tie it with some lines to the preceding scene, between Cassio and Jago; but you'll think about this later. In the meantime it's good to let this Otello rest awhile, for he is as nervous as we are. You perhaps more than I.

---

[1] Cf. Macbeth's words in Shakespeare's *Macbeth*, v. v. 24–8:

    Life's but a walking shadow, a poor player
    That struts and frets his hour upon the stage
    And then is heard no more. It is a tale
    Told by an idiot, full of sound and fury,
    Signifying nothing.

Boito marked these lines in his volume of François-Victor Hugo's French translation of Shakespeare's *Macbeth*.
    In Verdi's opera *Macbeth* to Piave's and Maffei's libretto, the protagonist's corresponding words in Act IV, Scene iii are:

La vita! che importa? è il racconto d'un povero idiota!
Vento e suono che nulla dinota!

[Life! What does it matter? It's the tale of a poor idiot!
Wind and sound that means nothing!]

If you come to St Agata later on, as you led me to believe, we can talk about it again, and this time with the necessary calm.[2]

Away, then, with any uneasiness. With Peppina's greetings, I am ever

Yours affectionately
G. Verdi

PS I have answered you late, because I have been at St Agata!

VERDI TO HENRI BLAZE DE BURY

[In French]   Genoa, 6 May 1884

[...] Don't believe a word of what the papers say about *Otello*! What is certain is: 1. That I haven't yet done a single bit of this opera, and that I probably won't write any more. 2. That one cannot say that even the *libretto* is completely finished, since Boito might still make a good many changes in case ... etc....

Under the circumstances, is it possible to think about the translation of an opera that does not yet exist, either dramatically or musically? Meanwhile I thank you, cher Monsieur Blaze, for your kind offer, which flatters me very much. One cannot build on the sand of the desert, and it is impossible to say anything definite about this *Otello*, which so far is only in *mente Dei* and in the fantasies of the journalists. [...]

VERDI TO FRANCO FACCIO

Genoa, 6 May 1884

In a few minutes we'll be leaving for St Agata, and I am taking a moment to drop you a line to thank you and to apologize for the painful commission I gave you. Boito has written to me at length and has explained to me how things happened. Certainly it would have been better if the papers hadn't talked; but that is *water under the bridge.*—Now then, must I in your opinion really finish this *Otello*? But why? For whom? To me it makes no difference! To the public even less. [...]

FRANCO FACCIO TO GIULIO RICORDI

Turin, 21 May 1884

[...] Tell me, rather, whether you have heard from *our* Maestro recently, whether he is in good health, and whether anyone knows if he is working on *Otello*. That is the shining beacon that our eyes are longing for. [...]

---

[2] By all indications, Verdi 'let this Otello rest' and did not see Boito again until their reunion in Giacosa's company at the end of September.

VERDI TO GIULIO RICORDI

St Agata, 23 May 1884

Dear Giulio,

Really, really! I have been in Milan for 24 hours!!!

And you tell me nothing about the Exhibition? About Faccio's triumph? About the Cantata? About the concerts?

I don't know yet whether I'll go to St Pellegrino or where in hell I'll be going! In case I accept you as a *messenger* with the payment of a cigar after each dinner, without talking about other things ... already past and gone forever!! Hamlet says ... 'Dead for six months and not forgotten yet!!'[1] Imagine! *Guglielm'Otello*[2] dead for so many centuries ... how to speak of him today?

In haste addio.

Yours,
G. Verdi

FRANCO FACCIO TO GIULIO RICORDI

Turin, 4 August 1884

[. . .] In Salsomaggiore, or rather in Tabiano, I have twice paid a visit to our great Maestro, who a week ago returned to the peace of St Agata. His health was flourishing, and I didn't fail to touch the *usual key*. [. . .]

VERDI TO CLARA MAFFEI

St Agata, 2 September 1884

Unexpectedly I have received the very sad news![1] Peppina knew it for 24 hours and wanted to hide it from me; but yesterday's mail brought me your letter and the family's announcement with its black border! Without grand phrases, you will well believe how deeply I regret the loss of that Saintly friend of ours. When I saw him in Milan a few months ago, I found him grown much weaker, but I hoped that he would recover and that I would see him again. Poor Carcano! I recall his last words. On a Sunday towards 1 o'clock I went to him and saw him getting ready to go out ... 'Don't bother,' I said to him. And with adorable simplicity he answered me, 'My dear Verdi, I am still one of those who go to mass on Sunday.' All right, all right, and so I accompanied him to the door of the church. 'Till we meet again' ... and I

---

[1] Shakespeare's text, III. ii. 138–9, reads: 'O heavens! die two months ago, and not forgotten yet?'

[2] Verdi is probably punning at Rossini's *Guglielmo Tell*.

---

[1] Of Giulio Carcano's death on 30 Aug.

won't see him again!! Alas, alas! You are quite right . . . having arrived at our age, we are surrounded by a void every day, and no matter how resigned, one doesn't always have the very strength that this last Saintly (really the last) friend of ours had to endure without grumbling. [. . .]

BOITO TO VERDI

Milan, 25 [September 1884][1]

Dear Maestro,

If you will have us, Giacosa and I shall arrive at St Agata during the day on the 29th, which is next Monday.[2]

We have planned this trip for three months now, and finally, to our great joy, we have both actually found two free days to do it.

Giacosa will arrive from Val d'Aosta, where there is no cholera, and he will meet me in Milan, where, thank Heaven, the public health is excellent. So we won't be bringing even the tiniest germ with us. We shall take a coach from Piacenza's most immaculate hotel and arrive at your home as uncontaminated as possible.

If, however, this plan does not fit in with your work and turns out to be inopportune, please send me a telegram in Milan the same day you receive this letter (I think you will receive it the day after tomorrow), so that I can postpone the trip and advise Giacosa accordingly.

Affectionate greetings to you and Signora Giuseppina.

Your
Arrigo Boito

VERDI TO BOITO

[Telegram]

Busseto, 26 September 1884

DO NOT TAKE COACH FROM PIACENZA—COME AT 2 BY THROUGH TRAIN TO FIORENZUOLA[1] WHERE YOU WILL FIND MY COACH

VERDI

---

[1] Postmark: MILANO 25/9/84.
[2] A probable previous communication concerning this visit is missing.

---

[1] Small railway station between Piacenza and Borgo S. Donnino, today's Fidenza.

VERDI TO BOITO

St Agata, 26 September 1884

Dear Boito,

Of course I'll have you here with Giacosa!¹

I sent you a telegram the moment I received your letter, but I am also dropping you this line to explain myself better.

You don't have to take a coach from Piacenza. You can leave Milan on Monday morning at 11.40 and without changing cars in Piacenza arrive in Fiorenzuola at 2.01; there you will find my coach. My coachman knows you. If Giacosa comes from Piedmont, he will arrive at Piacenza a few minutes after you. He will change cars and come with you to Fiorenzuola. I repeat, at 2.01.

We're not so afraid of germs around here! You won't even be tainted with chloride or carbolic acids.

Till Monday, then, and addio—no, not addio.

Your
G. Verdi

VERDI TO CLARA MAFFEI

St Agata, 16 November 1884

Dear Clarina,

Don't take it amiss if despite my long silence I can't write to you at length even today. These are laborious, unpleasant days, without poetry . . . days of business, figures, accounts with the peasants and administrators. Prosaic things, most prosaic ones, but unfortunately, without them one doesn't eat. Poor human nature! And we think we're so great . . . superior beings. Hm!! [. . .]

¹ Boito and Giacosa were guests at St Agata from 29 Sept. until 1 Oct. 1884. Giacosa spoke of this visit in a lecture about 'The Art of Reading' at Trieste in early May 1885. Excerpts from this lecture were quoted by La *gazzetta musicale* of 17 May 1885:

In the company of Arrigo Boito, I had the very high honour of being a guest at his [Verdi's] villa of Sant'Agata. It was last October. In my presence, the great Maestro was discussing with Boito some parts of the libretto which the latter had written for him, following the scenario of Shakespeare's *Othello* step by step. And while discussing it with deep dramatic perception, he came to read aloud entire scenes of the drama. His voice, the intonation, the cadence, the impulses and the rage revealed such emotional agitation and enlarged so immeasurably the sense of the words that we clearly perceived the origin of the musical idea. [. . .]

VERDI TO BOITO

Genoa, 9 December 1884

Dear Boito,

In what part of the globe are you? I hope this letter reaches you in any case. It seems impossible, but it's true!!! But!!!! I am busy writing! I am writing .... because I am writing without a goal, without preoccupations, without thinking about *later on* ... in fact, with a decided aversion to *later on*.

Listen, then:

In the scene *for four* in the second act, the dialogue between Jago and Emilia[1] ends too soon. The musical line is given to Desdemona; Otello speaks during the intervals; the others almost speak (notes and words), and since they finish too soon, as I have already said, I need four lines for each of them individually—Jago happy to have the handkerchief and Emilia frightened that it is in his hands. The metre is in 5. I am quoting the last strophe for you.

JAGO. *Ne mi paventi*?	[*You don't fear me*?
EM. Uomo crudel	Cruel man
JAG. A me ...	Give it to me ...
EM. Che tenti!	What are you trying to do?
JAG. *A me quel vel*!	*Give me that veil*!]

That's all.

Peppina greets you and I take your hand.

Your
G. Verdi

BOITO TO VERDI

[?, after 9 December 1884][1]

Maestro, I don't have a single piece of writing paper to hand, so I am using a blank page of yours to answer you; and I've found a nice little piece of cardboard on which I have transcribed the lines you want. I've added others in case these do not suffice. I had to think hard to remember how I managed the strophes between Jago and Emilia; I don't think I was wrong. The extras I'm sending you may be useful to you, since many lines are eaten up by the *notes and words* in a fast metre such as the five-syllable one. These extras are also good because for a few measures they put a new, almost playful colour into the *scene for four* and conveniently set up Jago's last violent gesture, permitting a certain economy in producing the effect. In short, see if it's good or bad.

Your letter brought me a joy that I have kept all to myself, but it came as

[1] In act II, Scene iv. (Cf. Shakespeare, *Othello*, III. iii. 304–25.)

[1] The envelope is missing. The contents of the letter suggest its date, and that it was written from the Villa d'Este.

no surprise. One does not escape one's own destiny, and through a law of intellectual affinity this tragedy by Shakespeare is predestined for you.

We'll have a talk in a few weeks. I'll be in Nervi for the Christmas holidays, or at the latest, for New Year's.

Poor Giacosa had to undergo a rather serious surgical operation: the extraction of a mucous membrane from his nose. He is in Val d'Aosta now, and he is well. How many times I have thought back on the beautiful days at St Agata!

Affectionate greetings to Signora Giuseppina and to you.

Your
Arrigo Boito

If the lines aren't suitable, write to me and I'll do some others.

Here are the concluding lines you wanted:

. . . . . .

A me quel vel![2]

JAGO. (*dopo d'aver carpito il fazzoletto*). (Già la mia brama
Conquido, ed ora
Su questa trama
Jago lavora!)
EMILIA. [[(Vinse l'orrenda
Sua mano impura
Dio ci difenda
Dalla sventura.)
JAGO. (Già il laccio l'agile
Pensier trovò.)
EMILIA. (Muta ma vigile
Scorta sarò.)]]

(Vinser gli artigli
Truci e codardi
Dio dai perigli
Sempre ci guardi.)

[*Give me that veil!*

JAGO. (*having snatched the handkerchief*). (Already my wish
I win, and now
On these meshes
Jago works!)
EMILIA. [[[(his horrible
Impure hand has won.
May God defend us
From misfortune.)

(The savage and cowardly
Claws have conquered
May God from danger
Always protect us.)

---

[2] After these words, the final text (II, 4) has this stage direction: *Con un colpo di mano Jago ha carpito il fazzoletto ad Emilia.* [*Abruptly, Jago has snatched the handkerchief from Emilia.*] instead of *dopo d'aver carpito il fazzoletto* [*having snatched the handkerchief*] alongside Jago's text. (Cf. Shakespeare, *Othello*, II. iii.320).

JAGO. (Already the agile thought
  Has found the snare.)
EMILIA. A silent but watchful
  Escort I will be.

And if these lines still aren't enough, here is an addition that can be put *in the middle of the section* between Jago and Emilia—after the first time Jago says: '*A me quel vel!*']]]

[[EM. No. Tu a colpevole
  Mister t'accingi.
JAGO (*quasi scherzosamente*). È un mio fuggevole
                Cappriccio.

EM. (*fissandolo*).   Fingi.
JAGO. Follie! quel morbido
  Lino m'adesca.
EM. V'è in te d'un torbido
  Fervor la tresca.
JAGO. (*incalzando*). Cedi.
EM.   No.
JAGO.   Taci.
EM. Punisce il ciel
  L'arti mendaci.
JAGO A me quel vel!]]
[[[EM. No. You set about
  A guilty mystery.
JAGO (*almost joking*). It's a fleeting
  Caprice of mine.
EM. (*staring at him*) You deceive.
JAGO. Madness! this soft
  Linen attracts me.
EM. There is the intrigue
  Of agitated zeal in you.
JAGO. (*insistently*). Hand it over.
EM.   No.
JAGO.   Be quiet.
EM. Heaven punishes
  Deceitful tricks.
JAGO. Give me that veil!]]]

VERDI TO OPPRANDINO ARRIVABENE

Genoa, 24 December 1884

Dear Arrivabene,
  I've been in Genoa since last night, back from St Agata, where I have been for a few days to see which jobs I had ordered have been done, and which ones can be done later on. Before I left St Agata, there were 4 or 5 centimetres

of snow, which will have melted by now, unless there has been a strong frost. There, as everywhere, they are complaining about the lack of water, and if that lasts much longer, we'll have a very bad harvest of grapes and fruit, and so we'll end up drinking no more wine. [. . .]

I'm not occupying myself with theatres and music at all, and it seems to me as though a century has passed since I lived in them. [. . .]

BOITO TO VERDI

[Nervi] 7 February [1885][1]

Dear Maestro,

I'll be returning to Genoa soon, but meanwhile, before I forget, here is the line that will help the audience avoid any misunderstanding of Cassio's words.

> CASSIO. Io qui credea di ritrovar Desdemona
> OT. (Ei la nomò)
> CASSIO. Vorrei parlarle ancora
> Per saper se la mia grazia è profferta

> [CASSIO. I thought I'd find Desdemona here.
> OT. He said her name.
> CASSIO. I'd like to speak to her again
> In order to know if my pardon has been offered.]

The rhyme is *certa*[2]—I've written it down.

Many greetings, and till we see each other again soon,

Yours most affectionately
Arrigo Boito

VERDI TO BOITO

[Genoa] Wednesday [18 February 1885][1]

Dear Boito,

If you don't mind, we'll postpone our little dinner for tomorrow until Saturday. Peppina is ill.

Addio, addio.

Your
G. Verdi

[1] The envelope is missing, but Boito's letter to Verdi in Dec. 1884 leaves no doubt that he wrote these lines at Nervi in 1885. During his sojourn at Nervi (12 kilometres south of Genoa) in Jan. and Feb. 1886, Boito obviously had several meetings with Verdi in Genoa.

[2] In the new verse (III. v), Cassio's last word 'profferta' rhymes with Jago's last word 'certa' ['certain']. ('*Fa cor, la tua causa è in tal mano / Che la vittoria è certa.*') ['Take heart, your case is in such a hand / That victory is certain.])

[1] Postmark: GENOVA 18/2/85.

VERDI TO GIULIO RICORDI

Genoa, 12 March 1885

Dear Giulio,

It really was a great pleasure for me and for Peppina to receive your short letter[1] telling me of your convalescence,[2] which your father also confirmed to me the next day.[3]

There is nothing else to be done now but to look after your health, take all possible care, and do little work. Do you understand?

Do little work. You say, 'In the most well-ordered life how could I happen to get such an illness. . . .'

Do you think that *working* too much is [living] a well-ordered life?

You are [engaged] in a feverish activity, which is still an illness . . . It must be cured! . .

I am glad, and greet you also from Peppina.

Addio, addio

Yours,
G. Verdi

PS Our health is fair . . .

BOITO TO VERDI

Milan.
Easter. [5 April 1885][1]

Dear Maestro,

I delayed my departure from Nervi yet another day: instead of leaving on Friday I left on Saturday. I saw Giulio a few hours after my arrival. He made an excellent impression on me. It didn't even appear to me that he had lost any weight—a small consolation, however, since he couldn't lose weight even if he wanted to. I had been told that he was very depressed emotionally, but I was not aware of this. We spent the evening together at Thomas Holden's marionettes and took immense delight in that marvellous show. When Holden comes to Genoa, do go to see him. He's the Listz[2] of puppets—such perfection cannot be believed unless it is seen. After the theatre we went to the café and left each other towards midnight. Today Giulio will spend the

---

[1] Missing.

[2] Giulio Ricordi had been bedridden since mid-Jan. 1885, and Verdi had repeatedly expressed his concern.

[3] Missing. Meanwhile, however, Tito Ricordi had sent Verdi an (inaccurate and incomplete) Italian translation of Heinrich Heine's essay 'Shakespeares Mädchen und Frauen'. Without dating it, he wrote on the margin: 'In case this could be useful to you or make you love your Desdemona even more.'

---

[1] Postmark: MILANO 5/4/85.

[2] Franz Liszt, the Hungarian piano virtuoso and composer (1811–86) misspelled.

day at the Villa d'Este. Tornaghi and other friends whom I had asked for news of Giulio before seeing him had told me, with some uneasiness, about a [certain] reluctance to work that he had shown after his illness; but then Giulio himself volunteered an explanation to me of this reluctance. He is still not completely recovered, and he must be very careful about his eating habits as well as his work; he confessed to me that when he tried to write, his arm swelled up immediately. It's natural, then, that he is reluctant to work at the moment; but this reluctance isn't due to any unhealthy moral or intellectual disposition, but rather to his physical condition, which still hasn't been perfectly restored. I believe that a good treatment during the summer, well planned and well carried out, will cure him completely.

This is my impression, and I don't think I am deceiving myself.[3]

Most cordial greetings to Signora Giuseppina. For you, Maestro, an affectionate handshake

> from your
> Arrigo Boito

AMILCARE PONCHIELLI TO TERESA BRAMBILLA PONCHIELLI

[Milan, end of April–early May 1885]

[. . .] Above all, I drove certain worries out of my head yesterday after a visit I paid to Verdi, who is still here in Milan. [. . .]

Then we talked about the opera by Puccini,[1] whose kind of music we don't like, because it follows in the footsteps of Massenet, Wagner, etc.—Then [we talked] about *Mefistofele*, in which he praised the duet 'Lontano, lontano,' the quartet, and certain instrumental details of the aria in the prison. But nothing else, and I understand that the fugue ending the act of the witches doesn't please him. He doesn't think Boito will finish *Nerone* so soon, since he told him that he was still composing the first act!!!!

Then he deplored the conditions that force the theatres to pay certain artists too much . . . and I could see that they planned to engage Masini, etc., at La Scala (therefore, in my opinion, [there is] the probability of having *Jago* . . . I believe!!).

I talked with him for about three-quarters of an hour. At a certain point he wanted me to go downstairs with him to see Field Marshal Moltke (Prussian),[2] who was leaving the hotel at that moment. [. . .]

---

[3] 'Also Giulio's illness is quite serious,' Verdi wrote to Clara Maffei from Genoa on 17 Apr. 1885. 'Boito wrote to me about it, as if the thing were over by now, but I am afraid it isn't so! Poor Giulio! This is a far greater misfortune than Filippi's illness—for his family, as for the firm and for many, many young artists. Let's hope, all the same!' (Autograph: Chiari; Ascoli, p. 409.)

---

[1] *Le villi*, opera in 1 act by Giacomo Puccini (1858–1924), his first; produced upon Boito's recommendation at the Teatro Dal Verme in Milan on 31 May 1884.
[2] Count Helmuth von Moltke (1800–91).

VERDI TO OPPRANDINO ARRIVABENE

Milan, 2 May 1885

[. . .] I am here with Peppina to . . . woe is me! have teeth pulled that for some time have been in a deplorable state! There is an American dentist here of great reputation, and I have put myself in his hands. Who knows what's going to happen. Meanwhile he pulled five and a root the other day! Monday I'll go to St Agata, and I'll return here after two months because of these damned teeth! I also received the booklet *Ars nova* which you sent me. I haven't had time to read it attentively, but from what I can make out, it's one of those typical publications that do not discuss, but that pass judgement with incredible intolerance. On the last page I read, among other things, this phrase: 'If you believe that music is the expression of feelings, of love, of pain, etc., etc., etc., forget about it . . . it is not for you!!!'

And how could I not believe that music is the expression of love, of pain, etc., etc.?? [. . .]

GIULIO RICORDI TO VERDI

Milan, 8 May 1885

[. . .] If, then, I am unable to profit from your kind invitation[1] for an extended visit, I can always be a guest at St Agata for a good week, which will be of the greatest help [for my recovery]. [. . .]

VERDI TO GIULIO RICORDI

St Agata, 10 May 1885

Dear Giulio,

Alas! Alas! You won't be able to stay here for more than about eight days? . . . That leaves no time to recover even from the boredom that will seize you in the first days after your arrival at our home. *Boredom* is a kind of fever which leaves a certain weakness when it's over, a weariness followed by a healthy and not disagreeable calm. After the crisis was over and calm had arrived, you would have taken up a bit of reading, playing the piano, writing music or something else, then a game of billiards, a few words with Peppina, a few more with me, grumbling about music, some walks along the banks of the Pò with a *crayon* or a *paintbrush*—and you would have found peace, calm, and health. But what can you do in eight days? . . However, you will do as you wish, and you will be welcome in any case. [. . .]

[1] Apparently, Verdi extended this invitation in person while staying in Milan from the end of Apr. until 4 May 1885.

OPPRANDINO ARRIVABENE TO VERDI

Rome, 24 May 1885

[. . .] I am very happy whenever I hear or read something praiseworthy about you; but I confess that since 'the new era of thought' has arrived I don't understand all the new theories. Even the *thesis* upheld by the honest Giacosa, your dear friend, I did not understand well. I have seen that he speaks of you with great sympathy and admires your reading; but I repeat, I did not understand the *thesis*. Far less did I understand the theory, solemnly expounded by someone else, that once a *type* has been created no other person must touch it, not even in a different art. But all our great painters have put their hands on types that had already been created, either by paganism or by Christianity. For example, he says that *Otello* belongs to Shakespeare and not to Rossini; this is true, but did Rossini perhaps create the type of the *Barbiere*? And yet it seems to me that (even after half a century) Rossini's *Barbiere di Siviglia* is more alive than the comedy from which it was drawn. As for *Otello*, it cannot be said that Rossini wanted to make it like Shakespeare. I know well that Filippi, that audacious judge, has said, 'Rossini did not understand Shakespeare,' but Rossini understood the *Otello* of the Marquis Berio; more than that he did not need to understand. Besides, anyone who has known Rossini knows that he had as much intellectual power to understand as Filippi has, and much more. On the other hand, I am not persuaded that music could not confront such a dramatic subject. Is it, perhaps, necessary to follow Shakespeare scrupulously? Can the Venetian element not be given greater development? Can the story not be modified? It's not Shakespeare who comes on stage but the Moor of Venice. Enough. You know more about this than I do and can better judge these absurd ideas. [. . .]

BOITO TO VERDI

Milan, Wednesday [9 September 1885]¹

Dear Maestro,

My desire to see you is great, but the fear I have of disturbing you is equally great. If you can assure me that I won't be bothering you, I'll decide to drop in at St Agata next Sunday. But if my coming would upset, even in the slightest, the lovely tranquillity of your home or—which would be even worse—the progress of your work, you must tell me this openly, with that frankness of yours which I admire so much, and I would be just as happy with your sincere words as with your kind hospitality.

And I make the same suggestion to Signora Giuseppina.

Most cordial greetings to the two of you from

Your most affectionate
Arrigo Boito

¹ Postmark: MILANO 9/9/85.

VERDI TO BOITO

St Agata, 10 September 1885

Dear Boito,

You could never disturb us! Come, and you will give great pleasure to me and to Peppina, too. And don't be afraid, either, of interrupting the progress of my work, as you say! Alas, alas! Since I have been here (I blush to say this) I haven't done a thing! The countryside, the baths, the excessive heat, and . . . let's admit it, my unimaginable laziness have stood in the way.

Well then, till Sunday. If you leave Milan on the *through train* at *11.40* a.m., get off at Fiorenzuola (I repeat, *Fiorenzuola*) at 2 p.m. and you will find one of my Bucephali,[1] which will bring you here.

Till we see each other soon. Peppina greets you and I take your hand. Addio

Affectionately,
G. Verdi

VERDI TO BOITO

[St Agata, September–October 1885?][1]

Here you have the fourth act.
Don't destroy anything of what you have already done.[2]
At the same time, I pay my little debt and greet you.

G. Verdi

VERDI TO BOITO

St Agata, 5 October 1885

Dear Boito,

I have finished the fourth act and can breathe! It seemed difficult to avoid the many recitatives, and to find some rhythm, some phrases for so many blank [*sciolti*] and so many broken [*spezzati*] verses. But in this way you were able to say everything that had to be said, and now I am as calm and happy as a lark. In doing the music for this ultra-terrible scene, I felt the need to leave out a strophe that I had asked you to add myself, and here and there to utilize a line, some half lines, and especially a most beautiful strophe that we had mistakenly abandoned. Consequently, there are some unconnected lines that you can easily *connect*.

You've overcome quite a lot of other difficulties!

---

[1] Italian plural form of Bucephalus, the war horse of Alexander the Great.

[1] The following letter might suggest the time of these completely undated lines.
[2] See *Carteggi* ii. 117–22 for substantial text in original libretto.

E gli occhi suoi piangevan tanto tanto
Da impietosir le rupi!

[*And her eyes cried so very, very much*
It made the rocks take pity!][1]

is more beautiful than the original.
I am transcribing the whole scene for you as it is now composed.[2]

Scene iii

. . . .
come stà fino all

. . . .
. . . .

Ami Cassio!

D. No! Sull'anima mia!!
O.   Quel fazzoletto
  Ch'io ti donai gli desti
D.   Non è vero!
O. Io lo vidi nella sua man!
D.   Fú inganno!.
O. Confessa
D.   Giuro
O.   Bada allo spergiuro!
  Pensa che sei sul tuo letto di morte!
D. Non per morir!
O.   Per morir tosto
D.   Aita!
  Cassio non amo .. Ch'ei qui venga .. ei parli . . .
O. Piú nol vedrai . . .
D.   Che dite? . . . . . Morto?!
O. ..   Morto!
D. Son perduta . . . Ei tradito! .
O.   E pianger l'osi?
D. Otello non uccidermi
O.   Giú . . . cadi
  Prostituta
D.   Pietà
O.   Muori
D.   Ch'io viva
  Questa notte
O.   Nò
D.   Un'ora
O.   Nò
D.   Un istante!

Aggiustate come volete que-
sto verso ma evitate una lun-
ga frase come era in prima:
'Chiusa per sempre è la sua
bocca.'

Conservate se potete *'Otello*
non uccidermi!'
È straziante!

[1] Cf. Shakespeare, *Othello*, IV. iii. 46: 'Her salt tears fell from her, which soften'd the stones.'
[2] Cf. Shakespeare, *Othello*, V. ii.

o. Nò!

D.   Sol ch'io dica un ave

                    E tardi È tardi . . .   *(Pausa lunga)*

o. Calma . . . come la tomba

EMILIA *(bussa alla porta)*.   Aprite!

o.   Emilia!!

EMILIA *(Entrando)* . . . [[Aprite! . . .]]

    Orrible delitto! . . . Cassio uccise

    Rodrigo

o.   E Cassio?

EM.   Vive!

o.   Cassio vive?!

D. Ingiustamente uccisa . . . ingiustamente

E. Ciel qual gemito! . orror

[D.]   Muojo innocente . . .

> *A me piacerebbe che Emilia dicesse ancora "Aprite! oh qual delitto!*

> *Forse è troppo dire tre volte "Cassio" ma stà tanto bene in Otello il Cassio vive*

E. Chi fú? chi fú?

    [D.]   Nissuno . . . io stessa . . . al mio . . .

    Al mio Signor . . . mi raccomanda . . . Addio! . . . *(muore)*

                                                va!

o.   Menti

                                        trice!

    Io l'uccisi

E.   Assassino!

o.   Fú di Cassio

    La druda! A Jago il chiedi! . .

E.   A Jago? . .

o.   A Jago!

EM. Soccorso . . . ajuto, ajuto! . . . All'assassinio! .

        Entrano *Lodovico Cassio Jago e soldati*

TUTTI. Quai grida . . . Cielo! . . . Desdemona uccisa!

EMILIA *(a Jago)*. Jago smentisci quel vile omicida . . .

    Credi la casta

    [[Credesti tu]] Desdemona infida? .

> *Mi piace poco in questo luogo la parola 'casta' Non potreste dire: Hai tu creduto et.*

JAGO. Tal la credea

E.   Tu?

J.   Sì

OTELLO *(interrompendo)*.   Quel fazzoletto

    Che un dì le diedi a Cassio essa donò.

E. Oh potenza divina!

J.   Taci

E.   Nò

    Tutto rivelo

J.   Taci

E.   Maledetto

    Dal Cielo

J.   Taci

E.   No

J.   Trema

E.   Costui

> Questo tratto pare lungo, ma in musica è riescito rapido, e breve piú che se fosse recitato.

Dalla mia man quel fazzoletto colse
  A viva forza!
CASSIO.   E nella mia dimora
  Trovai quel velo!
MONTANO *(entrando grida)*. Rodrigo morente
  Svelò di quest'infame opre nefande
OTELLO *(a Jago)*.
  Ah! Discolpati
JAGO *(con un'urlo) Nò! (e fugge)*
LOD.   S'insegua, e tratto
  Al carcer sia! .
OTEL *(con grida)*. E il Ciel non ha piú fulmini!!
LOD. *(a Otello)*.
  Tu sei mio prigionier! .
OT. . *(pausa lunga)*   Tutto è finito! . .
  La gloria è un lampo, un sogno menzogner!
        s'avvicina a Desdemona
  E tú . . . come sei pallida!—e stanca e muta e bella
  Pia creatura nata—sotto maligna stella
  Fredda, come la casta tua vita e in cielo assorta!
  Desdemona, Desdemona!—Ah! . . morta—morta—morta!!

*Dopo una lunga pausa corre al tavolo ove aveva deposta la spada . . .
      lo previene,
Cassio* [[*impedisce et*]] *e toglie la spada. Allora Otello estrae un
pugnale e dice*
        [[*rapidamente e si uccide*]]
  Questo pugnal mi resta! . *e si uccide.*
TUTTI   Ah sciagurato!
[OTELLO] Prima d'ucciderti et etc . . *come stà . .*

                    • — — — — — —

                    . . . .
                    [as it is up to the
                    . . . .
                    . . . .

                    You love Cassio!

D. No! By my soul!!
O.   That handkerchief
  I gave you, you gave to him
D.   It isn't true!
O. I saw it in his hand!
D.   It was a trick!.
O. Confess
D.   I swear
O.   Beware of perjury!
  Mind that you are on your deathbed!
D. Not to die!
O.   To die soon
D.   Help!
  I don't love Cassio . . Have him come here . . let him speak . . .

o. You will see him no more . . .

What are you saying? . . . . .

Dead?!

Adjust this line as you wish, but avoid a long phrase as it was before: 'Closed forever is his mouth.'

D.   Dead!

o.

D. I am lost . . . He, betrayed!.

o.   And you dare weep for him?

D. Otello, do not kill me

Keep, if you can, 'Otello, do not kill me!' It's heartbreaking!

o.   Down . . . fall down

   Strumpet
D.   Pity

o.   Die

D.   Let me live

   Tonight

o.   No

D.   One hour

o.   No

D.   One moment!

o. No!

D.   Just let me say a prayer

o.   Too late Too late . . . *(Long pause)*

o. Quiet . . . as the grave

EMILIA *(knocking at the door).* Open!

o.   Emilia!!

EMILIA *(entering)*. . .   [[Open! . . .]]
   A horrible crime! . .   Cassio has killed
   Rodrigo

I'd like Emilia to say once more, 'Open! Oh, what a crime!'

o.   And Cassio?

EM.   He lives!

o.   Cassio lives?!

D. Unjustly killed . . . unjustly

Perhaps it is too much to say 'Cassio' three times, but the 'Cassio lives' is so good for Otello.

E. Heaven, what a groan! . Horror

[D.]   I die innocent . . .

E. Who was that? who was that?

[D.]   No one . . . I myself . . . to my . . .
   to my Lord . . . commend me . . . Farewell! . .   *(she dies)*

o.   Go!

                         Liar!

   I killed her

E.   Assassin!

o.   She was Cassio's
   Mistress! I asked Jago about it! . .

E.   Jago? . .

o.   Jago!

EM. Help . . . help, help! . .   Get the assassin! .

       Lodovico, Cassio, Jago, and soldiers enter

ALL. What shouts . . . Heaven! . . Desdemona killed!

EMILIA *(to Jago)* Jago, deny this vile murder . . .
   Do you believe the chaste
   [[Did you believe]] Desdemona unfaithful?

I don't care for the word 'chaste' at this point. Couldn't you say: Did you believe, etc.

JAGO. Such I thought her

E.   You?

J.   Yes

OTELLO *(interrupting)*.   The handkerchief
   That one day I gave her, she gave to Cassio.

E. O divine power!

J.   Be quiet

E.   No
   I'll reveal everything

J.   Be quiet

E.   Cursed
   By Heaven

J.   Be quiet

E.   No

J.   Tremble

E.   This man
   Grabbed that handkerchief by force
   From my hand!

CASSIO   And in my home
   I found that veil!

MONTANO *(enters and shouts)*. Rodrigo, dying.
   Revealed the nefarious deeds of this infamous man.

> This passage seems long, but set to music it has become quicker and shorter than if it were spoken.

OTELLO *(to Jago)*. Ah! Vindicate yourself

JAGO *(with a suppressed howl)*. No! *(and flees)*

LOD.   Follow him and take him
   To prison! .

OTEL. *(crying out)*. And Heaven has no more thunderbolts!!

LOD *(to Otello)*. You are my prisoner! .

OT. . *(a long pause)*.   All is finished! . .
   Glory is a flash of lightning, a lying dream!
     approaches Desdemona
   And you . . . how pale you are! and weary and silent and beautiful,
   Pious creature, born under an evil star
   Cold, like your chaste life, and taken up into Heaven!
   Desdemona, Desdemona!—Ah! . . dead, dead, dead!!

After a long pause he rushes to the table where he had put the sword . . .
   stops him
Cassio [[prevents him]] and takes the sword. Then Otello pulls out a dagger and says
[[swiftly and kills himself]]
   This dagger is left to me! . *(and kills himself.)*

ALL.   Ah, unlucky man!

[OTELLO] Before I killed you, etc., etc., . . *as is* . .

· — — — — — — —]

Amen, and I greet you from the heart.

Affectionately,
G. Verdi

VERDI TO CLARA MAFFEI

St Agata, 9 October 1885

Dearest Clarina,

Today is the awful day![1] *I am 72!!!!* And how fast the years have gone by, despite so many sad and joyous events and so many, many hardships and labours! But let's put aside these thoughts which bring too much sorrow when we indulge in them ... to the point of despair! And how are you spending [the years], my dear Clarina, without the persons who surely were dear to you and who stood by you for so many years? At our age one feels the need for support. Until a few years ago I seemed to be self-sufficient and not to need anything. How presumptuous! .. Now I'm beginning to understand that ... I am rather old!!!! [. . .]

BOITO TO VERDI

Villa d'Este
Lago di Como, 9 October [1885][1]

Dear Maestro,

First of all, from the bottom of my heart, *Evviva!*[2] Next, I must confess to you that I have an irresistible desire to know what you have written on that page so full of terrors; that page is the most distressing ever conceived by the human mind.

I must add that without first hearing the accents and rhythms you have written, I cannot very well finish the little connecting job you expect from me in this scene; if they have captured the truth in all its horror, and with the power and simplicity with which they captured it in the preceding scenes, then one must really be afraid of hearing them, and doubtless this will be the case.

In just a few days I shall have the opportunity to be near you again. I must be in Rome on the morning of the 19th of this month. On the way there or back I can stop at Fiorenzuola and from there run over to St Agata. I'll be staying in Rome for about a week. If our *interview* works out on the way there, I would leave Milan on the morning of the 16th, stay at St Agata on the 17th, and leave again for Rome the morning of the 18th; if it works out

---

[1] Supposedly Verdi's birthday was 10 Oct. 1813, but his mother had told him that he was born on 9 Oct. 1814. Only in 1876 did he ascertain in the parish register at Le Roncole that he was a year less a day older than he thought. However, he continued to observe his birthday on 9 Oct. (Mary Jane Phillips Matz considers 9 Oct. 1813 the correct date. See her article *Le radici dell'albero genealogico verdiano*, and also Alberti, pp. 286–7.)

---

[1] According to the postmark of this letter—CERNOBBIO 8/10/85—Boito dated it one day later. Judging from his very clear handwriting, he was in no hurry and not as absent-minded as on other occasions. It seems more likely, therefore, that the clerk at the little post office of Cernobbio failed to advance the date of his stamp.

[2] On the occasion of Verdi's birthday (see note 1 to the preceding letter).

for my return, instead, our meeting would take place towards the 25th or the 26th, but then my friend Giacosa will be travelling with me, and I wouldn't have the heart to leave him alone on the train so close to the threshold of Schakespeare's kingdom. Please choose between these two alternatives.

But perhaps you would prefer to postpone our meeting until Milan, if you are going there again this year and will stop over for a few days before going on to Genoa. I'll stay at the Villa d'Este until the afternoon of the 14th, that is, through next Wednesday; then I'll go to Milan.

We are agreed.

I repeat: to do well what little I still have to do, I must have Shakespeare's text in front of me and your music close at hand. I await your reply. Many cordial greetings to Signora Giuseppina. For you, Maestro, a handshake, and once again: *Evviva!*

Your most affectionate
Arrigo Boito

PS Unless you wrote the wrong date,[3] I received your letter after a long delay.

VERDI TO BOITO

St Agata, 11 October 1885

Dear Boito,

All right, I'll expect you on the 16th. It wouldn't be possible later, since Peppina, as usual, must go to her sister's.[1] You will find one of my Bucephali in Fiorenzuola at 2 p.m. on the *1*6th. But send me a telegram the day before to confirm your arrival.

Till we see each other again ... till we see each other again,

Your
G. Verdi

BOITO TO VERDI

Milan, 23 [October 1885][1]

Dear Maestro,

I can say with Aristophanes: '*j'ai perdu ma fiole*'.[2] When I left St Agata I forgot the *Otello* volume and now, putting my papers in order, I notice that I

---

[3] Verdi's dating corresponds to the postmark on his letter of 5 Oct. 1885. The post appears to have been exceptionally delayed.

---

[1] Barberina Strepponi in nearby Cremona.

---

[1] Postmark: MILANO 23/10/85.
[2] Literally in French: 'I have lost my flask', in slang also meaning 'my head'. This quotation seems to derive from *The Frogs* by Aristophanes, in which Aeschylus pokes fun at Euripides.

also forgot the copy you made of the last scene,[3] which I had received at the Villa d'Este and on which we worked together a few days ago. I'm afraid that if you find this manuscript you might tear it up and throw it in the waste-paper basket. But I hope I'm still in time to rescue it. It is dear to me; it is a souvenir of our work. There is a letter from you to me attached to it, so please don't destroy it, but put it in the volume of our tragedy so that it won't be lost.

Giulio, who is well and whom I saw the day before yesterday, told me that the payment had been made on Signora Giuseppina's behalf. Nothing else remains for me to say but to greet you and once again to thank you very much for the powerful and elevated intellectual emotions I enjoyed at St Agata, and for your and Signora Giuseppina's good and dear hospitality.

Your most affectionate
Arrigo Boito

PS You needn't bother to send me the volume and the manuscript,[4] since we'll be seeing each other again very soon in Milan.

VERDI TO BOITO

St Agata, 27 October 1885

Dear Boito,

I found your French Shakpeare and your notebook, etc. . . . But what do you want [me?] to do with the latter? I think it should be burned, and I would have burned it if you hadn't asked me for it. But we'll take care of this transaction when I go from here to Milan in 15 or 20 days[1] to have *my teeth checked.*

I am still involved with the fourth act, which I want to finish completely, along with the instrumentation, so that I can seal it up and talk no more about it until the . . . the . . .

Addio. Give me your news and tell me if your poet has finished *Nerone*[2] . . .

Your
G. Verdi

---

[3] The copy that Verdi had sent to Boito on 5 Oct. 1885. A facsimile of the autograph in *Carteggio* i. 88–9 shows Verdi's and Boito's corrections. See also *Carteggi* ii. 117–22.

[4] Apparently, Verdi returned to Boito neither the manuscript, i.e. the copy of the last scene, nor his letter of 5 Oct. 1885, which Boito had left with him. Both are at St Agata.

---

[1] According to *La gazzetta musicale* of 29 Nov. 1885, the Verdis arrived in Milan only at the end of Nov., proceeding to Genoa on 5 Dec. 1885.

[2] Ironical remark, since Boito was his own poet.

VERDI TO GIULIO RICORDI

St Agata, 6 November 1885

Dear Giulio,

Do what you think best for *La traviata* as well as for the *Miller*.[1] I also point out that the *Miller* is almost a new opera for present-day theatregoers, and a kind of *début* for the music!

I add that la Bellincioni will never have the [same] success in the *Miller* as in *La traviata*,[2] and therefore it will be less effective for her, and a discredit to—or at least [cause for] *doubts* about—the music of the *Miller*, which they will find nice or ugly, young or old. . . . Old?!! As if *30* or *40* years ago one couldn't make good music without the exuberant orchestral and harmonic beauties of today. I don't mean to disapprove of the qualities of today's music, but I disapprove of the system . . . that is, the attempt to make a heavy, boring, more conventional system than before, and *poor* despite the luxuries mentioned above.

It's very well to search for young singers (as long as one finds them?), and it's very well to give new operas (I have always said this) by new composers. Only instead of one, you should give two or three——Why don't the young fellows who were awarded prizes two years ago[3] have a new opera ready? . . . In two years!!—Perhaps they will say that Mayerbeer was slow; but I reply that *Bach, Händel, Mozart, Rossini*, etc., etc., wrote *Israel in Egypt*[4] in *15* days, *Don Giovanni* in a month, the *Barbiere* in 17 or 18 days!

But so it is; these men, besides their inventiveness, did not have spoiled blood, had well-balanced natures, were level-headed, and knew what they wanted. They didn't need to be inspired by others, or to *do* like the moderns à la Chopin, à la Mendelson, à la Gounod, etc. They wrote spontaneously, as they felt; and they made masterpieces that had, it's true, imbalances, defects, even mistakes, which most of the time were strokes of genius . . . Amen.— [. . .]

VERDI TO BOITO

St Agata, 8 November 1885

Dear Boito,

There isn't the slightest doubt. The conclusion of your letter[1] is perfect.

---

[1] In a letter to Verdi of the previous day, Giulio Ricordi suggested these operas for La Scala in the forthcoming season.
[2] *Luisa Miller* was not included in the repertoire of La Scala in 1886. *La traviata* had a single unsuccessful performance with Gemma Bellincioni on 30 Mar. 1886.
[3] Unknown.
[4] Oratorio by Georg Friedrich Händel (1685–1759), not to be confused with Rossini's *Mosè in Egitto* which was composed with similar speed.

---

[1] The corresponding letter is missing.

Principal goal: *The Unity of the Diapason*.² Give in if you cannot do otherwise—but not without [first] declaring openly, loudly, and publicly that from the scientific point of view *870* vibrations is an error. You speak clearly and distinctly and will easily present the truth.

With the authority of our conservatories, it could very well be declared that we retain the diapason of 864 because it is more correct; but such firmness might seem like stubbornness, and [the sort of] childishness that could almost lend itself to ridicule and that your friends on the other side of the Alps would immediately seize upon.

Conclusion: *Give in*, I repeat, *if you cannot do otherwise*; and *the Unity*, etc.

Write to me about the outcome of it all from Vienna.³ With Peppina's greetings, I wish you a good trip and say addio.

Your
G. Verdi

OPPRANDINO ARRIVABENE TO VERDI

Rome, 16 November 1885

My dearest Verdi,

Today, leaving the house shortly after noon, I met our Piroli right at the door. I knew that he was well, since he had been seen at the Costanzi, where, after forty years, he again heard and applauded your *Ernani*, who—being more fortunate than we are—doesn't age at all. I told him that you were wrong to think me already dead. [. . .] I asked him about you, and he told me that you were well, and that it is said, hoped, and believed that the wicked Jago is about to leave St Agata for Milan. [. . .]

VERDI TO OPPRANDINO ARRIVABENE

St Agata, 20 November 1885

[. . .] As for the wicked Jago (not Jago but *Otello*), I have really worked a great deal these last months. This has diverted me, lifted me up, and given me, to say it all, the greatest pleasure. As for having it performed, that is a different kettle of fish. This will be more difficult than to finish it entirely. [. . .]

---

² Greek διὰ πασων, i.e. 'through all strings'. In Greek and medieval theory, the interval that includes 'all the tones', i.e. the octave. Verdi refers here to the standard concert pitch. A universal pitch was to be established at an international conference in Vienna, in which Boito participated. (See Appendix V.)

³ Boito apparently planned to write to Verdi from Milan; but on his return there, he seems to have met him unexpectedly. The dental treatment Verdi mentioned in his letter to Boito of 27 Oct. 1885 had obviously been postponed.

CLARA MAFFEI TO VERDI

Milan, 7 December 1885

These are not thanks, but blessings that my poor soul sends you for all the infinite, ineffable goodness you have lavished upon me in these very sad days;[1] you consoled me with your precious affection, which moves me and makes me proud; you supported me by giving my conscience ever more solace, and this is the greatest goodness! It is sweet to forgive; it is a hard, terrible punishment to recognize that one has been wrong or that one has done what one should not have done!

Kiss, bless also the dear and best Peppina. [. . .]

OPPRANDINO ARRIVABENE TO VERDI

Rome, 9 December 1885

My dearest Verdi,

From your last letter[1] I understand that by this time you will already have left for Genoa to spend the winter there. And how did the acquisition of the eating machines in Milan, of which you spoke to me, work out for you? I am sure that the pleasure of your excursion to Milan was ruined for you by Andrea Maffei's death, a death that has saddened me, too, since he was my friend for over half a century! But you were there and surely wanted to press his hand once more, mindful of the first *intimate ovations*, so to speak, by a most distinguished and intelligent society in his home at the dawn of your long and splendid day—but you could not bid him farewell! [. . .]

I am very glad that you are writing and, as you tell me, diverting yourself with *Otello*.

I hope that Filippi will not say of you, as he has said impertinently of Rossini, that you did not understand the English tragedian; besides, I believe that even if one understands him very well, it isn't necessary to follow him with scrupulous fidelity. It's a work of imagination, not history.

A propos your many *scores*, I was asked a question that I couldn't answer, of course. The question is this: 'Why has Verdi almost entirely suppressed the *contralto*? In the instrumental quartet we have a double-bass, violoncello, viola, and violin; so it must be, and so it would be good in the case of the human voice. Why suppress the viola?' I don't remember well whether I have asked you this at some time, but I don't think so. I would no doubt remember your answer. It's possible that you might not have answered me.[2] You aren't obliged to satisfy all the curiosity of other people.

That would be the last straw! [. . .]

---

[1] Andrea Maffei, Clara's former husband, had died unexpectedly in a hotel in Milan on 27 Nov. while Verdi happened to be in the city.

---

[1] Of 20 Nov. 1885. In that last letter, Verdi had mentioned the 'acquisition' of dentures in Milan.

[2] No answer to this question exists in Verdi's available correspondence with Arrivabene.

VICTOR MAUREL TO VERDI

[In French]   Paris, 22 December 1885

Dear and Illustrious Maestro!

In the world of music and theatre in Paris there is, at this moment, only one great news that the papers give; this is it:

VERDI HAS FINISHED HIS JAGO

I am, and will forever be, proud to remind myself of the honour of having been the first interpreter of the strange, complex figure whom the breath of your mighty genius was destined to endow with sublime musical thoughts and accents. In fact, you promised me after a rehearsal of *Simon Boccanegra* that to thank me for the zeal and enthusiasm with which I interpreted my role, you would write one entirely for me.

If God gives me health, you said to me, I will write Jago for you! I consider myself not unworthy of the honour you kindly allotted to the few qualities [I possess] as an artist of honesty and conviction. I am pleased to let you know—with the artistic conscientiousness you could appreciate in me—that my vocal resources have never been so powerful and secure as they are today [. . .]

I hope, dear and illustrious Maestro, that you will keep your promise to me. [. . .]

VERDI TO VICTOR MAUREL

Genoa, 30 December 1885

Otello is not completely finished, as has been said, but it is well on its way towards the end. I am in no hurry to complete the work, because thus far I have never thought, nor do I now think, of having it performed. The conditions in our theatres are such that the impresario, even when achieving a success, must always suffer a loss due to the exorbitant expenses for the artists and the *mise-en-scène*. Therefore I do not want to feel remorse for causing anyone's ruin with one of my operas. So things remain suspended between heaven and earth, like Muhammad's tomb, and I'm not deciding on any practical solution.

Before ending this letter I wish to clarify and explain a misunderstanding. I do not believe that I ever promised to write the role of *Jago* for you. I am not in the habit of making a promise that I am not completely sure I can keep. But I might very well have told you that the role of Jago would be one of those which perhaps no one else could interpret better than you. If I said this, I confirm what I said. This, however, does not include a promise; it would be only a wish, a most realizable one so long as unforeseen circumstances do not oppose it.

For the present, then, let's not speak of *Otello*. Allow me, my dear Maurel, to send you my good wishes for the new year, and to remain your sincere admirer. [. . .]

VERDI TO MARIA WALDMANN

Genoa, 1 January 1886

[. . .] You will forgive me, my good Maria, if I don't reply now to all the lovely things you say in your letter.[1] I will tell you only that it's really true that I have worked a lot on *Otello*, that the work is well advanced, but that it's very, very difficult for me to decide whether [or not] I should let it be performed. [. . .]

GIUSEPPINA VERDI TO GIUSEPPE DE SANCTIS

Genoa, 1 January 1886

[. . .] Verdi has almost finished *Otello*, and he will finish it, since he is enjoying this work, but I think he may never give it! Therefore the time, the theatre, the artists are all fantasies of clever journalists! *Amen*! [. . .]

ALPHONSE LEDUC TO VERDI

[In French]   Paris, 1 January 1886

[. . .] The moment *Jago* is completed I [shall] address myself to your kind remembrance, asking whether it would please you to transfer the rights for France, Belgium, and Switzerland to me. [. . .]

I need not tell you that from every point of view there is a very great interest in having *Jago* in the same publishing house as *Aida*. [. . .]

VERDI TO ALPHONSE LEDUC

[In French]   [Genoa, ? January 1886]

My *Othello* (not *Jago*) is not finished. It is true that towards the end of this past winter and at the beginning of autumn I worked a lot, but many things are missing to complete the score . . ., and I couldn't tell you if and when I will go back to work.

Permit me to tell you, also with my usual frankness, that—while I greatly appreciate the great interest in having *Othello* in the same publishing house as *Aida*—I really would not know how to refuse it to Ricordi (my publisher for 47 years!), who has a music firm in Paris himself. But for the moment one must not speak of *Othello*.

I hope you will find my reasons entirely just and honest, and that you will be kind enough to retain your good friendship for me. [. . .]

[1] Missing.

VICTOR MAUREL TO VERDI

[In French]   Paris, 10 January 1886

Dear and illustrious Maestro,

In view of your courteous benevolence, I hope you will do me the favour of taking note of this too long letter, which I am unable to shorten.

Through bitter experience, and at my expense, I have learned of the amounts to which theatrical budgets can rise, especially when the artists enjoy rather strong backing and can impose upon a management conditions which you so rightly term *exorbitant*.

I appreciate the full value of your sound reflections on the crisis that thwarts the theatres in Italy. For this reason be assured that the question of money would always be a secondary one for me, if on the day you decide to have the score of your new *Othello* performed, unforeseen circumstances do not oppose your assigning the role of Jago to me.

If apprised of the date of the first performance a few months beforehand, I will make myself available, and in this case my monetary demands will simply be those of any other singer engaged as a baritone at one of your leading theatres.

Among your great singers of both sexes, it seems improbable to me that a tenor and a soprano of your choice cannot be found who would be happy to limit their demands, in this most exceptional circumstance, to the resources at the disposal of the management that will have the honour to perform *Othello*.

What I have the honour of stating to you seems to me to be most realizable. I hope, then, and with all my heart: *that with or without me Othello* may soon see the footlights, conquering the hearts and minds of all. These are my wishes for the new year.

Having said this in all sincerity, I wish to explain a word in my previous letter which I am afraid you interpreted in a sense that was contrary to my thought.

In the promise that I recalled on the subject of the role of Jago, do me the favour of seeing only the great and sincere admiration I profess for your genius!

I consider that when an artist pleads in favour of his convictions, and not in favour of his purse, he must always say what he believes to be the truth! This is my case here: I sincerely believed what I had the honour of writing to you, I believe it still, and will believe it always; but I shall bow, and bow with a good grace, before unforeseen circumstances that—by actually altering your desire to hear me interpret the role of Jago—might give you the impression of even the slightest annoyance on my part.

My letter would end here if an unforeseen event—which, however, you might seriously consider—had not made it a duty to proceed. It concerns this:

Last night, at the office of M. Carvalho, there was talk of the notice that appeared in *Le Figaro* for Monday morning, the 5th of this month.

After the letter I had the honour of writing you, I thought that the erroneous news that had been appearing of late might have given you the idea that I was no stranger to this backstage gossip.

There is nothing to it, I assure you; however, as to the present question, I thought it my duty to make the truth known, but in such a way that no doubt could remain in your mind about the manner in which I am interpreting what has been confided to me when [as it happened then] I feel compelled to commit an indiscretion.

As I told you, the conversation in the director's office of the Théâtre Lyrique in the rue Favart was quite animated.

M. Carvalho, who was the first [director] to lend his great artistic expertise to the brilliant triumphs of *Rigoletto*, *La traviata*, [and] *Macbeth*[1] on a French, Parisian, stage (the old Théâtre Lyrique), expressed his doubt concerning this regrettable news; I convinced him by telling him that this notice contained the absolute truth, since I had it from you yourself, and that as soon as I came home I would write you to express all the regret I personally felt about it.

Well then, he said to me, you be my interpreter to the illustrious author of *Rigoletto*, and be sure to tell him that if later on his present intentions should change, and the theatre I direct at this time does not seem unworthy of his new work, we would be most proud to provide him with our collaboration, dedicating to the interpretation of *Othello* an uncommon heart and devotion.[2]

I am transmitting M. Carvalho's words to you with all the more artistic interest because at our last meeting, in your apartment in the Palazzo Doria in Genoa, I had occasion to inform myself about the role of Jago; on that subject you had expressed yourself a few months earlier on the stage of La Scala, in a way that was so flattering to me; at the same time I asked you in the name of the late M. Vaucorbeil whether the Opéra should not hope to give soon a companion piece to *Aida* with a new work of yours, and you answered me then:

'I have not done anything. Great business commotions are the reason for this; I had to dismiss the administrator of my properties and thus have a heavy load of material involvements again.'

And then—but confidentially—you did me the honour of adding: 'My work is not made for the vast resources of the Opéra; it is an intimate lyric drama for three characters; there is no luxury to be indulged in, simply the wits to employ the art of the *mise-en-scène*.'

The Opéra-Comique, which is rightly thought of as the theatre in Paris, where the spirit of the *mise-en-scnène*, thanks to M. Carvalho's exceptional

---

[1] In the critics' and Verdi's own opinion, Carvalho's production of *Macbeth* on 21 Apr. 1865 was not a 'brilliant triumph' at all (see *Carteggi*, iv. 159–60).

[2] According to *Copialeterre*, p. 338 n. 1, the director of the Paris Opéra had made the same offer to Verdi in a (missing) letter of 4 Jan. 1886.

talent, has the highest rating—this theatre today has no more than the title of Opéra-Comique, considering the kind of music that is played there; the truth is that the real opera of Paris is the one where they prefer to give works like *Roméo et Juliette, L'Étoile du Nord,* which are sung with recitatives, etc., etc.

You do me the honour of thinking that no one could interpret the role of Jago better than I; well then, permit me to tell you that you would find in M. Talazac an Othello whose equal no other French theatre could offer you. He cannot be unknown to you, after the continuous successes he has had on this stage.

As for Desdemona, M. Carvalho asks me to tell you that if you do not find her in his company, he would offer you the one you designate. To praise the orchestra and the chorus is unnecessary, I think, since you have already had occasion to appreciate them; I might add only that at the time of the performance of the *Requiem Mass* at the Opéra-Comique,[3] the chorus and orchestra were far from the perfection that they have attained under the direction of M. Danbé.

Finally, I conclude that with a manager who is as much an artist as M. Carvalho, nothing is impossible when [one is] dealing with the interpretation of a Maestro like you. Orchestra, chorus, artists, stagehands, tailors—be assured that all would enthusiastically work towards the same goal: to attain a height equal to that of the new masterpiece which you shall bestow upon the musical world.

I finish—it is time. Accept, dear great Maestro, the respectful and devoted sentiments of

V. Maurel

GIULIO RICORDI TO VERDI

Milan, 11 January 1886

[. . .] As for la Bellincioni, whom I did not know, and heard for the first time at the first [full stage] rehearsal and also at the dress rehearsal, I really must say that she made an extraordinary impression on me, one that put her on a par with la Patti at her best. Certainly her voice is not as round and velvety as la Patti's, especially considering, perhaps, that she has the good fortune of being only 21 years old! . . But the timbre is pleasant, and of sufficient size for La Scala. She must have an absolutely extraordinary talent, for I have *never* heard the recitatives spoken and recited with such delightful *nuances*! . . Although I could not call her a beauty, she has a lovely, expressive, tall, slender figure. I don't know what impression she will make on the audience; certainly a good one; however, it will change to an excellent one when, after a few nights, this artist's great intelligence and enchanting naturalness are understood in even the smallest details. [. . .]

---

[3] Verdi conducted performances of the *Requiem* at the Opéra-Comique between 9 and 22 June 1874, as well as in June 1875.

VERDI TO BOITO[1]

Genoa, 11 January 1886

Dear Boito,

. . . .

.... *Montano* comes on stage in the first act to get a good stabbing, and he returns in the last to accuse Jago. Why doesn't he appear in the third [act] finale? ... This is a very annoying question, because if you found it to be right, you would write eight lines for me and (now that the finale is done) I would be very much at a loss how to add another *real* role in this piece, since I wouldn't like to double the part of another bass. So what do you think? Write eight lines or let Montano sleep? I would wish him pleasant dreams, and I would be even happier than he.

I haven't finished.

It seems impossible! ... but in the passage [*squarcio*] preceding *the Concertato* there are two lines that ramble on, strain, and bother me!

Here they are:

. . . . . .

Onestamente nol potrei. Voi stesso	[*Honestly, I could not. You yourself*
Il suo contegno colla mente arguta	*Study and judge his behaviour with*
Studiate e giudicate.[2]	*A keen mind.*
OT. *Eccolo è desso*	OT. *Here he is, it is he.*
Nell'animo lo scruta	*Pry into his soul*].

I would ask you to make only two lines out of these four. It would be easy to use only the first and third, but it's all right for Otello to say '*lo scruta*', and I think it's easy to fit it in—

If you go to hear *Roberto*[3] tell me in all secrecy whether one might fish out a Desdemona from those two young girls (sopranos).[4]

Watch out for the quality of the voice, for *intelligence and sentiment* above all. Even if they sing poorly, never mind. On the contrary, so much the better! Then they are more likely to sing the way I want them to[5] . .

Addio, addio.

Affectionately,
G. Verdi

[1] The abrupt start of this letter suggests that previous ones are lost, since, according to all indications, Verdi and Boito had not met for some time. A few lines which Boito clearly addressed to Tornaghi in Milan on 3 Jan. 1886 tell of his whereabouts. Presumably, he spent all of Jan. and most of the month of Feb. at home in Milan.

[2] These two sentences (by Jago) were cut. Otello's '*Eccolo è desso*' became '*Eccolo! È lui!*' ['There he is! It's he!'] (III. viii).

[3] Meyerbeer's *Robert le diable* conducted by Faccio at La Scala on 14 Jan. 1886.

[4] Gemma Bellincioni and Ernestina Bendazzi-Secchi (1864–1931), daughter and pupil of the prominent Verdi singer Luigia Bendazzi (1833–1901).

[5] Among several remarks of this kind, Verdi wrote to Tito Ricordi on 22 May 1871 about the young tenor Roberto Stagno and Maria Waldmann: 'They may be inexperienced, but they are young; and when there is voice and sentiment, I am always for the young; you can always do with them whatever you want.' (Busch, *Aida*, p. 159.)

VERDI TO BOITO

Genoa, 14 January 1886

Dear Boito,
Thanks for the two lines.[1]

. . . .   *guerriero*

. . . .

È quel ch'Egli è
            Palesa il tuo pensiero
JAGO. *Meglio è serbar su ciò la lingua muta*[2]
OTEL. *Eccolo! È lui. Nell'animo lo scruta.*

[. . . .   *warrior*

. . . .

He is what he is.
            Reveal your thought.
JAGO. *It's better to keep a mute tongue about this.*
OTEL. *Here he is! It is he. Pry into his soul.*]

Scene viii

Amen

I am happy, very happy, that you didn't allow Montano to leave his bed
with the wound he had received. I worried like the devil that you might tell
me it would have been good to see Montano in the finale, too! I can breathe
again! There are just 11 real roles, including the chorus, and sometimes 12!
With Montano they would have become . . . . .!

Let's not talk about la Bendazzi any more.[3] Tell me something about la
Belincioni!

Oh, you surely won't hear all of *Otello* in just a month from now! I still
have a lot of retouching to do in the first act. . . In fact, I'm going to redo a
great deal! . .

I'm very sorry about Ponchielli![4] As soon as I received your letter I
telegraphed Giulio[5] to send me the news at once, which I expect any moment.
If you don't mind, drop me a line about this, too.

Poor Ponchielli! He is still young and strong! Let us hope! But three
physicians!!!! They will not have the courage to take a dozen ounces of blood

---

[1] Boito's letter containing these lines is missing.
[2] This line was slightly changed to 'Meglio è tener su ciò la lingua muta.' ['It's better to keep
quiet about this.'] (III. vii. Cf. Shakespeare, *Othello*, IV. i. 266–7.)
[3] In his missing answer to Verdi's letter of 11 Jan. 1886, Boito apparently reported negatively
on Ernestina Bendazzi.
[4] Obviously Boito had informed Verdi in his missing letter that Ponchielli was dying.
[5] Missing.

from his veins, which would relieve him right away, since pneumonia is involved!

Addio, addio.

G. Verdi

BOITO TO VERDI

[Milan] Saturday evening [16 January 1886][1]
7 p.m.

Poor Ponchielli has taken a turn for the worse since this morning, and the physicians fear that he may die from one hour to the next. If tomorrow brings an improvement I'll write; but only a real miracle of nature can save him! Poor friend!

Arrigo Boito

BOITO TO VERDI

[Milan, 18 January 1886][1]

Dear Maestro,

You already know that Ponchielli is dead;[2] the peace he did not have in life, on account of the wicked selfishness of his wife's family, he will have now, in one way or another.

I know that Giulio was in Genoa with Corti;[3] and Giulio, whom I have just seen, repeated to me bits of La Scala impresario's oratorical eloquence. I admire Corti's loquacity, but I do not admire his use of my name in the heat of inspiration to invent stupidly a silly story that hasn't even a shadow of a kernel of a beginning of an embryo of a foundation of truth. Corti told you that I had informed him that *Otello* was finished and that I had urged him to leave for Genoa. I didn't say this to Corti or Ricordi, or to anyone else, and I haven't breathed a word. What I regret is that this story coincides with the last letter you wrote me, and that in your eyes it therefore can take on an aspect of truth. Fate is sometimes a rogue, and this is a roguery of fate. But Corti has an effrontery that deserves to be corrected. I haven't even seen him for several months, and when I do see him in the street I always avoid talking to him so as not to be subjected to indiscreet questioning. I am certainly not the one who pushed him to Genoa to annoy you with useless words and arguments which will not have the power to hasten your work's end by a single hour. I spoke to Gailhard, who also went to Genoa for [the sake of] *Otello*, to try to discourage him, since I knew that you weren't thinking of the

---

[1] Postmark: MILANO 16/1/86.

[1] Postmark: MILANO 18/1/86.
[2] On 17 Jan. 1886.
[3] With Cesare or Enrico Corti on 17 Jan. 1886.

Opéra for the first performance of your score. But now the hunt for *Otello* is on, and everybody is trying to seize the prey. I keep silent, or I say only the vaguest, most reserved words in this matter; in your eyes, however, my name is being drawn into their greedy conversations, and this disturbs me, disturbs me, disturbs me. It disturbs me so much that now I disturb you by writing about it. I can't tell you anything concerning la Bellincioni; I didn't attend the performance of *Roberto*. When it is given again I'll go to hear her and write to you about my impression. Cordial greetings to you, dear Maestro, and to Signora Giuseppina.

> Your most affectionate
> Arrigo Boito

VERDI TO GIULIO RICORDI

Genoa, 18 January 1886

Dear Giulio,

After our conversation yesterday I wanted to look over once again what I have done with *Otello* . . . and the tenor's part frightened me. In many, many things Tamagno would do very well but in very many others not! There are broad, long legato phrases to be sung *mezza voce*, something impossible for him. And what is worse, the end of the first act and (worse still) of the fourth would be cold!! There is a short but towering melody, and then there are most important *mezza voce* phrases (after he has wounded himself) . . . . and one cannot do without them! This worries me a lot! If [only] I had finished! and if one could hear him . . . before deciding?   —   —   —

This must be considered.—

Addio, addio

> G. Verdi

GIULIO RICORDI TO VERDI

Milan, 19 January 1886

Illustrious Maestro,

I have the honour of replying to your letter of yesterday; and since you are so kind to take up the matter with me, I dare to reveal my observations to you! . . . . for what they are worth . . . although I never would have ventured to do so before you first mentioned it to me. If you only knew, Maestro, for how long I have been pondering in my poor head over all that would be needed, if that fortunate event should come about which we, and practically the whole world, desire so much! . . . . . Enough . . . . about this, but please bear in mind that I speak only hypothetically, and if I talk nonsense, I do not want to be responsible.

I, too, have thought that the only two possible tenors would be Masini or Tamagno; but I favoured the latter, considering that all in all Otello must lean towards force and violence. But after all that you wrote to me, other observations must be made. For delicacy of singing Masini certainly surpasses Tamagno by a thousand miles; but you will remember that his Bs and maybe also his B flats are a bit veiled, a bit weak; however, I have not heard him for many years and do not know if he still has this deficiency; what also worried me was that it would be Masini's début at La Scala, which would be complicated by the double trepidation of a first appearance and of the immense responsibility. It is true that with your instructions these defects and peculiarities that Masini shows in his interpretation of operas would be corrected; for this reason, then, a bold début is still preferable to overly cautious judgements.

But in Tamagno I have [also] observed singular anomalies, since sometimes he has been unable to phrase, as you tell me in your letter, whereas he did so at other times. Since I am writing to you in the evening, I shall send you first thing tomorrow morning two pieces you can look at (I send them because you certainly will not have them) which I have heard Tamagno sing very well, without pushing his voice, and with sweetness: the romanza of *Le Prophète*[1] and the one of the *Figliuol prodigo*.[2] You will be able to compare by the *tessitura*; I have heard these pieces with my own ears, and with great surprise, not believing Tamagno capable of going so far as this. — As for the management, it certainly makes no difference to them whether Tamagno or Masini is engaged, since the expense . . . . . . will be on the same level and the management is only interested in satisfying you. Tamagno, I think, happens to be leaving tonight or tomorrow morning for Madrid; he has been in Milan for about a month. What a pity, because *without any kind of commitment* the problem could easily have been solved!! . . . . . by broaching the question openly with him alone.

And since we are speaking of artists, I remind you that I asked you whether the part of Desdemona was like Aida, and that you answered me: less dramatic. This encourages me to speak to you again of la Teodorini and la Bellincioni. They are two excellent artists, but the second has more grace, more *charme*. La Teodorini certainly has lovely low notes; but in the middle there is a little flaw, for the notes are weak; then they become lovely and strong again; in short her voice is certainly greater in volume than Bellincioni's but altogether less sympathetic, less fresh. If a complete rest, for a whole year until December, could be arranged for la Bellincioni, I think the few deficiencies noticed today could be corrected and the power of her voice would increase. Remember, Maestro, what la Waldmann was like when I had you hear her? . . . . and I had the courage to have you hear her after a semi-fiasco at the very Scala itself! . . . You found an intelligent artist, one whose defects you corrected right away, and then she became the incomparable singer we all know. I am fully confident it will be the same with la Bellincioni; I wish I could tell you: Do you wish to hear her in Genoa without troubling yourself to come to Milan, or in the theatre? . . . . . . It could be arranged very easily, without anyone's knowing it.

[1] Opera in 5 acts by Meyerbeer.
[2] Opera in 4 acts by Ponchielli.

After all, you have frankly explained the state of affairs, whether you will want, and be able, to finish *Otello* ..... [whether] it will be given; but no commitment whatever for the time being; the management is fully informed and convinced of this. Therefore, Maestro, you have full freedom and every right of discussion without committing yourself to anyone; it is certain, however, that if matters are studied and prepared ahead of time they can be done well, and according to your rightful wishes; above all you will spare yourself continuous efforts, and us the grave displeasure of seeing you toil excessively, or dissatisfied; I need not repeat to you that Verdi can consider himself an absolute monarch; and for the love of justice I must say that at La Scala nobody is more adept than the Cortis, who have great and precise ideas.

Today our excellent mayor wanted a detailed report from me on what was done in Genoa, and I explained the true state of affairs to him, which, he found, conformed to what the management had related to him. Negri was overjoyed by the cherished hopes, so overjoyed that when the Council was in session half an hour later, several councillors pointed out the extraordinarily good mood of our Leader. He told me: 'Ah! .... if Verdi finishes and gives *Otello*, not only is our Scala safe, but then I can make her enter a real phase of prosperity! .... We shall also conquer the 3 or 4 continual opponents and shall vote for a subsidy of 10 years! .... I hope the Maestro will succeed in this. ...'

I confirm my letter of yesterday; I hope for good news; we are having horrible weather—it has been snowing for 10 hours and I cannot bear it any more! ..... My regards to Signora Peppina; always at your disposal, I remain

> Yours most gratefully,
> Giulio Ricordi

VERDI TO VICTOR MAUREL

Genoa, 19 January 1886

Dear Maurel,

In the midst of the many things I have had to do during these days, I could not answer your very kind letter of the 10th of this month. What you say about the well-known affair is all right, but at the moment I think it untimely to speak of *Otello*; I must finish it completely before making any decision whatsoever.

Thank Sig. Carvalho very much and tell him that I am quite convinced that his theatre would give me a perfect production, one that would satisfy any artistic need, from whatever point of view; but knowing Boito, you will be persuaded that he has made of *Otello* a libretto with the most powerful situations and verses. I have tried to give these verses the most truthful and accurate accent I could. This quality (which might also be a defect) would be lost in translation to a large extent. Therefore *Otello* must first be given in Italian . . . . But I repeat, to speak of it now would be untimely . . . .

With great esteem and friendship, always yours

VERDI TO GIULIO RICORDI

Genoa, 20 January 1886

[. . .] In a few days—when everything is over—you will tell poor Signora Ponchielli how much I share her grief! how I deplore the loss of that worthy man, that most distinguished artist!

If I sent no letters or telegrams of condolence, it is because of my feeling that it seems cruel to aggravate the wound of a heart already suffering enough, by repeating a thousand times over (in order to console) the tormenting reason for the grief! Maybe the way I feel is strange; but I believe that silence is the only comfort in great sorrows! [. . .][1]

BOITO TO VERDI

[Milan, 20 January 1886][1]

Dear Maestro,

Last night I saw and heard her.[2] If I were ten years younger I would already be in love with her. She's pretty, tall, slim, young, elegant, dark, supple; and with blonde hair she would perhaps be even more beautiful, for there is so much sweetness in that face, which is enveloped by an aura of attractiveness. The audience, too, feels this aura and enjoys applauding her, and does so more than she deserves, since this attractive girl is, after all, not yet an artist, and I don't know if she ever will be one.

The voice is pleasant, and slight, like her figure, but it isn't a true voice of the theatre; it has a thin timbre that penetrates into the crowd without filling the hall. The almost pastoral part of Alice suits this young lady well enough; here and there she projects some phrases well, and even with a certain impetuosity, or rather, with a certain fortunate audacity that comes, I believe, from the confidence she has in her own attractive appearance. I don't think she possesses true dramatic feeling, true spontaneity, or power of accentuation; her gestures have evidently been taught her by an acting coach, and her vocal phrasing must be the faithful imitation of what some Lamperti has taught her, and all this is clearly obvious. Everything she does on stage seems borrowed from someone else.

Let's note two good qualities: she has good pronunciation (but not very

---

[1] According to a newspaper clipping, which Verdi enclosed in his letter to Giulio Ricordi of 4 July 1886, he had agreed to be the godfather of a child Ponchielli's widow expected in that month.

---

[1] Postmark: MILANO 20/1/86.
[2] Gemma Bellincioni in the Italian version of *Robert le diable* at La Scala.

good) and she seldom looks at the conductor. If I were Faccio, I would object to this good quality, but in any case it proves that there's something musical in the girl. Something—but I don't think it's real artistic inspiration.

I was in a box near the stage and therefore in a position to judge the strength of her voice and the clarity of her intonation quite favourably. At the end of the evening I realized that I was always *looking at her when she was singing*, which goes to show the charm of her face and her figure, the whiteness of her teeth, and nothing more. Too bad! I don't believe la Bellincioni was born to be strangled on the island of Cyprus. Too bad! The account is over. Cordial greetings from

Your most affectionate
Arrigo Boito

VERDI TO BOITO

Genoa, 21 January 1886

Dear Boito,

Thank you for the news ... which I wish had been better.

Can you tell me now about la Teodorini? Do you remember her well? Tell me only about the voice, how her middle register is and how high she goes at the top.

The outcome of my long conversation with Corti and Giulio is this: I have not finished the opera and I don't know *whether I will finish it.* If I do, I shall give it [to La Scala], always assuming that the conditions are suitable. No formal commitment, absolutely none. In talking about it I indicated *Maurel, Tamagno, Teodorini.* But afterwards, thinking it over and looking at the score, I realized that Tamagno would be excellent in many places but that he wouldn't succeed in the final duet of the first act, and even less at the end of the opera, so that two acts would end coldly (as I wrote to Giulio). You don't know the first duet, but you do know the end of the opera. I don't think that he could effectively project the short melody '*E tu come sei pallida*' ['*And you, how pale you are*'], even less '*Un bacio, un bacio ancora*' ['*A kiss, yet another kiss*'] ... particularly since between this second kiss and the third, there are 4 measures for the orchestra alone, which must be filled with delicate, moving gestures that I imagined as I was writing the notes. It would be the easiest thing for a real actor to do, but difficult for ... anyone else.

As you know, Gailhard came to see me, and I'm surprised he didn't tell me that he had talked with you first. I told him the opera wasn't finished, that it was in Italian, written in good Italian, and that the first performance should be in Italian.

They always speak to me and write to me about *Jago!!!* I answer: *Otello, pas Jago, n'est pas fini!!,* and they continue to tell me and write to me about *Jago, Jago.* He is (it's true) the Demon who sets everything in motion; but Otello is the one who acts: *He loves, is jealous, kills, and kills himself.* For my part, it would seem hypocritical not to call it *Otello.* I prefer it if they say, 'He tried to fight a giant[1] and was crushed', rather than, 'He tried to hide behind the title of Jago'. If you are of my opinion let's start baptizing it *Otello*, then, and tell Giulio this right away.

And the appeal?[2] It's very kind . . . and I feel obliged; it's also 'kind if you want', but still an imposition. But no: it doesn't commit me at all, for I won't give the opera [to La Scala] if I'm not convinced . . . and furthermore I know quite well that all those who have signed will be, with few exceptions, the first to throw stones, in that spirit of undoing which characterizes our time, counteracting the kindness I have been shown. Isn't this true? *Amen.*

Addio

G. Verdi

VERDI TO GIULIO RICORDI

[Genoa] *Friday* [22 January 1886]

Dear Giulio,

I sincerely believe our tenor[1] could have managed well in the two pieces you sent me. In *Mayerbeer's* there are the B flats at the end which are so good for him. In the other, by Ponchielli, which is more *cantabile* than the first, he also has a few F sharps and G sharps and, at the end, also the final notes that lie well in his voice . . . It isn't so in *Otello.*—After he has ascertained that Desdemona has been killed [although] innocent, Otello is breathless; he is weary, physically and morally exhausted; he cannot and must not sing any more, except with *a half-muffled, veiled voice* . . . but with a *reliable* one. This is a quality that Tamagno doesn't have. He must always sing with *full voice*; without it his sound becomes ugly, uncertain, off-pitch . . . This is a very serious matter and gives me much to think about! I prefer not to give the opera if this point of the score isn't brought out . . . Oh, if you had come 8 days sooner, I myself could have talked with Tamagno and could have come to an understanding with him . .

Addio, addio

G. Verdi

GIULIO RICORDI TO VERDI

Milan, 23 January 1886

[. . .] Now I shall reply to your letter of yesterday, and forgive me if I do so briefly. I have seen Tamagno and, since he asked me, I explained the true state of affairs; and as though it were my own idea, I told him that the

---

[1] Weinstock, p. 418 n., relates this remark to Rossini's *Otello* rather than Shakespeare's *Othello*.

[2] To give the première of *Otello* to La Scala. This appeal is missing, but explained in Boito's answer of 23 Jan. 1886.

---

[1] Francesco Tamagno.

Maestro knew more and that he would receive exact information from him. Tamagno added: 'I am sorry I must leave for Madrid right away, but I'll be away for only about a month; if the Maestro is kind enough to receive me, I'll be happy to pay him a visit upon my return. Whether or not I am allowed such a coveted honour, I give you my word that I shall not accept any future engagement until after my return.'—Thus I believe I have interpreted your wish in the best possible manner and without any commitment on anyone's part. Leave it to the Cortis, who will, after all, be able to keep the negotiations with Masini and Tamagno going until you can decide. Speaking of the Romanza of the *Figliuol prodigo*, there actually are F sharps and G sharps; but on the whole it is not a high *tessitura*; for example, Tamagno sang the first bars very well, and with a really pleasant *mezza voce*; and therefore I wrote to you that I thought it was a question of study; certainly it will not be easy to achieve what you desire, but not impossible; but the way things stand at this time, you need not have any worries; and you can quite leisurely and freely see what you like best in every way. [...]

BOITO TO VERDI

[Milan, 23 January 1886][1]

Dear Maestro,

You ask me to speak only about the voice, *about the voice* of la Teodorini. I obey, but the question, posed within these limits, has a rather sad result. This artist's voice has never been her principal gift; for some time they have been saying that her vocal resources have deteriorated, and they claim that the impresario Ferrari was not pleased with her when he took her to America. If what they say is true, if this singer is losing the security and the timbre of those few effective notes she possessed *towards* the bottom and *towards* the top, the instrument would be almost unserviceable. The middle register was weak even when I heard her in Madrid,[2] and the extreme top register was without resonance, without carrying power. You ask me how high she goes: in the fourth act of *Mefistofele* there is a C that doesn't last long, in fact that lasts only a brief moment, and that C did not ring out; before that C there is a B flat, and it did not ring out well. As I write I ask myself, in order to be quite sure, if my memory isn't letting me down; but I put this doubt aside when I think that a beautiful voice, a real voice with beautiful and powerful high notes, can never be forgotten once it is heard. If I had to speak of la Teodorini's other gifts, praise would take the place of criticism, since she possesses theatrical, dramatic qualities—those that are real and true—and I owe to her many beautiful nights when she sang in my own opera.

But I could begin another long chat here, talking about this new subject, so I remain true to your instructions and come to a close.

[1] Postmark: MILANO 23/1/86.
[2] As Margherita in *Mefistofele* on 27 Jan. 1883.

In a month, dear Maestro, we shall see each other again, and then we can talk at length and in depth.

I knew nothing (I never see anybody), nothing about the appeal made to you by the Club dell'Unione and the fashionable Milanese. The day I saw Galliard,[3] however, I heard that the box-owners of la Scala and the gentlemen of the Club, alarmed by the news of the visit by the Director of the Opéra to Genoa, had decided to send this appeal to you; but I didn't know they had actually done so. I understand that this fact must not have an influence on the decisions you make, but one cannot deny that it was an act of lovely courtesy and noble homage, which does them honour.

Affectionate greetings to you and Signora Giuseppina.

Your
Arrigo Boito

GIULIO RICORDI TO VERDI

Milan, 26 January 1886

Illustrious Maestro,

I am replying right away to your esteemed letter[1] of yesterday. [. . .] In fact, the article by Fortis was the *only* one worthwhile under the circumstances; last night I sent *Il pungolo* with news of *Otello* to Signora Peppina![2] . . . . I think what Fortis writes about this matter is the *right note*, and that it will have your full approval. [. . .]

EMANUELE MUZIO TO GIULIO RICORDI

Nice, 28 January 1886

[. . .] I am writing to a trustworthy person in Paris to find out the present condition of Maurel's voice, and I shall transcribe for you what he tells me. Maurel cannot be judged by *Zampa*,[1] since he had the solo pieces transposed . . . There is a baritone of real dramatic talent and with a voice, and that would be Devoyod. Thin figure, high-strung, good musician. Well then, as you rightly tell me, he [a Jago] will be found; but how nice it would be if all the artists could be Italians. [. . .]

How many swindles the French papers have printed about *Otello*. Gailhard has told them all that it doesn't have the dimensions '*pour une grande salle comme le grand Opéra*'. That is [like] the fable of the fox who, not being able to have the grapes, said he did not want them because they were sour. You did well to say a few words to the Milan *reporters*. The journalists are

---

[3] Gailhard.

[1] Probably in the Biblioteca Palatina.
[2] Missing.

---

[1] Opera in 3 acts by the French composer Ferdinand Hérold (1791–1833).

the Hydra of today; they feed on errors, arrogance, and slander. The news that Verdi has promised *Otello* to *La Scala* I read in *The Times* of Monday in a long dispatch from Rome, in *L'Independence Belge*, and in others.

The Maestro is quite absorbed right now with scoring the quintet with chorus that comes after Otello has insulted Desdemona in the presence of all; it's one of the most beautiful pieces, with the off-stage chorus that Boito heard, and the jealousy duet between Otello and Jago. You will hear how much novelty there is, how much passion, vigour, and tears there are. '*Salce! Salce! Salce!*' ['*Willow!*'] in the fourth act gives you the shivers and makes you weep.

Let's cheer up—all will go well. Watch out for Emilia, who is a soprano (not a mezzo,[2] as you wrote to me[3]); a robust voice—and above all one *in tune*—is needed for the curses upon Otello in the fourth act. [. . .]

VERDI TO GIUSEPPE PIROLI

Genoa, 29 January 1886

[. . .] The impresario of La Scala and Giulio Ricordi were here and brought me a letter with many signatures asking me for *Otello*. I answered them that *Otello* is not completely finished, and that *If* I finish it I will give it at *La Scala*, provided always that there is a suitable company. No firm commitment.

To the Director of the Opéra in Paris I said that *Otello* is written in good Italian verses, which I have sought to give the best accent I could. This quality, and perhaps this defect, would be altered too much in a translation, and therefore *Otello* has to be produced, for the first time at least, in an Italian theatre. [. . .]

FRANCESCO TAMAGNO TO VERDI

Milan, 29 January 1886

Illustrious Signor Commendatore,

The gratitude I bear you encourages me to write these lines to you in order, somehow, to express the satisfaction I feel when thinking of the honour Your Excellency has deigned to grant me by choosing me as the protagonist *in the longed-for new opera Otello*, in which I hope to execute my part in the manner that such a great opera requires. [. . .]

---

[2] Nevertheless, this part is usually cast with a mezzo-soprano as listed in the orchestra score. Ginevra Petrovich was the first Emilia at La Scala, Italia Costa sang the role with Faccio conducting in Parma on 13 Sept. 1887. Other roles of these two unknown singers could not be ascertained. While Emilia's tessitura in the quartet of Act II is clearly that of a mezzo-soprano, her high notes in the ensemble of Act III and towards the end of Act IV might explain Verdi's intention to entrust this part to a soprano.

[3] In a missing letter.

VERDI TO GIULIO RICORDI

Genoa, 31 January 1886

Dear Giulio,

I enclose an embarrassing and compromising letter.[1]

As soon as you and Corti had returned to Milan I wrote to you that I had great doubts about Tamagno (as Otello), because there are passages nearly impossible for him, especially the last.

I am writing today to Madrid, declaring that he has been misinformed and that I have not definitely decided about giving the opera or about who must perform it. I don't know how Tamagno will take it . . . But so much the worse for the person who could not keep the secret!—Meanwhile I lose time with false rumours, discussions, and by answering annoying letters! [. . .]

VERDI TO FRANCESCO TAMAGNO

Genoa, 31 January 1886

Dear Tamagno,

I am pleased to hear of the satisfaction you would have in performing the part of Otello; but at the same time I must complain about persons who have made promises in my name that they could not make.

I have not finished the opera, and even if I should finish it, I have not absolutely decided to give it. I have written purely for my pleasure, without plans for publication, and at this moment neither I nor anyone [else] can say what will be convenient to do! Another problem arises, and that is to find artists suitable for the respective parts. You know better than I that no matter how capable an artist may be, not all parts are suitable for him, and I would not sacrifice anyone, and much less you! Now then, my dear Tamagno (and this shall remain a secret between us), when you return from Madrid let's meet in Genoa or elsewhere, and then we shall talk and discuss [matters] with frankness and fairness. For now, no decision, and so much more so because, I repeat, I have not *finished* and have not formally promised to give the opera.

I thank you for the most courteous letter you have written me and take this occasion to declare my feelings of cordial esteem. Yours

EMANUELE MUZIO TO GIULIO RICORDI

Nice, 1 February 1886

[. . .] As of yesterday, Verdi writes to me again,[1] 'I shall give *Otello* if I find singers to my taste.' In my reply[2] I expressed a doubt about Maurel's vocal

---

[1] Francesco Tamagno's preceding letter.

[1] Missing, probably destroyed as almost all of Verdi's letters to Muzio.
[2] Missing.

resources and told him that Devoyod was the only baritone among foreign artists who could sing and act the part of Jago... As for the others, I told him, 'You know who they are,' since we have talked about them several times in his room in Genoa. [...]

I think your father should write to the Maestro about *Otello*, without asking what his conditions are at this time, since, *strictly speaking*, it isn't finished; but he must ask him—which he can do well—whether in principle this opera, *which he hopes will not be the last one*, may, like Verdi's first opera, belong to his firm. Verdi will answer that it isn't finished, that he wants to find the artists, etc., and that there is time, but Tito must insist. [...]

TITO RICORDI TO VERDI

Milan, 3 February 1886

My dear Verdi,

A tactfulness which you will appreciate has kept me silent until today, but to be silent any longer is a burden to me.

From Giulio I had news of you and of *Otello*. I know quite well that you have not yet finished the work and therefore have rightly not entered into any definite commitment. But I hope that my most ardent wishes shall soon be fulfilled!..... and I say soon because my health is deteriorating, and before I leave this poor world, my greatest consolation will be to have the pleasure once more of applauding a new masterpiece of yours, which, by the way, is not going to be 'the last one', as you say!...

Now, I am expressing to you only the hope that when you have finished *Otello*, you may give to my House the honour of making it a companion of your other immortal masterpieces which you have already bestowed on my House.—Thus you will be giving me a double consolation with the thought that a new, solid foundation for the future will remain for my House and my children.—

But I do not say anything more to you, and I confidently await a benevolent, definite word from you.—

Meanwhile I embrace you from my heart and join my voice to the voices of others in urging upon you our theatre and our art, to which you alone bring glory and respect.

Remember me to your distinguished and peerless Signora Peppina, and let me embrace you with love and gratitude,

Your old friend
Tito Ricordi

PS My greatest wish would be that you might leave *Otello* to my House *for all countries*.[1]—Again yours most affectionately,

Tito Ricordi

---

[1] See Verdi to Alphonse Leduc, 1 Jan. 1886.

VERDI TO GIULIO RICORDI

Genoa, 4 February 1886

Dear Giulio,

No matter what you may say, the engagement of Tamagno was a mistake which can jeopardize everything. I have told you, and I repeat, that I don't believe he can succeed either in the duet that ends the first act, or in the last scene; this way, two acts would end coldly ... It's not possible!

And now, having settled the question of the tenor, we come to Desdemona. When is a good time to come to hear la Bellincioni? I think before the first performance of *Ballo*. When will that be? And tell me when I should come. If in *8* or *10* days from now, so much the better.

In haste addio

G. Verdi

GIULIO RICORDI TO VERDI

Milan, 5 February 1886

[. . .] Do not worry about the tenors, since everything will go as you wish.

You will also have time during all of February to hear la Bellincioni, since [. . .] the performances of *Robert* [*le diable*], also with the ballet on stage, will continue; the first and fifth, or the third and fifth, acts will be given, which are just those in which la Bellincioni sings. [. . .]

VERDI TO ANGELO MASINI

[Genoa, early February 1886]

In answer to your kind letter of 30 January,[1] I can only repeat what I have already told others concerning *Otello*.

I have not finished the opera. Whether I will finish it, and when, I could not say myself. As for the artists, I add that I cannot say who would be right for this opera until it is completely finished.

Therefore, Signor Masini, do what is in your best interests, without thinking of the uncertain possibilities of *Otello*.

I thank you for the kind words in your letter about me and beg you to accept greetings from

VERDI TO GIULIO RICORDI

Genoa, 7 February 1886

Dear Giulio,

It's not worth the effort to hear la Bellincioni in two acts. She must be heard in an entire opera to find out her good qualities, her defects, and how

---

[1] Missing.

she holds up . . . . I wouldn't judge her in *Traviata*! A mediocrity can have the good qualities to have a success in that opera and [can still] be very bad in all the others.—If you had written me *24* hours ago, I would have come to Milan tonight. It was the right time. Afterwards one could have come to some practical solution, and if I had not cared for la Bellincioni, one could have thought of someone else. This way we are always up in the air, time is lost, and I get no work done!

As for the tenors, you find everything easy, and I very difficult. I have not written for this or that artist, and now, in looking over the parts that I have done, I don't find any whom I like, or who are suitable.—Masini (as the Cortis suggested) has written to me . . . I answered that he should not think of *Otello* at all. Yesterday (still as the Cortis suggested) the baritone *Devoyod* came to me . . . I answered him[1] as I had Masini. Many others have written to me, and I haven't answered. Meanwhile no progress is made, and what is worse, all of this causes disturbances and upset, and so time is lost! Ah, the time! the time! . . . Watch out, dear Giulio, that we don't find, in the end, that we've let it slip by! If I don't manage to finish before summer the *more than a little* that I still have to do, *Otello* will not be possible.

Inform the Cortis of this letter, and save it. It must not be said later on . . . . . 'We hoped, we thought,' etc., etc.

Addio, addio

G. Verdi

EMANUELE MUZIO TO GIULIO RICORDI

Nice, 11 February 1886

Here is the Maestro's reply to me of yesterday, the 10th:[1] 'I am sorry to hear what you tell me about Maurel, for nobody could do that part like him. Nobody enunciates as clearly as he does; and in the part of Jago there are so many *parlandos* that need to be said quickly and *sotto voce*, which no one could do better than he.' [. . .]

TERESA STOLZ TO ROMILDA PANTALEONI

[Milan, mid-February 1886]

[. . .] I beg your pardon for not answering until now your very dear letter of 24 January.[1] I was away, and consequently I read your letter only last night on my return from Genoa. From the contents, I see that you were rather alarmed by all the rumours going around concerning la Bellincioni's contract

---

[1] Missing.

---

[1] Missing, but see Muzio to Ricordi, 1 Feb. 1886.

---

[1] Missing.

with La Scala, and even more concerning her singing Maestro Verdi's new opera. Just stay calm; all these were only false reports or, to put it better, pure humbug.

Maestro Verdi, when he read these inaccurate reports, became furious and said right away, 'All this gossip, this agitation, this kind of pressure gets on my nerves and makes me lose the desire to finish this work of mine.' It's true that Ricordi is much inclined toward la Bellincioni, but I know, after all, that when Maestro Verdi in the past wanted to choose some artist (whom he did not know), he first went to hear her; and so he will also do now, trusting only his own judgement. Stay calm, and don't be alarmed by anything, since nothing has been done up to now.

Maestro Verdi will arrive here in a few days and hear *this so highly extolled Bellincioni*, and he will persuade himself that she isn't nearly so good as Ricordi had tried to make him believe. For my part, speaking as a friend, I am very fond of you and hold you in the esteem you deserve as a great artist; consequently, ask yourself if I won't do what I can to speak to the Maestro about you and your true successes during the two seasons at La Scala. [. . .]

I have seen Maestro Faccio, who has told me everything, and who also says that you are unduly alarmed by this whole affair. [. . .]

GIULIO RICORDI TO VERDI

Milan, 18 February 1886

[. . .] If it is convenient for you, you can come to Milan on Saturday. On Saturday evening the first and fifth acts will be given, on Sunday the third and fifth, so you will hear la Bellincioni in the whole opera. Should these days not be agreeable to you, next Tuesday evening the third and fifth acts will be done. For my guidance, please just telegraph me as soon as you have received this letter; and since the famous secrecy of the telegraph is scarcely to be trusted, it is better to choose a conventional phrase, one indicating only the date of your visit, i.e. 20 all right—or 23 all right.

[. . .] For Heaven's sake, I would not now want la Bellincioni to be the *deus ex machina*. I already told you my impressions, for what they are worth, and I told you also that she is not without some defects; but I reminded you, on the other hand, of la Waldmann's many defects when you heard her in my father's home, and what an artist she became after she had studied a single part under your powerful guidance. But I dare to say even more: If we are extremely short of tenors and baritones, nevertheless we find ourselves at a time that is not at all unfavourable for sopranos: if la Bellincioni fails, I think I can assure you that there are two or even three others deserving of your attention.

For you to come to the opera unobserved, I have studied various means— the other times I had a fiasco; but now I venture to suggest this to you: enter the theatre from the dressing-room of the management, go to the box I will prepare for you, and have the blessed patience to stay there alone! [. . .] In a few days we shall pay you a visit; the doctor has ordered Ginetta[1] to spend 5 or 6 days at the Riviera; who knows, maybe we'll choose Nervi! .. In any case, we shall pass through Genoa. [. . .]

ROMILDA PANTALEONI TO ALCEO PANTALEONI

Rome, 27 February 1886

[. . .] Today I give you the news of my new contract with La Scala for next year! [. . .] Ricordi—true to his past persecution of me—tried to block the road for me this time also, only because he has found a new flame, the prima donna Bellincioni, whom he wanted to impose even on *Verdi*. But he had to deal with Verdi himself (who didn't trust Ricordi and went *in persona* to hear la Bellincioni at La Scala); he had to deal with the Cortis, who wanted me; he had to deal with la Stolz, who fought for the right cause—mine—and with D'Ormeville and Faccio, who united to make Verdi understand how great an aversion Ricordi has *honoured me with*. [. . .] So I will be Desdemona! [. . .]

FRANCESCO TAMAGNO TO VERDI

Milan, 27 February 1886

Esteemed Signor Commendatore,

I make it my duty to inform you that I have received your esteemed letter sent to Madrid.[1]

Tomorrow I shall finally leave for that city, since I am almost completely recovered.

On my return, towards the middle of April, I shall come to Genoa right away, and with every good will to satisfy you.

Forgive again the disturbance, and believe me with all respect and esteem

Yours most devotedly,
Tamagno, Francesco

EMANUELE MUZIO TO GIULIO RICORDI

Genoa, 14 March 1886

[. . .] Boito entered the Maestro's room[1] just as he was at the piano and let me hear for the second time the duet at the end of the first act, the only piece he [Boito] had not heard, since he had only finished it in the last few days.

After lunch, before Boito arrived, I spoke to the Maestro about the French

[1] Giulio and Giuditta Ricordi's daughter Gina, Verdi's young friend Ginetta, who accompanied him to his fields at St Agata. In 1890 she married Luigi Origoni.

[1] Verdi's letter of 31 Jan. 1886.

[1] At the Palazzo Doria, Verdi's home in Genoa.

translation, and he told me that he would be most happy to see it done by Boito himself; and he even added that he would not profit from the royalties on the translation, but would leave them to him. He will tell him himself at the right time and place.

I also told the Maestro that the opera should be printed [in time] for the rehearsals, just as you wrote to me, and he acknowledged this need; you yourself will have realized it from the ensemble piece which the Maestro let you hear and which is very clear, but complicated . . .

That's done, and if you have other things for me to tell him in Paris,[2] you will write to me about them. [. . .]

VERDI TO OPPRANDINO ARRIVABENE

Genoa, 17 March 1886

Dear Arrivabene,

I'm about to leave for Paris!!! What do you say to that? You will be astounded; but certainly not more than I!

I'll meet St Joseph[1] on the way and thank him for the good wishes you have sent me . . . . and don't you say that ugly word . . . . the 'last!' Who knows how many more you will still have to send! And that won't be bad either for you or for me! Well then, I'm going to Paris, and I really don't know exactly why. I'm going partly to hear Maurel, partly to see if they are crazier than before; partly also to get myself moving!

It will be a matter of fifteen days, twenty at the most! *Otello* goes slowly, but it goes! . . . Shall I finish it? Maybe yes. Shall I give it? It is difficult for me to answer this! Meanwhile we pull ahead and *amen*.

VERDI TO GIUSEPPE PIROLI

Paris, 4 April 1886

First and foremost, I am very happy to hear good news about your health. Ours is equally good, despite the fatigue of this trip of ours and, above all, of the sojourn . . . Never a moment's peace; moreover, I go to the theatre almost every evening. It's a necessity!! I must hear these young artists whom I didn't know. To tell the truth, they're not too bad! At the Opéra they have a tenor with a stupendous voice[1] . . . then two women with rather thin voices, but with talent. In short, I repeat, they're not bad!

We'll stay here the whole week. We'll leave Sunday or Monday, the 12th,

---

[2] The Verdis visited Paris from 19 or 20 Mar. until 11 Apr. 1886.

---

[1] In Italian San Giuseppe, Verdi's and his wife's patron saint (cf. Boito to Verdi, 5 Apr. 1883, n. 4).

---

[1] Possibly Léonce-Antoine Escalais (1859–1940), who sang at the Opéra from 1883 to 1891 and in 1905. He also recorded selections from *Otello*.

and go via the Gotthard.[2] We'll stop over in Milan for two days and be in Genoa towards the 16th. [. . .]

VERDI TO GIULIO RICORDI

Paris, 7 April 1886

Dear Giulio,

The answer you have given Tamagno[1] is the right one.

I keep repeating that now, as in the past, I want my complete freedom of action *vis-à-vis* the management as well as the artists. Let the one and the other do all that is useful to them, all that they want, as though not a single note of *Otello* existed. Besides (always the same story), the opera is not finished; and if things go on like this, I don't know how I'll be able to finish it! Too many distractions! Too many worries! Too much business! Too much trouble!

We are in fairly good health, but very, very tired. I think, I hope, we'll leave Sunday night and arrive in Milan Monday evening at 7 — —

Greetings to all.

Addio, addio

G. Verdi

I heard *Sigurd*![2] There are magnificent things in it! *Mise-en-scène* marvellous and (a big thing!) good performance. *Caron, Bosman, Figuet, Sellier*—you know them . . . A good *Sacerdote* (*Le Grand Prêtre*) who is an Indian. In short, a very, very good ensemble . . . I am greatly surprised by that! — — —

VERDI TO GIUSEPPE PIROLI

Paris, 7 April 1886

We leave Paris Sunday night in order to arrive in Milan Monday night. We'll go through Switzerland, because we want to see the *Gotthard tunnel.*

Everybody tells me here that the customs in Chiasso are excessively rigorous, and that they turn all the suitcases upside-down. I don't blame them, because one has to deal with Switzerland, but since we are good Italians and have nothing to declare, I would ask whether you could have one of our *officials* write or telegraph the head of the customs in Chiasso to check our suitcases by all means, but to take a little pity on them . . . There is no time to lose, since we'll be in Chiasso Monday at 5 p.m. Maestro Muzio will

---

[2] Railway tunnel in Switzerland, opened in 1882.

[1] Missing.
[2] Opera in 5 acts by Ernest Reyer (1823–1909).

be with us, and I guarantee that he, too, will have nothing to declare; therefore the permission should be extended *to Maestro Verdi and his family.*

Please. please, please excuse me!

We stop over in Milan for two days, then right away to Genoa.

Addio, addio, and again, excuse me. In great haste.

TITO RICORDI TO VERDI

Milan, 16 April 1886

Illustrious friend,
Signor Commendatore Giuseppe Verdi
Genoa

Our friend Muzio has given me the most comforting news, that you have been so kind as to grant my wish, which was to leave to me the rights to your *Otello* for all countries, and at the terms you want, of course; that is, whenever you finish composing the opera and decide to have it performed.

This very kind decision, and the terms of the transfer, of which our friend Muzio informed me, are a new proof of the precious friendship that for so many years has been the glorious banner of my House and a new testimonial of your most noble sentiments, as well as a worthy counterpart to the power of your genius.

I truly could not have wished for greater moderation in the compensation owed you for the transfer. I agree, then, with a happy and grateful heart to pay you the sum of *Two Hundred Thousand Lire* in four instalments of 50 thousand each, the first upon delivery of the score, and the others at terms to be agreed upon; plus the usual 40 per cent for rentals of the material and 50 per cent for sales, except in the case of France and Belgium, where the author's rights to the music and the words must be reserved for you in regard to the performances; while my House retains title to the orchestra score and the related right to print the translation, as well, which will be done by a person you choose and in the manner you wish, and to furnish scores and parts for the use of those theatres.

For the rest, I think one could hold to the other usual conditions of our last contracts, of which I can send you copies, in case you do not remember them.

I await only your order before having the pleasure of drawing up the act of transfer in legal form.

Meanwhile, reiterating my most sincere thanks for your many kindnesses, and assuring you that my House will be fully committed to responding in a worthy fashion to the trust with which you have honoured me, I remain with all my heart

Your affectionate old friend
Tito di Giovanni Ricordi

My and my wife's respects to your excellent Signora Peppina.[1]

---

[1] Tito Ricordi dictated this letter, but the last three lines are in his handwriting.

BOITO TO EUGENIO TORNAGHI

Quinto,[1] 16 April 1886

[. . .] Today I'll make a dash to Genoa to see the Maestro. [. . .]

GIULIO RICORDI TO VERDI

Milan, 23 April 1886

Illustrious Maestro,

I received your telegram[1] and communicated it to Tamagno, who asks me to pay you his respects and inform you that he will leave Milan for Genoa Monday morning instead of Tuesday, thus gaining a day. So he will be at your home on Monday at about 2 p.m.

Accept, Maestro, devoted greetings

from your affectionate
Giulio Ricordi

BOITO TO GIULIO RICORDI

Quinto, 24 April 1886

[. . .] I won't return to Milan until early June. Here I am well and work well (well doesn't mean fast) like a hermit in a clean, quiet hotel; I see the Maestro often, and for all these reasons I'm in no hurry to return to Milan. [. . .]

BOITO TO VERDI[1]

Quinto, 6 May [1886][2]

Dearest Maestro,

Yesterday I received a letter from Giulio[3] telling me that Edel would be leaving for Venice next Saturday and would take advantage of a few free days which he has to begin studies for the costumes, and he asked me for instructions. I answered that I couldn't give him the list of the costumes for two reasons: first, because it had to be made in accordance with your wishes, and then, because I didn't trust my memory without the libretto in front of me. I didn't refuse to give him general instructions, however, on which he

---

[1] Today Genova-Quinto al Mare, 10 kilometres south of Genoa.

---

[1] Possibly in the Biblioteca Palatina.

---

[1] Boito did not finish and post this letter, but apparently showed it to Verdi during one of his visits in nearby Genoa. The autograph was among Verdi's letters to Boito in the possession of the Albertini family.

[2] The year is inferred from Boito's letter to Verdi of 16 May 1886.

[3] Missing.

could base some preliminary studies. Among these instructions there is one most important point that you, Maestro, must decide: *the choice of the period*. See if my reasoning has been right. If it doesn't seem right to you, we still have time to correct it with a telegram to Giulio and a letter to Edel. What is the origin of Shakespeare's *Othello*? A story by Cinzio Giraldi in the Hecatommithi.[4] What is the date of the Hecatommithi? 1527, the year of the sack of Rome. What is the date of the story in question? Giraldi himself gives it: a few years before the approximate date which is found in the preface to his stories. Therefore it is a period of time which cannot exceed the following limits: 1520–5. These dates are of historical value to us, and in my opinion we can't find any others that are more likely. A battle between Venetians and Turks was very possible in those years: the Kingdom of Cyprus (that is, the inheritance of Catterina Cornaro[5]) had already become the possession of the Venetian Republic.[6] There is another observation to be made: short story writers such as Boccaccio, Sacchetti, and Cinzio Giraldi draw the material for their writings from their imagination, or from history, from the chronicles, or from popular accounts that are often based on history or the chronicles. Giraldi, then, took his own theme for the Othello story either from his own imagination or from an actual event. If we allow the first hypothesis, Giraldi's imagination becomes law for us, because in the absence of major laws, minor ones decide. If we allow the second hypothesis, we must be even more faithful to Giraldi's dates, in the belief that they are founded on fact. My own conviction is that this story was based on fact, if not in every particular detail, certainly in its general outline. A number of arguments could be produced to justify this conviction, but I already know that you must share my opinion.

Then, if our theatrical action can be limited to one of the five years between 1520 and 1525, there must be a far greater limitation to the pictorial presentation of the *costumes*. Today if we walk down our streets, we find the *gommeux*[7]

VERDI TO BOITO

St Agata, 8 May 1886
Dear Boito,
For three lines I did recently[1] I have consulted the original...

'For sir were I the Moor I would not be Jago'

Perché Signor fossi io il Moro io vorrei non esser Jago.

[4] See Appendix II.
[5] Caterina Cornaro (1454–1510), Queen of Cyprus from 1472 to 1489.
[6] From 1489 to 1571.
[7] French for fops.

[1] Words of Jago to Roderigo in Act I, Scene i of the opera. (Cf. Shakespeare, *Othello*, I. i. 55–7: '... for sir, / It is as sure as you are Roderigo, / Were I the Moor, I would not be Iago.')

Hugo, however, says it like this:

> *Si j'étais le More je ne voudrais pas être Jago*
>
> [*If I were the Moor, I wouldn't want to be Iago*]

And in Maffei's translation:

>   ... *Quand'io potessi*
> *Trasformarmi nel Moro essere un Jago*
> *Già non vorrei* ...
>
>   [... *If I could*
> *Transform myself into the Moor, a Iago*
> *I'd rather not be* ...].

And so Rusconi's translation isn't precise. ... Yet it didn't displease me ...

> *Vedermi non vorrei d'attorno un Jago.—*
>
> [*I wouldn't like to see myself around a Iago.—*]

Now then, what are you planning to do?
Do you want to leave the three lines?
Do you want to redo them?
Do you want to take them out, leaving things as they were?
I am moving ahead very slowly, but I am moving.
Answer me in a word to *Busseto* St Agata, and greetings and greetings.

Affectionately,
G. Verdi

BOITO TO VERDI

Quinto, 10 May [1886]

Dear Maestro,

What I am about to write seems like blasphemy: I prefer Rusconi's phrase. It reveals more than the text, it reveals Jago's evil mind, Otello's good faith, and proclaims an entire tragedy of deceits to whoever is really listening. Rusconi's phrase proves very useful to us, since we've had to omit the wonderful scenes that take place in Venice, where those sentiments are suggested. In my opinion we should keep it the way the translator gives it to us. This does not alter the fact that Rusconi was wrong to tamper with one of Shakespeare's thoughts. The faithfulness of a translator must be highly scrupulous, but the faithfulness of the artist who with his own work illustrates the art of another can, in my opinion, be less scrupulous. The translator's duty is not to change the letter; the illustrator's mission is to interpret the spirit. The one is a slave, the other is free. Rusconi's phrase is inaccurate: this is a translator's fault, but it matches the spirit of the tragedy very well, and the illustrator must take his own advantage of this virtue. By carrying this line of reasoning further, we arrive at the following result: *We do right in adopting Rusconi's fault.* This is the way I would suggest you resolve the *qualms* you discussed in your letter today.

I'll be staying in Quinto all of May. At the very beginning of June I'll be in Milan.

In Milan I'll await your go-ahead to come to St Agata. In any case I'll write to you when I get back home.

Many greetings to you, to Signora Giuseppina.

Your most affectionate
Arrigo Boito

VERDI TO BOITO

St Agata, 14 May 1886

Dear Boito,

Very happy that you have kept the three lines ..... '*d'attorno un Jago*' ['*around a Jago*'].

Still another little thing, and I'm finished ... That is, you'll be finished! You know that the storm (musically speaking) continues during Otello's entrance and until after the Chorus of six-syllable verses. There are too many lines in Otello's *solo*[1] and the storm gets too broken up. It seems to me that the scene wouldn't lose a thing if it were shortened by 4 lines, and then I could make a phrase for Tamagno, perhaps an effective one; in fact, it's already made ... thus:

Forza ai remi	[Strength to the oars
Alla riva!!	To the shore!!
Ancorate il vascello	Anchor the ship
Evviva Evviva!	Hurrah Hurrah!]

OTELLO (*sbarcato in fondo all scena: sull'alto ...*).
Esultate. L'orgoglio Musulmano

---

[1] Boito had originally written in Act I, Scene i (*Carteggi* II, 104):

TUTTI. Evviva Otello.
JAGO (*a Rodrigo*).   Sia dannato Otello.
OTELLO (*a Jago*). E Desdemona?
JAGO.   Attende nel castello.
OTELLO (*a Jago famigliarmente*). Onesto Jago, Cassio, buon Montano
E voi tutti esultate, e suoni *a festa*
  Tutta Cipro. L'orgoglio musulmano ...

[ALL. Long live Otello.
JAGO (*to Rodrigo*).   Damned be Otello.
OTELLO (*to Jago*). And Desdemona?
JAGO.   Is waiting in the castle.
OTELLO (*to Jago informally*). Honest Jago, Cassio, good Montano
  And all of you, exult, and *all of Cyprus*
  Ring out a feast. The Muslim pride ...]

(Cf. Shakespeare, *Othello*, II. ii–iii.)

Sepolto è in mar; nostra e del Cielo è gloria
Dopo l'armi lo vinse ... gano (*Entra nel Castello*)²
TUTTI. Evviva Otello! Vittoria vittoria!

[OTELLO (*having disembarked at the rear of the stage, high up ...*).
Rejoice. The Muslim pride
Is buried in the sea; ours and Heaven's is the glory.
After our arms, the hurricane defeated it. (*Enters the castle*)
ALL. Long live Otello! Victory, victory!]

Answer in a word. Cordial greetings from Peppina.

Your
G. Verdi

BOITO TO VERDI

Quinto, 16 [May 1886]¹

Bravo!!! I completely agree on this cut of four lines, which allows Otello's
entrance to be moved to the other three lines you mention. Now we've found
the entrance that didn't satisfy us and that we were hunting for, and it's
splendid. A powerful exclamation of victory that ends in a blast of the gale
and a shouting of the people! Bravo, Bravo! Excellent, too, is the idea of
having this phrase spoken from a high point of the stage!

Edel wants to start preparing his studies for the *Otello* costumes already;²
he has asked me for the list of the costumes, but I did not want to give it to
him, since you and I must make this list together at St Agata. He has asked
me for instructions about the historical period and the painters he must
study, and these I thought it advisable to give him, since I know Edel is as
lazy as he is gifted and needs a lot of time to complete a job. He will prepare
himself in the meantime, doing research, making sketches, and getting
photographs. I hope to bring Edel's preliminary work to St Agata; and with
those materials before our eyes we shall narrow our choice of costumes, and
then he can paint the sketches.

The period (in fact, almost the very date) of our tragedy presents itself,
without any need for us to rack our brains to find it. Cinzio Giraldi, who, as
you know, is the source of Schakespeare's tragedy, gives us two time limits
within which the date of Othello's story occurs. I have torn a page out of an
ugly, inexpensive edition of *The Hecatommithi* so that it might serve as a
document for you. It's a page from the introduction.³ In this, too, Cinzio

---

² Cf. Shakespeare, *Othello*, II. i 202: 'News, friends, our wars are done, the Turks are
drown'd ...'

¹ Postmark: QUINTO AL MARE 16/5/86.
² See Boito to Verdi, 6 May 1886.
³ Pp. 3–5 of vol. i in the first publication (*De gli Hecatommithi di M. Giovan Battista Gyraldi
Cinthio Nobile Ferrarese* (2 vols. in 4; Monte Regale: Lionardo Torrentino, 1565)). See
Appendix II. A translation of the page that Boito enclosed is printed after this letter.

Giraldi imitates the *Decameron,* by arranging the collection of his hundred *tales* in an historical framework. He pretends that these stories were told in the company of the fugitives from the sack of Rome in 1527, exactly as Boccaccio does in the introduction to his tales, where he imagines them to be told by the fugitives from the Florentine plague.

Therefore: 1527. This is not just a *date,* but a *fact* that serves us. You have another fact in hand: Open my volume of Schakespeare, which remained at St Agata; look for Giraldi's novel, which is translated there, and you will find in the first lines how the cruel story of Othello and Desdemona happened *a short while before.* Consequently Giraldi fixes the period thus: *a short time before 1527.* I don't think I was wrong in giving Edel 1525 as the extreme limit. A couple of years between the event and the narration of the event doesn't seem too much to me. In my opinion, then, Edel mustn't go beyond 1525 in his studies, but he must focus on a long period of years prior to that fixed date. The clothes of that time changed less rapidly than those of today. Today, wherever there are numbers of people, we see some thirty years of fashion represented; the Italian overcoat that you still wear is proof of this, and the high collars on your shirts another proof! Thirty years separate one from the other. I advised our Edel to study the Venetian painters of the last years of the fifteenth century through the first quarter of the sixteenth. Fortunately for us, the two great documents of those years are Carpaccio and Gentile Bellini! The clothing for our characters will come from their pictures.

Have I done well? Have I done badly?

If I've done badly, we still have time to correct the error.

Cordial greetings to Signora Giuseppina.

A good handshake for you.

Your
Arrigo Boito

ENCLOSURE

I say then that, since the fifteen-hundred and twenty-seven years had already gone by after the true Son of God was born among men for the salvation of mankind, a German nobleman,[4] filled with hatred against the holiness of the pope and the entire most sacred order of the holy prelates like many of his nation (incited by malicious minds, who armed tongue and quill against the holy and catholic Roman church), mustered a very large and mighty army of German folk. Stained by Luther's and his adherents' pestiferous heresy, he invaded Italy with the abominable thought not only to destroy Rome, the common fatherland of all nations, but with his own hands contemptibly to kill the pope by strangling him with a golden rope which he carried with him. When, having arrived in Italy, he came close to carrying out his wicked and eveil plan, he fell with a stroke, as though struck down by divine justice, so that he was unable to fight. But there was no lack of other barbarian commanders among those people who, stirred by the same hatred and greedy quest of reward, kept the German

---

[4] Georg von Frundsberg (1473–1528), a friend of Martin Luther, arch-enemy of Pope Clement VII, and an imperial captain in the service of Charles V of Spain.

army together in order to carry out that horrible and infamous enterprise. A commander, who was well experienced in warfare,[5] joined their forces, made himself leader of the whole army, and after many detours that he made, went with incredible speed to Rome where he found very few armed men; for although the pope had heard about this army, he believed the words of some powerful noblemen, by whose wishes he felt these people depended, and gave leave to all the men of arms he found in Rome for his defense. This heightened the desire of the enemy's commander and his whole camp to attack in firm hope of victory. On the sixth of May, after the very great commander had assembled his army around the town of St Peter and wanted to climb the wall to order the assault on the antique walls of Rome and thus to find the way to enter the city, he was, I believe, by divine will killed by a soldier's bullet. It penetrated the left side of his groin; his death, however, did not occur right away [...].

BOITO TO VERDI

[Milan] 4 June [1886?][1]

Dear Maestro,

I have been in Milan since last night, and already I'm hopeful I'll soon receive a line from you telling me to come to St Agata. Many greetings to Signora Giuseppina.

Your most affectionate
Arrigo Boito

VERDI TO GIULIO RICORDI

Montecatini, 28 June 1886

[...] Everybody coming from Rome tells me how wonderful la Pantaleoni is in *Delorme*.[1] Everybody, everybody! A real fanaticism, extraordinary!—Alas! The greater the fanaticism, the more I fear for Desdemona!! Such a passionate, fiery, violent artist, how will she be able to control and contain herself in the calm, aristocratic passion of Desdemona?

It's true that when one has real talent and feeling, one succeeds almost all the time; all the same   —   —   — [...]

GIULIO RICORDI TO VERDI

Milan, 30 June 1886

[...] As for Signora Pantaleoni, I am confident that she can satisfy your demands; no doubt she has a very great talent, a clear, effective pronuncia-

---

[5] Charles, Duke of Bourbon (1490–1527), led Frundsberg's 12,000 men against Rome in 1527.

---

[1] The year can only be guessed; 1886 seems to be the most likely (see Verdi and Boito Chronologies, 1886).

---

[1] *Marion Delorme*, opera in 4 acts by Ponchielli.

tion. You rightly observe that in *Gioconda* as well as *Delorme* her greatest success is in the fourth acts, that is, at the most dramatic points; but it is also true that in these two last acts the best music is found. I have never heard *Le villi*[1], but I know that the soprano part is that of a naïve young girl, and in this, too, la Pantaleoni had great success . . . . . *sed supremo judice sententiam manet.* [. . .]

VERDI TO GIULIO RICORDI

[Montecatini, 4 July 1886]

[. . .] I have read a letter by Faccio in *La fanfulla*![1] . . . Too much, too much!! If I were an intimate friend of Faccio's, as for example Boito is, I would tell him frankly that this is not nice, not dignified, and too provincial! But I don't care, as long as nothing of the kind happens to *Otello*! . . No luncheons—no dinners—no toasts . . . *and no letters!!!*
   Addio, addio

Affectionately,
G. Verdi

GIULIO RICORDI TO VERDI

Milan, 6 July 1886

Illustrious Maestro,
   Before all else, my congratulations for your remarkable progress in musical composition! . . . The piece I received[1] shows a certain facility, and deserves to be published; but to do this I expect something better! . . . . . . Certainly you will succeed in progressing even further, if you persist in your studies!! . . . . .
   As for the ink, even if it became white, there is little harm; let me inform you that I am keeping a special paper of Moorish Venetian colour in readiness, on which even white ink will show up very well! [. . .]
   I have not read *La fanfulla*—but I know very well that you are right. But when necessary I will do all I can not to let scenes take place that would be unpleasant for you; I have always done this when I was aware of things in time. And I will arm myself with a carbine and telescope in order to become a regular guard! [. . .]

[1] Opera in 1 act by Puccini, his first.

[1] A Roman newspaper. Faccio's letter has not been found.

[1] Probably in the Biblioteca Palatina.

FRANCO FACCIO TO GIULIO RICORDI

San Pellegrino, 14 July 1886

My dearest Giulio,

I read in *Il corriere della sera* that Giuseppe Verdi 'has closed the eyes' of our good and beloved Countess Maffei. [. . .] In these painful circumstances, too, our great Maestro showed the compassionate kindness of his noble heart; and I hope that in her last moments the poor dying one may have recognized the illustrious man at her side giving her the comfort of a long, proven, most tender friendship! [. . .]

VERDI TO BOITO

St Agata, 17 July 1886

Dear Boito,

I, too, am a little worried[1] about the printing of the libretto for the finale of the third act, because I would really like the reader to be able to see and understand everything at a glance.

Turn the page and you'll see what I propose, and you'll find it better . . . . so much better.[2]

The page where the three columns are, of course, should be completely in the middle of the libretto, with the seams where the *empty spaces* are.

It's all right to print Desdemona's solo at the end of the preceding page, so that the reader won't be distracted and will give all his attention to her. If he turned the sheet then, he would find himself in front of the whole muddle of the *Concertato*.[3]

Don't let Giulio bring up any problems concerning the more or less beautiful appearance of the edition. The important thing is to make the readers understand . . . if they want to understand!

Tomorrow I hope to have the head to go through and review what has been done . .

Addio, addio

Your
G. Verdi

[1] Presumably, Boito had expressed this concern orally while meeting Verdi in Milan on 13 July, the day of Clara Maffei's funeral.

[2] Verdi's wish was respected only in the early editions of Ricordi's *Otello* libretto. See Verdi's transcription, which he wrote on a separate sheet, on p. 224 (translated on p. 225), and the final text in the first printed libretto, representing minor corrections, on p. 226.

[3] A term used occasionally in the early seventeenth century in connection with various manifestations of the novel principle of 'contrast' or 'rivalry'. (Willi Apel ed., *Harvard Dictionary of Music*, 2nd edn 1969, p. 192.) In Italian nineteenth-century opera, a 'concertato' usually refers to an ensemble at the end of an act, in which the voices of the soloists, chorus, and orchestra compete.

ENCLOSURE

Come stà et.

. . . .

. . . .

. . . .

OTELLO. Noi salperem domani—A terra! e piangi!

e afferra Desdemona furiosamente e Des. cade. Emilia e Lodovico la raccolgon e sollevan pietosamente. Otello avrà nel suo gesto terribile gettata la pergamena al suolo, e Jago l'avrà raccolta e letta . .

DESDEMONA

A terra! . . sí . . nel livido
Fango . . percossa . . . io giacio . . .
Piango . . . m'agghiaccia il brivido
Dell'anima che muor.
E un dí sul mio sorriso
Fioría la speme e il bacio
Ed or . . . l'angoscia in viso
E l'agonía nel cor.
   Quel sol sereno e vivido
Che allieta il cielo e il mare
Non può asciugar le amare
Stille del mio dolor . .

[As it stands, etc.

OTELLO   We will sail tomorrow—To the ground! and weep!

and he furiously seizes Desdemona and Des. falls. Emilia and Lodovico take her up and support her with compassion. In his terrible outburst Otello has thrown the parchment on the floor, and Jago has picked it up and read it . . .

DESDEMONA

To the ground! . . yes . . in the livid
Mire . . struck down . . . I lie . . .
I weep . . . the shudder of my
Dying soul chills me.
And one day in my smile
Bloomed hope and a kiss.
And now . . . anguish in my face
And agony in my heart.
   The sun serene and bright
That gladdens sky and sea
Cannot dry the bitter
Tears of my grief . .]

Jago ad Otello accasciato su d'una sedia

Una parola

OTEL. E che!

JAGO. T'affretta! Rapido
Slancia la tua vendetta! Il tempo vola.

OT. Ben parli

JAGO. È l'ira inutil ciancia. Scuotiti!
All'opra ergi tua mira! All'opra sola.
Io penso a Cassio. Ei le sue trame espia.
L'infame anima ria l'averno inghiotte.

OT. Chi gliela svelle?

JA. Io!

OT. Tu?

JA. Tu?

OT. Giurai

OT. Tal sia

JAG. Tu avrai le sue novelle questa notte
abbandona Otello e si dirige verso Rodrigo
I sogni tuoi saranno in mar domani.
E tu sull'aspra terra

ROD. Ahi triste!

JAGO. Ahi stolto!
Stolto! Se vuoi tu puoi sperar, gli umani
Arditi orsù riafferra e m'odi

ROD. Ascolto.

JAGO. Col primo albor salpa il vascello. Or Cassio
È il Duce. Eppur se avvien che a questi accada
Sventura ... Allor qui resta Otello

ROD. Lugubre
Luce d'altro balen

JAGO. Mano alla spada!
A notte folta io la sua traccia seguito
E il varco e l'ora scruto, il resto a te
Sarò tua scolta. A caccia a caccia Cingiti l'arco
venduto

R. Sì t'ho [[donato]] [?] onore e fè!

JAGO. (*a parte*). (Corri al miraggio! Il fragile tuo senno
Ha già confuso un sogno menzogner.
Segui l'astuto ed agile mio cenno
Amante illuso, io seguo il mio pensier

ROD. Il dado è tratto! Impavido t'attendo
Ultima sorte, occulto mio destin
Mi sprona amor, ma un avido tremendo
Astro di morte infèsta il mio cammin

IL CORO
a gruppi dialogando
contemporaneamente ai dialoghi di Jago

DONNE

Pietà!

CAV.

Mistero!

DONNE

Ansia mortal bieca
Ne ingombra anime assorte in lungo orror

CAV.

Quell'uomo nero è sepolcrale, e cieca
Un'ombra è in Lui di morte e di terror

DAME

Vista crudel! Strazia coll'ugna l'orrido
Petto!

CAV.

Figge gli sguardi immoti al suol
Poi sfida il Ciel coll'atra pugna l'ispido
Aspetto ergendo ai dardi alti del Sol

DAME

Ei la colpì! Quel viso santo pallido
Blando si china e tace e piange e muor
Piangon così nel Ciel lor pianto gli angeli
Quando perduto giace il peccator

EMILIA

Quella innocente un fremito
D'odio non ha ne un gesto
Trattiene in petto il gemito
Con doloroso fren.
La lagrima si frange
Muta sul volto mesto.
No chi per Lei non piange
Non ha pietade in sen.

RODRIGO

(Per me s'oscura il mondo
S'anuvola il destin
L'angiol soave e biondo
Scompar dal mio cammin.)

CASSIO

(L'ora è fatal Un fulmine
Sul mio cammin l'addita
Già mia sorte il culmine
S'offre all'inerte man
L'ebbra fortuna incalza
La fuga della vita
Questa che al ciel m'innalza
È un'onda d'uragan.

LODOVICO

Egli la man funerea
Scuote anelando d'ira
Essa la faccia eterea
Volge piangendo al Ciel
Nel contemplar quel pianto
La carità sospira
E un tenero compianto
Stempra del core il gel

224

[EMILIA
That innocent one has no shudder
Nor a gesture of hatred.
She holds back a groan in her breast
With painful restraint.
Tears burst forth silently
Upon her sad face.
No, who does not weep for her
Has no pity in his heart.

RODRIGO
(The world grows dark for me,
My fate is clouded over;
The sweet and fair angel
Vanishes from my path.)

CASSIO
(The hour is fatal. A thunderbolt
Shows it on my path.
Already the summit of my destiny
Offers itself to my inert hand.
Drunken fortune spurs on
The flight of my life.
What raises me to heaven
Is a hurricane's waver.)

LODOVICO
He shakes his funereal hand,
Panting with wrath.
She turns her ethereal face,
Weeping, towards Heaven.
In contemplating those tears,
Pity sighs,
And a tender compassion
Thaws the frost of the heart.

THE CHORUS
talking to each other in groups,
simultaneously with Jago's dialogues.

WOMEN
Mercy!

CAV[aliers].
Mystery!

WOMEN
Sinister, mortal anguish
Encumbers our souls immersed in deep horror.

CAV.
That black man is sepulchral, and there is
A blind shadow of death and terror upon him.

LADIES
Cruel sight! He rends his horrid chest
With his nails!

CAV.
He fixes his glances motionless upon the
ground,
Then he defies Heaven with his dark fist,
Raising his shaggy face to the high rays of the
Sun.

LADIES
He struck her! That saintly, pallid, soft face
Bows down and is silent and weeps and dies.
Thus cry the angels in Heaven
When the sinner lies lost.

Jago to Otello, who has collapsed on a chair.
A word.
OTEL.   What?.
JAGO.   Make haste! Rapidly
Hurl forth your vengeance. Time flies.
OT. You speak well.
JAGO.   Anger is useless rubbish. Arouse
yourself!
Set your sights on the task! Only on the task.
I think about Cassio. He atones for his plots.
Hell engulfs the infamous guilty soul.
OT. Who tears it from him?
JA.   I!
OT.   You?
JA.   I swore.
OT.   So be it.
JAG. You will have his news tonight.

He leaves Otello and goes towards Rodrigo.

Your dreams will be upon the sea tomorrow
And you upon the harsh land.
ROD.   Ah, sad!
JAGO.   Ah, blockhead!
Blockhead! If you wish, you can hope; get hold
again
Of your manly daring, and listen to me.
ROD.   I'm listening.
JAGO. At early dawn the vessel sails. Now Cassio
Is the Commander. Yet if it happens that
Misfortune befall him . . . Then Otello remains here.
ROD.   Gloomy
Light of another lightning.
JAGO.   Grasp your sword!
In the thick of night I follow his tracks
And search for his passage and the hour; the rest is
up to you.
I will be your guard. . To the hunt, to the hunt! Gird
on
The bow.
R. Yes. I have [[sold]] [[given]] [?] you my honour and
faith!
JAGO. (*aside*). (Run to the mirage! Your fragile mind
Has already confused a lying dream.
You follow my astute and agile hint,
Deluded lover, I follow my thought.)
ROD. The die is cast! Fearless I await you,
My ultimate fate and hidden destiny.
Love spurs me on, but an avid, terrible
Star of death infests my path.]

EMILIA

(Quella innocente un fremito
D'odio non ha nè un gesto,
Trattiene in petto il gemito
Con doloroso fren.
La lagrima si frange
Muta sul volto mesto;
No, chi per lei non piange
Non ha pietade in sen.)

RODERIGO

(Per me s'oscura il mondo,
S'annuvola il destin;
L'angiol soave e biondo
Scompar dal mio cammin.)

CASSIO

(L'ora è fatal! un fulmine
Sul mio cammin l'addita.
Già di mia sorte il culmine
S'offre all'inerte man.
L'ebbra fortuna incalza
La fuga della vita.
Questa che al ciel m'innalza
È un'onda d'uragan.)

LODOVICO

(Egli la man funerea
Scuote anelando d'ira,
Essa la faccia eterea
Volge piangendo al ciel.
Nel contemplar quel pianto
La carità sospira,
E un tenero compianto
Stempra del core il gel.)

IL CORO

(a gruppi, dialogando)

DAME

Pietà!

CAVALIERI

Mistero!

DAME

Ansia mortale, bieca,
Ne ingombra, anime assorte in lungo orror

CAVALIERI

Quell'uomo nero è sepolcrale, e cieca
Un'ombra è in lui di morte e di terror.

DAME

Vista crudel!

CAVALIERI

Strazia coll'ugna l'orrido
Petto! Figge gli sguardi immoti al suol.
Poi sfida il ciel coll'atra pugna, l'ispido
Aspetto ergendo ai dardi alti del Sol.

DAME

Ei la colpì! quel viso santo, pallido,
Blando, si china e tace e piange e muor.
Piangon così nel ciel lor pianto gli angeli
Quando perduto giace il peccator.

JAGO. *(avvicinandosi a Otello che resterà accasciato su
d'un sedile).*
(Una parola.
OTELLO.   E che?
J.   T'affretta! Rapido
O. Ben parti.
J.   Slancia la tua vendetta! Il tempo vola.
                          È l'ira inutil ciancia. Scuotiti!
All'opra ergi tua mira! All'opra sola!
Io penso a Cassio. Ei le sue trame espia.
L'infame anima ria l'averno inghiotte!
O. Chi gliela svelle?
J.   Io
O.   Tu?
J.   Giurai.
O.   Tal sia.
J. Tu avrai le sue novelle in questa notte . . .)
                  (abbandona Otello e si dirige verso Roderigo)
J. *(ironicamente a Roderigo)*
(I sogni tuoi saranno in mar domani
E tu sull'aspra terra!
RODERIGO   Ahi tristel
J. Stolto! Se vuoi tu puoi sperar; gli umani,
Orsù! cimenti afferra, e m'odi.   Ahi stolto!
R.   Ascolto.
J. Col primo albor salpa il vascello. Or Cassio
È il Duce. Eppur se avvien che a questi accada
                  (toccando la spada)
Sventura . . . allor qui resta Otello.
R.   Lúgubre
Luce d'atro balen!   Mano alla spada!
J. A notte folta io la sua traccia viglio,
E il varco e l'ora scruto, il resto a te.
Sarò tua scolta. A caccia! a caccia! Cingiti
L'arco!
R.   Sì! t'ho venduto onore e fè.
J. (Corri al miraggio! il fragile tuo senno
Ha già confuso un sogno menzogner.
Segui l'astuto ed agile mio cenno,
Amante illuso, io seguo il mio pensier.)
R. (Il dado è tratto! Impavido t'attendo
Ultima sorte, occulto mio destin.
Mi sprona amor, ma un avido, tremendo
Astro di morte infesta il mio cammin.)

BOITO TO VERDI

Como per Villa d'Este
21 July [1886]

Dear Maestro,

While you were thinking about the typographical questions concerning the libretto and were resolving them in the best possible manner, I was ruminating over the remarks you made to me[1] regarding Desdemona's presence, which isn't sufficiently prepared for in the *big ensemble scene*.

At first your comment seemed a little too detailed to me; then it seemed right, and worthy of study. I've tried to correct this imperfection in the most concise and suitable way I could. See if I've succeeded:

I propose two additions: the first one being three lines in the scene between Jago and Otello in Act III, the second being two lines in the following scene.

JAGO (*s'incammina*	. . . .	Mio Duce
con Otello verso la	Grazie vi rendo.[2] Ecco gli Ambasciatori	
porta del fondo. Ma	Andiamo ad essi. *Ma . . . credo opportuno*	
ad un tratto s'arres-	(*Anche a sviar sospetti o uggiose inchieste*)	
ta).	*Che Desdemona accolga quei Messeri.*	
O.	*Sí Qui l'adduci.*	
(*Jago esce rapida-*		. . . .
mente dalla porta di	. . . .	
sinistra. Otello conti-		
nua ad avviarsi verso	. . . .	
il fondo per attendere		
gli Ambasciatori.)		

---

[1] Presumably, oral remarks by Verdi at the time of Clara Maffei's funeral in Milan, 13 July 1886.

[2] In the final text (III, vi):

> *Il tumulto è sempre più vicino. Fanfare e grida.*
> Ecco gli ambasciatori.
> Li accogliete. Ma ad evitar sospetti,
> Desdemona si mostri a quei Messeri.
> OTELLO. Si. Qui l'adduci.
> (*Jago esce dalla porta di sinistra; Otello s'avvia verso il fondo per ricevere gli ambasciatori.*)

> [*The uproar comes closer and closer. Fanfares and shouts.*
> Here are the ambassadors.
> Receive them. But to avoid suspicion,
> Desdemona should show herself to these Gentlemen.
> OTELLO. Yes. Bring her here.
> *Jago exits through the left door. Otello goes toward the background to receive the ambassadors.*]

(Cf. Shakespeare, *Othello*, IV. i.)

LOD.
(*a Desd. che sarà en-*   Madonna,
trata con Jago e se-   V'abbia il cielo in sua grazia.[3]
guita a breve distanza
da Emilia.)

DESD.   E il ciel vascolti.

EM.   (*Come sei mesta.*
(*a Desd. a parte*)

DESD.   Emilia! una gran nube
(*a Em. a parte*)   Turba il senno d'Otello e il mio destino.*)

[JAGO   . . . .   My Chief,
(*walks with Otello*   I give you thanks. Here are the Ambassadors.
towards the door at   Let's go to them. *But . . . I think it opportune*
the back. But sud-   (*Also to remove suspicions or irksome inquiries*)
denly he stops.)   *That Desdemona receive these Gentlemen.*

O.   *Yes.   Bring her here.*
(*Jago exits rapidly*   . . . .
through the door on
the left. Otello con-   . . . .
tinues to walk upstage
to await the Ambas-   . . . .
sadors.)

LOD.   My Lady,
(*to Desd., who has*   May Heaven keep you in its grace.
entered with Jago,
followed by Emilia
shortly after.)

DESD.   And may Heaven hear you.

EM.   (*How sad you are.*
(*aside to Desd.*)

DESD.   Emilia! A great cloud
(*aside to Em.*)   *Disturbs Otello's mind and my destiny.*)]

                       . . . .

The rest as it is in the manuscript.[4]

The libretto that Giulio transcribed is in Tornaghi's hands now, and he
will give it to Edel to read. I would prefer that no one else read this little
volume. Giulio told me that you already had almost finished the orches-

---

[3] In the final text (III, vii): 'V'abbia il cielo in sua guardia.' ['May heaven guard you.']
[4] See *Carteggi* ii. 111–15 for original text of Boito's libretto at St Agata.

tration of Act I! Be careful not to overtax yourself. You have time. Sometimes it is good to follow the advice of a lazybones.

Many greetings to Signora Giuseppina and to you.

From the heart,
Your
Arrigo Boito

PS Write just a line to me to let me know whether this letter has reached you.

VERDI TO BOITO

[St Agata] *Thursday* [22 July 1886][1]

Dear Boito,

I have received your last letter.—These lines fit, and I think they will do well. They upset the composer a little, who will be forced to suspend or prolong that little off-stage trumpet concert,[2] etc. ... But never mind.—Thank you and *addio*. Peppina greets you.

Your
G. Verdi

VERDI TO MARIA WALDMANN

St Agata, 23 July 1886

[...] I have lost a very dear friend whom I have known for 44 years! The Countess Clara Maffei, whom you might have known by name! Good, intelligent, affectionate ... and at the same time a friend one could count on!.. Poor Clarina! And so, one after the other all go away! [...]

Ah, *Otello*?!! Do not believe what the papers have said. It's likely, but not certain. I still haven't promised a thing ... and I'm very little disposed to promise ... We'll see!

Back just now from Montecatini, we're not going to move any more, except to go to Genoa in the winter and maybe to Milan. [...]

BOITO TO VERDI

[Como per Villa d'Este] 25 July [1886]

Dear Maestro,

It's better as follows; a line is saved:[1]

---

[1] Postmark: BUSSETO 23/7/86.
[2] Three groups of trumpets announcing the arrival of the Venetian ambassadors in Act III.

---

[1] See Boito to Verdi, 21 July 1886.

Ecco gli Ambasciatori	[Here are the Ambassadors.
Li accogliete. Ma ad evitar sospetti	Receive them. But to avoid suspicion
Desdemona si mostri a quei Messeri.	Desdemona should show herself to
OT. Sì, qui l'adduci.	these Gentlemen.
	OT. Yes, bring her here.]

Thus, without the long interpolation, the phrase can be spoken very rapidly by Jago.

Your
A. Boito

BOITO TO EUGENIO TORNAGHI

Villa d'Este, 28 July 1886

[. . .] Take care to let no one but Edel read the libretto of *Otello*, and to plug your ears when you read it. I am saying this because I know, unfortunately, that one word allowed to slip from the lips creates a hundred others that were never said, and the next day you see them in print. [. . .]

VERDI TO GIUSEPPE PIROLI

St Agata, 7 August 1886

[. . .] I was deeply upset by the death of Clarina Maffei. She was my friend for 44 years! ... A true and sincere friend! She certainly could not write her husband's verses ... but what a heart! And what nobility of character! And what loftiness of sentiment! [. . .]

GIULIO RICORDI TO VERDI

Levico [Trentino, Austria], 10 August 1886

Illustrious Maestro,

I thank you very much for your kind reply,[1] and we are very glad to have your good news. Ours is also good, and we are nearly finished with the cure, so that we leave Levico in three days.

This is the positive and happy part; but right away there is the law of compensation with the negative part, the hardly comforting news you give me concerning Faccio's visit[2] and your work.

Basically I understand Faccio's reservations; he is not very outgoing by nature, and in this case he found himself in a very delicate position ... *ad personam*[3] and also before you, Maestro. Whether you like it or not, he has always held you in great awe!! [. . .]

---

[1] Probably in the Biblioteca Palatina.
[2] Presumably at St Agata a few days earlier.
[3] In reference to Faccio's intimate relationship with Romilda Pantaleoni.

I think, however, that there is an easy way out: I myself shall ask Faccio for news . . . . . in order to know the truth; in short, I shall make him *sing like a blackbird*. [. . .]

I am scared by what you say: *status quo*! . . . . I am thinking of the reduction [piano–vocal score], of printing the orchestra and vocal parts!! . . . . and I wish I could fly to you and return with the . . . . . most precious manuscript! . . . . .

Edel, contrary to his habit . . . . . has worked, and is well along with the costume sketches, which I shall then submit to you for your approval. [. . .]

FRANCO FACCIO TO GIULIO RICORDI

Brescia, 14 August 1886

[. . .] What you have written to me about la Pantaleoni[1] was told to me at St Agata by our great and adored Maestro. What could I answer him? Together we examined the part of Desdemona, which seemed to me to be musically just as suitable for la Pantaleoni as for all other sopranos in similar parts in all Verdi operas. As for the *type* of part, la Pantaleoni would by her very nature be rather inclined to strongly dramatic ones; but this doesn't mean that she would dislike parts in which she would have to adapt herself to tenderness and sensitivity. I mentioned to the Maestro the honest and, I believe, deserved success she enjoyed in *Le villi*.[2] In this opera she had to perform just such a naïve, tender, idealistic personality; and I added (in spite of the uselessness of such an explanation) that in view of the great honour bestowed upon her, la Pantaleoni would dedicate herself to the part of Desdemona with *long study* and with *great love*, and that she would endeavour above all to fulfill the great author's just demands. I said further that la Pantaleoni—who is at Salsomaggiore at this time—would not sing any more until next winter [. . .] just to be at the Maestro's disposal whenever it should please him to let her study, whether in the country right away or in Genoa later on. The excellent Maestro showed that he was agreeable to these plans of the artist, adding that at the moment he had work to do but that he would write to me soon in order to invite la Pantaleoni to Genoa or St Agata. At that time she would be able to accept your kind and dear offer to accompany her; I informed la Pantaleoni of this offer, and meanwhile I send you her warmest thanks in advance.—I am unable to tell you here about the music of *Otello*, which I know almost entirely by now, and which I was so moved to hear, as you can easily imagine. This sublime subject must not be contained in the narrow confines of a letter. I will tell you only that Verdi's genius is inextinguishable, since this new creation doesn't resemble the others—also immortal ones—that preceded it. He still had work to do, as I wrote to you above. But that is work on the orchestration, not on the

[1] Missing.
[2] As Anna in the first performance of that opera at La Scala on 24 Jan. 1885 with Faccio conducting.

composition. At the moment, alas, I had to leave him, he had very little to complete in the orchestration of the first act; but he still had to orchestrate almost the entire second and third acts. The last, the wonderful last act is completely finished, and one might say [that it came] from Verdi's head already fully orchestrated—so ingenious and perfect is the whole composition. [...]

GIULIO RICORDI TO VERDI

Milan, 18 August 1886

[...] As I wrote to you, I not only sent a letter to Faccio in Brescia, but, passing through Brescia on our return, I also spoke to him; and then I found here a letter of *eight* pages in answer to mine. I had already foreseen the *impaccio*, illustrious Maestro, in which *Faccio* found himself!—please note the rhyme—and how in your presence—on account of his natural reserve and also his more than natural awe—he would not venture overly forthright assertions. He told me that if la Pantaleoni has appeared in dramatic roles, it is because the new operas were in that style. The only new one in which she interpreted a character of a sweet, naïve, affectionate young girl, was *Le villi*, whose success at La Scala, it is true, was due to la Pantaleoni, the other parts being mediocre. For my part I am sure that this artist will satisfy you, since she has great intelligence and musical instincts; furthermore she had the foresight not to accept any other contracts, in order to find herself in fresh voice at La Scala; and this proves how well she understands the importance of the commitment she has assumed.

In short, as for what Faccio told me in person and as for what he wrote to me, I believe you may do what you already had in mind, that is, to show the part to la Pantaleoni without fear of finding yourself in one of those delicate and unpleasant situations that are better avoided.

In any case, Maestro, command me; I suggest the following, because I know, of course, that if you should not approve, you would tell me so *frankly*—this not being an occasion to stand on ceremony.

Do you think that to remove that little *gêne* of a first encounter and to raise the morale of the Signora a bit, I myself might accompany her to you, when you think it opportune? ..... of course, I would then leave right away.

Do you think that if I then came another time to show you the costume sketches, I might be accompanied by Edel? .... If modifications or changes should be required, Edel himself could then make note of them while he was present, and thus the task would be facilitated.

These are the suggestions I dare to make, because, I repeat, if they disturb you in any way you only have to tell me: no—we will do this and that—and all will go very well. The conclusion is always: *I am entirely at your command.*

I will not even tell you what Faccio has written to me about the impressions he had!!! .... and with what moving words he speaks to me of *Otello*! .... These things are better left unsaid, but I will not leave unsaid

Giuditta's cordial, most cordial greetings to you and Signora Peppina, and even less will I leave unsaid my own greetings to both of you, with the assertion of the deepest feelings of devotion and gratitude.

Yours most affectionately,
Giulio Ricordi

GIULIO RICORDI TO VERDI

Cernobbio, 26 August 1886

Illustrious Maestro,

I am writing to you from Villa d'Este, where I have come to visit my family.

La Pantaleoni only left Salsomaggiore on Sunday, after a fall by her sister, who broke her arm while the visit was being planned. She will be in Milan Saturday night, and so we shall leave on the usual train at 11.40 a.m. in order to be in Fiorenzuola by 2 p.m. [. . .]

Boito, who asks me to give you his regards, shares my confidence in la Pantaleoni. Let us hope, then, that you can be satisfied, and we shall be most happy about it. I have talked with Boito about the translation,[1] and I shall have the honour to tell you in person what we have in mind. [. . .]

VERDI TO BOITO

[St Agata, about 29 August 1886][1]

Pro Memoria

1. What should the women be doing in the Act I drinking song? Should they also be drinking? . . And why not?   —   — .

2. If you don't mind, I'd like to redo four lines that were cut in the scene between Otello and Desdemona in the third act . .

. . . . . .

Pur già qui annida[2] il demone gentil del mal consiglio,
Che il vago avorio allumina del piccioletto artiglio
Mollemente alla prece s'atteggia e al pio fervore
Eppur con questa mano, io v'ho donato il core

---

[1] Of *Otello* into French.

[1] On this Sunday, Giulio Ricordi had accompanied Romilda Pantaleoni to St Agata. Verdi probably gave him this *Pro Memoria* for Boito, who was at the Villa d'Este in Cernobbio while the Ricordis were vacationing there.

[2] In the final text (III. 2) Otello says: 'Eppur qui annida . . .' ['And yet here nests . . .'] (Cf. Shakespeare, *Othello*, III. iv. 35–9.) See Verdi to Ricordi, 2 Dec. 1886 and Ricordi to Verdi, 4 Dec. 1886.

[OTELLO.] [*Yet here already nests the gentle demon of bad counsel,*
Which the lovely ivory of the little claw illuminates.
Softly it poses in prayer and pious fervour.
[DESDEMONA.] *And yet with this hand I have given you my heart.*]

Signor mi raccomanda[3] *... Emilia ... Addio*
[*Lord commend me ... Emilia ... Farewell*]

VERDI TO FRANCO FACCIO

St Agata, 2 September 1886

Dear Faccio,

Signora Pantaleoni left just now and gave me hope that she would return towards the middle of October, when her part will be completely copied and even printed. I have entrusted the fourth act to Giulio, in which Desdemona has the largest and most difficult part. The *Canzone del salice* [*Willow Song*] is causing the composer as well as the artist performing it the greatest problems. She should sing with three voices, like the most sacred Trinity: with one for Desdemona, another one for Barbara (the maid), and a third for the '*Salce, salce, salce*' ['*Willow*']. Signora Pantaleoni's voice becomes cutting at passionate points, and in high notes a little too biting; she gives too much metal, so to speak. If she could get used to singing with a little more head-voice, the *smorzato*[1] would come easier to her and her voice would also be more secure and natural. —I have advised her to study this way; and you, with your influence, should give her the same advice. Besides, it isn't always true that her D is such a bad tone, as she says. There is a point where she succeeds the best with it:[2]

3 Judging from Boito's answer of 6 Sept. 1886, Verdi seemed to have doubts about these last words of Desdemona. The end of the *Pro memoria* is apparently missing. In the final text (IV. iii) Desdemona says: 'Nessuno ... io stessa ... al mio Signor mi raccomanda ... Emilia ... Addio ...' ['No one ... I myself ... to my Lord commend me ... Emilia ... Farewell ...'] (Cf. Shakespeare, *Othello*, v. ii. 125–6: 'Nobody, I myself, farewell: / Commend me to my kind lord, O, farewell!').

1 Faded away.

2 Verdi writes the following quotation, which appears to be the second 'Salce' phrase of the 'Willow' Song, in the soprano key. Note the differences of dynamic notation in the corresponding phrase in the orchestral score, *Otello* (Milan *et al.*: Ricordi [1958], plate no. PR 155, p. 472).

This phrase is repeated three times. The last time she manages it well, the two other times less so.

I told you frankly what I think, and I tell you again that—with her great talent and theatrical instincts, with good will and study—she will succeed very well in the part of Desdemona, even though it is not completely suited to her way of expression and her voice ... Mind you, she does many, many things with the greatest ease. Addio; I don't know what I have written to you in such great haste. Try to make sense of it. Addio, Peppina sends her greetings.

Yours,
G. Verdi

BOITO TO VERDI

Villa d'Este [6 September 1886][1]

Dear Maestro,

Musical considerations must, in my opinion, decide the questions you have submitted to me.[2]

Can the women's voices help the effect of the drinking song? Let's add them. They will repeat the men's words in the refrain. And if they don't [help it], would you add them only because of the fact that they mustn't be idle on stage! This argument doesn't seem strong enough for me to devote two staves of the score to them, if these two lines don't bring about their musical effect and, worse yet, if the feminine timbre spoils even in the least the masculine boldness of this piece. I repeat: if you want to add the women because you are worried about the *staging*, don't add them. They won't be idle. There are forty-five women at La Scala; after the *fuoco* [*di*] *gioia* [fire of joy], about *twenty or more* gradually disperse; the remainder we divide into two parts. Some go to the rear to walk or sit down with their lovers, others can spread out fishing nets on the floor of the rampart. The prettiest and the least proper ones we'll have sitting with the men at the table, and these will be about *ten or twelve*, and they won't think of anything else but being pinched and eating and drinking. These girls and the ones who remain at the back, over twenty in all, will scream the two '*fuggiam*' ['*Let's flee*'] and the '*s'uccidono*' ['*They're killing each other*'] at the moment of the brawl; and if these don't suffice to produce a powerful scream, the other *twenty or more*, who had dispersed into the wings, can run in with all the noise of a few moments earlier, and at the sight of the drawn swords howl '*Fuggiam*' with the others. This is the approximate staging of the women's chorus during the time that elapses between the chorus of the *fuoco di gioia* and Otello's reprimand.

If the four lines already cut in the *Otello–Desdemona scene in Act III* are musically useful to you, use them; I have no objection. Who can be a better

---

[1] Postmark: CERNOBBIO 6/9/86.
[2] In the *Pro memoria*, supposedly delivered by Giulio Ricordi.

judge than you? The same may be said about the monosyllable '*Vien*' ['*Come*'] in lieu of the bisyllable '*Andiam*' ['*Let's go*'] at the end of the first act. In these matters I am neutral, like Switzerland.

If, while you are applying tone-colours to your opera, some doubt or some thought should come to you that might require my presence at St Agata, write to me about it, and I will fly to you.

Affectionate greetings to you and to Signora Giuseppina.

Your
Arrigo Boito

Regarding also the last words of Desdemona, you are the only arbiter and judge.

GIULIO RICORDI TO VERDI

Milan, 7 September 1886

Illustrious Maestro,

By now you will have had a letter from Boito in answer to the various questions concerning the libretto. Boito also showed me your model page of the third [act] finale.[1] It works very well; it is a great concept, one that gives a clear and exact idea.[2]

Tomorrow morning the reduction for voice and piano of the fourth act will be started; the copy of the orchestra score has already been made—and so I shall send the part to Desdemona tomorrow morning. [. . .]

FRANCO FACCIO TO VERDI

Brescia, 7 September 1886

[. . .] La Pantaleoni, while passing through Brescia on her way to Abano, could not resist the temptation to stop over for a few hours to tell me all the particulars of her memorable trip to St Agata.

She was radiant with joy, laughing and crying at the same time while she spoke of the affectionate welcome with which the great Maestro had honoured her, of her studies with the supreme author, of the generous encouragement, and of the precious counsel she received to correct vocal defects. In short, she told me every detail of what you, illustrious Maestro, in all your kindheartedness, wrote to me right away.

La Pantaleoni has every right to abandon herself fully to these new and fruitful emotions. I can find no words, then, to express my deep feeling and gratitude for what you had the kindness to write to me about this artist. [. . .]

---

[1] See Verdi to Boito, 17 July 1886.
[2] The third act finale was printed accordingly in the first editions of the libretto, but in later editions Verdi's wishes were no longer fulfilled.

VERDI TO GIULIO RICORDI

[St Agata] *Tuesday* [7 September 1886][1]

[. . .] Saturday morning at 9.05 I myself or a person I have put in charge will be in Piacenza with the package, etc. . . . It's understood: When the person whom you send sees an individual with a large package, he will ask him . . 'Is it from the Maestro?' . . And the other: 'Are you from the House of Ricordi?' etc. In this package you will find the whole first act . . . up to the entire Scene vi of the third act! . . Eternal God! How many notes!!! So your copying office will have work to do; and I shall rest for four or five days, because with those damned scores containing 32 lines my eyes get tired; . . and mine are really tired . . . Telegraph me if it's all right for Saturday and addio, addio

Your
G. Verdi

VERDI TO BOITO

[St Agata] *Thursday* [9 September 1886][1]

Dear Boito,

Let's do the *pinching*! This way I can keep the women quiet in the drinking song (they would have spoiled it) and I'll let them burst into laughter a couple of times in F♯ minor among themselves, about Cassio or about the pinches.

Tomorrow morning I shall send the House of Ricordi the whole first act completely finished and all of Scene vi of the third; and thus, with the fourth already sent, perhaps three-fifths of the Moor is ready. I can breathe a little!

I thank you! I can't tell you now if I'll have to bother you again (it won't be for anything serious), because I actually plan to do nothing for *6* or *8* days. My eyes are a little tired on account of that damned paper with 32 lines.

I have gone over the three major roles *one* by *one* to see if they are suitably dressed, without patches, if they stand up straight, and if they work well . . . *They work*!! And a curious thing! Jago's role, except for some *éclats*, could be sung entirely *mezza voce*!

But . . . all of this does no good if the *notes* don't please the respectable . . . Addio, addio.

Till we see each other, I hope soon.

Your
G. Verdi

---

[1] Postmark: BUSSETO 7/9/86.

[1] In answer to Boito's letter of 6 Sept.

GIULIO RICORDI TO VERDI

Milan, 9 September 1886

Illustrious Maestro,

In answer to your esteemed letter of Tuesday I telegraphed you right away.[1] Garegnani, the chief copyist, will come, and therefore I have taken the liberty of telling you that if you should decide to go to Piacenza, it would be useful. But I also repeat that if because of the weather or for some other reason you don't feel like going yourself, there is no urgency whatsoever, and everything can be taken care of later on.

I send you warm thanks for finishing the first act in such a short time! . . . . . . and for turning in Scene vi of the third at the same time. So there will be a good deal of work, and you can be at your leisure. In all of this, one always comes to the conclusion that you are a *marvellous* man! . . . . . .

Even that indolent and cynical tribe of music copyists changed at the sight of an orchestra score by Verdi!! . . . . . .

All are in a good mood—there are those who remember having made the first copy of *Aida*, others of the *Messa*, and still others of the *Ballo in maschera*, and so on!! . . . . In short, in four days they have made me a copy of the orchestra score, the singers' parts for the arranger [of the reduction], Desdemona's part, and they have extracted the string quartet! . . . . I was astounded.

I am enclosing a proof of the famous page as you had it in mind;[2] it came out very well, and also, Boito told me that no one could do better. I am taking the most jealous care of everything, and hope to avoid any knavish trick of clandestine copying or indiscretions of the journalists! The pages set into type are under lock and key, and the orchestra score, with all the work on the parts going on, is locked up in the safe every night. I imagine, Maestro, that this visit of your autograph to the safe may be a great good omen and may make it fertile for the future. [. . .]

We still have a heatwave!! . . . . . which might be good for the land, but is very bad for the sultry streets of Milan.

Yours most affectionately
Giulio Ricordi

VERDI TO GIULIO RICORDI

[St Agata] Sunday [12 September 1886][1]

Dear Giulio,

In the fourth act, after the *solo* of the double-basses, at the moment when Otello gives the kiss to the sleeping Desdemona, there are notes in the

[1] Missing.
[2] The three columns in the third act finale of the libretto.

---

[1] Postmark: BUSSETO 12/9/86.

orchestra [score] that are badly arranged, causing a poor mixture. Correct as [you will see] on the paper I enclose.[2] I have already corrected the original.

Addio, addio

Yours,
G. Verdi

GIULIO RICORDI TO VERDI

Milan, 15 September 1886

Illustrious Maestro,

I received your esteemed letter with the corrected piece you enclosed from the orchestra score—and the correction was made in the copy. I did not answer you right away, because the reduction of the fourth act was almost ready and I was waiting to write to you until I could inform you at the same time that I was posting it to you; I sent it this morning before handing it over to the typesetters.

As far as I can tell, the reduction came out well, clear and easy rather than difficult, except for two or three points that are not naturally easy by themselves. You will also find one or two questions on which I await your decision.

In a couple of days I can send a copy of part of the first act to Saladino.

I await your orders, then, and send you and Signora Peppina my most devoted regards.

Believe me, Maestro, always your most grateful

Giulio|Ricordi

PS Faccio has come to me just now and asks me to give you his affectionate regards. We are looking at the orchestra score to determine which comprimarii can be proposed for Rodrigo and for Emilia, the latter being most important. For the others we are set.

VERDI TO GIULIO RICORDI

[St Agata] Friday [17 September 1886]

Dear Giulio,

I am returning the reduction of the fourth act.—There was little to be done over. The one who did the reduction might have been wrong in the tempo, which is not quite as fast as he probably thought; and thus I have simplified too much when Desdemona says '*Cassio non amo*' ['*I do not love Cassio*'], etc. and thus also at '*Otello non uccidermi*' ['*Otello, do not kill me*'], etc., etc.

[2] Missing. Possibly at Biblioteca Palatina.

Correct in the score a G ♮ in the solo of the double-basses[1] and [also correct] the *clarinet*[2]

cielo [heaven]

Tomorrow I go back to work.—
  Addio, addio

G. Verdi

Pay attention to *Rodrigo* and *Emilia*: I'll be wild and inexorable! No pretext will seem true to me .... Just as none seemed true to Boito, who had to postpone *Nerone* to translate *Otello*.[3]

GIULIO RICORDI TO VERDI

Milan, 20 September 1886

Illustrious Maestro,

Having made the two corrections in the orchestra score, this very day I passed on to the engravers the reduction of the fourth act with the modifications marked by you; I thank you very much for them, even though I regret that they caused you trouble and work. As it is now, I think the reduction renders the orchestra quite successfully. So once more, a thousand thanks to you.

Everybody is working on *Otello*; and to keep you from finding the famous *pretext* ...... with which you threatened me, I tell you that we have fished out a first-rate Rodrigo!! ... So one of your pretexts is already well destroyed. Now we are fishing for the Signora Emilia, and today I shall hear one with Faccio. We have agreed with Cairati on the chorus: instead of 100, we'll have 104 voices, bringing the women up to 40 instead of 36. I shall also show Cairati the orchestra score so that he may plan for the voices as well as for the children's chorus.—

Edel has been sensible this time!!! .... That's another Verdi miracle!! ..... He has completed 53 of the 58 costume sketches; and so as not to let him slip away from me, I took him with me to the lake [of Como] and locked him up there until he finished everything. So yesterday we had a meeting of three and a half hours with Boito (who is ...... as accurate as a Benedictine monk!!); and since Giacosa was there, too, we thought of inviting him also to the exhibition of the designs; I hope you will have nothing against it—or do you? ... I am glad to tell you that the costumes were an immense success. Edel has really surpassed himself. We also solved the problem of Desdemona's last

[1] At the beginning of Act IV, Scene iii (PR 155, pp. 492–3).
[2] Cf. the first two bars in PR 155, p. 504.
[3] Boito was already working on the French translation of *Otello*.

costume. Edel completely accepted some observations that Boito and Giacosa made, and today he is working on the required corrections. Only one costume sketch for Otello, one for Emilia, and three for the chorus are still missing; I hope he will be finished in a few days—so that we can submit all the sketches for your approval.

In a few days a part of the reduction of the first act will be ready.

I think I have sufficiently abused your time, and therefore I shall now hold my tongue, but not without first sending to Signora Peppina and you my expressions of affection and everlasting gratitude.

Most devotedly
Giulio Ricordi

VERDI TO GIUSEPPE PIROLI

St Agata, 1 October 1886

[. . .] Giulio Ricordi was here with his wife for four days and left two hours ago. Of course, all the while we talked and planned for the etc. [. . .]

I'm almost finished and will rest for four or five days. [. . .]

VERDI TO GIULIO RICORDI

[St Agata, about 1 October 1886][1]

Pro Memoria

Assuming I am able to complete what remains to be done for the music of *Otello*, it will be well for the House of Ricordi to establish as of now the conditions above all with the management of La Scala.

1. The House of Ricordi shall, with the management, set the rental,[2] of which I shall realize my share, etc., etc., — —

2. I will assist in all those rehearsals (which I shall judge necessary); but I do not wish to commit myself in any way to the public, and consequently the poster shall simply say

Otello
Poetry by Boito
Music by Verdi

No one, *absolutely no one*, at the rehearsals, as usual.— I have complete authority to suspend the rehearsals and prevent the performance, even after the dress rehearsal, if
either the execution
or the *mise-en-scène*
or *anything else* in the way the theatre is run should not be to my liking.

---

[1] Apparently, Verdi handed these instructions to Giulio Ricordi at St Agata.
[2] Of the scores and orchestra material, etc.

The personnel connected with *Otello* shall answer directly to me ... the *conductor* of the orchestra, of the chorus, the producer, etc., etc.

The first performance may not take place without my authorization, and should anyone think he can circumvent this condition, the Ricordi Publishers shall pay me a fine of one hundred thousand (100,000) Lire.—

GV

—I request normal pitch in the theatres
—A box for opening night at the disposal of Signora Verdi[3]

GIULIO RICORDI TO VERDI

Cernobbio, Sunday, 3 October 1886

Illustrious Maestro,

I found that Boito, who is always the man of surprises, is still here! He is no longer going to the Lago Maggiore, but to Varese, and he, too, will be in Milan toward the 12th of this month. So when you come, Faccio, Boito, Edel and Ferrario will be there, and you can give all the orders you wish.

Yesterday I spoke to Muzio about Maurel, and we are in complete agreement. I have also seen Corti, who would not even dream of giving a new opera as a second one [in the repertoire]; he told me that he would be the most . . . . . . foolish of impresarios to commit a stupidity like that. I also clearly told him the general conditions ... which Corti accepts with his eyes closed, leaving everything, so to speak, in the hands of . . . . . where it belongs.

I have received the reduction of the third [act] finale; I am reviewing it and shall send it to you before handing it over to the engravers.

[...] *Thank you* for your warm and dear hospitality to us. [...]

GIULIO RICORDI TO VERDI

Milan, 5 October 1886

Illustrious Maestro,

Confirming my letter of the day before yesterday, I would like to inform you that in order not to leave you idle (!!!) I am sending you the reduction of the third [act] finale today. Recalling as well as I could how I heard you play it, I have corrected the transcription here and there. So you will see whether it works or not, and what changes must be made.

I have seen Muzio, who is in excellent health, and as I already told you, we are agreed on Maurel and also on the thunder machine.

From Faccio I had an answer to my last letter, and I think it is a good idea to enclose it.[1] Almost the entire part has already been sent to Signora Pantaleoni. [...]

---

[3] These last two lines appear to have been written by Giulio Ricordi.

---

[1] Giulio Ricordi's letter to Faccio and Faccio's answer are missing.

GIULIO RICORDI TO VERDI

Milan, 8 October 1886

Illustrious Maestro,

I have just received the reduction of the third act and thank you very much for your promptness. It has already been handed over to the engravers. Today I had the first proof of the entire fourth act engraved.

For your information, at the attack of the trumpets the metronome marking is missing also in the autograph; it can be put in at your convenience when you come.

And for that matter Caprara,[1] as I had foreseen, will only be in Milan the day after tomorrow, the 10th, instead of returning on the 2nd. But I have bombarded him with letters and telegrams, and I hope that if not by the 12th, then at least by the 14th the model of the first scene will be ready. I shall telegraph you on the 12th; so I shall see to what point the work has progressed, and you can plan for your journey here so that nothing will be upset that has already been arranged beforehand.

Edel is ready, having finished (unheard-of miracle) all his work—and the scenic designer Ferrario is already putting all the drops into place and is making the first traces. So as soon as you give the order *AVANTI!* everything will move in order and without any troubles.

Muzio leaves tomorrow, and we are in perfect agreement on what must be done in Paris. [. . .]

FRANCO FACCIO TO GIULIO RICORDI

Abano (Veneto), 9 October 1886

My dearest Giulio,

La Pantaleoni (who sends cordial greetings and will write to you) has shown me your letter,[1] to which I reply right away in so far as it concerns me. [. . .] You can be sure that I'll be back in Milan in time to receive our great Maestro. [. . .] La Pantaleoni has already written to him that she is *musically ready* and that, happily anxious, she is waiting for a sign from him to return to St Agata. [. . .] I am more and more convinced that Verdi's genius is perennially young and strong, and that *Otello*, like *Aida* and the Mass—not to mention his most recent creations—will be a new *masterpiece*. What good fortune this is for Italian art, and what immense joy for *us*, who honour the composer and so dearly love the man! [. . .]

---

[1] Presumably the head-carpenter of La Scala, which has no record of him.

---

[1] Missing.

VERDI TO GIULIO RICORDI

[St Agata] Wednesday [13 October 1886][1]

Dear Giulio,

To explain better my telegram,[2] I tell you that I am arriving tomorrow after five.

Don't bother to come to the station (it attracts too much attention), but come for dinner at six.

Inform Spatz of my arrival and tell him that I'll be alone; for this reason, and also because it's only a matter of a few days, it's unimportant whether or not the usual apartment is free. Inform him only after 2 o'clock, so that he'll have no time to get my name in the papers before my arrival. He will have lots of time later on. Order two dinners from him, if you would give me the pleasure [of your company]. Afterwards we can go to work, if there isn't too much, since after dinner it tires me. Perhaps it will be better to put it off until the next day after breakfast. We'll have time!! Prepare everything and inform everybody—*paintshop, machines, sets, lightning, thunder, poetry, music, Cairati—Faccio*, if he's in Milan, *Boito*, if he's in Milan.

Addio

G. Verdi

ROMILDA PANTALEONI TO ALCEO PANTALEONI

Abano, 14 October 1886

[. . .] I have studied a great deal with Faccio these last few days and can tell you that I know my part almost by heart; he was most demanding with me, because he somehow pretends that I must make myself immortal with Desdemona. How much I would give if you could come to hear me; I feel sure you would be content! In a few days, that is, the 17th or the 18th, I return to the illustrious Verdi; he invited me in a letter I had today![1] I assure you that I felt proud and happy to receive a letter . . . *all of it written in the hand* of that Great Man! [. . .]

GIULIO RICORDI TO VERDI

Milan, 18 October 1886

Illustrious Maestro,

[. . .] I come to you in the hope of news which, like that concerning Signora Peppina, I expect to be excellent.

---

[1] Postmark: BUSSETO 13/10/86.
[2] Missing. Possibly in the Biblioteca Palatina.

---

[1] Missing.

And in the meantime I will tell you that, together with Prof. Orsi,[1] we have studied and provided for the thunder machine; we have studied the largest dimensions at the *Opéra* and think the result should be excellent. The Mayor (regretting that he was unable to pay his respects to you, since he was away until yesterday) has authorized me to go ahead straight away and do what is necessary.

Yesterday I sent you the proofs of the fourth act; and in two days I shall send you those of the Desdemona–Otello duet in the first.

Kindly look at the original and indicate to me how Otello's last phrase should be; in the printed proof you corrected it like this:

ba   –   cio
[kiss]

In the copy of the score it is like this:

ba   –   –   cio
[kiss]

as if the last syllable were almost a sigh.[2]

Boito begs you to send him the volume of Hugo's French translation,[3] and asks me to pay his respects to you; so does Faccio.

And as I go back and hear again the erudite chatter, I thank you most cordially for the beautiful, happy, interesting and unforgettable hours I spent with you, and for all your kindness to me. Please give my regards to Signora Peppina and remember the deepest gratitude of

Yours most devotedly,
Giulio Ricordi

VERDI TO GIULIO RICORDI

St Agata, 18 October 1886

Dear Giulio,

I have received the fourth act, which I am not returning right away because I haven't decided with la Pantaleoni what is more suitable for the two *refrains*.[1] Maybe I'll send it tomorrow. Meanwhile, continue your work on *Otello*. Think about the last costume sketch for Otello. It's very beautiful,

---

[1] Unknown.
[2] Verdi opted for the second choice. Ricordi indicates neither the key nor the signature; his notes are a G sharp and an F sharp. (Cf. Ricordi orchestral score, plate no. PR 155, p. 530).
[3] For his work on the French translation of the opera.

---

[1] In the 'Willow' Song (IV. i).

but it isn't right! It's a Negus *Teodoros* .. a *Cetivayo*[2] (except for the belly), but not an Otello in the service fo *Venice*. One has to look very hard to find a trace of a Venetian costume. Addio, addio

G. Verdi

GIULIO RICORDI TO VERDI

City Hall of Milan   19 October 1886

Illustrious Maestro,

See what a counsellor of little zeal [I am]! . . . Even today I am leaving the session for a moment to bother you again.

In the second-act chorus you have used words that were then deleted by Boito. I am enclosing the piece in question![1] The second line contains the new words that Boito himself has put together, and you will see whether they work or not. But Boito also says that if you think the first go better with the song, he absolutely does not care about the new ones and in that case will put the first ones back into the libretto. [. . .]

VERDI TO GIULIO RICORDI

St Agata, 21 October 1886

Dear Giulio,

I am returning the printed fourth act and a small bundle of the Canzone where the *refrain* is changed.[1] I have also changed the timbres and the accents on the notes of '*Salce, salce, salce*' ['*Willow, willow, willow*'] . . . which will be better. Adjust them not only in the reduction but also in the orchestra score . . When you leaf through my orchestra score, which I am sending, you will find little papers indicating the changes.[2]

I have sent, that is, *I am sending*, Boito the French *Otello*.
Addio.

G. Verdi

GIULIO RICORDI TO VERDI

Milan, 23 October 1886

Illustrious Maestro,

I am sorry, Maestro, but today I am going to disturb you with a rather long letter; but since I must bother you, I might as well do it properly. I am

---

[2] According to *Carteggio* ii. 354–55, this *Cetivayo* was a pot-bellied king of the Zulus. He was captured by the British in 1879 and died in England in 1884.

---

[1] Missing.

---

[1] Missing. Possibly in the Biblioteca Palatina.
[2] Possibly in the Biblioteca Palatina.

proceeding in order. This morning I received: printed proofs of the fourth act and related little bundles of the autograph orchestra score. All is well, and the necessary corrections have already been made in all the parts. Yesterday I sent you: a bundle containing the autograph orchestra score of the quartet, plus an extract of the reduction of the trio. (Here I open a parenthesis to tell you that I read it with Faccio, and this piece is simply *marvellous!!!*—and I close the parenthesis right away.)

—News regarding the storm. With the kind co-operation of Prof. Orsi, I believe we shall have a superb storm!!! ..... Having made the necessary comparisons with the dimensions of the thunder [machine] at the *Opéra*, which Muzio sent us, we shall have at La Scala a kind of big drum with these measurements: 1.35 metres wide, 2 metres long. Try to note these measurements and you will see that perhaps not even God Almighty up there disposes of such majestic thunder!!—Now we shall perform some experiments to find out whether a roll by hand or by mechanical means is preferable.

—Backstage trumpets: After talking about them again with Faccio and Orsi, all three of us have reached the same decision, which is: to use 12 trumpets *ad hoc* that would be of the same timbre and sonority; and to solve the problem safely, I have given Orsi a trumpet part, asking him to write to Mahillon[1] in Brussels without telling him, of course, what it is about. Enclosed herewith is Mahillon's reply—marked with blue pencil.[2] He is certainly the foremost builder of instruments in Europe and a distinguished musician in his field. Will you, Maestro, please now decide the matter? In case [you approve] I would order all the 12 trumpets right away.[3]

—The Prefect of Brera[4] sends you his heartfelt thanks for the page of the Manzoni *Requiem*!! ..... only ..... he would like to have it right away for the opening of the hall at Brera.

—The painter and scenic designer Ferrario has for 26 years held the second professorship of perspective at Brera; now that Bisi is dead, he is competing for the first. He came to see me a moment ago, desolate because he had lost one of the most precious documents that could support his candidacy at the Ministry of Public Instruction. And that is the letter you addressed to the same Prof. Carlo Ferrario about the sets for *La forza del destino* when it was first given at La Scala. Also, the Secretary of the Academy of Fine Arts told Ferrario that such a letter would have been the best of all these documents. Poor Ferrario—who knows how many times he has prayed to St Michael since then—is always hit by bad luck, and to this day he has been unable to find that letter. To have only two lines from you would be his greatest fortune; your approving inspection of the *Otello* sets would also be a good

---

[1] Charles Mahillon (1813–87) or his son Victor (1841–1924).
[2] Missing.
[3] They were ordered and played in *Otello* at La Scala.
[4] The Prefect of the Palazzo di Brera in Milan, which was inaugurated as a Jesuit community in 1651, and has been seat of the Academy of Fine Arts since 1776. In addition to an art gallery, lecture rooms and auditoriums, the building contains a large library and an observatory.

pretext; in short, he trusts in you and would be most grateful to you; it's a personal letter, of course, to be added only to the documents of the competition.

—Enough?

—Not yet! . . . . I have sent for Edel and shall see him today or tomorrow; I shall explain to him your wishes regarding Otello's final costume and shall forward these to him, together with the changes for the other two or three.

And now I really do think I have finished . . . for today . . . .

Greetings and respects to you and your kind Signora Peppina, and I send feelings once again of affection and gratitude.

Yours most devotedly
Giulio Ricordi

Please return Mahillon letter.

VERDI TO GIULIO RICORDI

[St Agata] Sunday [24 October 1886][1]

Dear Giulio,

Today a day lost for the instrumentation of *Otello*! Alas! Alas!

I am returning Mahillon's letter.[2] I think it would be good to make the two highest parts of the trumpets *an octave* higher.—

I am frightened to hear that our trumpeters cannot even make the high G any more. And I have written the horns and trumpets high in many parts!! It's strange! I recall that in my youth in the little orchestra of Busseto (with the straight trumpets in G) I let them blow Ds and Es in abundance, and sometimes also Gs, namely these very notes[3]

Open, oh earth! It's incredible today, but true! Let Faccio take a look at the trumpets and horns in *Otello* and consult the player, etc. . . .

I am enclosing a letter from Muzio,[4] which you will give to Boito to read. I won't answer for a while, or with a letter (sounding the bell) that does not commit me as yet. But it's better to settle with Boito what can and must be done. I mentioned it to him recently *en passant*, but we didn't settle anything. Now, having read Muzio's letter, he may be able to tell whether this ballet

---

[1] Postmark: BUSSETO 24/10/86 or 25/10/86.

[2] Possibly in the Biblioteca Palatina.

[3] By 'straight trumpets in G' ('trombe diritte in *sol*') Verdi, presumably, means valveless instruments, approximately 34″ long, which could produce only a few tones of the harmonic row. Verdi indicates the real pitch, but not the particular notes to which he refers regarding the instrument.

[4] Missing. Evidently concerning a production of *Othello* in French requested by the Paris Opéra.

can and *must* be done. He should tell this to you or write to me about it. He can think about it for a few days, and then, when he has expressed his opinion frankly and decisively, I will give a decisive answer to those at the Opéra.

You will also find the letter for Ferrario![5] And then? . . Is there more?

Return Muzio's letter to me.

I think I have finished. Addio

G. Verdi

EUGENIO TORNAGHI TO VERDI

Milan, 25 October 1886

Illustrious Maestro
Signor Commendatore Giuseppe Verdi
Busseto
Giulio finds himself obliged to stay in bed today; I hope it may be a fairly little thing, perhaps caused by the inconsistency of the weather. He has asked me to send you bundle vi—which I am dispatching by registered post[1]—and to deliver your letter to the painter Ferrario.—He is keeping the Muzio letter to speak to Boito about it.—He will then write to you at length, as soon as he can. [. . .]

VERDI TO GIULIO RICORDI

[St Agata] Tuesday [26 October 1886]

Dear Giulio
Did you receive everything I sent to you the day before yesterday? . . .
Mahillon letter
Muzio letter
Ferrario letter
Requiem letter[1]
Who knows what . . . Letter?!
Today I am sending first act printed.
Trio third act in reduction . . .
A few notes are to be added in the orchestra score. Meanwhile, correct the copy; and put red marks in the original . . .

I hope I can orchestrate a bit today. But who knows! What will the post bring at *11* and *5*? Peppina is right: 'Blessed be the past. Post twice per week.' Addio

G. Verdi

[5] Missing.

[1] Missing.

[1] Missing.

VERDI TO EUGENIO TORNAGHI

[St Agata] Tuesday [26 October 1886][1]

Dear Signor Tornaghi,

From your letter I learn that Giulio is not well. I hope it is a little thing and that he may soon return to his work.

This morning I posted the reduction of a part of the third act and the galley proofs of the first act. In the final duet I made a correction that is no good. At Desdemona's words

> *Ed io vedea fra le tue tempie oscure*
> *Splender il genio che in fronte ti sta*[2]
>
> [*And I saw between your dark temples*
> *The genius shine that shows on your brow*]

I have changed an F to a C. Tell the *chief copyist* to leave the C as it *was before.*

Ever yours devotedly

G. Verdi

You won't believe it! But I still have had no time to read the form of the contract you sent me—

EUGENIO TORNAGHI TO VERDI

Milan, 28 October 1886

Illustrious Maestro
Signor Commendatore Giuseppe Verdi

I have the honour of acknowledging receipt of your precious letter of Tuesday. This morning the reduction of a part of the third act and the galley proofs of the first were delivered to me. In the final duet[1] I let the F remain on the '*tà*' of the '*eterea beltà*' ['*ethereal beauty*']. I have urged the chief copyist to pay great attention to your directions.

Giulio is still obliged to stay in bed but is much better. [...]

ROMILDA PANTALEONI TO ALCEO PANTALEONI

[?] 29 October 1886

[...] Last night I returned from Busseto, where I stayed for twelve days, enjoying the sublime harmony of the great old man! If you could hear the

---

[1] Postmark: BUSSETO 26/10/86.
[2] 'Splender del genio l'eterea beltà' ['The ethereal beauty of the genius shine'] in the final text of Act I. Scene iii.

---

[1] Of Act I.

heavenly things—and what strength of artistic fibre! It seems impossible that all this is the work of a man past *seventy*! And how much tenderness and depth there is in the look of the genius! He made me study twice a day, in the morning and the late afternoon! And I assure you that with him I thoroughly examined the immense beauties of those sweet and at the same time powerful melodies; I really believe that with this opera I shall arrive at the height of my glory! [. . .]

VERDI TO BOITO

St Agata, 29 October 1886

Dear Boito,

The ballet in the second act is well thought out,[1] and they will be happy with it. It goes without saying that the *ballet* must serve only for the *Opéra*. Elsewhere *Otello* will remain as it is now, or better, as it will be tomorrow or the day after tomorrow, when I hope to have the last note of the instrumentation finished . . .

So now, think about the translation.

As you know, Signora Pantaleoni has been here, and she left yesterday. She knows here entire part very well, and I hope she will obtain excellent effects in it. Only in the scene of the first act is something missing. It's not that she doesn't sing her *solo* lines well, but she interprets them with too much accentuation and too dramatically. We'll have other rehearsals, however, and I'll insist that she manage to find the right accent for the situation and for the poetry.

Yesterday, in *Il corriere*, I read the description of the *Otello* costumes and saw to my surprise that Desdemona is still wearing a splendid dress in the first act, and that in the last act Otello has a wild, savage costume with bare arms, like a *Cetivajo* without a belly.[2] Keep an eye on this, for to me these seem to be gross errors. And also keep an eye on that other costume, which you yourself christened a *Toreador*'s.

Addio—With Peppina's greetings, I affectionately take your hand.

G. Verdi

VERDI TO FRANCO FACCIO

St Agata, 29 October 1886

Dear Faccio,

As you know, Signora Pantaleoni left yesterday. She knows her entire part very well, and if the *stars*, and the whims of the audience, are not hostile to

---

[1] Presumably in answer to a missing letter from Boito in which he sent Verdi a draft of this ballet which was never composed; another ballet was interpolated in the third act later on. (See Verdi to Boito, 16 Aug. 1882.)

[2] Cf. Verdi to Ricordi, 18 Oct. 1886, where the spelling is *Cetivayo*.

the opera on that night, one can say that she will obtain effects everywhere. Very good ones in the quartet, and also in the duet and finale of the third act, and in the entire fourth. She need have no stage fright. Her tones will go very well if she makes them less biting and all in the *head*, as I have also advised her to sing at many other points. If there is anything to find fault with, it's the scene of the first act. There, something lighter, airy, and—let's say the word—voluptuous would be called for, as warranted by the situation and the poetry. She sings her *solo* phrases very well, but with too much accentuation and too dramatically. However, we shall have other rehearsals, and we'll manage to find the right expression.

This is between us, but if you should some time go over the part with her, tell her to sing as much as possible with head-voice.

And now, my dear Faccio, I earnestly beg you to make Tamagno (when he arrives) study his part. He is so careless in reading music that I really wish he would study the part with a true musician, one who can make him sing the notes with their real value and *in tempo*. As for the interpretation of the chorus, we'll take care of this when I explain all my intentions concerning the singing, staging, etc., etc. And now I greet you in haste and from the heart.

Your
G. Verdi

FRANCO FACCIO TO VERDI

Milan, 31 October 1886

Your letter reached me while in the silence of my little room I was admiring the marvels of the score of the first act—vigorous, overwhelming, imaginative in the scene of the tempest, sparkling in the *fuochi di gioia*, extremely effective in the scene of the drinking song and the brawl, heavenly in the final duet. The great figure of Verdi appeared to me in the fantasies of his genius; imagine how overjoyed I was to see his handwriting at the same time!

So you are not dissatisfied with la Pantaleoni! Oh, what a satisfaction for me, and what good fortune and honour for this very modest artist! And how grateful she is to you! If you read the letter she wrote to me[1] in which she spoke with the most tender emotion about you and the excellent Signora Peppina. You will hear, she tells me, how many subtleties the good, illustrious Man has taught me . . .

Do not doubt, Maestro, that I will repeat to la Pantaleoni the recommendations you gave me in your precious letter of yesterday[2] regarding the scene in the first act; but worth more than my words will be your presence later on, the presence that fascinates and transports all those who hear your intentions, such as la Pantaleoni, who feel the religion of art.

[1] Missing.
[2] In Verdi's preceding letter of 29 Oct.

As soon as Tamagno arrives (in a few days), I shall make him study and shall watch out above all, as you rightly desire, for his *musical precision*.

I am taking up your precious time with my talk: enough, I will try to finish. But first a correction. At the 31st bar (the fifth after letter Y) of the *allegro* in E of the *fuochi di gioia*, the sopranos of the chorus, in the last fourth, have two F sharps while the accompaniment has the diminished chord

Where is the oversight? In the voice or the accompaniment? You can tell Garegnani about it when he comes to get your manuscript. [. . .]

OPPRANDINO ARRIVABENE TO VERDI

Rome, 31 October 1886

My dearest Verdi,

For more than four months I have gone from country to country in search of better health, and instead have found it to be worse. Inevitably I carry with me a great obstacle to the desired improvement, and that is the date of my birth: 1807. [. . .]

I would be sorry to disappear from this world before hearing the echo of the applause, sure to be immense, that will greet the great finale to your artistic career, which you are preparing with your *Otello*; it will leave behind

A splendour that will have no sunset.[1] [. . .]

Remember me to Signora Peppina, and if this should be my last letter,[2] keep it as the testament of affection of one of your oldest and warmest friends, who sends you all the best wishes. Addio, addio, my dear friend, and again addio

Opprandino A.

VERDI TO BOITO

[St Agata, 1 November 1886][1]

Dear Boito,
It's finished!
Hail to us . . . .
    (and also to *Him*!!)
Addio
G. Verdi

---

[1] 'Uno splendor che non avrà tramonto.' Even with the assistance of erudite scholars I have been unable to determine whether Arrivabene quoted this line or wrote it himself.
[2] It was indeed Arrivabene's last letter to his great friend.

---

[1] No doubt Verdi gave this news to Boito the same day as to Giulio Ricordi in the letter that follows.

VERDI TO GIULIO RICORDI

St Agata, 1 November 1886

Dear Giulio,

From Tornaghi's last letter, saying, 'Giulio is much better', I deduce that you are completely recovered by now; and I am writing to tell you that *Otello* is completely finished!! Really finished!!!! .... Finally!!!!!!!! I don't dare send it by post, because there are too many new pages, and woe if they were lost!—Let's plan, then, as before. Send Garignani[1] as far as Fiorenzuola (since now it would be uncomfortable for me to get up too early and come home too late, in order to go to Piacenza). Let's settle for *Wednesday* the *3rd*. Garignani should leave Milan on the *11.40 through train* and arrive at Fiorenzuola at 2 p.m.—He would return right away on the *2.36* and would be back in Milan by 5.5 .. I myself would be in Fiorenzuola at 2 o'clock, and we would have a good half hour to *chat* if it should be necessary.

Have I made myself clear?

If it's all right this way, send me a telegram right away saying, 'All right,' and, I repeat, I'll be in Fiorenzuola with all the little papers Wednesday at 2 p.m.

Addio, addio, and stay well always.

G. Verdi

GIULIO RICORDI TO GIUSEPPINA VERDI

Milan, 2 November 1886

[...] So this prodigious *Otello* is finished, then!! .. Truly prodigious!! .... Faccio and I have been reading it almost every day, and every day we are even more astounded as we penetrate into this great masterpiece, great in its details, great in its general form!! And a colossus of Michelangelo refined by Cellini! ..

Ah! .. this dear Verdi of ours! What a man!! .... Boito is right in saying that these men are rare, in whom all physical and intellectual forces are so perfectly balanced as to make them the privileged beings of humanity.

Now our Maestro can rest quietly, and if the nice weather continues, relax in his favourite rustic occupations before going to Genoa. [...]

GIULIO RICORDI TO VERDI

Milan, 3 November 1886

Illustrious Maestro! ......

You must know that I have a contract with Mr Winter, who obliges me to catch a colossal cold every year; since I want to be absolutely free in the

---

[1] Garegnani, chief copyist of the House of Ricordi.

coming winter months, I agreed that I would catch it right away! . . . . . and so I managed to stay in bed for 5 days! . . . . . . Now I am free from this obligation, too, and completely ready for your orders. —

Proceeding in order with the communications I must impart to you, I inform you that the 12 trumpets were ordered from Brussels as agreed.

Boito will have written to you in answer to Muzio's letter;[1] I know that he is now hard at work on the translation and that the fourth act is very well under way.

Garegnani is bringing you the 5 new costume designs; I think, Maestro, these will please you very much and that Edel will thus have satisfied your wishes. — The orders to the tailor and the property man have *all* been given! . . . Tomorrow I shall take a look at the sets — and now, in order not to waste your time, I greet you devotedly . . . . . . and repeat a hosanna to you. I am, gratefully and affectionately,

Giulio Ricordi

VERDI TO GIULIO RICORDI

[St Agata] Wednesday, 4 o'clock [3 November 1886][1]

Dear Giulio,

I'm back already[2] . . . and am very glad to hear that you got your obligations to Mr Winter out of the way! . . but don't do any further business with him!

Garignani will shortly be in Milan with the Moor. —

I have seen the costume designs and still find Otello's final one too savage* . . not at all Venetian . . . also, Desdemona['s] is too rich in the first act. The others excellent, and Jago's stupendous.

*it also attracts too much attention and is distracting. If the audience gets to say, 'Oh, what a beautiful costume,' we are lost. Artists must have the courage *de s'effacer*!! I'll write again tomorrow . . Addio

Yours
G. Verdi

Peppina thanks you and says that she is fine.

---

[1] Both letters are missing.

---

[1] Postmark: BUSSETO 3/11/86.

[2] From the railway station at Fiorenzuola where Verdi had handed his autograph score of *Otello* over to Garegnani (see Verdi to Ricordi, 1 Nov. 1886).

VERDI TO GIULIO RICORDI

St Agata, 4 November 1886

Dear Giulio,

...... So now, let's seriously take care of the performance, and let's watch out that we don't fall on our faces. Here a serious question arises, more serious than it seems to be at first sight: I mean *the Tamagno question*.

La *Pantaleoni* knows her part by heart, and when we get to the piano rehearsals I'll have almost nothing to tell her about colours, accents, etc., etc. .

Maurel, once he has studied the music, will imagine the rest, and with him, too, little or nothing will have to be done.

Not so with *Tamagno*. Even when he has learned the music well, much will have to be said about interpretation and expression.— — I will have to make my observations directly to him, more so than to any of the others (and to him, the *5,000* Lire tenor!), and these (especially in front of Maurel) could *blesser* his self-respect and his feelings. In this way bad humours, irritations, *insults, quarrels* arise . . . and then *brrrrr* . . . . one no longer knows where it's going to end. This is a danger: a danger that must be avoided at all costs.

What to do?

If the season were less far along, I could ask him to come here to St Agata! But then how would he spend his day? I couldn't let him sing all day long; and after a few hours of study I would still have to take care of him in some way or other, chatting, playing billiards, going for a walk or going here and there. All these things would be very, very tiring for me; and at this moment I really have no need to tire myself any more! It would be impossible for me!—

Another possibility would be to ask him to come to Genoa. We could be there earlier than planned, between the *15th* and the *20th* of this month. In the meantime Tamagno could study the notes well with Faccio and come to Genoa around the 20th. He could stay at the *Londra* or the *Milano*—hotels nearby—and could come to me around *12* in the morning to study for a few hours; then he could go for a walk and return around *6* to eat soup with us. Afterwards we would drink a good cup of *coffee* and smoke a good *cigar*, and after 9 o'clock we could go through the study we did in the morning.—This would be an excellent plan, but I don't dare suggest it to him. I wouldn't have the nerve to make him spend a few hundred Lire, after having seen him travel with his little daughter, precisely between Genoa and Milan, in second class!

What do you say to that? What can be done? Could you, being a municipal counsellor . . . give counsel? . .

Think about this, and think about it seriously! Take care of this matter for me.

As I told you above: *there can be a danger*. Let's try to avoid it while there is time.—

Addio, addio

Your
G. Verdi

In the long scene between Otello and Jago in the second act finale, seven verses before Jago's account of the dream, correct Jago's part as follows:[1]

Ah! *Morte e dannazione!*   Ar-dua im – pre - sa   sa -

[OTELLO.] Ah! *Morte e dannazione!*	[Ah! *Death and damnation!*
[JAGO.] Ardua impresa sa-[rebbe] ecc.	An arduous undertaking it would be, etc.][2]

VERDI TO OPPRANDINO ARRIVABENE[1]

St Agata, 4 November 1886

Dear Arrivabene,

What the devil has gotten into you— . and what the devil are you saying?!!.—Chase away all the melancholies and be determined to get well. I understand about age, but after all, you are healthy, you are slender, without moods. . . . and today it's also the fashion to live to the age of 90, 115, 139, as I read yesterday about a woman of this age who left two sons, one 85 years old, the other 94!!.

Away, then, with these melancholies, and get well soon, since I hope to embrace you next spring, when my work will be finished and I'll come to Rome.—

I am a little tired, but my health is not bad. I have completely finished *Otello*! Now . . *à la grâce de Dieu*! Courage! I greet you in Peppina's name and take both your hands with the old affection.

Cordially
G. Verdi

---

[1] Cf. Ricordi orchestral score, plate no. PR 155, p. 269.

[2] Cf. Shakespeare, *Othello*, III. iii. 402–3: 'OTHELLO: Death and damnation ... O! / IAGO. It were a tedious difficulty ...'

---

[1] In answer to Arrivabene's letter of 31 Oct.

GIUSEPPINA VERDI TO GIUSEPPE DE SANCTIS

Busseto [St Agata], 5 November 1886

[...] The final note of *Otello* was written on All Saints' Day, and I am very happy that this opera is finished! As vigorous as Verdi is, in spite of his age, such a physically and spiritually great work is not the best recipe for the preservation of strength. Let's hope that art, at least, will have gained from this!

Morelli knows how logical Verdi is and will have guessed that Otello would wear not his traditional costume but Christian clothes; and that he would wear the armour of Venice and the coat created for the general in the service of the Venetian Republic. Tell Morelli this and give him our greetings, along with all the sympathy and admiration he deserves from the whole world. [...]

GIULIO RICORDI TO VERDI

Milan, 6 November 1886

Illustrious Maestro,

I have the honour of replying to your last two letters.[1] In accordance with your observations about the last sketches by Edel, I shall have the alterations executed as you wish. [...]

And now to your last important letter, regarding Tamagno. I think there is, and can be, no problem, for ever since I spoke to him (in August) he declared himself most happy to study in Genoa. He starts *today* studying with Faccio, to whom I have handed over the first and fourth acts; the day after tomorrow I shall give him the third, and in 4 or 5 days the second act. So just between the 15th and the 20th, I think, Tamagno will be ready to go to Genoa, where he can stay for 8 or 10 days; he can then return to Milan a few days before starting the season. This is the plan, and I think Tamagno has also talked it over with Faccio; so all that is needed is to set a convenient time, and I shall also tell Tamagno some of your ideas about the hours for study, etc.; and everything will go *comme sur des roulettes*.

But ..... there is a but .... Maestro! ..... If between now and the 20th the conditions regarding hygiene in Genoa do not change, is it wise for you to establish yourself in a place that is infected? ... Since early September I have known from a very important person in the army that the cholera in Genoa is of rather considerable proportions. [...] Think about it in time, Maestro, since while it is true that one must dance when at the ball .... there is no reason to plunge into it if one is on the outside!! [...]

[1] Of 3 and 4 Nov.

EMANUELE MUZIO TO GIULIO RICORDI

Paris, 9 November 1886

[...] I am desperate about this *Otello première* and I avoid friends and acquaintances as a debtor does his creditors. Just now the famous, great Clemenceau came to me asking for a seat, which I wasn't able to assure him.

Maurel already knows the music of the first act and almost the whole finale of the third. I have corrected his mistakes, of which there were many. He has understood Jago's part well, [as well as] the character, which with few exceptions is thoroughly ironic. Maurel ends his performance at the Opéra-Comique on 8 December and leaves the next day for Genoa on the Paris–Rome express via Nice. I have already arranged with the Maestro for him to stay there for two or three days to give the last touches to the part. I think that if he arrived in Milan on the 13th or 14th, instead of the 12th, the management wouldn't reproach him. He has sung *Aida* in Italian hundreds of times, so with one or two rehearsals he can do the performance.

The Maestro has written to me about the translation: 'I think Boito is already seriously working on it. Later I shall also ask you to have a letter written to Du Locle.' [...] As soon as the whole opera is printed, I think, Boito should call on Du Locle, and then they both should do the work. If Boito makes the literal translation, the other could prepare the verses, so that the Maestro could review the translation when he comes to Milan. [...]

Choudens was truly sorry that he could not get the business, but since the Maestro, in order to keep all the property rights for you, did not want to leave *Otello* for France to him or any other publishers, you cannot sell it [to him ...]

GIULIO RICORDI TO VERDI

Milan, 9 November 1886

Illustrious Maestro,

I am in receipt of your esteemed letter of yesterday.[1] You do very well to write to Genoa,[2] and I hope and wish that the person to whom you turn will tell you the truth! [...]

Meanwhile I will tell you that Tamagno is studying daily with Faccio with the greatest eagerness and love, and that Faccio is very pleased. Today I shall give him the whole third act. And today I am sending you the last piece of the reduction; I have looked it over with Saladino, and you will find some *alternatives*, so you will choose the preferable reduction. This way the edition [of the reduction] will be complete in a few days.

---

[1] Probably in the Biblioteca Palatina.
[2] Verdi probably wrote to his friend Giuseppe De Amicis about the cholera. The letter is missing.

Now, a nuisance, so to speak . . . . . . an editorial one. There still is [a part of] the public that cannot buy the complete opera but is content with and wants some excerpt. I have looked and looked again! . . . . But it is really difficult to pull one out, of course, without slashing the work in some way. For example: In the first act there certainly is a most popular piece, that fascinating *Drinking Song*; but who can sing it when it is detached from the rest? . . . . Take out the chorus . . . . but no, by Jove!! . . . . So let's leave it where it is. One must then stick to those pieces that can really be detached from the whole. What do you think, Maestro, of this list with first lines:

Excerpts for *Song*:

Act I	Desdemona–Otello (sop. and ten.)	Già nella notte densa— [Already in the dense night—]
Act II	Jago (bar.)	Vanne; la tua meta già vedo— [Go; already I see your aim—]
——	Desdemona–Emilia–Otello –Jago (sop., 1/2 sop., ten. and bar.)	Se inconscia, contro te, sposo, ho peccato [If against you, husband, I have sinned unconsciously]
——	Otello–Jago (ten. and bar.)	Desdemona rea! [Desdemona guilty!]
Act III	Desdemona–Otello (sop. and ten.)	Dio ti giocondi, o sposo [May God give you joy, O husband]
——	Otello (ten.)	Dio! . . mi potevi scagliar tutti i mali! [God . . you could hurl at me all evils!]
Act IV	Desdemona (sop.)	Scena, Canzone, and Ave Maria

Excerpts for pianoforte only:

Act I	Desdemona–Otello	Drinking Song and final duet
Act II	Chorus	Dove guardi splendono— [Where your glances shine—] the Jago solo—the quartet— However, I would not think the great Otello–Jago duet suitable.
Act III	The two pieces mentioned above—plus the finale	
Act IV	Desdemona's piece as above—	

Tell me your ideas frankly, Maestro, and any changes that might please you better.

But I am not finished yet! . . . When you were in Milan recently, I spoke with you about various projects for productions of *Otello*: among the first and most serious ones is that of the Costanzi in Rome for the spring. Now the impresario Canori is persisting in letter after letter, and he is supported by the most reasonable necessity of securing the artists who can be employed elsewhere from one day to another. He has given me *carte blanche* to engage artists of La Scala; this is all right for la Pantaleoni, Tamagno, and Paroli[3] (Cassio), but Maurel will probably be at the Opéra; hence one must look for another baritone; I think one might keep an eye on three who are the most suitable ones: Kaschmann—Devoyod—Battistini.—Faccio would be the conductor, of course; sets and costumes [would be] renewed, but those of La Scala—and 10 or 12 leading singers of our chorus would go along. Condition *sine qua non: normal diapason.* If you have nothing against this in principle and [if you can] find serious guarantees in these proposals, please authorize me to open official negotiations, since it is particularly urgent that the singers be engaged right away.

Later I shall write to you about Florence and Parma; today, I think, I have abused your time more than enough.

With affectionate regards to Signora Peppina, I remain ever yours gratefully and

most devotedly,
Giulio Ricordi

VERDI TO GIULIO RICORDI

St Agata, 11 November 1886

Dear Giulio,

I am returning the reduction with a few little changes. And while I remember it, tell Faccio not to let Tamagno study the very last phrase, *'quella vil cortigiana che è la sposa d'Otello'* [*'that vile courtesan who is the wife of Otello'*], of the duet between Otello and Desdemona in the third act .... I have done this phrase twenty times and cannot find the right tone ... and perhaps I won't ever find it ... but who knows ... perhaps I'll need Boito's help ... We'll see in Milan! I am quite content with the news you give me about Tamagno's study. Tell Faccio he should insist and not get tired of it. . . . . ; in spite of this study, I shall still have many things to say about the musico-dramatic interpretation, and I really ought to be with him [Tamagno] for *3* or *4* days, but alone, without the company of the other artists! But where? And how?—Damned cholera!! From Genoa they write to me as if it were slight, passing, nothing at all ... You are alarmed ... We'll see!

What you propose for the excerpts is all right.

The Rome affair is a bit muddled. I don't know the performers you propose to me. As far as I know, *Kaschman* and *Battistini* are two somewhat mawkish singers who require phrases that are not in Jago's part. The one is a Frenchman, and I much mistrust his enunciation, since Jago cannot be

---

[3] Giovanni Paroli, tenor; the first Cassio in *Otello* and the first Cajus in *Falstaff.*

performed, and isn't possible, without *Maurel's* extremely good enunciation. You heard Devoyod in a room; but for God's sake don't trust that. These rehearsals are always misleading. Who do you think is best (and also ask Faccio)? Always bear Jago's part in mind, however. In this part one must neither *sing* nor (with few exceptions) *raise one's voice*. If I were a singing actor, for example, I would speak it all in a whisper, *mezza voce*. Now then, consider this carefully ... As for the others, very well.

All right for Faccio (naturally). And pay great attention to the *diapason*. In fact, I would think that it would be good to have it published from now on that there is a clause in our contract that says, etc....

It would be a warning (and they would prepare themselves in the meantime) to the orchestras that must play *Otello*.

Remember that I care very much about this and will be most rigorous in insisting that these conditions be carried out——

And now addio, addio

G. Verdi

GIULIO RICORDI TO VERDI

Milan, 12 November 1886

Illustrious Maestro,

I am in receipt of your honoured letter of yesterday and the roll containing the reduction;[1] I shall see to the excellent changes you have patiently indicated.

Since Faccio came to see me, I informed him of your letter. He asks me *primis ante omnia* to pay his respects to you and to let you know that the phrase in the third act duet has already been studied, and that it works very well for Tamagno; this does not mean that you cannot change it as you think best.—Faccio confirms to you that Tamagno is studying daily with great zeal. He reads the first and fourth acts fluently and without errors; and yesterday he started to study the third.—Following your instructions, Faccio is limiting himself to teaching the notes exactly, mathematically—and nothing else.—

We talked about Rome; your observations on the danger of Devoyod's enunciation are absolutely right; the two others I proposed, Kaschmann and Battistini, would be considered excellent by Faccio, too; it is true they tend to be mawkish, but where one can be so, as in the *Favorita*, etc. etc.; but where there is nothing mawkish they will not, cannot, and cannot be made to be mawkish. They are both intelligent and very good actors. If well directed, we believe, they will not be unworthy of singing Jago.

All right for the *diapason*; on this subject I put four lines in *La gazzetta* that will certainly be reported by other papers. [...]

Always having some wild idea or other, I will suggest one to you: Why

---

[1] Probably in the Biblioteca Palatina.

don't you make a trip to Milan on about the 18th or the 20th? .... I understand what is inconvenient in all of this! .... But if you leave everything ready in Busseto and bring here only what is necessary for 6 or 7 days, you, and most of the things at Busseto, could leave for Genoa as soon as the news is reassuring. Your coming here would be useful, really incalculable.

You could coach Tamagno; you could come to a definite understanding with Boito about the translation; he has already translated ⅔ of the fourth act; and since at the moment he is not talking about going to the Riviera so soon, a lot of time could be used, and if you find that he is doing well, the translation would go at full steam. You could decide about the ballet, etc., etc., and also about who knows how many details which I do not remember at this moment, but which could be settled; this way, your final trip to Milan will just serve to fire up the machine and go ahead at full speed. [...]

—Oh! .... Gentlemen!! .... You make arrangements for me a little too freely!

This you can say, Maestro; but there is a very easy remedy: to consider that the above was never written!! [...]

GIULIO RICORDI TO VERDI

Milan, 13 November 1886

Illustrious Maestro,

In the end I think you will send me the licence for 'distinguished bore', and I shall accept it by going on to bore you with the enthusiasm worthy of .... another licence.

Well, I received your letter .... the musical one!![1] ... In order not to waste time, I let the engraving of the piece continue, but left out the two or three pages where the changes occur that you intend to make. And I ask you to allow me to wait two or three days before I return the orchestra score (Otello–Jago, second act) to you, only because the postal service is in great disorder on account of the railway disasters! ... Actually, your letters and [other] mailings have reached me regularly .... but it can happen that just the important roll is misdirected and makes a trip to who knows where!! .... As soon as I know that the postal service is functioning regularly again I shall send it; meanwhile no time is lost, since the engravers are working, and before they finish you will have the chance to review the orchestra score. In the meantime I am sending you a proof of the third act in which you will find two or three questions that require your answer.

As soon as I see Boito, I shall inform him of what you wrote to me. Boito is working with alacrity, sometimes until midnight, since he wishes to finish the fourth act translation, which he is anxious to show you so that it will serve him as a guide for the rest. He maintains that the fourth is the most difficult act to translate and therefore the greatest obstacle to overcome. [...]

---

[1] Probably in the Biblioteca Palatina.

Soon I hope to get the *thunder* [machine] for a rehearsal in the theatre; who knows if it will not warrant changing the tempo!! ... A real ruin! ....

I think this is enough for today!! ... But no: I also wanted to tell you that I agreed with Edel on the changes you mentioned—and that really is enough. [...]

VERDI TO EUGENIO TORNAGHI

St Agata, 13 November 1886

[...] One condition is missing that I indicated orally to Giulio,[1] and that is ... 'To publish the libretto *4* or *5* days (not more) before the first performance.'

'To put the piano–vocal score on sale right away on the morning after the first performance.' [...]

EUGENIO TORNAGHI TO VERDI

Milan, 15 November 1886

Illustrious Maestro
Signor Commendatore Giuseppe Verdi
Busseto
I have received your esteemed letter of the 13th. It is agreed that the House [of Ricordi] is pledged not to publish the libretto of *Otello* until 4–5 days before the first performance, and to put the piano–vocal score on sale right away on the morning after this performance. [...]

GIULIO RICORDI TO VERDI

Milan, 15 November 1886

Illustrious Maestro,
I am in receipt of your lines of Saturday,[1] and I hasten to inform you that—with the postal services being regularly re-established—I am sending you today your orchestra score of the second act, *Otello and Jago*, for the changes you wish to make there. Thus I shall be able to complete the entire engraving of the opera as soon as you return it ....

Meanwhile, tomorrow morning I shall also give Faccio the second act, with the exception of the last piece, which is not yet ready, and I shall send the same to Muzio. I am trying to keep the proofs, manuscripts, etc., well defended with all the art of warfare; you would not believe what sieges and what cunning are being used everywhere; fortunately until now all have remained badly disappointed! .. Also, to Tamagno I gave only the vocal part

---

[1] In Verdi's *Otello* contract with the House of Ricordi.

[1] Probably in the Biblioteca Palatina.

itself; and Faccio learned the opera by heart to accompany him; so there is no danger of indiscretions. Tamagno is enthusiastic about his study; I met him the other night, and he *fredonné* for me almost the whole part [he had] already studied.

Tornaghi informed me of your letter; all right for the libretto and the piano–vocal score, as you requested. [. . .]

Now I am anxious about the French edition, which must be completely ready, and *very quickly*, since time goes by so fast. I am arranging for the English and German translations—and I finish without boring you with anything else. [. . .]

VERDI TO GIULIO RICORDI

St Agata, 16 November 1886

Dear Giulio,

Yesterday I sent the printed third act; and today I am sending the corrected original . . . Act II.

I'll come to Milan either Sunday evening or Monday evening (whichever suits you better, in case you may wish to be away on Sunday) . . Inform Boito about it, with regard to the translation of the fourth act and [the need to] talk at length about the *Ballet*, since once we are well agreed, I will finally!! answer the directors of the Opéra.

Also inform Faccio regarding Tamagno. And where shall we have Tamagno study?

At the hotel? No; because we would have all the waiters at the door, and perhaps also the blond Spatz . . . and then what publicity! . . It would be a disturbance and an attraction for everybody [if we did it] in your father's room now that they have returned; and then (I don't know why), one rehearses badly in that room! . And where, then? Hmmm!!! You decide where you think it's less inconvenient, and I will go there . . . . .

Don't forget the two costume sketches about which I made those certain observations . . . . Imagine! . Not being content because they are too beautiful!

Keep my coming as secret as you can . . . . later on inform only the blond Spatz, and (like the last time)[1] don't come to the station, but come instead at six o'clock with an empty stomach . .

Addio, addio
G. Verdi

Write to me right away whether Sunday or Monday is more convenient for you.

---

[1] See Verdi to Ricordi, 13 Oct. 1886.

GIULIO RICORDI TO VERDI

Milan, 18 November 1886

Illustrious Maestro,

I am in receipt of the proofs of the third act and send you warm thanks for the patient accuracy with which you have gone over them; now I await the orchestra score of the final scene of the second act and, just so that I do not leave you idle, I am sending you the proofs of the first act. Only the second remains to be completed, and then the whole opera will be ready and in perfect order. As you requested, it will be published on the morning following the first performance; therefore we have all the time we need, since *15 days*, and no more, will suffice to prepare everything for the printing; so it is useless and imprudent to print it much sooner, also because of the danger that a copy might be smuggled out.

In the *Desdemona–Otello* scene in the third act you have indicated a correction to the E flat at the attack '*Tu di me ti fai gioco*' ['*You mock me*']. In the original orchestra score the E flat falls on the D at $\frac{6}{8}$ [time]; look at the little sheet attached, and if you decide on the correction as indicated to me in the proofs, I will follow it in the orchestra score and in the parts.

Yesterday I was in the theatre: *Aida* is almost ready,[1] and today Caprara starts work on the first act of *Otello*; I am glad to see that everybody is working with zeal and that the promises are being kept; in the theatre this is a miracle brought about by that Saint whom you know!!! .... and whose name is *Giuseppe Verdi*.

Well then, Maestro, may we or may we not hope to see you soon? .... Boito also awaits you anxiously, and so do Faccio and I. [...]

GIULIO RICORDI TO VERDI

Milan, 18 November 1886

Illustrious Maestro,

Just as I was about to end my letter, yours arrived!! ....

Pum! Pum! ... bang! ...

These are cannon shots, salvos of joy on the announcement of your coming!! .... But let's go on right away to the facts. Since Faccio was in my study, I informed him right away about what concerns him.

Now, it would be practical to settle for Monday, since last Sunday we came close to losing .... Otello. Tamagno took a trip to his property near Varese and found himself on a train almost colliding with another!! ... Miraculously, they came to a halt one metre apart!! .... The emotion and the cold he felt have made him a bit indisposed, and so he suspended his studies for 3 days. Faccio says that if he is made to study through Monday,

[1] *Aida* opened the new season of La Scala on 26 Dec. 1886 with la Pantaleoni, Tamagno, Maurel, and Navarrini under Faccio's baton.

Tamagno will have studied the *whole* opera, since all that is missing now is the second act, which he does not even have to complete.—Since it makes no difference to you, *Monday* would then be preferable, so on Tuesday you would have Tamagno all ready to study with you. I thank you warmly for your kind consideration, but now I shall no longer move from Milan.

All your observations about the rehearsal room are absolutely right; but my father is still in the country, so his apartment is empty!! ..... I understand that the room is gloomy, but on the other hand these premises offer the best guarantees of ..... secrecy. There would also be my little room, which is perhaps more suitable for music; no disturbance for us, since all the children are at school .... In short, you will see, and possibly we shall see together; one idea leads to another, and one can find something better.

I shall inform Boito as you tell me; but to inform the Cavaliere[1] and the blond Spatz, I will wait for you to telegraph me with the words, 'Sending everything Monday'. Then it will be understood that you will arrive on Monday on the usual train, that I shall advise Spatz on Saturday, and that I shall present myself at 6 o'clock as you command, that is, with an empty stomach!! ...

Will Signora Peppina come with you? .....

And now this really is enough! .... And tell me that the biggest bore is

> Yours most devotedly,
> Giulio Ricordi

VERDI TO GIULIO RICORDI

[St Agata] *Friday morning* [19 November 1886]

Dear Giulio,

1. Since I must stop over in Piacenza for half an hour, I'll definitely leave Monday and be in Milan after five o'clock the same day.

2. On second thoughts, it's better to rehearse with Tamagno at the theatre. Near the rehearsal room (the horrible room!) there is another room that would be very good. Have a *little piano* brought there, one with a light keyboard and normal tuning — —

3. I have just received a letter from Paris: Maurel is anxiously awaiting the second act. Make haste.

4. We'll speak with Boito right away about Du Locle, who is now not going to Genoa, so it's useless for him [Boito] to come to the Riviera. And then, where? We'll talk about this with Boito that very Monday evening so that I can write to Paris the next morning — —

I have finished ... No ... Last night I read a little article in *Il corriere* ... You laugh? .. But I don't laugh .... All this chatter will paralyse the effect of the first night — — and humiliate me!!

Addio, addio

> G. Verdi

[1] Not identified.

GIULIO RICORDI TO VERDI

[Milan] Saturday 20 November 1886

Illustrious Maestro,

Faccio has [just] come to me and informed me of Tamagno's attached letter,[1] which I am sending to you right away. Since the main purpose of your trip is to *give the last polish*, so to speak, to Tamagno, you might prefer to delay for two or three days; Faccio says that he can have him study the second act in a day or two; since it is only a question of a simple cold, he will be able to study tomorrow or the day after tomorrow, and you can leave the following day. If everything is planned, however, and you decide to come all the same, Boito's translation of the entire fourth act is ready, and the time could be usefully spent with this. Command me, Maestro, and telegraph me right away how I am to proceed. Always most devotedly

Giulio Ricordi

GIULIO RICORDI TO VERDI

Milan, 22 November 1886

Illustrious Maestro,

Yesterday I had your telegram:[1] *Wednesday* is all right. Now I have received your letter of Friday, and since you are a blessed man and are always right ...... you also found the best solution for the Tamagno business. Today I myself shall go to see if the little room is in order, and I shall have the piano brought there for you.

I have already sent the second act to Muzio 4 days ago, minus the last scene, which I had finished with great speed and am sending today. So Muzio will have *the whole opera*.

——I think Boito will go to Nervi in early December, but about all this when you come.

——I do not know to which little article in *Il corriere* you are referring; there is one every moment! ... And not just in the papers in Milan, but in Paris, London, Vienna, etc., etc., as well!! .... I cannot tell you how much I am doing to silence these barking dogs!! .. But .... the freedom of the press has brought us to these fine results, which by now are common practice all over the world!! [...]

EMANUELE MUZIO TO GIULIO RICORDI

Paris, 22 November 1886

[...] The persons who in my opinion merit a seat in the stalls are: Reyer, Ritt, Gailhard, Carvalho, Clemenceau, and Blaze de Bury. [...]

[1] Missing.

[1] Possibly in the Biblioteca Palatina.

I am awaiting the end of the duet between Jago and Otello that is interrupted by the most beautiful chorus celebrating Desdemona's feast-day and that ends with the oath, if I remember well. Maurel is deeply immersed in his part and will be a model Jago. He would even cut off his beard, saying that the full beard will make his face too gentle; but he will talk about this with the Maestro and Edel. In the second act he is playful, humorous, ironical, but terrible from the *Credo* onwards, and he says that the movements of his face must be seen.

When the Maestro hears him in fifteen or twenty days, he will know his part by heart. [. . .]

TORLONIA[1] TO VERDI
[Telegram]

Rome, 27 November 1886

EXPRESSING FEELINGS GENERAL REPRESENTATION ENTIRE COMMUNITY I BEG YOU AFTER PERFORMANCE SCALA MILAN ASSIGN YOUR OPERA OTELLO TO APOLLO ROMA FOR NEXT LENT—THUS OUR THEATRE WHICH EARLY NEXT MAY MUST BE DEMOLISHED [and which is] DEAR TO YOU AND ARTISTIC ITALY FOR FIRST SUCCESSES TROVATORE BALLO MASCHERA WILL HAVE GLORIOUS END WITH NEW TRIUMPH SHINING ACHIEVEMENT NATIONAL GENIUS—HAVE TELEGRAPHED RICORDI REQUESTING AUTHORIZATION FOR IMPRESARIO LAMBERTI[2] WHO I HOPE WILL ACCEPT CONDITIONS YOU AND PUBLISHER WILL ESTABLISH FOR PERFORMANCE RENT PRODUCTION ORCHESTRA SCORE

ACTING MAYOR TORLONIA[3]

EMANUELE MUZIO TO GIULIO RICORDI

Paris, 2 December 1886

[. . .] Today I posted to Camille Du Locle, *Hôtel de la Poste* in Rome the first act of the *Otello* libretto, informing him that you will send him the music, since he, like Nuitter and the other translators, always makes his translations to the music in order to follow its accents. As the Maestro told me, I wrote to him that later on he would meet Boito in Nervi or Milan, that Boito had finished the translation of the fourth act to the *Maître*'s satisfaction, and that he was working on the third and thought he [Du Locle] would translate the first and second acts. [. . .]

---

[1] Presumably Leopoldo Torlonia (1853–1918), a descendant of an ancient noble family; politician, mayor of Rome and, from 1909, senator of the Kingdom of Italy.
[2] If misspelled, apparently Giuseppe Lamperti (1834–98 or 99), the elder son of Francesco Lamperti.
[3] Neither Verdi's nor Ricordi's (negative) reply has been located.

GIULIO RICORDI TO VERDI

Milan, 2 December 1886

Illustrious Maestro,

Regarding your honoured letter of yesterday:[1] I am very sorry about what you write to me concerning Maurel. But I suppose that—however serious the affair might be—Maurel will have taken another residence where no cohabitation and therefore no illicit relations can be proved; if there is no other devilry behind it, he personally should not be in any danger. Of course, I will say nothing to Boito and will not risk a word about it, since you say that you will not give *Othello* in Paris without Maurel. It would nevertheless be distressing if, of all people, this were to befall a great artist, completely Jago off stage, as well!...

I am sending you the proofs of the first and fourth acts, so you [will] have the whole opera complete. Forgive me for telling you that the sooner you can return everything to me the better. Cairati has already started the chorus's study, and in about ten days they will know not only *Aida* but perhaps the *Flora*,[2] too!! So even before the theatre opens he will be able to begin reading rehearsals of *Otello*, gaining much time. I must hand over a complete part to Cairati in any case, but I think he is a man who can be trusted.

Tomorrow or the day after tomorrow we shall try the thunder [machine]—and I shall let you know about it.

The [cholera] conditions in Genoa have actually improved. [...]

VERDI TO GIULIO RICORDI

[St Agata] 2 December 1886

Dear Giulio,

I am sending the third bundle containing the printed reduction of Act III.

I have made a little change in Otello's scene. I don't think it has gained dramatically, but something [is gained] musically—*it goes better*; there is no change in tempo; and it's well that the violins take up the phrase with which Otello's song ends; it's also faster .. In short, tell Faccio to go over this little piece with Tamagno again, and if it goes well (it cannot go badly) return the bundle to me so that I can *orchestrate* it ....

On p. 43 you will find an ... '*è quello!*' ['*it's that one!*']. Adjust this page with all the rest.

At the end of the Trio[1] (here Boito was right) the trumpets enter six bars earlier; and the final word of the Trio coincides with the first attack of the

---

[1] Probably in the Biblioteca Palatina.
[2] *Flora mirabilis*, opera in 3 acts by the Greek composer Spiro Samara (1861–1917). (See Roosevelt, pp. 142–3.)

---

[1] In Act III, Scene v.

trumpet. This way a rest of only *4* bars will remain; and that's the time needed to rearrange the set a bit.

Soon we go to Genoa. Our servants will leave on Monday, and we'll leave on *Tuesday* or Wednesday. Just for your information, so that you may return the bundle to me before then.

What news in Milan? I haven't heard anything of late ..

By the way, *Maurel* finishes in Paris on the *8th* . . . he leaves the evening of the *9th*. If he still intends to pass through Genoa, the earliest he can be there is the 10th. He would come to me on the 11th, but in this case he could never get to Milan by the *12th*. Arrange with Faccio and Corti to give him a few days in Genoa and to enable me to keep him.—

Amen . . . and addio

G. Verdi

Turn over

I am sending you three whole bundles containing the third act; on account of the bad weather I was unable to go out, and so I corrected the entire first part of the act in the orchestra score.

Ask Boito . . . .

In Act III, Scene ii Otello says

Eppur qui annida, ecc. . .

[*And yet here nests*, etc. . .]

. . . .

and after three verses there is another

Eppur con questa mano, ecc. .

[*And yet with this hand*, etc. .]

Is it an oversight, or does he want it so?? In my orchestra score and in the first manuscript it is there.

Pur già qui annida, ecc.

[*Yet here* already nests, etc.].

GIULIO RICORDI TO VERDI

Milan, 4 December 1886

Illustrious Maestro,

I received part of the proofs of the third act with the change in *Otello*'s solo; I sent it right away to Faccio, who replied: *It is going stupendously well*! . . . . . . I had the piece copied for Tamagno and am sending the bundle back to you this very day so you can use it for the orchestra score; then we shall correct the orchestra parts as soon as we have the orchestra score. I shall wait until you return the bundle to make the correction at the end of the trio and at the attack of the trumpets.

Faccio has also let me know that Maurel can stay in Genoa until the 14th, since this would not hold up the rehearsals for *Aida*. I shall inform the management, then; and there will always be time to keep [him] one more day, if you should find it necessary.

Boito says that he actually made the change by putting in two '*Eppur*'; the '*Pur già*' was too obvious an artifice not to repeat the same word—and in dialogue the repetition of '*Eppure*' is natural and done often.[1]

Edel has redone the costume sketch of *Otello* [in the] fourth act; on the basis of my famous rough design, I think, it may now be good.

Ferrario has finished the second scene; also, yesterday he started the fourth—and shortly he will do the first.—I have frequent sessions with Caprara about the first scene; we are trying to do our best with the *fuoco di gioia*; yesterday I saw the *hull* of the admiral's ship! . . . . . today we tried the thunder, and this, too, I think, is going well. It sounds better with 2 big sticks that obtain better effects than with the double mallet, with which the hand grows tired and cannot do it.

As you see, I am also sending you work in these few days before you go to Genoa!! . . . . . how about it, Maestro? . . . . . Yes, you can say this is crazy. But the time passes very rapidly! . . . .

Tomorrow morning I shall send Du Locle the music of the first act as a guide to the translation; I shall urge him 10,000 times not to show it to anyone; but if you, too, would like to write him a line on the matter, it would be better yet. Du Locle is now in Rome—Hôtel de la Poste.

And now I wish you and Signora Peppina a good journey to Genoa, where by now everything seems to be normal again.

And for us I wish that the day may soon come when we shall have you both in Milan; I am already looking forward to this very great pleasure and meanwhile remain, with feelings of the deepest gratitude,

Yours most devotedly,
Giulio Ricordi

I never had time to draw up the contract with La Scala; I hope that I can do it in a few days—and think it very useful to send it to you before signing it, in order to be sure that nothing has been overlooked.

GIULIO RICORDI TO VERDI

Milan, 7 December 1886

Illustrious Maestro,

To your esteemed letter of yesterday:[1] for your information, the Corti brothers have never talked to me about a production of *Otello* at La Scala, and for the simple reason that their management ends this year! Signora

---

[1] *Eppure* remained both times in the final text.

[1] Probably in the Biblioteca Palatina.

Gabbi was already engaged four or five years ago at La Scala; I do not know too well why her engagement has been cancelled; there is a whisper that it is for the reason of . . . . . *pregnancy!!* After her success at the Dal Verme (truly deserved) the Cortis seem to have engaged la Gabbi once more; I do not know this *officially*, however, but I believe it is true; and I also believe they have done this to assure themselves in time of a good soprano, since la Pantaleoni already seems to have been negotiating with Naples. All the outlines of this come from la Gabbi's agent, I think, who has fed it to an editor of the *Perseveranza*, who for his part has fed it to his readers. [. . .]

And while on this subject—and since I am dwelling on it, I come to no end—it is my duty to inform you that after Rome there is a project for the Fenice in Venice, with the *identical company*, Faccio, Caprara, La Scala sets, except that Kaschmann would be substituting for Maurel. When it is more concrete, I shall notify you as soon as possible so that you may say whether or not you approve.

The Signori Corti leave it entirely up to you to arrange Maurel's stay in Genoa as you think best; if he has not finished by the 14th, he may also stay there the 15th—and even the 16th. So you will have time, Maestro, to do all you want. [. . .]

VERDI TO CAMILLE DU LOCLE

Genoa, 10 December 1886

[. . .] I received your letter[1] forwarded from Genoa yesterday the moment I was leaving Busseto . . . Now I am here permanently until the moment I go to Milan!

I'm the one who is very glad that you were willing to assume the task of making the translation of this *Otello* with Boito. I understand that towards the 20th you will be in Nervi. How nice it would be if I could arrange for Boito to come here at that time! [. . .]

GIULIO RICORDI TO VERDI

Milan, 10 December 1886

Illustrious Maestro,

Following your telegram,[1] I am sending you the first act proofs—not the last [ones] you sent me, however, since they are already in the hands of the engravers, but the first. In these, however, I had *all* the corrections made; as they are now, they correspond perfectly to the last proofs.

When I think about it a little, I fear it may be rather late to have the original in hand only when you come here. Could not just the bundle

---

[1] Missing.

---

[1] Possibly in the Biblioteca Palatina.

containing the change in Otello's *solo* be sent by registered post? But I am still afraid that this most important packet might become lost. On the other hand, we must prepare the orchestra parts, most of which have already been engraved; and they could not be completed and corrected in time by early January. What is to be done, Maestro? ... Do you want me to send Garegnani when it is convenient? ... That would not disturb me at all ... and you? ....

Plan for Maurel as you think best, so that you can complete the necessary studies with him. Faccio will then be sure not to tire him with the *Aida* rehearsals; and to tell the truth, one could not wish for a more beautiful and comfortable part than Amonasro.

I note your observations concerning Venice; but be assured that Faccio would not accept the engagement if they did not have the necessary elements in abundance; actually, this is the most important part, since the artists would be the same. But when the time comes I shall make it my duty to give you exact information. If it can be arranged, the *Fenice*, too, would be revived and could, according to the legend, rise from its own ashes.

I also had a letter from Du Locle[2] and informed Boito of it. I know nothing about the translation, because I have been so busy for 8 days that I cannot even leave the office until dinner.

I hope that you and Signora Peppina had an excellent trip[3] and are in perfect health; with my affectionate regards to both of you, I remain, full of profound gratitude

Yours most devotedly,
Giulio Ricordi

How much I would give
to hear Maurel!!! ...

GIULIO RICORDI TO VERDI

Milan, 14 December 1886

Illustrious Maestro,

I am in receipt of your esteemed letter announcing Maurel's arrival to me;[1] but ..... the cruel Maestro Verdi has made an omission ...... that fills me with curiosity!! ... It is quite true, however, that he who is silent confirms that Maurel is wonderful.

Garegnani is at your disposal; you only have to let me know a day before, and he will leave right away on the morning express train, a most comfortable train, giving him plenty of time to stay there.

Today or tomorrow I shall send you the contract with La Scala, which I do

---

[2] Missing.
[3] From St Agata to Genoa.

---

[1] Probably in the Biblioteca Palatina.

not want to sign before you have carefully examined it; I hope that nothing has escaped me, but in any case I shall feel safer after your observations, should you have any.

Paroli (Cassio) already knows his part very well. I have handed out the other parts (Montano, Lodovico, Roderigo), as well, and tomorrow I shall hand out all the parts for the chorus to Cairati to start the reading.

The 12 trumpets have already left Brussels, so they will be here within a few days.

We have tried the thunder [machine] again in two or three places, and the best seems to be between the wings on the left near the proscenium; the effect is *excellent*; but you will decide this when the time comes.

The sets are coming along well; soon the fabrics will arrive from Turin; I saw a sample of one; they are stupendous!—

Everything is ready for *Aida* and almost [everything] for the second opera;[2] the management is making every effort to put it on as quickly as possible.

The subscriptions have been closed. There are no more seats in the stalls for the first [performance of] *Otello*, and reservations are being taken for the second. [...]

VERDI TO GIULIO RICORDI

Genoa, 15 December 1886

Dear Giulio,

To satisfy your curiosity right away, I will tell you that the recent encounter with Maurel has convinced me that no one (allowing that he will do well) will perform and sing Jago as it should be. You will tell me, in your optimism ... but *he*, but *you*, but *she* ... No, no, no! No one!!.. And I am very sorry to have written this part! ... And also ... the opera!! .. And at least to have it made public knowledge, so to speak!—Oh, if I could turn back!! .. But let's not fall into a bad humour! The times are black enough! As for the contract, I believe you did not forget anything, but if I come to Milan I think I'll seem like an *intruder* ... And, for example, in a discussion with Corti he might very well say to me, 'Who are you?' I will go further: supposing there is a dispute, not with you, but with the House of Ricordi ... I could still be told ... 'Signor Maestro, if it doesn't please you, go away, we'll do without you.' .... Then, that kind of privilege for the family and others to assist at rehearsals doesn't work. The Ricordis aren't a family, they are a tribe in which there are the *Lions*, the *clever* ones, etc., etc., who after a rehearsal would be only too glad to bang some little piece on any old lady's piano ..... And then let's start off from a just, natural, and also legal principle: 'The House becomes the proprietor of the orchestra score after publication. Until then the property is entirely mine.' Therefore no one has the right to take *mon bien* before that time.

[2] *Flora mirabilis*, to be followed one month later by *Otello*. (See Ricordi to Verdi, 2 Dec. 1886.)

In any case, just leave the contract as it is (my feelings aren't hurt by it), but add an ample, comprehensive and clear clause: 'If Maestro Verdi comes to hold the rehearsals of his *Otello*, he will have at his disposal . . .' etc., etc., etc. . . . And thus, deleting the short clauses concerning the rehearsals, we can reach an agreement . . — —

It will be well to prepare the contracts before my arrival, or at least before I go to the first rehearsal. — —

I hope it will all be settled that there is to be no standing room in the stalls . . Remember I intend to make this a condition . . .

One last thing, and I'll be finished. I have read in the papers that the rental for *Otello* was set at *30 thousand* Lire! I am pleased to see that the rental is modest, and even more so because I believe that *Aida* cost Brunello only *20 thousand*. If Brunello paid that sum, Corti must be quite content with the sympathy you show him——

You can send Garignani whenever you want. Everything will be ready! . . . Addio, addio

G. Verdi

VERDI TO GIULIO RICORDI

[Genoa] Wednesday [15 December 1886]

Dear Giulio,

Maurel has left and will be in Milan at this hour.

Be sure that he has the part with him! . . He will tell you about his squabble with Tamagno! . Try to bring them together so that they may be good artistic comrades at the rehearsals.—

I am now adjusting other errors, and you can send Garignani whenever you want.—

In going over the part again with *Maurel* I saw that something is missing (in the vocal ensemble) at the end of the chorus in the second act:[1]

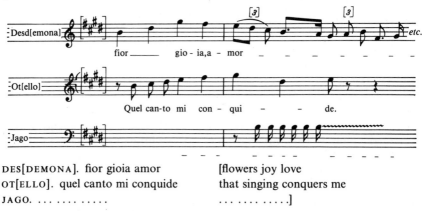

DES[DEMONA]. fior gioia amor   [flowers joy love
OT[ELLO]. quel canto mi conquide   that singing conquers me
JAGO. . . . .]

---

[1] Verdi does not give a signature in this quotation, as usual and unnecessary in this correspondence. See Ricordi orchestral score, plate no. PR 155, p. 224, for final solution.

Jago is on stage and should say something. For example, something in the way of the verses that were cut in the 1st act² . . .

Soave accordo . . .	[Sweet harmony
— — —	— — —
Io romperò, ecc., ecc.	I will break, etc., etc.]
— — —	— — —

Only two verses, preserving the metre of Otello's verses — — — *broken* [*tronchi*], *plain* [*piani*], as he likes . . . I am not writing to Boito, since when the letter arrived in the morning, it would distract him for the rest of the day and keep him from his work on the translation or something else. You talk with him about it over a drink of *Vermouth* at Cova.³ —
Another thing.—At the end of the *chorus* there are the two words

'Eccola!' ['There she is!']
'Vigilate' ['Watch']

. . . Originally they were said by Jago after the . . . '*Può affermare il sospetto*' ['*Can confirm the suspicion*']. There they went well, here they no longer fit the music. If Boito doesn't want to leave them as they were in the original, it would be better to take them out altogether, and the verse would become a seven-syllable instead of an *eleven-syllable* one . . . .
Addio addio

G. Verdi

BOITO TO VERDI

[Milan, 16–17 December 1886]

Dear Maestro,
Forgive the poor quality of these pieces of paper. Haste is my excuse, I have no others at hand. The page written in pencil¹ concerns the letter you wrote to Giulio.
An alteration to the lines added for Jago comes to mind:²

Beltà e letizia in dolce inno concordi
I vostri infrangerò soavi accordi.

[*Beauty and joy, harmonizing in sweet song,*
Your gentle chords I will break.]

---

² See Boito to Verdi, 17 June 1881, n. 7.
³ Boito's favourite restaurant in Milan. (See Document X, n. 3.)

---

¹ Missing. Apparently, Boito rewrote some verses in response to Verdi's second letter to Giulio Ricordi of 15 Dec. 1886. The final text (II. iii) corresponds to Verdi's wishes expressed in that letter.
² See Boito to Verdi, 17 June 1881, n. 7.

or:

> *Beltà ed Amor in dolce inno concordi*
> ecc., ecc. . .
>
> [*Beauty and Love, harmonizing in sweet song.*
> etc., etc. . .].

With the translation, we are at Cassio's entrance in the third act.[3] The translation of the third is better than that of the second, and it is just as difficult. I have written to Du Locle,[4] and I have had Giulio, in *La gazzetta musicale*, correct a report from *Le Figaro*, which might have displeased Du Locle; the correction will appear in the next issue of *La gazzetta*.[5]

Cordial greetings

> Your most affectionate
> Arrigo Boito

GIULIO RICORDI TO VERDI

Milan, 17 December 1886

Illustrious Maestro,

If I did not reply right away to your esteemed letter of the 15th, it is because all day long I awaited the return of the draft of the contract,[1] which I received this morning.[2] I am very glad to have sent it to you, so that you could make these observations which you found most opportune. Allow me, however, illustrious Maestro, to justify some parts of the contract.

In the extension of this contract the specifications of those for *Aida*, *Boccanegra*, etc., were followed; in those, you had requested that you personally not be involved in any manner, and therefore [you] were omitted purposely. In your above-mentioned letter you foresee situations that seem to me impossible; but really, Maestro, I believed I had done something that would meet with your complete approval. As I was sending you the draft of the contract, I said to myself: pacts or no pacts, I want something better; and the same day (as you will see from the enclosed letter)[3] I wrote to the Mayor, who by virtue of his office is president of the Commission of La Scala, telling him that the moral support of the Commission would be better than any contract; in the enclosed you will see, then, the very fine and explicit reply of our skilful Negri, completing the contract. Kindly return this letter to me to be put in the files.

---

[3] Boito and Du Locle translated *Otello* into French. (See Verdi to Du Locle, 10 Dec. 1886.)
[4] Missing.
[5] In *La gazzetta musicale* of 19 Dec. 1886 we read: 'Some papers have reported that the French translation of Verdi's *Otello* will be done by Arrigo Boito; this news is completely inexact: Maestro Verdi has entrusted this translation to the Messrs Arrigo Boito and Camille Du Locle, who began their work some time ago.'

---

[1] Between the House of Ricordi (also representing its authors) and the management of La Scala.
[2] Possibly in the Biblioteca Palatina.
[3] Missing.

The contract begins with one of the customary printed forms, and it was by a mere oversight, which you so well noted, that the last part of Paragraph 9 concerning the rehearsals was not deleted. That authority, however, was completely restricted in the subsequent manuscript, in which I put a ? . . . in blue pencil; but if you so desire, those parts contained between the pencilled words can very well be omitted; then I noticed that I had forgotten [about] Boito; his involvement in the rehearsals is more than natural, of course, but it had better be included in the paragraph.

Please see the earlier paragraph in regard to your own person[al involvement]; I drafted it in a manner that I think will correspond to your ideas.[4] I did not mention the *diapason* and *standing room* because the normal *diapason* has already been adopted for two years, and the matter of standing room has already been announced to the public; anyway, these matters can be included very well and will not hurt.

For all of that, I would like you to take note of these modifications, and I am returning the contract to you, which you can let me have again right away, giving it in a closed envelope to Garegnani. He will be in Genoa tomorrow, Saturday morning, and, in accordance with your telegram, will bring the proofs. I think you will have sufficient time to give Garegnani all the instructions you wish, but in any case it would not matter even if he returned Sunday morning.

I forgot an observation about the contract; if you will be kind enough to read it again, you will note that there are some repetitions; i.e. I [will] withdraw the orchestra score for this or that [reason], etc.; I believe it can be reduced, without, of course, touching its essence, and can thus be improved in clarity and in diction.

I heard a rehearsal of *Aida* with orchestra: excellent!! . . . . With regard to *Aida*, I have checked on the Brunello rental: 22,000 [for] *Forza destino* and *Aida*. Why, then, 22,000 now? . . . I thought I should account for this: The *Forza destino* was the first *revival*, whereas *Aida*, if I am not mistaken, is at least the fourth.

[In addition], the company at that time cost about half as much as that of today, while the subsidies have remained the same.

Did I do wrong? . . . I hope not; but if I did, give me absolution!! . . . .

You will be served with the panettone! . . . . It would be too bad if you delayed your coming here on its account!!! . . . .

And here I come to a stop, for I think I have bored you sufficiently; please remember me to Signora Peppina; we hope that your health is excellent, and in the meantime I remain most gratefully and devotedly

Yours,
Giulio Ricordi

Boito will have sent you what is needed for Jago;[5] he told me that the translation of the third act is going well.

---

[4] See Verdi's *Pro Memoria* of 1 Oct. 1886.
[5] See preceding letter from Boito to Verdi.

VERDI TO BOITO

Genoa, 18 December 1886

Dear Boito,

Thanks for the two lines.[1] I have just delivered the final acts of *Otello* to Garignani! . . . Poor Otello! He won't come back here any more!!!

If you go to hear Emanuel tonight, drop me a line tomorrow and tell me if I was very wrong! . . .

Addio, addio

G. Verdi

VERDI TO GIULIO RICORDI

[Genoa] Saturday [18 December 1886][1]

Here you have *Otello*!!!!!!
You went too far in deleting . . . .
Tell Tornaghi to do the contracts again and to send them to me, in agreement with your contract with Corti.
Thank Boito for the two lines, and I am glad that his work is coming along so well.
I am returning the letter of the Mayor; apart from *him*, there has never been a good . . . I'd say *understanding* between me and the management. Also, the last time with *Boccanegra* there was a little thing that I don't want to go into . . . forget about it . . . let's hope nothing will happen in these circumstances . . . I could hardly tolerate it.

Addio, addio

G. Verdi

GIULIO RICORDI TO VERDI

Milan, 19 December 1886

Illustrious Maestro,

Upon his return Garegnani handed over to me the orchestra score of the second and third acts and your esteemed letter with the form of the contract; I thank you for everything and for a certain kind deletion of ?[1] . . . . another proof of your goodness. In this matter of rehearsals, after all, with a throng

---

[1] Of 16–17 Dec. 1886.

---

[1] The dating of this letter in the Ricordi Archives and Abbiati, iv. 293, is 20 Oct. 1886. The four preceding letters, however, clearly establish this date.

---

[1] This question mark corresponds to the autograph.

of .... family, I have always swallowed grave displeasures, of which it is useless to talk, because they are .... small miseries.—I deeply, very deeply regret what you tell me about the management and your reference to *Boccanegra*; I do not know to which occurrence you mean to allude; but anyway, I am inclined to believe that there was some unintentional failure; I know the members of the management very well, and it seems impossible to me that *scientes* or *volentes* they could have failed to show you respect.—Also, in this last circumstance I could only ask *repeated, insistent* questions to find out if I might anticipate any wishes you might have—and these gentlemen could certainly have no greater satisfaction than to hear that everything proceeds as you want.—

At the first announcement that the actor Emanuel wanted to give *Othello* I felt annoyed .... and I was wrong. Perhaps I had not seen this drama for over 20 years; I was there last night, and I am glad I was there and that it is being performed.—It is colossal!! .... It is a wonder, and on stage it gains a hundred times over the reading; it made the deepest, [most] extraordinary impression on the audience, also because it is not known to most of them.—*Il corriere della sera* gives a somewhat severe, though generally just, review; and now I will tell you my impressions .... and may Verdi forgive me the nonsense I am about to utter.—Boito really has extracted its vital juices to form his libretto; excellent idea, to do without the 2 acts[2] in Venice, beautiful [though they are] as pictures and as an introduction to the characters, but less interesting than the other 4 that would correspond to those of the libretto.—In the music drama, with its condensed dialogues and more rapidly developing passions, the grandiose scenes are far superior to those of the drama: The first and third acts cannot be compared with the corresponding spoken ones.—The most important dialogues made the greatest impression on me when they reminded me of Boito's, and I was amazed and gratified to see that the *words* which hit the audience the most were faithfully preserved in the libretto. Need I tell you, Greatest Maestro, what I thought as I imagined the power those words, those scenes, will gain from the music? ..... I think it is unnecessary. All in all, these performances will be useful: they will be an initiation for the audience, which believes, or makes believe, that it has Shakespeare and *Othello* at its fingertips and instead doesn't know a thing about it!!! ...

Boito did not come, because he is no admirer of Emanuel; in fact, he was annoyed that artists of La Scala went there, saying that they would learn bad things! ... In my opinion he is wrong: Emanuel was fair in the first two acts, but excellent in the other four, and he had stupendous moments, especially in the scene with Desdemona and in the other with Jago.—Otello is far more pleasing in the Venetian costume than in Salvini's baroque Turkish one.—The costumes conceived by Edel will be very good.

Last night la Pantaleoni was at the performance in a box, Tamagno in another one, Maurel and Edel in the stalls, by chance near me.—They will

---

[2] Only the first act of Shakespeare's tragedy in 5 acts takes place in Venice.

find another interpretation, but this treatment of the drama before their eyes has certainly been most useful; for Tamagno (who watched with eyes wide open), *extremely useful!* . . .

And useful for la Pantaleoni, too; useless for Maurel, since the Jago was very bad; but it was good for him, too, to see the whole drama. It served us well for certain comparisons of the costumes, etc., etc., and tonight we shall hold a little session with Edel and Maurel to study a few more things for the costumes.

And now . . . . enough, in fact quite enough, don't you think so? . . .

You write to me to tell Tornaghi to send you the contracts; you mean the contract between you and the publisher? . . . In that case I may remind you of what we wrote to you, in October, I believe—when an outline was sent to you.[3] If you like, a new copy will be made; it was divided in two: the contract of transfer and a private writing concerning the agreements for the first production at La Scala; and this, because the latter had better not be included in the contract, in case it has to be reviewed for some suit [charging] infractions, alterations, etc., etc. And if you do not wish to trouble yourself at this time, it can very well wait until you come to Milan. In short, decide now, and always do what you prefer.

Devoted greetings to Signora Peppina and yourself from

> Yours most gratefully,
> Giulio Ricordi

BOITO TO VERDI

[Milan, 21 December 1886][1]

My dear Maestro,

The Moor will no longer knock at the door of the Palazzo Doria, but you will find the Moor at La Scala.

Otello is. The great dream has become a reality. What a pity! Still, in spite of the sadness that has followed the completion of the opera, I would also like the French translation to become a reality soon. A lot of work is being done, and unless I'm deceiving myself, it's being done well. In a week the trio will be finished. Then I'll probably leave for Nervi,[2] where I shall meet Du Locle and see what he has done, and he'll see what I've done. If Du Locle works hard until the middle of February or, at the latest, until the end of that month, the translation can be completed.

Meanwhile Ricordi can have the fourth act engraved, and then, very soon thereafter, the third, which, as I said, is already well along, and the first, which Du Locle did. The second will come last.

---

[3] No trace of such an outline has been found.

---

[1] Postmark: MILANO 21/12/86.
[2] Apparently, Boito went to Nervi only in March after the first performances of *Otello* in Milan.

I didn't go to see Emanuel; he is a very mediocre actor, cold, monotonous, unsympathetic. If no eagle can be born from a hen's egg, then out of Emanuel's head can come no kind of interpretation of Othello. Rossi and Salvini, there are the two giants! Tamagno could have learned something from them; but from Emanuel he could learn absolutely nothing, and I wouldn't have wanted him to go to that performance. The other actors, I hear, were even worse than Emanuel!

Now, Schakespeare's *Othello* has your mark, *and this you have done*; that's enough, and there is no need to beg for the effects of others.

So great was the haste in which I wrote my last letter[3] that I realized, after it had already fallen into the letter box, that I had forgotten to put on the stamp. I was afraid you might not receive it. The State's budget will have earned a ten-cent fine.

Cordial greetings to you and Signora Peppina.

> Your most affectionate
> Arrigo Boito

VERDI TO GIULIO RICORDI

Genoa, 24 December 1886

Dear Giulio,

I am sorry to trouble you, since unfortunately I know what troubles are like ... but I can't help it.

La Waldmann has written [to ask] me, with great insistence, to get a box for the first night of *Otello*, in the *first* or *second* tier, and she would resign herself even to the *third* ... Can you find it? . Talk about it with Corti or with whomever you think ... Answer me in detail, and in any case tell me the price.

Is it true that you have sent tickets to various people in Busseto and, among others, to the *Carraras*? That's a nuisance and a great effort for me, which you could have spared me .. For God's sake spare me any effort, apart from what is needed for the rehearsals. If I become ill ... I will allow *Otello* no longer——

I, too, am of Boito's opinion. The artists were wrong to go to Emanuel's *Othello*. One of the two: If we, Boito and I, have *hit* the mark correctly, there is no need of another interpretation; if we didn't *hit* it, wanting to modify or reshape the bad work we did would be worse.—

So you consulted *Maurel* about the costumes? . And why? ... That may be all right for his own, but there was no need concerning others! Don't be surprised by an announcement in *Le Figaro* one day or another that *Maurel* has enlightened the *mise-en-scène* at La Scala. — —

Addio, addio

> G. Verdi

[3] Of 16–17 Dec.

GIULIO RICORDI TO VERDI

Milan, 25 December 1886

Illustrious Maestro,

This morning, as soon as I received your esteemed letter of yesterday, I searched right away for the boxes, which are hard to find for sale, since they are private property, as you know.

Well, then: in the 1st tier—o!

in the 2nd tier—*only one*, very beautiful: last price for the première of *Otello*, Lire 1,200

in the 3rd tier—very good—Lire 1,000

But I cannot guarantee that they will still be there tomorrow or later, because they might be sold from one moment to the next, and they do not hold them, of course. In any case it would be good to telegraph me as soon as possible.

I have not sent either one or more tickets to those people in Busseto, for several reasons: *first*, because I don't have them; and that is Arlecchino's reason; *second*: even if I had them, I would not know for what purpose to send them! . . . *Third*: Because I don't know anyone in Busseto. A gentleman from Busseto came to me to find out, more or less, when *Otello* would be premièred, and I advised him not to come to the opening, if several people were involved, because they would not find seats! . . . Did I do well? . . . I think so.—Only Dr Carrara wrote to me that, since he did not want to disturb you, I should reserve 3 ordinary seats for him, which he duly paid for at the box-office, and nothing more. This I could not have refused to do. So, illustrious Maestro, do not listen to all the false news that people tell; for my part I may say that, *as much as I can*, I make superhuman efforts and try in every way to prevent anything that I could suspect of being an annoyance to you. But consider that I am 'Horatio alone against all of Italy'.[1] You cannot imagine the visits, the interviews, the traps they set for me to dig up something!! . . . A person even came from Rome, sent purposely by *Fracassa*!![2] I hope you will see with what jealous care everything is guarded, since until today one can say that nobody knows a thing, even though very many people have already worked on it, such as copyists, engravers, typographers, editors, vocal-score reducers, tailors, scenic designers, stagehands, etc.

As for the costumes and Maurel, I expressed myself badly, perhaps: the session with him and Edel was for the costume of *Jago*; there was no need for us to consult with Maurel about the other costumes, since you and Boito had approved them. You told me yourself: when Maurel comes, agree with him on the costume design; and this was done; only the session lasted . . . . . 3 hours!! . . . . The costume was to Maurel's complete satisfaction, except that a

[1] Giulio Ricordi alludes to the legendary Roman hero Horatius Cocles's single-handed defence of a bridge against an Etruscan army in the late sixth century BC.
[2] *Il Capitan Fracassa*, a Roman newspaper.

slight change in the belt, dagger, and sword for the first act was decided upon; these weapons were exchanged for others, and that is all. Maurel insists he should take off his beard; but there is time to decide this; using an old photograph, Edel has painted Maurel's head—Jago without a beard—and it seems most becoming to me; you will decide. Besides his own costume, Maurel has seen Otello's for the last act, since Edel had brought it along to show me and to find out if it went well in this final form; but to tell the truth, Maurel did not put his two cents in, and said nothing; in fact, he seems *very* [much] changed to me from some years ago!! . . . Maybe the lessons he received have done some good.

You know, Maestro, that in certain things, and perhaps in everything, I am an ass!! . . . Well then, allow me and also forgive me this time if I keep my opinion regarding Emanuel's *Othello*!! . . and if I repeat that especially for Tamagno it was a most useful thing. I admit that you and Boito would be able to make Tamagno understand the character and study it thoroughly, but you would never reach him with the power that the *visual* medium can have—and in the places that correspond to the opera Emanuel was excellent!— Oh! . . as far as the musical and dramatic performance of *Otello* is concerned, that will be your business, Maestro, [since] all this was conceived, envisioned by you! . . . and no one, including Boito himself, (!!!!!) can with a single word indicate and give the right note as Verdi can. But at least you will be spared the initial thankless fatigue of explaining to Tamagno who Othello was! If I am wrong . . . . I lower my head, or better, my blockhead, and won't open my mouth any more.

Last night, dress rehearsal of *Aida*: excellent performance and most splendid staging. For la Pantaleoni it is perhaps not the most suitable opera; but she exceeded my expectations and does many things beautifully. Principal remark: she is singing with more ease, more legato; her intonation is no longer as uncertain on some notes as before!! . . . You are a *MAGICIAN*!!. Maestro! . . I know what I am saying: *Beautifully dressed!* La Novelli[3] (Amneris) not very intelligent or refined, but splendid voice and beautiful woman; one of the best, leaving la Waldmann aside, of course. Tamagno has even more voice than usual!! . . . Magnificent Radames. Maurel magnificent . . . and in *excellent* voice, far better, incomparably so, than the last time; Navarrini a cannon, and Limonta excellent (King. . . . then *Montano*). With such a performance, the season seems assured to me. All are working feverishly; *Flora* is already ready with singers and chorus, and Faccio, with extraordinary activity, has already read the entire opera with the orchestra. Ferrario is giving the last touches to the first set for *Otello*; so all the sets will be finished in a few days, rolled up and put away to be pulled out at the right time. The 12 trumpets have arrived from Brussels; we shall try them one of these days in the theatre; but Orsi has tried them already and informs me that they are very good.

But I seem to hear you exclaim: enough! . . enough! . . . and it really is

[3] Nouvelli.

enough; but all the same, affectionate, infinite wishes for you and Signora Peppina from

> Yours most grateful and devoted for life
> Giulio Ricordi

A cordial greeting to Muzio, to whom I hope to write tomorrow.

VERDI TO GIULIO RICORDI

Genoa, 26 December 1886

Dear Giulio,

Yesterday I received a stupendous letter from you,[1] full of your heart. You tell me so many, many good and beautiful things that I would never know how to answer you in kind, except to tell you that I thank you from the heart for everything you say, reciprocating the wishes of happiness for you and for the entire family.

Today I received your other business letter.[2]

I telegraphed la Waldmann,[3] and I hope she answers right away with a telegram, which I shall relay to you right away.[4] I have advised her to send boxes, and *Otello*, to the devil.

I like Jago without beard very much; in fact, we spoke about this. But *with* or *without*, it will always be all right.

I am glad about the news concerning la Pantaleoni; and if I can find some hours in Milan to be with her, alone and free, I hope she will find still better things.—

You ... come on ... you know well that you are no dolt!! Perhaps you have, I'd say, a few extremist obsessions, but a dolt you are not.— *The visual medium* is all right if Emanuel was right; but if Emanuel made a *weakling* of Otello, and in some places almost a whimpering *old man* (as they reproached him), it would be a bad lesson for Tamagno.

Tomorrow at 9.25, at the time you will receive this letter, I shall be on my way to St Agata for some urgent personal business. See to it that I find in Busseto by 4.00 p.m. a telegram giving me news about this evening.[5] News that is exact, severe, and sincere.

With Peppina's regards and wishes addio, addio

> Yours,
> G. Verdi

PS Is it true that at the head of the *Otello* edition you want to put the

---

[1] Missing.
[2] Of 25 Dec.
[3] Missing.
[4] Missing.
[5] The opening night of *Aida* at La Scala. The telegram is missing.

painting by Boldini in pastel with hat, scarf, etc.?[6] However great the
similarity, and whatever the merit of the work may be, I think it's a joke
rather than a serious painting to be put at the front of the edition, etc. . .

VERDI TO MARIA WALDMANN

Genoa, 26 December 1886

The moment I received your very dear letter,[1] the day before yesterday, I
wrote to Milan. It was useless to contact the management, and so I turned to
Giulio for a special box, and herewith I am enclosing the card with which he
answered me.

You already know from the telegram I sent you a few hours ago what is
going on. These are exaggerations, abuses . . . and I—excuse me—would send
boxes, and *Otello*, to the devil. [. . .]

GIULIO RICORDI TO GIUSEPPINA VERDI

Milan, 29 December 1886

Kindest Signora Peppina,

Your good, courteous, dear letter of the day before yesterday[1] has moved
me deeply, and I really could not find adequate words to thank you. I am
awaiting your coming here with immense pleasure. [. . .]

I know, distinguished Lady, how much our House and, in the *most
particular* way, the writer owe to you!! . . I know it, I will *never forget* it,
and you, most kind and exquisite woman, may bear the necessary
consequences. [. . .]

GIULIO RICORDI TO VERDI

Milan, 30 December 1886

Illustrious Maestro,

Excuse me if I can only give a brief answer to your honoured letter of
yesterday.[1]

Flora opens next Thursday, the 6th.[2] The rehearsals for *Otello* could then
begin *when you wish*; I would say the 2nd or 3rd; therefore the sooner you

---

[6] Giovanni Boldini made this well-known painting of Verdi on 9 Apr. 1886 in Paris. It did not
appear in Ricordi's scores of *Otello*.

---

[1] Missing.

---

[1] Probably in the Biblioteca Palatina.

---

[1] Probably in the Biblioteca Palatina.
[2] *Flora mirabilis* opened only on 8 Jan. 1887.

come to Milan, the better it will be, so you will also have time at your disposal for la Pantaleoni. If the *Flora* barely, barely has a fair success, the management will repeat it Saturday and Sunday, the 8th and 9th, thus leaving the artists of *Aida* completely free—and this will allow you to dispose of them as you think best. As soon as the *Flora* has opened the management will make every effort for the ballet; they reckon they will open with this on the 11th; but I think it is impossible. But in any case the ballet will open *soon*; from that day on you will have the stage, technical personnel, etc., entirely *free*; and I think this coincides very well with the period in which the musical studies will be completed. Today, the 30th, and Saturday, the 1st *Aida* will be given; then, I believe, the artists can be free for the whole week, that is, from the 2nd to the 10th—except, of course, in absolutely unforeseen cases. The management knows its own interests only too well not to understand that the more days they leave la Pantaleoni, Tamagno, and Maurel free, the more days will be gained for the opening of *Otello*.

From what I have revealed to you, Maestro, I think that all is going well in accord with your wishes and provisions. I hope, then, to have good news about your arrival right after the end of the year.

Today I am sending you the *complete proofs of Otello! ... Hosanna in excelsis*!! ....

And here I end, without repeating the wishes I had the pleasure to send you a few days ago, but asking your permission for an act that for me will be a happy sign, and that is to embrace you with the full breadth of the heart and soul and with all those feelings of deference, gratitude, and reverence from

Your most devoted
Giulio Ricordi

GIUSEPPINA VERDI TO GIUSEPPE DE SANCTIS

Genoa, 2 January 1887

[. . .] Forgive me if I answer briefly. Apart from the many commitments these days, during which everyone feels obliged to tell us, more or less sincerely, the most lovely, the best things in this world, we are about to leave for Milan. With the preparations for the departure, the instructions to those staying behind, etc., etc., our tongues are hanging out from fatigue, worries, and troubles!

Let's hope things will go well in Milan. For the first, second, and third performances—whether *Otello* goes well or badly—the theatre is sold out, and so sold out that there would be no room for a grain of millet! [. . .]

EUGENIO TORNAGHI TO VERDI

(from London) [about 2 January 1887]

This morning I had a long talk with Mr Harris about *Otello* for Drury Lane. In addition to Maurel, he has engaged Paroli and Navarrini, three of the performers in Milan. Mancinelli would be ready to go immediately to Verdi. Chorus and orchestra are splendid. He has three or four Desdemonas. Tonight the tenor will be proposed. In the telegram he sent to Muzio this morning, Harris told me, he suggested Runcio, who was very successful in *Trovatore* in English on Saturday evening. Mancinelli and I intend to propose De Restke[1] to you, who is much more intelligent. Please see if it might be possible to settle. This would make a very fine impression. Certainly Harris would put it on as he alone can put on operas in England. Upon receiving affirmative replies, he would leave everything that is needed with Mancinelli.

GIULIO RICORDI TO VERDI

Milan, 2 January 1887

Illustrious Maestro,
Forgive me if the many occupations at the end of the year, in addition to official and ceremonial visits, have prevented me from answering you right away.[1] Now I am all yours. *In primis*, I shall be very careful not to contradict you as to your evaluations regarding the success of *Aida*; that would be audacity on my part; I tell you only that the management, Faccio, and all are very content; that the performances are going well, considering that at La Scala the first 15 or 20 days are always very cold, whatever the work, and the attendance light; this is not happening this year; so? [. . .]
Faccio has really worked like . . . . a martyr; so much so that from yesterday on he has begun the rehearsals for *Otello*, with all the other secondary parts, since he is free every day and occupied only at night. Tonight I have a meeting in the costume shop to approve the fabrics, all of which arrived yesterday from Turin; so tomorrow the sewing of costumes will start, since the costume shop has finished the opera and the ballet that must be produced, which is a miracle.
You can imagine with what joy I read the news of your arrival on Tuesday. I shall have the piano (a good one, of course) brought to the rehearsal room; please tell me whether you want a good little upright piano in the drawing room of the Hôtel; I think it will be useful to have it, in case it is needed to try the translation, etc., etc. If this is so please telegraph me so it can be put into place before your arrival, and you will not have the trouble of moving it. Boito is here, always keeping it a secret whether he will go or stay! But

---

[1] The Polish tenor, Jean De Reszke.

[1] To a letter in the Biblioteca Palatina?

however it may be, he will make only one trip and return to Milan right away; I hope to see him today. He has almost finished the third act and tells me that he is content with it. I am glad to read what Du Locle has written to me![1] . . I have already sent what was needed.

The trumpets sent from Brussels work very well. Well, then, bon voyage! . . . . I am happy to say to both of you: till we see each other soon.

Yours most devotedly and gratefully,
Giulio Ricordi

A million thanks to Signora Peppina.
In view of your imminent arrival, I think that sending you the biannual accounting is superfluous——

VERDI TO MARIA WALDMANN

Milan (Albergo Milan) 7 January 1887

Dear Maria,

Your letter[1] arrived only last night, since it was forwarded to me from Genoa.

I have already started rehearsals and hope that we'll be ready by the end of the month. In matters concerning the theatre nothing can be certain, but I repeat that we shall open during the last days of January or the very first of February.

As for the box, Giulio, on my behalf, immediately paid the 1,200 Lire, since it was wise to pay right away. There is a receipt that says for the *first performance* of *Otello*. Send the money to me or to Giulio, or better still, bring it along when you come . . .

Peppina sends you many, many greetings. Regards to your husband, and till we see each other again soon!

G. Verdi

VERDI TO GIUSEPPE PIROLI

[Milan] Sunday . . . [9] January 1887

Poor Arrivabene! He, too, is gone!! I heard of his death straightaway, from a telegram sent to me by his family,[1] that is, by Giovanni.[2] [. . .]

---

[1] Missing.

---

[1] Missing.

---

[1] Missing.
[2] Arrivabene's nephew.

VERDI TO DOMENICO MORELLI

Milan, 11 January 1887

Excuse me, my dearest Morelli, if my many and weighty commitments at present have not permitted me to write to you before now.

For three or four days I have been in possession of the photographs of your magnificent paintings—one more beautiful than the other. But for me the wonder of wonders is the Madonna, whose head is turned upwards among the clouds, and who holds the hand of the child in her own. What pure thought, what poetry, and, to put it better, what divinity there is in that *human* head. I am not playing with words, with 'human' and 'divine'. It's a deep impression I feel in contemplating that woman in human form with the divine expression. [. . .]

VERDI TO MARIA WALDMANN

Milan, 12 January 1887

Dearest Maria,

Yesterday I received the bank check for *1,200* Lire for the box bought for you. I have *endorsed* it to Ricordi, who at this hour will have the exact amount! So we are square, and upon your arrival you will get the key to the box from me or Giulio!

For your information, I hope to open the *29th* or the *30th*. You know, however, that nothing can be certain in this kind of thing. I'm losing no time . . . and am actually going to rehearsals this very moment. [. . .]

TOMMASO SALVINI TO VERDI

Florence, 24 February 1887
Gino Capponi, 17.

Maestro!

The great composer of the lyric *Otello* will be kind enough to the little interpreter of the prose *Otello* to put his signature on the pen and ink portrait by the Pole Sadowsky,[1] which I acquired in New-Jork as a tribute to the great and deeply felt admiration I nourish for all those who raise themselves up as *giants* among the dwarfs of the country. I do not congratulate you on the new triumph you have won! A voice in the desert is not heard, the grain of sand is not found in the sea. You have been, you are, and always will be the same *Verdi*! That says everything! May God keep you for the fatherland, which is in need of *light* in the midst of such low morale.

Yours most affectionately,
Tommaso Salvini

[1] Unknown.

TEATRO ALLA SCALA

17ª Rappresentazione.

Questa sera, Sabato 5 Febbraio 1887 alle 8¼ precise

PRIMA RAPPRESENTAZIONE

del Dramma lirico in 4 atti, versi di A. Boito:

OTELLO

Musica di GIUSEPPE VERDI.

(Proprietà Casa Ricordi)

OTELLO, moro, generale dell'Armata Veneta	Sig.ª	TAMAGNO FRANCESCO
JAGO, alfiere	"	MAUREL VITTORIO
CASSIO, capo di squadra	"	PAROLI GIOVANNI
RODERIGO, gentiluomo veneziano	"	FORNARI VINCENZO
LODOVICO, ambasciatore della Repubblica Veneta	"	NAVARRINI FRANCESCO
MONTANO, predecessore d'Otello nel governo		
dell'isola di Cipro	"	LIMONTA NAPOLEONE
Un ARALDO	"	LACONARSINO ANGELO
DESDEMONA, moglie d'Otello	Sig.ª	PANTALEONI ROMILDA
EMILIA, moglie di Jago	"	PETROVICH GINEVRA

Dopo l'opera si daranno i primi due quadri del ballo di L. Manzotti:

ROLLA

Le Sedie e le Poltrone sono esaurite. - Nella Platea non
vi sono posti in piedi ed il piccolo atrio e chiuso al Pubblico.

PREZZI PER QUESTA SERA

Biglietto d'ingresso alle Sedie ed ai Palchi	. Lire	5
»	»	al Loggione	» 5
»	»	pei sig.ⁱ Militari in uniforme	» 2,50

il Teatro si apre alle ore 7¼   Il Loggione alle ore 7

The poster for the Première of *Otello* in Milan
(Museo Teatrale alla Scala, Milan)

VERDI TO THE PRESIDENT OF THE INTERNATIONAL
ARTISTIC CIRCLE IN ROME

Genoa, 7 March 1887

Several newspapers are announcing that the *International Artistic Circle* is collecting signatures to invite me to Rome for the first performance of *Otello*.[1]

I do not know if this is true, but if it were so, permit me to inform you, Signor President, that I cannot and must not go to Rome under these circumstances.

My presence, from an artistic point of view, would be perfectly useless; why, then, should I go to Rome? ... To display myself? To let myself be applauded?

My feeling is one neither of modesty nor of pride; it is a feeling of personal dignity that I would be unable to renounce.—[...]

GIULIO RICORDI TO VERDI

Milan, 11 March 1887

[...] The performances of *Otello* proceed and resemble each other; it is an incomparable success!! [...]

I have written to Venice for those songs;[1] very difficult to find them; but they managed to track down something, which I shall send in a few days. [...]

VERDI TO GIUSEPPE PIROLI

Genoa, 12 March 1887

[...] I am going to Nervi, where Boito and Du Locle are staying and are still at work. The thing begins to be a little long.[1] [...]

VERDI TO GIULIO RICORDI

[Genoa] Monday [14 March 1887]

Dear Giulio,

Yesterday, descending the long staircase of the Hôtel Eden in Nervi with Boito and Du Locle, I said, 'Here is the set of the 2nd act of *Otello*!'

The lobby of this hotel is grandiose, and most beautiful. It has three great windows; behind them a garden (still young), beyond the garden the sea.

---

[1] At the Teatro Costanzi on 16 Apr. 1887.

---

[1] Verdi considered antique Venetian melodies for the ballet required at the Paris Opéra.

---

[1] Possibly on account of Boito's love affair with Eleonora Duse (see Boito Chronology, 1887).

For *Otello*, therefore: a shallow set, almost down to the curtain, and on the backdrop, many large windows, separated by little Moorish or Venetian columns, etc., etc. Beyond the large windows, a great park with a great square and a great avenue, and smaller streets crossing it.... and plants, plants, plants; the sea, yes or no, as you like. The large glass windows of metallic, very transparent fabric, without fear for the voices! This way the action required by the drama could take place, and the audience would understand, and even hear, that in this moment two events, two actions happen simultaneously: A *feast* for Desdemona, a *conspiracy* between Jago and Otello——

Zuccarelli's set may be as beautiful as you like, but it's still wrong. Give in; I repeat for the thousandth time that in my opinion there is nothing to be made but a glass wall. The big palaces in Venice also have completely transparent reception halls and always with large windows. Finally, to say it all in one word, this scene must present to the audience two distinctly different premises .. *a large park for Desdemona's feast, a lounge for Otello and Jago.* I have said this before.

By God! It's so easy! But I foresee the *ifs* and the *buts*——
In haste addio

G. Verdi

Boito has left——[. . .]

GIULIO RICORDI TO VERDI

Milan, 15 March 1887

Illustrious Maestro,

No sooner did I receive your esteemed letter this morning than I immediately called the scenic designer Zuccarelli, and fortunately he had not yet begun the set for the second act. I have communicated your ideas to him, and I am happy to tell you that I think we shall succeed completely in making the scene as you have indicated. Also, the problem of the gauze as glass has been eliminated by adopting another fabric that will give the idea of windows and remain transparent enough [for one] to make out the garden. So now the scenic designer Zuccarelli is fully persuaded and will do the scene as it must be. I have also seen the *ground plan* for the last scene, with the modifications you suggested, and I think it is all right; I liked the third scene, as well, which he presented to me entirely in a model.

[. . .] Like Diogenes I am always searching for a good Emilia for Rome and Venice! It seems impossible, but it is difficult to succeed in this; but we must succeed; also, we have found a good Rodrigo. I saw Boito this morning, who with great joy brought me the first and fourth acts of the French edition all complete, and I passed them on to the shop straight away. [. . .][1]

---

[1] Other pages of this long letter concern Giulio Ricordi's preoccupation with the complicated reorganization of his firm, which he had discussed during Verdi's recent sojourn in Milan.

VERDI TO THE PARENTS OF CAMILLE BELLAIGUE[1]

[In French]   Genoa, 15 March 1887

Monsieur and Madame Bellaigue,

I am the one who ought to be glad to have made the acquaintance of your son, so frank, so amiable, so lively, and so full of talent. Full of enthusiasm, as all young people should be, he has perhaps seen too much golden colour in this *Otello*, of which he speaks in such an exalted way. But it is certainly not I who must complain about his enthusiasm; on the contrary, I must pay him the warmest and most sincere compliments and thank him for his splendid article in the *Revue des deux mondes*. [. . .][2]

GIUSEPPINA VERDI TO GIUSEPPE DE SANCTIS

Genoa, 21 March 1887

The amount of letters, cards, poems, books, music, etc., etc., sent to Verdi during the past three months is such as to make it impossible to read them, even if one were able to live without sleeping and eating, but could only read continuously!! In this jumble it is possible that your letter might have eluded him and suffered the fate of so many others. Enthusiasm is nice, but when it takes the proportions of—I would almost say—immense and repeated avalanches, the man who is the cause of so much enthusiasm remains almost oppressed and confused in the midst of his satisfaction and gratitude.

Verdi thanks you and sends you his greetings, and have patience if he has not written to you and is not writing directly to you now. Also, at this moment, while I am writing to you, he is busy with the poet who is translating *Otello* into French. [. . .]

VERDI TO GIULIO RICORDI

Genoa, 25 March 1887

Dear Giulio,

I am returning the orchestra score[1] [illegible]. Let them print it (the modern way) with the violins below and the flutes above, etc., etc.

Giulio's father Tito, still officially in charge of the House of Ricordi, was opposed to his son's ideas of keeping pace with new industrial and technical developments. Considering the Maestro 'a second father', Giulio asks him to support his ideas in a letter to his father. There is no record of such a letter, but Verdi himself became a member of the new firm 'G. Ricordi & C.' after Tito's death in 1888.

---

[1] In answer to a missing letter.
[2] See Document VII.

---

[1] Anticipating an early production of *Othello* in French at the Paris Opéra, Ricordi had sent Verdi the orchestra score of *Otello*—presumably a handwritten copy—in which he expected Verdi to include the ballet required by the Opéra. The last word of the first sentence in this letter is underlined. It is illegible, but might suggest 'straight away'.

I would have liked first to take a final look at the orchestra score to see whether any part is incorrect or not quite in order, or whether any connection is bad, etc., etc. I didn't think you'd be so quick.

As for the ballet, or rather, *Divertissement*, why print it?[2] It's a concession (a *lacheté*) that the authors wrongfully make to the Opéra; but artistically it's a monstrosity. In the heat of the action, to interrupt with a ballet!!! The opera must stay as it is, and therefore it's useless to print the ballet.——

Those miserable dances of the seventeenth century are no use to me whatsoever. Still, there must be something a bit closer [to our time]!: What were the *Sarabands*, the *Gavottes*, the *Gigues*, etc.? Can you find them for me? They can be found in Corelli,[3] but they are too well done, too masterly . . . they have never served for dancing!! .

Search, then, and addio

G. Verdi

PS If Boito is in Milan, or when he comes, urge him to come here quickly. Also, the second act is finished,[4] but Boito must see (and approve) the verses of this act.—

Du Locle wants to leave, I must go to St Agata for a few days, and meanwhile Boito is going to dinners! Everything ends in banquets![5] [. . .]

GIULIO RICORDI TO VERDI

Milan, 26 March 1887

[. . .] All right for the orchestra score, and the dances will be made as you wish, that is, written by hand.—For my own benefit, I ask you this: If the dances must serve only for France, I understand that you do not want them in Italian theatres, and that is very well. But the *Russian* Imperial Opera would like to give *Othello* in Russian with the dances. Do you think this might be allowed?—As you know, the Russian translation has already been arranged.—[1]

As soon as I received your telegram[2] I searched for Boito, found him, and telegraphed you.—[3]Boito asks me to tell you that he must stay in Milan only

---

   [2] With great reluctance, Verdi only wrote this ballet seven years later for the first performance of *Othello* at the Opéra on 12 Oct. 1894.
   [3] Arcangelo Corelli (1653–1713), considered the finest composer of Italian instrumental music of his time.
   [4] Of the French translation by Camille Du Locle in nearby Nervi.
   [5] Presumably Boito interrupted his work with Du Locle in Nervi in order to meet Eleonora Duse in Milan.

   [1] The first performance of *Otello* in Italian at the Imperial Opera in St Petersburg was given without the ballet, which Verdi did not write until 1894, on 8 Dec. 1887. The first *Othello* in Russian took place in Moscow on 8 Apr. 1889.
   [2] Possibly in the Biblioteca Palatina.
   [3] Missing.

4 more days, or 5 at the most; he will then again be at your disposal in Genoa. He lets you know *in confidence* that he is working; he did not succeed with Du Locle in translating two phrases he considers very important; he wanted to translate them together with Solanges, who happened to be ill; but today he went back to work. When he goes to Genoa he will compare these two phrases with the translation that has already been made, and he hopes that you will be pleased.

[. . .] On Thursday I went to *Otello* and wrote a few words about it to Signora Peppina.[4] Tamagno and Maurel splendid, as always; chorus and orchestra good. La Pantaleoni steadily getting worse. I am taking steps, have actually taken them!! . . but much diplomacy is needed to succeed in this without bringing about a catastrophe. [. . .]

VERDI TO CARLO D'ORMEVILLE[1]

Genoa, 28 March 1887

Dear Signor D'Ormeville,

It may well be as you say in your telegram,[2] and that is all right.

I regret having to tell you that in spite of your protests it will be impossible for me to go to Rome for *Otello*.

Never, never in my too long career have I presented myself to the audience only to let myself be seen! In this very city of Genoa, where for the revival of my first opera, *Oberto di S. Bonifacio*, at the Carnival of 1840[3] (47 years ago!) I had to assist with the rehearsals from the first to the last, thus assuming responsibility for the performance, it was natural that I faced the judgement of the audience. So I did at that time and so I have done later on, every place and every time, never in any other way.

Signor Canori also knows that, besides having advised him against such a dangerous enterprise, I have told him and repeated to him many, many times that I would never go to Rome under these circumstances, not at any price.

To you, Signor D'Ormeville, I shall repeat the words I spoke to Maestro Marchetti, who in spite of the well-known refusal insisted that I should go to Rome: 'You, who are an artist,' I told him, 'hear a voice in your heart that approves of my resolution!'

With all esteem I am

Most devotedly,
G. Verdi

[4] Missing.

---

[1] The Istituto in Parma dates the autograph of this letter 23 Mar. 1887.
[2] Missing.
[3] At the Carnival of 1841.

CAMILLE BELLAIGUE TO VERDI

[In French]   Paris, 29 March 1887

Dear and great Maestro,

Your letter[1] has overwhelmed me and left me in confusion. But as I said to Madame Verdi, you do not understand all the beauties of *Otello*!!! You pretend that I see too much golden colour in it. Not at all, it is you who do not see in it enough of this colour. Your modesty is unbelievable, and if I were to tell you all that I think of you, I would be scolded.

I am beginning to know *Otello* by heart. I play it wherever I go, and in three weeks or a month from now I shall have large sections of it performed at my house. La Krauss will be Desdemona, the two Reszkés Otello and Jago; we shall also have a good little Cassio, and I hope all will go well, including the pianist, whom you know and who will try to do his best.

[. . .] Thank you again for your letter, and thank you for your benevolence and for your works. I cannot hope to see you in Venice in May; later this summer, when I am at Lake Como, I shall greet you at St Agata, if you permit it.

Please pay my respects to Madame Verdi, and believe me your deeply devoted

                                                   Camille Bellaigue

When you see Boito, reproach him for not writing to me and for not sending me his portrait, as he had promised, and also another portrait! He will know well what I want to say, and you will tell him.

VERDI TO EMANUELE MUZIO

[Genoa] 2 April 1887

After lengthy and, for me, unusual negotiations for *Othello* at the Opéra, I think it would be proper for everyone to come to a solution. If the directors of the Opéra, in addition to so many difficulties, find Madame Caron's voice deteriorated, weak in the low notes, deficient in the top ones, and, what is more, *off pitch*, I cannot and must not insist on engaging an artist who has their complete disapproval.

I don't insist any more; but since I don't find another artist among the personnel of the Opéra who could please me in the part of Desdemona, I charge you to give the directors of the Opéra formal notice that as of this moment all negotiations in regard to *Othello* are broken off.[1] [. . .]

---

[1] Presumably of 15 Mar. to Bellaigue's parents concerning his review of *Otello* (Document VII).

---

[1] These negotiations were resumed only in 1894.

VERDI TO BOITO
[Telegram]

Genoa, 14 April 1887

EXPECTED YOU YESTERDAY—WILL NOT BE IN GENOA TODAY—COME TOMORROW
IF YOU CAN

VERDI

BOITO TO EUGENIO TORNAGHI

Nervi. Eden-Hôtel, 14 April [1887]

[. . .] The translation of *Otello* is completed and transcribed. [. . .]

OSCAR CHILESOTTI TO VERDI

Bassano [Venice], 15 April 1887

[. . .] In accordance with the letter from Signor Giulio Ricordi,[1] who asked me
for ancient Venetian dances for you, I find, after searching through my
papers, two Galliards[2] by two Italian composers who are not at all unknown:
Ortensio Perla of Padua[3] and Pomponio of Bologna.[4]

They are lovely and curious in many ways. I am taking the liberty of
sending them directly to you, in the hope that they may interest you. I did not
publish them in my little book on Besard, since at that time I had not found
the explanation for two misprints in the original. [. . .]

VERDI TO BOITO
[Telegram]

Genoa, 17 April 1887

AND WHEN FOR THE TWO OF YOU[1]

VERDI

---

[1] Missing.
[2] The galliard (*gaillarde* in French) was one of the most popular dances in the sixteenth
century, normally paired with the pavan.
[3] Unknown.
[4] Unknown.

[1] This might suggest an invitation to Boito and Du Locle. Piero Nardi copied this telegram as
well as that of 22 Apr. 1887. The address (Eden Hotel-Nervi), however, disagrees with Nardi's
account of Boito's journey to Nantes for the first French performance of *Méphistophélès* (Nardi,
Vita di Boito, p. 453). The date of this performance was 23 Apr. In all probability, Boito
attended at least the final rehearsals. Presumably, he met Giacosa in Turin during his trip from
Nervi to Nantes, and certainly on his return from Nantes. (Nardi's statement that Boito had not

VERDI TO FRANCO FACCIO

Genoa, 19 April 1887

I thank you for your concern and for the news you give me,[1] but among so many precious sentences, among so many *ifs* and *buts*, I won't know anything until after the sixth performance.

Let's speak of something else. Why did the directors of the theatre in Brescia not consult anyone before arranging for *Otello*?[2] To tell me that it will be splendidly performed is to use a phrase that is of no significance to me. How can the part of Otello be entrusted to someone whom nobody knows except by what has been said about him? A mere debutant will always be impossible for this part! Giulio heard him in a room!! But my God, let's not joke; who is able to judge in such a way? For example: Devoyod had to be the first Jago in the world!! You saw that in Rome! And Lecherie[3] for Jago? No, no . . . that isn't possible! Ah! For three months, and even longer, this *Otello* has given me a lot of trouble! What need was there to publish it! [. . .]

VERDI TO GIULIO RICORDI

Genoa, 22 April 1887

Dear Giulio,

Before Brescia, let's talk about Rome.—Faccio telegraphed me after the second [performance][1] about the good success, without going into details. Other letters, confirming the success, spoke not very favourably of la Gabbi, who despite the freshness of her voice was much, very *much inferior* to la Pantaleoni.[2] From the reports, I had already arrived at the same appraisal, and I don't consider la Gabbi equipped for a subtle part like that of Desdemona. Also, la Pantaleoni, in spite of her dramatic instinct for high-strung parts, could not feel and understand Desdemona. To judge *terre*

---

yet returned from Nantes by 4 Apr. is obviously wrong.) In view of the vicinity of Nervi and Genoa and Verdi's likely awareness of Boito's journey to Nantes, his telegram of 22 Apr. should have been addressed to Nantes rather than Nervi. On 26 Apr. Verdi writes presumably to Milan. Without a doubt, Boito would have seen Verdi in Genoa, had he returned from Nantes via Turin to Nervi. Boito's whereabouts between 14 Apr. and 25 May 1887, however, cannot be completely ascertained. All we know is that he accompanied Rossini's remains from Paris for reburial in Florence on 3 May 1887. (See Boito Chronology, 1887.)

[1] About the first performance of *Otello*—with the Scala ensemble, except for la Pantaleoni—under Faccio on 16 Apr. at the Teatro Costanzi in Rome.
[2] Faccio conducted the first *Otello* in Brescia with a different cast on 11 Aug. 1887.
[3] Paul Lhérie.

[1] Missing.
[2] Romilda Pantaleoni had become ill during the first twenty-five *Otello* performances in Milan, and the Corti brothers, managers of La Scala, threatened her with a lawsuit. Verdi's letter to Giulio Ricordi of 15 May 1887 seems to have prevented it, but in Rome, Venice, and also in Brescia, la Pantaleoni was replaced by Adalgisa Gabbi.

à terre, the character of Desdemona, who allows herself to be mistreated, slapped, even strangled, who forgives and commends herself [to God], seems a bit stupid! But Desdemona is not a woman, she is a type! She is the type of goodness, of resignation, of sacrifice! Such beings are born for others, unconscious of their *own self*! Beings that partly exist and that Shaespeare has put into poetic form and has deified by creating *Desdemona*, *Cordelia*, *Juliet*, etc., etc.—these are types that perhaps can only be compared to the Antigone of the ancient theatre.—

This is the way Desdemona ought to be understood! But who could do it? Goodness knows!!! Perhaps la Teodorini, la Borghi-Mamo, la Ferni!!? They have much talent, and apart from the question of voice and *tessitura*, to them, perhaps, I could make myself clear and make myself understood. And perhaps (this would be even better) they could find out on their own. La Gabbi certainly could not; and therefore her coming here would be useless, above all for such a short time. It would be said: 'The Maestro didn't know how, wasn't able to do her any good!'

So we would have *la Gabbi* in Brescia . . . a little thing!

Leherie[3] affected, with a voice that is no voice!

A debutant!! For that part, a *debutant*?! . Or almost one?! Therefore, in spite of everything, even in spite of a success, *Otello* will never be performed and presented well in Brescia!

But you've gone soft!! Well then, do as you wish, but on one condition: that even if it's a success, no one will come to tell me . . .

'You see, Maestro?!'

By the same token, I'll be generous in case it's a fiasco, and won't say . . . 'You see,' etc.

I'll add a word and will be done: Watch out for la *Gabbi* in Venice! Watch out for *Battistini* in Naples. He, too, cannot be a good Jago. The San Carlo is a most curious theatre, not for intelligence and the greatest musical instinct; but because in that theatre they are now, more than anything, enjoying scandals they themselves are provoking.

And then, the chorus? . . Remember last year's Mass!

Finally, Maurel could really have been engaged at the San Carlo at least for *10* or *12* nights. Think about it! [. . .]

VERDI TO BOITO
[Telegram][1]

Genoa, 22 April 1887

A THOUSAND THANKS—PEPPINA GETTING BETTER[2]—GREETINGS

VERDI

[3] Paul Lhérie.

---

[1] Probably addressed to Nantes.
[2] After her surgery in mid-April, Boito had obviously inquired about her condition.

VERDI TO BOITO

Genoa, Tuesday [26 April 1887][1]

Dear Boito,

I read it in the papers yesterday; and today I received a letter confirming the excellent success of your *Mefistofele* in Nantes.

Wonderful.

Accept the sincere congratulations of your

G. Verdi

Peppina getting better.

VERDI TO GIULIO RICORDI

Genoa, 27 April 1887

[...] In answer to your letter of yesterday,[1] I have direct news about *Oxilia*. Not much voice, not much else! Let's not even talk about la Tetrazzini! . Also, about la Gabbi I have straightforward news (don't think it comes from Faccio), and it isn't very favourable—fresh voice, weak in the middle, and nothing dramatically. Therefore in Brescia it's an absolutely deplorable cast. I said to you, 'you take care of it,' it's true; in spite of this I will say a last word. Since one can only have *Oxilia* and *Leherie*, I would still take la *Pantaleoni* for Desdemona!! La Pantaleoni will always have a greater authority than the others. She has done it for 25 nights at La Scala .... No matter how she may be, I still think she is better than the other ones proposed — — Just leave la Gabbi for Venice, since those gentlemen don't want la Pantaleoni; but believe me, with that company in Brescia la Pantaleoni could be better than all of them — — — Write to me about this matter right away—

I have seen that the Cortis have given up the theatre! They are shrewd!

Don't let yourself be seduced, and whoever the new impresario may be, no *Otello* at La Scala, absolutely not...

Addio, addio

G. Verdi

[1] Presumably, Verdi sent these lines—three days after the first performance of the French *Méphistophélès* in Nantes—to Paris, from where Boito accompanied Rossini's coffin to Florence, arriving there on 2 May. (See Boito Chronology, 1887.)

[1] Missing.

VERDI TO GIULIO RICORDI[1]

Genoa, 29 April 1887

Dear Giulio,

Muzio was here and left again straightaway. We don't need Muzio to know what la Gabbi is like. A mediocre Desdemona. Nothing more ... Everything proves it.

Lately I have wondered whether it might be possible to find a Desdemona to my liking, and la *Teodorini*, la *Borghi-Mamo*, la *Ferni*, etc., etc., occurred to me; but the results of appropriate information from all over are: 'Talent *yes*; voice *no*.' All of them impossible for the part of Desdemona.—Who is left? La Tetrazzini?—La Cattaneo? La Damerini? Blocks of wood, impossible for the portrayal of that most poetic part, one too poetic for hunks of meat without talent. Only la Gabbi would remain! She alone, and mediocre! With all this scarcity, and in spite of everything, I go back to la Pantaleoni. She's not my ideal for Desdemona, and this I have always said, even when you spoke so highly of her to me; but she has qualities, after all, that the others don't have. Now then, I think (always assuming, however, that she regains her health) it would also benefit *Otello* to have her engaged in Brescia. There everything is of modest proportions. There are no giants who could squash each other. *Oxilia, Leehrie, Pantaleoni* form a well-balanced whole. Besides, la Pantaleoni is respected in Brescia, and she may very well have her first success there. You speak of singing off pitch! But she has always sung off pitch; and that has never prevented her successes. Besides, by engaging la Pantaleoni for Brescia a *cruel act* would be redressed, one which circumstances might have demanded, but which was a *cruel act* all the same; it could have and should have been avoided or mitigated!

. . . .

You trust your judgement when hearing voices in a room?!! I for one have never understood anything in a room!

I care very little whether the Cortis return to La Scala or not. Perhaps they're no worse than the others; but it is certain, more than certain, that they, too, don't know how to form companies, prepare performances, and put together a season. This occurred last year; the same thing happened this year! They got away with it, it's true ... but only just, and they deserve no credit for that at all!

I wish *Otello* in Naples would come to naught[2]. You are quite wrong if you believe you can establish reforms from now up until the Carnival [season]. I know that town very well. There are so many obstacles that a reform is impossible! Remember the performances of the *Mass* and of *Mefistofele*! .. Truly the fault was general!—Besides, what need is there to give *Otello* in Naples? Beware of the so-called first theatres that have many pretensions and

---

[1] See draft of this letter in *Carteggi* iv. 87–8.
[2] The first performance of *Otello* in Naples was given at the San Carlo on 4 February 1888.

insufficient means. At La Scala itself not everything was good ... Badly conceived *sets*, badly organized *staging* ... The *fire* of joy ... *The ship*, the storm, etc., etc., very, very poor ... and on and on!—Poor Otello! I am sorry that he came into the world ... The success? What does it matter to me! Amen.

Answer me right away, since on Monday I'll probably go to St Agata. Addio, addio

G. Verdi

PS Peppina is all right. She is up and sends you her regards.

. . . .

. . . .

PS I had forgotten the bundle containing Act II of *Otello*! I'll do it, I'll do it .. though reluctantly![3]

VERDI TO ROMILDA PANTALEONI

[Genoa; after 29 April 1887][1]

The sad case that strikes you causes me grief, too, and since you speak to me with such frankness about very delicate matters, don't take it amiss if I answer with equal frankness.

You definitely did not feel well in Milan; I was aware of this from the very first rehearsals, I was at first alarmed by it, but after thinking about [it] and considering everything, I was determined to stay calm, to remedy every inconvenience as much as I could, and to go on *coûte qui coûte* to the end. For that matter, I did not reveal my anticipations and my doubts to anyone, not even to Faccio.

The audience was courteous, but don't be deceived by the kindnesses shown on the last night. Grateful for the past, it wanted to be dignified and well behaved; it was so, and that is all right.

But after you have fulfilled this engagement at La Scala, it would be most dangerous to undertake others. Just imagine the disapproval in Rome or, more likely, in Venice! What a scandal, and what damage! Therefore I approve of the decent and honest decision that you have made to resign.

Perhaps it would have been even better if on the last five nights, when you yourself said that you were not feeling well, you yourself had declared: I am not well, but I will sing until the end in order to hurt no one; and if you had requested absolute rest and a release from Rome and Venice.[2]

---

[3] A revision of the end of Act II. Julian Budden, *The Operas of Verdi* (3 vols; London: Cassel; New York: Oxford University Press, 1973–81), iii. 370, describes this change, pointing out that the original version still exists in later piano–vocal scores.

[1] Undated draft.

[2] On 17 May 1887, the first performance of *Otello* in Venice took place at the Teatro Fenice under Faccio's baton, as in Rome with the Scala cast except for la Pantaleoni, replaced by la Gabbi.

Such a gesture would have been very nice! Anyway, the result is the same, and as great as the damage might be at present, it is but momentary.

Think now only of getting well, and don't be angry with anyone. *Stay calm and rest until you feel completely restored; I say *completely*, and don't let yourself be misled by any *perhaps*, *buts*, or *ifs*.

Recover completely, and then, when you return to the stage with one of your favourite operas, your health and voice being restored, you will again be the distinguished artist you have been.

Forgive this frank language. I could not do otherwise; anyway, I think I am giving you a proof with this of the esteem and friendship I feel for you.[3]

VERDI TO FRANCO FACCIO

Genoa, 29 April 1887

I deplore, deeply deplore what has happened! Let's for a moment draw a veil over this painful event and speak to each other openly and with sincerity. I don't know whether la Pantaleoni has spoken to you of a letter of mine in answer to one from her. Perhaps I told her some not very agreeable things, but I thought that I should tell her everything that seemed just and true to me.

I shall do the same with you. You cannot be unaware that when *Otello* came about, I said that I did not think la Pantaleoni, an excellent artist in what I would call high-strung parts, would be suitable for the part of Desdemona. La Bellincioni (a new Patti, they said!!) was proposed to me. I went to Milan to hear her; I did not approve of her, and that same night, in the corridor of the third tier, I said precisely these words to Giulio and Corti: 'Settle your programme and engage la Pantaleoni. With her and with Tamagno you can have a repertory, even without *Otello*! ... *Otello* will be given or not be given; it makes little difference ...'

La Pantaleoni was engaged. For some time there was no more talk of *Otello*. You know what happened later on. You came to St Agata; la Pantaleoni came with Giulio for 48 hours; finally la Pantaleoni alone. Even though I was always of the opinion that Desdemona did not suit her, by studying the part, I hoped, she would be particularly successful in the solo of the third [act] finale and in the duet of the same act, even more so than in the fourth act. La Pantaleoni herself was hoping for this success and missed it! ...

When we arrived at the first rehearsals at La Scala I became aware of a deficiency I had not noticed at St Agata: the break in the voice. I did not write about this to la Pantaleoni. Being a bit familiar with the theatre and with voices, I became seriously alarmed by this, and worried for several days. I

---

[3] On the same page of this draft Verdi wrote:
  1. Concerning Peppina's operation: 'I have spent two terrible days of anxiety, but now I am—in fact, we are—content. [. . .]'
  2. To the management of the theatre in Brescia: 'Grave domestic worries' upset him, but for *Otello* he requests artists, in whom he has complete faith.

seriously pondered what should be done, and among the many thoughts that ran through my head, I resolved not to say anything to anybody, to continue the rehearsals, to stay calm (and I managed to do this, although with some difficulty), and to endure everything that was not to my liking . . .

The moment came and went well! In spite of this, let's not have any illusions, la Pantaleoni did not do well. I'm not talking to you just about the voice, which by nature has always been flat; but she recovered when she reached the top notes, which became ringing and beautiful. Not so now. Also in the top notes, the voice remains tight and thin. Well, then! . . . as I wrote to her, I think a rest is absolutely necessary! She must remain calm, tranquil, without anger, without agitation; and when she regains her strength and her voice, no one can prevent her from resuming her career. You see things in too grim a light to speak of a broken career. No, she can return to the theatre with the operas she considers most suitable to her voice and her way of feeling; and since you believe that I can be useful to her, I give you my solemn and sincere word that I will do what is possible to fulfil your wishes. [. . .]

VERDI TO FRANCO FACCIO

Genoa, 1 May 1887

I don't know what impression my letter of the day before yesterday might have given you. I thought that I should not conceal anything and should say everything I considered to be the pure truth. Nothing else, nothing else. It is possible that the Cortis have written to la Pantaleoni about some performances of *Gioconda* in Venice! I am anxious to tell you that I have not advised [them to make] this proposition, that I have nothing to do with it, and that it is not what I would have, and have, requested for her. This may serve for your guidance. [. . .]

VERDI TO GIULIO RICORDI[1]

Genoa, 1 May 1887

Dear Giulio,

This isn't a matter of a 'kind heart',[2] but of redressing in some way a cruel act, as I have said! It's an act in which I myself can be suspected of having taken part; and I am anxious to clear things up.

You, it's true, were severe towards la Pantaleoni at the beginning, severe to the point of being unfair; but later, when I had heard la Bellincioni and in your presence had advised Corti not to engage la Pantaleoni for *Otello*, but to form a company and establish a repertoire, 'with or without *Otello* . . . it matters little,' as I said, you told me that I could not have found anyone better than la Pantaleoni, and you yourself refused [to give] *Marion*[3]—I don't

---

[1] Presumably in answer to a missing letter of 30 Apr.
[2] Romilda Pantaleoni's replacement.
[3] *Marion Delorme* by Ponchielli.

recall for which theatre—without this artist! At that time I was the only one who did not believe in la Pantaleoni for Desdemona; but after considerations, observations, regards, etc., etc., etc., I made the mistake of giving *Otello* at La Scala and of tolerating many, many things (and there were many) that were not to my liking! [It's] always so.

You tell me, 'Once la Pantaleoni has been accepted in Brescia she can no longer be refused in any other theatre'?!! Well, then?.. If she is successful and regains her former voice, what harm would there be? Despite all the scarcity of artists we'll have yet another Desdemona, and I will say as you once did that 'You won't find anyone better', apart from la Gabbi, who, as I see it, will be the perpetual, inevitable Desdemona!.. But what others?

Do what you think best for *Gioconda* in Venice, but under those conditions I wouldn't blame la Pantaleoni if she didn't accept. But do what you think best.—As for Naples, the second cast in Brescia has been re-engaged! Why are they planning *Otello*? I am sorry you don't believe in what I told you seriously. I repeat, nobody can make general reforms in that theatre. It's organized that way, and so it must be, and so it will be. I do not approve at all, not at all, of *Otello* at the San Carlo in Naples.

Not tomorrow, but only on Tuesday, shall I go to St Agata, where I'll arrive about 4 p.m. and can receive the post about 5 o'clock. I mention this for your information.

Peppina still well.

Addio, addio

G. Verdi

GIULIO RICORDI TO VERDI

Milan, 2 May 1887

Illustrious Maestro,

I received your esteemed letter of yesterday, and, as you indicate to me, I answer by writing to you at Busseto—and by asking you to let me know whether it is all right for me to propose la Pantaleoni for Brescia straightaway, as I mentioned to you in my previous letter. When you rightly found la Bellincioni vocally deficient, in truth only la Pantaleoni remained and was free of engagements; but who could foresee the condition of her health and voice?... When she sang at La Scala two seasons earlier, she was not so, and for all her defects of intonation, she had a strong and penetrating voice, was sure of herself, and evidently was not as worried as she is now; therefore I thought I could tell you in good conscience that nothing better would be found among the available artists—and no one, I repeat, could foresee her present condition from one year to another. But I certainly do not want and must not discuss this matter today; and I can only say with you that nothing better can be found for another Desdemona; so I await only your definite approval to propose la Pantaleoni's engagement in Brescia. Among good artists for this part, I think la Teodorini would succeed, but she is still engaged abroad; and la Borghi-Mamo, if she took a rest, would have all the qualities of voice and talent for this part. She is a little ugly, it is true, but on stage she is right! .... for example, she, and she alone, was so fascinating in the part of Elena in *Mefistofele*, which should also require a beautiful face! ... so that it remains a mystery to me that she was able to make [the audience] shout with enthusiasm!! ... me included.

As for *La gioconda* in Venice, I thought that I did well to telegraph the Cortis to find out at least if the negotiations with la Pantaleoni were continuing or not.

Let me say, Maestro, that I am extremely mortified and very saddened by what you write to me regarding Naples! ... But how can you think, even for a single moment, that anyone in the firm would have made even the slightest commitments without your permission? ..... When Villani put in for the San Carlo and asked to plan *Otello*, I mentioned it to you right away, during your sojourn here in Milan. You did not object, but only mentioned the need for an absolute improvement of the whole company and called to mind the obligation of the *diapason*; and this was done, in so far as by authorizing Villani to propose *Otello*, all conditions regarding the performance were stated; the obligation of the *diapason* and of the reform of the whole company was imposed; later, during the negotiations, in every telegram to Villani I did not fail to keep hammering away at these *absolute* conditions, without which nothing would be concluded. I know very well not only the actual obligations, but also the moral ones, which for me are greater, and because of which no commitment could be made for *Otello* unless you were first consulted. So it was done for Naples, and, if you recall, even Maestro Gialdini[1] was discussed, who had to hear the opera in the theatre, as you said; and so it was done, since he went to Rome.

Villani will come to Milan, after all, now that you have decided against his theatre; I shall hear from him what he intends to do regarding the whole company, and I shall take care to inform you right away. You will see whether the guarantee he may make is sufficient, and [you will see] what modifications will be necessary, and they will be made; and if they are not made, so much the worse for the management. Certainly this *Otello* is the only chance the San Carlo, too, has to come up with something good. I remember the successes of *Don Carlo* and *Aida*!! ... But it is true that at that time a certain person was present who makes the crippled walk upright and the blind see![2] .... But you, who know him so well, will also know if it is possible to take on a similar project!! ... ?? ....

Unfortunately I must be away for two days, having been unable to get out of repeated invitations from Florence; but I shall be back on Wednesday evening and shall thus again be ready to receive your orders, which I

---

[1] Gialdino Gialdini (1843–1919). Neapolitan conductor and composer of operas between 1886 and 1910.

[2] In reference to Verdi's personal staging of those operas at the San Carlo in 1872–3.

anxiously await. Meanwhile I hope you will let me know that you had a good stay at St Agata; please tell me also when you will be back in Genoa, and whether you will be staying there for some time yet.

Accept, Maestro, all my devotion, while I remain always

> Yours most gratefully and most devotedly,
> Giulio Ricordi

The engraver in Leipzig asks me for the bundles containing the second act which we are still withholding; I am answering that for now the third and fourth are complete and that the end of the second will be sent later.[4]

VERDI TO GIULIO RICORDI

Genoa, 2 May 1887

Dear Giulio,

Today I am sending the *Stretta* of the second [act] finale.[1]

Of course, the first one will now become better.

See to it that it is performed in Venice; and tell Faccio that he shouldn't say anything to anybody, since perhaps no one will be aware of it. Otherwise *they will shout* that I have redone *Otello*!!

I don't know Bottesini's address in London. Your correspondent there will know it; ask him to forward it [the letter] to him straightaway.[2]

Addio, addio

> G. Verdi

VERDI TO GIULIO RICORDI

St Agata, 5 May 1887

Dear Giulio,

In a few moments I leave for Genoa! Having received your letter of the *2nd*, I think it will be good from every point of view to propose la Pantaleoni for Brescia; first, however, ask Faccio about the state of la Pantaleoni's health and voice. If you don't want to do this, I will; in which case give me Faccio's address.

Ah, this Desdemona is quite a difficult part, and I dreamt of artists of talent, or at least of instinct, for this part, and I don't see them and don't find them! Muzio writes to me that la Gabbi (in good voice) sings the Willow

[4] Ricordi had not yet received the new end of Act II mentioned in Verdi's letter to him of 29 Apr. and in the following one.

---

[1] See Verdi to Ricordi, 29 Apr. 1887.
[2] Dissatisfied with the playing of the double-basses in the fourth act of *Otello*, Verdi had asked his friend, the double-bass virtuoso, composer, and conductor of *Aida* in Cairo, Giovanni Bottesini for advice. (See Verdi to Ricordi, 22 May 1887.) Verdi's letter to Bottesini and Bottesini's answer are missing.

Song badly ... she hurries the first triplet too much and holds the final *C*
following *F* too long. The usual *provincialisms* of those who have no talent.
For this part I wanted either la *Teodorini* or *Borghi-Mamo* or *Turolla* or
perhaps *Ferni*, who have instinct; but everybody gives me the saddest
information about their voices.

Poor Desdemona!

Now we come to Naples!!!!!! [...] *Otello in Naples is a fiasco!!*—In music
the Neapolitans are the French of Italy .. 'We are we ... Here music was
born ... Here we can do it as well as elsewhere ... in fact, much better!' Note
that ... 'elsewhere!!'—[...]

VERDI TO GIULIO RICORDI[1]

Genoa, 11 May 1887

Dear Giulio,

Alas, alas! . The business in London[2] causes me real displeasure. Poor
[illegible]! Poor *Otello*! ... — And when another great personality asks you
for other pieces will you have the guts to refuse? — I would definitely deny it
... but I don't want to jeopardize your publishing interests ... so do as you
think best.—

Otello in Parma in September is real madness! In September?[3] Did I
understand well? .. But as you say, an answer can wait until after Brescia.

And as to Brescia, the Pantaleoni business absolutely must be straightened
out. Corti protesting her, 'because you refuse' [to let him have] the score, is
an ugly thing! *An error* has been committed from the beginning, and it must
be remedied. It's justice! And on the other hand: it can also be in our own
interest to have la Pantaleoni as Desdemona! [...] From all the reports I
have, la Gabbi is absolutely not a good Desdemona. Mediocre; nothing
more.— 'The *Ave Maria*?' you will say! .. My God! But the effect there stems
from the mutes that make the audience so deaf [to what it hears] that it no
longer understands the deficiencies of the composition and execution. Ask
the many Neapolitans who went to hear her in Rome, and they will tell you
few goods things about her weak and insecure voice even in the middle
register.—Ask the many people in Milan who went to Rome, and they will
tell you that they were rather dissatisfied with la Gabbi. Ask also Tamagno
and Maurel, and if you can make them talk, they, too, won't have many good
things to say about her. In short, the true Desdemona has yet to be found.
The only capable ones would still be Teodorini, Borghi-Mamo, Turolla, but
the reports about their voices are very bad! For me the only excellent one
would be la Ferni. La Ferni can sing, and she sings more than all the others.
Desdemona is a part in which the thread, the melodic line never ceases from

---

[1] Apparently in answer to a missing letter.
[2] See Eugenio Tornaghi's undated letter to Verdi of Jan. 1887. Faccio conducted the first
Otello in England at the Lyceum Theatre in London on 5 July 1889.
[3] Faccio conducted the first *Otello* in Parma on 14 Sept. 1887.

the first note to the last. Just as Jago has only to declaim and *ricaner*, and just as Otello, now the warrior, now the passionate lover, now crushed to the point of baseness, now ferocious like a savage, must sing and shout, so Desdemona must always, always sing. So I have done it, so I would do it again in spite of the learned precepts of the critics. I repeat, Desdemona sings from the first note of the recitative, which is also a melodic phrase, until the last note of '*Otello non uccidermi*' ['*Otello, do not kill me*'] . . . which is also a melodic phrase. Therefore the most perfect Desdemona will always be the one who sings the best. [. . .] My conclusion for Desdemona: 1. La Ferni—2. La Pantaleoni, if recovered—3. La Gabbi. [. . .]

VERDI TO GIULIO RICORDI

Genoa, 15 May 1887

Dear Giulio,

I was writing to you just as your telegram[1] arrived.

Apart from faults and reasons on the part of everyone: my first, only, and invariable opinion is that this lawsuit should be stopped.

It will be ugly to retell in court how la Pantaleoni was prevented from going to Rome!

Ugly to tell how, although ill, she sang the last five performances of *Otello* in order to keep the management from losing about 600,000 Lire; and out of gratitude the Cortis bring a suit against her! I understand that one must be rather naïve to believe in the gratitude of impresarios, but even so, this thing is very ugly! On the other hand, this suit, which you describe as indecent, I find only deplorable. If la Pantaleoni, with contract in hand, and believing herself recovered, presents herself to her impresario, saying 'I am ready,' and the impresario responds by bringing an action against her, it is the management that causes the suit, and it is in the wrong.

To sum up, I am still of the opinion [that it is best] to start new procedures and to telegraph Faccio about this matter. Fix things, fix them! . . .

We leave tomorrow, Monday, and we'll be in St Agata by 4. Peppina is well and sends her regards to all.

Addio, addio

G. Verdi

VERDI TO ROMILDA PANTALEONI[1]

Genoa, 15 May 1887[2]

Pardon you?!! But dear Signora Romilda, there is nothing to pardon! If you are the victim of a lawsuit, one that I deplore and that you could not

---

[1] Missing.

[1] In answer to a missing letter.
[2] The date given by Giuseppe Morazzoni (15 Mar. 1887) is in error. He obviously read 'Marzo' instead of 'Maggio'.

avoid, it's not your fault at all. Moreover: even if you yourself had brought this suit, I would not reproach you, for if I were in your shoes I myself might have done the same, even if convinced that it would not have done any good.

I understand everything: I understand how great your sorrow must be; but you, who did not bend before so much humiliation—which (as you say) proved no stronger than you—will find the strength in your nature to fight against this blow which strikes you so unmercifully. Don't let yourself be knocked down and don't speak of an irreparable collapse. This is certainly a difficult moment, but no one can know what will happen tomorrow! Who ever knows! . . .

Peppina is most grateful and sends you her most cordial greetings. Tomorrow we leave for St Agata, where I hope to find the tranquillity I have been seeking for more than four months.

Affectionately I take your hands.

> Most devotedly,
> G. Verdi

GIULIO FERRARINI TO GIULIO RICORDI

> Parma, 16 May 1887

Illustrious Signor Commendatore
Giulio Ricordi
Milan
Most illustrious Signore,

On behalf of the Communal Authority of this city, I am honoured to address this letter to you, which follows the telegram of the day before yesterday.

In the unceasing desire to give *Otello* on the stage of this Royal Theatre next September, there are two possibilities that could facilitate the agreement:

1. Delay the opening of the Exhibition.
2. Put on another opera before the first performance of *Otello*.

I ask Your Honour to consider these two likely circumstances and to inform me in the meantime whether—if one or the other were possible—the company performing the opera by Verdi in Brescia would *definitely be approved* for Parma, as well. [. . .][1]

> Your most obedient servant,
> Giulio Ferrarini

[1] Giulio Ricordi annotated this letter: 'To be safe, I'll inform the Maestro that in Parma they believe even now that la Gabbi will sing in Brescia. In case, I'll ask him to tell me which rule to follow if they propose la Gabbi—only, of course, if the Maestro considers negotiations convenient.'

GIULIO RICORDI TO VERDI

Milan, 18 May 1887

Illustrious Maestro,

After a few days of tranquillity I cannot help disturbing you today with the enclosed;[1] would you be kind enough to tell me how I should act and what replies I should give in the matter.

Regarding the Pantaleoni affair in Venice, I am now awaiting other replies, having written again on this matter.[2]

In a few days I shall send you a part of the printed proofs of the first act orchestra score; I hope a truly beautiful edition will come out.

After sending you the telegram this morning,[3] I had three others from Venice, all unanimous in announcing a great, immense success. Theatre not full, however, because the prices are considered too high!! The management says, on the other hand, that it cannot lower them; but I think it would be in its best interest to reduce them. [. . .]

VERDI TO GIULIO RICORDI

St Agata, 19 May 1887

[. . .] Ah, this *Otello* gives me great troubles! And I almost curse the moment I gave it away! On my desk it was a consolation, and now it is hell!

A bad project, that one in London! The worst, the one in Parma. I didn't know it would be for an exhibition! There's nothing worse than giving a new or important opera during an exhibition.[1] People are tired, or they don't come, or they yawn! The impresarios always make a bad calculation and do bad business during an exhibition! You see an example in Venice! The saying 'because of the price' doesn't hold. No, the reason is very different. I for my part am most displeased with the success in Venice! The first, the one and only barometer of success is the box-office! By God, the preceding [performances] in Milan and Rome weren't good enough to fill the theatre in Venice!

Getting back to Parma, I think I prefer London, though with a heavy heart. And if you grant it, mind you well, I don't want to talk with Mancinelli or with anybody else. Do as you wish and leave me in peace. What do you want me to tell you? I was displeased with the *mise-en-scène* and with many musical matters in Milan. A little better, but very little, in Rome. Now I'm most distressed by this . . . . . 'success' in Venice. So do, do, do, and addio.

G. Verdi

---

[1] The preceding letter.
[2] Missing.
[3] Missing.

---

[1] Apparently, Verdi had not forgotten the lukewarm reception of his *Don Carlos* on 11 Mar. 1867 during the exhibition of that year in Paris.

VERDI TO CESARE VIGNA

St Agata, 22 May 1887

[...] I know about *Otello* in Venice ... An evening within the family! ... That's all right. If the public didn't hurry to the first performance, it means that in Venice there wasn't the trust that, for example, existed in Milan. And there were no preceding [performances] in Milan! [...]

VERDI TO GIULIO RICORDI

St Agata, 22 May 1887

Dear Giulio,

Again about *Otello*!! So we'll never be finished with this damned Moor!

Realizing that everybody's out of tune, and the double-basses worst of all, I am sending the fingerings (which are Bottesini's!!); put them in the score, then, and put the enclosed card[1] in the original so that I can write them into the original the next time I come to Milan.

The barometer[2] is doing well now; but who will compensate me for the first [performance].—

In haste addio, addio

G. Verdi

VERDI TO BOITO

St Agata, 24 May 1887

Dear Boito,

Du Locle has accepted his half (*5,000* fr.) of the sum I offered to you and to him *sur vos droits d'auteur* of the *Otello* translation. If you accept the other half, as I offered you before, I would be most happy and, as I've said already, *more calm*! ... So write to me *yes* and I will have your *5,000* Lire paid to you right away![1]

Peppina is getting better; actually I can say she is cured. I'm spending my time going up and down the fields, cursing this horrible weather ... but after all, after four months of ... I am calm and can breathe.

I take your hand and say addio.

Your
G. Verdi

---

[1] This card is missing and Bottesini's fingerings for the solo passage of the double-basses in Act IV do not appear in the Ricordi orchestra score (PR 155). Whether or not Verdi wrote them into his autograph score, as he intended, is still to be investigated. Today's double-bass players can no longer appreciate the problem.

[2] The box-office receipts at the Teatro Fenice in Venice, where six performances of *Otello* took place.

---

[1] No correspondence between Verdi and Du Locle pertaining to this arrangement has been found.

BOITO TO VERDI

Milan, 26 May [1887][1]

Dear Maestro,

Since you so desire, and since Du Locle has accepted, I reply: *Amen* and thank you.

If I didn't reply in this way I think I would appear to be haughty towards you (which isn't possible) and also towards my collaborator. Therefore I accept the good and kind offer you have made me. I appreciate your scruples about this kindness, but I insist that they are scruples. I accept under the conditions that were established on the page you wrote from Genoa.[2] May your will be done, then, in everything.

I'm glad about the good news regarding Signora Giuseppina, who refuses to believe that I will visit St Agata; but I'll make her a believer before the summer is over.

At present the summer is cold and rainy.

Well, then, Otello triumphs in his adopted country, too, in front of the real Lion of S. Marco. And he will continue his great flight into space and time more than the human mind can foresee.

Dear Maestro, stay healthy and strong and happy, and continue to care for me a little bit.

Your most affectionate,
Arrigo Boito

Most cordial greetings to Signora Peppina.

Yesterday I had dinner with Morelli, that great artist and sympathetic man, and our talk was about only one thing. Morelli will stay in Milan for several days; he's here as a member of the Commission for the façade of the Cathedral.

VERDI TO BOITO

St Agata, 27 May 1887

Dear Boito,

Ricordi will pay you on my account *5,000* fr. I say *francs*, that is to say, the equivalent of 250 gold Napoleons.

All you need do is declare to the agent of your *Droits d'auteur* in Paris (I imagine it's Roger) that when *Othello* is performed in France, your *Droits d'auteur* for the translation belong to me up to the sum of 5,000 fr. Amen.

When we get to the end of the summer I'll be able to tell if you're a man who keeps his word. Give my very, very best to Morelli, really a great artist.

Oh, if he . . . !

---

[1] Postmark: MILANO 26/5/87.
[2] Missing.

Oh, if you . . . !
St Agata! You can arrive at Fiorenzuola at 2 p.m. and be at St Agata by 4!
Addio, addio. Greetings from Peppina. I take your hand.

G. Verdi

BOITO TO VERDI

30 May [1887]
Milan

Dear Maestro,
Now you can sleep peacefully. Tornaghi delivered the 250 twenty-franc
pieces to me today. If you, good and dear Maestro, had all of them, as well as
Du Locle's, on your stomach, I assure you it would be some weight. A weight
to make your pockets burst, literally, I say, and that's not just an expression.
Thank you again with all my heart. But now this *Othello* must really go
well in France; otherwise I'll be in your debt for those five thousand francs
for all eternity, and that weight on your stomach will be passed on to me. I've
tried to lure Morelli to St Agata, but until now he has resisted, suffering like
his S. Antonio.[1]
I'll try to tempt him once more.
I'm sending you a copy of the letter I have written regarding the *Droits
d'auteur*.[2] I hear that Maestro Muzio is in Milan, and I've told Tornaghi to
ask him to convey this letter himself to the appropriate person.
Affectionate greetings to you and Signora Giuseppina.

Your
Arrigo Boito

ENCLOSURE
[In French]   Milan 30 May 1887
Monsieur . . . . .
Having received from Maestro G. Verdi an advance of 5,000 francs for my part of
the French translation of *Otello*, I ask you, cher Monsieur, to transfer to Maestro
Verdi my *Droits d'auteur* for *Othello* when this opera is performed in France, up to the
above-stated sum of 5,000 francs.
You would greatly oblige me by taking note of this declaration, cher Monsieur, and
please forgive the trouble I am causing you.
Believe me, etc., etc.

AUGUSTE VACQUIRIE TO VERDI
[Telegram, in French]

Paris, 30 May 1887

THE COMMITTEE OF THE PRESS FOR THE VICTIMS OF THE OPERA-COMIQUE ASK YOU
KINDLY TO GIVE YOUR CONSENT FOR THE PERFORMANCE OF THE CREDO FROM

---

[1] A painting by Domenico Morelli.
[2] Printed after the text of this letter.

OTELLO—MAUREL HAS OFFERED TO SING IT—AT THE SAME TIME CAN YOU ASK SIGNOR RICORDI TO LEND US THE ORCHESTRA PARTS WHICH HE SHOULD SEND TO PARIS—YOUR GENEROUS CO-OPERATION FOLLOWING SUCH A DISASTER[1] WOULD BE PARTICULARLY PRECIOUS TO US

    PRESIDENT OF THE COMMITTEE VACQUIRIE—DIRECTOR OF THE RAPPEL
    SECRETARY CARTHEUR MEYER—DIRECTOR OF THE GAULOIS

VERDI TO AUGUSTE VACQUIRIE
[Telegram, in French]

[Busseto, 31 May 1887][1]

MAUREL IS WRONG—ERROR TO SELECT THIS PIECE OUT OF CONTEXT IN A FOREIGN LANGUAGE—BUT UNDER THE CIRCUMSTANCES I CANNOT REFUSE CONSENT—AM WRITING RICORDI IN THIS REGARD ALTHOUGH RICORDI AS REAL PROPRIETOR CAN REFUSE

VERDI

VERDI TO GIULIO RICORDI

[St Agata] 31 May 1887

Dear Giulio,

Here you have the telegram I received from Paris and here is my reply.

The circumstances are so grave that I do not think it possible to refuse. You, however, in spite of everything, are still the proprietor. Artistically this is certainly a very, very ugly thing! Damnedest *Otello* (and I say this with all my heart) how many troubles! How many troubles! If only I had never written it. Addio

G. Verdi

FRANCESCO TAMAGNO TO VERDI

Milan, 7 June 1887

Dear Maestro,

I received your most precious letter of the 30th of last month[1] after a short delay, since it had to be forwarded to me in Milan on account of my early departure from Venice.

First of all, permit me to thank you for your kind and speedy reply, and allow me also to tell you that if I was mistaken about the circumstances, the

---

[1] 131 persons had perished in a fire on 25 May.

---

[1] This date is inferred from the letter that follows.

---

[1] Missing.

fact is, however, that someone is attempting to defame me to you, for what reason I do not understand.

I gather this from your last words, which report that you were told that on the nights of my successes I exaggerated some sounds to the point of making them *no longer musical*.

Well then, Maestro, I have done neither more nor less in Venice than I did first in Milan and then in Rome; and frankly I think that as for the voice (I say this because I do not ascribe it to merit) nature has treated me well enough not to have to resort to forcing of this kind!

As for the artistic part, I have always and everywhere done my best, and I will always try to be as worthy as I can be of the art I profess; and also on this point, my illustrious Maestro, since I have been accepted as your interpreter, your flattering words on my behalf—while they keep me from being too modest—show me the path I must follow and from which I do not think I have strayed.

I do not speak of my indisposition on the last night in Venice; I think it would be unworthy of you for me to tell you how such a thing can happen to an artist even a hundred times greater than I without his artistic value being lessened.

There remains to be considered the extreme maliciousness of the kind of Jago[2] that takes pleasure in putting me so charitably in ill-repute; but Jago is essentially honest, and rather than direct his artistic observations to me, trying for the sake of art to correct the defects that I might have, he prefers instead to make his poison work near you.

I think, however, I would be offending my dignity if I were serious in revealing these insinuations; and only the fear that they could take root in your mind compels me to bother you with my letters and to try to set things straight.

I am sure that your good sense and sound judgement will absolve me; meanwhile, greeting you with affectionate respect, I beg you to keep me in your precious benevolence and declare myself

Yours most devotedly,
Tamagno, Francesco

BOITO TO VERDI

[Milan?] 9 June [1887][1]

Dear Maestro,

Here is a letter from our able English translator,[2] Signor Hueffer, the reporter for *The Times*, whom you know. He suggests that we adopt the Latin text for the first part of Desdemona's Ave Maria, where the words are

---

² Victor Maurel.

---

¹ The year corresponds to the first edition of *Otello* in English translation (July 1887).
² Missing.

whispered on the repeated   ♭𝅗𝅥   . Then the English version would start again, where the prayer expands, taking on an entirely personal religious character. I like the idea. See if it appeals to you, and please let me know your opinion so that I can send it on to the translator.[3]

The contrast between Latin and English would, I think, help to enhance the dramatic and musical concept of this episode.

I was pleased to hear that Jago's Credo would not appear in the evening [concert] at the Opéra.[4] It would have been a big mistake.

Most cordial greetings to the inhabitants of St Agata, among whom I'll soon be for a few days. An affectionate handshake

from your
Arrigo Boito

VERDI TO BOITO

[St Agata] *Sunday* [12 June 1887][1]

I'm waiting for you. Write to me or send me a telegram when you'll be arriving at Fiorenzuola (day and hour), and I'll send one of my Bucephali to bring you to St Agata.

Addio, addio, addio

Your
G. Verdi

VERDI TO GIUSEPPE PIROLI

Milan, 28 June 1887

Our illustrious Mancini wrote to me eight or ten days ago recommending the conductor Mascheroni. Not knowing Mascheroni, I had to reply to Mancini (and I was sorry) that I could not comply with this request. Now a very intelligent and serious person here has openly told me about Mascheroni's qualities and defects: 'Suddenly emerged with little experience on the conductor's chair, he is a bit hotheaded and thinks a little too highly of himself. He neglects [the opportunity to reach] an understanding with the singers, the so-called *piano* rehearsals. and prefers to take care of the orchestra.'

This is a very grave fault!! There can be no good performance if early rehearsals with the singers haven't been prepared well. The musicians in the orchestra have the music before their eyes; generally they know music better than singers, and they have the conductor in their midst, who guides them,

---

[3] Verdi seems to have declined the proposal when he met Boito a few days later. Francis Hueffer's translation does not include any Latin text.

[4] See Verdi to Ricordi, 31 May 1887.

---

[1] Postmark: BUSSETO 12/6/87.

etc., etc. The singer is left to himself, is preoccupied with the stage, his movements, his voice; and also with those 3 or 4 thousand eyes fixed on him. Therefore the experienced and skilled conductor must first of all take care of the vocal ensemble.

Publishers and composers sometimes accuse him [Mascheroni] of negligence and indifference, and Ricordi puts him in charge of the performance of *Don Carlos* in Rome. Another grave, very grave misfortune is his lack of authority with the orchestral and choral forces, that is to say, his deficiency in discipline.

On the other hand, Mascheroni has good qualities as a conductor. A good musician, a good memory, a firm beat. In spite of this, will Mascheroni be able to regain that authority and prestige which—there's no point in concealing it—have by now been quite shaken? What guarantees can one have? What is public opinion like, apart from personal sympathies that may exist regarding the person rather than the artist? [. . .]

FRANCIS HUEFFER TO BOITO[1]

[In English]   London, July 1887

My dear Maestro,

As I put down the pen, which has just traced the last lines of the translation of your *Othello*, my feelings towards you are not altogether of an amicable kind. You had set me a task which, if interesting in one way, was on the other hand one of the most difficult I had ever undertaken, and now that I have finished that task, I apprehend, that it is not likely to please anybody, least of all myself. You had placed me, as we say in familiar phrase, between the devil and the deep sea; while following your work from line to line, from word to word, I had on one side of me the ocean depths of Shakespeare's thought and tragic passion, and on the other hand the sonorous beauty of the *lingua di si*, as wielded by your hand and wedded to Verdi's strains; the devil having after his wont chosen the most attractive form of disguise. How to shape my course between these two formidable difficulties was what puzzled my poor brain for many anxious days, and nights as well, knowing as I did that failure in this case would be commensurate with the length of life which Verdi's and your genius secured for this musical *Othello* in the country of Shakespeare. As to the result of my labour, others must judge and probably will judge not in the most friendly spirit; for those who know Shakespeare without knowing music will say that I have taken all manner of liberties with the sacred original; and those who know music without knowing Shakespeare will be staggered at a style of diction so entirely different from that of the ordinary libretto. The only person whom I have a faint hope, and at the same time the greatest desire to satisfy, is yourself; and by entertaining that hope I at the same time pay you a great compliment, or rather I should say, express that

[1] Open letter, published in English piano-vocal scores of *Othello*.

profound esteem in which I hold you and your devotion to, and, where necessary, self-abnegation in, the cause of all that is highest and purest in art. That devotion you have shown in many fields and on many occasions. The masterpieces of various languages are familiar to you. Goethe's great poem has found in you the most and, omitting the finale of Schumann's *Faust*, I might almost say, the only congenial interpreter. Hero and Leander, two of the sweetest creations of antique myth, have excited your poetic, I wish that I could add, your musical genius; and we are all anxiously expecting your embodiment of that lurid but essentially dramatic nightmare of Roman history—Nero. To hear a good singer declaim the words '*quantus artifex pereo*'[2] to your music will alone be a treat that may console one for many platitudes of modern opera. To the work of our own Shakespeare, also, you are not a stranger. Hamlet and Othello have passed through the alembic of your imagination and have come forth from it dramatic poems, not mere librettos. A man of your stamp—to return once more to the aforesaid compliment—will understand and perhaps appreciate my motive, when I say that I have to some extent sacrificed your poetry to that of your great original. What I mean is this: Knowing that it was your intention to reproduce the spirit of Shakespeare as far as the divergent genius of the two idioms and the two nations would allow, I have restored the words of Shakespeare even where you, for good and sufficient reasons, had somewhat modified their purport. Let me give you an instance. In the third act, where Othello asks for the loan of Desdemona's handkerchief on the pretence of suffering from 'a salt and sorry rheum', your keen southern susceptibility was perhaps a little shocked by this touch of realism: and you place the seat of the pretended illness for the second time in the forehead instead of in the nose. Here I have unhesitatingly restored the cold for the head-ache. Again, you have moved some of the *dramatis personae* one step upwards in the scale of military rank. Cassio with you is a captain, and Iago a lieutenant. Here also I have ruthlessly cancelled their promotion. Cassio as in Shakespeare is the lieutenant, and Iago, God bless the mark!, his moorship's ancient. These are small matters, but they are cited here in illustration of my method of restoring Shakespeare's text when retransferring his ideas to Shakespeare's tongue. That I was able to do this in so many cases, that so many of Shakespeare's salient words appear in my libretto, is at the same time the best proof of the care and reverence with which you have treated *Othello*. I could cite such lines as 'Think'st thou I'ld make a life of jealousy.' 'The fountain from the which my current runs, or else dries up,' almost the entire plea of Othello before the senate, which (as the first act of the play had to be sacrificed) you have ingeniously used in your love duet; and innumerable others.

In the matter of form I have carried out a similar process of restoration. In the dialogue I have discarded the rhyme altogether, and have returned to blank verse, the recognized medium of the English poetic drama. Only in the

---

[2] 'What an artist dies with me', last words of the Emperor Nero.

lyrical pieces and in the *ensembles* where Shakespeare is altogether out of the question, and where your diction occasionally and faintly suggests the libretto proper, I have used such rhymes as readily suggested themselves.

My remarks hitherto refer to the poem in its separate condition. When it came to adapting that poem to the music, another consideration even more powerful than reverence for Shakespeare asserted itself. The finest poetry in the world would in opera be valueless if it did not fit the music, if it could not be sung; and if this applies to the work of other composers, how much more so to this *Othello* in which Verdi has adhered to dramatic and declamatory truth with a consistency and a beautiful, I might almost say pathetic self-abnegation, worthy of so great a master. To make the metrical accent coincide in every instance with the musical accent, to alter the phrasing as little as possible, to give to each important word and thought the musical emphasis intended by the composer, has been my earnest endeavour; and, in these respects at least, I am prepared to challenge the most searching investigation of intelligent critics.

To the same supreme duty even the language and the metre of Shakespeare had to yield. If rather than destroy the balance of the cantilena I had to stretch the line already quoted 'The fountain from the which my current runs' on a Procrustean bed, and let it take the form of 'The crystal fountain from the which my current ever runs,' I inserted those two meaningless words with a pang; but I did insert them.

But I must conclude, having, I fear, claimed too much of your attention already. Let me finally assure you that the trouble and anxiety, which this translation has cost me, are more than amply repaid by the consciousness of being connected in ever so humble a way, with a work which, in my opinion, marks an epoch in the development of Italian opera—showing, as it does, that the feeling for truth and beauty, the two vital components of all art, is still alive in the land of song.

>Believe me,

>your sincere and admiring friend,
>Francis Hueffer

VERDI TO GIULIO RICORDI[1]

Montecatini, 9 July 1887

[. . .] Give Tornaghi a good position;[2] together you will see to it that the shop may prosper also in the future; it will certainly prosper with an accurate administration, without unnecessary luxuries, and without being partial to or against any music. Giulio Ricordi can have hatred and love for certain composers and certain music; the publisher Ricordi must neither love nor

---

[1] In answer to a letter of 8 July in regard to the reorganization of the House of Ricordi. (See Ricordi to Verdi, 15 Mar. 1887, n. 1).

[2] Eugenio Tornaghi had appealed to Verdi to intervene concerning his position in the reorganized firm.

hate; he must do honestly what is useful to his firm... not working with fantasy, but being practical... Oh dear, oh dear! . I realize that I am preaching! .. The fault of old people!! . Excuse me! [...]

GIULIO RICORDI TO VERDI

Milan, 14 July 1887

[...] With your other letter[1] you meant to give me another proof of all your great and precious benevolence; I shall treasure your advice, Maestro, and I shall save your letter religiously so that it may serve me as a precious guide in the new and important responsibilities which I am about to assume. [...]

I have completely finished the staging [i.e. Production Book] of *Otello*,[2] and the manuscript was checked by Boito; when a corrected proof is ready I shall send it to you so that you can see whether any changes have to be made.

In case you have orders to give me, my address is: Villa Prunner, LEVICO—Trentino.

Again, as always, thanks and more thanks, and renewed feelings of everlasting gratitude.

Yours most devotedly,
Giulio Ricordi

GIULIO RICORDI TO VERDI

[Levico, 29 July 1887]

[...] A dear acquaintance of mine is here, Commendatore Artom, the Inspector General of the civil engineers, *chief* of all the layouts of the railroads. Since the one from Borgo San Donnino to Cremona must still be changed, he requests that I ask you where the layout and the station would be most convenient for you; perhaps it could also give good service to Villanova, which could be useful for your hospital.—Do you recall whether you once sent him the plan of your farms? It would help if you could have a copy of it made. This way he can try to give you the least possible trouble in the changes that are to be made. [...]

VERDI TO GIULIO RICORDI

St Agata, 1 August 1887

[...] Please thank Commendatore Artom for his great kindness and consideration.—Senator Piroli told me some time ago about this railroad from Borgo to Cremona.

For my part I only wish that the railroad won't go through my fields; the station in *Busseto* is as convenient for me as *Cortemaggiore* or *Villanova*,

---

[1] The preceding one.
[2] See Document II.

etc. . . It seems to me, therefore, that the layout—already established, as I was told—would be very good ... from Borgo to Busseto, Cortemaggiore, Monticelli, Pò . ., etc., etc. [. . .][1]

VERDI TO EUGENIO TORNAGHI

St Agata, 12 August 1887

[. . .] I thank you also for the telegram concerning *Otello* in Brescia.[1]—In Brescia, as in Venice, few people the first night!—A sign of trust in those two towns!—If they want something better, they are quite right! . . [. . .]

VERDI TO EUGENIO TORNAGHI

St Agata, 13 August 1887

Dear Signor Tornaghi,
    I thank you for the news about *Otello* in Brescia.[1]
    The success?.—You will tell me from the barometer of the box-office after the fourth or fifth performance! — —
    I am returning the preface to *Otello*.[2]
    Excellent! Nothing better!—But ... those gentlemen ... will they read it, will they understand it ... will they follow the advice?
    In any case, it's good that it has been done. — — —

    Believe me always your

G. Verdi

VERDI TO FRANCO FACCIO

St Agata, 19 August 1887

    I thank you for the telegram and your letter,[1] and apologize for not having answered right away. I am very busy, even though I'm not writing operas, putting all my things, all my affairs in order so that afterwards I can .... take it easy, if I can!
    Well, then! So *Otello* is running even without the 'creators?!!'[2] I had become so accustomed to hearing the glory of those two proclaimed that I

---

[1] The railroad was laid out as established.

---

[1] Missing.

---

[1] Missing.
[2] Boito's Preface to Giulio Ricordi's Production Book (Document II).

---

[1] Missing communications in regard to *Otello* in Brescia.
[2] Cynical reference to Tamagno and Maurel, who had appeared in all previous performances of *Otello* in Milan, Rome, and Venice.

had almost persuaded myself that they had made this *Otello*! You disillusion me now by telling me that this Moor works even without stars! Is it possible? I will say also that I was quite consoled when I learned that in Brescia, as earlier in Venice, the audience was scarce on the first night ... 'Bravo,' I said to myself, 'those are progressive audiences!' It was an act of mistrust towards the composer of former times, an act that demonstrated a most praiseworthy, most ardent desire for the new, the beautiful. All this was logical and right; but if people now go to the theatre and applaud .... ah, me! my heart sinks to my boots .... Now I'm the one who is losing all trust! In short, I cannot but be glad with you, if you got the leaky boat going!

Addio, my dearest Faccio! Peppina, who is well, sends her greetings, and I take your hands affectionately.

GIULIO RICORDI TO VERDI

Milan, 24 August 1887

Illustrious Maestro,

Your kind letter to Levico[1] was very dear to us; if I did not answer right away, the reason was a slight inconvenience, Giuditta having been ill and under the threat of one of her usual angina attacks; fortunately it was a minor illness, which, however, delayed our departure for a week.—On our return we stayed in Brescia, where I heard the fourth performance of a certain opera entitled *Otello*; it would be worth your while to hear it one of these days so that you might learn something for the time when you will write another opera!!! .....

Joking aside; general comparisons useless: altogether a fine performance, executed with care and passion. La Gabbi a bit cold in some places, excellent in others, such as the quartet, the third [act] finale, and the last act. Oxilia good: a bit lacking in the low register; pleasant in the middle register; in the

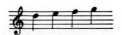

he recalls Masini's voice; the high notes secure and on pitch; more than sufficient as an actor, who will improve because he is intelligent; altogether a good Otello; also very good in the final scene.—Lherie[2] seemed awkward to me in the first act; excellent, however, in the second and third; very good [in] the *Credo* and Cassio's *Dream*; very good in the quartet and in the trio with Cassio and Otello. The usual others good; the whole company good; the staging more than sufficient. The big theatre full to bursting; great attention, applause scarcely held back. Faccio wrote to me that the performances continue like this and that the famous Verdian barometer (*vulgo: box-office*) shows constant good weather!! .....

---

[1] Presumably written after the first *Otello* in Brescia. Autograph in Biblioteca Palatina?
[2] Paul Lhérie (Jago).

Do you know, then, Maestro, what the truth is? . . . . . That the music is so perfect, so extraordinary and interesting that (of course with the exception of a shoddy performance) all fairly good artists will succeed in performing it and that every audience will enjoy it with enthusiasm; make this known to that *Author* whom you know.

I am sending you this letter through our friend Muzio; also the final completed proof of the staging [i.e. Production Book[2]]. Kindly read a little of it every day, and if you should have observations to make, mark them in the margin. Boito has also corrected it; what's missing now is the review of the *summum judex.*

Maurel has made some observations to me; some I found very good; you will hear about this from Muzio.

We had the very great pleasure of finding our boys in excellent health!—Yesterday Tito completed the very difficult examinations of his penultimate year at the polytechnic institute; he has passed them very well; so he was compensated for two months of indefatigable study, really by day and by night; you can imagine how glad we are.

My mother is well now, and so is my father; so this is a fine moment, which will be finer still if I receive excellent news from you and Signora Peppina. [. . .]

VERDI TO GIULIO RICORDI

[St Agata, after 24 August 1887]

Comments on *Otello* Production Book:[1]
  Hiding his face in his hands, etc., etc.,
  seems like repentance and should not be, since he says later:

> *Forse onesto tu sei, ma tante volte ti credo un birbo* . . . . .[2]
>
> [*Perhaps you are honest, but many times I believe you are a scoundrel* . . . . .]

Otello's attitude should be one of supreme scorn.
Nothing else.
Just to say something
  I would not like Jago to say the phrase '*Temete Signor, la gelosia*' ['*Be fearful, my Lord, of jealousy*'][3] *molto sotto voce*
  1. Because the orchestra plays *au grand complet*
  2. Because the accent of this phrase should be—rather than mysterious—*dark, fatal, pointed,* almost *prophetic* . . . what do I know!
  Talk about this with Boito, and if he agrees find a word to substitute for *sotto voce.*

  [2] See Document II.

---

  [1] Document II.
  [2] Cf. Shakespeare, *Othello*, III. iii. 391: 'I think that thou art just, and think thou art not.'
  [3] Cf. Shakespeare, *Othello*, III. iii. 169: 'O, beware jealousy.'

This last *threatening gesture* isn't forceful enough, but is rather cold. After Otello has sworn and cursed so much, he has other things on his mind than stopping again to make another gesture.

I would stop with the annotation '*S'incamminano rapidamente verso la porta*' ['*They walk quickly towards the door*']——and the curtain falls.

GIULIO RICORDI TO VERDI

[Milan] 30 August 1887

Illustrious Maestro,

I would have been able to put together another company for *Otello* that I think could equal the one in Brescia. But there is trouble with the theatre! ... whose city can be a bother to you: Genoa! ... To tell you the truth, if this were to cause you to hurry to Milan for a fortnight ....., I would make the arrangements straightaway; for your peace of mind, Milan will be one of the few centres where there will be no *Otello* this winter!! ... Well, then? .... Joking aside, illustrious Maestro, if you think that planning for Genoa might be a nuisance to you, nothing will be done. You have only to tell me so bluntly. But since the decision is urgent, I beg you to answer me right away by telegram upon receipt of this letter: either 'Go ahead' or 'Wait for another year,' if the affair is not to be brought to completion.[1] [...]

Fabulous box-office in Brescia!! ...

GIULIO RICORDI TO VERDI

[Milan] 6 September 1887

Illustrious Maestro,

All right for Genoa[1]—and very well for the indicated corrections in the staging [i.e. Production Book]. I send you warm thanks for this. [...]

VERDI TO FRANCO FACCIO

St Agata, 16 September 1887

Dear Faccio,

I was in Milan with Peppina for 36 hours, and returning here I found your telegram concerning *Otello*.[1]

I am very, very grateful to you for this affectionate solicitude, which is

[1] Such a telegram has not been found.

[1] The first performance of *Otello* in Genoa took place at the Teatro Carlo Felice on 24 Nov. 1888. Verdi did not attend.

[1] The missing telegram apparently concerned the first *Otello* performance conducted by Faccio in Parma on 14 Sept.

dearer to me than the success itself, for which we await the *irrevocable sentence* of the severe audience after the fourth performance.

How many demands, how many pretensions, and how much ...!!!

To you I send sincere compliments, knowing with what authority and with what love you have made even a lame one walk.

Addio, my dear Faccio. I greet you for Peppina and take your hands.

Addio
G. Verdi

VERDI TO BOITO

St Agata, 16 September 1887

Dear Boito,

Just back from Milan, I found your letter here.[1]

You will always be welcome, you and Giacosa, when you feel like running here to St Agata. Just tell me the day and the hour.

Up till now everything has gone well; but I am very disturbed by the request for the French manuscript of the third act of *Othello*.[2] I don't recall this manuscript at all! I don't have it here; it might be in Genoa, but who knows! Perhaps it doesn't exist any longer! You must know that there was quite a flood in my room in Genoa. A pipe of the great Nicolai water reservoir burst, ruining carpets, walls, furniture, and a very beautiful antique cabinet with a writing desk underneath. There were a lot of papers in this piece of furniture, and when I went to Genoa[3] and tried to open the drawers with the keys, everything fell apart: the veneer, the gum or the glue, and the wet papers presented only a stinking pulp. It could be, though I don't think so, that the French manuscript was among those papers! But I don't think so because there should only have been papers of earlier dates in that piece of furniture! Do you know what you have to do? Don't think any more about that translation, which will always go well. Don't waste your time with this kind of work, and don't waste time searching for the impossible in Caccini, in Peri, etc., etc. You have far better things to do!

Oh, excuse me, excuse me ... I realize that I've been giving you advice ... I, who detest advice and advisors! ...

Excuse this chatter. Greetings, till we see each other.

Your
G. Verdi

---

[1] Missing.
[2] The manuscript of the French translation completed in Apr. 1887.
[3] From St Agata between 9 and 12 Aug.

GIULIO RICORDI TO VERDI

Milan, 1 October 1887

Illustrious Maestro,

The management in Genoa came to me not once, but twice, every day to learn the news regarding the result of the letter which the mayor of that city addressed to you; since I know nothing about it, of course it is very easy for me to respond; but the impresario will not give up and tells me that I am the one who does not want to make arrangements for *Otello*, since Maestro Verdi must have answered favourably.[1] And since I know nothing about this, either, this reply, too, is easy for me. If I continue to be negative I will get rid of the management; if, however, you think the arrangement is possible, I shall get all the appropriate guarantees regarding the company as a whole, which, as you wrote to me, is mediocre. The management, however, is prepared to form the chorus and orchestra from the major part of the companies in Venice and Parma, which were excellent, indeed; and for our guarantee I would have them give me the list of the artists to be engaged, which I would have Faccio examine. [. . .]

BOITO TO VERDI

Cernobbio Villa d'Este
Lago di Como
4 October [1887]

Dear Maestro,

First of all, I thank you again for the beautiful and inspiring days I spent at St Agata.[1]—Next I beg you for a favour, and don't scold me for having again accepted an assignment; it will be the last.—The Minister of Education[2] wishes to confer with me about the musical institutions of the Kingdom. We know that in Italy music is being studied badly these days; the Minister's invitation is a good occasion to try to straighten out the studies in the governmental schools, and therefore I have consented to the desire of the person who governs them. It will mean an excursion to Rome and a couple of lost days (perhaps not uselessly); then I'll return to my work. I do not intend to recommend to the Minister a reform of the statutes of the music schools or a union of their various constitutions. These questions are as big as they are futile and difficult. Let them keep the statutes that they have; it's not from them that good or bad scholars come. The natural intelligence of the student

---

[1] No such correspondence has been found. The first *Otello* in Genoa was given only on 24 Nov. 1888.

---

[1] Boito and Giacosa had been guests at St Agata for three days in late Sept. (Nardi, *Vita di Boito*, p. 533).

[2] Michele Coppino (1822–1901), Professor of Italian Literature and Chancellor of the University in Turin.

takes highest advantage of good studies and can be derailed by bad ones. This is the point: *the direction of the studies.*

The opportunity presents itself to put into practice the advice that you were able to put into three words with antique clarity, wisdom, and conciseness: *Tornate all'antico.*[3]

So let's return to the antique, but the schools must be obliged to return there; they will never return if they're not obliged. In the governmental programmes of the high schools and colleges, the study of Virgil, Horace, Lucretius, and Cicero is obligatory. So, also, I think, in the conservatories the study of Palestrina and the other greatest Italian musicians of the sixteenth, seventeenth and eighteenth centuries must be *obligatory.* This is the right way, this is what should be studied in the schools and in vocal exercises. Vocal art must be raised again and restored to the full wave of sound of Palestrina's parts. The young students, who, hardly born, babble abstruse ideas, must be *obliged* to wash themselves in that wave and in that purity. Composers would change their minds, and it would be good for singers, too.—Composers and singers—there is the rottenness of today's studies, and this must be remedied. The instrumentalists are there, they manage by themselves. There are plenty of good and cultivated pianists; Naples has given us excellent ones in recent years, also Milan; Bologna always produces good strings, and Naples good woodwind players. But the study of composition is falling into decay. The young students of composition are full of presumption and ignorance.

They must be instructed in the great music of the great Italian centuries. Once instructed, they will be less puffed up and will see art more clearly. They must also be obliged to study a little history, in well and simply written texts, so that at the same time they may learn the great dramas of mankind and the beautiful style of the language. They must be obliged to study a little prosody and declamation, so that they may learn to give a human accentuation to dialogue, as is required by the truth, since music is nothing else but the sound of sentiment and passion.—I have learned all these things from you, who have put them into practice, and you may tell me if I have learned them well. I, too, would like to be able to put them into practice in my work and suggest them to the person who governs the studies, in order to offer students the possibility of studying well.

Now, this is the favour I am asking of you:

Please give me a short list, a list of six names, no more—six names of composers you believe most suitable to be studied by the young people.

These six names, beginning with Palestrina, should represent the six brightest lights of *vocal art* in the sixteenth, seventeenth and eighteenth centuries. I am asking you this favour because I trust your judgement so very much more than anybody else's. There's no one better than you to compile this list, which will serve as the programme of the studies.[4]

[3] Boito quotes from the famous sentence that Verdi had written to Francesco Florimo on 5 Jan. 1871: 'Torniamo all'antico; sarà un progresso.' ['Let us return to the past; it will be progress.']

[4] The end of the letter is missing.

VERDI TO BOITO

St Agata, 5 October 1887

Dear Boito,

If you promise to give me no credit or blame for it, I am sending you some names that first come to my mind. There are more than six, but there are so many good ones in that era that I don't know which to choose.

Palestrina (in primis et ante omnia)

———

Victoria[1]

———

1500   Luca Marenzio (purest composer)[2]

———

Allegri (that of the Miserere)[3]

———

and so many other good composers of that century, with the exception of Monteverde,[4] who led the voices badly.

———

*Carissimi[5]

In the
beginning
of the 17th   Cavalli[6]

———

[1] Tomás Luis de Victoria (*c.*1548–1611), Spanish composer, presumably disciple of Palestrina, whose friend and temporary successor he was in Rome.

[2] Luca Marenzio (1553–99), considered the most outstanding composer of madrigals. His works display particular contrapuntal wealth.

[3] Gregorio Allegri (1582–1652), Roman composer and singer in the papal chapel; best known by his *Miserere*, originally performed in the Sistine Chapel of the Vatican and published only in 1771.

[4] Claudio Monteverdi (1567–1643), the most celebrated, widely travelled church and opera composer of his time, considered the creator of music drama and a new musical style.

[5] Giacomo Carissimi (1605–74), the first great master of oratorios and cantatas, who initiated the development of non-liturgical church music.

[6] Francesco Cavalli (1602–76), organist and composer of sacred music in Venice, distinguished pupil of Monteverdi. He wrote 42 operas which were most successful in their time.

Later {
  Lotti[7]

  ———

  *Scarlatti, Alessandro[8] (who has treasures also of
  harmonies)

  ———

  *Marcello[9]

  ———

  Leo[10]

  ———
}

For the
beginning   { *Pergolesi[11]
of the 18th   { Jomelli[12]

Later   *Piccinni[13] (the first, I believe, to write quintets and
              sextets, etc. Author of the first true *opera
              buffa, Cecchina.*)

If you really want only six, I think those marked with * are to be preferred.

Later we have Paisiello[14]
               Cimarosa[15]

[7] Antonio Lotti (*c*.1667–1740), distinguished composer of sacred music as well as operas in
Venice and Dresden.

[8] Pietro Alessandro Gaspare Scarlatti (1660–1725), the father of Domenico Scarlatti, was a
descendant of an Italian family of musicians, the main exponent of Neapolitan opera, and
conductor at the chapel of Queen Christina of Sweden.

[9] Benedetto Marcello (1686–1739), composer and poet. He wrote a satire about operatic
activities of his time, numerous concerts, masses, oratorios, and one or two operas. Verdi
particularly admired his recitatives.

[10] Leonardo Leo (1694–1744), significant representative of the Neapolitan School, composer
of comic operas, many oratorios, masses, and other works.

[11] Giovanni Battista Pergolesi (1710–36), renowned for his *opera buffa La serva padrona*, a
Stabat Mater for strings, and the abundance of his vocal and instrumental compositions.

[12] Niccolò Jomelli (1714–74), Neapolitan composer of 82 *opere serie e buffe*, countless
masses, oratorios, and other ecclesiastical works; conductor at the court of Stuttgart from 1753
to 1768.

[13] Niccolò Piccinni (1728–1800), favourite student of Leonardo Leo. He wrote sacred music
and was an important contributor to the *opera seria* and *buffa* of the eighteenth century; his
opera buffa La Cecchina was internationally acclaimed. Before and after the French Revolution,
Piccinni was active in Paris where an artistic quarrel came about concerning his type of opera
and the opposite style of Gluck (1714–87).

[14] Giovanni Paisiello (1740–1816), composer of *opera seria* and *buffa*, Piccinni's and Cimarosa's rival in Naples. As conductor at the court of St Petersburg, he wrote, among other operas,
a most successful *Barbiere di Siviglia* (1782). In addition to approximately 100 operas, he
composed piano concertos, quartets, secular oratorios, cantatas, and sacred music.

[15] Domenico Cimarosa (1749–1801), eminent opera composer of the Neapolitan School,
Paisiello's successor in St Petersburg and Antonio Salieri's as conductor at the court of Vienna
where he wrote *Il matrimonio segreto*, his best-known work.

Guglielmi, Pietro,[16]
etc., etc...
then Cherubini,[17] etc.

I wish you good success; and if you succeed you will be doing a blessed work; because (I'm not speaking of schools, which can all be good) the young people study the wrong way; in fact, they've gone astray; and if music is—and it is—as you define it, one really must know a little prosody and declamation and have enough culture to understand what one must understand. When one well understands what one has to compose, and when one has to compose, and when one has to shape a character or to portray a passion, it is more difficult to be derailed by oddities and extravagances of any vocal or instrumental kind whatsoever.

Give me your news about what you have done and achieved.—

I press your hand in haste and greet you from Peppina.

Your
G. Verdi

GIULIO RICORDI TO VERDI

Milan, 12 October 1887

[...] The purpose of my letter is to inform you that today I have the pleasure of sending you by rail the first copy of the printed orchestra score of *Otello*, and I will be glad to know that you are satisfied with this edition. Mind you, however, Maestro, that if you should use it in any way to make a copy or something else of it, I would bring a terrible lawsuit against you!!

I do not repeat the congratulations and thanks which I telegraphed you;[1] you must know what is in my heart and soul for you! [...]

BOITO TO VERDI

Villa d'Este
31 October [1887][1]

Dear Maestro,

Here is what has happened: The textbooks (sixteenth, seventeenth, and eighteenth centuries) were unanimously voted for by the principal directors

---

[16] Pietro Alessandro Guglielmi (1728–1804), Tuscan composer of 103 operas and, as conductor of the Church of St Peter in Rome, also of sacred music.

[17] Luigi Cherubini (1760–1842), held in high esteem by Beethoven and Goethe. Among 15 Italian and 14 French operas he wrote—mostly in Paris—innumerable sacred and other works manifesting masterful technique and purity of style. From 1821 to 1842 he was the director of the Paris Conservatory.

---

[1] On the occasion of Verdi's birthday. The telegram is missing.

---

[1] Postmark: CERNOBBIO 31/10/87.

of the royal conservatories. We'll see what will follow. After this voting I left Rome, leaving those gentlemen to come to an agreement on their statutes (there aren't even two that resemble each other) and on their regulations.—Of course, as you wished, I made no use of your letter, even though I had it with me in my pocket and was tempted more than once to make use of it. In a few days I'll be in Nervi, and if you are in Genoa I'll come, as usual, to the Palazzo Doria to spend an hour together.

Affectionate greetings to you and Signora Giuseppina.

Your
Arrigo Boito

VERDI TO GIULIO RICORDI

Genoa, 5 December 1887

Dear Giulio,

Here I am back from St Agata, where I spent three days in the rain, the fog, the cold, and worse yet ... with figures! *Figures* and *Composer* both are very, very much out of tune; but there's no remedy .. yet one must submit to the necessities of life, which are mainly material ones and always reduce themselves either *de trif* or *de traf*[1] to one, to two, to three, etc., etc., etc. . . . . .

And since we are tuned to numbers, I must speak to you once more about the business between me and the House of Ricordi that is to be arranged by the end of the year. I believe I have made myself quite clear to you before, and I believe you have understood just as well; nevertheless I must repeat that within a *week* or *ten days* you should send me a more precise accounting of the current term and of all the rest of my holdings, and I would bring with me the amount necessary to complete the *200* thousand Lire.[2]———Since this is (for a composer, of course) a rather important amount, it will be well to draw up a regular deed, and you should have it prepared straightaway so that no time will be lost later on. I would plan to be in Milan on the 27th and would like to leave again for St Agata the morning of the 28th. Therefore it would be necessary to have the deed prepared for that day. I would come to you right away, either about 3 p.m. or in the evening, to read the deed and sign it. Have I made myself clear?

Nothing else for now but greetings from your

G. Verdi

[. . .]

---

[1] Unknown and untranslatable—probably French—expression in the autograph (Ricordi) and also the copy (*Copialettere*, p. 346) of this letter.

[2] A loan Verdi made to the House of Ricordi to be repaid after his death to the still existing Casa di Riposo [Old Age Home], which he founded in Milan. (See Biographical Note on Giulio Ricordi and Ricordi to Verdi, 15 Mar. 1887, n. 1.)

VERDI TO GIULIO RICORDI

Genoa, 26 December 1887

Dear Giulio,

Today, too?!! Yesterday the *monstrous* Panettone; today the little bags!! Why? But why, why, why? . . .

Peppina and I thank you very, very much, but we must make a pact for the future! You will always send us a Panettone, as long as we last . . . but let its weight never be more than a kilo.

Are we agreed . . ?!—

As planned, I'll be in Milan tomorrow by the *through train*; and let me find a card at the hotel telling me the hour.

Best wishes and addio

Affectionately,
G. Verdi

3 o'clock. Received telegram *D. Carlos* Naples . . . Bad for *Otello*. I seem to hear them screaming at the first performance . . . 'But here are none of the melodies of *Otello*!!' So it was the first time for *D. Carlos*! . Ah, audiences, audiences [!]

VERDI TO FRANCO FACCIO

Genoa, 2 January 1888

[. . .] I had the good fortune to see Boito and Giacosa for a quarter of an hour.[1] They stopped by the hotel in great *toilette* and, knowing I was there, came up . . .

We saw la Pantaleoni, and you can't imagine Peppina's and my pleasure to see her in such flourishing health. Signora Stolz told us that her voice was in excellent condition, too, and if that is so, she cannot miss having a great success here,[2] which Peppina and I wish her with all our hearts; we are hoping for it; in fact we are almost certain of it. [. . .]

VERDI TO FRANCO FACCIO

[Genoa, ? January 1888]

[. . .] This telegram,[1] which touched me very deeply and was most dear to me, brought back memories of that first night, and then the third, when, leaving the theatre amid affectionate greetings on stage, I met the orchestra musi-

[1] Probably on 27 Dec. 1887 in Milan.
[2] As Gioconda at the Teatro Carlo Felice in Genoa.

[1] Missing, probably containing wishes for the New Year.

cians on the staircase, who—moved, without uttering a word—shook my hand, and in their faces were engraved these words: 'Here, Maestro, we won't see each other again . . . never again!! . . .'

Never again is a phrase, perhaps, that sounds like a death knell! Weaknesses, weaknesses! Let's not talk about it any more! I thank you for speaking to me in this manner about *Otello*, but let's leave him in peace, too, and let him go on his way as long as his legs will hold him up; besides, it's not going to hurt anyone . . . Today in music there is symphonic abstruseness on the one side, and *marqueterie*, in various colours, on the other, which makes the elegant public shout: '*c'est distingué, c'est de bon goût*', as though a fashion shop were involved. Our composers are fishing a bit here, a bit there, concerned only with harmonic blendings and combinations, ignoring the art of writing for the voice, and forgetting that more than anything, there is need for ideas. How content I would be if I could get to hear even a badly orchestrated opera that contained some great phrases—just one heroic, clear-cut phrase, or one of great jollity, as, for example, '*Largo al factotum*,' etc.[2] [. . .]

VERDI TO BOITO
[Telegram]

Genoa, 5 January 1888

THANKS FOR MOST WELCOME NEWS[1]—SENDING TELEGRAM TO GIACOSA[2]

VERDI

VERDI TO GIULIO RICORDI

Genoa, 22 January 1888

[. . .] And now we speak German! I don't understand that language; nevertheless a few things in the German translation of *Otello*[1] caught my eye that aren't good. Not at all! In the Willow Song the repetition of the word does not, and must not, make any sense; it's a vague voice, one that's neither Desdemona's nor Barbara's; it's a sound which one hears but which, I would say, is stiff . . . And therefore one must not, at that moment, say, 'Green Willow', green or yellow! Have them say only, '*Weide, Weide, Weide*' ['*Willow, Willow, Willow*'].

---

[2] Verdi expressed the very same ideas in a letter to Du Locle of 8 Dec. 1869 (*Copialettere*, pp. 219–22, and Busch, *Aida*, pp. 4–5).

---

[1] About the success of the first performance in Milan of Giacosa's play *Tristi amori*. Probably, Boito telegraphed this news to Verdi from Nervi to where this telegram is addressed.
[2] Missing.

---

[1] By Max Kalbeck (1850–1921), music critic and writer in Vienna, known for his many German translations of operas in various languages.

Worse yet at the end when Otello says, '*Desdemona, Desdemona ... ah morta morta morta!*' ['*Desdemona, Desdemona ... ah, dead, dead, dead!*']. A heartrending and true exclamation! The translator has made a phrase of it that's neither beautiful nor true ... '*Dolce morta cara*' ['*Sweet dear one, dead*'] or something similar.[2] Here there must be neither a poetic nor a musical phrase; even I myself had the good sense to make only sounds that have almost no tonality! ... Have the translator adjust the verse as he wants, but always have him say three times, '*morta morta morta!*' [...]

GIULIO RICORDI TO VERDI

Milan, 23 January 1888

Illustrious Maestro,

I hasten to answer your most honoured letter of yesterday. I am writing straightaway to the German translator about the modifications you indicate to me, and I shall have the edition corrected not only for the reprints, but also in the existing copies.[1]

Regarding *Otello*, you touch a grave and painful key, one that has been upsetting me for several months, as I wonder how similar infamies are possible!! ... I am certain you will imagine that I have left no stone unturned in order to discover where and in what manner the reductions are being falsified. But what can be done?! ... Even some theatrical agents aid and abet the thieves, and we are unable to make them squeal, not even with promises of money. Our lawyer, the Deputy Panattoni, came expressly to Milan, and we considered every possible and impossible way to prevent such thievery and such distortion of art as is done with falsely orchestrated scores; but unfortunately our laws are powerless, and the American ones ..... do not exist. On my return from Naples[2] I shall stop over in Rome expressly to request an audience with the Minister of Justice, to reveal to him the state of affairs and to see if it is not possible to change the law. To Mexico we have sent telegrams, protests ..... but without getting any satisfaction. I fear that in Buenos-Ayres nothing can be achieved with the present laws; but you rightly say: the thief must be hit with publicity; this has already been done to some extent: I have telegraphed the Italian Consul and have written to the Argentine Consul in Genoa, who seems to have taken the matter very much to heart. But there is still one step to be taken that might be decisive, and that is for you to send a telegram there; I think that for the protection of your

---

[2] '*Mein süsses, totes Liebchen!*'

[1] Evidently to no avail. Verdi's wishes were fulfilled only by Walter Felsenstein (1901–75), the artistic director of the Komische Oper in East Berlin, who made a new German translation of *Otello* for his noteworthy production in 1960 (see Verdi, *Othello* Klavierauszug. Milan and Frankfurt/M. G. Ricordi and Co., 1963–4, Plate no. 130619, rev. by Mario Parenti, new German translation by Walter Felsenstein), p. ix.

[2] Presumably after attending the first performance of *Otello* with Tamagno, la Gabbi, and Kaschmann, conducted by Gialdino Gialdini at the Teatro San Carlo in Naples on 4 Feb. 1888.

artistic creation you have every right to do it, and if you agree with this line of reasoning, I would have a telegram devised like this:

His Excellency President Republic of Argentina—Buenos Ayres—In order to avoid public deception and an insult to art I am honoured advise Your Excellency I recognize my *Otello* granted only to the impresario Ferrari by Publisher and sole proprietor Ricordi.

VERDI[3]

If all moral sense has not been lost, this should have great weight; it seems impossible that the Argentine authority would lend itself to subsidizing a thief!! [. . .]

VERDI TO GIULIO RICORDI

Genoa, 26 January 1888

Dear Giulio,

I hear that the Quartetto Italiano[1] is to perform that *Quartet* of mine, etc.!!!!

I get no pleasure from this at all; but if it must be performed, I would like it to be done well.

You will have no time to occupy yourself with this, but if you happen to have the chance, you should tell the director of the Quartet to watch out that the andante in 3/4 [time] is not taken faster than indicated, as happened before.

Further: [tell him] to modify the shadings in the final fugue, meaning that it is to be played *pianissimo*, all *staccato* [and] *a punta d'arco* until six bars before the letter E, where it says *Più forte*. From this moment until the end, do the shadings as they are indicated.

I've experimented with this effect in *Cologne*[2] and found it good. Well, they can try it [and see] if it works well; if not, it's [to be] done as it was before.

Always sorry to cause you to lose time, I greet you and remain

Affectionately,
G. Verdi

---

[3] There appears to be no record of such a telegram.

[1] No reference of a Quartetto Italiano in Verdi's day could be traced. Apparently, the first string quartet by that name was formed after the First World War by the violinist Remy (Ressigio) Principe, born in Venice in 1889, with Ettore Gandini, Giuseppe Matteucci, and Luigi Chiarappa.

[2] At the Festival where Verdi conducted the *Requiem* on 21 May 1877.

EUGENIO TORNAGHI TO VERDI

Milan, 11 February 1888

Illustrious
Signor Commendatore G. Verdi
Genoa

Giulio, who received your precious note of yesterday[1] the moment he was leaving for Reggio for the first [performance] of *Asrael*,[2] has left to me the honour of answering you.

The representatives of the House in Berlin[3] had written to us that the management of the Theatre of Weimar hoped to be able to give *Otello* if the House allowed them quite reasonable terms. We replied by offering a rental contract of one year for a *thousand florins*, or a sale of the material for *two thousand florins* and 6 per cent royalties from the box-office, as is customary in Germany. [. . .]

Giulio has charged me to inform you that the House will in any event be quite happy to arrange this as you will think suitable. [. . .]

VERDI TO EUGENIO TORNAGHI

Genoa, 13 February 1888

I don't like to be embarrassed by the rentals of my operas; but this time I gave in, since they wanted to persuade me that the performance would be a good one on the part of the singers, too. A rather rare thing in Germany! . . . Also, in Munich the Othello and Jago are a couple of hoarse voices.[1] [. . .]

EUGENIO TORNAGHI TO VERDI

Milan, 14 February 1888

Illustrious Maestro
Signor Commendatore G. Verdi
Genoa

Honoured by your esteemed note of yesterday, I have informed Giulio right away. In order to assure us of a good performance in Weimar also on

---

[1] Probably in the Biblioteca Palatina.

[2] Opera by Alberto Franchetti (1860–1942), premièred in Reggio Emilia. In addition to various successful operas compared to Meyerbeer's, Franchetti wrote symphonic and chamber music. From 1926 to 1928 he directed the Conservatory in Florence.

[3] Bote & Bock, since 1838 distinguished music publishers in Berlin.

---

[1] Exactly one year after the première in Milan, Hermann Levi (1839–1900), who conducted the first *Parsifal* in Bayreuth, introduced *Othello* in German to Munich. None less than Heinrich Vogl (1845–1900) sang the title role. He was the first Loge and Siegmund in Bayreuth where, between 1876 and 1897, he appeared also as Tristan and Parsifal.—Eugen Gura (1842–1906), the Jago, was the first Donner and Gunther in Bayreuth, thereafter also King Mark and Hans Sachs. A certain Frau Schöller appeared in the role of Desdemona.

the part of the singers, we have written to obtain exact information. If this should be reassuring, we could agree to the conditions of the management of that theatre, and we would not fail to mention your esteemed recommendation. We hope thus to have interpreted your intentions correctly; but if this is not the case, you have only to tell us. [...]

GIULIO RICORDI TO VERDI

Milan, 16 February 1888

Illustrious Maestro,
   Concerning the business in Weimar, everything will be arranged straightaway according to the instructions received from you. In this so-called century of progress, it is really distressing to see that thieves can profit from the works of genius, and with the consent of governments!! ....
but that's the way it is.——There is a new piracy in Amsterdam about which nothing can be done.[1] [...]

GIUSEPPINA VERDI TO GIUSEPPE DE SANCTIS[1]

Genoa, 18 February 1888

   Your impressions are worth more than so many others, for they are conceived with artistic feeling, with deep observation, and with that mark of pure truth that is so desirable and so rarely found. Your poor father would surely have found ineffable consolations in this success of *Otello*![2] .... May the big box-office please the management, as it appears that *Otello* gave musical enjoyment to the intelligent Neapolitan audience. [...]

EUGENIO TORNAGHI TO VERDI

Milan, 22 February 1888

Illustrious Maestro
Signor Commendatore G. Verdi
   Genoa
   We are taking the liberty of enclosing the letter we received today from our representatives in Berlin concerning the company proposed for *Othello* in Weimar.[1] Giulio, who is occupied, has charged me to ask you to let us know if in your opinion we can agree and make the contract with that

---

[1] Translated into Dutch, *Othello* was performed on 10 Mar. 1888 in Amsterdam. The conductor and composer Johannes Meinardus Coenen (1824–99) furnished an orchestration based on the vocal score.

---

[1] In answer to a missing letter.
[2] On 4 Feb. at the Teatro San Carlo in Naples.

---

[1] Missing.

management. Would you at the same time kindly return to us the letter from Bote & Bock. [. . .]

VERDI TO EUGENIO TORNAGHI

Genoa, 23 February 1888

Signor Tornaghi,

The news concerning the singers in Weimar given by *Bot Botte*[1] doesn't say and doesn't clarify what I wished to know. In fact the phrase '*Artistes d'un bon renom*' could also mean, 'they had a name and have no more voice'. I think this translation is correct.

I was interested [in the possibility] that *Othello* would be given at least once in Germany with dependable artists; and in this case I would have asked the House of Ricordi to yield a bit on the financial terms. Being unable to attain this goal, I wash my hands of the affair and inform the House of Ricordi that it can do whatever it likes . . .

Believe me always

Cordially,
G. Verdi

GIULIO RICORDI TO VERDI

Milan, 25 February 1888

Illustrious Maestro,

This roguery in Amsterdam[1] is the one about which I have already had the honour to write to you, and for which we have sent a protest to be published in that city. Still, if you intend to reply directly,[2] it will always be an authoritative announcement to the public, and you can then say that a protest has already been sent, also in your name, by the publisher. The public, however, stupid as it is, will run to the theatre all the same, just to see *Othello*! [. . .]

MELCHIORRE DELFICO TO VERDI

[Portici,[1] 1 March 1888
Villa Friozzi]

Dear Maestro,

After so many years I present myself to you!!!! Who knows what you will say?!!! Do you remember me??!! I heard your *Otello* . . . I am full of

---

[1] Bote & Bock.

---

[1] See Ricordi to Verdi, 16 Feb. 1888.
[2] Presumably Verdi did not.

---

[1] A suburb of Naples.

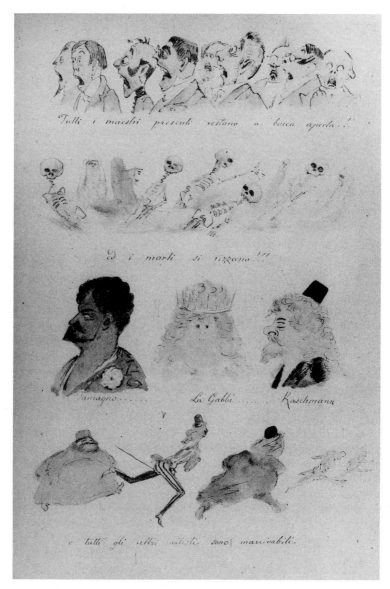

Delfico's caricatures (George Martin)

Tutti i maestri presenti restano a bocca aperta!!
Ev í morti si rizzano!!!
Tamagno . . . . La Gabbi . . . . Kaschmann . . . .
e tutti gli altri artisti sono inarrivabili.

[All the attending composers remain with their mouths open!!
And the dead ones rise!!!
Tamagno . . . . La Gabbi . . . . Kaschmann . . . .
and all the other artists are unsurpassable]

enthusiasm for it!!!!! ... the way it begins ... the way it ends ... it's
something very great!!!!! The Baron Genovesi,[2] Florimo, and I got
goose-pimples in the last scene!!!!!
[. . .] All the attending composers remain with their mouths open!!! ... and
the dead ones rise!!!

Tamagno ... la Gabbi ... Kaschmann ... and all the other artists are
unsurpassable. The orchestra marvellously performs embellishments, nuances, ornamentation, and cannon shots!! Next to *Otello* all your other
operas seem small!! ... I wish I could fly to you to embrace you and press
your hand. [. . .]

Forgive the liberty I am taking in sending you these scrawls[3] ... My very
best compliments to Boito, too, for his splendid libretto. [. . .]

VERDI TO BOITO
[Telegram]

Genoa, 3 March 1888

PLEASE PLEASE PLEASE—TOMORROW AT SIX[1]

VERDI

GIULIO RICORDI TO VERDI
[Telegram]

Milan, 15 March 1888

WITH IMMENSE JOY I ANNOUNCE TO YOU RESOUNDING COMPLETE GREAT TRI-
UMPH OTHELLO VIENNA[1] SEVEN CALLS AFTER FIRST ACT SIX SECOND EIGHT THIRD
ELEVEN FOURTH IMMENSE IMPRESSION CORDIAL GREETINGS

GIULIO

---

[2] Baron Giovanni Genovesi, who belonged to the circle of Verdi's Neapolitan friends.
[3] Caricatures enclosed with the letter. See p. 342.

---

[1] Presumably an urgent invitation for dinner.

---

[1] Performed in German and conducted by the renowned Hans Richter (1843–1916), Wagner's
collaborator, on 14 Mar., and considered the greatest sensation at the Hofoper since the
introduction of electric lighting on its stage in the previous year. Hermann Winkelmann (1849–
1912), Bayreuth's first Parsifal and Vienna's first Tristan, sang Othello; Theodor Reichmann
(1849–1903), Bayreuth's first Amfortas and of international fame, sang Jago. In Vienna, too,
however, the Desdemona seems to have been a problem. She was 'Antonia Schläger, a Viennese,
not exactly slim at the best of times, who was later particularly well known for her Santuzza in
Cavalleria rusticana. "Toni", as she was always called, was very popular for a while, but
unfortunately she grew stouter and stouter and left the stage to run a restaurant, which she did
equally well.' (Marcel Prawy, *The Vienna Opera.* New York: Praeger, 1970, p. 55.)

VERDI TO MELCHIORRE DELFICO

[Genoa, 22 March 1888]

I am doubly glad, since I know now where to address my reply[1] and can thank you for the beautiful, most beautiful caricatures of *Otello*. I will even tell you that Maestro Muzio was here when they arrived, and, leaving for Milan, he wanted to take them along to show to Giulio Ricordi. Everyone found them most beautiful. They are still in Milan (the caricatures), but I hope they will be returned to me soon so that I can enjoy them, too. [. . .]

VERDI TO BOITO

[Milan] Sunday [8 April 1888][1]

Dear Boito,
I am in Milan for a few days.
Today I go to the Swiss concert and won't be at home tonight.
Till we meet again later, either at your home or at mine.

G. Verdi

EUGENIO TORNAGHI TO VERDI

Milan, 2 May 1888

Illustrious
Signor Commendatore G. Verdi
Genoa
We regret having to disturb you again on account of the *Otello* affair in Buenos Ayres.[1] We had sent Signor Ferrari a copy of the contract which the House had the good fortune to make with you;[2] but it seems that a legal snag has been hit, since Ferrari has asked us by telegraph to have you send a telegram of confirmation to the Italian ambassador. [. . .]

---

[1] To Delfico's letter and enclosure of 1 Mar.

---

[1] This data is inferred from two concerts given by the Zurich Männerchor at La Scala on 8 and 9 Apr. 1888.

---

[1] See Ricordi to Verdi, 23 Jan. 1888.
[2] Missing.

VERDI TO GIULIO RICORDI

[St Agata, ? May 1888?][1]

[. . .] Signora Ferrari[2] came to see me and told me about the theft of *Otello* by Ciacchi.[3] The affair is so grave and wrongful that I am sure you will do what is possible and impossible to prevent this evil. It seems to me that it can be done; but if the laws of that country should not suffice to give satisfaction, in fact to give justice, it seems to me that we can hit the thief morally, at least, with publicity. [. . .]

VERDI TO ROMILDA PANTALEONI
[Telegram][1]

[Busseto, ? May 1888?]

DO WHAT IS IN YOUR INTEREST AVOID LAWSUIT[2]

VERDI

GIULIO RICORDI TO VERDI

Milan, 16 June 1888

[. . .] We are negotiating with that Sieni,[1] who presented a falsified *Otello* in Mexico,[2] to put him in his place and have him make amends; I hope to succeed, and that will set a good precedent. The time will come for that rogue Ciacchi!! . . . unfortunately I am informed by a telegram that the roguery was

---

[1] Abbiati (iv. 351) gives this excerpt from Verdi's letter, which is not in the Ricordi Archives, and the following telegram without any date. Judging from Tornaghi's preceding communication and the period of the Italian season in Buenos Aires, Verdi wrote this letter in May 1888.
[2] Wife of the impresario Angelo Ferrari.
[3] The impresario Ciacchi planned to produce the first *Otello* in South America at the Teatro Politeama in Buenos Aires.

---

[1] Presumably to Buenos Aires, in answer to a missing telegram.
[2] After a successful return to the stage in *La gioconda* at the Teatro Carlo Felice in Genoa in early 1888, applauded and encouraged by Verdi, Romilda Pantaleoni had left for a South American tour arranged by the impresario Ciacchi. When he conspired to present *Otello* in Buenos Aires without Ricordi's authorization, la Pantaleoni refused to participate. Ciacchi threatened her with a lawsuit, but she followed Verdi's advice and shared in the triumph of the first South American *Otello*—without Faccio—in Buenos Aires on 12 June 1888.

---

[1] Another unknown Italian impresario.
[2] Alfred Loewenberg states in *Annals of Opera*, p. 1127, that *Otello* was presented in Mexico on '18 November 1887 (in Italian; pirated, orchestrated from the vocal score by P. Valline; the original was given there only on 18 January 1890)'. According to Gerónimo Baqueiro Foster (ed.), *Historia de la Musica en Mexico* (Mexico: Instituto Nacional de Bellas Artes, 1934), iii. 279 and 293, Paolo Vallini conducted Rossini's *Otello* in Mexico in 1886, and Francisco Vallini conducted the first performance of Verdi's *Otello* in Mexico in 1897. The pirated performance of 18 Jan. 1890 is not mentioned in that publication.

committed recently, with the performance of *Otello* in Buenos Ayres. It is an unheard-of infamy! .... And as soon as possible we will give a first-class lesson to that gentleman who can only be a thief or a counterfeiter. [...]

GIULIO RICORDI TO VERDI
[Telegram]

Milan, 7 September 1888

JUST THIS MOMENT SIX O'CLOCK I LOST MY FATHER.—HOPE YOU WILL RETAIN GOOD MEMORY FAITHFUL FRIEND BRAVE MAN AND THAT MY GREAT SORROW WILL HAVE COMFORT OF YOUR BENEVOLENCE

GIULIO[1]

VERDI TO FRANCO FACCIO

St Agata, 23 September 1888[1]

Dear Faccio,
    Thank you for your good letter.[2]
    The loss of poor Tito was sad also for me; for me in particular, after so many events and mutual interests. And so all the friends and acquaintances of my youth in Milan, all the most intimate ones, those I saw constantly every day, all, or almost all, have disappeared in these last years!! What a desolate emptiness!!
    You are still young, but when you are as old as I am you will not just understand, you will feel how desolate this emptiness is!!

GIULIO RICORDI TO VERDI

Cernobbio, 24 September 1888

[...] You will be able to understand everything when I tell you that relations with my family are getting worse every day, and that the unworthy behaviour of all the members of my father's family, with no exceptions, is downright monstrous. To think that for 26 years I have worked like a dog, wearing out brain and health with an unselfishness that, unfortunately, I now call stupidity, only to arrive at this beautiful result. [...]

[1] No telegram or letter of condolence from the Verdis has been located. But Verdi wept upon hearing the news.

[1] Postmark: BUSSETO 22/9/88.
[2] Missing.

BOITO TO VERDI

(Ivrea) San Giuseppe
9 October [1888]¹

Dear Maestro,

The nice project has gone to the mountain,² and I, too, have returned to the mountain. The nice project was to go to St Agata with the Ricordis, but Giulio's illness has prevented its realization.—There's always next year, but we'll certainly see each other again before then, in Milan or Genoa.

The cold won't dislodge me from the place where I'm writing to you until November. Meanwhile, dear Maestro, I have seen your writing again, on the little card that Signor Mariotti³ has brought me. I could not accept his kind, flattering, and most honourable offer,⁴ and I know that you had foreseen my refusal.

If I were one of those most enviable and distinguished creatures who know how to attend simultaneously to several occupations, I might have accepted.

But to withdraw for a little work, I had to isolate myself up here. If you saw this place you would admire it and enjoy its peace. Still, as I am writing to you, a devilish wind is blowing, one that penetrates and whistles through the windows, and I feel as though I were lodged inside the pipe of a piccolo during a forte of the orchestra.

I have such a great desire to see you again and to talk with you that in writing you I'm already allowing myself to chatter.—Enough. I wish the time would again come when the theme of each of our letters was the study of a great work of art. Mariotti gave me excellent news of your health, and this comforted me. I beg you to give many greetings to Signora Giuseppina from me.—A cordial embrace from

Your
Arrigo Boito

VERDI TO BOITO

St Agata, 14 October 1888

Dearest Boito,

Ah, ah! Your meagre excuse!

The Ricordis have come and gone¹ ... and since you're enjoying yourself

---

¹ Postmark: IVREA [Piedmont]: 9/10/88.
² Literal translation of the Italian saying for 'come to nothing', required to explain Boito's play on words.
³ The little card is missing.
⁴ The direction of the Conservatory in Parma. In his search for a director of distinction, Mariotti had approached Verdi, who suggested Boito or Bottesini.

---

¹ After a visit of two or three days. See Ricordi to Verdi, 18 Oct. 1888.

in the middle of the orchestra of piccolos in the Canavese Mountains,[2] it's all right .. and there's always next year!

Signor Mariotti, who came to you in vain, later went to [see] Bottesini in London, and with good results, it seems.[3] Now Mariotti is very busy providing for the rest. I have suggested a few names; among others, la Mariani,[4] a good musician and one of the best artists. She would work out well.

And now *addio* .. Here nothing either new or nice. After two splendid days it's raining, raining, raining today!—

I greet you from Peppina, and if you are *working*, I absolve you from all your sins[5] and press your hand.

Affectionately,
G. Verdi

GIULIO RICORDI TO VERDI

Milan, 18 October 1888

Illustrious Maestro,

That dear and splendid hospitality one receives at St Agata always leaves the most charming and pleasant impressions. [. . .]

Otello, it seems, will be performed in Genoa between the 15th and the 20th of this coming November;[1] I have already arranged for the 6,500 Lire, which will be at your disposal within a couple of days' notice.

On my return,[2] *Otello* had already been performed in Rome,[3] with triumphant success. [. . .]

VERDI TO GIULIO RICORDI

St Agata, 9 November 1888

Dear Giulio,

I see that the papers are talking of a jubilee!![1] ... Good heavens! . Among the many useless things that are done in the world this is the most useless one of all, and I, who have committed so many, detest all useless things *en masse*. Moreover, it's an impracticable thing, and it's a foreign imitation, which

[2] In western Piedmont.
[3] Bottesini accepted Mariotti's offer, but he died on 7 July 1889.
[4] The soprano Maddalena Mariani-Masi did not teach in Parma.
[5] Verdi seems to be alluding to Boito's affair with Eleonora Duse, who had stayed with him at San Giuseppe from early July until the end of August.

[1] On 24 Nov. at the Teatro Carlo Felice in Verdi's absence.
[2] From St Agata.
[3] In a revival at the Teatro Costanzi.

[1] The fiftieth anniversary of the première of *Oberto, Conte di San Bonifacio*, Verdi's first opera, at La Scala on 17 Nov. 1839.

makes us imagine something that doesn't exist, that cannot exist and must not exist! In theatres organized around a repertoire, however, this always useless jubilee would be feasible, but with us it can only turn out as a meagre event without importance.

They also talk of star artists!—Hmm!!.. La Patti, who is a true artist, could probably in a moment of madness say *yes*; but the others, even without answering *no*, would at an opportune moment find excuses, engagements even in an unknown world.

You, who are a reasonable man when you want to be, fight this useless and unrealizable idea with two lines in print. You, being authoritative in this business, will be believed; and should it still be necessary to make some concession, propose to hold the jubilee 50 days after my death!

Three days suffice to cover men and things with oblivion! The great poet says, 'Heavens! Dead for two months and not yet forgotten!!'[2] . . .

I believe in the three days——
Addio

Yours,
G. Verdi

VERDI TO GIULIO RICORDI

[St Agata?, after 9 November 1888][1]

I have been told that Maurel wants to propose that you present Otello *seated*!! What a horror!..

Imagine Otello's state of mind at that moment after so many sufferings, so many rages, so many oaths; and tell me whether a man can be *seated* in such a state! I would understand him upset, moved, and even with a little of *St Vitus dance*, but seated!!! . . . Oh!!

BOITO TO VERDI

Milan, 6 December [1888][1]

Dearest Maestro,

I am so sorry to have missed your greeting that I can't help saying so to you.—I thought you had been gone since Monday,[2] and yesterday a thousand chores obliged me to remain away from home all day long.

---

[2] See Shakespeare, *Hamlet*, III. ii. 138–9, and Verdi to Ricordi, 23 May 1884.

---

[1] In the Ricordi Archives these undated lines are listed after the preceding letter. Maurel's proposal was apparently related to a revival of *Otello* at La Scala on 17 Feb. 1889.

---

[1] Postmark: MILANO 5/12/88. Apparently, Boito misdated these lines.
[2] Verdi and his wife had been in Milan in early December for negotiations concerning the purchase of a lot for the building of the Casa di Riposo. They returned to Genoa on Tuesday, 3 Dec.

When I returned I found your kind card.[3]

I hope to see you often in Genoa in January.

Many good greetings to you and Signora Giuseppina from me and my brother.

> Your most affectionate,
> Arrigo Boito

VERDI TO GIULIO RICORDI

Genoa, 14 December 1888

Dear Giulio,

Monday I'll be in Milan about 1.10 p.m.[1]—I can come to you at the hour you wish, as soon as I've washed my face and had a little lunch—

> Addio
> G. Verdi

Regards to all also from Peppina who is fairly well.

VERDI TO GIULIO RICORDI

Genoa, 1 January 1889

Dear Giulio,

Corti was here, as you know. The Sindaco and Faccio wrote to me,[1] as you also know!

And why didn't you write to me? ——

I have no right to oppose, nor do I oppose, the performance of *Otello* at La Scala.

I am, however, convinced as before that Oxilia doesn't have the vocal timbre needed for the part of Otello, but I am sure that he has excellent qualities as an artist; therefore, with *Maurel*, la *Cattaneo*, la *Borlinetto*, and a good Cassio, together with the others who should be good, you will form a good ensemble.

And since you speak to me of *Otello*, I will make some observations to you . . . . .

First of all, the sets did not convince me. They may have been so many masterpieces, but they did not serve the action that unfolded in the drama. Too small and short the first scene, and therefore the action clogged up. Too long the scene in the garden. I would change the third [act] and make two [scenes] out of it; a small inner room for the first scenes between Otello,

---

[3] Missing.

---

[1] Probably concerning the Casa di Riposo.

---

[1] Missing.

Desdemona, Jago, and Cassio. Then an open change for the rest. Boito should be consulted about this.

Furthermore, something better should be found than that measly '*fuoco di gioia*'.—

As for the music, no corrections would be needed in shadings and tempi. It's all very well for people to pretend (and they are wrong) that allowances should be made for the different qualities of vocal timbre. No: There is *only one* interpretation of a work of art, and there can be *only one*.

The solo of the double-basses until now has been unbecoming to La Scala; and I reproach myself for not having prescribed a remedy, one which was easily found. One had [only] to charge the most capable musician with marking the fingerings and with holding some section rehearsals. Now that the fingerings have been marked by *Bottesini*,[2] all Faccio has to do is to have them executed exactly, without listening to the chatter, the objections that will be made by all those who don't know how to play well.

I would try something else for the chorus in the garden. I would have the soloists sing from one side only:

1. A good boy for the first *solo*
2. A good baritone for the second *solo*
3. A good soprano for the third *solo*

accompanied by a single mandolin and a single guitar, with only 8 choristers for the notes of the accompaniment, and even without them!

Heavens! I seem to hear protests, doubts, and objections from everybody, etc., etc., etc... All I'm saying is, '*Rehearse*, but *rehearse* with goodwill, without prejudices — —on the contrary, with the faith to succeed.'

Amen. I greet you

Yours,
G. Verdi

VERDI TO GIULIO RICORDI

Genoa, 6 January 1889

Dear Giulio,

Tell Signor Corti that if *Otello* is in need of 'important modifications!'[1] .... he may make them himself.

I am sorry I allowed myself to give advice for this *revival* at La Scala.

The harm is done ... but there is a remedy: not to pay any attention to the letter I wrote to you on the matter or to the most useless conversation I had with Signor Corti.

I would now, for my petty vanity, like *Otello* to be produced as before,

[2] See Verdi to Ricordi, 2 May 1887.

[1] Obviously, Corti had made this remark to a journalist interested in the revival of *Otello* at La Scala on 19 Feb. 1889. (See the two following letters.)

even with the double-basses out of tune, with that wretched Emilia, and with etc., etc.

Always your

G. Verdi

[. . .]

GIULIO RICORDI TO VERDI

Illustrious Maestro,

I received your honoured letter of yesterday . . . . and what do you want me to tell you, you're right, not just once, but a hundred thousand times! . . . You can well imagine how angry I am about that stupid journalist; fortunately I have arranged for a denial right away, although no one with whom I spoke had taken the news seriously.

I also complained to Corti, but he, too, was beside himself because of what had happened. [. . .]

VERDI TO GIULIO RICORDI

Genoa, 7 [8] January 1889[1]

Dear Giulio,

Your letter reached me after mine had left—

I had read *Il corriere*, and today *La perseveranza*.

The fault is Corti's, who couldn't keep quiet, and the *reporter*, of course, has added, altered, etc. [. . .]

This wouldn't be so bad if there weren't an *implication* in the whole affair: that *Otello* is in need of important modifications, and that, poor little pupil that I am, I have bowed to the judgement of the experts and the infallibility of the public! . . . Poor things! . . and

po - ve -ro an - chi - o!

povero anch'io!   [poor me, too!][2]

——————Meanwhile the great news, the marvellous discovery, is beginning to get around . . . and that's all very well — —

[1] Presumably 8 Jan. 1889, since this letter appears to be the answer to Giulio Ricordi's preceding one of 7 Jan.
[2] Verdi's hastily scribbled notes suggest a personal exclamation of grim humour or a quotation from an existing opera.

I approve of what you tell me; but be very careful before you decide to make experiments, and *rehearse, rehearse, rehearse* until you find the effect . . . because alas, alas; . . pandemonium if it were to go badly! Then one would have to turn to some horn player to make a new orchestration; to some new conductor to discover an unknown interpretation; . . . and I don't know to whom else . . . to send them all to the devil!!

Meanwhile, addio—

Yours,
G. Verdi

VERDI TO GIULIO RICORDI

Genoa, 9 January 1889

[. . .] Now I think I should inform you of a very serious problem I noticed last night at the performance of *Asrael* at the Carlo Felice. Here they have heaped all the double-basses together like sheep, and the result is deplorable beyond all belief. When the double-basses, I would say, surrounded the whole orchestra, their dark sound partly covered the shrill sonority of the brass and the out-of-tune sounds of the woodwinds, and the sonority in the fortes was full and grandiose. This way it's shrill and empty. Furthermore, in the passages where only the quartet of strings dominates, half the audience hears only an indistinct humming and the other half hears too much. All of this, I think, was done in view of the *solo* in *Otello*; but the double-basses were out of tune all the same. The seating and distribution of the orchestra, I believe, was done here as it was in Milan for *Aida*.[1] It went well, but these blessed conductors always have something to do; and their vanity isn't satisfied unless they undo even what is going well. It's not enough for them to accept the applause on the stage like other prima donnas; and to thank the audience from the podium if it applauds four bars of the prelude, as if they had written them!— . All of this is ridiculous! And I'm not going to talk about it now, because I'm no longer involved and am just a simple *amateur*.

I know that Faccio planned to make changes in the orchestra. I will permit myself to say that it would be an enormous error to follow the example of Genoa for the double-basses. [. . .]

GIULIO RICORDI TO VERDI

Milan, 12 January 1889

[. . .] As I wrote to you, as soon as *Zampa*[1] has been performed I shall reach an understanding with Faccio about everything that concerns *Otello*; in the

[1] See Busch, *Aida*, pp. 96, 106, 133, 151, 160–1, 163, 181, 183–4, 212–16, 218–19, 229, 237, 239–41, 262, 323, 356, 427.

[1] French opera in 3 acts by Ferdinand Hérold (1791–1833).

meantime I will inform you, Maestro, that except for a change in the seating, the orchestra remains exactly the same as before; the change concerns only the 1st violins and seems to have had a fairly good result; all the others, woodwinds, double-basses, etc., are in the usual place.

Zampa will be performed next Wednesday with the ballet *Teodora*; if these two productions go well, as is hoped, it will be fortunate for the theatre and the management, and for us, who will be able to rehearse *Otello* well and calmly. [. . .]

VERDI TO [?] BORIANI[1]

Genoa, 16 January 1889

Esteemed Signor Boriani,
    I think it well to inform you that I have received news about the Hospital of Villanova, and I want to believe and to hope that it is not accurate. Here is what is said:

1. That food is scarce.
2. Even more scarce is wine (which is provided in the cellar).
3. That more is paid for milk than it is worth and that it is of poor quality.
4. That the oil is of the most common kind and is therefore harmful for the food as well as for the lighting.
5. That there was an attempt to purchase half spoiled rice and homemade black pasta.
6. That funeral expenses must be paid even by those who are without any means.
7. Many other things I do not mention, for the sake of brevity.

Being away, I cannot say anything, I can neither believe nor disbelieve; but in any case, this news saddens me a great deal when I think that I have not reached the goal I had set for myself by dedicating a part of my fortune to erect this Pious Place.
    I believe that the Hospital is well provided for, and that there is no need for excessive economy; but to tell you the truth, rather than suffer these dissatisfied people, I would prefer that the Hospital be closed and nothing more be said about it.
    But I hope that all this is not true, and that you will assure me of this as soon as possible with a couple of words.
    With all esteem, I remain devotedly.

[1] President of the hospital at Villanova.

VERDI TO GIULIO RICORDI

Genoa, 22 January 1889

Dear Giulio,

Othello at the *Opéra* would be a fiasco such as it hasn't been up to now . . apart from the one in Palermo!!![1]

There are no singers for *Othello* at the Opéra. There is no one who could interpret it musically; and I don't want to go to the *Big Shop*. It's really the business of a shop, not of art, the proposition of those gentlemen. Let me make myself clear:

1. By giving *Othello* they would fulfil a contract of the *cahier des charges* or at least gain credit with the minister.

2. Since it's a short opera, after a few performances they would count on a *Lever de rideau*. Since, by not spending large sums, they no longer have worthy artists, they lean on and count on the ballets! *Othello* would be under fire!!!

3. For them a fiasco or a success means the same. They know that *Othello* has been performed in [twenty?] places, and they know that at the time of the Exhibition many people will want to hear it to make comparisons. Therefore twelve or fifteen performances for curiosity's sake, then a *Lever de rideau!*—This is *art* for those gentlemen.—

I also think that exhibitions are very bad for new operas—always in artistic terms. As far as I am concerned, if in the past I was hostile ten times over, now I am so a hundred times!

Without going into details, I will answer that we believe the Exhibition would not be favourable for the new opera. People go to the theatre tired from the fatigue of the day, and they are bored and they go to sleep[2]——

I couldn't be briefer.

Forgive me — Addio, addio

Yours,
G. Verdi

GIULIO RICORDI TO VERDI

Milan, 25 January 1889

Illustrious Maestro,

Here I am disturbing you. They would like to give *Otello* in London; but fortunately, that Signor Harris is not involved, who has always made unsuitable proposals. It is the manager of the *Lyceum Theatre*, Signor Meyer,[1] who, I am assured, is capable. The ensemble for the project is based

[1] In Dec. 1888.
[2] Cf. Verdi to Ricordi, 19 May 1887.

[1] Otherwise unknown.

on the present company of La Scala, provided, of course, that everything is as successful as we think it will be. Conductor Bevignani. New sets, costumes, props made by those who supply La Scala. No other opera would be given, only 10 or 12 performances of *Otello*.

I beg you to tell me, illustrious Maestro, if you approve of the project in general, so that I will then also ascertain all the details.[2] [. . .]

VERDI TO GIULIO RICORDI

Genoa, 2 February 1889

Dear Giulio,
Il caffaro[1] reports two articles, by *D'Arcais*[2] in *L'opinione* and by *Tom* in *La fanfulla*, about the well-known jubilee!!

I won't repeat what I wrote you in my letter of last 9 November, but I will tell you only that if two years ago I could have imagined a similar project, I would have put a special clause in the *Otello* contract preventing the plan from being carried out. Now I can only ask you as the proprietor of my operas not to hand over the scores for a performance. It doesn't take much to publish two lines, even mentioning me: 'Due to the Maestro's insistent wish I cannot hand over the music for,' etc., etc. [. . .]

VERDI TO GIULIO RICORDI

Genoa, 3 February 1889

Dear Giulio,
There has been too much chatter, and there would be too much if I came to Milan even for 24 hours!—

If you found that by reducing the number of the chorus in the second act the effect is better, then reduce again, again, and again! You must be quite certain that at La Scala a unison chorus of six people will always sound empty, and even unpleasant. Either a hundred voices or a single one, as long as it's in tune. A single voice does not produce emptiness; it imposes silence. Therefore I think that in this chorus one voice for the *soli* would be enough, with eight accompanying voices, two guitars, two mandolins. Then all with the *full orchestra*.

And while we're on this *subject*, I would also propose that the orchestra be reduced in the *concertato* of the third [act] finale, at the 38th bar in E flat minor[1]

---

[2] Verdi's reaction is unknown.

---

[1] A newspaper in Genoa.
[2] Francesco's D'Arcais (1830–90), composer and music critic of the newspaper *L'opinione* in Rome.

---

[1] This quotation shows the beginning of the eleven bars from letter M of the orchestral score (Ricordi, plate no. PR 155, p. 424).

Cellos

for eleven bars; then again for another eleven bars from C minor[2]

until the *più mosso!* ♩—♯82[3] with only *six* first violins, *six* seconds, *four* violas, *two* cellos, *two* double-basses. At the same time I would have the chorus well assembled on stage, entirely isolated, and very far upstage, so that Jago can dominate and hold the interest with his movements, with his actions, and with his infamous words to Otello and Rodrigo without being disturbed by the dark noise of the orchestra. And here it is really the case of making *emptiness* in the orchestra; an *emptiness* that should be dramatic—I seem to hear all the *ifs* and *buts* of the opposition, also because of the problem of the ensemble, the chorus being so far away. But I will add and will say that if instead of having rehearsals with the orchestra alone—always useless rehearsals, even harmful to the ensemble—one, two, three, four, etc., etc., rehearsals were held of all together, including stage action in these passages, one would perhaps achieve some effect in the end. I will be told that this finale, like the chorus of the second act, isn't effective. Maybe.—Someone else would have done better, but I couldn't have done so; and worse yet, I am unfortunately convinced that the effect is missing because for one reason or another the execution has never been good, or at least the interpretation was not according to my ideas. Afterwards I deplored, and I still deplore, not having been more severe and demanding to begin with! But what can I say! There were so many, many things not to my liking, but I thought that at 74 years of age I shouldn't allow myself the fits of rage of the *Aida*—and, even more, of the *Forza del destino*—years. I wanted once, just once in my life, to *behave* like a great man, and I didn't succeed ... I won't go back there again! — —

In conclusion: rehearse the way I have indicated to you. *Rehearse*, I repeat, and don't say straightaway ... '*It isn't possible*' ... and why?. *Rehearse, rehearse*, it can't do any harm —

Oh excuse me, excuse me!—Poor Giulio! With all that you have to do, to be obliged to read so many useless words!!! —

Addio, addio

Yours,
G. Verdi

---

[2] This quotation shows the beginning of the eleven bars from letter O of the orchestral score (Ricordi, plate no. PR 155, p. 435).
[3] Note the metronomic difference ♩=92 in the orchestral score (Ricordi, plate no. PR 155, p. 440).

VERDI TO GIULIO RICORDI

Genoa, 5 February 1889

Dear Giulio,

Too laudatory, that article, but very nice![1]

Too much with kid gloves; .. but perhaps it could only be done this way!

Thank you, thank you! . Oh, if only one could have a little rest! ..
Imagine!—the students want to take part in this *jubilee*, too[2] .. and they
threaten to invite the other universities to do the same! .. Yet another
madman proposes to christen a main street with the name of ... (I dare not
say it!) .. but this I have prevented right away by sending someone to the
mayor, who promised me he would turn down the proposal if it were ever
made. Now I'm a bit calmer, in hopes that it all may cool down; and I'm
already prepared to be called a 'bear' and 'ungrateful!' ..

I have just received your telegram, and I'm very glad that the effect has
improved.[3] Don't *tire* of *rehearsing* in this way, so that something better may
result. And Oxilia? That alarms me a bit! These are bad signs! You should
give them some careful thought.—And couldn't one have De Negri? That
would be a *masterstroke* and a sure, a very sure success. I haven't talked to
anyone with either intelligence or a good ear who didn't praise this tenor with
enthusiasm. Now, after this revival,[4] they no longer say, 'Tamagno may be
first, but this fellow isn't second ...'; instead they are now saying, 'Superior
to all!' This might be a bit exaggerated, but there must be something very
good about it. And that crazy Tamagno comes here for a special
performance just 48 hours later!![5] He must either be mad or disgustingly
greedy!! He gives the impression of saying, 'I, I will let them hear how *Otello*
must be performed!' That makes him disagreeable, and he will find a very
severe audience. Certainly he will have his effects in the 4 bars of his entrance,
in the *Addio*, and in some other passages of vocal display; but De Negri was
also applauded after the entrance; he repeated the *Addio* and also the
Giuramento finale of the second act, and certainly not thanks to the two very
unfortunate Jagos; he was also much admired in the *parlante* of the third act
with the lament of the violins; and he was heavenly in the Duet of the first act

---

[1] Draft of an article written and published by Giulio Ricordi in *La gazzetta musicale* of 10
Feb. 1889. See the two letters that follow.

[2] The students of the University of Genoa organized a ceremony, which took place in Verdi's
absence.

[3] The missing telegram apparently related to Verdi's preceding letter.

[4] Of *Otello* at the Teatro Carlo Felice in Genoa on 24 Nov. 1888. De Negri appeared in
subsequent performances until early Feb. when he left for Turin.

[5] Tamagno replaced De Negri on 7 Feb.

(Tamagno wasn't) and in the last act .... I'm quite curious to see, that is, to hear, what the success will be like! — —

Again a long letter!—Addio, addio

Affectionately,

G. Verdi

PS I've written worse than usual! Excuse me!

I am returning the article...

Keep the money for the time being; we'll talk about it—

GIULIO RICORDI TO VERDI

Milan, 8 February 1889

Illustrious Maestro,

These days I have had a great many troubles and nuisances! ...... and consequent fits of anger; little troubles, little nuisances, but when added up ..... they amount to a heavy load!—Good for me that in the midst of these clouds your welcome letters arrived; you may say, Maestro, that they are long! ..... They will never be long enough, so great is the pleasure they give me. To the little troubles was added the very great one of Oxilia's illness! .... We had really rehearsed with passion and love!—and one could have had a first-rate dress rehearsal! ...... Now all the care and effort have become useless. The worst part of it is that it seems to be a serious matter, that is, a throat infection! .... Corti didn't stand around doing nothing, and left the other night for Turin to get De Negri; he should have returned last night; but, not having seen him yet this morning, I am persuaded that he did not succeed, as I had foreseen, since *Otello* is also announced in Turin![1] I shall see Corti later on and hear the news. A pity! .... A pity! ..... A pity! ..... If you had seen the beautiful scenes, all four of them!—The storm is marvellous, and also the clear sky is so well done that it looks absolutely real. I seem to hear you say: 'Why didn't you do all these beautiful things while I was around? ......' Because they did not have the head-stagehand that they have this year; he is from Trieste and has studied a lot at the theatre in Vienna; excellent not only as a stagehand, but also on account of the new lighting, which improved the sets by 50 per cent. I am really, really sorry that you did not attend at least one rehearsal; also, you could have told me whether the musical interpretations you indicated were well executed, as I flatter myself [they were]. And now, when and how will it be possible to give *Otello*? ...... Two rehearsals must still be held .... Here is the opportunity for the famous 24-hour trip. Decide, ... Maestro, and your presence, as always, will bring good luck to the theatre, to the artists .... to all!! Don't laugh! ...... It is so.

On Sunday, then, I shall publish the article — — Jubilee. But ... it will not

---

[1] A revival at the Teatro Regio on 14 Feb. 1889.

do any good, since I fear, illustrious Maestro, that it will not be possible to stop such a great movement! .... Good, as you say, the publisher will also refuse [to allow] the operas! ...... *Something else will be done*!—For this, too, what a comfort it would have been to me to have you and your advice present here. I repeat, I shall not allow the operas ...... but that will not stop the manifestation of a *national feeling*. Meanwhile I will be a mastiff; I shall gnash my teeth, I shall bark; but when nobody hears me, I will come back shouting at the top of my lungs: '*Long live our Verdi*!!' And I am starting right now. [...]

Corti was here just now; he would have made arrangements with De Negri, but could not come to an understanding with Borioli;[2] he will undertake new negotiations; Oxilia has an abscess in the throat, a question of days; the physicians agree, however, in asserting that once it has burst, the voice will not have suffered at all. Corti says that he has kept the promise he made you for a beautiful staging.

VERDI TO GIULIO RICORDI

Genoa, 9 February 1889

Dear Giulio,

Well, then, I think the article tomorrow won't hurt, and that they'll persuade themselves that at least, at least it's an unattainable thing.

I regret and am alarmed by the Oxilia business! . The symptoms are not good! Let us hope!

My coming would be useless, and I'd be nothing but a *trouble ménage*. Have them do as I say and, if you agree, follow my modest suggestions. Thinking about it again, I am persuaded that in the chorus of the second act, the *soli* must really be executed by a *single voice* with a small accompaniment of voices and sounds. It would become quieter, more modest, simpler, and I'd say more innocent, thus going along with Desdemona's personality. For instance: one boy offering flowers makes a kind and innocent gesture; six boys become coarse. So for the rest——

Getting back again to the third [act] finale. Here, too, there can be no dramatic truth or effect if one doesn't succeed in completely isolating Jago, so that the eyes of the audience focus only on him, so that his words, not his voice, dominate everything, and so that beneath his words only an indistinct and, if you like, even *inexact* murmur is heard! *Inexact*! These words would make the hair on a musician's head stand on end, but never mind.

Conclusion!

A large and long set... Chorus far away, very far away.

Jago clearly visible. Orchestra reduced, as I told you, and even more so. I say again, *rehearse, rehearse*. And now that you have time, why don't you hold a rehearsal of only these two pieces in the theatre with the sets, the action, and an upright piano? (These are the useful rehearsals.) Then another

---

[2] Daniele Borioli, impresario of the Teatro Regio in Turin.

rehearsal of these two pieces with orchestra, repeating until the effect comes about?—Amen——

Tamagno has had a real success here! They say...

Yours,
G. Verdi

VERDI TO FRANCO FACCIO

Genoa, 10 February 1889[1]

[...] That hollow, dark, monotonous sound, always on one side, cannot produce a good effect. If the double-basses could be arranged in a single row [facing the conductor], as in Vienna, very well; but if that can't be done, it's better to leave half of them on one side, half of them on the other. You will say that in a *solo* they won't play together. The *solo* in *Otello* is an exception, and one must not think only of that; and do you know why the double-basses didn't work well in Milan? First of all, because various musicians weren't very capable, second, because the first double-bass player had no authority.

As there is no composer (with few exceptions) who doesn't believe his own music to be the best of all, so there isn't an orchestra musician who doesn't believe himself to be a Beethoven *manqué*. Consequently the concert masters must have authority, energy, and the ability to say, 'Do it this way.' I don't even approve of the division of the violas, the cellos, and the [second] violins. These three instrumental groups are precisely the ones which weave the harmony and always accompany together. For the first violins it matters little whether they're on one side or the other, as long as they play well. [...]

VERDI TO GIUSEPPE PIROLI

Genoa, 10 February 1889

Tell me something, you, who find yourself in the turmoil of a revolt![1] Sad matters that, unfortunately, will have consequences! It will be put down, arrests will be made, people sent into exile, but that won't do any good. Among the masses, certainly, there are always the instigators, the wicked subjects, the thieves, but there is almost always *hunger*.

I don't like politics, but I admit its necessity, the theories, the forms of government, patriotism, dignity, etc., etc., but first of all *one must live*. From my window every day I see a ship, and sometimes *two*, each of them loaded with at least a thousand emigrants! *Misery and hunger!* In the fields I see proprietors of some years ago now reduced to peasants, day labourers, and emigrants (*misery and hunger*). The wealthy, whose fortunes decrease from year to year, can no longer spend as before, and therefore *misery and hunger!*

---

[1] Faccio was rehearsing *Otello* at this time for its revival at La Scala on 19 Feb.

---

[1] See Biographical Note on Francesco Crispi.

And how can one go on? Our industries will certainly not save us from ruin!

You will say that I am a pessimist? . . . No, no . . . I believe I am right in saying that I am deeply convinced that at the end of this road we shall find complete ruin. [. . .]

GIULIO RICORDI TO VERDI

Milan, 15 February 1889

Illustrious Maestro,

Oxilia really seems to be recovered; he was prepared to perform tomorrow, but the management was prudent and postponed until *Tuesday*. Tonight, rehearsal of several details; tomorrow during the day, stage rehearsal; Sunday evening, dress rehearsal.———

Let's hope that for once there may be no more mishaps!

In Turin last night, *Otello* a complete triumph; it seems that another excellent Jago has been found in Dufriche; so much the better. When will some other tenor be found? [. . .]

VERDI TO BOITO

Genoa, 17 February 1889

Dear Boito,

Writing this letter is a shot in the dark, but I'm certain that it will reach you somehow.[1]

I am sorry to keep you, even for a few minutes, from your work, but I feel the need to talk to you about that . . . jubilee, which I find useless and without any possible good results.

Let's put aside my *own self*, my modesty, my pride, and all the rest . . . . then I ask:

What are you going to do on that night of the 17th of November? A concert of various operatic pieces?

My God! What shabbiness!

Or performances of some operas?

But then, to give significance to these performances, three or four [operas] would have to be performed. The *first*, the *last*, and another one in between these two. The performances of these two wouldn't be difficult, but the first would be difficult and costly, since four first artists would be required (who would also be able to sing), *mise-en-scène*, and all the rehearsals as for a new opera.

And the result?

Imagine whether our audience, with inclinations that are so different from

---

[1] Verdi addressed this letter to Boito's home in Milan, from where it was forwarded to him at the Hôtel des Anglais in San Remo.

those of 50 years ago, would have the patience to listen to the two long acts of *Oberto*! Either they would be politely bored in silence (always a humiliating thing) or they would manifest their disapproval. In this case it would no longer be a feast, it would be a scandal.

As for the other project, that of founding a permanent institution with a national subscription,

I ask again:

What sum could be collected? A small sum would serve only to give one of those customary competition prizes that are of no use to art or to the winner. A sum that could truly be useful—hard to collect in these very critical times—would have to be considerable, very considerable, in order to form a capital whose interest might be sufficient to support a young person in his first experiment in the theatre.

And here, how many difficulties arise!

1. The impresario should be given a guarantee for the value of the opera.
2. Guarantee a conductor who will give a good performance.

To succeed in this, there would be no other way (though not a sure one) than to nominate a committee . . . even two. One to examine the poetry. The other to examine the music. It would be easy to find the first, and I would indicate right away: *Boito* and two others. More difficult the second: Again *Boito* . . . and then?

Furthermore, these committees would have to take upon themselves the ungrateful and difficult task of severely watching over the *mise-en-scène* and the musical and dramatic performance, so that the impresario could not present the opera like a *pis aller*, with the only purpose being to pocket whatever the sum.

And here another question arises: Where will the opera be performed? In Milan?—But if it is by national subscription, why couldn't the Romans, for example, demand to have it in Rome? The Neapolitans in Naples . . and so on.

How many difficulties!

I finish (breathe again) and conclude by telling you what I've been telling Giulio since early November, that this jubilee, apart from being extremely unpleasant for me, is neither useful nor practical.

If you share my opinion, you—as a composer and poet with greater authority than the others have—see to it that all of this is quickly silenced, without leaving a pretext to come back to it—and you will be doing an excellent thing.

Obviously this letter is confidential. There is nothing I couldn't say out loud; but still it's useless for me to let my voice be heard about this.

I have made you lose some time, and I'm sorry: Excuse me!

Addio. With Peppina's greetings, I cordially press your hand and remain

Affectionately,
G. Verdi

VERDI TO GIULIO RICORDI

Genoa, 18 February 1889

Dear Giulio,

I foresaw it!

I never had any faith in this revival of *Otello*. One should have left the first impressions at La Scala and not have given it again for many years——To speak of mishaps, of illness doesn't hold. No, no—it's all the same.

This revival was neither fitting nor useful.

And now, what do the author and publisher gain?——And what does Corti himself gain? He can be sure of half a fiasco . . . . at the least!

Your telegram[1] makes me assume—in spite of the *excellent elements*, as you say—that not everyone is suitable for his part, except, as always, Maurel; and I think that la Cattaneo herself isn't worth very much in the fourth act! And then? If the Otello is inadequate, if the fourth act falls short, what remains?

In short . . . it has been a big mistake! You will say that I, too, approved it. No—I was drawn into it, never convinced — —

Amen——

Give me frank and straightforward news, and believe me always

Yours,
G. Verdi

BOITO TO VERDI

San Remo.
20 February [1889]
Wednesday

Dear Maestro,

I have just this moment received your letter.

As soon as I read in the papers that I was part of the Commission for the Jubilee, I wrote to Giulio to let me know when the first session would be. I am anxious to attend it, precisely to prevent the approval of proposals that could displease you. You see, Maestro, before I received your letter I prepared myself to act as if I had already read it.—Trust Giacosa, Negri, and me. I cannot promise you to let the Jubilee fall by the wayside; the country wants it.

But I assure you that we will do our best not to be faulted by you or by any other wise judge.

If a telegram from Giacosa doesn't call me to Milan before Sunday, I'll be

---

[1] Missing. Apparently, Giulio Ricardi telegraphed Verdi after the dress rehearsal of 17 Feb.

in Genoa on Sunday, if you permit, to collaborate on the destruction of your dinner.

Affectionate greetings to you and Signora Peppina.

Till we see each other soon.

> Your
> Arrigo Boito

VERDI TO BOITO

Genoa, 21 February 1889

Dear Boito,

Ah me! Ah me!

I had hoped for a different answer from you! I have nothing more to add, after writing repeatedly to Giulio and to you; I only say again that I have been, I am, and shall always be against the celebration of this Jubilee—

Till Sunday, then, to eat soup with us—

Sans adieu

> Affectionately,
> G. Verdi

VERDI TO FRANCO FACCIO

Genoa, 24 February 1889

[. . .] You would have done well to have written to me before, since you might have been a little embarrassed after the disaster.[1] I know what extenuating circumstances you could mention to me, but by God, when one knows the theatre just a little, one must mistrust an artist quite a lot who, after a few performances, is sadly deteriorating, who goes to San Remo for many days and returns without being cured; one must then really think that that artist has either lost his voice or has been stricken with an illness requiring long hours to cure.[2]

I foresaw the scandal . . . I repeatedly wrote about it to Giulio. The warning had no effect, and so be it. [. . .]

VERDI TO GIULIO RICORDI[1]

Genoa, 3 March 1889

Dear Giulio,

I understand everything! . . Yet you propose to sacrifice the opera a second time without being able to bring the slightest remedy to the theatre.

---

[1] Of the *Otello* revival at La Scala on 19 Feb.
[2] Oxilia in the role of Otello.

---

[1] In answer to a missing letter, in which Giulio Ricordi proposed a change of cast for the performances of *Otello* during the present season.

It isn't true to say that the one disastrous performance did not prejudice the music. I myself have heard from different persons, whom I could also name to you, these very words: 'It no longer seemed like the same music.' Three or four nights with De Negri and (don't be surprised) la Pantaleoni, since la Cattaneo is a bit stupid, even quite a bit. She revealed herself as such when she told you, 'They told me not to move,' etc. . . By God, if she had had a bit of good sense, she would have answered that in an *Ave Maria* one doesn't shout or gesticulate.

This is my straightforward, honest opinion — — You'll sacrifice the opera. This sentence implies that the effect produced the first time was excessive, [even] if it was not confirmed. In any case, the sentence includes a doubt as to how genuine the first success was.

It's madness to trust Oxilia, even after a rehearsal.

Another madness, that of Giannini.[2]

The theatre won't gain a thing and will sacrifice *Otello* a second time!

There was only one remedy; and you won't do the theatre the least bit of good——[. . .]

VERDI TO BOITO

Genoa, 6 March 1889

Dear Boito,

Upon leaving Milan[1] I threw some papers into the fire, among them that awkward[2] scale. I have the first part of this scale, but of the second, which I wrote then and there, I've forgotten the modulations and the voice-leading of the parts, particularly of these three notes

If you didn't burn it, send me the A sharp and G sharp chords.

You will say that it isn't worth the trouble to occupy oneself with these trifles, and you are quite right. But what can I say! When one is old, one becomes a child, they say. These trifles remind me of my teacher,[3] who amused himself by racking my brains with similar *basses* when I was eighteen years old.

I also think that with this scale one could make a piece with words—for example an *Ave Maria*, adding for the tenor or the soprano, however, the same scale with different modulations and voice-leading at the subdominant.

    [2] Presumably the tenor Francesco Giannini.

---

    [1] After a presumably short stay.
    [2] A *scala enigmatica* invented by Professor Adolfo Crescentini (1854–1921) at the Liceo musicale in Bologna. This unusual scale employs C, D♭, E, F♯, G♯, A♯, B, C, as it ascends, and the same notes descending, except that the F♯ becomes natural.
    [3] Presumably Vincenzo Lavigna. (See Verdi Chronology, 1832–5.)

It would be difficult, however, to return naturally to the tonic. Another *Ave Maria*! It would be the fourth!⁴ So I could hope to be beatified after my death.

Ever your

G. Verdi

BOITO TO VERDI

Milan, Thursday [7 March 1889]¹

Dear Maestro,

I did well to copy the two little pages containing the broken scale in which you went up and down with so much ease.

Any problem solved without effort is a blessing.

In those contrapuntal passages that sing, there is a melancholy charm which brings the evening prayer to mind.—May this fourth *Ave Maria* come forth.

I won't mention it to anyone, trust me. Many *Ave Marias* are needed, so that you may be pardoned by His Holiness for Jago's Credo.—On Saturday night I want to hear *Otello*.

I'll give you news about it. Played at the piano, those two little pages please me even more than when I thought of them with my memory's ear.

Affectionate greetings

from your
Arrigo Boito

PS The Mayor² has forwarded my letter to Cambiasi,³ who, having read it, has hidden it, however, and keeps it a secret and has not presented it to the Commission—I have asked Aldo Noseda⁴ to request that it be read at the next session.

GIULIO RICORDI TO VERDI

Milan, 10 March 1889

[...] As I telegraphed you after the dress rehearsal and after last night,¹ I confirm that Giannini managed well in the difficult step.² De Negri's voice is

---

⁴ The first ('Salve Maria') appears in Act I of *I Lombardi alla Prima Crociata* (1843), the second is an 'Ave Maria' (after words by Dante) for soprano and strings (1880), the third is Desdemona's 'Ave Maria' in Act IV of *Otello*.

¹ Postmark: MILANO 7/3/89.
² Gaetano Negri.
³ Missing, apparently dealing with the afore-mentioned Jubilee. Pompeo Cambiasi (1849–1908) wrote theatrical chronicles. (See Bibliography.)
⁴ President of the *Società Orchestrale* of La Scala (1852–1916); under the pen-name *Il Misovulgo* [The enemy of the vulgar] for many years music critic of *Il corriere della sera* in Milan.

¹ Missing telegrams concerning the change of cast for *Otello* at La Scala.
² Presumably in the '*Esultate*' at his first entrance (I. 1).

as usual, and that is without missing the high notes, which are not as strong as the others; middle and low registers splendid; suitable figure, fair on stage; squarely on pitch. If we could have had him 15 days earlier, much more could have been done, since he had not studied the part with subtlety; the strangest thing is that the piece he sings best, really very well, actually beyond comparison with Tamagno, is the duet with Desdemona in the first act!! . . . But with that robust voice, he is less effective in the forceful phrases.

La Cattaneo very good, incomparably better than on the first night; and all the others good, orchestra and chorus excellent. Altogether a production that has satisfied the audience, with applause and calls after every act. [. . .]

VERDI TO GIULIO RICORDI

Genoa, 11 March 1889

Dear Giulio,

All things considered, it would have been better if this *Otello* had not been given.—I really would have preferred, as I told you, that this opera were not performed in the present season, not even with Oxilia, unless it could have been arranged with Tamagno and [unless] you could have excluded la Cattaneo, who, let's face it, is a stupid little thing with six nice high notes from the E to the C——

I understand that an arrangement with Tamagno would have been unfair to the tenor of the season, and to other interests, which I also understand; but from an [artistic] point of view, *Otello* should only have been given in this revival with Tamagno. [. . .]

VERDI TO BOITO

Genoa, 11 March 1889

Dear Boito,

On the contrary, thank you for paving the way for me with Signor Edwards.[1] This way it'll be easier for me to give a negative reply.

In Shaspeare's country they will reproach us for omitting the first act, but they aren't going to hold Jago's Credo against you. And by the way: You, you are the principal culprit who must ask pardon for that Credo! Now you must at least compose a Catholic *Credo* for four parts in the style of Palestrina, after you have finished that certain . . . . . which I dare not name.[2]

As for me, I hope I have taken good care of my affairs with the Blessed Lord. The *Ave Marias* have become five instead of four!! But how? That particular Scale wasn't enough for the whole Prayer; so I thought of

[1] In a missing letter, card or telegram, Boito mentioned the English musicologist Henry Sutherland Edwards, who seems to have made an urgent appeal for Verdi's and Boito's presence at the first performance of *Otello* in England at London's Lyceum Theatre on 5 July 1889.
[2] *Nerone.*

adding the same scale beginning on the fourth of the note to the Soprano part
... but later, it was impossible to get back to the principal note with grace
and simplicity (and it seemed so easy). So, I added another Scale in C to the
Alto part; and another one in F to the Tenor part. And thus, I've made the
two *Ave Marias*. Strangely enough, with that unhinged Scale, the
modulations turn out well, and so does the distribution of the parts!!

I had no close contact with Paolo Ferrari, but heard with deep regret about
the loss of this great playwright of ours, who was truly the foremost.

Addio. With Peppina's greetings, I cordially take your hand.

Your
G. Verdi

BOITO TO VERDI

[Milan] Wednesday [13 March 1889][1]

Dear Maestro,

I won't go back there.[2] That opera, where each note has a spiritual
meaning, cannot be performed by idiots. One leaves there with a liver
ailment. That tenor is a mad dog.[3] I've never seen a more beastly scoundrel
on the stage. The ass has a good voice, but what an ass! The prima donna is a
well-fed, fat nonentity, a zero.[4]

When Maurel appeared, however, I again had the great, full, and deep
artistic impression of two years ago. He also seemed to be more serious, more
perfect than he was then, and equally powerful.

His voice seemed stronger to me, too. That man will go on singing for
some fifteen years.

The theatre was so crowded I had to ask for a place in the boxes. The
audience peacefully swallows the tenor and the prima donna, and its
attention isn't distracted by them.

So much the better. We are more exacting and we want the exquisite
impression of art, and our fault is our punishment. Never mind.

I'm very eager to see the fifth *Ave Maria*. The next time we see each other
I'll ask you to satisfy me. As I thought again about the design you sketched
for me in your letter, I doubted whether that maligned scale for the soprano
part and the other voices could be sung by human beings. But then, as I
thought it over and looked at the two little sheets you left me, I understood
that the surrounding harmony which tempers and governs them, transforms
that scribble into a line that really sings and is easily adapted to the
modulation of the ensemble. And so one learns something every day.

I simply don't understand those Englishmen of mine.[5] They've returned to

[1] Postmark: MILANO 13/3/89.
[2] To another performance of *Otello* at La Scala.
[3] Francesco Giannini.
[4] Aurelia Cataneo Caruson.
[5] Unknown except for Henry Sutherland Edwards.

me for a new assault. They are full of good and serious intentions and are no vulgar speculators. But their insistence knows no bounds. After saying 'No' twenty times, in order to get rid of them, I had to say that, time permitting, I'd go to London!

But I added that in all probability my time would not permit. And with this phantom promise, which equals 'No', I freed myself.

Four more lines and I'll be finished.

The end of the second act of *Otello* is much clearer and more effective now than it was before,[6] or so it seems to me, even though I haven't forgotten the violent artistic impression that finale made on me when I saw it in the first sketch.

Many kind greetings to Signora Giuseppina and to you.

> Your most affectionate
> Arrigo Boito

GIUSEPPINA VERDI TO GIUSEPPE DE SANCTIS

Genoa, 19 March 1889

[...] I did not know who followed Tamagno in *Otello*.[1] and I hope this Durot[2] may come out victorious in the dangerous comparison.

Verdi knew this tenor Durot in Paris many years ago, when he had not yet trod the boards of the stage and Verdi had not yet written *Otello*.

Afterwards he didn't see any more of him and, consequently, can't have advised him how to perform that imposing part. [...]

VERDI TO GIULIO RICORDI

Genoa, 28 March 1889

Dear Giulio,

I received your letter from Signor Mayer[1] . . . It's absolutely impossible for me to do what he wishes.

He also tells me that on Saturday there will be a new appearance by Oxilia (evviva) at La Scala!!! . Poor *Otello*! Destined this year for the experiments of hoarse voices and the worst screamers in the province!

I hope you don't mind sending me—simply out of curiosity—a telegram

---

[6] See Verdi to Ricordi, 29 Apr. and 2 May 1887.

---

[1] In a revival of the opera at the Teatro San Carlo in Naples.
[2] See Verdi's letter to him of 5 Jan. 1891.

---

[1] Missing. (See Ricordi to Verdi, 25 Jan. 1889.)

on Sunday morning.[2] Just tell me the bitter, bitter truth. I'm expecting anything; nothing will surprise me.———

Believe me always

Yours,
G. Verdi

PS I have just this moment received a letter from Muzio,[3] who writes to me that in Naples you have imposed a second performance with Durot and have *suspended the subscription!* Ah, permit me this time to tell you that you are wrong! How? At La Scala (where *Otello* is known) you allow a scandalous performance (foreseen) with Oxilia! You allow that other tenor![4] For next Saturday you allow another almost certain scandal with Oxilia!

You are indulgent with a too mediocre Desdemona.[5] And you don't allow Durot, after a success, to the subscribers of the San Carlo?!!
Oh, by God, I really don't understand anything any more.

GIUSEPPINA VERDI TO GIUSEPPE DE SANCTIS

Genoa, 29 March 1889

[...] Verdi would be quite anxious to have exact, trustworthy news of the success of the tenor Durot on the two nights he has sung *Otello* at the San Carlo after Tamagno's departure.

Probably you will not have been to the theatre, but it won't be difficult for you to find out what success Durot may have had, keeping a great distance from Tamagno, of course, and without comparisons.

He wants to know only the pure, purest truth. [...]

GIUSEPPINA VERDI TO GIUSEPPE DE SANCTIS

[Genoa] 11 April 1889

Just a word to thank you in Verdi's name for all the reports you have kindly furnished concerning Durot.[1] [...]

GIULIO RICORDI TO VERDI

Milan, 30 April 1889

[...] Today Durot was booked for London; I was charged to try Tamagno again, but I don't think it can be arranged;[1] I shall make it my duty to keep you informed. [...]

---

[2] Missing.
[3] Missing.
[4] Francesco Giannini.
[5] Aurelia Cataneo Caruson.

---

[1] Missing.

---

[1] However, Tamagno was to sing Otello at the Lyceum Theatre in London on 5 July 1889.

GIULIO RICORDI TO VERDI

Milan, 8 May 1889

[. . .] As I have already written to you, I tried in every way to cancel the London affair,[1] to the point where the impresario, Mr Mayer, expressly made a trip to Milan; it was not possible to reach the goal, since he had already engaged the artists and contracted the orchestra, chorus, sets, costumes, etc., etc. I also told him that we negotiated with Tamagno, with whom nothing was concluded. Now, however, it seems that he would be disposed to appear, and I had him questioned; but then, I do not know whether Mayer, who has three tenors, would be so disposed!! .... In a few days I shall know something positive and will inform you right away.

You know the popular edition of the operas of Giuseppe Verdi!! .. 10 volumes are published; now I would like to complete the collection, adding to it: *Oberto—Finto Stanislao—Giovanna d'Arco-Alzira—Il corsaro—La Battaglia di Legnano—Attila—Masnadieri*. Thus the collection would be really complete. Besides the above-mentioned ones, however, there would be: *Gerusalemme* and *Stiffelio*. But especially for the latter one, I would appreciate hearing your opinion, since I believe that the orchestra score belonging to it no longer exists in the archive! ... What a pity!!! .. A real pity!! . [. . .]

VERDI TO GIULIO RICORDI

St Agata, 10 May 1889

Dear Giulio,

If I were a Neapolitan I would tell you: *Neh! Voi pazziate*!! [No! You're crazy!!] What do you want the poor public to do with *Oberto*, the *Finto Stanislao*—and other similar works, etc.?—And what good will reprinting them, etc., etc., etc., do for art and for the publisher?—

Not even I could tell you what has become of the *Stiffelio*! It's not a pity, absolutely not a pity, if there's no longer a trace of it!

But there's no need for my opinion; you know what you must do, since as far as I am concerned, I would make an *autodafé*[1] of it all; and for such an occasion I would even write a funeral march! And I'd make a nice one for you, too, that is, a *hearty* one!! .

---

[1] The first *Otello* in England on 5 July 1889.

[1] The Spanish term *auto de fé*, derived from the Latin *actus fidei*, applied to the burning of heretics at the stake. Such sentences of the Inquisition were carried out with pompous ceremony in Spain and Portugal until the end of the eighteenth century. One of the most impressive features of Verdi's *Don Carlos* is the scene of the autodafé.

Ah me, the London affair! But let's not talk about it any more! *À la grâce de Dieu!* .

And now I shake your hand and greet you also from Peppina.

Addio, addio

Yours,

G. Verdi

EMANUELE MUZIO TO CARLO D'ORMEVILLE

London, 6 July 1889

[Hotel address illegible]

Dear D'Ormeville,

Otello great success . . . a great sensation.[1]

Tamagno good in the forceful phrases, but in the duet in the first act, which must be sung, he didn't satisfy everyone. Maurel immense, sustaining the jealousy duet of the second act as a great artist. The audience was breathless. La Cattaneo was accepted, that's all. The tremolo in her voice and her guttural low notes are unpleasant. The comprimario parts, chorus, and orchestra very good. Altogether a success for the music and the artists Maurel and Tamagno. [. . .]

VERDI TO FRANCO FACCIO

Montecatini, 14 July 1889[1]

From the telegrams and Muzio[2] I had news of *Otello* in London. Now you confirm this news, and it pleases me, even though at my age, and with the present conditions of our music, a success is of no use. You speak of the 'triumph of Italian art'!! You deceive yourself! Our young Italian composers aren't good patriots. If the Germans, starting with Bach, have arrived at Wagner, they make opera like good Germans, and that's all right. But we descendants of Palestrina commit a musical crime by imitating Wagner, and we do useless, even harmful work.

I know that they spoke very well of Boito, and that gives me the greatest pleasure, since praise attributed to *Otello* in Shakespeare's homeland is worth a lot. [. . .]

---

[1] Under Faccio's baton at the Lyceum Theatre on 5 July. (See Document XI.)

---

[1] Four days after Verdi had written to Boito, 'So let's do Falstaff!'

[2] Missing.

VERDI TO GIULIO RICORDI

Genoa, 17 January 1890

Dear Giulio,

Boccanegra, too, won't be in the interest of the management of La Scala![1] Nor could one have better hopes with a Boccanegra who is such a mediocre actor,[2] and with Cattaneo and Navarrini so poorly equipped for those parts! But this is not the purpose of my letter. I wanted to tell you, instead, that if after De Negri's more or less successful performance[3] someone should get the idea of reviving *Otello*, it would be a great error to do it! After the torture it was put to last year, I think it would be helpful from every point of view not to speak of it for a long time.—

Give me your news, which I hope will be good! Ours isn't bad, but apart from the *flu*, there is something very sad in the air![4]

Regards to all, also from Peppina.

Affectionately,
G. Verdi

GIULIO RICORDI TO VERDI

[Milan] 18 January 1890

Illustrious Maestro,

Again I am writing to you from my home, from which I haven't moved for 4 days on doctor's orders!!—Imagine what mood I'm in . . . . not being able to go to my studio or to take care of the business.—How long will it last? . . . It's really time for things to change.—As you say, the world is overcome by a mysterious, universal sadness. Meanwhile the business suffers from it . . . . and an increasingly difficult future is ahead of us. Enough: Let us keep going as best we can, and with courage. I was quite sorry not even to be able to stage *Boccanegra*; unfortunately Faccio . . . is no longer himself; it is already an enormous effort for him to conduct the orchestra, and he no longer occupies himself as before with the singers and the stage, and so everybody does as he pleases.

---

[1] *Simon Boccanegra* had been revived on 15 Jan. with Faccio conducting for the last time.
[2] Mattia Battistini.
[3] As Gabriele Adorno.
[4] 'The 1890s, for Italy, were a time of fierce, even bloody social strife.' (W. Weaver, *Duse: A Biography*. London: Thames and Hudson, 1984, p. 82.) It exploded in the spring 1898 when—after Italy's defeat in Africa in 1896—government troops fired on unarmed strikers and demonstrators. Italy was not alone in such a struggle. All of Europe saw the rise of socialism in the wake of the Industrial Revolution. Other events contributed to Verdi's prophecy of the First World War. Already on 30 Sept. 1870, he had written to Clara Maffei: 'We shall not stay out of the European war, and we shall be swallowed. It will not happen tomorrow, but it will happen. A pretext is found right away.' (Busch, *Aida*, p. 73.) See also Verdi to Piroli, 10 Feb. 1889 and the Biographical Note on Francesco Crispi.

What you write to me concerning *Otello*, however, is all right; until now nothing has been said about it; maybe after De Negri's very great success the idea may occur to someone—for the time being, I repeat, nothing is being said about it. In [that] case they can re-engage De Negri for another year. [. . .]

EMANUELE MUZIO TO VERDI

[Paris, 22 October 1890][1]

My dearest Maestro and friend Verdi,

There is a little trouble with my will; please do as I say.[2] I shall soon depart for the other world, full of affection and friendship for you and for your good and dear wife. I have loved you both, and remember that ever since 1844 my faithful friendship has never diminished.

Remember me sometimes, and till we see each other again later on in the other world. Many kisses from your faithful and affectionate friend

E. Muzio

VERDI TO GIULIO RICORDI

St Agata, 4 November 1890

Dear Giulio,

At the moment I have no mind for anything and am almost unable to grasp it. This poor Muzio wrote precisely these words to me on 25 of October: 'I have put my things in order.'[1] I know him as a man of order, and he will certainly have thought of everything; still, if anything should be missing, ask Signor Pisa[2] to do on my account, in such a grave circumstance, everything that must be done, in the most convenient way.

Peppina and I are absolutely desolate! If I weren't 77 years old . . . . and in such a harsh season . . . ., but I am 77 years old!!!

Addio

VERDI TO THE MAYOR OF VILLANOVA

St Agata, 16 November 1890

Esteemed Signor Mayor of Villanova,

I was unable to see either the President or the Vice-President of the hospital, since they were away; but if you, Signor Mayor, can make out a certificate of poverty for her, Ferretti will be received.

[1] This dating is based on two notes in *Copialeterre*, pp. 359 and 361.
[2] Muzio had named Verdi the executor of his will.

---

[1] Missing. Muzio died on 27 Nov. in Paris.
[2] Unknown.

Thinking over our conversation of the day before yesterday, even though at a sad moment, I repeat, after mature reflection, what I told you in person, that is: if you think that the sum contributed for the maintenance of the hospital is a burden on the Municipality of Villanova, you have only to take the necessary steps to exempt it from this expense, assuring it that there will be no objection whatsoever on my part.

I am leaving tomorrow morning. With my respects, I remain devotedly.

VERDI TO EUGÈNE DUROT

Genoa, 5 January 1891

Signor Durot, artist—now in Madrid.

You know that in the will of our poor friend[1] I have been charged to withdraw from you the third of the proceeds from his writings.

Our poor late friend speaks of you with these words of praise: 'My dear student Eugenio Durot, who is now singing in Madrid, an honest and brave man. ...'[2] After such phrases I should have nothing else to say to you but simply to [ask you to] send me the sum; but since I must and want to give an exact account to the executors of the will and to the heirs, I beg you to send me, together with the sum owed to the heirs, the amount of your present and future engagements in Madrid until the end of August, 1891.

I do not add another word, so as not to sadden you and sadden myself even more.

The loss is grave! You have lost a good maestro, I, a friend of almost 50 years. Let us honour his memory by scrupulously fulfilling his will. I press your hand and remain devotedly.

VERDI TO GIULIO RICORDI

Genoa, 11 March 1891

Dear Giulio,

It's destiny! ...

I'll never be able to rid myself of the troubles of my operas!

Roger[1] has written to me . . . . . 'et de m'indiquer la proportion du partage des Droits entre Vous et M. Boito' . . . . . etc.——

He is surely alluding to the performances of *Otello* in Nice.[2]

I don't have the contract of *Otello* here; and therefore I turn directly to you so that you may tell me what my rights for that opera are and whether I can have Boito participate.—— [. . .]

[1] Emanuele Muzio, who had left to Eugène Durot a sum he had lent him in 1881, as well as some jewellery and an endowment to Durot's son Ernest. (*Copialeterre*, p. 361[1]).
[2] The corresponding letter should be at St Agata, but has still not been located.

[1] Agent of the Société des Auteurs et Compositeurs Dramatiques in Paris.
[2] The first *Otello* (in Italian) in France had been given with Tamagno at Nice in February.

VERDI TO GIULIO RICORDI

Genoa, 15 March 1891

[. . .] Panattoni[1] also tells me that Roger has asked him how the profits from *Otello* in Nice should be established. I have already answered, but I'll write again when I have a letter from you — — [. . .]

VERDI TO GIULIO RICORDI

Genoa, 21 March 1891

Dear Giulio,
   I have read Panattoni's memorandum,[1] which is nice and clear, as plain as the first, and more detailed. [. . .]
   Yesterday I went to hear Salvini (I haven't set foot in the theatre for two years, I believe), who did Jago in *Otello* with Drago.[2] Well; success with the audience . . . but I, who am never content, found a Jago who wasn't *Jago*. They say that he was the true *Jago*, and to me he seemed . . . I wouldn't know what! A few lines, a few phrases . . . said very well ∴. No character. — — — Now too tragic, now too comic. — — —
   Addio, addio

Affectionately,
G. Verdi

GIULIO RICORDI TO VERDI

[Milan] 31 March 1891

[. . .] I received a long letter from Tamagno,[1] who proposes to give *Othello* in Paris, and also asks me to turn to you for your consent; it is understood that he will form a company and everything else as the occasion requires. I beg you, therefore, to telegraph me if, as at other times, I must say that for the time being it is impossible to arrange, or if—since Tamagno is involved—I can at least find out which company he plans to form, etc., etc.[2] [. . .]

VERDI TO [?] BORIANI

Genoa, 22 April 1891

Esteemed Signor Boriani,
   Returning from St Agata, I found here your most honoured letter, in which you ask to be relieved of the office of the President of the Hospital at Villanova!

---
[1] Attorney of the House of Ricordi.

---
[1] Missing.
[2] Unknown.

---
[1] Missing.
[2] Verdi's response could not be traced, but it was obviously negative.

I understand that (to judge from the troubles I suffer myself) that office had to become a heavy burden upon you.—Perhaps you could not reduce the frictions of the higher personnel of this establishment, especially between the physician, the parish priest, the sisters, etc., etc., and from that all the bad .... I do not want to know whose fault it is, but unfortunately (you know this) those frictions exist and are very marked!—Well then: in a charitable shelter one should only breathe calm, peace, and the greatest harmony for the relief of the unfortunate who are suffering, and there should not be irritations, rancour, nervousness and childish feelings, which would be ridiculous if they were not harmful to the sick. The very respect that everyone should feel for an establishment in the presence of suffering humanity should have inspired higher, more blessed sentiments, especially in those who have the noble mission of curing and healing the sick. All this is deplorable! ... and unfortunately it will still go on! ... I am grateful to you for continuing in your office until the appointment of the new President, and I thank you for having given of yourself with zeal and intelligence in these two long years, and also for having gone to so much trouble during the construction of a part of the building.

In hopes that, in spite of these slight disagreements, our personal relations will not change at all, I remain, with true esteem, Signor President,

Your devoted

GIULIO RICORDI TO VERDI

Milan, 22 May 1891

[...] For February and March of next year they are requesting *Othello* in French at the theatre of Monte Carlo, and they propose Duc, Maurel, and Caron; of course, I have not made any reply and am awaiting your orders in the matter. [...]

VERDI TO GIULIO RICORDI

St Agata, 25 May 1891

[...] *Monte Carlo*!! Open, O earth! Do you know that place?[1] . It's a thing that has no name, and I understand why those who direct the gambling are interested in causing a sensation ... Othello, Maurel, Caron, Duc bring them business. But artistically speaking, that really wouldn't be the place to give *Othello* for the first time in French! .. [...]

---

[1] Verdi had 'known' it in 1878 (see his Chronology for that year).

GIULIO RICORDI TO VERDI

Milan, 18 July 1891

[. . .] A letter from our representative in London[1] confirms the great success of *Otello*.[2] [. . .]

VERDI TO EUGÈNE BERTRAND

[In French]   St Agata, 27 October 1891

Very honoured by your kind request to give *Othello* at the Opéra, I am unable to give you an answer at this time, since I do not know all the artists who should perform this opera. — You speak to me of Mlle Melba, who is an artist, as I know; but I do not think that the role of Desdemona would be suitable to the nature of her talent. And who would be Othello? That is the important thing. In addition, you tell me that I could see M. Maurel in a little while. With him I could then talk about it at length. I shall be in Milan in fifteen days and later in Genoa. I can easily be found in one of these two cities. [. . .]

VERDI TO GIULIO RICORDI

Genoa, 26 January 1892

[. . .] Ah, you can't imagine what a nuisance the *Othello* affair at the Opéra is to me.

Let's talk frankly *inter nos* and for our eyes only.

I'm convinced that *Othello* at the Opéra would have no success without (modesty aside) my taking an active part at the rehearsals; and I don't feel like taking on such an exertion! Even less could I tolerate, in these days of political–national activity,[1] the inevitable disagreements in that theatre. — On the other hand, I know well that they don't care to have another *opera* in their repertoire, above all one by a foreign composer! For those gentlemen it's enough to have something new for a *lever de rideau* on the nights of the ballet ... something, you will understand, that would not be to my taste! . Then, then, then ... and precisely for these *thens*, it's difficult to reply without one of these *thens* causing us to collide!

You, with your talent, will find the way to make a suitable reply ... For

---

[1] Missing.
[2] On 15 July, for the first time at Covent Garden, with Jean De Reszke and Victor Maurel under Luigi Mancinelli's baton. See Document XI.

---

[1] Tension between France and Italy, largely caused by their conflicting pursuit of colonial expansion in North Africa. (See Biographical Note on Francesco Crispi and Verdi to Ricordi, 17 Jan. 1890.)

example: that I am busy, half-sick (and this is the truth); that for the time being I couldn't decide . . . Say, after all, what you think best to pull us out of this difficult situation. I repeat again that *Othello at the Opéra* would be a fiasco! It's a true and deep conviction of mine!

Stay well, and addio

Cordially,
G. Verdi

GIULIO RICORDI TO VERDI

Milan, 29 January 1892

[. . .] What you write to me regarding Paris is all right, and consequently I shall know how to behave. I wanted to write to you not only for this, but also to give you news which I hope will not annoy you. Since Maurel is free in February, the management of La Scala has engaged him to perform *Otello* with De Negri, who is now in very good voice and is having a true and great success; he certainly will be an Otello who need not fear comparison with Tamagno. I would have liked to write to you first, but for fear of an engagement elsewhere the management has negotiated so urgently with Maurel that I had no time to do it. Also, I happened to be in bed [with the flu]. [. . .]

VERDI TO GIULIO RICORDI

Genoa, 31 January 1892

Dear Giulio,

Again *Otello* at La Scala?!!! After the massacre done to it the last time,[1] it should have been left alone for ten years before being taken up again!

But that impresario of yours[2] imposes himself and imposes . . . also disposes of your stuff without even saying 'Hello!!' At least punish him for such boldness! . . If I were the proprietor of *Otello*, I would have asked for 100,000 Lire (I say one hundred thousand) for the rental [of the] material, just to make true the insolent phrase that one of his clerks hurled behind my back in the lobby of the Carlo Felice: 'To Maestro Verdi we pay hundreds of thousands of Lire for the rental [of the] material; so let him pay for his servant's ticket'; and this because my servant had permitted himself to look into the auditorium through the glass in a door.

It was a scandal!

Your impresario in Milan will do good business with two artists: *Maurel* and *De Negri*. The rest will be as God wishes! Moreover, one must agree that *Otello* was badly produced at La Scala ever since the first time. The fault was

---

[1] In Feb. and Mar. 1889.

[2] Luigi Piontelli (?–1908), double-bass player, important impresario, friend and promoter of Arturo Toscanini; in charge of La Scala from 1892 to 1893.

largely mine, because I had obliged myself to stay calm and to restrain myself in everything that didn't convince me. Neither Desdemona nor Emilia nor Roderigo convinced me; and the sets perhaps even less so, which may have been well painted and well designed, but didn't serve the scene and the drama at all. To mention just one: the set of the second act was arranged in such a way that one couldn't understand a thing: one didn't understand how and where the dialogue between Cassio and Jago took place; nor did one understand whether in the serenade Otello and Jago were apart from the others or together with them. So, more or less, in all the acts. In short, *Otello* was badly produced at La Scala, and since in the theatre bad traditions remain, the evil has remained, and endures. And it seems impossible that we have never been able to find a Desdemona who could take advantage of the duet in the third act and of the quite dramatic *solo* in the finale of the same act. And so also in this reprise there will only be a kind of a concert with duets and the soli of Otello and Jago for the consolation of your critics, who will continue to shout that the music drama, the true drama, the lofty drama must be sought in Germany and in France!!—

Let's cheer up, then, and amen!

Our health is as usual .... Little improvement!!—Peppina and I had decided to go to Milan for a few weeks to have a change of atmosphere and to get away from this environment, which is now so sad for us .. But *Otello* puts an obstacle in our plans.——Later on, who knows!!! Meanwhile, if *Otello* is decided upon, give it as soon as possible; break your neck, and let's talk no more about it. [. . .]

GIULIO RICORDI TO VERDI

Milan, 1 February 1892

[. . .] Your esteemed letter of yesterday distresses me greatly, above all because of the announcement that a probable trip of yours to Milan would now be delayed. It also distresses me because of all your troubles in regard to *Otello*; it distresses me also in view of the incident you mention. [. . .] Of course, I never considered myself authorized to make even a vague allusion to Piontelli as to what happened; I am sure that the vicious reply must be attributed to some lout employed by him. [. . .] Piontelli may be a scoundrel like all the other impresarios, but—for the sake of pleasantry or his business interests—he is a man who shows himself to be the most obsequious in the world; and since in his theatres everywhere he presents operas by a certain Verdi, it is really not conceivable that he could do something that rude!— Judged by the theatre's progress, he is certainly the most capable impresario I have seen at La Scala up to now. [. . .] But having said this for the sake of the truth, I believe I can also tell you that *Otello* will certainly not be given under the same conditions as last time, which, as I wrote to you then, I was forced to endure in spite of myself .... At that time nothing less than the protagonist was missing, and unfortunately the first symptoms of poor Faccio's terrible illness manifested themselves!!¹ ... Already there was no direction any more!! ..

Today there are only two tenors who can perform *Otello*: Tamagno and De Negri; let's hope another one will appear! ... But in the meantime he cannot be found, and in this very carnival [season] I have had to turn down 7 proposals for *Otello*, since there are no possible tenors around, even if one were content with half—if not complete—dogs!!² ....

The idea of *Otello* is not new to the management; not knowing whether De Negri would be in really good health, they have talked with me about Tamagno since last summer—just for *Otello* and perhaps for some more performances of *Le prophète*, too; they were disposed to pay up to 3,000 Lire per performance; but Tamagno—whether he had other plans or was not satisfied with the offer—stuck to the 5,000!! .. and I myself advised the management against this, since figures like these are the true ruin of the poor theatres!!—

Now De Negri is not only well, but the true Benjamin³ of the audience, which hears him sing and pronounces him a true artist. Last night I also learned that De Negri himself pushed for *Otello*, and a note I had from him this morning confirms this to me; in it he thanks me for not having opposed him and tells me that he hopes to do himself honour in his favourite part. As for the sets, they were modified for the second time, and precisely according to your instructions; especially those of the second and third acts; I thought then that they corresponded to all your demands, and they will be done in the same way now.

For Emilia and Cassio, not *good secondary singers*, but *good* leading ones; Signora Arkel has sung *Otello* in several theatres already, and always with success. I myself hope to make a complete recovery very soon, and so I shall growl, beginning with the first rehearsals, if something doesn't go right! ... I do not speak of Mascheroni; for him it's a solemn occasion!! [. . .]

VERDI TO GIULIO RICORDI

Genoa, 2 February 1892

Dear Giulio,

.... He may very well be the most capable impresario (the others are so stupid!!), but it is certain that the unseemly rudeness, if it wasn't uttered, was inspired by him. [. . .]

What I'm now anxious to know is when you will be rid of *Otello*. I know

---

¹ In view of G. B. Shaw's glowing review of Franco Faccio's conducting of *Otello* in London in July 1889 (see Document XI), Ricordi's remark seems surprising. Two years before his death, however, Faccio must have had an extraordinary spurt of energy to achieve the success of *Otello* in London before his final triumph with *Die Meistersinger* in Milan.

² Italian opera fans call inferior tenors 'cani', i.e. (barking) dogs.

³ In the Old Testament (Genesis 35:18) the younger and favourite son of Jacob by Rachel.

that the sets have been modified, but from what I'm told the improvement wasn't remarkable.

It matters little that la *Arkel* has done *Otello*; the point is whether she has done it, and can do it, well.

I repeat ... *Otello* in Milan was originally produced badly (by my fault) and now you can hardly put it back on its feet and get it off to a good start ..

You will have *duets, soli*, and ... I don't know what else!

As far as I'm concerned, I only want it to be performed soon, since I need to get myself going, to have a change of atmosphere, and to take care of and conclude many affairs in Milan.

So then, when will it go on? [. . .]

GIULIO RICORDI TO VERDI

Milan, 5 February 1892

Illustrious Maestro,

Today I have finally resumed my usual office hours.

I was unable to reply straightaway to your honoured letter of the 4th[1] of this month to tell you anything definite about the performance of *Otello*. From what I read in your abovementioned letter, I wish it could be tomorrow, since this, unfortunately, is a reason for the delay in your coming to Milan!! [. . .] Since we must see to it that everything goes well, I am advising you that *Otello* will not be ready to be performed until the 12th or 15th of this month—not later, I hope, unless there are illnesses of the artists or other similar and unforeseen causes, which we hope will not be the case.

This morning Maestro Mascheroni came to me to ask me for an opinion ... which I did not have and did not risk giving. In all the theatres where he has conducted *Otello*, he has put the double-basses together in the fourth act, thus obtaining a secure ensemble in the *solo*. Mascheroni mentions that at La Scala the distance between the basses on the right and the left is so enormous that a tight and homogeneous execution becomes even more difficult. Therefore he asked me whether it was suitable to unite all the double-basses in the fourth act on the left; he also said that when he talked with you about *Otello*, you mentioned this union of the basses to him, since he had done it in other theatres.[2] [. . .]

GIULIO RICORDI TO VERDI

Milan, 9 February 1892

Illustrious Maestro,

Of a man who speaks and writes excellent things, it is said: 'He speaks like a printed book!' But this proverb is really wrong, since one reads so much nonsense in printed books . . . . .

[1] Apparently the 2nd.
[2] See Verdi to Ricordi, 9 Jan. 1889, and to Faccio, early Feb. 1889.

To affirm something true, however, one should say: 'He speaks like Giuseppe Verdi'——and that goes for the letter of the 6th of this month,[1] which you kindly addressed to me and of which I informed Mascheroni. He asks me to thank you warmly, and he thinks it is superfluous to tell you that it will be done exactly as you indicate. Maurel has already arrived, two days ago, and so the rehearsals are regular and complete. [. . .]

GIULIO RICORDI TO VERDI

Milan, 16 February 1892

Illustrious Maestro,

Forgive me if I briefly follow up my telegram[1] and confirm to you that everything went really well, well, well. However, I have never seen similar *shivers* before the start . . . . and I no longer knew what to do to instil courage from left to right, so great was the responsibility that everyone felt towards the author. I can also give you exact news, since you must know that I am actually directing the complicated mechanism of the new lighting!! . And so I am obliged to bury myself below the stage, precisely at the prompter's feet . . and that is an excellent place to hear the whole performance. I absolutely place the orchestra above all; in the whole opera it was superior, beyond all praise. De Negri a great success; certainly he cannot achieve effects with his top notes, but on the whole he is really an excellent artist due to the accentuation and nobility of his phrasing; he pleased without reservation; in some places he was better than Tamagno, as in the third act; not inferior in the fourth. Maurel himself, as always, except that even he was so preoccupied that he ran out of breath in the drinking song in the first act; but later he vindicated himself. La Arkel is without question the best Desdemona up to now; she, too, was paralysed in the beginning; very good in the third and fourth acts. Excellent Emilia—la Guerrini; very good also Cassio,[2] who exaggerated in some places which he had never done in the rehearsals. The chorus altogether good, very good in the *concertato* of the third [act] finale. This we rehearsed 7 or 8 times by itself, also inviting Boito, and I think we almost reached the effect you want; it would be even better if Maurel restrained his voice a bit in all his *parlandos*. Costumes altogether stupendous; altogether good sets.

I won't tell you about the lighting effects!! . . . They are my solo pieces, and I modestly assert!! that in the first act I do extraordinary things!!! . . . . and in the fourth . . . . there is a certain pink reflection . . . . enough, let's forget it.[1]

Magnificent house . . I believe the best box-office of the season. Tomorrow, second performance. The audience, to judge from what I heard this morning, most content.

---

[1] Missing.

[1] Missing, concerning the performance of *Otello* at La Scala on the previous night.
[2] P. Pelagalli-Rossetti, the first Dr Cajus in *Falstaff*.

I am also really most content with Mascheroni; he has acquired a great quality: surprising calm once he is on the podium! Encores of the *Credo* and the *Ave* [Maria] were requested; but we had already agreed to proceed.

I shall give you news of the second performance, because for two nights at least I must be like Radames under the stage, until I am certain that the electricians are quite sure about the lighting cues.

The result, on the whole, is a fine *Viva Verdi*, and the wish to see you here very soon!!—Now, illustrious Maestro, you're *rid*!! . . . as you wrote to me, of *Otello*.

Well, then? . . . .

Always with the warmest gratitude

Yours most devotedly,
Giulio Ricordi

VERDI TO HARICLEA DARCLÉE

Busseto, 29 May 1893

Please accept my apologies for not answering your kind letter[1] any sooner. I had thought that it was a question of a French translation of *Otello* to be performed at a theatre in France; but now that I know that it is a question of an Italian *Otello* to be given at Monte Carlo, there can be no difficulty on my part;[2] and I am very glad that you will assume the part of Desdemona, and wish you the success you deserve. [. . .]

GIULIO RICORDI TO VERDI

Comerio,[1] 31 July 1893

[. . .] The director of a Belgian theatre (not Brussels . . . the name of the city escapes me at the moment . . .) has asked for *Othello*—in French! I think you will agree to wait for a better occasion. [. . .]

VERDI TO GIULIO RICORDI

Genoa, 4 August 1893

[. . .] *Othello* in Belgium! If it were in Brussels it might work, but in the provinces I don't think so. [. . .]

---

[1] Missing.
[2] See Verdi to Ricordi, 25 May 1891.

---

[1] Village near the northern shore of the Lake of Varese north-west of Milan.

GIULIO RICORDI TO VERDI

Comerio, 10 September 1893

[...] Two persons were in Milan on matters concerning the House [of Ricordi] in Paris, and, in the name of Bertrand of the Opéra, they spoke to me of *Othello*—obviously in French. I replied, of course, that this was a matter involving the Maestro, and that I would speak to him about it. [...]

VERDI TO GIULIO RICORDI

St Agata, *Thursday* [14 September 1893][1]

Dear Giulio,
   Boito has left and will tell you everything about the translation, which is excellent.
   Regarding *Othello* at the Opéra, there is nothing to talk about at this moment. And in the first place, who would sing it? [...]

GIULIO RICORDI TO VERDI

Milan, 20 September 1893

[...] Ah! .... Maestro!—what a chore my profession has become at this point! [...] I can't stand it any more and don't know how I can go on with this infamous life!—But let's forget it now; meanwhile I see what you are writing to me about *Othello* at the Opéra; I believe you sense also a question concerning [its] advisability in view of the unfortunate political conditions at present;[1] but these can change. It remains to be seen how the Opéra intends to put on *Othello* and what means it has at its disposal; and of this only you can be the judge. But between 20 and 30 October I must go to Paris and on that occasion hear several performances and report to you on the matter. [...]

VERDI TO GIULIO RICORDI

St Agata, 21 September 1893

[...] *Othello* in Lyons! Oh, dear! The theatre of that city may well be the first, the second, or the third theatre of France, but without doubt it's a bad theatre. *Othello* and *Falstaff* (I speak as an artist) should be given first in

---

[1] This date is inferred from a letter Verdi wrote to Boito on 15 Sept. 1893, in which he mentions 'the beautiful [French] translation' of Boito's *Falstaff* libretto to be handed over to Giulio Ricordi.

[1] See Biographical Note on Francesco Crispi.

Paris .... Tomorrow I'll write to you with all my reasons at length and in detail . .

Addio, addio

Yours,
G. Verdi

VERDI TO GIULIO RICORDI

St Agata, 21 [22] September 1893

Dear Giulio,

..... To continue my letter of yesterday, I will say in two words that 'my operas in France will never be successful without my assistance'——

This is a phrase that seems exaggerated and unpleasant; but it's also true, very true.

My age now would not permit me to go to Paris for this purpose: Nothing except my age—Not our sad political conditions; not the hostility of colleagues with their respective newspapers, whom I could still fight with my strong armour of 'indifference'!

The conclusion?—Not to permit the operas!—This would be my wish; but I know that there are the interests of the translators, of the publisher, etc., etc., and therefore I hesitate to cast a veto, and tell you to *do as you think best*!

Addio, addio

Yours,
G. Verdi

GIULIO RICORDI TO VERDI

Milan, 29 September 1893

Illustrious Maestro,

I have a double regret: my delay in answering two of your very kind letters, and the cause of the delay. It may suffice for you to know that from Sunday until yesterday, Thursday, at 7 o'clock in the evening, I was buried in the midst of 4 lawyers, arbitrators, and similar ..... filth!—I touch myself to find out whether I am dead or alive!—[...]

As always, what you say or write is gold, even a genuine diamond; therefore, when you write to me that your presence in Paris is necessary, I answer: Maestro, you are right. When you tell me that the political reasons or the hostilities do not count for you, I repeat: It is true. There are a thousand facts to prove it. When you conclude that your wish would be not to permit the performance, I would say right away, 'Let your will be done'!! And I would say this because I feel it in my heart, I feel it in my mind, and the one and the other tell me what I owe to Verdi, and that my only ambition should be not to cause him—even unwillingly—the slightest trouble. But I am counting on little at this point, not to say zero! .... How can I fulfil such a wish without hurting (and this you anticipate with the greatest fairness) important interests? On the other hand, how can I agree with your conclusion, 'Do as you think best'! What I think best is to do what is agreeable to you!! . . . . . And here I am walking on two parallel lines that will never meet!! . . . Don't you think, however, that a way might be found to make them touch a bit, by trying to reconcile everything in the best way possible? I understand perfectly how tiresome, exhausting, enervating it could be for you to put on *Othello* at the Opéra, where everything moves at a snail's pace, while you would also expend an enormous amount of spiritual and physical strength; but I do not think this would happen at the *Opéra-Comique*, where so much less would happen by minimal degrees. And this idea of mine is confirmed by the fact that you had decided to go to Paris this coming November, when Carvalho was to put on *Falstaff*. Thank Heaven no different reason exists today, compared to the period in which the first *pourparler* with Carvalho took place; and even if he had really planned to give *Falstaff* in November, there would have been serious obstacles, since the translation was like the building of a cathedral without the materials, and it would have been impossible to begin the rehearsals of the opera. So it was good that Carvalho delayed. But what has not been done can perhaps be done a little later, and perhaps also in a more favourable season with regard to the climate? . . . Kindly read the enclosed letter by Grus,[1] who was in Milan to talk to me about various affairs, among them *Othello* and *Falstaff*. As for the first at the Opéra, I think it would be difficult to put together a suitable company, apart from the defects already mentioned; for the second however, it is quite easy to find lively and intelligent personnel at the Opéra-Comique for an excellent interpretation. And, speaking of art, would it be useful if 2 masterpieces like *Othello* and *Falstaff* were exiled from France? . . .

I have written to you already about the insistent requests for *Othello* in *Lyons*; I am enclosing two letters on the matter that I have just now received;[2] I will hear your orders for a definite reply. Meanwhile, I'm sure . . . a silly thing: since we no longer talk of *Othello* at the Opéra, could Maestro Luigini not come to Genoa later on to receive instructions directly from you? . . . . . If this is a silly thought, let's send it to the Devil straightaway. [. . .]

VERDI TO GIULIO RICORDI

St Agata, 2 October 1893

Dear Giulio,

Ah me, let's speak of business!—On the first days of my stay in France[1] I heard performances in *Lyons*, *Marseilles*, and in *Brussels*! . . . . Maybe, under

---

[1] Léon Grus, a music publisher in Paris, wrote to Ricordi about Carvalho and *Falstaff*.
[2] Missing.

---

[1] Presumably in 1847.

Gevaert's influence, this last theatre has improved a little bit; but I don't think so about the other two.

Therefore I am horrified to hear that *Othello* should be given for the first time in France in Lyons!![2]

I refer to my last letter and repeat that if the interests of others demand it, let God's will be done, but I personally don't want to be involved in any way, and I don't want to assume any responsibility. [. . .]

VERDI TO GIULIO RICORDI

Milan [Genoa], 4 December 1893

Dear Giulio,

Here we are in Genoa about 20 minutes late . . Good trip, with Peppina in a bit of a *funk*; and with *10* degrees of fog from Milan to Pavia, *20* degrees from Pavia to Novi. After Novi, a serene sky with Venus shining splendidly before us, and a violent wind that persists . .

I speak again of Paris with you, in order to protect us from a blow that threatens us; and after thinking about it well, I think that the shortest and safest way is the one I mentioned to you before I left Milan: *Boito* should come to an agreement with Du *Locle*, and the two of them should ask and authorize *Nuitter* to speak with the directors of the Opéra in order to hear what modifications they want. All this before another translation is made, above all *made from a* [illegible] *piece!* .

And now, thank you for the kindnesses extended to us; excuse us the troubles we have caused you, with the promise to cause you greater ones another time . . .

Peppina and I send our greetings to all.

Yours,
G. Verdi

GIULIO RICORDI TO VERDI

Milan, 7 December 1893

[. . .] Boito came to me the morning following your departure; I informed him of the correspondence concerning Paris, and he told me that he would write to Du Locle right away. Boito will certainly inform you of the reply.[1] [. . .]

---

[2] *Otello* had been given with Tamagno in Italian at Nice in Feb. 1891. The first performance of the work in French, however, was to take place in Paris on 12 Oct. 1894.

---

[1] Missing.

VERDI TO GIULIO RICORDI
[Card]

Genoa, 14 [12] January 1894[1]

Dear Giulio,

I still haven't received the letter from Gailhard.[2] Maybe he'll tell you tomorrow what he thinks and what he wants—Ah, I've known for a long time that I *smell a rat!* [. . .]

VERDI TO GIULIO RICORDI

Genoa, 12 January 1893 [1894]

Dear Giulio,

Gailhard's letter[1] reached me late and I'm sending it on to you right away——

The *Othello* affair is delicate and embarrassing. One can see that Gailhard has had a translation made, and he says so . . . . 'ceci fait je le soumettrais à vous, Boito, Du Locle, etc.'—Now, even if this translation were a thousand times better than the one by Boito and Du Locle, I cannot and must not accept it. The direct path to take is to turn first to Boito and Du Locle. I reserve for myself [the right] to look into it *later*. And when they have told me that the controversies with the director of the Opéra are settled, then I'll come in, too . . . always *later*.

So write to Gailhard and tell him that since I have asked Boito and Du Locle to make this translation for me, I cannot cause them the displeasure of having somebody else put a hand to their work; and I'll never accept any change unless they, Boito and Du Locle, are content. It also seems to me that to move quickly, you should show this letter to Boito right away so that he might write to Du Locle right away so they can make the decision they think best.

But they shouldn't waste time.

Addio, yours
G. Verdi

[1] Judging from the contents and sequence of the correspondence, Verdi dated this card in error.
[2] Verdi expected to hear from Gailhard concerning his interference with Boito's and Du Locle's French *Otello* translation.

[1] Missing.

GIULIO RICORDI TO VERDI[1]

Milan, Saturday [13 January 1894]

[. . .] I received a telegram from Gailhard,[2] who tells me that he wrote to you concerning *Otello* and . . . . the translation. Here I absolutely smell a rat. The two letters I wrote, in agreement with you, to the management of the Opéra,[3] made things very clear! You will see, then, what Gailhard has to say now. [. . .]

VERDI TO GIULIO RICORDI

Genoa, 14 [13] January 1894[1]

Dear Giulio,

Ugh! How many letters!

1. Yesterday I wrote you a card.

2. Last night I wrote you a long and boring letter, enclosing one from Gailhard.

3. And now a third one!!! . . To tell you that I've written to Du Locle[2] [telling him] to come to an agreement with Boito; and that I would be of the opinion that (unless they would like to go to Paris) they both should trust Nuitter to reach an understanding with Gailhard and to see whether his proposition is acceptable. Nuitter can be trusted! I repeat again that I don't want to enter into this question of arrangements. And therefore, as a matter of fact, I won't answer Gailhard at all. I leave this task to you, and above all to the translators.

I will talk to him only about the company and about the baritone, whom I don't know——

Return Gailhard's letter to me, and addio.

Yours,
G. Verdi

---

[1] Apparently Giulio Ricordi had received Verdi's card of 12 Jan., but not yet the preceding letter and its enclosure (Gailhard's letter to Verdi).
[2] Missing.
[3] Missing.

---

[1] Since Verdi refers to a card and a letter he wrote 'yesterday' and 'last night', he might have misdated this letter.
[2] Missing.

EUGENIO TORNAGHI TO VERDI

Milan, 14 January 1894

Illustrious Maestro
Signor Commendatore G. Verdi
  Genoa

Giulio received your 2 esteemed letters[1] together with Gailhard's the moment he took a train to hear an artist in Berne. He has charged me to make an appointment for him and Boito for tomorrow evening. Giulio also plans to make a trip to Genoa the day after tomorrow, Tuesday to report to you what has been arranged. [. . .]

BOITO TO VERDI

Milan [18 January 1894][1]

Dear Maestro,

The question of the *Otello* translation threatened to drag on indefinitely, and became very complicated. I thought I had to straighten it out by writing to Gailhard yesterday. I've kept a copy of the letter and am transcribing it for you:[2]

Cher Monsieur,

I learned about your letter to Verdi[3] only the day before yesterday from M. Ricordi; this explains my delay in answering you. The negotiations concerning the Otello *translation must not, in my opinion, drag on any longer. If all the persons interested in this affair had to consult each other* on every detail, a telephone network would have to be established between Paris, Genoa, the Isle of Capri,[4] and Milan. For my part, I will take advantage of circumstances which permit me to simplify the question. The passage in question (recit. and Willow Song) is in my domain, since I translated the third and fourth acts; therefore I can dispose of this fragment without interfering with the work of my collaborator, M. Du Locle, and without upsetting propriety. I have just read it again, and it is detestable. I would like to redo it, but since you seem to be satisfied with your own substitution, I authorize you to present it to the Maestro; his approval will [also] be mine.

Please accept, cher Monsieur, the expression of my deep regret at the fire in the Opéra warehouses. Believe me, etc., etc., etc., etc.

Well then, on the most incriminating point, the concession has been made; other little details of minor importance will remain, and it will be easy to come to an agreement on them. Gailhard's letter to me[5] speaks of *legères*

---
[1] Presumably Verdi's letters of 12 and 13 Jan.

---
[1] This date is inferred from Verdi's following reply.
[2] In French.
[3] Missing.
[4] Du Locle was staying there at this time.
[5] Missing.

critiques, so it's not a question of a new translation of the entire opera. Gailhard's motive, I believe, is sincere.

The recitative and the Willow Song really are *detestable* (they were the first lines, the first attempts, in collaboration with Solanges), and they must be redone. I like to be correct. The interest of a work of art must come first. If the variant offered by Gailhard is good, so much the better; if it's bad, Solanges and I will do another one and will say once more: *So much the better*.

I have now received a letter from Du Locle in which he asks if he must write to Nuitter for information. I would answer that he should ask for it—this way we'll know everything in detail. I'm convinced that in all these negotiations there is no danger that threatens our particular interests, and that the good faith of the directors of the Opéra is complete.

I am enclosing a little sheet[6] on which the new entrance of the Fairies in Act III of *Falstaff*[7] is transcribed.

Affectionate greetings to you and to Signora Giuseppina.

Your
Arrigo Boito

VERDI TO BOITO

Genoa, 19 January 1894

Dear Boito,

Allow me to tell you that you've been too accommodating and too optimistic in your reply to Gailhard! I don't think it was necessary to tell him that you were the translator of the third and fourth acts and Du Locle of the rest. Furthermore, I wouldn't have left the right to anyone to change a single word; and for that matter, I will even declare to you that I shall never assume the responsibility of being the first to approve those changes! They must be submitted to me by the translators I have recognized, Boito and Du Locle . . . And by no one else!

I am also less optimistic than you . . . '*convinced*', as you say, '*that in all these negotiations there is no danger that threatens our particular interests*' . . .

I know nothing about it!! But I ask myself: 'Why did they take the liberty of making a translation without asking your permission?' . . .

I think those few lines will go very well in French. Now translate them into Italian, without adding anything, of course, etc., etc.[1]

Greetings, and greetings also from Peppina, and believe me Your

G. Verdi

---

[6] Missing.
[7] Changes made in the French version of the opera, with slight alterations incoroprated into the final Italian score.

---

[1] See note 7 to the preceding letter.

VERDI TO GIULIO RICORDI

Genoa, 19 January 1894

Dear Giulio,

Boito has written to me and has transcribed the letter he sent to Gailhard!

I found the letter (as I wrote to him) too indulgent and optimistic! He accepts the changes that Gailhard had ordered, as long as they're agreeable to me. But I don't want to assume this responsibility. I don't want to recognize translators other than Boito and Du Locle ... Boito tells me then at the end, 'I'm convinced that in all these negotiations there is no danger that threatens our particular interests, and that the good faith of the directors of the Opéra is complete'. *Amen* .... But I, who am not an optimist, am asking myself, 'Why have they made a translation, or part of one, without saying anything?' ....

I have written these things to Boito this very day. If he speaks of them to you, tell him your opinion, too, and let that be the end!—I add that I wrote to Boito declaring that I would not accept changes made by others who aren't Boito and Du Locle. If Boito doesn't speak to you about it, don't say anything. [. . .]

GIULIO RICORDI TO VERDI

Milan, 19 January 1894

Illustrious Maestro,

Boito informed me of his letter to Gailhard; I found that it greatly facilitated the matter, but I still mentioned to him that one had to dot the i's and that he should certainly be aware of any mess in the *Droits d'auteur*. But if, on the whole, I am naïve, because I believe even .... a scoundrel honest, it seems to me that Boito scores points on me!!—In any case, before a decision is made, things must be made quite clear.—

I am sending you the French *Othello* libretto. [. . .]

VERDI TO EUGENIO TORNAGHI

Genoa, 25 January 1894

Dear Signor Tornaghi,

Very sorry about Giulio's illness, but as you indicate, it will, I hope, be a little thing and cured soon.

Meanwhile I beg you to tell me whether the House [of Ricordi] has answered Gailhard. If not, let me know the same day it answers so that I, too, can afterwards (but afterwards) write to Gailhard.

Health and health.

Yours,
G. Verdi

EUGENIO TORNAGHI TO VERDI

Milan, 26 January 1894

Illustrious Signor Maestro
Commendatore G. Verdi
  Genoa
  In receipt of your welcome page of yesterday, I am glad to inform you that
Giulio is better, that he will leave his bed today, and will write to Gailhard
tomorrow or the day after tomorrow.[1] [...]

VERDI TO PIERRE GAILHARD[1]
[In French]

Genoa, 31 January 1894

My dear M. Gailhard,
  Otello at the Opéra in Italian?!!! That surprises and amazes me!
  I am not discussing your right to give works at the Opéra in Italian; but
when I think of the Opéra, your great *Théâtre National*, I cannot envision in
that theatre a work that is not French! There is something out of tune and
shocking in this mixture...: the *Opéra* and an *Italian work*.
  It is perfectly true that *Aida* was given in Italian before it was given in
French; but that is a different case. *Aida* was first given in Paris in an
exclusively Italian theatre.
  If *Otello* must now be given at the Opéra, I think it must be given
translated into French.
  I regret, my dear M. Gailhard, that I am not of your opinion, but this will
not hinder you, I hope, from accepting my feelings of esteem and friendship.

VERDI TO GIULIO RICORDI

Genoa, 31 January [1894]

Dear Giulio,
  I received the telegram.[1] I answered Gailhard right away, right away, like
this.....[2]

  [1] Missing.

---

  [1] In answer to a missing letter, whose contents are explained in *Copialettere*, p. 388, n. 2:
  "Gailhard proposed these participants for *Otello*: La Tetrazzini [-Campanini], Tamagno
  and Kaschmann, Italian orchestra and chorus, conductor Duschamps of Monte Carlo
  [unknown]. But Verdi observed to Giulio Ricordi in a telegram: 'The company would be
  excellent, but the whole thing would be little dignified and raise an inferno in that theatre,
  which would do no good to anyone except perhaps the directors getting rid of a nuisance. If
  Otello must be given at the Opéra, it must be in French. This is my opinion. Tell me yours.'
  With this *Otello* project, the directors of the Opéra were anxious not to lose ground in their
  competition with the Opéra-Comique, whose director Carvalho had assured himself of the
  Falstaff performance in French (18 April 1894)."

---

  [1] Missing.
  [2] In French.

.... 'If Otello must now be given at the Opéra, I think it must be given translated into French', etc. [...]

VERDI TO CAMILLE DU LOCLE

Genoa, 8 February 1894

Dear Du Locle,

I am extremely embarrassed by our musical affairs in Paris. Affairs that concern not only me, but also my collaborators on *Othello* and *Falstaff*.

You know that *Falstaff* will soon be given at the Opéra-Comique; and later, *Othello* at the Opéra. It's an important and perhaps serious thing, and one must not take a false step.

In Paris they are saying that Carvalho no longer is the Carvalho of old; that his theatre is in decline; that his associates complain about the choice of productions and about poor profits, etc., etc. These rumours are echoed by some papers, and they're creating a gloomy background. You will say that all of this doesn't concern you! Not at the moment, it's true, but since *Othello* must be given afterwards, it's in everybody's interest, including yours, that the background not be black.

I no longer have a reliable friend in Paris to give me frank information on this matter. Nuitter would be the person to whom one might turn; but I'm not close enough to him and would have no right to ask him about such a delicate question.—And you?—You, who for so many years have been an intimate, sincere, loyal friend. Could you do it? Would you do it? If so, you would do me the greatest favour, you would get me out of so many embarrassments, and then I would come to a decision that could not hurt our artistic reputation and our personal dignity. Nuitter could be sure of my word of honour, my silence, and my discretion.

I wish you the very best and send you Peppina's greetings.

Yours affectionately,
G. Verdi

PS In this case I beg of you to be as prompt as you can; there's no time to lose.

VERDI TO BOITO[1]
[Telegram]

Busseto, 8 May 1894

HAVE BAD COLD AND CANNOT TALK—DELAY YOUR ARRIVAL FEW DAYS—WILL TELEGRAPH

VERDI

---

[1] In answer to a missing letter. See Verdi's following lines to Giulio Ricordi.

VERDI TO GIULIO RICORDI

St Agata, 10 May 1894

[...] Boito wrote to me about coming to talk to me—alas!—about this *Othello* at the Opéra. But I had and still have a cold and cannot speak, I have no voice! I'll write about it later. [...]

BOITO TO VERDI

11 May [1894][1]
Milan

Dear Maestro,

Yesterday I read in *Le Figaro* that the *thousandth* performance of *Mignon*[2] will take place in the Sunday *matinée*, that is the day after tomorrow. Assuming that you might not be aware of this date, I wanted to tell you about it in case a telegram should leave Sant'Agata to the Conservatory in Paris.[3]

And now, as to Paris, this is what it's about: Gailhard and Bertrand have an immense desire to give *Othello* at the Opéra. Their desire is so ardent that they would like to produce it *in the month of October*, in order to be able to give a large number of performances over the entire theatrical season.

To reach this goal, it is necessary to start preparing the opera soon, and in order to start, the following things are indispensable:

I. that you approve the idea of producing *Othello* in October rather than in April.

II. that you review the translation as it is now.

III. that you agree to hear Mme Caron, who would come to Italy especially to have you hear her in the fourth act.

I stayed in Paris an extra day (after completing the changes in the translation) to hear la Caron, who is back in voice, in *Salambô*,[4] and I liked her immensely.

I'm making a clean copy of the translation. After we have checked it together, I'll send it to Du Locle. He will make his comments from the literary point of view and will fill in some gaps in Acts I and II, left purposely to give him some problems to solve, too. I'll write to him that this revision of the translation, being most useful to the whole of the work, won't in the least impair the integrity of our author's rights (and this is true). Besides, the entire lyrical part, with rare exceptions, has been left as it was.

---

[1] Postmark: MILANO 11/5/94.

[2] The première of this opera by Ambroise Thomas had taken place at the Opéra-Comique on 17 Nov. 1866.

[3] Verdi's good friend Ambroise Thomas had been the director of the Conservatory in Paris since 1871.

[4] *Salammbô*, opera in 5 acts by the French composer and critic Ernest Reyer (1823–1909) to a libretto by Camille Du Locle based on the novel of the same title by Gustave Flaubert (1821–80).

I hope, dear Maestro, that your cold is about over. Now you know everything I wanted to tell you. When you're completely cured I shall arrive with the translation transcribed, and we'll look it over carefully together.

Many good greetings to you and to Signora Giuseppina.

> Your most affectionate
> Arrigo Boito

VERDI TO BOITO

St Agata, 12 May 1894

Dear Boito,

My voice has returned a bit, but the whole city of Paris still weighs on my stomach and on my legs.[1]

Come here when you want.

Don't forget that the *through train* that stops at Fiorenzuola leaves Milan at 1.30 p.m. and arrives at 3.27.

Till we see each other. Greetings to all.

> Affectionately,
> G. Verdi

BOITO TO VERDI

Monday, 14 May [1894][1]
Milan

Dear Maestro,

I'll arrive at St Agata on Thursday and will be at Fiorenzuola on the train you mention. By Thursday I hope you'll be able not only to speak, but also to sing, and I hope to be able to sing and talk myself, since for three days I've also had a cold in the head, throat, and chest.

Well then, till we see each other this Thursday.

To be on the safe side, I'll reconfirm my arrival by telegram the day before. Many good greetings

> from your affectionate
> Arrigo Boito

VERDI TO BOITO

St Agata, 16 May 1894

Dear Boito,

I left the libretto of *Otello* in Genoa, the very one on which the altered lines in the third [act] finale were written. If you come tomorrow, as I shall learn

---

[1] After the performances of *Falstaff* at the Opéra-Comique.

---

[1] Postmark: MILANO 14/5/94.

from the telegram I'm to receive later on,[1] bring an Italian libretto of *Otello* with you.

Till we see each other again. Addio

Addio
G. Verdi

VERDI TO BOITO

[St Agata, about 17 May 1894][1]

1. I don't find it quite proper that *Tristan und Isolde*—established by contract for the autumn—is now being suspended in order to give the opera of another author! How much chatter and animosity could this stir up!

2. To perform two operas by the same author within six months, even though in different theatres, cannot be useful either for the directors or for the author.

3. I wish to hear *Caron*, as you yourselves have planned.

4. As to Delmas, an outstanding artist in every way . . . his voice is really that of a middle bass. With a powerful, fresh and young vocal organ, it is understandable that he can easily climb to an F, even a G; but his voice is not of a baritonal character. He can hardly unite his beautiful *middle* notes with the high ones. For example, he will be excellent in the 'Credo', but not in the *hypocritical* phrases in the rest of the part.

5. My *rêve* would be two artists, who impress themselves with *authority* on the audience. 'Authority' is a word that makes no sense in the theatres of Italy, but very much so in Paris. Caron and Maurel—that is my *rêve*. As for Maurel, he said to me when I saw him the last time for 5 minutes at the Opéra-Comique: '*Maitre, si vous avez besoin de moi*, je suis à vos . . .' I answered him: 'All right, but at the moment one must not talk about it, and I even beg you not to let this conversation of ours leak out . . .' From this you will understand that Maurel would like to come to Paris, but I think only next March . . .

But why could Gaillard now not speak directly with him about it, and hear what might be possible either in *October* or *April*?—

As for myself, I would much rather wish for March or April, in order to have a long time to do everything comfortably for the ballet and for the rest, etc., etc. . . .

Lastly, I also say that if it should not be convenient for the directors of the Opéra to wait, why couldn't you also give *Othello* without me?—

You handle it . . .

---

[1] Missing. However, Boito arrived at St Agata on 17 May as planned.

[1] Presumably Boito received these observations concerning Verdi's *Otello* negotiations with the Opéra upon his arrival at St Agata on 17 May 1894.

VERDI TO BOITO

St Agata, 25 May [1894]

Dear Boito,

Just now I replied by telegram[1] to the directors of the Opéra ... 'Vous pouvez engager Maurel pour la première d'*Othello* en octobre ... Si Madame Caron est encore dans l'intention de venir en Italie je dois aller Lundi ou Mardi à Milan hotel Milan ou pourrions nous encontrer' ... etc., etc. I need your help in this matter, and you should send a telegram to Paris right away. To tell the truth, this thing is very delicate, and if I were Madame Caron I wouldn't go to Milan to be judged ... On the other hand, I want to be fairly certain about la Caron's voice. All in all, the affair is more serious than it might appear to be. If Caron is in good voice everything will go *comme sur des roulettes*, but if she shouldn't be ... then some serious problems would develop on my part ... Let's avoid these scandals, then, and send a telegram to Paris to settle it all ...

Addio, addio in haste.

Affectionately,
G. Verdi

VERDI TO BOITO

[St Agata] Saturday [26 May 1894][1]

Dear Boito,

I have received your telegram.[2] Don't *by any means entrust the solution to chance*!! No! That would be cowardice on my part, especially since Gailhard himself had proposed having Caron come to Italy. I telegraphed the directors on this matter[3] ... I'm afraid that this affair is getting entangled. Du Locle is ill. We'll settle or spoil it all in a few days in Milan.[4]

Addio
G. Verdi

GIULIO RICORDI TO VERDI

Milan, 9 June 1894

[...] I have written for Cyprian songs or dances,[1] and as soon as I have a reply I will hasten to inform you of it. [...]

---

[1] Missing.

---

[1] Postmark: BUSSETO 26/5/94.
[2] Missing.
[3] Missing.
[4] From the end of May until early June, Verdi was there to confer with Gailhard, Boito, and Giulio Ricordi.

---

[1] Material for Verdi's composition of the ballet for *Othello* required by the Opéra.

OSCAR CHILESOTTI TO GIULIO RICORDI

Bassano, 10 June 1894

Illustrious Signore,

In all the works I have transcribed I could not find Greek–Cyprian dances; I would almost be inclined to believe that there are no antique (authentic) ones. But research in the *Thesaurus harmonicus* of Besardus (a real emporium) would not be inopportune.[1] The oldest dances of Latin origin have been listed by Neusidler[2] and are transcribed at the beginning of my book *Liutisti del 500*.[3] See *Welcher Tantz*[4]—*welche* is the word in German that indicates the Latin race. [...]

GIULIO RICORDI TO VERDI

Milan, 11 June 1894

Illustrious Maestro,

Here is Dr Chilesotti's answer, and as you will see, there is nothing you want—and if Chilesotti says that he found no Greek or Cypriot melodies or dances, I would not know to whom to turn. It is up to you, then, to find them in that unique library that is the head of Maestro Verdi!——

With the most affectionate greetings

Yours most gratefully,
Giulio Ricordi

VERDI TO GIULIO RICORDI

[St Agata] Tuesday [12 June 1894][1]

Dear Giulio,

Something other than the library of my head is needed .. If nothing is found, I'll do nothing!

In the meantime one can research to see if anything is to be found in that *Thesaurus harmonicus* by Besardus ....

And where is that book *Liutisti del 500* by Chilesotti?

In short, if somebody doesn't help me search, I won't do anything.

Yours,
G. Verdi

PS And where are the Venetian arias and dances to be found?

[1] See Biographical Note on Jean-Baptiste Besard.
[2] Hans Neusidler (1508–63) or his brother Melchior (1507–90), who were among the earliest German lutenists.
[3] See Biographical Note on Oscar Chilesotti.
[4] 'Wälscher Tanz' in correct German. (See Appendix IV, n. 1.)

---

[1] Postmark: BUSSETO 12/6/94.

VERDI TO BOITO

St Agata, 12 June 1894

Dear Boito,

I hope this letter reaches you before your departure[1] ...

You ought to know that at one time the management of the Opéra paid so-called *Primes*, especially to foreign authors, for their travel and hotel expenses. Rossini had them, too, as did Mayerber, I believe; and I myself had them for all my operas, except *Aida*, which, as GRAND SEIGNEUR, I renounced.

In the case of *Othello*, it's not a question of *Primes*, but of guaranteeing all our rights and, above all, of preventing the opera from being tampered with and mutilated by the caprice of an artist, as is happening now to *Falstaff* with Maurel (I'm very irritated by this ... also with Giulio, who didn't assert himself.)[2]

I also add that apart from the *Droits d'Auteur*, established by law, there are the so-called *Billets d'Auteur*, too, which must be controlled.

Roger will be able to give you all the necessary instructions to guarantee
1. Our *Droits d'Auteur*
2. *Billets d'Auteur*
3. *Unaltered performance* of the opera.

Ask him in my name, and I hope he will take an interest in this matter, which is important to us.

Bon voyage, and have a good time.

Greetings from Peppina and from me.

Affectionately,
G. Verdi

PS Will you be going to the *Grand Hôtel Capucines* again?

BOITO TO VERDI

Wednesday [13 June 1894][1]
Milan

Dear Maestro,

I leave tomorrow morning. I'll tell Roger everything you told me to tell him.

I have prepared for the work I have to do with Gailhard as best I could.[2]

I don't know yet at which hotel I'll be staying. Not at the Grand Hôtel.

I'll write to you from Paris.

[1] For Paris.
[2] After Verdi's and Boito's departures from Paris, Maurel had taken it upon himself to make major cuts and changes in subsequent performances of *Falstaff* at the Opéra-Comique.

---

[1] Postmark of arrival: BORGO S. DONNINO 13/6/94.
[2] Preparations for the first performance of *Othello* at the Opéra.

I'm afraid I'll find the hotels very crowded because of the *grand prix*,[3] which takes place on Sunday, but I'll find myself some cubbyhole. I'm sorry I won't see Bellaigue in Paris; he has already left for Switzerland.

In his last letter to me (ever more enthusiastic about *Falstaff*) he asks me to give you and Signora Peppina many regards, to which I add my own most affectionate ones.

Your
Arrigo Boito

VERDI TO GIULIO RICORDI

[St Agata] 13 June 1894

Dear Giulio,
For your information I am sending herewith the third act finale completely orchestrated and the printed orchestra score.[1]
A note for my peace of mind.
Addio, addio

Yours,
G. Verdi

GIULIO RICORDI TO VERDI

Milan, Friday [15 June 1894][1]
[...] As for the research for melodies and dances you desire, I have now written to Naples, where the library is one of the richest in Italy; I am awaiting the answer, but with little hope! ...... what does it matter? ... Do you really think it necessary to have this blessed music in your hands? And if it cannot be found, do you mean to refuse to do the dances? ... And let them make a mess of the night with one of their usual ballets? .. On the other hand, Gailhard has said that no more than 5 minutes are required—he intended to take advantage of the famous scene with the columns for the entrance of the dancing procession!! .... It would be a real pity to give all of this up! Do it, Maestro, do it without waiting for *savants* and non-*savants*, and music of the 1500s, 1600s, 1700s!!—You will have a great idea, which they'll all eat in a salad, and in spite of what you write to me I would not be at all surprised to hear, after your return to St Agata, that Turks, Greeks, and Venetians are all cooked up and served by Maestro Giuseppe Verdi—may God bless him!—
[...]

[3] At the horse races.

[1] French version of *Othello*.

[1] Date inferred from the contents of the correspondence.

GIULIO RICORDI TO VERDI

Milan, 15 June 1894

[. . .]
PS I received your other letter, which informs me of the posting of the
finale;[1] I'll let you know the moment it reaches me. Yesterday I sent the third
and fourth acts, with corrections, to the Opéra.

VERDI TO GIULIO RICORDI

St Agata, 16 June 1894

[. . .] The music sent to me is of no use.[1] It has no importance at all.
    Keep searching, since I can't do without it.
    Addio, addio

Yours,
G. Verdi

GIULIO RICORDI TO VERDI

Milan, 21 June 1894

[. . .] Today I am sending you the reduction,[1] with the request please to return
it as soon as you can so that it can be engraved without delay. I am enclosing
a telegram from Paris.[2] I will try to write to Tebaldini to see if he can find
something that you desire.[3] [. . .]

VERDI TO BOITO

St Agata, 23 [22] June 1894[1]

Dear Boito,
    Since I don't have your address, I am asking Giulio to send you these two
lines.
    In case you have finished the work with Gailhard, come to Milan quickly.
I'm going there tomorrow,[2] and I'll stay there until the moment I go to

---

[1] On 13 June.

---

[1] Music to serve as a model for the composition of a ballet in *Othello* at the Opéra.

---

[1] Of the French *Othello*.
[2] Missing.
[3] For the ballet in *Othello* at the Opéra.

---

[1] Judging from the two letters that follow, Verdi actually wrote this one on 22 June.
[2] According to Giulio Ricordi's letter of 23 June the Verdis did not go to Milan before the
24th; their arrival there on the 23rd without Giulio Ricordi's knowledge is most unlikely.

Montecatini, on the evening of 1 July. If you could be in Milan on about 27 June, there would be time for us to examine the notes on the translation, and everything would be finished.[3]

Greetings and greetings.

Affectionately,
G. Verdi

If you happen to see some kind of Cyprian–Greek dance . . . Look into it![4]

VERDI TO GIULIO RICORDI

[St Agata] Friday 23 [22 June 1894]

Dear Giulio,

I have received reduction [of the] finale and hope I can return it to you this very day.

There are still some mistakes in the original orchestra score. Meanwhile I'll adjust the reduction: the reduction[1] when I come to Milan. [. . .]

I don't know where in Paris Boito is staying. Please put his address on the enclosed [envelope], since you know it, and send it to him as soon as possible. In any case your representative will know it.

In haste addio

Yours,
G. Verdi

GIULIO RICORDI TO VERDI

Milan, 23 June 1894

Illustrious Maestro,

I received the reduction with the corrections marked, and what you tell me about the orchestra score is all right. In the meantime I am transferring your corrections to the French text; I shall give it to the engravers right away and send the copies to Paris.

Boito's address in Paris is the Hôtel Continental, to which I posted your letter.

Tebaldini will be in Venice on Monday and will occupy himself right away with research at the Marciana Library.

I hope to see both of you soon in Milan. [. . .]

---

[3] Presumably Boito returned to Milan only in early July.
[4] For the ballet requested by the Opéra.

---

[1] Verdi inadvertently repeats 'the reduction' ['la riduzione'].

VERDI TO GIULIO RICORDI

Montecatini, 3 July 1894

[. . .] The trip was good.[1]—Peppina is as usual, and is not eating!! What a remedy!! Hard to find [one], given her repugnance to physicians, to medicines, to cures, etc., etc. So you see what good cheer? I'm in the middle of a hospital! [. . .]

GIULIO RICORDI TO VERDI

Milan, 9 July 1894

Illustrious Maestro,
    I received your esteemed letter, which, to my displeasure, does not bring me happy news!—Not just for reasons of health, but for many others, I could answer with a litany of unpleasant things!—Never before have I felt as tired, disgusted, and fed up as now—persuaded that a gentleman and a fool are really synonymous! . . . . But let's put all this aside in hopes of happier news from you, along with a good result of that cure for Signora Peppina.
    Yesterday I posted you the book from Paris.[1] I am enclosing herewith what Tebaldini sent me[2]—it seems there is nothing else. [. . .]

VERDI TO GIULIO RICORDI

Montecatini, 9 July 1894

Dear Giulio,
    I received the Greek melodies.[1] There's nothing I can use, even though they are interesting, while I don't believe they are from Greece and the Orient.— [. . .]
    Now I need something *Venetian* besides the Furlana.[2] There is something

---

[1] From Milan to Montecatini on 2 July.

---

[1] Apparently 'the Greek melodies' mentioned in the letter that follows and in Giulio Ricordi's letter of 11 July.
[2] One music sheet containing a dance of sixteen bars in praise of a Venetian princess in 1597, and a few annotations. See Verdi's comment in his letter of 10 July.

---

[1] See note 1 to the preceding letter.
[2] Also Forlana.
    'A dance from northern Italy (*Friuli*). In dance collections of the 16th century (Phalèse, *Chorearum molliorum Collectanea*, 1583) it is similar to the *passamezzo* (in duple meter), whereas in the baroque period it is a gay dance in triple meter (6/4, 6/8) with dotted rhythms and characteristic repeats of motifs. It became associated with festive activities in Venice, e.g., in the ballets of Campra (*L'Europe galante*, 1697; *Le Carnaval de Venise*, 1699; *Les Festes Vénitiennes*, 1710). Bach's orchestral Suite in C major includes a *forlane*. [. . .]' (Willi Apel, *Harvard Dictionary of Music* 2nd edn; Cambridge, Mass.: Harvard University Press, 1969, p. 326).

by *Bizet*,[3] but it's not enough. Look for it as quickly as possible, since there's no time to lose.
   Addio, addio

Yours,
G. Verdi

VERDI TO GIULIO RICORDI

Montecatini, 10 July 1894

Dear Giulio,
   I am returning the third act finale. It's all right, unless there are any wrong notes that I am unable to correct — —
   What miserable music Tebaldini has sent you! Even at that time there was much else, much else!
   Something of an even later period would be needed. Search, search! . It seems that all these *savants* don't know any more about it than I do! But then, what need is there to be a *savant*?! It isn't worthwhile. Meanwhile, send me a nice *Furlana*—there must also be a *Farandole* by Bizet.[1]—Courage, courage! Keep on going straight on your way without looking right or left.
   Greetings and greetings

Yours,
G. Verdi

GIULIO RICORDI TO VERDI

Milan, 11 July 1894

Illustrious Maestro,
   All right: The volume of Greek melodies will be noted. But meanwhile you must excuse me if you find a bill inside!—I had given the order for this volume to be posted to you the moment it arrived from Paris—and unfortunately the zealous storekeeper did not open the volume but sent it right away as it was!—
   Today I am sending you the 2nd part. [...]

---

[3] See the following letter.

---

[1] Verdi probably knew of the Farandole in the Suite no. 1 extracted from Bizet's music to *L'Arlésienne* in 1872. The Farandole is 'a Provençal dance performed by men and women who, holding hands, form a long chain and follow the leader through a great variety of figures to music played on the pipe and tabor. The dance seems to be of very ancient origin (symbolic celebration of Theseus' escape from the labyrinth?) and is still danced today. Similar dances are the branle and cotillon. The music of the farandole is usually in moderate 6/8 meter. The dance has been introduced into opera by Bizet (*L'Arlésienne*) and Gounod (*Mireille*).' (Apel, *Harvard Dict.* p. 308)

VERDI TO GIULIO RICORDI

Montecatini, 12 July 1894

Dear Giulio,

Alas! Alas! I'm half desperate! — — I received the *Farandol* and the *Furlana*! . . There's nothing for me, and I don't understand a thing!—But is it possible that there are no popular Venetian songs even from a more modern period? In short, I would need:

Something *Turkish*! . .

Something *Cyprian–Greek*!

Something *Venetian*!

If it isn't found, rather than do something inconsequential, it's better to do nothing! Consider also the fatigue I would encounter: the heat of the season and, let's just say it, the slight will to work. I believe the best solution would be to write to Gailhard that he should think of something else and give up this ballet; or, . . . I was about to say, let him have it done by whomever he wants . . . . No . . . not that!

So let's again give it some thought. Help me to find it: search, ask, and if it's not possible . . . . we'll write to Gailhard, as I said above . . In any case there's no time to lose! [. . .]

PS For now, think, and think seriously, what *is* to be done, what *must* be done, for the *Othello* ballet.

VERDI TO GIULIO RICORDI

Montecatini, 17 July 1894

Dear Giulio,

Tonight we are leaving for St Agata. [. . .]

Gailhard has written to me about the *ballet*.[1] Good Heavens! I'm completely at a loss and don't know what to do! Try to send me what you have been searching for me—but I'm quite afraid not to do anything. In haste addio

Yours,
G. Verdi

PS   Our health *idem*.

GIULIO RICORDI TO VERDI

Milan, 18 July 1894

[. . .] All my research . . . . . . alas! . . . has been successful[1]—Nothing in Naples, where they advise me to turn . . . . or in Venice; and you already

[1] Missing.

---

[1] This can only be meant cynically.

know of the treasure that has been found there. Well, then? . . . Rummage in the Verdi library!! · . . . There you will find all you want!!—With all my gratitude

Yours most devotedly,
Giulio Ricordi

VERDI TO PIERRE GAILHARD[1]
[In French]

Busseto, 19 July 1894

I have just this moment arrived from Montecatini, a little tired, sweltering, and in great need of rest. Since we met in Milan I have given no more thought to the dances for *Othello*.[2] You know that I would have liked to find something characteristic, very short, and tolerable. Neither then nor at the present time was I able to find anything! But after a few days of rest I shall think about it some more, and I hope to find something and to do it on time.

The model of the second act is very good, and it will be possible to hear the chorus in the serenade. Delighted that Mme Caron and M. Saléza are working ardently on *Othello*, in which, I am sure, they will give a superior interpretation. [. . .]

VERDI TO GIULIO RICORDI

[St Agata] Thursday [19 July 1894]

Dear Giulio,

I'm not sure whether I wrote to you the other day, so just in case I repeat that we are here. —

Gailhard has written to me about the dances, but if you don't give me a hand by indicating something, I won't be able to do a thing——

In short, we are here. Write to me.

Addio
G. Verdi

---

[1] In answer to the letter mentioned in Verdi to Ricordi, 17 July.

[2] See Verdi to Ricordi, 12 and 16 June and 9, 10, 12 and 17 July 1894, as well as the postscript in his letter to Boito, 23 June 1894, which sharply contradict this assertion.

VERDI TO GIULIO RICORDI

[St Agata] Saturday, 20 [21] July 1894

Dear Giulio,

Here is the receipt[1]——

You're joking about the ballet of *Othello*[2] . . . but joking aside, I'm most embarrassed, and shall perhaps finish with 0000.

Addio, addio

G. Verdi

GIULIO RICORDI TO VERDI

Milan, 23 July 1894

Illustrious Maestro,

I received your esteemed letter with the enclosed receipt.

Truly, Maestro, I am not joking in regard to the dances of *Othello!*—If we have been unable to find anything, you mean to give up? . . . This really seems impossible to me—and I was not joking when I repeatedly told you that the best of the *savants* was still you—so much more so since only two or three little numbers are involved, and not a real ballet such as in the *Vespri* or *Don Carlos*. Since nothing exists, who can create better than you? . . . . Send the *savants* and their *trouvailles* to the Devil, and with a spark of your imagination you will let Venetian dancers and Greek maidens jump forth and will then intertwine them all—and I am not joking. [. . .]

VERDI TO GIULIO RICORDI

[St Agata] Thursday [26 July 1894]

Dear Giulio,

I've been working at examining all the hymns. All of them are modern; the oldest one is by Haydn, and it's also the most beautiful one. So then, nothing, not a thing for me!

Now that I remember, Félicien David must have something of the kind I'm looking for in the *Désert* . . Either a hymn to Allah! . or the song of *Muezzin!*?

Have someone search, and if it's there, send it to me on a page.

Addio, addio

Yours,
G. Verdi

---

[1] Unknown.
[2] See Ricordi's letter of 18 July.

GIULIO RICORDI TO VERDI

Comerio, 29 July 1894

Illustrious Maestro,

I sent you straightaway what you requested of me in your note. [. . .]

I hope the heat will ease up so that without discomfort you can think about the dancing entrance of the lovely girls of the Opéra. [. . .]

VERDI TO EUGENIO TORNAGHI

Busseto, 5 August 1894

Dear Tornaghi,

I received the paper[1] from Paris and I thank you.

Now I would need (not having the big orchestra score here) some bars of the big orchestra score in which to insert the ballet.[2]

So ask the head of the copying office to transcribe for me, on a little sheet of music paper, the first 8 bars of page 26 in the reduction; that is, the bars

JAGO. Desdemona si mostri a quel messere

[OTELLO.] Si, qui l'adduci.

[JAGO. Desdemona should show herself to this gentleman

[OTELLO.] Yes, bring her here.][3]

plus another five bars. I repeat, in the orchestra score. He should send them on music paper, by post.

Believe me always

Devotedly,
G. Verdi

[1] Apparently music paper.
[2] Act III, Scene vi.
[3] In the actual text:

JAGO. *Desdemona si mostri a quei Messeri.*
OTELLO. *Si, qui l'adduci.*

[JAGO. . . . Desdemona should show herself to these Gentlemen.
OTELLO. Yes, bring her here.]

VERDI TO GIULIO RICORDI

St Agata, 21 August 1894

Dear Giulio,

I hope you have returned from Levico and that the cure has done you good, as I warmly wish for you.

This very day I'm sending the registered package containing the *ballet* for *Othello* in Paris—Your doctors of music were unable to find me a thing . . . but I found a *Greek song* of 5 thousand years before the coming of Christ! . . . . If the world had not existed then, so much the worse for the world! Then I found *a Muranese* that was composed 2000 years ago for a war that took place between Venice and Murano, which the people of Murano won. Never mind if Venice did not exist then. With these *discoveries* I have composed my clever ballet, imagining how it must be performed, and I've written an outline for it that you'll find together with the orchestra score.[1] When you send the ballet, please send this outline and a full orchestra score to Gailhard, so that the ballet master won't have many people dancing the *soft passages* of the orchestra and few people in the loud ones, etc.—

As soon as you've received the package, write to me, or better yet, telegraph me straightaway, 'I have received it.'

Greetings and addio

G. Verdi

ENCLOSURE
     (*5 minutes and 59 seconds*)
With the splendid third act set of the columns before my eyes, I thought of writing the music as follows: Right in the beginning at the start of the trumpets should appear a group of female *Turkish Slaves* who, being slaves, dance lazily and in a bad mood.

At the end of this 1st tempo, however, they gradually become animated while hearing the *Arabian Song*, and they end up dancing in a frenzy.

At the *Invocation to Allah* they all prostrate themselves . . . At this moment a group of beautiful Greek maidens appears between the columns, and after 4 bars yet another group they move forward and, on the 13th bar, intertwine in a quiet, aristocratic, classical dance . . .

There follows right away *La Muranese* Allegro Vivace $\frac{6}{8}$, and between the columns advances a group of male and female Venetians . . . after 8 bars a second group. At the fortissimo (*bar 18*) they meet and dance downstage.

After this fortissimo there is a piece of very gentle music in F sharp which should be danced only by *two*. The motive is repeated in louder orchestration, and then all the Venetians join the dance. The first $\frac{6}{8}$ motif is resumed, and there I should like to see another group of Venetians appear from the background.

The dance to the *Warriors' Song* should be performed only by men. The first motif is resumed and all the Venetians can dance; then, at the *più mosso*, Venetians, Turks, Greeks and everybody can dance . . . *Amen.*

---

[1] The outline is printed after the text of this letter.

GIULIO RICORDI TO VERDI

Milan, 22 August 1894

Illustrious Maestro,

Our letters have crossed and before leaving for the country, I have the good fortune to receive your esteemed letter of yesterday and the package containing the orchestra score. I have had work started on it immediately, and I shall send the copy to Paris (already informed beforehand) on Saturday morning, together with your most useful choreographic instructions.

I would have liked to read the score to give myself very great pleasure and to verify the authenticity of the antique melodies that you have so expediently dug up!—This time the *savants* will be badly disappointed, not once, but ten times!! .. Also *bouché* will be some researcher of Apollonian hymns, who will be able to discover the sources from which you have drawn!! But I did not want to delay the work by even half an hour, and so I handed over the manuscript to the head copyist immediately; when the copy has been made, then the period, the origin, the tetrachords, the Doric tones, and the percussion section will be verified. [. . .]

GIULIO RICORDI TO VERDI

Milan, 14 September 1894

Illustrious Maestro,

Today I received the first proofs of the ballet; the reduction has been corrected as you indicated. I also hope to be on time in sending the engraved orchestra parts of this new section to the Opéra; thus everything will be complete. I was right, then, when I said that the best of the *savants* was Maestro Verdi!! . . . . You've put all the mice and *chercheurs* of libraries in your hip pocket . . . . and good night. Meanwhile, tell Maestro Verdi that I am sending him a '*Viva*'——[. . .]

[PS] I still don't have the whole libretto! Oh, Boito!! .. Boito!!

VERDI TO GIULIO RICORDI

St Agata 17 September 1894

Dear Giulio,

If Boito hasn't finished correcting the translation, how can they hold the rehearsals at the *Opéra*!? These rehearsals will be badly organized, incomplete, and purposeless.

Ah!! I have never been forced to submit to the composition of a ballet with a downpour of notes! . . . so that *à la rigeur* as far as I'm concerned and for my own use, I could have done without them!

L'Art musical[1] says that this week the orchestra rehearsals will start . . this would probably be tomorrow! But what shall I come to do in Paris, then? . . To show my ugly face? No! Certainly not!

I had indicated to Gailhard some change in interpretation, in accent, in colouring, especially in the quartet and elsewhere![2] But if no [piano] rehearsals are held, this would be impossible! — — And then my trip to Paris would be impossible.

Our servants have left for Genoa today; tomorrow we leave, so I can busy myself with particular, rather serious affairs of mine.

Keep me posted, for [the sake of] my plans, on what is happening, and believe me always

Yours,
G. Verdi

VERDI TO BOITO
[Telegram][1]

Genoa, 19 September 1894

DO NOT UNDERSTAND WELL WHAT PRELIMINARY STUDIES TERMINATED MEANS— COMING TO PARIS I WISH TO MAKE SOME CHANGES IN ACCENTS OF COLOURING AND TO SETTLE SERENADE AND OTHER MATTERS—THIS CAN ONLY BE DONE AT PIANO REHEARSALS MORE OR LESS AS WAS DONE AT OPERA-COMIQUE[2]—IF REHEARSALS TOO FAR ALONG AND DO NOT ALLOW THIS IT IS USELESS FOR ME TO COME TO PARIS—TELEGRAPH ME ABOUT THIS[3]—IN ANY CASE I CANNOT BE IN PARIS BEFORE TUESDAY OR WEDNESDAY

VERDI

VERDI TO GIULIO RICORDI

Genoa, Wednesday [19 September 1894][1]

Dear Giulio,

Yesterday, the moment I was leaving St Agata, I received a telegram from Gailhard.[2] Last night, arriving here, another one from Boito.[3]—I answered Boito with a long telegram and, to better explain myself to you, I am telling you that I won't go to Paris to show my ugly face or to read *my name* in the

[1] *Art musical, musique, théâtre, beaux arts*, journal in Paris.
[2] Missing.

[1] In reference to a missing letter or telegram.
[2] For the rehearsals of *Falstaff* in April.
[3] No such telegram has been located.

[1] Date inferred from the letter that follows.
[2] Missing.
[3] Missing.

papers. I wish to hold some rehearsals of details at the piano; but now, if the rehearsals with the singers and the orchestra are so far along, it will be difficult, I would say, to *turn back* without offending those ladies and gentlemen—

The conclusion: I would like for example: one intimate rehearsal of details at the piano with only *Caron* and *Saléza*.

Another one with *Saléza* and *Maurel*. Another with all the artists. Another on the stage to try out the voices for the serenade, the placement of the chorus, guitars and harps. Once this is done (well, of course) the orchestra rehearsals will be very short——

At any rate, the opera cannot be withdrawn, and since Boito must go to Paris, he should go straightaway and ask Gailhard if what I have said above is possible. If so, he should send a telegram, and I will be in Paris on Tuesday or Wednesday, or Thursday morning at the latest, to hold a rehearsal on the morning of the same day. If not, I'll stay at home, since I don't want to *show myself* or cause *useless* talk about me.

Addio, addio

G. Verdi

PS I have no time to reread the letter. Guess anything you don't understand———

VERDI TO GIULIO RICORDI

Genoa, 20 September 1894

Dear Giulio,

As I telegraphed you,[1] I am writing to you that if you will come to Paris it will give me great pleasure, but do what you think useful for your affairs and for yourself——

I have written to the Minister for a *laissez passer* at the customs.[2]

Have also written to the hotel to have the usual rooms;[3] and so everything I need is taken care of.

Can you tell Boito, if he goes to Paris straightaway, as he wrote to me,[4] that I'll arrive in Paris at seven (I believe) on Wednesday morning; that at about 1 o'clock on the same day a rehearsal can be held; a rehearsal of details, that means a rehearsal with Caron and Saléza (alone) or with Saléza and Maurel—And perhaps these two rehearsals can be done in a single day from *one* to *three*: From *three* to *five*.

Write to me what you plan to do and addio—

G. Verdi

[1] Possibly in the Biblioteca Palatina.
[2] Missing.
[3] Missing.
[4] Missing.

Les Bureaux ouvriront à **7** h. **1/2** — On commencera à **8** heures

AUJOURD'HUI VENDREDI 12 OCTOBRE 1894

RENTRÉE DE **M. MAUREL**

PREMIÈRE REPRÉSENTATION

OTHELLO

Drame Lyrique en QUATRE actes, de M. Arrigo BOÏTO

Musique de **M. G. VERDI**

Version française de MM. C. DU LOCLE et A. BOÏTO

Décors : 1er acte, M. JAMBON ; 2me acte, Mrs AMABLE et GARDY ; 3me acte, M. CARPEZAT ; 4me acte, Mrs RUBÉ et CHAPERON

Costumes de M. BIANCHINI

Desdémone	Othello	Iago
Mme ROSE CARON	M. SALÉZA	M. MAUREL
Emilia	Cassio	Ludovic
Mme HÉGLON	M. VAGUET	M. GRESSE
Rodrigue	Montano	Un Héraut
M. LAURENT	M. DOUAILLIER	M. CANCELIER

Au 3me Acte, **DANSES** réglées par M. HANSEN

Mlles **SANDRINI, VIOLLAT, BLANC, H. RÉGNIER, SALLE**

Mlles GALLAY, J. RÉGNIER, CHASLES, PERROT, MESTAIS, P. RÉGNIER
MANTE, MONNIER, MONCHANIN, IXART, CARRÉ, CHARRIER
MM. LECERF, STILB, GIRODIER, MARIUS, RÉGNIER, JAVON.

DEMAIN SAMEDI 13	LUNDI 15
ROMÉO ET **JULIETTE**	**OTHELLO**

Le Bureau de Location est ouvert à l'Opéra, côté gauche de la façade, de 10 heures à 7 heures.

The Poster for the première of *Othello* in Paris (Bibliothèque de l'Opéra, Paris)

And whether Boito is going or not, and when?———

It's three o'clock, and I've received the telegram[5] after having written the letter!———

So as not to write another one, I confirm what I have written above———

I'll be arriving Wednesday morning, I believe about seven.

Bon voyage

VERDI TO FRANCESCO CRISPI

Paris
Grand Hôtel, 13 October 1894

Excellency,

Last night, at the first performance of *Othello* at the *Opéra*, I was honoured with the Great Cross of the Legion of Honour.[1] The President of the Republic[2] himself—surrounded, I believe, by all the ministers—offered me the decoration. All this with great warmth and cordiality. The audience took part in this with the same warmth.

Now I believe it would be an excellent idea if Ambroise Thomas, the author of *Mignon* and *Hamlet*, were to receive the same grade in the Order of S. Maurizio and Lazzaro, of which he is already a great officer. I would also wish that the two co-directors of the *Opéra*, Gailhard and Bertrand, who spared nothing to obtain a marvellous performance of *Othello*, together with the conductor of the orchestra,[3] might receive the same decoration that the directors of the *Opéra-Comique* received on the occasion of *Falstaff*; that is, for the two directors of the Opéra, the grade of Officer; for the conductor, the grade of Cavalier.

I am turning directly to Your Excellency so that you, with your authority, may eliminate all the difficulties, should there be any.

I would be most happy if I could show my gratitude for the honours received and for the many, many courtesies extended to me by all.

I shall stay here for about 8 more days, and I would be most happy if I could give the same good news to the illustrious maestro and the directors.

Please accept my apologies, Your Excellency, and be assured of my most profound esteem and admiration.

[5] Missing.

[1] On the same occasion Boito and Giulio Ricordi received the grade of Cavalier.
[2] Jean Casimir-Périer (1847–1907), 5th President of France from 1894 to 1895.
[3] Paul Taffanel.

VERDI TO GIULIO RICORDI[1]

Paris, Sunday [21 October 1894]

Dear Giulio,

I leave tomorrow night, Monday——

Box-office at the Opéra on Friday 23,000 Francs or more!! Enormous! And there was no Caron[2] . . she will sing tomorrow night.

Crispi's telegram, which I myself gave President Périer to read, will be returned to you from Genoa.[3] It was enclosed with a package of other papers that would be hard to find now——

Greetings—in haste addio

Yours,
G. Verdi

VERDI TO GIULIO RICORDI

[Paris] Monday [22 October 1894]

Dear Giulio,

Here is Crispi's telegram, and I still believe it would have been better not to give it to the papers,[1] but to communicate it only to the ministers.

I read it to President Périer myself.[2] Kind words . . . that's all — —

I am leaving tonight.[3]

Tonight Caron, whom I saw yesterday, will sing . . and not at all [illegible]!!

In haste addio

G. Verdi

Greetings to our poet, your colleague, as Cavalier of the Legion of Honour.

---

[1] Giulio Ricordi had returned to Milan shortly after the opening night at the Opéra.

[2] Her substitute was Rose Bosman, a French soprano at the Opéra from 1885 to 1898.

[3] This appears to be the telegram published by Abbiati (iv. 556) without a date and the name of the addressee: 'Proud that the Italian name has been highly honoured in that great and pleasant city, I send wishes of fraternal affection between the two neighboring peoples and bless the art that has provided the occasion. Glory to Verdi, whose harmonies have crossed the Alps and opened the way to an accord of hearts.' This telegram was presumably received in Paris by Giulio Ricordi, who left it in Verdi's hands.

[1] Crispi himself seems to have requested the publication. Verdi, Italy's most successful ambassador of good will, however, reiterated his objection on 25 Oct. in a letter from Genoa to Giulio Ricordi: 'All is well in the end.—I only regret *Crispi's* telegram. . . Apart from those who christened it a "Crispinada", *Le Ménestrel* writes this morning "Crispi-girouette—Quelle lyrisme! . . . . Entre l'affection des deux peuples latins il n'y a que l'épaisseur d'un Crispi. . ."' ['Crispi-weathercock—What lyricism! . . . . There stands nothing in the way of affection between these two Latin peoples but that blockhead Crispi. . . . .']

[2] Probably on the occasion of a banquet Périer offered Verdi and his wife in the Elysée Palace.

[3] After a performance of *Falstaff* at the Opéra-Comique, which greatly pleased him, Verdi had attended a memorial service for Gounod and the third performance of *Othello* on Friday, 19 Oct. at the Opéra. His letter to Giulio Ricordi of 25 Oct. reflects his final farewell to the 'grande boutique': 'I left the Opéra Friday night; and I greeted the artists, one and all, who gave me the most cordial, pleasant, and moving welcome. And I myself was a little bit bouleversé.'

GIULIO RICORDI TO VERDI

Milan, 24 October 1894

Illustrious Maestro,

From Signora Stolz I heard about your excellent journey from Paris to Turin—and I do not doubt that it will have been excellent from Turin to Genoa, where you and Signora Peppina will now be able to rest in tranquillity—and in the excellent health in which I had the pleasure to leave you.

I will not repeat to you, Maestro, the overpowering, yet sweet, emotions I experienced while attending such great events, nor the joy in the highest honours bestowed upon our greatest and beloved Maestro. [. . .]

I think of the rehearsals, of the miracles of physical energy you accomplished, putting to shame so many youngsters made of rancid whipped cream!—Summing up, everything was so beautiful that it seems like a dream to me, since almost all the realities of life are dull or sad!—But . . . wherever you are present, everything changes: everything becomes refined by lively colours, and the mind and heart rejoice with respectful admiration. [. . .]